LIBRARY
AND
INFORMATION
SCIENCE
ANNUAL

VOLUME 4

1988

LIBRARY AND INFORMATION SCIENCE ANNUAL

VOLUME 4

1988

Bohdan S. Wynar EDITOR

Ann E. Prentice ASSOCIATE EDITOR
Anna Grace Patterson ASSOCIATE EDITOR

1988

LIBRARIES UNLIMITED
ENGLEWOOD, COLORADO

Library and Information Science Annual (formerly *Library Science Annual*) is a companion volume to
American Reference Books Annual.

Libraries Unlimited books are bound with Type II nonwoven material that meets and exceeds National
Association of State Textbook Administrators' Type II nonwoven material specifications Class A
through E.

Contents

Part III
REVIEWS OF PERIODICALS

Part IV
ABSTRACTS OF LIBRARY SCIENCE
DISSERTATIONS
by Gail A. Schlachter

Publications Cited

FORM OF CITATION	PUBLICATION TITLE
ARBA	American Reference Books Annual
BL	Booklist
BR	Book Report
Choice	Choice
CLJ	Canadian Library Journal
C&RL	College & Research Libraries
EL	Emergency Librarian
JAL	Journal of Academic Librarianship
JOYS	Journal of Youth Services in Libraries
LAR	Library Association Record
LJ	Library Journal
Online	Online
RBB	Reference Books Bulletin
RQ	RQ
SBF	Science Books & Films
SLJ	School Library Journal
SLMQ	School Library Media Quarterly
TN	Top of the News
VOYA	Voice of Youth Advocates
WLB	Wilson Library Bulletin

Introduction

For many years our own literature — specifically the literature of library and information science — was somewhat neglected by the reviewing media. In spite of the increasing amount of monographic material, periodicals, and serials in library and information science produced each year, only a small portion was ever reviewed in our own periodicals such as *Library Journal, Choice, Wilson Library Bulletin, American Libraries, Library Quarterly, College and Research Libraries*, etc. This problem was more fully analyzed by Ching-Chih Chen and Thomas J. Galvin in "Reviewing the Literature of Librarianship: A State of the Art Report," published in *American Reference Books Annual 1975* (pp. xxxi-xlv). The report indicates that from January 1971 to June 1973 more than one-fourth of the current publications of potential interest to those in the profession had not been reviewed in any of the most significant professional journals. These findings were confirmed by Susan J. Webreck and Judith Weedman in "Professional Library Literature: An Analysis of the Review Literature," published in *Library Science Annual 1986* (pp. 3-12). Their conclusion indicated that "the number of reviews which appeared in the selected journals has increased over the past twelve years, but that this increase is not proportionate to the increase in the number of titles published. This suggests that the reviewing media have not been able to keep pace with the growth of the professional materials."

Because of this existing situation, in 1970 *American Reference Books Annual* started to review books in library science published in the United States in order to offer more comprehensive coverage than the periodicals provided. To provide better access to such materials reviewed in *ARBA*, a separate bibliographic guide was published in 1987, namely Donald G. Davis and Charles D. Patterson's *ARBA Guide to Library Science Literature 1970-1983*. Their work constitutes the first step in a retrospective bibliography covering 1,728 titles of library science books published in the United States or English-language titles that have exclusive distributors in the United States. This compilation has received positive comments in professional literature and hopefully will be followed by a companion volume of retrospective library reviews covering the nineteenth century to 1970. When this is completed, the library profession will have made a good start toward bibliographic control of its own literature; the library profession will have done for itself what it has long done and encouraged for others.

Starting with 1984, Libraries Unlimited decided to produce a separate annual entitled *Library Science Annual* to provide a more comprehensive reviewing service for all books dealing with library science published or distributed in the United States. In addition, *Library Science Annual* began to evaluate more systematically all library science periodicals and indexing services, and highlighted research trends in library science by providing abstracts of the most significant doctoral dissertations produced each year. Each annual contained a number of essays by library educators, practitioners, and publishers. Volume 1 presented six such essays, including Eric Moon's essay "The Scarecrow Press" and Claire England's "The Canadian Library Press." Published also was Norman Stevens's article "The History and Current State of Library Publishing in the United States: An Impression."

This first volume and the two subsequent volumes were favorably reviewed by such journals as *Journal of Academic Librarianship, Wilson Library Bulletin, American Libraries, Canadian Library Journal, College and Research Libraries, Journal of Library History*, and many others. With volume 3, the title was changed to *Library and Information Science Annual* (*LISCA*), which reflected the expanded scope of the annual as it covers the closely related field of information science in more depth. To facilitate this expansion of materials included and the broadening of *LISCA*'s focus, Ann E. Prentice, Director of the Graduate School of Library and Information Science, University of Tennessee, agreed to assist as the new associate editor.

Volume 4 of *LISCA* has somewhat broader objectives than the first three volumes. They are as follows:

1. To review all English-language monographs and reference books in library and information science published each year, not just selected or recommended titles. Volume 1 reviewed 253 titles, principally U.S. works, a few Canadian imprints, and other imprints distributed in the United States. Volume 2, extending coverage of Canadian imprints, reviewed 305 titles. Volume 3, with coverage of Canadian and British imprints, reviewed 382 titles. Volume 4, with coverage of Canadian, British, and some Australian imprints, reviews even more titles for a total of 549. This recent total reflects a 30 percent increase in material over the previous volume and an increase of over 50 percent since the first volume was published in 1985.

2. To evaluate systematically all English-language library and information science periodicals and indexing services. Each year, the editors of *LISCA* select titles for review, including some of national or regional interest and some that are subject-oriented. The total number of periodicals and indexing services reviewed in *LISCA* 88 is 48, bringing the total number reviewed in the last four years to 153.

3. To highlight research trends in library science by providing abstracts of the most significant doctoral dissertations produced in a year. Gail A. Schlachter has contributed abstracts of 159 dissertations over the first four years of *LISCA*.

4. To report on significant trends in library information science literature through a number of essays by prominent library information science professionals. The current volume contains six essays including "Keeping up in Information Science" by Trudi Bellardo, "The Library as Publisher: Desktop Publishing in ARL Libraries" by William C. Robinson, "Controlled Circulation Serials" by Nancy J. Butkovich and Marjorie Peregoy, and "The Research Efforts of Major Library Organizations" by Sharon L. Baker and Ronald R. Powell.

5. To attempt, over time, a permanent record of the intellectual activity in library and information science and to impose bibliographic control over the literature.

6. As we noted earlier, *LISCA* now covers more Canadian and British materials. In contrast to previous volumes that included foreign titles only if available from U.S. distributors, all Canadian titles known to the publisher are included here, as well as many British titles and some Australian titles.

Certain categories of materials are not covered in *LISCA*. Those include specific periodical articles, publications of vanity presses, and certain in-house publications that are institution-specific. For the time being, research reports of limited distribution, audiovisual materials, and some continuing education "kits" produced by ALA divisions or affiliates will not be covered.

REVIEWING POLICY

The editors of *Library and Information Science Annual* have applied the same rigorous reviewing standards that *American Reference Books Annual* is noted for. The *LISCA* staff keeps an up-to-date list of well-qualified library educators and practitioners so that books may be assigned for review appropriately. This year *LISCA* has used the services of approximately 200 librarians and scholars at libraries and universities throughout the United States and Canada; their names are listed following this introduction. Reviews in *LISCA* are signed as a matter of editorial policy.

Standard instructions for *LISCA* reviewers, prepared by the editorial staff, are briefly summarized here: Reviewers should discuss the work and then provide well-documented critical comments, positive or negative. Such things as the usefulness of the given work; organization, execution, and pertinence of contents; prose style; format; availability of supplementary materials (e.g., indexes, appendices); and similarity to other works and/or previous editions are normally discussed. Reviewers are encouraged to note intended audience and/or level, but the review need not conclude with specific recommendations for purchase.

All the materials reviewed are given full bibliographic description, and citations to other review sources are given for books.

ARRANGEMENT

LISCA is arranged in four parts. Part 1 contains 6 essays contributed by authors well known in Canada and the United States, treating various library and information science publishing areas. Part 2, comprising reviews of 549 books, is arranged into subjects, including such areas as automation, cataloging, comparative and international librarianship, information technology, school library media centers, and special libraries and collections. Reviews of 48 periodicals, arranged under the headings National, Subject-oriented, and Regional, compose part 3. The fourth and final part has abstracts of 37 dissertations listed alphabetically by author's name.

AUDIENCE

It is our goal that users benefit from *LISCA*. It has been created with the needs of students and researchers, practitioners and library educators in mind. We believe that publishers and other information professionals will also find much of interest. We urge librarians to contribute their suggestions for improvement, and to support our efforts to create an outstanding annual review for librarians in the United States and internationally.

ACKNOWLEDGMENTS

In closing, we wish to express our gratitude to the many contributors, as well as to associate editor Ann E. Prentice, without whose support this fourth volume of *LISCA* could not have been compiled. We would also like to thank the members of our staff who were instrumental in the preparation of *LISCA*: associate editor Anna Grace Patterson, as well as David V. Loertscher, Judy Gay Matthews, Kay Minnis, Carmel Huestis, Sharon Kincaide, and Patti Leach, who compiled the author/title index.

Bohdan S. Wynar

Editorial Staff

Bohdan S. Wynar, Editor-in-Chief
Ann E. Prentice and Anna Grace Patterson, Associate Editors

Contributors

Robert D. Adamshick, Librarian, U.S. Army Corps of Engineers, Chicago.

Chris Albertson, City Librarian, Tyler Public Library, Tex.

Ann Allan, Assoc. Professor, School of Library Science, Kent State Univ., Ohio.

Walter C. Allen, Assoc. Professor Emeritus, Graduate School of Library and Information Science, Univ. of Illinois, Urbana.

(Christina) Young Hyun Allen, Director of Support Services, Beloit Public Library, Wis.

Mohammed M. Aman, Dean, School of Library Science, Univ. of Wisconsin, Milwaukee.

Charles R. Andrews, Dean of Library Services, Hofstra Univ., Hempstead, N.Y.

Susan B. Ardis, Head Librarian, Engineering Library, Univ. of Texas, Austin.

Marcia L. Atilano, Reference Librarian, Eastern New Mexico Univ., Portales.

Bill Bailey, Reference Librarian, Newton Gresham Library, Sam Houston State Univ., Huntsville, Tex.

Sharon L. Baker, Asst. Professor, School of Library and Information Science, Univ. of Iowa, Iowa City.

Robert M. Ballard, Professor, School of Library and Information Science, North Carolina Central Univ., Durham.

Gary D. Barber, Coordinator, Reference Services, Daniel A. Reed Library, State Univ. of New York, Fredonia.

Susan S. Baughman, Univ. Librarian, Goddard Library, Clark Univ., Worcester, Mass.

Carol Willsey Bell, Genealogist, Youngstown, Ohio.

Trudi Bellardo, Asst. Professor, School of Library and Information Science, Catholic Univ. of America, Washington, D.C.

Ron Blazek, Professor, School of Library Science, Florida State Univ., Tallahassee.

Marjorie E. Bloss, Manager, Resource Sharing, OCLC, Dublin, Ohio.

George S. Bobinski, Dean and Professor, School of Information and Library Studies, State Univ. of New York, Buffalo.

Carol June Bradley, Music Librarian, State Univ. of New York, Buffalo.

Robert N. Broadus, Professor, School of Library Science, Univ. of North Carolina, Chapel Hill.

Ellen Broidy, History Bibliographer, and Coordinator of Library Education Services, Univ. of California, Irvine.

Barbara E. Brown, Head, General Cataloguing Section, Library of Parliament, Ottawa.

Judith M. Brugger, Serials Cataloger, City College, City Univ. of New York.

Betty Jo Buckingham, Consultant, Iowa Dept. of Education, Des Moines.

Robert H. Burger, Assoc. Professor of Library Administration, Univ. of Illinois, Urbana.

G. Joan Burns, Principal Art Librarian, Art and Music Dept., Newark Public Library, N.J.

Nancy J. Butkovich, Science and Technology Reference Librarian/Instructor, Sterling C. Evans Library, Texas A & M Univ., College Station.

Lois Buttlar, Asst. to Director, Center for the Study of Ethnic Publications, School of Library Science, Kent State Univ., Ohio.

Esther Jane Carrier, Reference Librarian, Lock Haven Univ. of Pennsylvania, Lock Haven.

Dianne B. Catlett, Graduate Assistant/Teaching Fellow, Dept. of Library and Information Studies, East Carolina Univ., Greenville, N.C.

Connie Champlin, Coordinator of Media Services, MSD, Washington Township Public Schools, Indianapolis, Ind.

John Y. Cheung, Assoc. Professor, Univ. of Oklahoma, Norman.

Boyd Childress, Social Sciences Reference Librarian, Ralph B. Draughon Library, Auburn Univ., Ala.

Margaret E. Chisholm, Director, School of Librarianship, Univ. of Washington, Seattle.

Larry G. Chrisman, Technical Services Librarian, Univ. of South Florida Medical Center Library, Tampa.

Gary R. Cocozzoli, Director of the Library, Lawrence Institute of Technology, Southfield, Mich.

Bonnie Collier, Principal Reference Librarian, Yale Univ. Library, New Haven, Conn.

Barbara Conroy, Educational Consultant, Santa Fe, N. Mex.

Jean L. Cooper, Technical Services Librarian, Science and Engineering Library, Univ. of Virginia, Charlottesville.

Paul B. Cors, Collection Development Librarian, Univ. of Wyoming, Laramie.

Camille Côté, Assoc. Professor, Graduate School of Library Science, McGill Univ., Montreal, Que.

Nancy Courtney, Reference Librarian, Roesch Library, Univ. of Dayton, Ohio.

Milton H. Crouch, Asst. Director for Reader Services, Bailey/Howe Library, Univ. of Vermont, Burlington.

Anna L. DeMiller, Humanities/Social Sciences Librarian, Reference Dept., Colorado State Univ. Libraries, Ft. Collins.

Donald C. Dickinson, Professor, Graduate Library School, Univ. of Arizona, Tucson.

Carol A. Doll, Assoc. Professor, College of Library and Information Science, Univ. of South Carolina, Columbia.

G. Kim Dority, G. Kim Dority Editing & Publishing Services, Denver, Colo.

Eliza T. Dresang, Manager, Library Media Services, Madison Metropolitan School District, and Lecturer, School of Library and Information Studies, Univ. of Wisconsin, Madison.

Esther R. Dyer, Director, Public Affairs Research and Information Services, Empire Blue Cross Blue Shield, New York.

Judy Dyki, Library Director, Cranbrook Academy of Art, Bloomfield Hills, Mich.

Marie Ellis, English and American Literature Bibliographer, Univ. of Georgia Libraries, Athens.

Claire England, Assoc. Professor, Faculty of Library and Information Science, Univ. of Toronto, Ont.

G. Edward Evans, Univ. Librarian, Charles Von der Ahe Library, Loyola Marymount Univ., Los Angeles, Calif.

Evan Ira Farber, Librarian, Lilly Library, Earlham College, Richmond, Ind.

Theresa Farrah, Graduate Assistant, Univ. of Washington, Seattle.

Adele M. Fasick, Professor, Faculty of Library and Information Science, Univ. of Toronto, Ont.

Patricia Fleming, Assoc. Professor, Faculty of Library Science, Univ. of Toronto, Ont.

Susan J. Freiband, Asst. Professor, Graduate School of Librarianship, Univ. of Puerto Rico, San Juan.

Elizabeth Frick, Assoc. Professor, School of Library Information Studies, Dalhousie Univ., Halifax, N.S.

Ronald H. Fritze, Asst. Professor, Dept. of History, Lamar Univ., Beaumont, Tex.

Edward J. Gallagher, Professor of English, Lehigh Univ., Bethlehem, Pa.

Ahmad Gamaluddin, Professor, School of Library Science, Clarion State College, Pa.

Mary Ardeth Gaylord, Reference Librarian, Kent State Univ., Ohio.

Edwin S. Gleaves, Librarian, Tennessee State Library and Archives, Nashville.

Frank Wm. Goudy, Assoc. Professor, Western Illinois Univ., Macomb.

Suzanne K. Gray, formerly Coordinator of Science, Boston Public Library.

Laurel Grotzinger, Dean and Chief Research Officer, Graduate College, Western Michigan Univ., Kalamazoo.

Leonard Grundt, Professor, A. Holly Patterson Library, Nassau Community College, Garden City, N.Y.

Blaine H. Hall, Humanities Librarian, Harold B. Lee Library, Brigham Young Univ., Provo, Utah.

Roberto P. Haro, Asst. Vice Chancellor, Univ. of California, Berkeley.

Marvin K. Harris, Professor of Entomology, Texas A & M Univ., College Station.

Thomas L. Hart, Professor, School of Library and Information Studies, Florida State Univ., Tallahassee.

James S. Heller, Director of the Law Library and Assoc. Professor of Law, Univ. of Idaho College of Law, Moscow.

Mark Y. Herring, formerly Library Director, E. W. King Memorial Library, King College, Bristol, Tenn.

Susan D. Herring, Reference Librarian, Univ. of Alabama Library, Huntsville.

Joe A. Hewitt, Assoc. Univ. Librarian for Technical Services, Univ. of North Carolina, Chapel Hill.

Shirley L. Hopkinson, Professor, Dept. of Librarianship, San Jose State Univ., Calif.

Renee B. Horowitz, Assoc. Professor, Dept. of Technology, College of Engineering, Arizona State Univ., Tempe.

Helen Howard, Director/Assoc. Professor, Graduate School of Library and Information Studies, McGill Univ., Montreal, Que.

William E. Hug, Professor, Dept. of Instructional Technology, Univ. of Georgia, Athens.

Janet R. Ivey, Automation Services Librarian, Boynton Beach City Library, Fla.

John A. Jackman, Entomologist, Texas Agricultural Extension Service, Texas A & M Univ., College Station.

Joan W. Jensen, Head, Reference Dept., Univ. of Connecticut, Storrs.

Richard D. Johnson, Director of Libraries, James M. Milne Library, State Univ. College, Oneonta, N.Y.

Thomas A. Karel, Asst. Director for Public Services, Shadek-Fackenthal Library, Franklin and Marshall College, Lancaster, Pa.

Sydney Starr Keaveney, Professor, Art and Architecture Dept., Pratt Institute Library, Brooklyn, N.Y.

Dean H. Keller, Curator of Special Collections, Kent State Univ. Libraries, Ohio.

Sharon Kincaide, Production Editor, Shepard's/McGraw-Hill, Inc., Colorado Springs, Colo.

Thomas G. Kirk, Library Director, Hutchins Library, Berea College, Ky.

Amey L. Kirkbride, Kent State Univ., Ohio.

Susan E. Kotarba, Branch Library Manager, Ross-Barnam Branch, Denver Public Library, Colo.

Shirley Lambert, Staff, Libraries Unlimited, Inc.

Brad R. Leach, Records Technician, 18th Judicial District, Englewood, Colo.

Hwa-Wei Lee, Director of Libraries, Ohio Univ., Athens.

Richard A. Leiter, Librarian, Littler, Mendelson, Fastiff and Tichy, San Francisco, Calif.

Elizabeth D. Liddy, Asst. Professor, School of Information Studies, Syracuse Univ., N.Y.

David V. Loertscher, Staff, Libraries Unlimited, Inc.

Elisabeth Logan, Asst. Professor, School of Library and Information Studies, Florida State Univ., Tallahassee.

Sara R. Mack, Professor Emerita, Dept. of Library Science, Kutztown State College, Pa.

Judy Gay Matthews, Staff, Libraries Unlimited, Inc.

Susan V. McKimm, Business Reference Specialist, Cuyahoga County Library System, Maple Heights, Ohio.

Margaret McKinley, Head, Serials Dept., Univ. Library, Univ. of California, Los Angeles.

Peter F. McNally, Assoc. Professor, Graduate School of Library and Information Studies, McGill Univ., Montreal, Que.

Philip A. Metzger, Curator of Special Collections, Lehigh Univ., Bethlehem, Pa.

Jerome K. Miller, President, Copyright Information Services, Friday Harbor, Wash.

Connie Miller, Coordinator, Computer Assisted Information Services, Main Library, Indiana Univ., Bloomington.

P. Grady Morein, Director of Libraries, Univ. of West Florida, Pensacola.

Lynn Morgan, Systems Librarian, Ontario Legislative Library, Toronto, Ont.

Andreas E. Mueller, Mathematician, Univ. of Illinois, Chicago.

K. Mulliner, Asst. to the Director of Libraries, Ohio Univ. Library, Athens.

James M. Murray, Director, Law Library/Asst. Professor, Gonzaga Univ. School of Law Library, Spokane, Wash.

Necia A. Musser, Head, Acquisitions and Collection Development, Western Michigan Univ., Kalamazoo.

Jo-Anne Naslund, Media/Reference Librarian, Curriculum Laboratory, Faculty of Education, Univ. of British Columbia, Vancouver.

Danuta A. Nitecki, Assoc. Director for Public Services, Univ. of Maryland Libraries, College Park.

Christopher W. Nolan, Reference Services Librarian, Maddux Library, Trinity Univ., San Antonio, Tex.

O. Gene Norman, Head, Reference Dept., Indiana State Univ. Library, Terre Haute.

Judith E. H. Odiorne, Librarian and Secretary/Treasurer, Barnabas Ministries, Thomaston, Conn.

Jeanne Osborn, formerly Professor, School of Library Science, Univ. of Iowa, Iowa City.

Berniece M. Owen, Coordinator, Library Technical Services, Portland Community College, Oreg.

Joseph W. Palmer, Asst. Professor, School of Information and Library Studies, State Univ. of New York, Buffalo.

Miranda Lee Pao, Assoc. Professor, School of Information and Library Studies, Univ. of Michigan, Ann Arbor.

Jean Parker, Humanities Reference Librarian, St. Olaf College, Northfield, Minn.

Judith M. Pask, Reference Librarian, Purdue Univ., West Lafayette, Ind.

Maureen Pastine, Director of Libraries, Washington State Univ., Pullman.

Anna Grace Patterson, Staff, Libraries Unlimited, Inc.

Marjorie Peregoy, Original Cataloguer, Serials/Assoc. Professor, Sterling C. Evans Library, Texas A & M Univ., College Station.

Daniel F. Phelan, Media Librarian, Ryerson Polytechnic Institute, Toronto, Ont.

Edwin D. Posey, Engineering Librarian, Purdue Univ. Libraries, West Lafayette, Ind.

Ronald R. Powell, Professor, School of Library and Informational Science, Univ. of Missouri, Columbia.

Ann E. Prentice, Director, Graduate School of Library and Information Science, Univ. of Tennessee, Knoxville.

Gary R. Purcell, Professor, Graduate School of Library and Information Science, Univ. of Tennessee, Knoxville.

Kristin Ramsdell, Asst. Librarian, California State Univ., Hayward.

Micaela Marie Ready, formerly Staff, Libraries Unlimited, Inc.

James Rice, Assoc. Professor, School of Library and Information Science, Univ. of Iowa, Iowa City.

Sandra A. Rietz, Professor of Education, Eastern Montana College, Billings.

Stan Rifkin, Director of Research and Development, Master Systems, McLean, Va.

William C. Robinson, Assoc. Professor, Graduate School of Library and Information Science, Univ. of Tennessee, Knoxville.

Ilene F. Rockman, Librarian, California Polytechnic State Univ., San Luis Obispo.

Antonio Rodriguez-Buckingham, Professor, School of Library Service, Univ. of Southern Mississippi, Hattiesburg.

JoAnn V. Rogers, Assoc. Professor, College of Library and Information Science, Univ. of Kentucky, Lexington.

Samuel Rothstein, formerly Professor, School of Librarianship, Univ. of British Columbia, Vancouver.

Michael Rogers Rubin, Attorney, United States Dept. of Commerce, Washington, D.C.

Edmund F. SantaVicca, Head, Collection Management Services, Cleveland State Univ. Libraries, Ohio.

Gail A. Schlachter, President, Reference Service Press, Redwood City, Calif.

Isabel Schon, Professor, College of Education, Arizona State Univ., Tempe.

Mark E. Schott, Serials/Reference Librarian, Eastern New Mexico Univ., Portales.

Anthony C. Schulzetenberg, Professor, Center for Information Media, St. Cloud State Univ., Minn.

LeRoy C. Schwarzkopf, formerly Government Documents Librarian, Univ. of Maryland, College Park.

Ralph L. Scott, Assoc. Professor, East Carolina Univ., Greenville, N.C.

Ravindra Nath Sharma, Asst. Director for Public Services, Univ. of Wisconsin Libraries, Oshkosh.

Gerald R. Shields, Assoc. Professor and Asst. Dean, School of Information and Library Studies, State Univ. of New York, Buffalo.

Marilyn L. Shontz, Chair, Library Science Dept., Shippensburg Univ., Pa.

Bruce A. Shuman, Assoc. Professor, Library Science Program, Wayne State Univ., Detroit.

Kari Sidles, formerly Staff, Libraries Unlimited, Inc.

Stephanie C. Sigala, Head Librarian, Richardson Memorial Library, St. Louis Art Museum, Mo.

Robert Skinner, Music and Fine Arts Librarian, Southern Methodist Univ., Dallas, Tex.

Nathan M. Smith, Director, School Library and Information Science, Brigham Young Univ., Provo, Utah.

Samson Soong, Manager of Catalog Dept., Alexander Library, Rutgers Univ., New Brunswick, N.J.

Barbara Sproat, Librarian, Denver Public Library, Colo.

Patricia A. Steele, Head, School of Library and Information Science Library, Indiana Univ., Bloomington.

Cynthia A. Steinke, Director, Institute of Technology Libraries, Univ. of Minnesota, Minneapolis.

Norman D. Stevens, Univ. Librarian, Univ. of Connecticut Library, Storrs.

Steven L. Tanimoto, Assoc. Professor, Dept. of Computer Science, Univ. of Washington, Seattle.

Alix Thayer, Editorial Assistant/*Journal of Library History*, Univ. of Texas, Austin.

Andrew G. Torok, Asst. Professor, Northern Illinois Univ., De Kalb.

Betty L. Tsai, Senior Assoc. Professor/Technical Services Librarian, Bucks County Community College, Newtown, Pa.

Dean Tudor, Professor, School of Journalism, Ryerson Polytechnic Institute, Toronto, Ont.

Carol J. Veitch, Director, Onslow County Public Library, Jacksonville, N.C.

Louis Vyhnanek, Reference Librarian, Holland Library, Washington State Univ., Pullman.

Kay Vyhnanek, Head, Circulation and Interlibrary Loan, Washington State Univ., Pullman.

Mary Jo Walker, Special Collections Librarian and Univ. Archivist, Eastern New Mexico Univ., Portales.

Jean Weihs, Course Director, Library Techniques, Seneca College of Applied Arts and Technology, North York, Ont.

Darlene E. Weingand, Assoc. Professor and Director, Continuing Education Services, Univ. of Wisconsin, Madison.

Lucille Whalen, Dean of Graduate Programs, Immaculate Heart College Center, Los Angeles, Calif.

Robert V. Williams, Assoc. Professor, College of Library and Information Science, Univ. of South Carolina, Columbia.

Wiley J. Williams, Professor Emeritus, School of Library Science, Kent State Univ., Ohio.

T. P. Williams, Head, Social Sciences Dept., Mississippi State Univ. Library, Mississippi State.

Nancy J. Williamson, Professor, Faculty of Library and Information Science, Univ. of Toronto, Ont.

Hensley C. Woodbridge, Professor of Spanish, Dept. of Foreign Languages, Southern Illinois Univ., Carbondale.

Bohdan S. Wynar, Staff, Libraries Unlimited, Inc.

Virginia E. Yagello, Head, Chemistry, Perkins Observatory and Physics Libraries, Ohio State Univ., Columbus.

A. Neil Yerkey, Asst. Professor, School of Information and Library Studies, State Univ. of New York, Amherst.

Arthur P. Young, Dean of Libraries, Univ. of Rhode Island, Kingston.

Marie Zuk, Language Arts Coordinator, Carman-Ainsworth School District, Flint, Mich.

Anita Zutis, Government Documents Special Collections Librarian, State Univ. of New York Maritime College, Fort Schuyler.

Part I
ESSAYS

Keeping up in Information Science

Trudi Bellardo

INTRODUCTION

The normally challenging task of keeping current with the literature in any area is made even more daunting in information science by the problem of defining the content and scope of the field. As has been said before, there is little consensus as to what sort of discipline or profession information science really is. That it contains many diverse elements is evidenced by the fact that the American Society for Information Science, a relatively small professional organization, is divided into over twenty special interest groups, about one for every 150 members. In contrast, the huge American Library Association is organized into eleven divisions, or about one for every 3,640 members. The subject interests of the members of ASIS and of the broad field of information science include bibliometrics, scientific communication, information transfer, retrieval evaluation, document analysis, information systems and technology, expert systems and artificial intelligence, automated language processing, telecommunications, classification research, publishing, education for information, information management, marketing and commercial aspects of information, information dissemination and use, library automation and networks, databases, office information, government information programs and policies, international information systems and agencies, and information resources and services for many different populations including medicine, law, education, biology, chemistry, the arts and humanities, and others. Clearly, it is an impossibility to keep current in all these specialties.

The difficulty in knowing where to look for cutting edge developments is further compounded by the variety of jobs that information professionals perform. They include research,

teaching, service, management, design, and development. The professionals in each of these jobs have different needs. Researchers need to know about other researchers' theories and empirical investigations. Teachers need to maintain a basic understanding of the principles underlying current practice and developments. They also need to keep abreast of a wide range of social, economic, political, and ethical issues and trends and need to identify readable, current, and substantial textbooks for their students. Managers and other practitioners need to understand the implications and applications of research findings and new technological developments as well as changes in the information industry. Designers must understand not only the potential of technological advances and prototype systems, but also the personal and societal needs of the potential users of their new products and services.

Describing how to keep current in information science is difficult also because to a certain extent it depends on the individual's background and training. If one has been prepared to read and understand the technical and scholarly literature of the field and to interpret the mathematics and statistics used by the researchers, it is much easier to skim the literature and quickly glean the most useful elements. Many information professionals, however, have been educated for engineering, electronics, communications, linguistics, chemistry, library science, history, law, or something else. For all those who have not been educated in the mainstream of information science (if there is such a thing), much of the current literature is quite abstruse. This phenomenon has been noted by some members of ASIS who admit they cannot or will not read their own journal, *JASIS* (*Journal of the American Society for Information Science*). What they usually say is that it is not relevant to their current interests or work, but what they probably mean is they simply do not have the background to understand the technical content.

What follows is an overview of the mainstream information science source literature, as well as some suggestions for beginners and bystanders to help them extract what is most useful to them.

The cross-disciplinary sources in management, computer science, engineering, communications, etc., that could be potentially interesting for information science have not been included. To do so would be an endless task.

JOURNALS

The mainstream information science journals can be divided into several categories, none of which is mutually exclusive and, in fact, many journals fall into more than one classification. The groups are characterized either by the major mission of the journal or by some special feature that is particularly useful for certain readers.

The first category includes those that are primarily scholarly whose purpose is to report scientific research studies. These journals have editorial boards, they referee contributed papers (always with a blind and sometimes a double-blind referee system), and the published papers have the scholarly hallmarks of presentation format and cited references. Most of the editorial or advisory boards are composed of representatives from different countries and many of these journals regularly publish papers from outside the United States or Great Britain. Included here are those that publish primarily in English. Full bibliographic information is given in the appendix.

Government Information Quarterly
Government Publications Review
Information Processing and Management
International Forum on Information
    and Documentation
International Journal of Information
    Management
Journal of Documentation
Journal of Information Science; Principles
    and Practices
Journal of the American Society for
    Information Science
Library and Information Science Research

The following group occasionally publish research papers, but they also serve as forums for descriptive and tutorial papers and news

items. All but Aslib proceedings have an editorial board and presumably referee contributed papers for quality control. In any particular issue, there is likely to be no more than one genuinely scholarly paper.

Aslib Proceedings
Microcomputers for Information
    Management
Online Review
Program

The third group of journals is aimed at practicing information professionals. Their contents include project descriptions, interesting operations, innovations, as well as tutorials on how to solve problems, take advantage of new products and services, increase productivity, or provide benefits to users of information.

Aslib Proceedings
Byte
Database
Inform
International Journal of Information
    Management
Microcomputers for Information
    Management
Online
Online Review
Optical Information Systems
Program

For keeping up with news in the field, the following journals provide timely reporting on technical developments, new products, market and industry changes, legislation, government policies and controversial issues, as well as events and people, including job changes.

Bulletin of the American Society for
    Information Science
Byte
Database
Datamation
FID News Bulletin
Government Publications Review
InfoWorld
Inform
Information Today
Online
Online Review
Optical Information Systems
Program

A special subset of these provides calendars of upcoming conferences and other special events.

Datamation
FID News Bulletin
Inform
Information Today
*International Journal of Information
    Management*
Online Review
Optical Information Systems
Program

Another way of keeping informed of new information products and services is by scanning the advertisements in the journals and magazines. Each of the following has a considerable number of pages of informative ads.

Byte
Datamation
InfoWorld
Inform
Information Today
Online
Online Review
Optical Information Systems

Making choices of new books to acquire and read would be difficult without the guidance of the critical book reviews in both the scholarly and the popular journals. Each of the following journals includes reviews that are lengthy, substantial, critically evaluative, and written by experts whose names appear on the reviews.

Byte
Database
Datamation
Government Information Quarterly
Government Publications Review
Inform
Information Processing and Management
*International Forum on Information and
    Documentation*
*International Journal of Information
    Management*
Journal of Documentation
*Journal of the American Society for
    Information Science*
Library and Information Science Research
Online
Online Review

The best reviewers use their reviews as forums to discuss issues and ideas in the field, to succinctly describe the state of research and the current schools of thought, and to suggest new avenues of research or stimulate fresh ideas and projects.

BOOKS

The number of books published each year in information science that report on research is actually quite small. Of the seventy-four books reviewed in *Information Processing and Management* in 1986, only three could be said to be scientific research reports of original investigations and two were historical studies. This small sample suggests that in information science, as in most scientific fields, the monograph is not an important vehicle for disseminating original research results. The journal fills that function. Most of the published monographs are descriptions of techniques or operations, are syntheses of previously published literature, are reference books of some type, or are textbooks of useful knowledge for the field. Only some of these are worthy of a straight reading-through; many are better used for occasional reference for specific needs. Some contain information that quickly becomes dated. Considering how expensive these books are, those containing ephemeral information should be avoided if possible. Some of the others, however, can be worthwhile to buy and keep.

Because the quality and intended audience varies so much, it would be prudent for the consumer to read at least one review before making the decision to buy. If a review is not available, the next best guidepost for quality and usefulness is probably the reputation of the author, rather than the reputation of the publishing house. The publishers in this field seem to offer a wide range of quality (judging from the variation in the reviewers' assessments of different books from the same publisher).

Some of the books published each year (twelve of the seventy-four reviewed in *Information Processing and Management* in 1986) are proceedings of conferences or seminars at which scientific studies were reported. If one needs to keep on the cutting edge of progress in research, one should attend the conferences, as most of the published proceedings do not appear until almost two years after the event. If one wants a recent retrospective overview of research, published conference proceedings are a satisfactory choice.

One book published annually that merits individual attention is the well-known and well-respected *Annual Review of Information Science and Technology* (*ARIST*). Published annually since 1966, this remarkable series has chronicled not only most of the theories and empirical investigations of the past twenty years, but also the technological advances and innovations, the important social and economic issues, information policies, applications and services in the field. The major criticism of the *ARIST* essays has been that they are difficult to read, being too succinct and too superficial. They never seem to offer as much analysis, synthesis, interpretation, and evaluation as one would want. On the other hand, they do an excellent job of identifying the recent literature and trends in many areas. Again, it may not always be appropriate to sit down and read these essays straight through, but they are useful to have at hand for occasional reference.

CONFERENCES AND SEMINARS

Staying on the cutting edge of research and development, and trends and issues is much easier if one has the opportunity and resources to attend the conferences and seminars of the various large and small professional societies and associations and those conferences, workshops, and institutes sponsored by consulting firms and publishing houses. One can choose from among the many scheduled each month by scanning the calendars in the journals listed above. Calls for contributed papers and descriptive articles on upcoming events also appear in these same issues. At these events, one can hear papers on both completed research and projects as well as work in progress. They afford one the opportunity not only to hear well-organized formal presentations, but also to probe interesting points in question-and-answer dialogues, both

in the meeting rooms and in more informal and relaxed settings. The large conferences offer the additional benefit of exhibits where one can see demonstrated the latest innovations in information products and services.

INDEXES

Because of the broad scope of the field, it is not surprising that literature searching in information science is seldom straightforward and can never be comprehensive in a single index. On almost any topic in the field, however, one could start a search in *Library and Information Science Abstracts* and find something of interest. The ERIC index also would be a likely source. Depending on the topic, one could carry the search further in indexes such as *INSPEC, NTIS, SSCI,* or *Library Literature.* See the appendix for fuller information on these sources. All are available both as online databases and in printed index form.

CONCLUSION

Despite the broad scope of the information science discipline or field, there is a finite number of mainstream sources for keeping abreast of the latest research, technological developments, and applications. As one goes into cross-disciplinary areas, a vast number of additional sources must be reviewed and placed in the context of information science.

APPENDIX

Journals

Aslib Proceedings. London: Aslib, The Association for Information Management. ISSN 0001-253X. Monthly.

Byte: The Small Systems Journal. Peterborough, N.H.: McGraw-Hill. ISSN 0146-5422. Monthly.

Database: The Magazine of Database Reference and Review. Weston, Conn.: Online Inc. ISSN 0146-5422. Bimonthly.

Datamation. Newton, Mass.: The Cahners Publishing Corporation. ISSN 0011-6963. Twice monthly.

FID News Bulletin. The Hague, Netherlands: Federation Internationale d'Information et de Documentation. ISSN 0014-5874. Monthly.

Government Information Quarterly. Greenwich, Conn.: JAI Press. ISSN 0740-624X. Quarterly.

Government Publications Review: An International Journal of Issues and Information Resources. New York: Pergamon Press. ISSN 0277-9390. Bimonthly.

InfoWorld: The PC News Weekly. Menlo Park, Calif.: InfoWorld Publications. ISSN 0199-6649. Weekly.

Inform: The Magazine of Information and Image Management. Silver Spring, Md.: Association for Information and Image Management. ISSN 0892-3876. Monthly.

Information Processing and Management: An International Journal. New York: Pergamon Press. ISSN 0306-4573. Bimonthly.

Information Today. Medford, N.J.: Learned Information, Inc. ISSN 8755-6286. Monthly.

International Forum on Information and Documentation. Moscow: All-Union Institute of Scientific and Technical Information (VINITI). (Also published in Russian.) Subscriptions available through the FID General Secretariat, The Hague, Netherlands. Quarterly.

International Journal of Information Management. Guildford, England: Butterworth Scientific Limited. ISSN 0268-4012. Quarterly.

Journal of Documentation. London: Aslib, The Association for Information Management. ISSN 0022-0418. Quarterly.

Journal of Information Science: Principles and Practices. Amsterdam: Elsevier Science Publishers (North-Holland) for the Institute of Information Scientists. ISSN 0165-5515. 6 issues/yr.

Journal of the American Society for Information Science (JASIS). New York: John Wiley & Sons. ISSN 0002-8231. Bimonthly.

Library and Information Science Research: An International Journal. Norwood, N.J.: Ablex Publishing Corporation. ISSN 0740-8188. Quarterly.

Microcomputers for Information Management: An International Journal for Library and Information Sources. Norwood, N.J.: Ablex Publishing Corporation. ISSN 0742-2342. Quarterly.

Online: The Magazine of Online Information Systems. Weston, Conn.: Online Inc. ISSN 0146-5422. Monthly.

Online Review. Oxford, England, and Medford, N.J.: Learned Information Inc. ISSN 0309-314X. Bimonthly.

Optical Information Systems. Westport, Conn.: Meckler Corporation. ISSN 0886-5809. Bimonthly.

Program: Automated Library and Information Systems. London: Aslib, The Association for Information Management. ISSN 0033-0337. Quarterly.

Monographs

Annual Review of Information Science and Technology (ARIST). Martha Williams, ed. Elsevier Science Publishers on behalf of the American Society for Information Science.

Indexes

ERIC. Consists of two subfiles: *Resources in Education* (*RIE*) and *Current Index to Journals in Education* (*CIJE*). Educational Resources Information Center of the U.S. Department of Education.

INSPEC. The printed indexes are three *Science Abstracts* publications: *Electrical and Electronics Abstracts, Computer and Control Abstracts,* and *Physics Abstracts.* Institution of Electrical Engineers.

Library and Information Science Abstracts (*LISA*). The Library Association (London).

Library Literature. H. W. Wilson Company.

NTIS. The printed version is *Government Reports Announcements & Index.* National Technical Information Service of the U.S. Department of Commerce.

SSCI. Full name: *Social Science Citation Index.* Institute for Scientific Information.

The Library as Publisher
Desktop Publishing in ARL Libraries

William C. Robinson

THE PROBLEM

Library as Publisher

When publishing for libraries and librarians is mentioned, most librarians think of such specialized publishers as the American Library Association, Greenwood Press, Meckler Publishing, Oryx Press, and Libraries Unlimited. It is difficult to think of the library as a publisher. Yet libraries have historically published a rich variety of works. Many of these library publications may have been ephemeral (bookmarks, short bibliographies, annual reports, and acquisition lists), but other publications (substantial bibliographies, including catalogs, manuals, reports, and periodicals) have been of considerable value. Inglewood [California] Public Library is one of the few to consider itself a publisher. Its manuals with their CIP statements and ISBNs are widely sold.[1] The Ohio State University Libraries have also made publishing a successful commercial venture.[2] Many larger libraries have issued technical reports of continuing value on a variety of important, topical issues. Some have been published as occasional papers while others have been "published" by ERIC in their microformat deposit collection.

Visibility of Library Publications

The visibility of library publications is often low because of poor bibliographic control. Rarely are these publications distributed or known beyond the home library. Many important reports, for example, evaluations of particular collections or automation planning documents, may not be well known in the library where they are produced.

In the past, some library publications looked informal and that may have contributed to the feeling that libraries were not really publishers because their products simply did not look professional. Anyone who has read library technical reports on ERIC microfiche or examined some of the sample library policy and procedure documents included in the ARL SPEC kit publications, has encountered at least a few library publications in typescript which are unattractive, difficult to read, and do not reproduce well.

Enter the Personal Computer

Today's personal computing hardware and software allows any library to produce quality publications at a reasonable cost in equipment, time, and effort. The personal computer has had an enormous impact on most larger libraries, particularly in the automation of circulation and cataloging functions. Curiously, it has had much less impact on the quality of internal and external communication. In some libraries, professionals still stand in line to use the one manual or electric typewriter in their department. Librarians with inadequate clerical support find themselves producing final drafts of technical reports with hunt-and-peck typing at a time when contemporary word processing software provides the library with the opportunity to produce printed material that is attractively designed and includes a variety of graphic material, such as dazzling graphs and crisp illustrations. Built-in spelling and style checkers can be used to create error-free reports.

In fact, word processing software such as Microsoft *Word, Word Perfect,* and *Full Write Professional* includes page design or layout features formerly associated with more expensive and complicated page layout software. However, desktop publishing promises even more.

Desktop Publishing

Desktop publishing produces near professional quality copy with equipment that occupies no more than a standard desktop. Typically, a personal computer with considerable memory, page layout software, and a laser printer are required. Note that true professional quality printed output requires printing technology with more than 1,000 dots per inch (dpi) while the Apple LaserWriter provides 300 dots per inch. However, even "mainstream publishers are finding that 300-dpi laser typesetting provides sufficient quality of certain applications."[3] Some of the more sophisticated dot matrix printers can produce output that is attractive and quite readable.[4]

The camera ready output of desktop publishing may be printed using photo duplication equipment in the library or the machine readable document file may be sent to a composition house where it will drive photo composition equipment. Linking desktop publishing with phototypesetters may be the best of both worlds: "the control and convenience of desktop publishing plus the quality of true typesetting."[5]

The prophets of desktop publishing argue that this increasingly inexpensive technology allows anyone or any institution to be its own publisher, creating material of considerable quality at reasonable cost. "The benefits of DTP are many, ranging from reductions in typesetting charges to improved turn-around time."[6] Jesse Berst says that "by the next decade, many—some would say most—American books will be published from the desktop."[7] This technology also allows material to be published on demand—that is a copy of a document can be printed when requested rather than producing stock for inventory—or published electronically to be disseminated over telephone lines.

Having a publishing house on the librarian's desktop should result in more attractive, more visible, and more widely used publications. By making it easier to incorporate graphic materials, the impact of technical report literature could be much greater. Higher quality publications should also have more impact on the community which the library serves.

Purpose

The survey discussed below began with the question: To what degree are members of the Association of Research Libraries using desktop publishing, how are they using it, and how satisfied are they with it? A literature search failed to locate information that would answer these questions.

METHOD

Since desktop publishing technology was not well established until 1986 and is only now being adopted by many colleges and universities, it seemed reasonable that desktop publishing would likely appear first in larger research libraries much as was the case with library automation.[8] As one expert said, the technology is still new enough so that "we're still somewhere between the innovator and early adopter stages."[9] Thus, the population surveyed consisted of members of the Association of Research Libraries. Because of problems with self-addressed stamped return envelopes and a sense that the Canadian situation might be different, the thirteen Canadian members of ARL were excluded from the population. A sample of fifty-one ARL member libraries was selected by the use of a random number table. With forty usable questionnaires returned, the response rate was 78 percent and represents a 39 percent sample of ARL members. Given the small size of the population, the forty cases may not be enough to make statistically valid generalizations. Both responding and nonresponding libraries were briefly examined and they appear to be similar in terms of such variables as size and geographic region. However, one might assume that those libraries not responding were less likely to be interested in or presently involved with desktop publishing.

FINDINGS

Professional staff size was the only demographic variable used in this study. About 98 percent of the responding libraries had a professional staff of twenty-one or more librarians. Again, this is a reminder that these are large research libraries.

Hardware and Software

Since desktop publishing is a microcomputer phenomenon, libraries were asked if they had a computer suitable for desktop publishing. Responses are summarized in figure 1. Desktop publishing began with the Apple Macintosh computer and the Apple LaserWriter

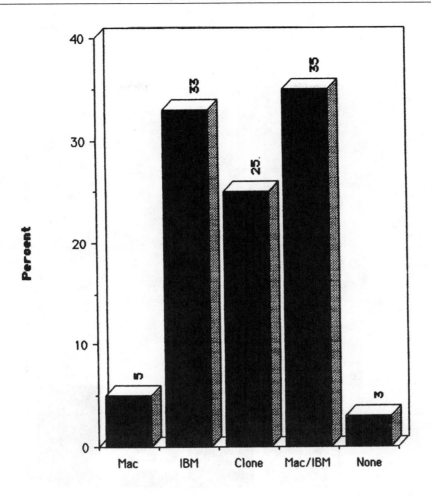

Fig. 1. Computer type.

printer. Beinhorn notes that the "Macintosh, unchallenged for nearly two years in the desktop publishing market, remains the 2-to-1 favorite in sales of desk top publishing software."[10] Although few research libraries have only the Macintosh, 40 percent do have a Macintosh while 93 percent have an IBM or compatible. If as some experts suggest, the Macintosh is the better machine for desktop publishing, then most research libraries are at a disadvantage. Nearly 77 percent of those ARL libraries presently active in desktop publishing have a Macintosh. This suggests that libraries with the Macintosh computer are more likely to be desktop publishers.

While the laser printer does not produce truly professional quality documents, its output is substantially better than that produced on dot matrix or daisy wheel printers. Most laypeople find laser printer output to be professional in appearance and most attractive. As figure 2 (page 12) indicates, nearly two-thirds of the responding libraries had laser printers and another 21 percent hope to have them within one year. Most of these libraries, then, can produce publications of considerable quality on their laser printer and then print copies using photo duplication equipment. About 85 percent of the libraries presently active in desktop publishing had laser printers and 100 percent

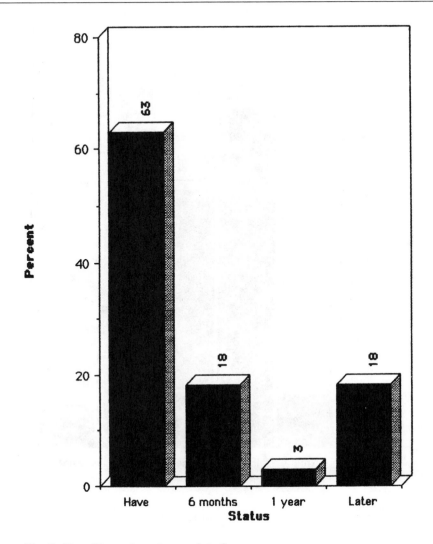

Fig. 2. Does library have laser printer?

would have them within six months. It is difficult to know if desktop publishing creates a demand for the laser printer or if availability of the laser printer creates a demand for desktop publishing, but they are associated.

Page Layout Software

Although virtually all libraries had the computer hardware required for desktop publishing, and most had the laser printer, only 33 percent had the page layout software usually associated with desktop publishing. Figure 3 indicates which page layout software packages are held. *Pagemaker* is clearly the most commonly used and is found in 77 percent of these libraries active in desktop publishing. Beinhorn, in his survey of desktop publishing for independent presses, says that *Pagemaker* "remains the standard that other desktop publishing packages must surpass."[11]

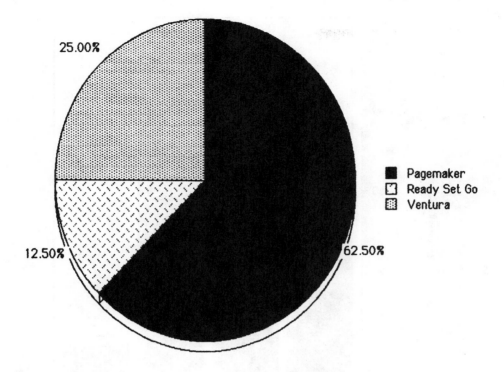

Fig. 3. Page layout software held.

While some word processing software does multiple column page layouts and allows text and graphic material to be mixed, it is not as sophisticated nor as professional as page layout software. However, two of the twelve libraries active in desktop publishing mentioned that Microsoft *Word* could be used for desktop publishing and was quite adequate. Still, it is clear that most research libraries do not now have the software to permit near professional quality publications.

Of those without page layout software, 48 percent plan to have it within one year (see figure 4, page 14). At that time, about 65 percent of the respondents would have it. We seem to be about one year away from a time when most of these research libraries will have the preconditions for desktop publishing—computer hardware and software plus the laser printer. ARL libraries appear to have recognized the value and utility of desktop publishing in their decision to purchase the necessary software.

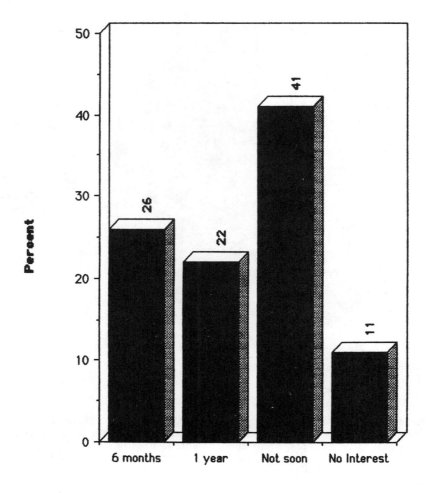

Fig. 4. When page layout software expected.

However, not everyone is ready to hop onto the bandwagon. There are thoughtful rationales for delaying entry into desktop publishing or postponing it altogether. One research librarian noted:

> We follow developments in desk top publishing very closely. We're very interested. However, our strong impression of the current state of the art is that the level of difficulty involved is too high for all but the most dedicated users. In our environment a trained operator would be required. That level of investment is out of the question.

Another librarian noted that at her library all publications were designed by professionals in a first-rate university publications office. With these experts available, there was little incentive to invest in desktop publishing. Another librarian noted that her library created high quality documents that included graphics, multiple columns, and typographic accents using Microsoft *Word*. In summary, most research libraries will soon have page layout software, but others are reluctant because of the cost of professional time and effort, attractive alternatives in the community, and satisfaction with word processing software.

Desktop Publishers

The following comments apply to those libraries that presently have and are using page layout software (N = 12 or 30 percent of the 40 respondents; another library has recently received the software, but has not yet used it).

Besides the page layout software, drawing, painting, and graphing software are often used to create high-quality illustrations and graphs which can then be imported into the page layout. About 83 percent of these libraries had drawing software, 75 percent had painting software, and 83 percent had graphing software. Digitizers may be used to scan graphic material, and make it machine readable so that it can be used in documents of one's own design. About 42 percent of these libraries had digitizers that would allow them to capture a wide variety of professionally produced illustrations and use them in their documents.

Page layout software may be used to produce camera ready copy which can be printed in the library or outside of the library. It may also be used to create machine readable documents which can then be composed and printed outside the library using such equipment as the Linotronic L300 typesetting machine for truly professional results.[12] Most (75 percent) of the libraries with page layout software use it primarily to produce copy which will be printed in the library using the laser printer and photo duplication machines. About 17 percent use page layout software primarily to produce camera ready copy to be printed outside the library. Only 8 percent use page layout software primarily to produce material which will be composed and printed outside the library.

Desktop Publishing Products

Presentation graphics were the products most (83 percent of the libraries) frequently produced using page layout software. Nearly 75 percent of the libraries produced pathfinders, bibliographies, brochures, or pamphlets. The same percentage used page layout software to produce signs. About 58 percent produced newsletters or magazines, but 76 percent hoped to do so in the future. Fifty percent produced handbooks or manuals, but 61 percent hoped to do so in the future.

Satisfaction and Ease of Use

How satisfied are these libraries with the quality of the output of their page layout software? Figure 5 (page 16) indicates considerable satisfaction, with 92 percent satisfied or strongly satisfied.

Page layout software has received considerable attention in the literature and some of these comments have indicated that the software is complex and often difficult to use, even for those quite familiar with microcomputers.[13] Reaction to software ease of use is found in figure 6 (page 17). In contrast to the difficulty suggested in the literature, 75 percent of the libraries found page layout software ease of use to be satisfactory or strongly satisfactory. This may reflect the sophistication and experience of the librarians using the software, but it is quite a positive finding for those considering purchasing page layout software.

Technical Support

It is difficult to discuss ease of use without introducing technical support. Some software is sold with inadequate documentation while other software is so complex that even good documentation is not enough. Where do these research librarians find technical support for page layout software? Nearly 75 percent found support available within their library. Fifty-eight percent had software support available on campus. About 42 percent were able to get technical support from the software company itself. Nearly 25 percent gained technical support from the published literature. Twenty-three percent were able to secure technical support from a local user's group. None of these libraries went to a local computer or software dealer for technical support. A summary evaluation of the quality of technical support for page layout software is found in figure 7 (page 18). With 75 percent characterizing support as good or excellent, getting help does not seem to be a problem. It may also be that these libraries employ professionals who are sophisticated users who require little help and puzzle things out by themselves. Berst notes that "most desk top publishing users still have a pioneer mentality—they blaze their own trails, unaware that consultants, colleagues or competitors may already have solved the same problems."[14]

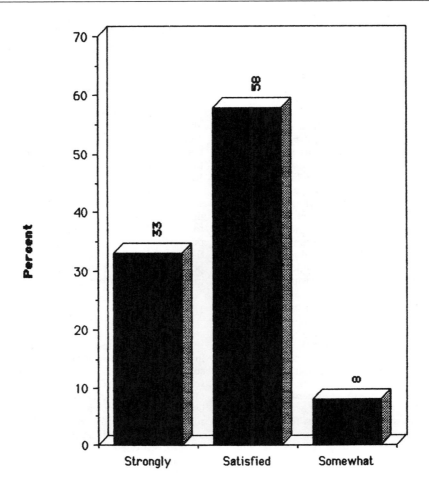

Fig. 5. Satisfaction with output quality.

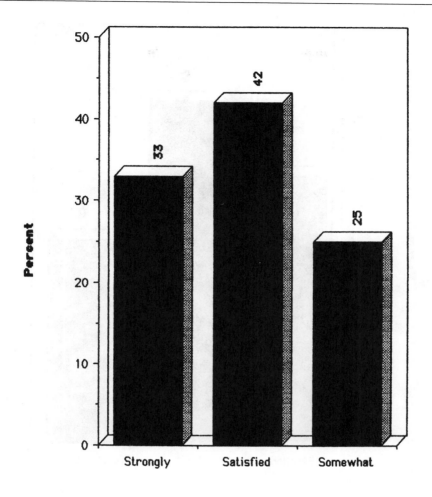

Fig. 6. Satisfaction with software ease of use.

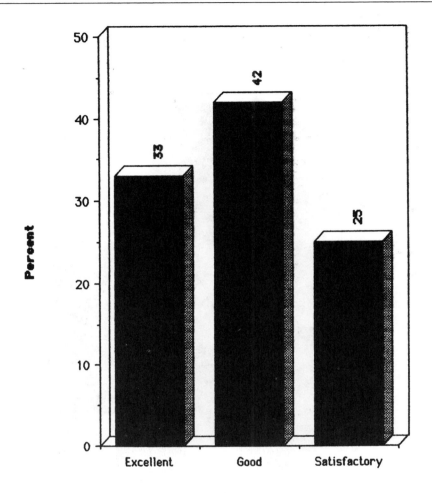

Degree of Satisfaction

Fig. 7. Quality of technical support.

Designing a page or a document with several pages may require considerable skill. The software provides the user with many options. It does not provide taste or experience in graphic arts design, including typography. Librarians using page layout software may need help with graphic arts design as well as in using the software. Nearly 73 percent of these libraries had graphic arts support available on campus. Fifty-five percent found support in the published literature. About 36 percent had support in the library and 36 percent in local user's groups. Eighteen percent found support through the software company and 9 percent through dealers. In comparing technical support for the software itself and for graphic arts design help, we find that in both cases campus and library support is widely available. The major difference is that software companies are more important sources for software support while the published literature is a much more important support for graphic arts design support.

Impact

What impact has desktop publishing had on the publication program of these libraries? The impact on the number of publications issued is seen in figure 8. About one-half of these libraries issue more publications than before. The availability of desktop publishing does seem to stimulate output and suggests that there will be more library publications in the future. The impact on the quality of publications is seen in figure 9 (page 20). About two-thirds of these libraries felt that desktop publishing had improved the quality of their publications. The impact on publication cost is seen in figure 10 (page 21). With only 17 percent of the libraries finding publication costs notably less than before, desktop publishing is hardly a cost-saving measure. This is somewhat of a contrast with the published literature which suggests that desktop publishing can save money.[15] However, with only 25 percent finding publication costs notably more than before, desktop publishing may be nearly neutral in its publication cost implications for most libraries. The final impact deals with timeliness of library publications. Nearly 75 percent of these research libraries issued their publications notably more timely than before because of desktop publishing.

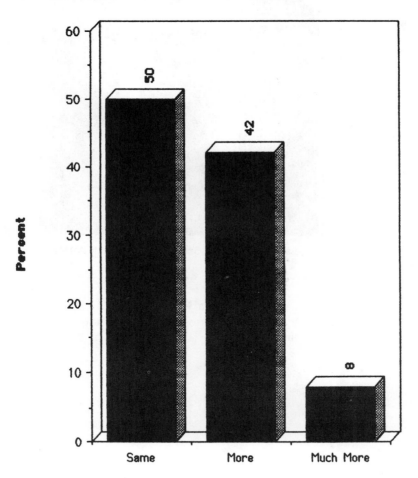

Fig. 8. Impact on number of publications.

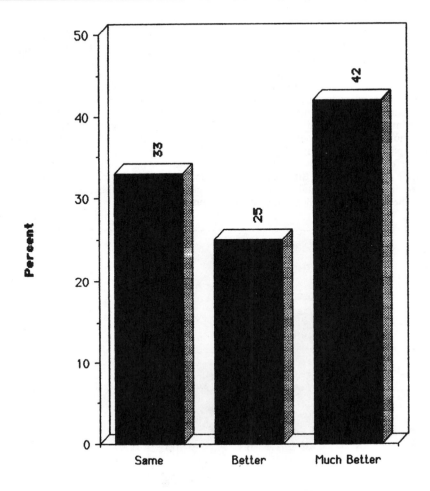

Fig. 9. Impact on publication quality.

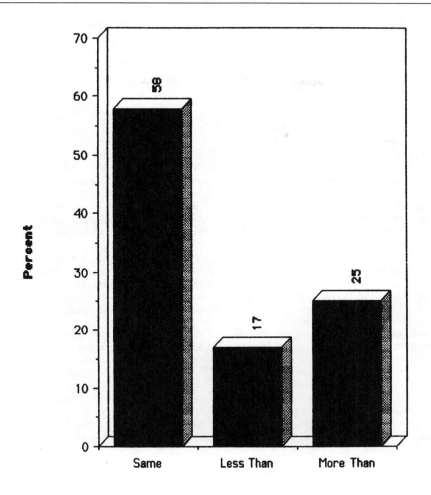

Fig. 10. Impact on publication cost.

CONCLUSIONS

It seems reasonable to assume that the desktop publishing currently seen in these ARL research libraries will trickle down to smaller, less research-oriented libraries over time. How long this might take is difficult to predict, but the relatively low cost of the computer and printer hardware suggests that it will not be long. Most academic, public, and special libraries already have an IBM or IBM clone suitable for desktop publishing, although perhaps requiring an increase in memory. Given the fact that desktop publishing began on the Macintosh and that most of the ARL libraries active in desktop publishing use the Macintosh, it seems appropriate to suggest that more libraries seriously consider acquiring the Macintosh computer. Given the importance of the laser printer in desktop publishing, libraries should also begin to plan to purchase one, particularly now that they are beginning to drop in price. If, as seems likely, library desktop publishing becomes a widespread phenomenon, library directors will need to begin planning now if desktop publishing is to be effective and efficient. Besides purchase considerations and budgeting, staff and staff education will need to receive attention, as will space. Simply buying page layout software and a laser printer and placing them on someone's desk is not likely to yield a professional publication program.

Libraries with desktop publishing also used drawing, painting, and graphing software to add illustrative material to their documents. Some of them used digitizers to scan published graphic material so that it could later be added to their publications. This suggests that there is a need to acquire this software and be proficient with it if desktop publishing is to be used to its fullest potential.

Composition and Printing

Most libraries are likely to follow the example of the libraries discussed here, doing composition on the computer and printing camera ready copy on the laser printer. Final printing is then done using photo duplication equipment. However, the computer may also be used as a front-end terminal which sends the machine readable document to a compositor for fully professional results. Libraries considering desktop publishing will need to evaluate the quality of their photo duplication equipment. They should also identify composition firms, perhaps in the local community, which can set type directly from the machine readable document. Being able to compare the cost and the quality of in-house versus professional composition and relate these to a particular publication function and audience is important in a well-managed publication program.

Future Products

It was surprising to discover that presentation graphics were the product most frequently produced by desktop publishing. Perhaps this is because several libraries acquired desktop publishing systems primarily to support bibliographic instruction programs. The popularity of bibliographies, including pathfinders, was expected and will probably account for most use of desktop publishing in the average library. While newsletters and magazines, as well as handbooks and manuals, were less popular, they remain important. With more attractive and sophisticated design and appearance, these publications should have more impact on the community served and may make the library more visible. It is hoped that more professional looking publications will encourage libraries to make them more widely available to the profession and to have them included in appropriate secondary publications.

The finding of considerable satisfaction with the quality of the product produced by desktop publishing is important. It suggests that the hoopla surrounding desktop publishing has considerable truth to it, that desktop publishing really does make a difference. Certainly the positive experience of these ARL libraries should encourage other libraries to follow their example.

Problems

While the ARL libraries using desktop publishing found ease of use to be satisfactory, this finding may need to be accepted with some caution. These larger libraries may have on their staff professionals who are more experienced, interested, and comfortable with computer software than the designated computer person in the smaller library. There is no doubt that page layout software is complex and requires considerable attention to detail. It is not intuitive and a considerable learning curve may be required before suitable products are produced. It seems important to note that many librarians will require a reasonable amount of education if they are to use page layout software efficiently and effectively. This may be an appropriate challenge for our professional associations: to implement a series of workshops on desktop publishing for libraries that will provide hands-on experience and provide others with an opportunity to learn from the mistakes and successes of the pioneers.

When software is complex, availability of technical support is important if use is not to be frustrating and painful. Snags are inevitable. These ARL libraries were able to find help in the library or on campus. Library help may be less likely in smaller libraries where the person using the software is the only computer "expert" on the staff. Certainly, a library considering desktop publishing would be well advised to identify others on campus presently involved with it and attempt to develop an appropriate relationship to facilitate learning.

It is important to stress that technical support is also needed to answer queries about graphic arts or design issues. Without some graphic arts training or advice, desktop publishing could be used to produce absolutely dreadful material. Widespread personal reading in the literature, discussions with graphic designs specialists on campus, and considerable experimentation may be necessary for effective use of desktop publishing. Libraries need to consider how they will meet these needs before they purchase the hardware and the software. It is particularly important that the individual who is asked to use the page layout software be given adequate released time to develop strength in the graphic arts.

Impact and Planning

The impact of desktop publishing in these libraries is clear:

- More publications are being produced.

- Better publications are being produced.

- More timely publications are being produced.

Surely this is a persuasive call for the more widespread use of desktop publishing in libraries. The impact of desktop publishing on cost is muddied, but the literature suggests that over time publishing costs may be reduced if the library had previously composed and printed its publications outside the library. If the function of the publication and the audience allow it, using the laser printer and photoduplication to compose and print in-house should be less expensive than having these done elsewhere.

Given the likelihood that many more libraries will become involved with desktop publishing, it is necessary to stress the importance of publication planning. As more and more librarians become familiar with the quality of the product, demand for in-house publications will increase substantially. One of the respondents made this point most effectively:

> Because our desk top publishing setup is the only one available in a large academic library, we have been contacted for many graphic applications beyond our primary responsibilities [library instruction]. Suddenly we are in the unenviable position of saying no to valued peers who have made requests for flow charts of job duties, preparation of personal professional materials, production of graphics for a grant. Desk top publishing is a wonderful thing that apparently everyone needs! Beware the lucky library unit that gets such a system. It's great to be popular, but ...!

Without planning and coordination, this situation seems inevitable and it could produce morale problems if some librarians feel that colleagues receive special treatment in having access to desktop publishing while they do not. Libraries need to consider the likely demand for desktop publishing products and plan accordingly. If there is to be but one workstation, then publication priorities need to be decided upon and widely shared with the staff.

Desktop publishing in libraries has arrived. We are probably one or two years away from its widespread use, but it seems inevitable that most larger libraries will soon be able to produce timely, attractive publications in-house. Most of these publications will be presentation graphics, bibliographies, pamphlets, and signs. But there should be some handbooks and manuals too. With better bibliographic control, these items could be used by and useful to a large number of librarians. Desktop publishing may even strengthen research and development in libraries by allowing timely, attractive, and inexpensive dissemination of results to the professional community.

NOTES

[1] John W. Perkins, "The Public Library as Publisher," *Library Journal* 103 (May 15, 1978): 1031.

[2] Jane L. Nelson, "An Academic Library Publications Committee: Twelve Years Later," *College and Research Libraries* 38 (July 1977): 317.

[3] Jesse Berst, "The Latest Word in Desk Top Publishing," *Publishers Weekly* 232 (November 13, 1987): 26.

[4] Charles Anderson, "Using Software," *Wilson Library Bulletin* 62 (January 1987): 48.

[5] Berst, 28.

[6] Berst, 28.

[7] Berst, 29.

[8] Berst, 26; Thomas J. DeLoughery, "Personal Computers and Laser Printers Are Becoming Popular Tools for Creating Documents on Campuses," *Chronicle of Higher Education* 34 (September 16, 1987): A115.

[9] Scott W. Tilden as quoted in DeLoughery, A115.

[10] George R. Beinhorn, "Desk Top Publishing for Independent Presses," *Publishers Weekly* 232 (November 13, 1987): 32.

[11] Beinhorn, 30.

[12] Ibid.

[13] Scott W. Tilden as quoted in DeLoughery, A115.

[14] Berst, 29.

[15] Greg Holden as quoted in DeLoughery, A116.

Controlled Circulation Serials

Nancy J. Butkovich and Marjorie Peregoy

The 1980s have been a decade of professional belt-tightening among serials librarians. In response to economic pressures manifested by static or declining budgets combined with rapidly rising costs, librarians have been forced to reexamine their serial subscriptions and identify publications of greatest value to libraries and patrons.

One category of publication that might come under close scrutiny is the controlled circulation serial. This article provides a definition of these special publications, analyzes their characteristics, and examines their roles, particularly in academic libraries.

Controlled circulation serials are serial publications in that they are "issued in successive parts bearing numerical or chronological designations and [are] intended to be continued indefinitely."[1] They are, however, a distinct subclass of serials in that they have specific restrictions placed on them concerning distribution, intended audience, and, depending on the definition, amount of advertising.

The ALA Glossary of Library and Information Science defines a controlled circulation journal as

A serial financed largely by advertising and available (usually without charge) only to those specified by the authors or publishers. According to the U.S. Postal Service [it is] a journal which is issued at regular intervals of four or more times a year, each issue of which consists of at least 24 pages containing no more than 75% of advertising, and which is not conducted as an auxiliary to and essentially for the advancement of the main business or calling of the business organization or individual who owns or controls it.[2]

For the purposes of this article, we will use the *ALA Glossary* definition because it identifies the criteria which are common to nearly all the definitions examined. These include availability to a specific audience designated by the publisher, a continuing subscription at little or no cost, and the presence of advertising. Other definitions examined include those in Brownstone and Franck,[3] Prytherch,[4] and *Ulrich's International Periodicals Directory.*[5]

The U.S. Postal Service identifies classes of mail for determination of correct postage rates and requires that all serials have an identifying number, preferably the International Standard Serial Number (ISSN), in order to qualify for second class postage rates.[6] The Postal Service definition is necessary because controlled circulation serials have special rates within the second class schedule.[7]

Controlled circulation serials exist because they are perceived to be effective vehicles for advertisers to present their products to potential buyers, although usually informative articles of interest to the readers are also present. Vendors subsidize publication costs so that the journal can be made available at little or no cost to persons whose professional connections put them in positions to purchase advertised items. Tiered pricing systems are often used for those who do not meet the publishers' criteria for free distribution.[8] Reader response cards are frequently included in order to facilitate the transfer of requests for information about advertised products from the reader to the vendor.[9]

Nearly all controlled circulation serials spell out the exact terms of eligibility. In addition to control by job description, geographic location can be a limiting factor. A fairly typical statement is the one appearing in *Construction Plant & Equipment*:

Applications for free copies of *Construction Plant & Equipment* are considered within the UK from specifiers and buyers of the construction team; main contractors; sub contractors; plant hire companies; local authorities; government departments and quarry and mine operators.[10]

Persons who wish to subscribe but who do not meet the specifications must pay the full subscription rate. However, a few journals, such as *Drilling*, add a third tier for those who do not meet the stated criteria, but who are actively employed in related positions within the industry. These people may receive the journal at a rate lower than that quoted to persons outside the industry.[11]

Since the journal is essentially the product of an agreement between the publisher and the vendor, vendors have a large degree of control over the journal's distribution. It is in the best interests of the publisher to keep an up-to-date mailing list of recipients of free subscriptions, since vendors frequently examine these records to ensure that the correct audience is being targeted. Records are kept current by periodic requests that the readership express its interest in and eligibility for free subscriptions by using reader response cards.[12]

Whether or not a library can receive a controlled circulation journal and at what cost depends on the case made by the library to the publisher for meeting the subscription specifications set by the publisher and vendors. In this respect a corporate library might be seen as having an advantage over a public or academic library in that the publisher is not as interested in having a wide readership as in having the right readership.[13]

The Sterling C. Evans Library of Texas A & M University is a medium-sized research library of approximately 1.6 million volumes serving a patron base of about 32,000 undergraduates, 7,000 graduates, and 2,000 faculty members. It currently subscribes to approximately 14,000 serial titles, which are housed in open stacks. Because of the traditional strengths of the university, the majority of these titles are in fields related to the sciences, technology, and agriculture, and many have controlled circulation. We have tried to select a representative sample from the "T" schedule (technology) of the Library of Congress Classification system, which we will analyze and compare with an earlier study of controlled circulation medical journals.

Our criteria for use and value evaluation included whether or not the title was indexed, number of holding libraries, listing in *Ulrich's*, mention in *Science Citation Index*, and availability of microformat versions. The number of holding libraries was established using OCLC records, while the availability of microformat versions was determined using a combination of OCLC records, *Ulrich's* listings, and notices in the journals themselves.

For local use data we considered the treatment given to the title at Evans Library. These factors include length of time copies are retained and whether or not older volumes are bound. We recognize that the reasons for retaining a title for the current year only can be two-sided, indicating either relatively little value, or that the information contained in the journal is of great value for a short period of time but rapidly becomes obsolete. Other factors examined were the number of subscriptions to a given title and whether or not microform holdings were kept. Informally, we also looked for missing pages, reader response cards, degree of "tatteredness," and other similar indications of patron use. The titles selected for study are arranged in figure 1 by LC classification.

LC Classification	Serial Title
T (General technology)	*High Technology* *Informationweek* *Iron Age Metal Producer*
TA (General engineering; General civil engineering)	*Civil Engineering* *Construction Plant & Equipment* *Consulting-Specifying Engineer* *Engineering and Mining Journal* *Materials Handling News* *Test Engineering and Management*
TD (Environmental technology; Sanitary engineering)	*Better Roads* *European Water and Sewage* *Pollution Engineering* *Water and Waste Treatment*
TE (Highway engineering)	*Highway and Heavy Construction* *Roads and Bridges*
TF (Railroad engineering and operation)	*Railway Age*
TH (Building construction)	*Equipment Today* *Multi-Housing News* *Wood 'N' Energy*
TJ (Mechanical engineering)	*Machinery and Production Engineering* *Power*
TK (Electrical engineering; Electronics; Nuclear engineering)	*Electrical Engineer* (Australia) *Electrical World* *Electronic Engineering* *Government Computer News*
TN (Mining engineering; Metallurgy)	*Drilling* *Materials Engineering* *OG&PE: Oil, Gas and Petrochem Equipment*
TP (Chemical technology)	*Ceramic Industry* *Food Processing* *Process Engineering* *Processing*
TS (Manufactures)	*European Rubber Journal* *Textile World* *Timber Harvesting*
TT (Handicrafts; Arts and crafts)	*Industrial Finishing*
TX (Home economics)	*Food Manufacture* *Prepared Foods* *Resort and Hotel Management*

Fig. 1. Controlled circulation serials by LC Classification.

The value of a journal is greatly reduced if there is no convenient way to gain access to its intellectual content. A frequently used form of access is the indexing or abstracting source. These publications, serials in their own right, most commonly arrange bibliographic citations according to subject or author, allowing order to be imposed on the content of the journals indexed. Figure 2 is a breakdown of the frequency of appearance of the sampled journals in indexing sources. Data for figure 2 were collected from OCLC records,[14] *Ulrich's* entries,[15] and the journals themselves.

# journals (n = 40)	% of total journals	# of indexing sources
6	15.0	over 15
7	17.5	11-15
8	20.0	6-10
13	32.5	1-5
6	15.0	0

Fig. 2. Frequency of journals in indexing or abstracting sources.

Because of the emphasis given to advertising by the publishers of these journals, we did not expect many of them to be indexed. An earlier study on controlled circulation medical journals by Key, Sholtz, and Roland suggested that a sizable percentage would not be.[16] They reported that of the twenty-five journals they examined, thirteen (52 percent) were not indexed at all, and only four were indexed by the major medical source, *Index Medicus*. Our study, on the other hand, produced only six titles (15 percent) out of forty which were not indexed, while 85 percent were indexed in at least one source. Over half (52.5 percent) were covered by six or more indexes, and one, *Food Manufacture*, was included in twenty sources.

Figure 3 looks at the same question from a different perspective. In it, the number of indexing and abstracting services are arranged by the number of journals in our study which are included in each source. As with figure 2, the data for this table came from OCLC records,[17] *Ulrich's*,[18] and the journals themselves.

# of indexing sources	# of journals in each source
1	19
1	17
1	15
1	14
1	12
2	11
1	9
2	8
5	7
3	6
5	5
8	4
7	3
15	2
22	1

Fig. 3. Indexing and abstracting sources arranged by number of journals included.

Thirty-four of the forty journals examined were indexed by seventy-five indexing and abstracting services. Just under half of these sources (49.3 percent) each listed only one or two of the journals. On the other hand, *Chemical Abstracts* indexed nineteen titles. *Engineering Index* was close behind, covering seventeen titles, and *PROMT* and *Excerpta Medica* indexed fourteen and twelve titles, respectively. This would suggest that, unlike the medical journals, controlled circulation technology journals are well represented in the indexing and abstracting sources.

With this high level of coverage, we expected to find a much higher percentage of articles cited for these journals than did Key, Sholtz, and Roland, who noted little evidence that the journals were cited, although they were frequently read.[19] Instead, an examination of the *Science Citation Index* yielded only three titles cited, *Engineering and Mining Journal, Food Manufacture*, and *Electronic Engineering*.[20]

There are several reasons why this low citation rate could occur, including journal title changes and journals which only recently began publication. Although we took these factors into account, we suspect that, like those in Key, Sholtz, and Roland, our journals "are seldom quoted in primary scientific journals but may be widely read and used."[21] This is confirmed by the impact factors of the journals which were cited in 1986. *Science Citation Index* defines the impact factor of a journal as

a measure of the frequency with which the "average article" in a journal has been cited in a particular year. The *JCR* impact factor is basically a ratio between citations and citable items published.[22]

Engineering and Mining Journal had the highest impact factor, 0.03, while the other two were listed as 0.01, indicating a very low impact on technical literature.[23]

All journals examined were in the OCLC database,[24] and all had ISSNs. However, not all were listed in *Ulrich's International Periodicals Directory*, a major information source for librarians published by R. R. Bowker.[25] Five (12.5 percent) were absent, possibly as a result of title changes, of being newly published, or because the publisher of the journal did not send the publishing information to *Ulrich's* for inclusion. Only eleven of the titles included mentioned controlled circulation, most likely the result of the journal publishers not having provided Bowker with the information.

Reader response cards were present in all but one of the titles, that being *Information-week*. This was slightly more than the 80 percent noted by Bottle and Emery in their study of response times of reply cards in selected controlled circulation chemical and technological journals.[26] The response cards have a dual purpose in most journals, serving not only to provide a convenient way for readers to express interest in the products being advertised, but also for readers to fill out if they are interested in receiving the journal free. The card, then, can act as a vehicle for determining the eligibility of the reader to receive the journal within the conditions of the controlled circulation. Several journals had their conditions of control on the reader response card and not in the publishers information block with the other subscription information.

We chose not to do a survey of other libraries asking for their policies concerning retention of controlled circulation journals. Our primary reason was the problem of obtaining a sample that would be sufficiently large to be representative without becoming unwieldy. Instead, we would like to indicate what has been done at the Sterling C. Evans Library.

Since journal subscription costs are based on the job descriptions of the subscribers, the question arises of how institutional costs fit into the pricing structure. The assumption prior to examining our records was that most controlled circulation serials would be "freebies." Upon examining acquisition records, however, we found this to be erroneous. Evans Library receives only three of the forty titles at no charge. These are *European Water and Sewage, Government Computer News*, and *Well Servicing*. For the remaining thirty-four titles, Evans Library pays the full subscription rates. The titles are received through our serials vendors with any jobber discounts which may apply.

A second assumption was that these titles would, for the most part, be retained only a short time because of their emphasis on advertising rather than on scholarly work. We began to suspect that this might not be the case when we realized the degree of indexing given the journals in our sample. An examination of acquisitions and binding records confirmed this. Only three titles, *Government Computer News, Informationweek,* and *Well Servicing*, are retained for the current year only; the other thirty-four titles are bound and placed in the stacks. Evans Library currently does not have duplicate subscriptions to any of the forty titles.

Twenty-four (60 percent) of the titles surveyed are also available in microformat;

however, Evans Library maintains microfilm holdings of seven of these (17.5 percent). These seven are retained in both formats, indicating a fairly significant demand for at least some of the titles. All titles examined are routed to the Current Periodicals Department (CPD) rather than directly to the stacks, indicating that immediate access is a factor in their usefulness to our collection.

At Evans Library journals which are sent to the CPD remain there for one year prior to being either bound or discarded. Current journals circulate without any restrictions within the building; they circulate outside the building only to faculty and graduate students for four-hour blocks of time. Bound journals may be checked out for four-hour time blocks by faculty, graduates, and undergraduates. Records are not available for determining the frequency of circulation by call number or title for any serial publication; however, informal examination of current issues in the CPD and bound issues in the stacks indicate that the controlled circulation journals in our sample are used. This informal observation includes such factors as missing reader response cards, appearance on re-shelving trucks, and general level of "tatteredness" of the issues.

Key, Sholtz, and Roland noted that there was little demand for controlled circulation medical journals after one year.[27] Without having any specific quantitative evidence to support us, we would like to suggest that this may not be the case for the journals in our study. We offer two reasons for this claim. First, the medical journals were examined in the context of a medical special library, while ours were studied from the standpoint of an academic research library. This rapid rate of obsolescence is fairly common in special libraries, where older materials are regularly weeded.[28] Academic libraries, on the other hand, are seen as depositories which "*preserve*, and make available the full record of human knowledge."[29] Second, the level of indexing given each of the two categories of journals suggests that the older volumes of technology journals would receive higher use in an academic library simply because there is greater access to the intellectual content of the journals. This question of usage of older volumes of controlled circulation technology journals in academic libraries would be an interesting area for further research.

A study of controlled circulation journals can be of value in assessing the composition of a library's total serials collection. The wide variety of subject matter covered and emphasis on current technology make these journals valuable; however, the level of value will vary depending on the purposes of the library in which they are being evaluated. These include curricula support and research in academic libraries, local industry and the general population for public libraries, and corporate goals and objectives for special libraries. Since controlled circulation journals are aimed at a specific professional audience and serve both as an advertising medium and as a vehicle for substantive articles, they have a definite place in all three types of libraries.

These journals, at least in the various fields of technology, are widely indexed in a substantial number of major indexes, thus providing convenient access to the content of these journals. However, the journals themselves appear to have only a minimal impact on scholarly literature, if frequency of citation is used as a criterion.

Controlled circulation journals are generally thought of as being "freebies." This is not true for most libraries, since they usually have to pay the full cost of subscriptions, because they do not meet the control specifications set by the publishers and the vendors.

In conclusion these journals blend unobtrusively into library collections and are not usually considered as a separate category of serial publication. Neither their formats, nor the ephemeral nature of much of their contents make them necessarily any less valuable to a collection, nor should they be automatic candidates to succumb to budget cuts. Controlled circulation serials, taken as a group, are worthy of study, since they are of value to libraries as well as patrons.

NOTES

[1]*Anglo-American Cataloguing Rules*, ed. Michael Gorman and Paul W. Winkler (Chicago: American Library Association, 1978), 570.

[2]*The ALA Glossary of Library and Information Science*, ed. Heartsill Young (Chicago: American Library Association, 1983), 58-59.

[3]David M. Brownstone and Irene M. Franck, *The Dictionary of Publishing* (New York: Van Nostrand Reinhold Co., 1982), 76.

[4]Ray Prytherch, *Harrod's Librarians' Glossary* (Brookfield, Vt.: Gower Publishing Co., 1984), 195.

[5]*Ulrich's International Periodicals Directory* (New York: R. R. Bowker, 1986), xii.

[6]National Serials Data Program, *ISSN Fact Sheet* (Washington, D.C.: Library of Congress, 1982), 1.

[7]"New Rates and Fees," *Postal Bulletin*, no. 21493 (January 9, 1985): 13.

[8]Paul Mayes, *Periodical Administration in Libraries* (Hamden, Conn.: Linnet Books, 1978), 15.

[9]Donald Edward Davidson, *The Periodical Collection* (London: Andre Deutsch Ltd., 1978), 64.

[10]*Construction Plant & Equipment* 15, no. 11 (1987): 3.

[11]*Drilling* 48, no. 3 (1987): 1.

[12]R. J. Findlay and W. Streatford, "Controlled Circulation Journals," *ASLIB Proceedings* 23, no. 6 (1971): 279.

[13]Ibid., 285.

[14]*OCLC* (Dublin, Ohio: Online Computer Library Center), OCLC nos. 1448176, 1519687, 1553730, 1567749, 1569649, 1642767, 1753088, 1762742, 1776298, 1798500, 1855790, 1969615, 2065189, 2242332, 2355166, 2421457, 2566889, 2619162, 2704067, 2850415, 3536224, 3773862, 4433661, 5137935, 7013136, 7079509, 7804475, 7811258, 8538292, 9369246, 9423548, 9901500, 10665942, 11552104, 11636008, 11660022, 12995889, 13507890, 14584358, 15127428.

[15]*Ulrich's International Periodicals Directory*, 36, 213, 215, 218, 372, 470, 588-89, 628-32, 638, 644, 688-89, 693, 707, 841, 1027-28, 1177, 1208, 1258, 1270, 1274, 1277, 1419, 1505, 1610, 1615, 1623, 1693.

[16]Jack D. Key, Katherine J. Sholtz, and Charles G. Roland, "The Controlled Circulation Journal in Medicine: Rx or Rogue?" *Serials Librarian* 4, no. 1 (1987): 17.

[17]*OCLC* (Dublin, Ohio: Online Computer Library Center), OCLC nos. 1448176, 1519687, 1553730, 1567749, 1569649, 1642767, 1753088, 1762742, 1776298, 1798500, 1855790, 1969615, 2065189, 2242332, 2355166, 2421457, 2566889, 2619162, 2704067, 3536224, 3773862, 4433661, 5137935, 7013136, 7079509, 7804475, 7811258, 8538292, 9369246, 9423548, 9901500, 10665942, 11636008, 13507890.

[18]*Ulrich's International Periodicals Directory*, 36, 213, 218, 372, 470, 588-89, 628-32, 638, 644, 688-89, 693, 707, 841, 1027-28, 1177, 1208, 1258, 1270, 1274, 1277, 1419, 1505, 1610, 1615, 1623, 1693.

[19]Key, Sholtz, and Roland, 17.

[20]*Science Citation Index: Journal Citation Reports, Cited Journal Listing*, ed. Eugene Garfield (Philadelphia: Institute for Scientific Information, 1987), v. 20, 1828, 1833, 1865.

[21]Key, Sholtz, and Roland, 17.

[22]*Science Citation Index: Journal Citation Reports, Cited Journal Listing*, ed. Eugene Garfield (Philadelphia: Institute for Scientific Information, 1986), v. 18, 12A.

[23]*Science Citation Index: Journal Citation Report, Cited Journal Listing*, v. 20, 1828, 1833, 1865.

[24]*OCLC* (Dublin, Ohio: Online Computer Library Center), OCLC nos. 1448176, 1519687, 1553730, 1567749, 1569649, 1642767, 1753088, 1762742, 1776298, 1798500, 1855790, 1969615, 2065189, 2242332, 2355166, 2421457, 2566889, 2619162, 2704067, 2850415, 3536224, 3773862, 4433661, 5137935, 7013136, 7079509, 7804475, 7811258, 8538292, 9369246, 9423548, 9901500, 10665942, 11552104, 11636008, 11660022, 12995889, 13507890, 14584358, 15127428.

[25]*Ulrich's International Periodicals Directory*, 36, 213, 215, 218, 372, 470, 588-89, 628-32, 638, 644, 688-89, 693, 707, 841, 1027-28, 1177, 1208, 1258, 1270, 1274, 1277, 1419, 1505, 1610, 1615, 1623, 1693.

[26]Robert T. Bottle and Betty L. Emery, "Information Transfer by Reader Service Cards: A Response Time Analysis," *Special Libraries* 62, no. 11 (1971): 469.

[27]Key, Sholtz, and Roland, 20.

[28]Ellis Mount, *Special Libraries and Information Centers: An Introductory Text* (New York: Special Libraries Association, 1983), 132.

[29]G. Edward Evans, *Developing Library Collections* (Littleton, Colo.: Libraries Unlimited, 1979), 219.

Collection Development for Government Publications

Gary R. Purcell

The concept of collection development, as applied to government publications, is relatively new to the practice of librarianship in the United States. The literature concerned with this matter only dates back to the latter part of the 1970s, and the first publication to deal with this as the central topic was a special issue of *Government Publications Review*, published in 1981.[1] Thus, only a small body of literature addresses the need for and the problems associated with the development of collections of government publications. This article will define the concept of collection development as it applies to government publications, identify and characterize the major factors that affect it, and discuss various methods that have been proposed for improving the quality of collection development for government publications, particularly in federal depository libraries.

DEFINITION OF COLLECTION DEVELOPMENT

The concept of "collection development" as used and understood in the 1980s has been described as the result of an "evolution in the thinking about the role of the library and its staff in relation to the library collection."[2] This concept has evolved from and represents a conceptual expansion of the earlier concepts of "selection" and "collection building."[3] A general definition of collection development by McClure provides a useful context for this examination of the application of the concept to government publications. McClure defined it in this way:

> Collection development is more than the selection and acquisition of materials. It is a decision making process that determines specific materials that will be obtained in terms of subject content, format and other criteria. A collection development policy is a plan that provides guidelines to the selectors as to the appropriateness of various types of materials for a particular collection. As such, it is a framework by which all the various departments in the library work toward common collection goals and standards.[4]

The broader concept of collection development was not applied to government publications until later than other components of library collections. However, various authors have established the need to integrate collection development principles for government documents holdings into the overall collection development plan for the library.[5] Thus, the priorities that govern the development of other components of the collection of a library should also govern the choice of government publications to be added to the holdings of the library. The same should be true of decisions regarding the retention of materials. The ideal government publications collection development policy is one that is totally integrated into the general policy of the library.

TOTAL LIBRARY INTEGRATION OF GOVERNMENT PUBLICATIONS

The notion of integrating government publications into a library's general collection development policy is actually part of a larger issue, namely the total integration of government publications into the library's collection. This level of integration is defined by Hernon and McClure to include (1) equality of bibliographic accessibility, (2) equality of physical availability, (3) equality of the level of professional service provided for government publications, and (4) equality of the status (or level of resource support) provided for government publications.[6] Although this level of equality has been achieved in some libraries, it is still a distant goal for most. The integration of government documents into the general collection development policy for any library is a significant first step to achieve total integration.

The notion of integrated collection development for government publications is gaining acceptance, at least in the literature of the profession. However, two major, seemingly contradictory circumstances tend to mediate against the actual implementation of this goal, at least in U.S. federal depository libraries. The first is the fact that the majority of depository libraries, and many nondepository libraries give government publications separate treatment.[7] This results from the fact that government publications are acquired in a different fashion from other library materials. In the case of federal depositories, government publications are acquired in a "passive" manner, through selection from a list of more than 6,000 categories (called item numbers). The selection and reception of government publications through this passive mechanism results in the acquisition of many publications that receive little or no use. Closely related to this is the fact that depository libraries are not charged for the publications, thus giving the illusion of the potential for increasing the collection at little or no additional cost.

The second barrier is the fact that both depository and nondepository libraries must acquire many of their government publications by purchase. This includes federal government documents not distributed through the depository system and most publications issued by levels of government other than the federal government (e.g., U.S. state and local government, foreign governments, and intergovernmental organizations). As the quality of bibliographic control for many of these publications is poor, adequate information for the identification and acquisition of most government documents of this type is lacking. The resources that provide current awareness of government publications tend to give fragmented and incomplete coverage. This situation results in a lack of awareness of the pertinence of many of these publications to collection development goals of libraries, and thus, most publications from these sources are overlooked. The result is that many libraries either overlook government publications as possible information resources or determine that their acquisition is too costly.

FACTORS AFFECTING GOVERNMENT PUBLICATIONS COLLECTION DEVELOPMENT

As the library profession has come to accept the notion of collection development for government publications, the major issue to be addressed in the last five years has been how to implement it in an effective, economical fashion. Five major factors that have an impact on the effective implementation of a government publications collection development program are identified below, with a brief characterization of this impact. Some of these are closely related to the barriers mentioned previously.

Federal Depository or a Nondepository Library

Perhaps the most significant factor pertinent to government publications collection development is whether or not the library is a depository for U.S. federal government publications. This is significant for most libraries because federal depositories typically have more staff members assigned to work with public documents than do nondepositories. This is justified by the additional volume of documents they deal with. With a larger number of staff members assigned to work with public documents, many depository libraries can give increased attention to a collection development policy for government publications. The greater volume of government publications received by depository libraries provides an increased justification for separate attention in the collection development policy to this component.

Level of Government of Publications Collected

A second factor relevant to library government publications collection development policies is the level of government for which official publications will be collected. To what extent will state, federal, local government, intergovernmental, and international documents be collected?

The needs of the clientele of the library, the resources available, and the nature and size of the library must be governing factors in determining the levels of government from which official publications will be collected. For example, a municipal public library should have the primary responsibility for collecting publications of the city and county government in which it is located. Similarly, an academic library with a strong curriculum in South Asian Studies should collect the official publications of countries in this region of the world.

Acquisition of Nondepository Publications

A third factor is the large number of government publications published by the U.S. federal government, and most of the state, local, foreign, and intergovernmental organizations that are not distributed through any type of depository system. This means that even federal depository libraries must make a conscious effort to identify and acquire these publications if they fall into the library's collection development profile. Librarians in federal depositories have a distinct advantage over their colleagues in nondepository libraries because of the large percentage of documents distributed through the depository system. However, in the collection of nondepository publications, much of that advantage disappears.

Microformat Distribution

A fourth factor that has an impact on collection development of government publications is the increasing percentage of items distributed in microform by the U.S. federal government and by private publishers such as Congressional Information Service. This also applies to publications of state and local governments, foreign governments, and intergovernmental organizations. The questions faced by libraries that relate to this issue are: whether to acquire publications in microform or paper copy, and whether

it is cost-effective to purchase large, often expensive sets of microform collections of government publications (some of which are duplicates of items that the library might already receive without cost as depository items). In considering the policy collecting government publications in microform, the same criteria should be applied as with paper copy publications.[8]

Cost of Government Publications Compared to Their Use

A fifth factor pertinent to collection development is the question of the volume of use of government publications compared to the effort necessary to acquire and make them available for use. The question is whether it is cost-effective to acquire government publications. Although these publications are usually inexpensive to purchase, the cost of identifying and maintenance can be substantial. If documents are not used at a level comparable to other materials, as some studies show, their acquisition might not be cost-effective.[9] This, of course, raises questions about inclusion of public documents in a collection development policy. The answers to these questions are closely related to the differences that exist among libraries, in their treatment of government documents, and particularly on the extent to which each library provides bibliographic and/ or physical integration of government publications with the main body of the collection.

These factors in many cases are intertwined, thus complicating the government publications collection development decision making process. The result is that, even with increased attention to the issue of collection development, there is still no clear-cut consensus among documents librarians about the preferred approaches to collection development. However, there is a discernible increase in the realization that methods are needed to facilitate collection development. Various approaches that deal with the factors mentioned above have been implemented or proposed to make collection development more rational and better suited to the individual needs of the clientele served by each library. Hernon and McClure have proposed a good strategy for designing and implementing a government publications collection development policy.[10] Examples from specific libraries as well as a model documents collection development policy can be found in the work by Hernon and Purcell.[11] These two sources can be useful for libraries considering the development of a documents collection development policy.

ISSUES RELATED TO GOVERNMENT PUBLICATIONS COLLECTION DEVELOPMENT

The remainder of this article provides a discussion of issues related to various aspects of government publications collection development.

The U.S. federal government constitutes only one of the several levels of government which libraries consider for collection development. Nevertheless, for most libraries in the United States, it is the most important in terms of both the number of titles acquired and the type of information obtained.

The most important factor relevant to collection development for this level of government is whether the library is a federal depository library or a nondepository library.

The differences in collection development strategies for depository publications faced by these two classes of libraries are striking. Selective depository libraries (which constitute the vast majority) must select from more than 6,000 categories (known as "item numbers"), which will then be sent on a "standing order" basis, without cost. The depository library does not pay for the titles received, and they do not own the publications. Ownership of the publications resides with the U.S. government, and stringent policies regarding the discarding of these publications apply.

Depository libraries have a wide range of choices in terms of the publications they can receive. However, their decision making is restricted by the fact that frequently two or more publication series are grouped together within a single item number. In order for a library to receive a desired document series, it might be necessary to receive one or more that are not desired. Thus, the depository library must select its collection based on item number categories rather than individual series. Although the Government Printing Office, the agency responsible for administering the depository system, has split many of the series in recent years, many are still grouped together in this fashion.

Depository libraries are faced with another collection development problem. The information about existing or new document series is often limited, and with more than 6,000 choices available, librarians faced with the responsibility of making the choices are often ill-prepared to make informed ones. This has prompted the development of a number of strategies to assist documents libraries in making choices. The major strategies are discussed below, following a characterization of the nature of nondepository collection development.

Nondepository libraries are varied in nature, ranging from small libraries to some that are very large. They also include all types of libraries (public, academic, special, and school). The characteristic that is common to all nondepository libraries is that they do not benefit from the automatic distribution program of the Government Printing Office. However, they do retain the right to discard any government publications without having to follow federal guidelines.

Because nondepository libraries do not receive publications through an automatic distribution system, they must acquire their publications in one of the following ways. They can purchase them from the GPO (Government Printing Office), they might be placed on the mailing list of a federal agency and receive publications through a limited system of automatic distribution, they might acquire them from a federal document distribution agency such as that maintained by the Department of Agriculture, they might acquire them directly from the publishing agency, they might acquire them on a standing order basis from a vendor of paper copy documents such as UNIPUB-Bernan, or they might acquire them from a microform publisher. For out-of-print documents, they must go through the normal out-of-print vendors. Depository libraries, of course, have all of these same options for duplicate copies or for nondepository items, but nondepository libraries must use these sources for all of their U.S. government publications.

Depository and nondepository libraries alike are faced with a difficult task in identifying and acquiring nondepository publications. These publications are varied in nature, and are less likely to be reported in standard bibliographic publications. The *Monthly Catalog*, the most comprehensive bibliographic record of newly published U.S. government publications, lists many nondepository items.[12] However, others are only listed in the catalogs or other announcements of the publishing agencies. It is particularly difficult to identify publications produced by agency printing plants located in regional or district offices. The consequence is that identification and acquisition of nondepository items is a time-consuming and often frustrating activity for depository and nondepository libraries.

A notable exception to this problem is the distribution of technical report literature, particularly through the National Technical

Information Service. Technical report literature will not be discussed at length here, except to note that a substantial amount of government-sponsored research and development results are reported through this medium. For a fuller discussion of technical report literature see McClure, Hernon, and Purcell.[13]

Depository librarians have articulated several strategies for facilitating the selection and collection development process. These strategies, which can also be used by nondepository libraries, include the creation of core lists, circulation studies, and user studies.

The creation of *core lists* of document series or item numbers has been developed as a strategy to enable depository libraries, particularly medium and small depositories, to maximize their selection of those government publications that have high reference value or are likely to have high usage. The basic and "official" core list is one developed by the Depository Library Council and published in the *Guidelines for the Depository Library System, Appendix A*.[14] This list includes titles recommended for all depositories, but compliance in the acquisition of these titles is not mandatory.

Other core lists are identified in a recent article by Moody. She notes that "Some of these lists have been developed specifically as core lists, whereas others have been an outgrowth of documents use studies and research."[15] The article identifies three suggested core collections, found in the *Federal Depository Library Manual*.[16] The three are the "Suggested Core Collection: Small/Medium Public Library" (372 items); the "Suggested Core Collection: Small Academic Library" (545 items); and "The Suggested Core Collection: Law Library" (443 items).[17] Each of these is based on a selected documents collection and each includes only a fraction of the total number of items available for selection.

A variant of the core list concept, based on research, and actual selection of titles by depository libraries is reported for all depositories and for law libraries. The study that reports these data was the result of an analysis of the Government Printing Office's computer-based records of the distribution to depository libraries.[18] The series titles of the 200 most frequently distributed depository items during January 1981 were analyzed. The series titles were ranked, and include the actual number of libraries selecting each series title, and the percentage of selective depository this number represents.[19] A similar study, reported in 1985, was conducted for law libraries that are depositories.[20] The core list derived for law libraries demonstrated greater consensus among depositories as to the series titles considered to be most important. The study of law library depository selection showed a consensus of 74.1 percent in the choice of the 200th most highly ranked title,[21] whereas the general study showed that the consensus among all depositories for the 200th most highly ranked title was only 60.8 percent.[22]

Another resource that can be used to derive a core collection is the *GPO Depository Union List of Item Selections* which lists by depository number the total number of depositories that have selected each item number.[23] This resource also identifies the libraries that make the selection, and this in turn can be used to determine if there is a similarity between the library considering an item for selection, and those that have already chosen to select the item.[24]

The value of core collection lists is that they provide a beginning point in the difficult task of selecting from among more than 6,000 item numbers. The core lists bring to the surface the most popular and visible document series, thus giving those responsible for collection development a sound basis for decision making. The disadvantage is that use of a core list derived from items selected by other libraries cannot fully reflect the information needs of the clientele of each individual library. Nevertheless, the more homogenous the group of libraries used to derive the core list, the more reliable the list is for collection development purposes.

Circulation studies of government publications provide another strategy for identifying the series titles or item numbers suitable for collection development. Several studies that focus on the use of federal government publications suggest ways that this can be achieved. Watson and Heim studied use of federal documents at the University of Illinois at Urbana-Champaign. This study, conducted in two phases, surveyed users who circulated government publications, and then analyzed machine-generated circulation records.[25] The features of this library that made the study distinctive were that it had a recently centralized collection with machine-generated records. Because of the high level of bibliographic access to government publications, it was possible to demonstrate which classification areas in the Superintendent of Documents Classification system were most frequently used. Also, the results of the study seemed to demonstrate that when good bibliographic integration of government publications exists, the circulation of documents is roughly proportional to their numbers in the collection.[26] The findings of this study have important implications for justifying the concept of total integration of government publications.

Sears and Moody, in a study of documents use at the library at Miami University (Ohio), were able to discern the areas of the collection that accounted for the majority of collection use.[27] From this, they derived a list of most frequently used individual documents and series. The study of document circulation and in-library use by Cook was reported for the purpose of identifying publications that generated high use which might be placed on the list of titles recommended by the GPO.[28]

The studies of current library use as a means of deriving data for collection development indicate that use of public documents is likely to be influenced by local variables, which in turn, are likely to have an impact on the nature of the collection development policy of the library. The Watson and Heim study suggests that the most important factor in affecting use may be the quality of bibliographic access to government publications.[29] In the library they studied, fully integrated bibliographic access was available for government publications, with the consequence that the publications were heavily used, and in proportion to the number of documents in each component of the collection. The other two studies were conducted in libraries that did not have the same level of bibliographic integration and the results were different. It is, therefore, difficult to find a common standard in these strategies that would be useful for all libraries in collection development.

Numerous *user studies* have been undertaken to obtain an indication of the preference of users for government publications in selected areas. The most complete review article on this topic, by Weech, identifies user studies up through the 1970s.[30] The most comprehensive user study, conducted by Hernon, identifies the characteristics of information needs of social scientists.[31] Hernon's study provides considerable insight into the way in which academicians in several social science disciplines acquire and use government publications. The results of the study serve as a model for studies of other disciplines, indicating factors that should be taken into consideration in the development of a collection development policy for government publications.

In a later study, Hernon and Purcell reported the results of two studies of the use of government publications by academic economists.[32] The first was a survey of libraries that served academic economists, in which library staff members were asked to indicate which

agencies of each of the major departments of the federal government published titles that would be of use to academic economists.[33] The second study, reported the results of a survey of selected academic economists at the institutions surveyed. The results of this study identified frequently used titles, names of government agencies most frequently consulted, and types of information needs experienced most frequently by the respondents.[34]

One objective of the user studies has been to identify those areas of greatest demand among users of government publications and to use the results as a basis for developing and implementing a more informed collection development policy for government publications.

For example, among federal publications, documents published within the recent past (three to seven years) were most heavily needed. Also, statistical publications and publications dealing with the legislative process were heavily in demand as were publications emanating from the Department of Health and Human Services.

User studies that demonstrate these demands are helpful in a general sense because they provide additional information for government publication collection development. The next logical step is to attempt to tie together the expressed user needs with specific series titles or item numbers, for a number of subject fields, and for a variety of types of libraries. To date, most of the studies of the use of federal documents have been conducted in academic libraries. The logical step is to expand this to other types of libraries and to a greater range of subject areas or disciplines.

CONCLUSION

Although the concept of collection development applied to government documents collections is of relatively recent origin, the implementation of the concept is now an accepted goal of many documents libraries. The extension of this concept to include the integration of government publications into the overall collection development goals of the library, and further, to create an environment for overall integration of government publications with the general collection, is not as widely accepted. In fact, most depository and nondepository libraries have not implemented either of these options. The increasing attention given in the literature to these extensions of the concept of collection development holds promise that they will be assimilated into the practice of the library profession over the next few years. Currently collection development and collection integration for government publications is, for most libraries, a goal yet to be articulated and is far from being achieved.

NOTES

[1] *Government Publications Review* 8A (1 and 2, 1981).

[2] Peter Hernon and Gary R. Purcell, *Developing Collections of U.S. Government Publications* (Greenwich, Conn.: JAI Press, Inc., 1982), 1.

[3] Ibid., 1-4.

[4] Charles R. McClure, "An Integrated Approach to Government Publication Collection Development," *Government Publications Review* 8A (1 and 2, 1981): 5.

[5] Perhaps the best statement of this can be found in Peter Hernon and Charles R. McClure, *Public Access to Government Information: Issues, Trends, and Strategies* (Norwood, N.J.: Ablex Publishing Corp., 1984), 87-99.

[6] Ibid., 87.

[7] Peter Hernon, Charles R. McClure, and Gary R. Purcell, *GPO's Depository Library Program: A Descriptive Analysis* (Norwood, N.J.: Ablex Publishing Corp., 1985), 65. The results of a survey of federal depositories show that 81.7 percent of the libraries "place most of their depository publications in a separate collection." This is a clear indication of special treatment of the government publications holdings.

[8] Peter Hernon, *Microforms and Government Information* (Westport, Conn.: Microform Review, 1981), 31-32.

[9] Jean L. Sears and Marilyn K. Moody, "Government Documents Use by Superintendent of Documents Number Areas," *Government Publications Review* 11 (1984), 104. The results of the study reported in this article show that circulation of government documents accounted for 1 percent of the total collection of the library whereas book circulation accounted for 24.66 percent of the total collection. These data indicate that documents account for a significantly lower percentage of the total use of the library than their percentage of the total collection.

[10] Hernon and McClure, 78-99.

[11] Hernon and Purcell, 124-208.

[12] Superintendent of Documents, *Monthly Catalog of United States Government Publications* (Washington, D.C.: Government Printing Office, 1895-).

[13] Charles R. McClure, Peter Hernon, and Gary R. Purcell, *Linking the U.S. National Technical Information Service with Academic and Public Libraries* (Norwood, N.J.: Ablex Publishing Corp., 1986).

[14] Superintendent of Documents, *Guidelines for the Depository Library System, Appendix A* (Washington, D.C.: Government Printing Office, 1977).

[15] Marilyn Moody, "Government Information: Selecting Documents: Using Core Lists of Item Selections," *RQ* 27 (Spring 1986): 305.

[16] Superintendent of Documents, *Federal Depository Library Manual* (Washington, D.C.: Government Printing Office, 1985).

[17] Ibid.

[18] Hernon and Purcell, 39-67.

[19] Ibid., 209-16.

[20] Sara Holterhoff, "Depository Document Selection in Academic Law Libraries: A Core List of Items Selected," *Government Information Quarterly* 2 (1985): 275-89.

[21] Ibid., 278.

[22] Hernon and Purcell, 216.

[23] Superintendent of Documents, *GPO Depository Union List of Item Selections* (Washington, D.C.: annual).

[24] Ibid.

[25] Paula D. Watson and Kathleen M. Heim, "Patterns of Access and Circulation in a Depository Document Collection under Full Bibliographic Control," *Government Publications Review* 11 (1984): 269-92.

[26]Ibid., 287.

[27]Sears and Moody, 101-12.

[28]Kevin L. Cook, "Circulation and In-Library Use of Government Publications," *The Journal of Academic Librarianship* 11 (July 1985): 146-50.

[29]Watson and Heim.

[30]Terry L. Weech, "The Use of Government Publications: A Selected Review of the Litera-ture," *Government Publications Review* 5 (1978): 177-84.

[31]Peter Hernon, *Use of Government Publications by Social Scientists* (Norwood, N.J.: Ablex Publishing Corp., 1979).

[32]Hernon and Purcell, 69-114.

[33]Ibid., 69-84.

[34]Ibid., 85-114.

Additions to the Personal Bookshelf

Ann E. Prentice

Like the shoemaker's child, librarians support the research of others and seek out information to enable others to do their job better but may not take the time to do the same for themselves. Focusing on the tasks at hand is necessary, but also may limit professional growth and will certainly narrow the individual librarian's ability to see daily activities in their broader context. The following selections are connected in that they provide a broader perspective or a new way of approaching an issue. Continued personal professional growth is the key to professional success and satisfaction. It is with this in mind that I offer the following windows on the world of communications, management, and the world in which librarians work.

What effect does color have on the individual? How should you arrange study areas so that most individuals will feel protected and comfortable? What are the boundary lines, visible and invisible, between private and communal areas? Architects and interior design specialists are sensitive to human needs for comfort and security. Those who are responsible for serving the public benefit from understanding the relationships between environmental forms and human behavior. Sommer, *Personal Space: The Behavioral Base of Design* (1969) discusses spatial behavior, human reactions to certain environments, and methods for managing that behavior. For example, people have their own sense of personal space and object to others who invade that space uninvited. Crowding too many people in a room may raise anxiety and will certainly reduce productivity. Why are long tables often a waste of space? How many people will sit at a table for eight or four? Carrels may be the most efficient use of space because they are protective of individuals at work. Sommer, a

psychologist, is never dull. Through him, you will gain insights into your own behavior in public places—why you do or do not feel comfortable in certain environments—and will become more sensitive to those elements that contribute to the comfort of others.

Within the book *Sign Systems for Libraries: Solving the Wayfinding Problem* (Pollet and Haskell, 1979) is a chapter by Roger Downs entitled "Magic, Minds, and Maps." This is the first time the study of maps has been applied to finding your way around a library. A library with its stacks and cubicles is indeed a maze to many a wayfarer, who would welcome any help. The ideal is to design the library with relationships between areas easily determined. When this is not possible, maps and other types of guides are necessary. Color schemes, signs, or architectural details are all helpful. In reading this chapter, you become aware of personal techniques for avoiding becoming lost and sensitive to those elements that make others comfortable or uncertain about their surroundings. The remainder of the book describes techniques for developing and installing sign systems and gives examples of sign systems appropriate to different environments. After reading *Personal Space* and *Sign Systems for Libraries* you may have the strong urge to redesign public spaces for patrons and then go on to redesign staff space. You will certainly be more sensitive to the individuals' response to the library as a place to visit and a place to work.

We all find it necessary to ask questions in order to solve problems, do a better job, or just learn additional information. Asking the right questions in the right way is an art. If you are conducting research, it is imperative that your questions be designed appropriately and asked in specific ways, for if the question is asked in a sloppy or ambiguous way, the answer will be equally sloppy and ambiguous. *The Art of Asking Questions* (Paine, 1951) tells you how to ask questions so that you will receive usable answers. Paine warns against using words like *could* or *should* and tells why you only ask one question at a time. You do not ask if the patron wants *Time* or *Newsweek* in the same question, and you do not assume the person from whom you are requesting information knows your jargon or even cares whether or not you plan to automate serials check-in. Paine, in very clear prose, describes how to ask questions correctly. Although this is necessary as part of research strategy, it is also useful for sharpening asking skills. If we ask better questions, we may get better answers.

Because social processes within the scientific community greatly affect the research effort, a sociological study of science provides insight into the ways information increases and is diffused. Research areas within the sciences are also social circles. Sociometric studies have identified networks of collaborators who are at work on similar problems. With leadership, researchers in the group will communicate their findings and exchange ideas, which causes the field to grow rapidly. Scientists may search for very specific types of information or may seek information of a general nature. The type of search depends on the discipline, the collaborators, and the prevailing attitudes toward research in an area. Through Crane's work, *Invisible Colleges: Diffusion of Knowledge in Scientific Communities* (1972), we may gain insights into the development of knowledge in a discipline and the kinds of areas explored, by being aware of the research communities at work. Who better than the information professional can map the publications of a field of research and conduct citation studies to show the ways in which information travels and is used? For whom is it more essential to understand these processes?

According to Schiller in *Communication and Cultural Domination* (1976, p. 9), cultural imperialism is "the sum of the processes by which a society is brought into the modern world system and how its dominating stratum is attracted, pressured, forced and sometimes bribed into shaping social institutions to correspond to or even promote the values and structures of the dominating center of the system." Since World War II, U.S. cultural artifacts and values from Disney to "Dallas" have been exported world wide and have served as a kind of war of ideas with battles fought using technology as weapons to transmit ideas. The conse-quences of this free and nearly instant flow of information are that the unique character of a region or nation may be altered as new ideas and ways of doing things are incorporated into the existing culture. Those who object to the cultural domination of one society over another may be called old fashioned or conservative when they are trying to preserve what is unique to a culture.

Technology that transmits levels of mass communication not previously possible permits new ideas to invade a society at all sociological, economic, and cultural levels at the same time. Different groups will see different applications for new ideas. For some, a new political view will be of intellectual interest; for others, it signals social change; and for still others, it is the beginning of revolution.

Engineers are urged to consider the social implications of the structures they build. What are the implications of building a bridge across a river and thus connecting towns or countries? What are the social effects of a poorly built auditorium when the roof caves in, killing many of those inside? Those of us involved in communicating ideas need to consider the implications of what we communicate and what the results may be in order to see our role in the information world in its broader context.

For those working in academic libraries, it is useful to take a look at the political environment of which they are a part (Brown, 1982). Academics depend upon a structure (the administration) so that they can be independent to pursue scholarship. Their obligation is more to their discipline than to the college or university. Administration is seen as the servant of the faculty and the library is part of the administrative structure that serves the faculty and enables them to teach and do research. Faculty members see administration as more powerful than it really is and spend a fair amount of time insisting on being involved in decision making while at the same time objecting to the amount of time their involvement requires. They may not understand how bureaucracy works and therefore consider it undesirable. From the administration, faculty members expect a good environment in which to work, a salary equal to their abilities, and treatment as individuals. Administration, while dealing with faculty as individuals, must also deal with the institution as a whole, through the planning, budgeting, and evaluation process. Individual concerns must be considered within the context of the institution and the larger society that controls it. Particularly in the case of the publicly supported institution, administrators rarely forget that conservative voters and legislators control the purse strings.

The academic library is in the midst of the political environment. Its resources are used by all disciplines. There is competition over levels of information support. The quality of service is defined very personally by faculty by the level of support the individual faculty member gets. This personal relationship expected by faculty and the way in which library faculty develop that relationship is one key to success of overall library service.

Major changes have occurred in higher education in the past decades. The student body has changed and tends to be more mature. Curricula in the liberal arts are forced to make room for professional programs. The faculty is aging and substantial numbers will retire in the next decade. Pressures come from an increased competition for students, the need to automate large areas of campus administration, and the continuing problem of maintaining adequate funding. Faculty often refuse to assume responsibility for dealing with these issues and say that these are administrative issues that they have neither the time nor inclination to address. Those institutions that ascribe to the tooth fairy syndrome, believing that if they muddle along, something good will come along to help, are often badly disappointed.

Keller, in *Academic Strategy: The Management Revolution in American Higher Education* (1983), recommends an active strategy for dealing with changes and for charting future actions. He suggests that administrators get people thinking about a few important concepts and then develop specific operational goals. Once there is an overall umbrella, specific goals can be determined. Those who will implement the plan also work it out, collect data as needed, and adjust it to take into consideration, but not necessarily to follow, market trends.

Higher education has had more than a decade of experience with strategic planning and has adapted this business process to its needs. Keller's discussion of how strategic planning works in academia is clearly written and takes into account the many social and cultural elements necessary to its success. Most institutions are already, to some degree, involved in strategic planning. Understanding the process is essential to those who plan library service within its context. On a second level of planning, academic libraries would do well to have their own strategic library plan.

A decade ago Christopher Lasch's reaction to the 1960s *me generation* and *now generation* was a national bestseller. In *The Culture of Narcissism: American Life in an Age of Diminishing Expectations* (1978), he characterized the journey into the self as not productive of self-awareness because it was more of an exhibitionist's journey than a true search for self-knowledge. Narcissism, extreme self-absorption, may be the neurosis of the decade where the emphasis is on style rather than content and on image rather than decisions. Appearances are dominant. What brand shoes you wear or which car you drive is more important than comfort or economy. Information is evaluated by the measure of *does it sound true* not *is it true*. Boorstein commented that we live in a world of pseudo events and quasi information. The concern is not *what is reality* but *how do we relate to reality*. To those outside that particular individual, this complacent self-preoccupation is boring.

Looking at Lasch's criticisms ten years later, are we still wallowing in self-involvement or have we developed a new neurosis? How much of the earlier neurosis remains? How much of it was evident in the first place? One way of charting where we are and how we arrived in our current condition is to select the social critiques of the past decade, identify the prevailing concerns, read the predictions, and see if they came true.

Lasch called the 1970s the *me decade*. Neil Postman, in *Amusing Ourselves to Death: Public Discourse in the Age of Show Business* (1985), calls the 1980s the *entertain me* culture. On this downward slide, we have descended into trivia where how one looks is more important than one's actions. Culture is transmitted visually by television and much of its programming is trivial. Without visual media, much of the trivia would die for lack of a vehicle.

Television as a form of media has changed the way we learn. As the alphabet shifted language from oral to written communication, television is shifting our learning to visual perception. After centuries of the printed word our new vehicle is television. We have gained an immediacy in experiencing events. We have lost the opportunities for reflection, weighing ideas, and sorting alternatives afforded by reading.

Who is in charge of our media? We need to understand the assets and liabilities of delivering information via television and to accept its benefits while being aware of its liabilities. For nearly a century writers such as H. G. Wells and Aldous Huxley have cautioned against unhesitating acceptance of media and message. Huxley in *Brave New World* was "trying to tell us that what afflicted the people ... was not that they were laughing instead of thinking, but that they did not know what they were laughing about and why they had stopped thinking."

Much effort is spent to assure that we are a literate population. Of equal value is becoming numerate so that we can measure and account. Numbers developed much later than letters and it was not until 1543 that the first English books of Arabic arithmetic were available. Roman numerals, which were used to express quantity but could not be manipulated, had been supplemented by Arabic numbers in the previous century. The need to measure and calculate increased. In *A Calculating People: The Spread of Numeracy in Early America* (1982), Patricia Cohen traces the use of numbers to manage trade, then to collect vital statistics, and finally to serve as a tool of scientific inquiry. Prior to 1776, science was descriptive, observational, and devoted to classification of things based on observed similarities.

Arithmetic was not part of the curriculum in colonial America. By the early nineteenth century it was taught generally but was seen as a man's domain. The idea that women could not figure and thus had no head for business was culturally imposed and is still with us. Arithmetic was also a political tool, being used to collect census data, determine the relative wealth of cities, or assess the damage caused by fire or epidemics.

As we review the growth of numeracy in the United States, we see how far we have come in a very short time. Only two hundred years have elapsed since science adopted mathematical methods. The first U.S. Census is less than two hundred years old. We have learned that numbers like words can illuminate our world by describing it in new ways. We have also learned that numbers, like words, can be used to build lies and to influence our actions in negative ways.

Change is the alteration from one state to another. Planned change is a method of organizing events and adapting to environments. Paul Goodman (1987) reviews themes in change literature such as intervention, survey, feedback, and quality of worklife as change mechanisms. He discusses means of assessing change, including models, standardized measures, designs, and analytical measures. Contributors to his work include Chris Argyris who emphasizes behavioral change—how learning and reasoning processes affect organizational change. Argyris questions whether we remain unaware of change because we are suppressing certain learning experiences. This may be why some individuals are more resistant to change than others. Perhaps we have invested so much in one course of action that we fear too great a loss if changes are made. A person can be trapped socially in a course of action. Change may be someone else's idea, and for one reason or another we resist it. Many individuals resist

change because the old behaviors still produce results. It is possible to ride a horse from coast to coast or to send smoke signals to a business associate but there are more efficient methods.

How do we change ourselves and our organizations? We change ourselves by understanding that attitudes are critical to change and change begins with understanding individual value systems, educating the individual, and building interpersonal relationships. We change the organization by maintaining an environment in which change can take place. Who initiates change? Individuals may be change agents. Management, labor unions, or other groups may initiate change. Change may be motivated by changes in the marketplace, the political arena, or the larger environment. In most cases change comes from the combination of all these. To be successful, people must change their way of doing things and they must be comfortable with the change.

Nearly all library managers work with consultants and many have experience as consultants themselves. Blake and Mouton (1976) discuss the ways in which psychology and psychiatry can be used in the workplace by the consultant operating as "industrial, business psychiatrist." Discussing issues with the client, determining what is needed to solve a problem or manage more efficiently, and then implementing the solution is one form of psychological counseling. Their conclusions can be generalized to nearly all types of consulting because the human element is part of all organizations. Although automating a circulation system may be a mechanical task for a consultant, implementing it requires people. People work better in the organization if they are included in the change process and understand the purpose of the change.

Most libraries are nonprofit organizations. They have a service mission, are structured to preclude self-interest or profit, and are exempt from paying federal taxes. Most nonprofit organizations are managed by individuals with skills and experience related to the mission of the organization rather than experienced managers who understand planning, personnel, budgeting, and related activities. Wolf (1984) has prepared an excellent guide on how to manage the nonprofit organization that would be useful for those responsible for managing libraries and other information centers.

Wolf's guide to successful fundraising is particularly useful and begins with the directive to put your own house in order, know your financial status, and develop with staff and board your long-range plans. The ten commandments for successful fundraising are a distillation of volumes of writing and years of experience.

1. only prospectors find gold

2. courtship precedes the proposal

3. personalize the pitch

4. if you want money, you have to prime the pump

5. when requesting money, assume consent

6. in writing a proposal, if you can't scan it, can it

7. in developing budgets be sure the numbers add up

8. when in doubt, communicate in plain English

9. don't take "no" personally

10. no matter how many times you say "thank you," say it again.

These authors (Unterman and Davis, 1984), Harvard Business School graduates, say that private business techniques are useful to the management of not-for-profit agencies. Their approach is geared toward the volunteer organization with a paid director and some staff. Although staffing differs from that of the library, many other elements are similar. There is an emphasis on planning, with the development and maintenance of a dynamic plan that can be evaluated and that fits into the sociological, political, and economic environment.

Marketing of services for nonprofits includes many of the same strategies as are used in business, such as how one prices services. Some services should be offered at no charge while others should have a fee. Which services are offered at no charge depends on the mission of the organization. For example, a library circulates books and offers basic references at no cost because that is the mission of the library. For those services demanding a fee, what is a fair price? Business techniques can be used to determine this. A marketing plan can be developed that will include both fee and free services and that will be in accord with the mission of the organization. Such a plan should be tested with the same rigor as would be used in the for-profit sector.

Numerous studies of leadership have been published in the past decade. We are told what constitutes good leadership, who is a good leader, and how to become a good leader. Sayles (1979) gives us a behavioral approach to being a good manager based on the expectation that good managers plan ahead, select qualified staff, reward good performance, and communicate well. Middle managers are both manager and managed and must come to terms with performing both roles at the same time and finding themselves restrained in their own activities by directives from above.

Good managers/leaders do not try to implement simplistic management models but look at the situation, the staff, and the resources to build a realistic model. New managers must learn quickly that reality differs from expectation, and they must learn to deal with reality. One reality is that the manager's time is fragmented. Many things need to be accomplished at the same time. There is never enough time to focus for long periods on any one problem. The good leader/manager manages personal time and staff time with equal care and efficiency.

All people have knowledge but not necessarily the same knowledge. There is sacred and profane knowledge, theoretical and practical knowledge, and formal and informal knowledge. Formal knowledge (Freidson, 1986) is rational, that is, sustained by reason and is organized into disciplines such as chemistry or physics or into structures such as bureaucracy. It is not a part of everyday knowledge as is informal knowledge, often labeled common sense. Formal knowledge is the basis for technical decisions and these decisions are a step in translating knowledge into action. Those who develop formal knowledge are the intellectuals, the professionals, and they are responsible for turning knowledge into power. Because of this, they should be mistrustful of authority, sensitive to ethical implications of action, and impartial to political or religious belief.

What is the role of the information professional in translating knowledge into power? Is it to locate the information on which decisions are made? Is it to make decisions? The information professional, as gatekeeper, holds a particularly sensitive position in the transformation of knowledge to power.

REFERENCES

Blake, Robert, and Jane Mouton. *Consultation*. Reading, Mass.: Addison-Wesley, 1976.

Brown, William R. *Academic Politics.* Tuscaloosa, Ala.: University of Alabama Press, 1982.

Cohen, Patricia Cline. *A Calculating People: The Spread of Numeracy in Early America.* Chicago: University of Chicago Press, 1982.

Crane, Diane. *Invisible Colleges: Diffusion of Knowledge in Scientific Communities.* Chicago: University of Chicago Press, 1972.

Freidson, Eliot. *Professional Powers: A Study of the Institutionalization of Formal Knowledge.* Chicago: University of Chicago Press, 1986.

Goodman, Paul S. *Change in Organizations: New Perspectives on Theory, Research, and Practice.* San Francisco: Jossey Bass, 1987.

Huxley, Aldous. *Brave New World.* New York, Harper and Row, 1979.

Keller, George. *Academic Strategy: The Management Revolution in American Higher Education.* Baltimore, Md.: Johns Hopkins University Press, 1983.

Lasch, Christopher. *The Culture of Narcissism: American Life in an Age of Diminishing Expectations.* New York: Norton, 1978.

Paine, Stanley. *The Art of Asking Questions.* Princeton, N.J.: Princeton University Press, 1951.

Pollet, Dorothy, and Peter Haskell. *Sign Systems for Libraries: Solving the Wayfinding Problem.* New York: Bowker, 1979.

Postman, Neil. *Amusing Ourselves to Death: Public Discourse in the Age of Show Business.* New York: Viking, 1985.

Sayles, Leonard R. *Leadership: What Effective Managers Really Do ... and How They Do It.* New York: McGraw-Hill, 1979.

Schiller, Herbert I. *Communication and Cultural Domination.* White Plains, N.Y.: M. E. Sharp, Inc., 1976.

Sommer, Robert. *Personal Space: The Behavioral Base of Design.* Englewood Cliffs, N.J.: Prentice-Hall, 1969.

Unterman, Israel, and Richard H. Davis. *Strategic Management of Not-for-Profit Organizations: From Survival to Success.* New York: Praeger, 1984.

Wolf, Thomas. *The Nonprofit Organization: An Operating Manual.* Englewood Cliffs, N.J.: Prentice-Hall, 1984.

The Research Efforts of Major Library Organizations

Sharon L. Baker and Ronald R. Powell

Several national associations have programs to stimulate research for the profession and for introspection. This article gathers together in one listing the various research mechanisms of these organizations.

THE AMERICAN LIBRARY ASSOCIATION

ALA has a Committee on Research which was established in January 1968, and which serves in an advisory capacity for the ALA Office for Research. The functions of the ALA Committee on Research are to facilitate research and related activities in all units of the association; to advise the ALA Council and Executive Board on programs, policy, and priorities regarding research; to recommend procedures to achieve expeditious consideration of all ALA unit proposals for research and related activities by the ALA Executive Board; to encourage the establishment of divisional committees for the purpose of stimulating research; to maintain liaison with all units of the association regarding research and related activities in the units; to identify questions regarding library service which need to be answered through research and promote the conduct of research to answer those questions; and to serve as an advisory committee for the Office for Research.[1]

The 1988 chair of the ALA Committee on Research is Charles R. Martell, Chair, Assistant Library Director, California State University, Sacramento, CA 95819.

In addition to the Committee on Research, ALA has an Office for Research, which is directed by Mary Jo Lynch. This office has three functions: (1) to collect, analyze, and interpret data about the membership of ALA and users of ALA products and services on an ongoing basis for organizational decision making; (2) to collect and/or promote the collection of statistics about libraries and librarians so that ALA and other organizations will have pertinent and consistent data available to them; and (3) to monitor ongoing research related to libraries and disseminate information about such studies to the profession. In carrying out these functions, the Office for Research will provide advice regarding research and statistics to the Executive Board, Council, and other units of ALA requesting such advice.[2]

Division Research Committees

A number of ALA divisions also have research committees, each with their own charges and activities. The following are the constituted committees with their respective chairs for 1988.

American Association of School Librarians
Research Committee
Chair: David V. Loertscher
P.O. Box 266
Castle Rock, CO 80104

Association for Library Service to Children
Research and Development Committee
Chair: Leslie M. Edmonds
Graduate School of Library and Information
    Science
University of Illinois
410 David Kinley Hall
1407 West Gregory Drive
Urbana, IL 61801

Association of College and Research Libraries
Bibliographic Instruction Section, Research
   Committee
Chair: Sandra G. Yee
Media and Instruction Supp. Serv.
University Library
Eastern Michigan University
Ypsilanti, MI 48197

Association of College and Research Libraries
Research Committee
Chair: Jerry L. Parsons
4504 Marble Way
Carmichael, CA 95608

Association of College and Research Libraries
Research Discussion Group
Chair: Melena Rowan
BRS Information Technologies
1200 Route 7
Latham, NY 12110

Association of College and Research Libraries
Western European Specialists Section, Research
   and Planning Committee
Chair: To be appointed

Association of Specialized and Cooperative
   Library Agencies
Research Committee
Chair: Ruth M. Katz
Director of Academic Library Services
Joyner Library
East Carolina University
Greenville, NC 27834

Library Administration and Management
   Association
Statistics Section, National Data Collection
   and Use Committee
Chair: Linda L. Parker
1000 Carriage Way
Lincoln, NE 68510

Library Administration and Management
   Association
Statistics Section, Using Statistics for Library
   Planning and Evaluation Committee
Chair: Burton M. Clark
University of Illinois
246A Library
1408 Gregory Drive
Champaign, IL 61821

Library History Round Table
Chair: Wayne Wiegand
School of Library and Information Studies
University of Wisconsin-Madison
Madison, WI 53706

Library Instruction Round Table
Research Committee
Chair: Patricia S. Vanderberg
University of California Library
Reference Department
Berkeley, CA 94702

Library Research Round Table
Chair: Barbara Immroth
Graduate School of Library and Information
   Studies
University of Texas at Austin
Austin, TX 78712

Library Research Round Table
Research Forums Committee
Chair: M. Lisa DeGruyter
6109 Vassar Drive
Austin, TX 78723

Public Library Association
Research Committee
Chair: Joan Coachman Durrance
School of Information and Library Studies
University of Michigan
580 Union Drive
Ann Arbor, MI 48109

Resources and Technical Services Division
Cataloging and Classification Section, Policy
   and Research Committee
Chair: Janet Padway
Meir Library
University of Wisconsin-Milwaukee
P.O. Box 604
Milwaukee, WI 53201

Resources and Technical Services Division
Planning and Research Committee
Chair: Pamela Bluh
8594 Hayshed Lane
Columbia, MD 21045

Resources and Technical Services Division
Preservation of Library Materials Section,
   Policy and Research Committee
Chair: Carolyn Morrow Manns
National Preservation Program Office, LM-G07
Library of Congress
Washington, DC 20540

Resources and Technical Services Division
Reproduction of Library Materials Section,
   Policy and Research Committee
Chair: Nancy E. Elkington
Preservation Officer
Hatcher Graduate Library, Room 7
University of Michigan
Ann Arbor, MI 48109

Resources and Technical Services Division
Resources Section, Policy and Research
    Committee
Chair: Linda Pletzke
8214 Beechtree Road
Bethesda, MD 20817

Resources and Technical Services Division
Serials Section, Policy and Research Committee
Chair: John J. Riemer
462 North Bluff Road
Athens, GA 30607

Young Adult Services Division
Research Committee
Chair: Lesley S. J. Farmer
135 Golden Hind Passage
Corte Madera, CA 94925

Research Awards

In addition to the various committees, offices, and round tables, there are a number of awards given which promote research in the field.

1. *(Carroll Preston) Baber Research Award.* This annual award of $10,000 is presented to a person doing research focusing on improved library services, new uses of technology, or cooperative projects. The award is donated by Eric R. Baber and is administered by the ALA Awards Committee. For more information, write Elaine K. Wingate, staff liaison for the ALA Awards Committee, at ALA Headquarters.

2. *Association of College and Research Libraries, Doctoral Dissertation Fellowship.* This annual award of $1,000 is presented to a doctoral student in the field of academic librarianship whose research indicates originality, creativity, and scholarship. The award was designed to encourage the dissertation work of doctoral students who have completed all their coursework and have had their proposals accepted by their institutions. The award is donated by the Institute for Scientific Information and is administered by ACRL. For more information write JoAn Segal, executive director of ACRL, at ALA Headquarters.

3. *Frances Henne YASD/Voice of Youth Advocates (VOYA) Research Grant.* This annual award of $500 was established to provide seed money for small-scale research projects that will have an influence on library service to young adults. Applicants must belong to

YASD. Grants will not be given for research leading to a degree. The award is donated by *VOYA* and is administered by YASD. For more information, write Evelyn Shaevel, executive director of YASD, at ALA Headquarters.

4. *Samuel Lazerow Fellowship for Research in Acquisitions or Technical Services.* This annual award of $1,000 is given to provide librarians in acquisitions or technical services with a fellowship for research, travel, or writing. Proposals are judged on their potential significance, originality, and clarity. The award is administered by ACRL. For more information, write JoAn Segal, executive director of ACRL, at ALA Headquarters.

5. *Jesse H. Shera Award for Research* (formerly the Library Research Round Table Research Award). This award of $500 is given annually for an excellent research paper. Entries are judged on definition of the research problem, application of research methods, clarity of the reporting of the research, and significance of the conclusions. The award is administered and donated by the Library Research Round Table. For more information, write Mary Jo Lynch, staff liaison for the Library Research Round Table, at ALA Headquarters.

6. *Justin Winsor Prize Essay.* This award of $500 is given to encourage excellence in research in library history. Essays should be original historical research on a significant subject of library history, and should be based on primary source materials and manuscripts if possible. The award is administered by the Library History Round Table. Manuscripts should be forwarded to Wayne Wiegand, School of Library and Information Studies, University of Wisconsin, Madison, WI 53706.

Research is published by ALA in a variety of ways. Some reports are published by ALA Publishing and released as books. Most research is reported in the various journals published by the association, either as research articles or in research columns. Journals which regularly report research findings include *School Library Media Quarterly, Library Resources and Technical Services,* and *Public Libraries.*

THE SPECIAL LIBRARIES ASSOCIATION

Founded more than seventy years ago by John Cotton Dana, SLA provides special support, services, and opportunities for special librarians and information managers. This year, a special committee has been formed to determine the role that SLA should play in promoting or conducting research in the area of special libraries or librarianship.

The 1987 Research Committee is chaired by James B. Tchobanoff, Pillsbury Company, Research and Development, Technical Information Center, 311 Second Street Southeast, Minneapolis, MN 55414.

Individuals and groups may also apply for money to conduct research through the Special Programs Fund, which supports programs and services that will further the scientific, literary, and educational purpose for which SLA is organized and operated. The amount of funding available varies from year to year. Recently, research monies have been granted to study corporate library excellence and education for special librarianship. For more information, write Sandy Morton, Director of Government Relations and Fund Development, SLA, 1700 18th Street NW, Washington, DC 20009.

SLA also publishes *Special Libraries*, a quarterly journal which periodically includes reports of research related to special libraries.

ASSOCIATION FOR LIBRARY AND INFORMATION SCIENCE EDUCATION

The Association for Library and Information Science Education (ALISE) promotes and facilitates research through a variety of activities and organizations. The Research Committee is the coordinating unit of the association for all research activities. It is also responsible for reviewing any research-oriented programs planned for the annual conference and for recommending to the board of directors all awards for research-related activities. George D'Elia (University of Minnesota, Management Science Department) is the 1988-89 chair of the committee.

The Research Interest Group is responsible for developing research-related programs for the annual conferences. Conferences regularly include doctoral forums and forums for current issues/research, both of which are opportunities for researchers to share their work informally with small groups.

ALISE annually awards one or more grants totaling $2,500 to support research broadly related to education for library and information science. The association also sponsors an annual research paper competition. Papers may concern any aspect of librarianship or information

studies. Winning papers receive honorariums of $500 and are presented at the annual conference. Recipients of these two awards must be personal members of ALISE. In addition, two outstanding doctoral dissertations completed during the preceding year are selected to be presented at the annual conference. Each winner of this competition receives a $400 award plus conference registration and personal membership in ALISE.

The *Journal of Education for Library and Information Science* is the official publication of ALISE. Each quarterly issue regularly includes research-type articles and other scholarly papers. The journal also contains the "Research Record," a column devoted to research-related issues and listings of recently approved proposals for doctoral dissertations in library and information science. The association continues to compile and publish its *Library and Information Science Education Statistical Report* as well.

AMERICAN SOCIETY FOR INFORMATION SCIENCE

The American Society for Information Science (ASIS) engages in numerous activities to promote and honor research efforts in the field of information science. The Research Committee, a standing committee that serves in an advisory capacity to the Board of Directors, bears the primary responsibility within ASIS for assessing the role of ASIS in the evolution of the field and profession; for identifying potential relationships with research foundations and other funding agencies; and for recognizing the role of research and researchers within ASIS and the field of information science. The 1988 chair of the ASIS Research Committee is Dr. Jeffrey Katzer, Professor, School of Information Studies, Syracuse University, Syracuse, NY 13244.

In 1987, the Research Committee initiated a new program, entitled Student Mini-Conferences, for students in graduate programs of library and information science, as well as in related fields in other schools and departments. The conferences, which are run by and for the students, provide opportunities for students to share their research and to meet their future professional colleagues. The Student Mini-Conferences are scheduled regionally in the spring.

Other research activities and interests within ASIS are represented within many of the twenty-one ASIS Special Interest Groups (SIGs). Included among the SIGs with the greatest research interests are Classification Research, Foundations of Information Science, Arts and Humanities, Medical Information Systems, Information Generation and Publishing. Many of the other SIGs also foster theoretical and research efforts.

Several awards are presented each year to honor or promote research efforts in information science. The Award of Merit, the society's most prestigious award, is presented annually to an individual who has made noteworthy contributions to the field of information science. Though the award is not specifically for research, it frequently honors individuals whose primary contributions have been based on research activities. The ISI Information Science Doctoral Dissertation Scholarship fosters research in information science by encouraging and assisting doctoral students with their dissertation research. The scholarship recognizes outstanding proposals for doctoral dissertations submitted by graduate students who have completed the coursework for their doctoral degrees. The Doctoral Forum Awards honor outstanding doctoral research work in the information field.[3]

NOTES

[1] *ALA Handbook of Organization: 1987-88.* Chicago: American Library Association, 1987.

[2] Ibid.

[3] The authors would like to thank Linda Resnik, Executive Director, for contributing information about the research activities of ASIS.

Part II
REVIEWS OF BOOKS

Reviews of Books

GENERAL WORKS

Essays and Proceedings

1. De Gennaro, Richard. **Libraries, Technology, and the Information Marketplace: Selected Papers.** Boston, G. K. Hall, 1987. 432p. index. $36.50; $28.50pa. LC 87-7568. ISBN 0-8161-1855-8; 0-8161-1869-8pa.

This collection of writings by a well-known and highly respected librarian-author consists of six unpublished papers and thirty-three reprinted papers. The latter span a period of two decades, and many have become the classics in library literature. Following a foreword by Thomas J. Galvin and a preface by the author, the papers are divided into two parts: "The Future in Perspective," which contains the six new papers from "Surviving Technological Revolutions" to "Libraries and Computing Centers in the Wired University," and part 2, which groups all the thirty-three reprinted papers in four categories: "Libraries and the Information Marketplace," "Managing the Library in Transition," "Library Technology and Networking," and "Library Automation: The Early Years." Within each category, papers are arranged in reverse chronological order.

Drawing on the author's rich experience in academic and research libraries, his knowledge of library technology, and his keen perceptions of the changes in librarianship, all of the papers are worth reading. As Tom Galvin states in the foreword, De Gennaro has "an instinct for choosing topics that are timely" and "of enduring value."

This book is highly recommended for all library and information professionals as well as every library science collection.

Hwa-Wei Lee

2. **Information '85: Using Knowledge to Shape the Future. Proceedings of a Conference....** London, Aslib, The Association for Information Management, with Library Association; distr., Medford, N.J., Learned Information, 1986. 173p. $30.00pa. ISBN 0-85142-198-9.

In 1980, three British information/library associations collaborated on a conference on information. The results of this conference were so successful that the organizers were urged to plan further such conferences. The second conference (this one held in 1985) was cosponsored by five associations: the Joint Consultant Committee of Aslib, the Institute of Information Scientists, the Library Association, the Society of Archivists, and the Standing Conference of National and University Libraries. Again, the results are most informative, providing wide perspectives on the future directions of information; hence the subtitle "Using Knowledge to Shape the Future."

Five major topics divide the conference: "See Ourselves as Others See Us," "The Public *versus* Private Debate," "Who Pays the Piper?" "The International Dimension," and "The Future." Although the speakers are predominantly from the United Kingdom, their views and perspectives are broad enough to make this volume germane to those in other countries as well. The issues as seen by the presenters of these papers deal with information in social, ethical, educational, and economic contexts. All of these topics are most relevant to those who consider themselves managers both of present-day and future information, be they in libraries or the more commercial side of the information industry. The articles in this volume are thought-provoking. They provide a good summary of where seers in the field feel we are and where we are going. One anticipates that the next conference (1990) will offer an update based on these presentations of 1985. The proceedings of the 1990 conference will be awaited with eager anticipation, especially if they are as well presented as this volume.

Marjorie E. Bloss

3. Information for All: Access and Availability. Proceedings of the Annual Conference of the Institute of Information Scientists, Peebles, 1986. Brenda White, ed. London, Taylor Graham, 1987. 245p. £15.00pa. ISBN 0-947568-16-6.

The papers that comprise this volume are as wide-ranging as the title of this work suggests. Seven broad topics divide the work, ranging from "Co-operation in Making Information Available," to "The Role of Information." The two keynote addresses were presented by Maurice B. Line in "Information Availability and Access: Issues and Approaches," and by Royston Brown in "The National Information Policy Framework." Line's concerns focus more on access to specific types of information, access to information issued in various electronic media, cooperation between the public and private sectors, and between nations. Brown's address deals with these issues against a backdrop of the development of libraries and information services in the United Kingdom as envisioned by the Library and Information Services Council. These two thought-provoking presentations provide the framework for the articles that follow.

The wide range of topics in this volume gives the reader much to choose from. In some cases, however, the subjects appear too broad (or the articles too short) to cover the subject matter adequately. This superficiality can be frustrating. Furthermore, there is no index — a major omission. Brief biographical data on the presenters/authors also would have been helpful. Given these concerns, it is difficult to give this work a glowing recommendation. It is interesting, especially for comparisons with parallel situations in the United States. It supports and enhances collections, but it certainly is not a basic text in its own right.

Marjorie E. Bloss

4. Josey, E. J., ed. **Libraries, Coalitions & the Public Good.** New York, Neal-Schuman, 1987. 174p. index. $29.95pa. LC 87-1642. ISBN 1-55570-017-9.

Libraries, Coalitions & the Public Good presents sixteen original papers on the theme of libraries and the public good; the economic impact of libraries on American society; and the emergence of alliances between libraries, educational institutions, and other related groups. Many of the papers were commissioned for E. J. Josey's 1985 Presidential Program of the American Library Association. Recent trends toward privatization and restrictive interpretations of the concept of public good are cited as reasons for intense reappraisal and reaffirmation of the

library as a key supporter of the Information Age and a major guarantor of an informed citizenry. Each of the chapter authors subscribes to a social vision which includes free library service and maximum accessibility to information.

Essays are arranged in three sections. Part 1, "Libraries and the Public Good," features papers by John N. Berry, III, Fay M. Blake, Virginia A. Hodgkinson, Arthur Curley, and Virginia Hamilton. Part 2, "Issues in Defining the Public Good," contains the work of Winn Newman, Gordon M. Ambach, Mary Hartwood Futrell, and Gerald R. Shields. The final section, "Coalitions and Libraries," offers the views of William Eshelman, Joan C. Durrance, Robert Theobald, Patricia Glass Schuman, Suzanne H. Mahmoodi and Roger D. Sween, and Nancy Kranich. Participants' comments are edited by Joseph A. Boisse and Carla J. Stoffle.

The papers are brief, generally thoughtful expositions which highlight the library's interdependent mission and consequent need for creative alliances. Perhaps Arthur Curley says it best when he postulates that libraries "are part of the essential fabric of our society — its fragile cultural and social ecology." If the president's program and resultant essays stimulate the profession to conduct research on the concept of the public good and to forge effective coalitions for the support of libraries, the vision will be sustained.

Arthur P. Young

5. Libraries 2000: A Futures Symposium. Proceedings, Toronto 1985. Richmond Hill, Ont. Ontario Library Service/Trent, 1986. 128p. illus. bibliog. $15.00pa. ISBN 0-9692554-0-3.

These proceedings are the result of a conference sponsored by the Canadian Ministry of Citizenship and Culture, held in Toronto in September 1985. The subject was "The Future," always fun because everyone has opinions (or should) about it, and may speak them with comparatively little fear of contradiction. Anyway, with the new century only fifteen years away (now it's more like twelve), it seemed high time for Canada to convene a blue-ribbon panel of futurologists to examine what lies ahead (may lie ahead?) for libraries and other information services. Technology and change, naturally, were cussed and discussed, as librarians, trustees, and administrators heard a number of challenging papers and then split into groups for analysis and discussion.

After opening ceremonies, there are papers on forecasting life in the twenty-first century. There follows a panel discussion on developments, new and anticipated, in fields which bear on libraries, such as robotics, home access to information, new media, and automated workplaces. Finally, the implications for Canada in all this conjecture are brought out in open forum, with questions and answers. The upshot of all this is that the future looks bright for the Canadian information industry, but, as always, with certain reservations and warnings. Most of the papers in this collection have general applicability to Western nations, while a few are specifically concerned with problems unique to bilingual Canada.

The book is attractively produced, with green headers against blue print on high-quality paper. Some of the exhortations belabor (belabour?) the obvious (e.g., "We are going to have to find new ways of doing things in the future"), but we neglect studying the future at our peril, lest we be caught completely unprepared for it. Essential reading for Canadian librarians; worth a look to the rest of us. [R: EL, May/June 87, pp. 35-36]

Bruce A. Shuman

6. **Library Lit. 16—The Best of 1985.** Bill Katz, ed. Metuchen, N.J., Scarecrow, 1986. 419p. $22.50. LC 78-154842. ISBN 0-8108-1926-0.

I always look forward to a new volume of the best of library literature, edited by Bill Katz. Here in one handy source are the articles representing the best thoughts and ideas of librarians for the most recent year available. The volume for 1985 continues a fine tradition as well as a good service for our profession.

Twenty-nine articles have been selected out of some 150 candidates by a jury consisting of John Berry, Mary K. Chelton, Arthur Curley, William R. Eshelman, Pat Schuman, and Bill Katz. For 1985 the majority of the selected articles emphasize two issues: the role of our government in hindering the flow of information and the negligence of libraries in assigning the wrong priorities to service.

Among my favorite articles were: "Information Practice and Malpractice," by Anne P. Mintz; "The Report of the First Librarian *in* Congress," by Major R. Owens; "Library Use, Reading and Economy," by Murray L. Bob; and "Why People Really Hate Library Schools," by Samuel Rothstein. Other authors represented include Michael Gorman, George D'Elia, Margaret F. Stieg, Carlton Rochell, Mary Niles Maack, and Elfreda A. Chatman.

Looking back over sixteen years of these compilations, I detect a growing strength in the literature of our field. I'm already looking

forward to the next volume. [R: JAL, July 87, pp. 176-77; WLB, May 87, p. 60]

George S. Bobinski

7. **"Next to Mother's Milk...."** (An Engelhard Lecture on the Book Presented by Lawrence Clark Powell at the Library of Congress on Tuesday, April 8, 1986). Washington, D.C., Library of Congress, 1987. 25p. (Center for the Book Viewpoint Series, 17). free pa. LC 87-4160. ISBN 0-8444-0551-5.

Powell is one of the most venerable names in modern librarianship (University Librarian at UCLA from 1944-1961, first Dean of UCLA's Graduate School of Library and Information Science, prolific author) and even the slightest piece of writing by him is worthy of the profession's attention.

The pamphlet under review is the transcript of a lecture delivered by Powell at the Library of Congress in April 1986. It is a brief and charming memoir of Powell's exposure to books and libraries, his ongoing relationship with the Library of Congress, and a tribute to some influential book-oriented people in his past. He takes his title from the proclamation of one of his college teachers, Carlyle Ferren MacIntyre: "Books, next to mother's milk the best food." Powell delivers a strong defense of the book, and grumbles a bit about the overly technological emphasis in library schools today. "Who will prepare librarians to serve children, young people, middle-aged dreamers, and old folks?" he asks.

After digesting this particular morsel of Powell's wit and wisdom, many readers (and librarians) will wish to pursue his major autobiographical works—*Fortune and Friendship* (R. R. Bowker, 1968) and *Life Goes On: More Years of Fortune and Friendship* (Scarecrow Press, 1986)—or a fine anthology of his writings, *Books Are Basic*, edited by John D. Marshall (University of Arizona Press, 1985).

Thomas A. Karel

8. Nicholson, John B., Jr. **Reading and the Art of Librarianship: Selected Essays of John B. Nicholson, Jr.** New York, Haworth Press, 1986. 281p. index. (*Collection Management*, Vol. 8, Nos. 3/4). $29.95. LC 86-18442. ISBN 0-86656-585-X.

According to volume editor Paul Z. DuBois, the essays of John B. Nicholson "offer a window into the mind of a librarian who believes that reading is one of the most precious of our freedoms and that no calling is more worthy than sharing the fruits of that experience."

Nicholson, a graduate of Washington and Lee University, received the master's degree in library science from Columbia University and spent the majority of his career as director of libraries at Kent State University (1945-1966). Seventy of his more than 300 essays were selected for this collection, and arranged in five sections: "Nature of Reading"; "Literary Creation and Types of Literature"; "Eleven Authors"; "Book Collecting"; and "Libraries, Librarianship, and the Freedom to Read."

Nicholson's essays capture the literary reflections of an eclectic, sensitive reader. He dashes from Plutarch and Thoreau to Dickens and C. S. Lewis with wit and insight. Overrated books, unappreciated books, feared books, and forged books all receive due consideration. Favorite authors who merit special attention include Constance Holme, John Buchan, Dorothy Sayers, C. S. Lewis, Rudyard Kipling, Charles Dickens, Austin Wright, Charles Williams, Stephen Donaldson, Hugh McLennan, and Edwin Teale. Most of Nicholson's reflections on libraries and computers are rather conventional, but his sketches of bibliographer Edwin W. Willoughby and librarian Blanche McCrum redeem this section.

These graceful essays reaffirm the act of reading as the central tenet of a free society. It is useful to be reminded that reading is also the heart of the bibliothecal enterprise. Perhaps no other librarian save Lawrence Clark Powell has consecrated the book with such debonair eloquence. [R: LAR, June 87, p. 297; RQ, Fall 87, p. 157; WLB, May 87, p. 59]

Arthur P. Young

Festschriften

9.   Line, Maurice, ed. **The World of Books and Information: Essays in Honour of Lord Dainton.** London, British Library, 1987. 214p. price not reported. ISBN 0-7123-0125-9.

Brought together to celebrate the achievements of Lord Dainton on the occasion of his retirement as Chairman of the British Library Board, these eighteen essays approach the worlds of books and libraries from a variety of perspectives and experiences. The authors are prominent individuals from many types of libraries and library-related environments. Among the topics are essays on the British Library and its clientele, problems of national information policy, libraries and the electronic campus, the nature and future direction of scholarly publishing, professionalism and librarianship, the costs associated with published research, the relationship between the scholar and the library, gradual evolution of the

British Library's research policy, and library preservation strategy at the local and national levels. Two fascinating bibliographic essays—" 'Unto the Hills'—A Personal Bibliography of Scottish Mountaineering," by Anthony E. Ritchie, and "Welsh Authors and Their Books, c. 1500-c. 1642," by Glamor Williams—embellish the collection with their warmth and uniqueness. A final section highlights "Papers and Lectures by Lord Dainton on Science, Education, Libraries and Information."

This volume should make fascinating reading for professionals in many countries. The essays are solid, and varied in length and scope. Recommended for all professional collections.

Edmund F. SantaVicca

Philosophy and Theory

10.   Blahut, Richard E. **Principles and Practice of Information Theory.** Reading, Mass., Addison-Wesley Publishing, 1987. 458p. index. $45.95. LC 86-20554. ISBN 0-201-10709-0.

Information theory is a highly complex subject "centered around a common mathematical approach to the study of the collection and manipulation of information." The author's objective is to make that subject more widely understood without deleting its content, and his assumed audience is the engineer who needs a working familiarity with performance requirements and the need to use mathematical models to design systems.

Shannon laid the foundation for information theory in the 1940s, and the author builds on that foundation to answer questions such as: What is information and how do we measure it? What are the limits on transmission? What are the problems? And what is our rate of progress?

The author, associated with both IBM and Cornell University, assumes a relatively high level of mathematics on the part of the reader. It is not for the beginner, nor is it a first book for the individual who has come to information systems design from a direction other than mathematics/engineering. This is the edge of the discipline of information science as it overlaps with mathematics and engineering. Its value is in serving as a link between the two disciplines and those who work with information in different ways.

Ann E. Prentice

11.   Flynn, Roger R. **An Introduction to Information Science.** New York, Marcel Dekker, 1987. 793p. index. (Books in Library and Information Science, Vol. 49). $39.75. LC 86-24369. ISBN 0-8247-7508-2.

This book, intended as a textbook for undergraduates, addresses questions relating to three themes: (1) the reduction of uncertainty in using information; (2) methods of data organization, indexing, and querying databases; and (3) the use of data in decision making. The text consists of several sections, each containing an overview and two or more chapters. These sections, entitled "Data Collection and Analysis," "Data Organization and Use," "Coding the Data," "Storing the Data," "Retrieving the Data," "Displaying Data," "Communication of Data," "Data Manipulation," and "Decision Making and Problem Solving," follow a useful process model of data use, rather than an externally imposed paradigm for discussion of the topics. An author index and a subject index are provided. Bibliographies are given at the end of each chapter.

Although the book is comprehensive in covering what it intends to cover, there are several anomalies. For example, in defining the subject of the text, Flynn states: "Information science is a relatively new field with at best a sketchy definition at the present time — it requires a knowledge of concepts and skills from various disciplines." But Flynn's presentation of a mix of research methods, information retrieval, computer science, and statistics does not cohere into a field, but instead remains atomized, in spite of his best, or anyone else's efforts.

As far as his order of presentation is concerned, sections on chi-square and correlation are given prior to a section on the normal distribution. This will certainly confuse the uninitiated. Furthermore, for a book this size, on this topic, the two indexes combined fail to meet the minimum index size (1/50) suggested by the *Chicago Manual of Style*. In addition, topics such as correlation and chi-square are given only as subentries under data analysis. The publisher's press release describes the book as an "introduction to manipulating, retrieving, transmitting and applying information in a database." Flynn tries to make it much more, with mixed results.   Robert H. Burger

12.   Mansuripur, Masud. **Introduction to Information Theory.** Englewood Cliffs, N.J., Prentice-Hall, 1987. 149p. bibliog. index. $35.00. LC 86-17033. ISBN 0-13-484668-0.

Texts abound on information theory, and the saving grace of this book is that the author targets the beginning graduate student familiar with the techniques of probability theory and adheres to that prescription in each chapter. Mathematical expertise needed to understand the book is provided in chapter 1, while entropy, variable-length and universal source coding, mutual information, channel theorems, rate-distortion theory, and error-correcting

codes comprise major topics of subsequent chapters. Each chapter closes with a set of problems that reinforce or complement the text and enhance the opportunity for the reader to intuitively develop concepts regarding information theory, the latter being a principal goal of the author. The mathematical rigor is adequate to bolster development of concepts. The short bibliography and index show the teaching background of the author, where time is short and clutter must be kept to a minimum. This book informs without overwhelming. [R: Choice, May 87, p. 1432]   Marvin K. Harris

13.   Meadows, A. J., ed. **The Origins of Information Science.** London, Institute of Information Scientists and Taylor Graham, 1987. 261p. (Foundations of Information Science, Vol. 1). £24.00pa. ISBN 0-947568-13-1.

The realization that industrialized societies are experiencing profound changes in their ways of doing things and solving problems becomes clearer in the writings of scholars as the century progresses into the Information Age. To look back into the origins of change and to reflect on the merits of earlier forecasts are endorsements that the Information Era has come of age. Starting with the question, "What is information science?" the present book goes on to outline the short but dramatic history of the origins of the Information Age through early writings. A direct line can be traced back from modern information work to the 1950s, when there was an explosion of activity in this field. Thus the chosen cut-off date for the materials included in this book is 1950. Pre-1950 literature is examined for themes which, in retrospect, can be viewed as contributions to the field of information science. Included in the book are a total of seventeen papers clustered under five parts: the growth of the literature; the use of citations leading to modern bibliometrics; statistics in communication; publishers, libraries, and readers; and a look forward provided by the classic article by Vannevar Bush, "As We Think." Each part is preceded by an editorial commentary and recommended further reading. This book is a must for all academic libraries and for every educated person who feels the need to have a sense of the future by looking at the past.   Antonio Rodriguez-Buckingham

14.   Pylyshyn, Zenon W., and William Demopoulos, eds. **Meaning and Cognitive Structure: Issues in the Computational Theory of Mind.** Norwood, N.J., Ablex Publishing, 1986. 264p. bibliog. index. (Theoretical Issues in Cognitive Science). $39.50. LC 86-10801. ISBN 0-89391-372-3.

An excellent addition in the Ablex Publishing series Theoretical Issues in Cognitive Science. The contents of this book are actually position papers and commentaries of a conference-workshop held at the University of Western Ontario Center for Cognitive Science in 1981. The papers included here deal with theoretical and philosophical issues of knowledge and meaning, issues in the computational theory of the mind as suggested by the title. More specifically, four major topics are presented, including the modularity of mind, written by Jerry Fodor, the symbol level and the knowledge level, written by Allen Newell, problems in procedural semantics, written by William A. Woods, and computational psychology and interpretation theory, written by Hilary Putnam. Equally important are transcripts of various comments made after the delivery of the papers and the discussions that occurred during the workshop afterwards. These discussions help to sharpen the understanding of the presented ideas from different angles. For anyone interested in the more theoretical and philosophical aspects of cognitive science, this book is a must.   John Y. Cheung

15.   Rubin, Michael Rogers, and Mary Taylor Huber, with Elizabeth Lloyd Taylor. **The Knowledge Industry in the United States 1960-1980.** Princeton, N.J., Princeton University Press, 1986. 213p. index. $40.00. LC 85-43307. ISBN 0-691-04235-7.

This book is an update of an earlier study, *The Production and Distribution of Knowledge in the United States* (Princeton University Press, 1962) by Fritz Machlup. In that book, Machlup gathered a statistical profile of a group of knowledge industries using a classification system in five categories: education, media of communication, information machines, information services, and other information activities. Machlup further divided these categories into about fifty individual information branches. He had intended to continue his work in a series entitled "Knowledge: Its Creation, Distribution, and Economic Significance" but his death prevented him from completing this plan.

The authors of this volume have continued Machlup's research by using tables, correspondence, and "at least 20 large file drawers" of data which he had gathered. Having been involved in the original plan for the series of ten books on the subject, the authors adhere to the methodology of Machlup's study. It is of great value that the book is structured for easy comparison with the earlier work, and the authors frequently summarize the results of such comparisons for the reader.

The work is very well organized and well written. Tables are explained and interpreted for the reader. There are sections on the general categories of the classification system and a good index. Often, where there are flaws in the presentation because of inherent confusions in the classification system, the authors bring this to the reader's attention.

One of the authors of this work, Michael Rubin, was also involved, along with Marc Porat, in a nine-volume work, *The Information Economy* (Government Printing Office, 1977), which uses a slightly different and more detailed classification system. Therefore, this work, apart from its independent value, is part of a much larger picture. The interpretive text certainly reflects the depth of background which was brought to the effort.

This book is indispensable to any library planning to have a basic collection on the economics of information and knowledge industries.   James Rice

16.   Slack, Jennifer Daryl, and Fred Fejes, eds. **The Ideology of the Information Age.** Norwood, N.J., Ablex Publishing, 1987. 277p. index. (Communication and Information Science). $37.50. LC 86-17423. ISBN 0-89391-139-9.

As we enter the Information Age we are as confused about our future as were those who entered the industrial age over a hundred years ago. More significantly, the information as opposed to the industrial age is a contested terrain whose very definitions differ remarkably from field to field. The essays compiled in this book, while differing in approach, share the theme that the Information Age is an ongoing articulation of political, economic, and ideological relations. The essays are clustered around two main subjects concerning the Information Age: the role of ideology critique, containing two essays, and the challenges to the dominant ideology, which is the largest part of the book. This subject is subdivided into "Philosophical and Theoretical Assumptions," containing essays on information and history and on the sociology of information; "Images of the Future," represented by six essays; and "The International Dimension," under which are listed essays on worldwide implications of the Information Age. The essays in this section which deal with Third World countries are especially interesting. This book is a must for academic and relevant special libraries and for the library of any educated person.

Antonio Rodriguez-Buckingham

17. Stillings, Neil A., and others. **Cognitive Science: An Introduction.** Cambridge, Mass., MIT Press, 1987. 533p. illus. index. $25.00. LC 86-27420. ISBN 0-262-19257-8.

This undergraduate text begins with a chapter describing the interdisciplinary field of cognitive science. In the next seven chapters, basic concepts in the five fields at whose intersection cognitive science lies are discussed: psychology, artificial intelligence, linguistics, neuroscience, and philosophy. The text concludes with four chapters on interdisciplinary research topics: language acquisition, semantics, natural language processing, and vision. Each chapter includes additional suggested readings. Technical concepts in the five fields are explained understandably with excellent examples relating to the everyday world. Cognitive science is concerned with information processes from a variety of perspectives and is clearly a subject relevant to the interests of information scientists. A review of this text would be a good means of familiarizing oneself with basic concepts in this field.   Margaret McKinley

18. Vickery, Brian, and Alina Vickery. **Information Science in Theory and Practice.** Stoneham, Mass., Butterworths, 1987. 384p. index. $59.95. LC 86-29913. ISBN 0-408-10684-0.

It is a pleasure to review this excellent book written by two eminent British researchers. Brian C. Vickery has a distinguished career as a researcher in information science and as a practitioner of information retrieval. In 1948, he was the first to point out the ambiguity between the verbal and graphic formulations of Bradford's Law of Scattering in an article published in the *Journal of Documentation.* He has subsequently made other important contributions to our field. Alina Vickery has made her mark in recent years in applying artificial intelligence techniques to information retrieval, specifically in referral systems.

In the broadest sense, this book seeks to further the understanding of communication and the processes of information transfer in society. This transfer is viewed in the context of society or social groups, individual knowledge states or "private knowledge," and structures of the relevant subject domains or "public knowledge." The key in the information communication process is the transfers of meaning. The essence of information retrieval is the transfer of meaning from sources to recipients. The ultimate aim of the theory and practice of information retrieval is to help optimize this process.

The book can be roughly divided into three major parts. The first four chapters explore the complexities found in the communication activi-

ties of people and their social context. Specific research studies are reported. Retrieval and information systems are covered in chapters 5-8. From the standpoint of information organization, problems, particularly those involved with semantics, are treated in-depth. Although much promise has been shown by many extensive investigations, enormous problems still remain to be resolved. With brutal frankness, the authors note that there is very little understanding of the knowledge structures which could be realistically modeled and captured in retrieval systems or expert systems. Thus, the current systems based on these imperfect semantic models are bound to produce modest and limited results. Query formulation and representation are equally complex and are also dependent on a variety of semantic factors. Areas of cognitive and behavioral studies are also not exact sciences. The last part of the book is devoted to evaluation of systems and a general discussion of information in society, including the impact of technology.

The preface indicates that this is not a manual of research methods nor a handbook of information systems design. It does contain a good deal of solid research findings as well as many critical evaluations of good and bad research. Indeed, the potential usefulness of much "cutting edge" research are discussed. One of the many strengths of this book is the inclusion of many specific research studies supporting the accomplishments of this field. The authors leave no doubt that human communication of information is complex and that information required by individuals or social groups is diverse, varied, and influenced by many factors. Yet clearly, Vickery and Vickery have conveyed the intellectual excitement and dynamism of information science. Although many examples are taken from British sources, the authors are by no means parochial in their approach. Important contributions to information retrieval and information science and key experimental studies are well represented.

The authors have produced a scholarly text. It is clearly written and its content well supported by carefully selected research findings. Anyone interested in information retrieval or the broader area of information science will want to read this book. Although it may not be suitable as a textbook for a single course in many library information science curricula in the United States, it most certainly should be an indispensable supplementary text. Finally, this is a handsome book published by Butterworths. It is a pity that its steep price of $59.95 will deter some, especially students, from purchasing it.

Miranda Lee Pao

Reference Works

ABBREVIATIONS AND ACRONYMS

19. Montgomery, A. C., comp. and ed. **Acronyms & Abbreviations in Library & Information Work: A Reference Handbook of British Usage.** 3d ed. London, Library Association; distr., Chicago, American Library Association, 1986. 220p. $10.00pa. ISBN 0-85365-946-X.

This is the third edition of a work first published in 1975. The author is Head of Library Services at the British Aerospace in the Naval Weapons Division. The book is a straightforward alphabetical listing of more than six thousand "acronyms and abbreviations encountered in the English language literature." The selection is therefore tied directly to those systems, organizations, resources, terms, etc., which have received notice in that literature. There are cross-references to changed names and to variations. The format is paperback. The print is easily read, using boldface capital letters for the acronym/abbreviation, and regular upper- and lowercase type for the expanded name. There is no reverse listing by expanded version.

Since 1975, when this title was first published, the number of entries has doubled and the layout has been made considerably more legible. As ever, there is entertainment for the happy browser: amusing entries (e.g., a Swedish entry, "BUMS ... now BICEPS"), depressing entries (e.g., "FOG—Future of Groups"), inappropriate acronyms (e.g., "RUSTIC—Regional and Urban Studies Information Centre"), and stunning self-awareness (e.g., "CACUL—Canadian Association of College and University Libraries"). Some entries may exceed what one wanted to know (e.g., "BNBCC—British National Bibliography Cricket Club"). The vast majority are of a more ordinary cast.

While, as the subtitle suggests, this book is intended for the British market, many of the entries are American and Canadian. This fact, together with the detailed British entries and the reasonable price, make the book a good purchase for libraries called upon to decipher the growing morass of ugly letter groups.

Elizabeth Frick

BIBLIOGRAPHIES

20. Davis, Donald G., Jr., and Charles D. Patterson, eds. **ARBA Guide to Library Science Literature, 1970-1983.** Littleton, Colo., Libraries Unlimited, 1987. 682p. index. $65.00. LC 86-27712. ISBN 0-87287-585-7.

"This work," according to the editors, "provides a foundation for the coverage which *Library Science Annual*, devoted to book reviews along with other bibliographical surveys, has continued from 1985 onward. It also constitutes the first step in a retrospective bibliography. The second step anticipates a work that reviews the literature of library science from the nineteenth century to 1970."

Of the many spinoffs from *American Reference Books Annual*, this hefty volume should be one of the most useful to the practicing librarian and the library educator. Surprisingly, we have precious few monographic bibliographies of the literature of library science, especially of reference books. The rather early cut-off date of 1983 for the present volume excludes one of the most notable of those bibliographies, *Reference Sources in Library and Information Services: A Guide to the Literature*, by Gary R. Purcell and Gail Ann Schlachter (1984). A combination of these two provides a measure of the breadth of reference publications in library science; the *ARBA* volume includes 1,728 entries, the other 1,193. While overlap is unavoidable, both contain a relatively high percentage of unique items, with Purcell and Schlachter being the more international of the two. The subject coverage in both works is truly impressive.

The arrangement of the current work follows that of *ARBA*, with some modifications. The reviews are taken, of course, from annual volumes of *ARBA*, with little if any revision or updating. Thus the reviews tend to be more substantial than the annotations in Purcell and Schlachter, but because of the diversity of authorship they are also more uneven. (An excellent perspective on *ARBA* itself is provided on pp. 32-33 in the review of volume 15, 1984, by the late A. Robert Rogers.)

All in all, this work reflects very well how librarians view their own, very substantial reference literature, and as such will be an indispensable item for virtually all libraries with professional collections. [R: Choice, Oct 87, p. 279; JAL, Sept 87, p. 234]   Edwin S. Gleaves

21. Herring, Mark Youngblood. **Controversial Issues in Librarianship: An Annotated Bibliography 1960-1984.** New York, Garland, 1987. 698p. index. (Garland Reference Library of Social Science, Vol. 342). $45.00. LC 86-12098. ISBN 0-8240-8578-7.

For the purpose of this annotated bibliography, "controversial" includes ongoing, often vitriolic, subjects as well as less emotional "gentlemen's debates." The topics covered range from the pedestrian (volunteers in libraries, networking) to the truly controversial (one year versus two year MLS degrees, censorship). Herring, director of King College Library in Bristol, Tennessee, has included only works pertaining to controversial topics in the book.

The bibliography has eleven broad chapters dealing with, in order, acquisitions and collection management, library facilities, "the human factor," technology, networking, library education, reference services, management, librarians and society, a librarian's view of the profession, and the future of librarianship. Each chapter is divided into specific categories, and items are arranged alphabetically by author. Whenever possible, Herring has drawn at least part of the annotations from the article itself. There are separate author/name and title indexes. Each chapter is introduced by brief remarks surveying the debate or debates.

This is not a comprehensive bibliography (the faculty status section lists twenty items, for example, while a recent online search yielded over eighty) but it is a good place to find a selection of major works on the selected topics. [R: LJ, 1 June 87, p. 88] Jean Parker

BIOGRAPHIES

22. Munford, W. A. **Who Was Who in British Librarianship, 1800-1985: A Dictionary of Dates with Notes.** London, Library Association; distr., Chicago, American Library Association, 1987. 91p. bibliog. $30.00. ISBN 0-85365-976-1.

Biographical information can often be difficult to find when it concerns those various groups of people who have traditionally been considered insignificant, such as librarians. Fortunately that situation has been changing recently, and the appearance of *Who Was Who in British Librarianship* provides an example of just how good the products of that change can be. W. A. Munford has sketched the careers of the approximately two thousand people who served as senior librarians in the United Kingdom after 1800 and who died before December 1985. Each entry supplies the birth and death dates and the dates and duration of professional appointments when available. In the case of those more famous and accomplished librarians, the entry includes a biographical annotation ranging in length from 25 to 350 words (e.g., Sir Anthony Panizzi), which annotation is sometimes accompanied by a brief bib-

liography. Among the librarians receiving biographical annotations are Henry Bradshaw (1831-1866), chief librarian of the Cambridge University Library, and Barbara Kyle (1913-1966), a leader of Aslib and an editor of the *Journal of Documentation*. While entries for most librarians simply contain the brief facts of vital dates and professional service, that is all this pioneering volume ever intended to do. It provides quick (once one has read the brief "Elucidation" section on page x) access to basic information from which further research can proceed if needed. All of which comes in an attractive and relatively inexpensive volume. This publication helps to make up for the absence, until relatively recently, of an ongoing series of current biographical reference publications about librarians. [R: LAR, 9 Sept 87, p. 473] Ronald H. Fritze

23. Trejo, Arnulfo D., ed. **Quien es Quien: A Who's Who of Spanish-Speaking Librarians in the United States, 1986.** Tucson, Ariz., Hispanic Books, 1986. 74p. $8.50.

The volume is a printed version of a database containing 325 Spanish-speaking librarians in the United States. Each entry contains the name of the person, name of spouse, birthdate, university where library science/doctoral degrees were obtained, fluency in reading and speaking Spanish, type of library where the librarian is employed, work experience, professional and honor society memberships, biographical sources in which the librarian is included, publications, honors, home address, and present position and place of employment.

The method of data collection is not certain, nor are attempts to systematically collect the data; however, the directory is easy to read and interpret. Since the scope now covers Spanish-speaking librarians rather than librarians of Spanish descent, the tool is developing into a more useful and practical one for a profession dealing more and more with diverse patrons. Recommended for personnel directors and others needing this type of information.

David V. Loertscher

CATALOGS AND COLLECTIONS

24. Parks, Stephen. **Elizabethan Club of Yale University and Its Library.** New Haven, Conn., Yale University Press, 1986. 280p. illus. index. (The Elizabethan Club Series, 8). $35.00. LC 86-7789. ISBN 0-300-03669-8.

This is a splendidly produced and valuable catalog and history of the library of the Elizabethan Club at Yale. It contains detailed descriptions of 318 books and manuscripts in the library, an excellent history of the development of the library, and individual histories of many of the books in it, all embellished with sixty-nine illustrations. Each entry in the catalog contains the author, title, imprint, collation, height in centimeters, statement about the edition, a description of the binding, notes about previous ownership, an indication of who gave the book to the club and when, and the citation of appropriate bibliographies. Cross-references to editors, translators, etc., are provided.

Alexander Smith Cochran was the principal benefactor of the club's library, donating three-quarters of its major holdings, and tribute to his generosity is paid by Alan Bell in his introduction. This introduction is valuable in its own right, and is a fine example of the uses of provenance. The illustrations are of the exterior and interior of the Elizabethan Club, title pages, significant pages of text, bookplates, signatures and other indications of provenance, and bindings. There is a full-page portrait of A. S. Cochran and the frontispiece is a color portrait of Elizabeth I. An index to binders and former owners of the books is also provided.

Scholars will welcome this description of an important collection of Elizabethan literature, and the catalog is also a fine example of how such a project can be planned and carried out.   Dean H. Keller

DICTIONARIES

25. Prytherch, Ray, comp. **Harrod's Librarians' Glossary (of Terms Used in Librarianship, Documentation and the Book Crafts) and Reference Book.** 6th ed. Brookfield, Vt., Gower Publishing, 1987. 855p. $79.50. ISBN 0-566-03538-3.

This handsome volume, the sixth edition of a glossary, the credibility of which has grown in the years since its first edition in 1938, appears just three years after the fifth edition. The author explains that the need for a new edition was hastened by the wider range of skills becoming appropriate for librarians with the more flexible range of roles assigned to them. "Over 400 terms from the fifth edition have been revised or removed, and over 600 new entries included." Prytherch was, apparently, tempted to restructure the book, for example, splitting the "book craft and printing terms from the database jargon." He decided against that: the volume is arranged in one alphabet, as were its predecessors.

The author is a well-known lecturer and information consultant who has acted as compiler since the fifth edition, when L. M. Harrod, its

first compiler, became the advisory editor. This edition covers librarianship in a broad sense, including "authorship, editing, printing, publishing, document delivery, collection management, conservation, database and catalogue production, thesaurus construction, system design and management, on-line computing and searching, the management of resources, records and archives, information analysis and repackaging, question and answer services, marketing, research, advice, brokerage, signposting and referral, exhibitions and consultancy."

As has been noted of previous editions, the British tone is evident (e.g., *catalogue, card cabinet*), but this edition covers North American concerns and organizations very well. There is, for instance, the addition of such acronyms as RASD (Reference and Adult Services Division) and CARL (Canadian Association of Research Libraries). The addition of definitions for newer technologies such as *optical digital disk* and *CD-ROM* are most welcome. There are occasional slips. For instance, the new entry *user education* is given no cross-references from possible terms like *library instruction* or *library orientation*.

Harrod's is a solid contribution, unmatched elsewhere. Despite the high price, it is a necessary addition to large and medium-sized collections. [R: JAL, July 87, p. 177; LAR, May 87, p. 244]
                                         Elizabeth Frick

DIRECTORIES

26. **American Library Directory 1987-88.** 40th ed. Judy Redel, ed. New York, R. R. Bowker, 1987. 2v. index. $149.95/set. LC 23-3581. ISBN 0-8352-2339-6; ISSN 0065-910X.

The fortieth edition of this annual provides up-to-date information on public, academic, government, and special libraries in the United States (and areas administered by the U.S. government) and Canada. It is alphabetically arranged by state, city, and name of library within the city. Highlighting each state entry are statistical facts such as total number of volumes, circulation, and expenditures in public libraries. An entry for a library generally includes an address, Standard Address Number (SAN), telephone number, key personnel, founding dates, users served, holdings, automation information, subject interests, special collections, branches, and other information. A single letter on the side designates the type of library (e.g., "P" for public and "S" for special). More than thirty-one thousand libraries and their holdings are listed in the two volumes. Information has been secured through questionnaires from library staffs and from some public sources (noted by an asterisk) when questionnaires were not returned. Some interesting facts emerged in this volume: less than 25 percent of libraries use some form of automation, and New Hampshire has the largest number of books in its public libraries of all states. Because of its currency, *American Library Directory* is a good source for information on individual libraries covered and seems to be reasonably accurate as well.

Anna Grace Patterson

27. Block, David, and Howard L. Karno. **A Directory of Vendors of Latin American Library Materials.** 2d rev. ed. Madison, Wis., SALALM Secretariat, Memorial Library, University of Wisconsin, 1986. 46p. index. (Bibliography and Reference Series, 16). $12.00pa. ISBN 0-917617-09-6.

This second edition of a directory of vendors of Latin American library materials includes information on 137 vendors. It is arranged in alphabetical order by vendor including the address, telephone number, and geographic and subject coverage for each vendor. In addition, it includes an index of geographic coverage and an index of vendors by country. Neophytes might find some basic information on vendors of Latin American materials. It is important to note, however, that important U.S. and Latin American vendors of Latin American materials have been inexplicably omitted and that other less reputable vendors are included. This disparity in coverage severely limits the usefulness of this directory.

Isabel Schon

28. **The CLASS Directory of Interlibrary Loan Policies.** 3d ed. San Jose, Calif., CLASS, 1986. 1v. (unpaged). index. $35.00 looseleaf. ISBN 0-938098-11-X.

This directory, produced by the Cooperative Library Agency for Systems and Services (California), lists the interlibrary loan policies of over six hundred OnTyme and RLIN institutions.

The main listing, alphabetical by name of institution, includes information for each entry that is useful to an interlibrary loan librarian: address, ILL staff, telephone numbers, network affiliations, lending policies, photocopy charges, OnTyme codes, RLIN codes, OCLC codes, NUC codes, WLN codes. The directory has three indexes: (1) OnTyme code, (2) RLIN code, and (3) geographic. The two code indexes, also arranged alphabetically, list the name of the institution and the city and state in which it is located. The user must then turn to the institution section for additional information. The geographic index is arranged alphabetically by

state and then city. Various departmental libraries are entered individually so that the number of institutions listed as included may be somewhat inflated, and most of these are located in the Western section of the United States, with over one-third from California.

This directory may be useful to libraries working with OnTyme and RLIN institutions. Current information on interlibrary loan policies is always useful. However, much of this material is available in other sources which cover a larger group of libraries or online where it can more easily be kept up-to-date.

Esther Jane Carrier

29. **International Directory of Library, Archives and Information Science Associations.** 2d rev. ed. Paris, General Information Programme and UNISIST; distr., New York, United Nations, 1986. 160p. index. price not reported.

Information on nearly four hundred library, archives, and information science associations is provided in this revised trilingual directory (English, French, and Spanish), originally published in 1983 by UNESCO. The descriptive information has been updated for 110 associations, based on responses to a questionnaire.

Part 1 lists twenty-nine international associations. Part 2 delineates national associations, arranged by country in French alphabetical order with English and Spanish translations. For example, if one is looking for German associations, they are listed under Allemagne (Republique Federale D')/Germany/Allemania. Within each country, associations are arranged alphabetically by title. Look for American associations under Etats-Unis d'Amerique; then subdivided by state, according to address. For example, the American Library Association is listed under Illinois.

Entries vary from simple addresses, such as the entry for the American Library Association, to detailed descriptions including date of founding, membership, main activities, bulletin/review, and other publications. All entries include association abbreviations when appropriate. There is also an alphabetical index of associations; the language of the country of origin is used. For example, Deutsche Bibliotheks Konferenz (German Standing Conference on Libraries) is found under Allemagne in the directory and "Deutsche" in the index. While the trilingual format is a bit awkward at times, this directory does provide a useful listing of difficult to locate international associations.

Esther R. Dyer

30.   Johnson, Jane G., ed. **Library Buildings Consultant List.** Chicago, Library Administration and Management Association, American Library Association, 1987. 120p. bibliog. index. $15.00 spiralbound. ISBN 0-8389-7086-9.

This paperbound book lists consultants who met minimum criteria established by the Buildings and Equipment Section of the ALA's Library Administration and Management Association, though the organization disclaims endorsement or certification of these persons.

There are two alphabetical (by name) lists of consultants: (1) librarians, and (2) architects and interior designers. For each individual, skeleton-type information is provided, including address, affiliation, experience, geographical limits, availability, fees, etc. The three indexes are by personal name, type of library, and state. Many of these names are widely recognized for their extensive work on building projects. Information was gathered by inviting candidates to apply and to submit a completed form.

For its specialized purpose, this update of the 1985 list is fully satisfactory.

Robert N. Broadus

31.   Makower, Joel, and Alan Green, eds. **Instant Information.** New York, Prentice Hall Press, 1987. 705p. index. $29.95; $19.95pa. LC 86-43169. ISBN 0-13-467804-4; 0-13-609413-9pa.

Condensed from the computerized databases at the Library of Congress, this fascinating directory contains nearly nine thousand listings of organizations which can provide up-to-date information on nearly any subject. The editors extracted the material from the LC database, edited it, organized it, and added more organizations to produce this book. From the Comet Information Center and the U.S. Botanic Gardens to the Association of Railway Museums and the Catholic Medical Mission Board, the variety of sources for information seems endless.

The listings include libraries, universities, trade associations, citizens' action programs, committees, resource centers, corporations, "think tanks," foundations, and basically any sort of organization that can provide information. Arrangement is alphabetical by state, including Canada and Puerto Rico. Addresses and telephone numbers are provided; there is a brief paragraph describing the organization's interests and services. Indexes by subject and organization enhance usability.

This compact, easy to use volume is a great source of information for any reference department. [R: Choice, Sept 87, p. 88; RBB, 15 Sept 87, p. 124]

Shirley Lambert

32.   Smith, Catherine, comp. and ed. **Inside Information 1987/88: A Directory of Organisations, Products and Services in the Information Sector.** 2d ed. London, TFPL Publishing, 1987. 194p. index. £30.00pa. ISBN 1-870889-06-1.

The title of this work aptly describes the contents, namely a broad range of organizations offering products and services to the information world. Entries include library schools, special library interest groups, library associations and library cooperatives, as well as major chambers of commerce, embassies, and academic and public libraries with special collections. Major vendors of computerized information services such as DIALOG and BRS are included as are hardware manufacturers such as Apple computers, Hewlett Packard, and IBM. Booksellers and book publishers are also included.

Unfortunately the scope of the volume primarily is limited to organizations headquartered or with branch offices in the United Kingdom. Thus, while one finds an entry for the American Library Association (ALA, Chicago) and the Special Libraries Association (SLA, Washington, D.C.), there is no entry for the American Society for Information Science. Addresses for international organizations such as IBM are provided only if they have an office in the United Kingdom, although there is a listing for Staatsbibliothek Preussischer Kulturbesitz with a Berlin address.

Entries generally include an address, one or more contact persons, and a brief description. The entries are arranged alphabetically, supplemented by a subject and keyword index. A listing of acronyms and abbreviations is also provided for some of the organizations. A separate section lists major conferences and events for 1988 although this too is incomplete. For example, SLA's annual conference is noted but no mention is made for ALA.

The compiler of this volume notes in the introduction that it is not fully comprehensive and that other directories complement it. This caveat notwithstanding, the potpourri of entries in the volume will serve only the user hoping to locate primarily British organizations linked in some way to the information industry.

Andrew G. Torok

33.   Whiteley, Sandy, comp. **Marketing to Libraries through Library Associations.** Chicago, American Library Association, 1987. 48p. index. (American Library Association Publishing Services Marketing Survey). $24.95pa. ISBN 0-8389-0470-X.

This small publication lists seventy-eight national, international, regional, state, and province library associations and contains "information on mailing list rental, advertising, and conferences." The compiler sent questionnaires "to more than 90 library associations," but at least 11 did not respond. Information contained in each entry includes name of association, address, telephone number, name of contact person, description of membership, number of members, mailing list rental information, availability of journal advertising, and availability of conference exhibits and advertising. The arrangement of the directory is alphabetical by name of library association within the two separate parts—national and international associations in the front and state, province, and regional in the back. The subject index is tucked away on page 20 between the two parts.

Marketing to Libraries was compared with *The Bowker Annual of Library & Book Trade Information 1987* (see entry 38) which lists library associations from all states and Canadian provinces, including the eleven which did not respond to the questionnaire. Entries in *The Bowker Annual* provide the number of members and the name, address, and telephone numbers of association officers, and a separate calendar of association meetings is also included. Many publishers and vendors may find *Marketing to Libraries* more appealing for their needs in publicizing their materials and services for two reasons: it includes marketing data and it costs less than one-third the price of *The Bowker Annual*.   O. Gene Norman

---

HANDBOOKS AND YEARBOOKS

34. Advances in Librarianship. Volume 14. Wesley Simonton, ed. Orlando, Fla., Academic Press, 1986. 320p. index. $37.50. LC 79-88675. ISBN 0-12-024614-7.

The 1986 edition of *Advances in Librarianship* consists of nine contributed papers, the first four constituting a thematic grouping on the subject of information use and policy. The first paper, written by Norman D. Stevens, provides a historical background. Nancy Freeman Rohde's critical review of user studies excludes few of the seminal works on the subject. Martha L. Hale identifies the methods used by information professionals in diagnosing information needs. Pamela Spence Richards reviews developments which influenced current information policy in the German Democratic Republic.

In other papers, Richard D. Johnson discusses collection development in four-year college libraries. Robert A. Seal reviews the literature on academic branch library collections. Michael H. Harris surveys and evaluates

library research and development in the United States. Richard C. Berner discusses the relationships between archivists, librarians, and records managers. Jean M. Perreault identifies problems caused by current trends and attempts at systematization of indexing and cataloging policy. Inadequate and difficult to locate catalog entries could be the end result.

While each paper is generally well written, those by Rohde, Harris, and Berner may have added significance for possible future professional development. Perreault's paper may be the most difficult to read, as he discusses problems which are not well understood. [R: JAL, Mar 87, p. 39]   Robert M. Ballard

35. Annual Review of Information Science and Technology. Volume 21: 1986. Martha E. Williams, ed. White Plains, N.Y., published for American Society for Information Science by Knowledge Industry, 1986. 432p. index. $52.50. LC 66-25096. ISBN 0-86729-209-1; ISSN 0066-4200.

The stated purpose of *ARIST* "is to describe and to appraise activities and trends in the field of information science and technology." This has been its purpose since Carlos A. Cuadra issued the first volume in 1966. Rather than cover the spectrum of possible topics each year, the annual has major topical reviews on a rotating basis. Thus, most authors will pick up their review of the literature where a previous author left off. Such a practice provides some continuity in the field, and as such provides an invaluable theory building/review mechanism.

The current volume concentrates on information needs and users, subject analysis, software interfaces for electronic information systems, business databases, a review of electronic publishing, a discussion of computer-mediated communication systems, a description of U.S. congressional efforts to implement a technological information system, a review of environmental information, and a view of the information resource management professional.

The articles, no matter the quality of writing, provide some sort of guide to the literature of the time span covered. This function is an important one to scholars and students alike. Particularly good essays in the current volume include Richard H. Lytle's discussion of the emergence of the information resource manager, which should be read by every librarian as well as information professional. Chartrand's article on the information revolution in Congress makes one wonder what role the Library of Congress is carving out for itself in the information process. Hjerppe's article on electronic publishing is one of the most current overviews, far beyond a review of electronic word processing/typesetting trends.

Like its predecessors, this volume gives one pause to look beyond the pressures of the day toward function, theory, ideas, research results and possibilities, and trends. A number of annuals in the field of library and information science are being produced which look at single topics within the field, but this tool retains its importance and significance to the profession.

David V. Loertscher

36.   ASIS Handbook and Directory, 1986. White Plains, N.Y., American Society for Information Science/Knowledge Industry, 1986. 128p. $50.00pa. LC 59-24244. ISBN 0-87715-517-8; ISSN 0066-0124.

As an official publication of the American Society for Information Science (ASIS), this handbook not only provides names and addresses of members of the organization but provides essential information about the organization itself. Sections on the organization's leadership, structure, chapters, special interest groups, historical information, and constitution and bylaws, complete with indexes, make this an indispensable publication for all wanting organizational information.   David V. Loertscher

37.   Berkman, Robert I. Find It Fast: How to Uncover Expert Information on Any Subject. New York, Harper & Row, 1987. 260p. index. $14.95; $6.95pa. LC 86-45640. ISBN 0-06-055061-9; 0-06-096153-8pa.

This is a useful book, designed to help "writers, businesspeople, job seekers, entrepreneurs, students or anyone who needs facts, data, answers or advice." But the reader needs to devote some time to it: it should first be read from beginning to end, because it is about information gathering strategy and about finding subject experts fully as much as it is about published information sources.

Part 1, "Unlocking the Information Vault," provides a brief overview of types of libraries and the obvious basic published sources: directories, indexes, abstracts, etc., and online search services. Most sophisticated reference librarians might quibble that many excellent guides or directories are not discussed. However, a less skilled researcher will find the described sources helpful. One particularly good chapter discusses in detail the types of information available from the U.S. government. Part 2, "Experts Are Everywhere," is a particularly good section. It should be read first as a complete unit. The author takes the reader through the process of identifying subject experts, making connections, and then talking with them.

Part 3, "Two Sample Searches," should be helpful to anyone embarking on an information gathering process for the first time. Public service librarians would offer much the same advice, which is clearly presented.

The index is more useful after one has read through the entire book and understands its tone and organization. It is less useful as a starting research point. The entries are usually listed by source (e.g., ERIC) rather than by subject (education). A researcher looking for sources of information about deceptive advertising needs to look under "consumer affairs"; information about retired executives willing to consult for new entrepreneurs is found under SCORE (The Service Corps of Retired Executives).

This handy volume provides practical and sensible advice in an easy to read style. It is recommended for college, public, and large high school libraries. [R: LJ, 1 Mar 87, pp. 67-68]

Susan S. Baughman

38.   The Bowker Annual of Library & Book Trade Information 1987. 32d ed. Filomena Simora, comp. and ed. New York, R. R. Bowker, 1987. 740p. index. $89.95. LC 55-12434. ISBN 0-8352-2333-7; ISSN 0068-0540.

The Bowker Annual, for the thirty-second time, performs its indispensable role for librarians and booksellers by providing statistical information, summaries of news, and coverage of the most important issues of the field. Serving as the "Bible" of the two professions, the breadth and depth of the information it covers are amazing. The structure of the current edition remains the same as the previous ones, with "Reports from the Field"; "Legislation, Funding, Grants"; "Library/Information Science Education, Placement, and Salaries"; "Research and Statistics"; "Reference Information"; and "Directory of Organizations." A special feature of this edition is the essays on access to information by major theorists and practitioners in the field.

For the most part, the information is as current as one could expect for such a massive undertaking. Statistics are covered for the previous calendar year, as are officers of organizations. Addresses are given for president-elect officers so that correspondence can usually be directed to the current year's president. Some lists, however, need to be more current. For example, "The Librarian's Bookshelf" contained only 1984 and 1985 titles. The "High Technology Bibliography" contained titles through 1985. However, the "Basic Publications for the Publisher and the Book Trade" contained titles through 1986.

While its $90.00 price has taken it out of the reach of many smaller library budgets, the annual continues as *the* major handbook for librarians and booksellers. [R: JAL, Sept 87, p. 236; LJ, 1 Nov 87, p. 71]

David V. Loertscher

39. Library and Information Science Annual 1987. Volume 3. Bohdan S. Wynar and others, eds. Littleton, Colo., Libraries Unlimited, 1987. 265p. index. $37.50. ISBN 0-87287-596-2; ISSN 8755-2108.

As a companion volume to *American Reference Books Annual*, this book (formerly *Library Science Annual*) includes a greater number of book reviews than its earlier volumes on information and library science. The volume provides a wide array of current reference sources which can be particularly useful for collection development. Part 1 presents essays of current interest on topics such as CD-ROM, micro hardware, and the research efforts of ALA and ALISE. Part 2 contains nearly 390 reviews covering general reference works, information technology, and special libraries and collections, among others. Periodical reviews of publications comprise part 3. The final part is devoted exclusively to a survey of library and information science doctoral dissertations listed alphabetically by author's name. Overall this volume has a much broader coverage of British and Canadian titles than the earlier volumes.

Wynar and Prentice provide an excellent, up-to-date guide to important reference sources for books and periodicals. The reviews can assist library educators and practitioners in information gathering activities. Complete citations precede each review. Although this material is somewhat less valuable to library students, it is an important source of reference tools for practitioners. The work is extremely accurate, with no misspellings found from the sample checked. As the editors have pointed out, *LISCA* is an indispensable reference guide for any librarian who wants to touch base with the current publishing trends in the library and information field, thereby to benefit from future innovations.

(Christina) Young Hyun Allen

40. The Library Association Yearbook 1987. R. E. Palmer, comp. London, Library Association; distr., Chicago, American Library Association, 1987. 393p. $30.00pa. ISBN 0-85365-857-9; ISSN 0075-9066.

Everything one would like to know about the Library Association of the United Kingdom may be found here. Included is information on the Library Association Council and staff; committees, branches, groups, and sections of the Library Association; publications; the charter, by-laws, and election regulations; medals, awards, and research grants administered by the Library Association; and a current list of members.

Personal members are listed alphabetically with current professional position. Dates are also given indicating when a member joined the association and another date following the letter "F" (Fellow) or "A" (Associate) is the year of election to the professional register as a Chartered Librarian.

In many respects this book is very similar to the *ALA Handbook of Organization and Membership Directory*, which also comes out yearly.

George S. Bobinski

41. Wertsman, Vladimir F. The Librarian's Companion: A Handbook of Thousands of Facts and Figures on Libraries/Librarians, Books/Newspapers, Publishers/Booksellers. Westport, Conn., Greenwood Press, 1987. 166p. index. $35.00. LC 86-29591. ISBN 0-313-25500-8.

The eclectic information about libraries and librarians gathered into this handbook reflects the compiler's affection for his profession. The first part of the book, "The Librarian's World Digest," is an alphabetical list of countries with subheadings "General Background," "Library Network," "Publishing Output and Distribution," "Noted Libraries," and "Librarians' Organization." Sufficient information is provided to give the reader an overview of the country and its level of literacy. Data are drawn from several basic reference sources such as the *World Guide to Libraries* (Saur, 1983) and UNESCO's *Statistical Yearbook*. By combining library and population statistics, the author provides a unique *LHO ratio*, that is, library holdings (in volumes) ratio per inhabitant. The principal value of the digest is to assemble a variety of information that makes it possible to compare one country with another. It is not ideal as a directory, however, because the information is dated (the cut-off dates being 1982-1983), and users would be well advised to consult updated versions of the cited sources for current data.

The second part of the book, entitled "The Librarian's Special Interests," contains four lists, each preceded by a brief bibliography. They are: "Noted Librarians, Past and Present," which provides birth and death dates, a sentence or two stating the relationship to libraries, and a source of reference for 118 people as diverse as Daniel Boorstin and Ptolemy I; "Who Said What on Books, Libraries, and Librarians," which consists of 125 quotations, some translated; and "Librarian's Belle Lettres," which cites and provides one-sentence annotations for ninety-five books or plays featuring librarians, however marginally. The final list is an uncommon list of 116 entries on "Librarian's Philately: Books, Newspapers, and Libraries on Stamps, by Country." An index of countries and personal names completes the volume.

In publishing this handbook Greenwood Press has enabled Wertsman to share his active curiosity about aspects of librarianship and his diligent compilations of unusual facts. Although not a general reference book, it should appeal to others with similar interests.

Joan W. Jensen

42.   Woodworth, David, ed. **Year's Work in Serials 1985.** New York, K. G. Saur, 1986. 143p. index. $28.00. ISBN 0-86291-567-8.

The 1985 literature on serials in libraries and on serials publishing and distribution is reviewed in six bibliographic essays plus a general overview and introduction. Of unique interest in the general overview essay is a section on the problems encountered by Third World countries in gaining access to information. In a collection management essay, there are discussions of weeding, cancellations, resource sharing, collection evaluation, use and user studies, citation analysis, interlibrary loan, newspapers, and microfilm. In an essay on bibliography the literature on serials lists, union lists, serials bibliographies, abstracting and indexing, and online databases is reviewed. A chapter on acquisition and administration covers the practical aspects of acquiring and maintaining a serials collection, including pricing, subscription agents, resource sharing, access, and storage. In an essay on automation, the literature on commercially available serials control systems as well as local development or data conversion efforts in UK or U.S. libraries is reviewed. In an essay on publishing, uses of citation data are discussed as well as pricing (once again), electronic publishing, and the proliferation of new journals. Essays are accompanied by extensive bibliographies whose entries consist primarily of journal articles from UK and U.S. periodicals. The literature on serials in 1985, in all of its many aspects, is well and carefully analyzed in each of the essays. A general emphasis on the international aspects of serials publishing and serials librarianship is especially worthy of note.

Margaret McKinley

INDEXES

43.   **Index to Free Periodicals: An Author, Title, and Subject Guide to Current Issues and to Research and Development Activities ... Volume 11, Number 2: July-December 1986.** C. Edward Wall, ed. Ann Arbor, Mich., Pierian Press, 1987. 57p. $15.00pa.

Designed to supplement *Readers' Guide to Periodical Literature*, this index offers author, title, and subject access to articles appearing in free periodicals. While one certainly should applaud the effort to collect and make accessible fugitive material, *Index to Free Periodicals* is not without some serious shortcomings, both with respect to content and indexing practices.

Modeling itself after *Readers' Guide*, the index purports to offer "a balanced coverage of subjects encompassing the humanities, social sciences, science and technology." In spite of this stated goal, the periodicals indexed lean heavily towards business titles, some sponsored by research organizations, others published by a particular company (*Ford Times* and *Friends*, a publication of the Chevrolet Division of General Motors, are two examples). The thirty-eight periodicals indexed in the July-December 1986 issue are an uneven mix of publications, with few covering any aspect of the humanities.

The introduction states that "like *Readers' Guide*, it is one of the few indexes providing an author, title, and subject approach" (p. ii). Title indexing is as inappropriate here as it would be in *Readers' Guide* (if *RG* bothered with that type of indexing). In *Index to Free Periodicals*, the title approach simply serves as filler, turning a rather flimsy publication into a somewhat more substantial one, at least in number of pages.

Although a case can be made for a publication that provides subject access to free periodicals, neither the format nor the journals represented indicate that *Index to Free Periodicals* adequately addresses that need.

Ellen Broidy

44.   **LCPA's Index to the** *Library of Congress Information Bulletin* **1986 (Volume 45).** By Betsy Reifsnyder. Washington, D.C., Library of Congress Professional Association, 1987. 51p. $10.00pa.

The *Library of Congress Information Bulletin* (*LCIB*) is the chief medium of communication between the Library of Congress (LC) and its staff as well as other libraries worldwide. It includes descriptions of past and future events at LC, announcements of LC projects and programs, bibliographies, photographs, summaries of national and international conferences, and staff news both professional and personal. In recent years, LC has been lacking resources to compile an annual index on a regular basis. In view of the research value of *LCIB* to a wide audience, the Library of Congress Professional Association (LCPA) undertook the project of preparing an index starting with the 1984 volume. It expects to continue the index on an annual basis, and hopes to compile cumulative indexes. This index is not an official LC publication, and those issuing *LCIB* are not involved in its preparation or distribution. It is copyrighted by LCPA. This index was prepared using terms from a special thesaurus which was created specifically for this project and is based chiefly on *Library of Congress Subject Headings*. Name headings are modeled after established forms in AACR2 and the LC authority file. A number of collective headings have been used for such items as acquisitions; concerts, plays, readings, and lectures at LC; and visitors to LC. In most cases, items collected under these headings are also indexed separately. A separate appendix, "Personnel Changes," lists permanent staff appointments, promotions, resignations, etc. Temporary appointments are not listed. Because the "blue pages" of the *LCIB* (called "Staff News") are not numbered, these are referred to by the page number immediately preceding the blue section, with the addition of a lowercase letter (a, b, c, etc.) referring to the first, second, third, etc., blue page. New with this edition are listings for grants from foundations and other monetary contributions. LeRoy C. Schwarzkopf

45. Organizations Master Index: A Consolidated Index to Approximately 50 Directories, Handbooks, Yearbooks, Encyclopedias, and Guides.... Denise M. Allard, ed. Detroit, Gale, 1987. 1120p. bibliog. index. $120.00. LC 86-27129. ISBN 0-8103-2079-7.

This work is an index to forty-five directories of organizations and institutions. In a single alphabet, *Organizations Master Index* (*OMI*) has approximately 150,000 entries for national and international associations, government agencies and advisory organizations, and foundations, plus many others listed in the above directories. Most entries in *OMI* contain the title of an organization, the sponsor or parent affiliation when needed, a geographical location if needed, and the abbreviated source code with publishing year for directories where organizations are listed. The user will find the annotations of the directories helpful in determining which sources to use. In developing this index, written and telephone surveys with librarians were conducted. The final list of sources included in *OMI* was selected from these surveys. The editors attempted to be consistent in their listing of organizations, but do encourage users to check for variant possibilities. Some of the source material indexed includes *American Art Directory* (see *ARBA* 85, entry 888), *Encyclopedia of Associations*, *The Foundation Directory* (see *ARBA* 86, entry 41), and *The United States Government Manual* (see *ARBA* 84, entry 456). Granting that the emphasis is probably on English-language titles, the inclusion of works from Great Britain, West Germany, and Canada assures some degree of international coverage. The number of organizations included is outstanding. Although the price seems unusually high, larger libraries, particularly, will want to acquire this title for their reference collections. [R: Choice, May 87, p. 1382; RBB, 1 June 87, p. 1508; WLB, Apr 87, p. 68]

Anna Grace Patterson

46. Special Libraries: A Cumulative Index 1981-1986: A Cumulative Author/Title/Subject/Member Information Index to All Issues of *Special Libraries* from 1981 through 1986. Joyce A. Post, comp. Washington, D.C., Special Libraries Association, 1987. 40p. $20.00pa. ISBN 0-87111-327-9.

This index provides access to articles appearing in *Special Libraries* from 1981 to 1986 by author, subject, and title. Book reviews are indexed by title, author, and reviewer. Software reviews are listed together under "Software." Letters are indexed under the name of the writer and, if written in response to an article appearing in *Special Libraries*, also indexed with that article.

This index offers coverage for only five years (1981-1986), while the last separate index to *Special Libraries* covered a decade of issues (1971-1980). Producing such an index every five years rather than every ten years should guarantee greater usefulness to those whose research requires timely access to literature on these types of libraries. Unfortunately, the price remains the same for half the time coverage, reflecting the effect the last five years have had on the cost of publishing.

The index should prove useful in tracking down information about the Special Libraries Association (SLA) and the individuals active in its functions, as these are included either under subheadings of SLA or the individual's name.

Elizabeth D. Liddy

ACQUISITIONS

47. Lee, Sul H., ed. **Pricing and Costs of Monographs and Serials: National and International Issues.** New York, Haworth Press, 1987. 109p. (*Journal of Library Administration*, Vol. 8. Suppl., No. 1). $29.95. LC 86-33653. ISBN 0-86656-620-1.

This publication is the result of a national conference held in February 1986 on the pricing and costs of monographs and serials. Included in it are informative perspectives about book and serial vendors, approval plans, and acquisition costs of both serials and monographs. The timing of the conference was especially opportune given the fact that it was the beginning of the decline of the U.S. dollar abroad. This would culminate ten months later with one of the steepest increases in non-U.S. published titles in the last decade.

The presenters represent not only librarians but vendors and publishers as well, and provide an in-depth assessment of why the costs for library materials have risen more steeply than the cost of other goods and services. A number of the articles refer back to Charles Hamaker and Deana Astle's excellent article, "Recent Pricing in British Journal Publishing" (*Library Acquisitions: Practice and Theory* 8 [1984]), and Marcia Tuttle's article in *LRTS* 30 (January/March 1986), "The Pricing of British Journals for the North American Market." Since a fair number of the presentations in this work do deal with the British/U.S. price differential, readers are referred to these works as well.

For the most part, the articles found in this work are reactive. They describe why vendors add on service fees; they describe why discounts (except, perhaps, for the bestsellers) have diminished so noticeably in recent years. A few of the articles, notably the ones by Christian M. Boissonnas and Lenore Clark, take a more proactive approach in that they offer some suggestions for ways in which librarians can fight back when they feel they are being unfairly gouged.

Although the volume lacks an index, the titles of the essays provide a reasonable overview of their contents; nor is the volume so large that the omission of an index is critical. The overall subject is one that is not about to dissipate. The topics are relevant today and will continue to be so in the future. This volume is recommended to any library that has a limited acquisitions budget. [R: JAL, Nov 87, p. 318]

Marjorie E. Bloss

ARTIFICIAL INTELLIGENCE

General Works

48. Aleksander, Igor, and Piers Burnett. **Thinking Machines: The Search for Artificial Intelligence.** New York, Alfred A. Knopf/Random House, 1987. 208p. illus. (part col.). index. $17.95pa. LC 86-2876. ISBN 0-394-74459-4.

Thinking Machines deals with the topic of artificial intelligence in a fashion that allows almost anyone to achieve an understanding of this complex subject. This is accomplished with the use of over one hundred color diagrams and the authors' limited use of the computer-industry jargon that so often clutters up other works. Nor do the authors include long and tedious excerpts of actual programs that mean little to the layperson. However, this book should not be overlooked by the expert. Much of it focuses on the theory of how people and machines approach problem solving, what intelligence is, how success in machine intelligence should be gauged, etc.

The book begins with a brief history of thinking machines, and then moves on to more fundamental questions. After laying this groundwork, the authors consider how computer languages and knowledge structures allow the computer to put problems into terms the machine can deal with. The work concludes with an intense look at computer handling of visual images and other sensory input and the impact of graphics and the visual world on computer intelligence. A three-page subject/topic index is included to assist in research.

Overall, the work is a success and stimulates thought not only about machine intelligence, but about human thought processes as well.

Brad R. Leach

49. Boden, Margaret A. **Artificial Intelligence and Natural Man.** 2d ed. New York, Basic Books, 1987. 576p. bibliog. index. $14.95pa. LC 86-47739. ISBN 0-465-00456-3.

Artificial intelligence (AI) has the potential for counteracting the dehumanizing influence of science, for proposing solutions to problems of the philosophy of the mind, and for illuminating the hidden complexities of human thought and psychology. AI is not a study of computers, but of intelligence in thought and action. The first edition of this book (1981) described AI in a way that stresses its human relevance and its role in the understanding of the human animal. The second edition underscores the implications of the dramatic growth of AI since the book first appeared. Growth, the author notes, does not necessarily mean development. The technology craze of the 1980s is due more to commercial and political factors than to intellectual advances in the field. The central problems of AI and the theoretical basis of its achievements have remained essentially the same. While there has been some advance, most of it has been in technological efficiency rather than in basic scientific understanding. Thus the main message of both editions is still timely.

Written in understandable language, and assuming no previous knowledge of computers or mathematics, this book reveals the impact that computers are having on our visual world, learning, creativity, problem solving, and the general understanding of our humanity. A must in all academic libraries and on the shelves of every modern educated person from artists to philosophers.

Antonio Rodriguez-Buckingham

50. Chadwick, Michael, and John Hannah. **Expert Systems for Microcomputers: An Introduction to Artificial Intelligence.** Blue Ridge Summit, Pa., TAB Books, 1987. 234p. $19.95; $14.95pa. ISBN 0-8306-0438-3; 0-8306-2838-Xpa.

This well-written, comprehensive introduction to aspects and techniques of creating and understanding expert system programming is not only directed to the active programmer, but also to the layperson who wants to grasp the hidden secrets behind artificial intelligence.

A short, informative introduction describes the applications and trends of today's and tomorrow's artificial intelligence and gives an insight into five major expert systems. Principles and strategies are presented independently from system and programming language. While the book describes differences between and advantages of the four high-level languages LISP, PROLOG, BASIC, and LOGO, it uses the language most programmers are familiar with, BASIC, to illustrate the theory with ready-to-enter program segments throughout most chapters. Because of LOGO's popularity, LOGO programs that parallel the BASIC listings included are provided with helpful comments. Forward- and backward-chaining techniques, applied expert systems, and learning systems are discussed, explained with easy-to-understand examples, and illustrated with standard flowcharts, numerous line drawings, and

computer output of the program listings for improved comprehension. Indexed.

Andreas E. Mueller

51. Davies, R., ed. **Intelligent Information Systems: Progress and Prospects.** Chichester, England, Ellis Horwood; distr., New York, Halsted Press/John Wiley, 1986. 300p. index. (Ellis Horwood Series in Artificial Intelligence). $44.95. ISBN 0-470-20726-4.

The Ellis Horwood Series in Artificial Intelligence is an extensive and growing list of books concerned with expert systems, their construction, and their use. Now numbering over thirty titles, this British series is consistently excellent in its coverage and treatment, provided that the reader has the technical background to understand and assimilate the material. Davies's book is no exception; it is a contribution to the vast literature of information science dealing with the intellectual, physical, and economic opportunities and pitfalls of putting information to its best use.

Editor Davies is a librarian at the University of Exeter, and his book describes varied applications of expert systems and artificial intelligence to the storage and retrieval of information. The overall effect of the work is intended to introduce librarians to the ways in which AI can be used to solve informational problems. The ten contributors discuss differing aspects of the overall problem: creating acceptance of machines in areas which were until recently thought to be the sole province of the human mind.

The contributors are international: Portuguese, British, Canadian, Danish, and American, and their papers are uneven in scope and complexity; some may be read by any intelligent reader, others require some knowledge of engineering, programming, or at least a logical orientation. Much is said about "cognitive science," a term not heard much on this side of the Atlantic, but all authors earnestly wish to convey strategies for dealing with a sea of information and turning it into knowledge. In all, this book is another useful British contribution to managing information and to creating "thinking machines." It is therefore recommended for library administrators with at least some prior understanding of artificial intelligence and computer science.

Bruce A. Shuman

52. Ford, Nigel. **How Machines Think: A General Introduction to Artificial Intelligence.** New York, John Wiley, 1987. 206p. bibliog.

index. $29.95pa. LC 86-15953. ISBN 0-471-91139-9.

This book presents a simplified introduction to the area of artificial intelligence and more specifically to expert systems. The notion of an intelligent machine is clearly presented and richly illustrated by many simple real-life scenarios. The author is particularly skillful in interacting with the reader by soliciting the reader's hands-on participation throughout the presentation. This is done through simple user exercises embedded in the text with answers printed upside down, and through provocative philosophical questions enclosed in boxes entitled "THINK!" Some exercises are given in the form of sliding cutout cards included at the back of the book. The book can be divided into three main sections: a basic introduction of an expert system; a more serious examination of various strategies for intelligent behavior; and a description of some of the current intelligent systems including STRIPS, ABSTRIPS, MOLGEN, SAVOIR, HEARSAY, EXPERT-EASE, AM, EURISKO, and ACT. There is also a brief tutorial on the PROLOG language. This book provides a balanced view of expert systems by presenting not only the power but also the limitations of intelligent machines. Aimed for the general public, the book is fun to read and easy to understand, requiring no particular technical background on the part of the reader. This book is highly recommended for the general library.   John Y. Cheung

53.   Forsyth, Richard, and Chris Naylor. **The Hitch-Hiker's Guide to Artificial Intelligence: IBM PC BASIC Version.** New York, Chapman & Hall/Methuen, 1986. 261p. illus. bibliog. index. $19.95pa. LC 85-26934. ISBN 0-412-28140-6.

Forsyth and Naylor have written a useful little book that makes artificial intelligence (AI), computer science's "department of clever tricks," accessible to the PC enthusiast. The book, legitimately touted as a do-it-yourself guide, not only provides material for the conceptual understanding of AI, but also gives examples of programs in IBM PC BASIC that actually work.

The book begins with a brief historical sketch of AI development, followed by chapters on expert systems, natural language, computer vision, machine learning, knowledge representation, problem solving methods, computer game playing strategies, computer creativity, and future trends for AI.

The programs provided as examples include "painting" an image with the computer, a robot maze learner, and others relating to knowledge

representation and computer game playing strategies. The book also includes a list of further reading, a general name and subject index, and an index of program listings.

The guide is a well-designed, well-written one that will be very useful for anyone interested in AI who has access to a PC. It is also available in Applesoft BASIC, BBC BASIC, and Amstrad BASIC versions.   Robert H. Burger

54.   Gill, Karamjit S. **Artificial Intelligence for Society.** New York, John Wiley, 1986. 280p. illus. index. $34.95. LC 85-29596. ISBN 0-471-90930-0.

How artificial intelligence (AI) will affect society in the near and remote future is a question that was asked at the 1985 Artificial Intelligence for Society Conference. Many social, educational, economic, cultural, and moral issues resulting from the implementation of AI programs were discussed. This work is a compilation of papers from that conference.

Each of the twenty-seven chapters was written by a British specialist in fields such as computer ethics, sociology, and psychology. Discussions cover the issues of knowledge transfer, the role of ethnic minorities in the information process, the effects of AI on women's lives, the role of educational software in schools, and the potential applications of AI for the benefit of human services.

This is a thought-provoking work and has potential for some controversy. It is recommended for public and academic libraries. A comprehensive bibliography is included for further reading. There is an index.

Andreas E. Mueller

55.   Goldenthal, Nathan. **Expert Systems and Artificial Intelligence.** Chesterland, Ohio, Weber Systems, 1987. 354p. bibliog. index. $19.95pa. ISBN 0-938862-91-X.

The intent of this book is to explain the basic concepts of expert systems and to demonstrate several working models. The examples are in Turbo Pascal or Turbo Prolog; familiarity with these languages is assumed. Approximately one hundred pages of the text are devoted to categorized annotations of existing expert systems such as FOREST, which diagnoses faults in electronic equipment; TAX-ADVISOR, a legal expert system; and HEME, a system designed to diagnose hematological disorders. Each listing includes a description of the system; the name of the developer; and a category called "Staging," in which each system is characterized by type of prototype (demonstration, field, production, or research) or commercial availability.

Nearly one hundred pages of text are devoted to an "Elaborate Prolog Expert System" called the Sierra Nevada Flower Base. The text shows the creation of an inference engine in Turbo Prolog in explicit detail. The intent is to allow the user to input various plant names, descriptions, growth habits, etc., and the system would name the plant and describe it.

A weakness of the book is the limited discussion of the analysis steps necessary to develop a system. Several times the author states that the first steps are to define the task, then analyze the problem, and extract the knowledge from the experts. No time is spent on "how" a task is defined and analyzed or the knowledge extracted. These are truly monumental tasks which no amount of programming expertise will overcome. The book, like many others, focuses almost entirely on lists of existing systems, available languages, and relevant terminology.

Susan B. Ardis

56. Grimson, W. Eric L., and Ramesh S. Patil, eds. **AI in the 1980s and Beyond: An MIT Survey.** Cambridge, Mass., MIT Press, 1987. 374p. index. (MIT Press Series in Artificial Intelligence). $24.95. LC 87-3241. ISBN 0-262-07106-1.

An excellent addition to the MIT Press Series in Artificial Intelligence. This book is a survey of artificial intelligence (AI) research interests and activities currently in progress at MIT. The presented material is a collection of twelve papers written by MIT researchers who originally presented this material at the "Artificial Intelligence: Current Applications, Trends and Future Opportunities" conference sponsored by MIT. The topics covered in this book include a general perspective of AI, knowledge-based systems, expert systems tools and techniques, system building as seen in medical diagnosis, AI and software engineering, intelligent natural language processing, automatic speech recognition, intelligent vision, seeing robots, robot programming, robot tactile sensing, and autonomous mobile robots. The purpose of this book is to present by way of survey to other researchers and students of AI the current research interests, future directions, and possible potential applications in AI, particularly at MIT. All the papers are tutorial in nature and are written in a style that is easy to read. Extensive references are also provided for the astute and more technically inclined reader. Technical knowledge is not a necessity to understand the presented material but may be helpful at times. This book is highly recommended for

the general public with a college-level education. [R: Choice, Dec 87, pp. 650-51]

John Y. Cheung

57. Hyde, Margaret O. **Artificial Intelligence.** Hillside, N.J., Enslow, 1986. 127p. illus. bibliog. index. $12.95. LC 85-20573. ISBN 0-89490-124-9.

Artificial Intelligence is a revision of *Computers That Think?* (1982), also by Hyde. It discusses artificial intelligence, the current extent and limitations of computer "intelligence," the development and use of robots in such areas as the automobile industry, "reading" machines, and who (or what) is in control, for children from the middle grades up.

The author defines intelligence, and reports on what scientists have learned about animal intelligence and the "learning" levels of computers. She covers the history of computers briefly and the importance of transistors and microchips. Hyde addresses the fear some people have of computer or robot takeover by telling the story of the clay creature created by a rabbi in Prague in 1580. The creature, "Joseph Golem," was brought to life by prayers and incantations and writing God's name on its forehead. When the Golem seemed to be taking control, it was destroyed by its creator. Hyde also touches on the more eminent threat to job security presented by industrial use of robots, citing a Japanese factory where 97 percent of the tasks are automated.

Computers that have sensitive enough touch to "read" braille; robots that can see well enough to vacuum airports; and Kurzweil readers that "recognize the letters of the alphabet in almost all printed materials" (p. 87) and read aloud, skipping part of the text or returning to a section previously read, are described. Artificial intelligence projects that feed enough background into a computer that it can make inferences are also mentioned.

Another topic relates to expert systems that are "described as the closest thing to cloning a human mind" (p. 108) and which are developed by having a scientist or group of scientists work with computer specialists. The result might be, for example, a machine that can diagnose illnesses, but is not much good at anything else or in recognizing its own limitations.

This is a broad and technical field. The author covers it somewhat superficially but keeps the reader's attention. It presents a middle ground in depth of coverage between *The Science of Artificial Intelligence*, by Fred D'Ignazio and Allen Wold (Watts, 1984) and

The Quest for Artificial Intelligence, by Dorothy Hinshaw Patent (Harcourt Brace Jovanovich, 1986). Both other volumes include glossaries, an important omission in Hyde's book. Hyde does offer a brief, fairly up-to-date bibliography, and an index which helps overcome the lack of a glossary.

This second edition of *Computers That Think?* does update the first edition, but the changes are relatively slight. Libraries with copies of the first edition may find another title, such as D'Ignazio's or Patent's, more useful than the 1986 edition of Hyde's book.

Betty Jo Buckingham

58.   Tanimoto, Steven L. **The Elements of Artificial Intelligence: An Introduction Using LISP.** Rockville, Md., Computer Science Press, 1987. 530p. illus. index. $35.95. LC 86-31044. ISBN 0-88175-113-8; ISSN 0888-2096.

Tanimoto's work is intended as an introductory textbook in artificial intelligence (AI) for undergraduate or graduate students. By integrating LISP programming techniques with explanations of AI principles, Tanimoto "presents elements of artificial intelligence as they are, describing their limitations as well as their assets." After a brief introduction to AI and a sizable chapter introducing LISP programming, topics such as productions and matching, knowledge representation, searching, logical reasoning, probalistic reason, learning, natural language understanding, vision, and expert systems are covered. Tanimoto gives predictions concerning the future state of AI in a concluding chapter. Access to the book's contents is made easy not only by a detailed table of contents but also by separate, well-constructed author and subject indexes. An appendix gives all LISP functions presented in the book with an explanation of their use and relation to other functions.

The text, which is clearly written and well organized, "grew out of the perception that hands-on experimentation coordinated with textbook explanations of principles and of actual programs can provide an ideal learning combination for students of artificial intelligence." This work, which incorporates this perception, succeeds admirably well both for a beginning AI student and for a more experienced practitioner who needs ready-reference access to techniques and principles. [R: Choice, July/Aug 87, p. 1722]   Robert H. Burger

Applications

59.   **Applications of Artificial Intelligence V.** John F. Gilmore, ed. Bellingham, Wash., SPIE, International Society of Optical Engineering,

1987. 616p. index. (Proceedings of SPIE — The International Society for Optical Engineering, Vol. 786). $79.00pa. LC 86-641430. ISBN 0-89252-821-4.

This volume contains about eighty papers presented at the Fifth SPIE (International Society for Optical Engineering) Applications of Artificial Intelligence Conference held in Orlando, Florida, 18-20 May 1987. This forum was specifically arranged for the presentation of applications work and for "identifying the contributions of this work to current technologies." The papers were delivered during ten topical sessions: "Expert Systems" (two sessions), "Image Understanding," "Artificial Intelligence Tools," "Knowledge Based Systems," "Heuristic Systems" (two sessions), "Manufacturing Applications," "Image Analysis," and "International Applications." The volume also contains an author index that includes the title of each author's paper.

This proceedings is invaluable for those wishing to know and become familiar with the latest developments in applications of AI. As with any conference of this size the papers are of varying quality, but many are excellent and together indicate some interesting trends, as pointed out in the introduction by the conference chair, John Gilmore. One of the most surprising trends is the development of organizations' own expert system tools, as opposed to licensing an existing product. Overall the editor has produced a significant and useful collection.

Robert H. Burger

60.   **Artificial Intelligence and Man-Machine Systems. Proceedings of an International Seminar Organized by Deutsche Forschungs- und Versuchsanstalt für Luft-und Raumfahrt (DFVLR), Bonn, Germany, May, 1986.** H. Winter, ed. New York, Springer-Verlag, 1986. 211p. illus. maps. (Lecture Notes in Control and Information Sciences, 80). $23.00pa. ISBN 0-387-16658-0.

Springer-Verlag's series Lecture Notes in Control and Information Sciences is a vehicle for disseminating lectures, research reports, and meeting proceedings in a timely manner. The current volume contains nine papers presented by scholars from the United States and Europe at the third applied engineering sciences seminar hosted by the DFVLR. Heinz Winter's paper appropriately begins the volume and is an overview of the various ways in which AI can be applied to automated processes, ranging from where the human does all of the planning and decision making to a final level where machines function in an autonomous mode. In four separate articles, J. Mylopoulos, et al.,

B. Radig, W. Wahlster, and L. Zadeh discuss knowledge representation in AI. Several of the articles contain specific examples relating to man-machine systems and others of which are more general. Two papers deal with robotics: G. Fischer's "Cognitive Science: Information Processing in Humans and Computers" and A. Meystel's "Knowledge-Based Controller for Intelligent Mobile Robots." The two remaining essays discuss specific applications of AI to a field: S. Cross, et al., on "Knowledge-Based Pilot Aids: A Case Study in Mission Planning," and U. Völckers's "Dynamic Planning and Time-Conflict Resolution in Air Traffic Control." The volume is softbound and the printing of each paper was apparently the responsibility of the authors, as demonstrated by the different typefaces and reproduction methods used (all of which are satisfactory). There are useful bibliographies accompanying the articles, but there is no index. Robert Skinner

61. Baird, Patricia, ed. **Expert Systems for Decision-Making.** London, Taylor Graham, 1987. 79p. £15.00pa. ISBN 0-947568-22-0.

This slim volume is a collection of six articles presumably based on papers delivered at an unnamed conference. The authors and their papers are D. R. McGregor, "Expert Systems in Information Management: A Timely Review"; Donald Michie, "Six Points Concerning Knowledge-Based Systems"; T. R. Addis, "Knowledge for the New Generation Computers"; Mike Turner, "Expert Systems for Information Management"; Alexander D'Agapeyeff, "The Exercising and Sharing of Decision Know-how in Business"; and David Hannaford, "Designing Expert Systems for DP Development Users." Patricia Baird edited the volume and wrote the introduction. While useful information and insights are presented (for example, Donald Michie's elaborations of his six points and D'Agapeyeff's description of Expertech XI), the papers and accompanying bibliographies are so general or brief as to make this collection a necessity only for libraries forming comprehensive collections on expert systems or those particularly interested in European applications of these systems. There are several figures, incidentally, most of which have not reproduced well. Robert Skinner

62. Brodie, Michael L., and John Mylopoulos, eds. **On Knowledge Base Management Systems: Integrating Artificial Intelligence and Database Technologies.** New York, Springer-Verlag, 1986. 660p. bibliog. index. (Topics in Information Systems). $38.00. LC 86-11889. ISBN 0-387-96382-0.

This is an excellent book covering the concepts and techniques of artificial intelligence in database applications. It is part of the series Topics in Information Systems, published by Springer-Verlag. The contents of this book are actually papers presented at the Islamorada Workshop on Large Scale Knowledge-Based Systems in 1985. The purpose of this book is to lay a foundation for further research interactions between two major research areas: artificial intelligence and databases. Seven major areas are addressed, including knowledge base management systems, knowledge bases versus databases, retrieval/interface/reasoning, extending database management systems, extending knowledge-based systems, knowledge-based system design issues, and advanced hardware for knowledge-based systems. Contributed papers are written by leading researchers in their respective research areas and are aimed at presenting in a tutorial fashion an overall introduction of the present and future research directions. Special emphasis is given to outline problems currently under investigation and directions for future extensions. Materials in this book, though originating from the workshop, have been superbly edited to present a balanced overall view of the scope. An excellent list of references and an extensive index have also been added to further enhance the utility of this book. Transcriptions of discussion on the papers, complete references on the authors, and detailed bibliographies make this book a valuable reference both for a graduate course and for a professional library in computer science. John Y. Cheung

63. Forsyth, R., and R. Rada. **Machine Learning: Applications in Expert Systems and Information Retrieval.** New York, Halsted Press/John Wiley, 1986. 277p. bibliog. index. (Ellis Horwood Series in Artificial Intelligence). $57.95. LC 86-3054. ISBN 0-470-20309-9.

Artificial intelligence and expert systems refer to intelligence on computer disks, capable of providing advice, playing games, developing strategies, and learning from mistakes. The Horwood Series now boasts over thirty titles with international authorship. Forsyth is Technical Director for Warm Boot, Ltd., in London. Rada, a physician, is with the U.S. National Library of Medicine. Their contributions are presented *seriatim*, rather than in collaboration. Forsyth's section deals with concepts and methods of machine learning, while Rada presents case studies of attempts to build programs which may be said to reason, remember, and learn. Together, they comprise an overview of artificial intelligence/expert systems, and ways in which machines create evolutionary learning strategies.

The book does an extremely competent job of defining terms and explaining procedures whereby, for example, programs may be devised which, once taught the rules of a game (e.g., poker, go, chess), can develop increasing skill through trial and error, just as (one hopes) people's minds do. The case studies get a bit technical, but do an equally admirable job of showing how attempts to build expert systems and trainable programs have succeeded or failed, and why. The reader becomes aware that programs exist which can replicate human thought processes with such fidelity that experts cannot distinguish a human opponent from a mechanical one. This leads to possibilities of artistic creativity, knowledge synthesis, theory formation, and even optimal selection among alternatives, a prospect at once irresistible and frightening.

From its brightly colored cover, depicting unseen forces at work upon familiar geometric shapes, to its illustrations, glossary, and bibliography, this book is a gem, very complicated but lucid.   Bruce A. Shuman

64. Gibb, Forbes, ed. **Expert Systems in Libraries. Proceedings of a Conference of the Library Association Information Technology Group and the Library and Information Research Group, November 1985.** London, Taylor Graham, 1986. 97p. bibliog. $25.00pa. ISBN 0-947568-10-7.

Expert systems (ES) is the current buzz-word for what was formerly called artificial intelligence. ES is an attempt to put on a disk a "consultant" sufficiently informed and capable of emulating the decision processes of a subject expert in a specific field of knowledge. The trick is to define and delineate the empirical domain in which the computer program is to have its expertise. When a clearly delimited field can be encapsulated into a few hundred explicit rules, says Gibb, of the Department of Information Science at the University of Strathclyde (England), the resultant program can perform at least as well as (and often better than) a human expert. It would appear that the time is right for ES development, because human experts tend to be increasingly scarce, expensive, busy, fallible, inconsistent, and mortal, while an expert-on-a-disk is only (occasionally) fallible.

The papers in this volume were presented at a one-day conference on ES held in Birmingham, England in late 1985. After Gibb's general overview of the subject, papers cover ES developments and trends in reference work, classification, and cataloging. While much of the

pioneering work in ES has been conducted in the United States, the emphasis of this series of papers is on the current problems of libraries in Great Britain. Still, the applications are universal, which makes this book both interesting reading and valuable for libraries looking for ways to get expert consultants' advice without paying airfares, hotel bills, and meal tabs. Highly recommended. [R: LAR, June 87, p. 293]   Bruce A. Shuman

65. Partridge, D. **Artificial Intelligence: Applications in the Future of Software Engineering.** Chichester, England, Ellis Horwood; distr., New York, Halsted Press/John Wiley, 1986. 239p. index. $37.95. LC 86-7171. ISBN 0-470-20315-3.

The relationship between software engineering and artificial intelligence is a two-way street. Software engineering techniques are helping AI developers create their large, complex, and "intelligent" programs. At the same time, AI techniques are helping software engineers build their business applications programs by partially automating the software development process. This book by well-known researcher Derek Partridge gives a lucid account of the influences each of these disciplines has upon the other.

The book is directed more towards the software engineering community than AI community, and it attempts to predict what the role of AI in software design and construction will be in the future. The book describes examples of AI techniques and applications here and there, but it is not to be considered a tutorial either on AI or on software engineering. The author, like many scientists, is disturbed by the sales hype currently found in the commercial community (and to some extent, in the academic community), and wishes to give a more realistic evaluation of AI's prospects for software engineering than one would otherwise get.

While this book would not normally be classified as a reference work, it should play a valuable role in any reference collection on artificial intelligence or software engineering, and it should be valuable to readers in computer science libraries in general.

     Steven L. Tanimoto

66. Townsend, Carl, and Dennis Feucht. **Designing and Programming Personal Expert Systems.** Blue Ridge Summit, Pa., TAB Books, 1986. 258p. bibliog. index. $27.95; $18.95pa. LC 85-30407. ISBN 0-8306-0692-0; 0-8306-2692-1pa.

Intended as an introduction to artificial intelligence and expert system concepts, this book describes how to build a knowledge system for problem solving. Methods of representing knowledge and using a knowledge base to solve problems are explained in part I, as are the components of a knowledge system. The reader is assured that "very little mathematical or programming experience" is needed for these chapters.

In part II, the authors construct a knowledge system that can be used on a microcomputer. Although, as they indicate, other computer languages can be used to program knowledge systems, the authors chose Forth (an interactive, interpretive language) for its versatility. They describe Forth in detail, but also incorporate other computer languages: LISP, Prolog, and Smalltalk. Chapters on list processing and other techniques needed for artificial intelligence are included. Appendices provide source code listing, diagnostic routines, Forth vocabularies, and lists of expert system tools and expert systems in use today. Organized as a tutorial or textbook with examples and exercises in each chapter, the book also contains helpful, well-presented graphics. Renee B. Horowitz

67. Wenger, Etienne. **Artificial Intelligence and Tutoring Systems: Computational and Cognitive Approaches to the Communication of Knowledge.** Los Altos, Calif., Morgan Kaufmann, 1987. 486p. bibliog. index. $32.95. LC 87-3170. ISBN 0-934613-26-5.

This is an excellent introduction to the emerging field of computer-aided instruction and more specifically intelligent tutoring systems. As suggested by the title, the author examines the state of the art of communicating knowledge from the computational and cognitive standpoints. Knowledge communication is more encompassing and involved than mere presentation or instruction of information. In the design of an intelligent tutoring system, in addition to accurately representing the knowledge domain, the student model must also be adequately accounted for. After briefly introducing the basic issues, a panoramic view of people, ideas, and systems is discussed, including dialogs, interactive simulations, coaching, diagnostic methodologies, student models, and problem solving. These topics are richly illustrated by existing systems such as SOPHIE, STEAMER, LOGO, WUSOR, BUGGY, GUIDON, etc. After a comprehensive and interpretative survey of existing intelligent tutoring systems, the author next presents a synopsis of the state of the art, covering the computer, the knowledge domain, the student, diagnosis, didactic operations, and knowledge communication. In addition to its comprehensive survey

and synopsis that serve as a basis for this emerging area, this book is particularly useful because it is easy to read and because of its unusually extensive bibliography and index. Annotated references are also provided at the end of each chapter. This book is highly recommended for professional libraries.

John Y. Cheung

68. Wolfgram, Deborah D., Teresa J. Dear, and Craig S. Galbraith. **Expert Systems for the Technical Professional.** New York, John Wiley, 1987. 314p. illus. bibliog. index. $32.95. LC 86-33970. ISBN 0-471-85645-2.

Expert systems and artificial intelligence have long since left the drawing boards and the research laboratories and are now used in a great variety of industrial situations. Concomitantly, more people are turning away from expensive and limiting "packaged" AI systems and are attempting to design and operate their own systems. This book's intended audience is industry, rather than libraries and other information-provision agencies. It is the cash-value applications of AI which concern the authors, and the intended audience should have prior training in or understanding of technical systems, as the title implies. What the reader will get here is advice and assistance in designing, programming, and using an expert system to its best commercial advantage.

The three American authors are all corporate executives, although one, Galbraith, seems to hold a joint academic appointment. They provide important and practical information, sound pragmatic advice, an excellent bibliography and index, and, perhaps best of all, a directory of names and addresses, furnishing the "who" and the "where" of getting started, if one intends to build a system from out-sourced components.

For the reader with the requisite technical background and an ability to withstand a competent but dry writing style, relieved somewhat by good illustrations, this book provides much significant material. If your firm seeks to build or adapt its own AI or expert system, this will help you plan, design, cost, and implement its various provisions. Library administrators, however, might find other works more germane, as this treatment keeps one eye on "the bottom line" at all times. Come to think of it, that might not be so bad for library administrators!

Bruce A. Shuman

69. Yazdani, Masoud, ed. **Artificial Intelligence: Principles and Applications.** New York, Chapman & Hall/Methuen, 1986. 348p. illus.

index. $49.95; $25.00pa. LC 85-22375. ISBN 0-412-27230-X; 0-412-27240-7pa.

In the past twenty-five years specialists have devoted much energy and thought to the development of a computer that could imitate human behavior. Breakthroughs in the artificial intelligence (AI) field have resulted in computerized robots and intelligent systems that help in decision making for the business and medical communities.

This excellent work is in a textbook format that shows the general principles and implementations of various expert systems. It is divided into five sections that discuss different aspects of the artificial intelligence research field. After a brief introductory chapter that presents the various theoretical models in the field, the various tools (programming languages and hardware) and techniques (lists and computations) are clearly presented. Following chapters discuss the potential applications of AI, including speech synthesis, vision and object identification, and robotics, and expert decision making systems are presented. A chapter on machine learning discusses theoretical machine learning and memory models for both man and machine. Final chapters discuss the social implications of AI, including possible unemployment, the negative computer image, and other potential societal threats. Each of the thirteen chapters is written by an active researcher on subjects such as computer vision, speech processing, robotics, natural language processing, expert systems, and machine learning.

Each chapter has a comprehensive annotated bibliography, and an extensive annotated bibliography completes the text. An excellent choice for public and academic libraries. It is indexed.

Andreas E. Mueller

Biographies

70.   Kernoff, Alan. **Who's Who in Artificial Intelligence: The AI Guide to People, Products, Companies, Resources, Schools and Jobs.** Woodside, Calif., published with Tom Schwartz Associates by WWAI, 1986. 261p. $95.00pa.

This unique reference guide contains well-organized information about institutions, companies, and individuals connected with U.S. artificial intelligence (AI). For easy reference, the field of AI is divided into expert systems, natural languages, visual recognition, speech recognition, robotics, supercomputers, and tools.

For each of the approximately four hundred individuals useful information on educa-

tional background, research interests, special projects, and affiliation is provided. AI projects and the persons involved in thirteen schools and laboratories are discussed in detail.

The last third of the book is a useful compilation of hard to find information about twenty-six projects—including NASA's first expert system for the space shuttle—of thirteen companies such as Kurzweil Applied Intelligence and Texas Instrument. The information on the projects and the companies are printed as supplied by the companies, which results in a sloppy presentation. However, the information provided is excellent and of primary value.

Other features include a job guide consisting of contact addresses; an informative table indicating growing departments of companies, and company advertisement; a comprehensive bibliography of over 150 volumes for AI students and researchers; and a helpful list of contact addresses for further information. There are page headers but no index. [R: Choice, Jan 87, pp. 749-50]

Andreas E. Mueller

Catalogs

71.   Bundy, Alan, ed. **Catalogue of Artificial Intelligence Tools.** 2d rev. ed. New York, Springer-Verlag, 1986. 168p. index. $27.50pa. ISBN 0-387-16893-1.

This catalog, the purpose of which is "to promote interaction between members of the AI community," provides a guide to AI tools available for a variety of jobs. The editor's hope is that it will "promote a common terminology, discourage the reinvention of wheels, and act as a clearinghouse for ideas and software." The cataloged techniques are arranged alphabetically. Access to them is enhanced by a subject index at the back of the catalog, and by their arrangement under nineteen subject groupings, such as computer architecture, expert systems, inference and reasoning, knowledge representation, natural language, pattern recognition, theorem proving, and vision.

Each entry consists of the name of the technique, a list of aliases for the technique, a brief description of it, and the contributor and references where it has been more fully described. Another valuable feature of each entry is the addition of cross-references in boldface type to other techniques in the catalog. The abstracts are clearly and concisely written, and are therefore easy to understand. The catalog itself is very likely to fulfill the editor's intent and expectations. [R: Choice, Mar 87, p. 1026]

Robert H. Burger

Encyclopedias

72. Encyclopedia of Artificial Intelligence. Stuart C. Shapiro, ed.-in-chief. New York, John Wiley, 1987. 2v. illus. index. $175.00/set. LC 86-26739. ISBN 0-471-80748-6.

This reference work contains 170 full-length articles on varied topics in artificial intelligence (AI). It is intended for use by professionals who are not AI specialists. AI is a field which contains elements of computer science, psychology, philosophy, mathematics, and linguistics; this work covers all of these aspects quite comprehensively, although it focuses on computer science and computer implementations of AI techniques, since this is where the bulk of AI research has been conducted. In addition to the 170 full-length articles, the work contains over 90 very brief articles discussing particular AI computer systems and tools.

The only comparable reference work is the three-volume *Handbook of Artificial Intelligence*, edited by Avron Barr, Paul Cohen, and Edward Feigenbaum (William Kaufmann, 1981 and 1982).

The articles in the encyclopedia were written by 205 AI researchers and reviewed by 180 AI researchers. The publisher claims that the authors are "authorities in the field" and that the reviewers are "experts." This is likely the case, since many of the names are recognizable as those of people who have contributed significant results to the field. The author(s) of each article is identified at the end.

The articles are organized alphabetically. They are extensively cross-referenced, and each article includes a bibliography. The bibliographies are up-to-date and well composed, containing both specific references from the text and references of general interest. Illustrations are used where appropriate, and are both clear and aesthetically pleasing. A single fifty-three-page index, containing entries for subjects, names, and computer systems, is quite complete.

The encyclopedia is a useful reference for a range of readers, from the educated layperson to the AI researcher. It is of most use as a starting reference for a technically oriented person, with some background in computer science and AI, who needs or wants to know about some particular aspect of AI. At the same time, its alphabetical organization and cross-referencing encourage browsing. Although many articles contain formal presentations of technical ideas, these all begin with a section providing a thorough overview which is accessible to the casual reader. In addition to articles on specific topics, the article "Artificial Intelligence" provides

an excellent conceptual overview of the field, and "AI Literature" is a good pointer to other sources.

The encyclopedia is also useful, although in a more limited sense, to people in business, education, the social sciences, and the humanities. They would generally be uninterested in the technical details which comprise approximately half of the average article. However, they may benefit greatly from such articles as "Limits of AI," "Anthropomorphic Robots," "Expert Systems," "Social Issues of AI," "Problem Solving," "Intelligent Computer-Aided Instruction," and "Philosophical Questions." Many of these articles cover important topics in a balanced and nonsensationalistic manner that is uncommon in the popular literature. In addition, the less technical of these topics are not covered at all in Barr et al.'s handbook.

One component missing from the encyclopedia which would make it more useful to all nonspecialists is a glossary of terms. Most articles use some specialized terms for which there are no corresponding encyclopedia articles.

Finally, the encyclopedia can also be very useful to the AI researcher who wishes to learn about a subject within AI which is outside of his or her specialty. The articles do not talk down to the specialist by overgeneralizing. Many articles (e.g., those on grammars and on logic) provide good technical introductions to important topics. However, the AI researcher often wants to know the details of particular AI systems, and the encyclopedia is not the best resource for this purpose. The brief articles on particular systems do not go into any detail; some system details are given in the full-length articles, but the coverage is scattered and uneven. On the other hand, Barr et al.'s handbook devotes many chapters to descriptions of individual AI systems. For this reason, the handbook is probably the more important reference for AI specialists, even though it is slightly obsolete.

The physical and visual format of the encyclopedia as a whole is excellent. The dimensions of the volumes (9 by 11 inches) are large enough to allow the encyclopedia to fit into two volumes, but not so large that the books are awkward to handle. The books conveniently lay flat when opened to any page. The paper and binding are of good quality. The type and the two-column page layout are comfortable to read.

Theresa Farrah

Handbooks

73. Hunt, V. Daniel. **Artificial Intelligence & Expert Systems Sourcebook.** New York, Chapman & Hall/Methuen, 1986. 315p. illus. bibliog. $34.50. ISBN 0-412-012111.

Terms and phrases once common only in computer science publications are now used in many other areas, including medicine, business, libraries, and even newspapers and newsmagazines. The increased public awareness of the topics of artificial intelligence and expert systems led to the production of this book, with the stated intention being to "clarify the terminology for artificial intelligence and expert system activities."

The book consists of five sections: an introduction or overview to the field, a dictionary, a list of software vendors, a bibliography, and a glossary of acronyms and trademarks. The overview covers the historical developments, basic attributes of the field, current applications, principal participants, and future applications. The overview leads logically into the largest section of the book, the dictionary. Included, along with expected use in the field of artificial intelligence and expert systems, are relevant terms from the related areas of natural-language processing, smart robots, machine vision, and speech synthesis, along with personal and trade names. The inclusion of trade names makes it possible to look up the word *rulemaster* and discover that it is not a term at all, but rather a trademarked expert system available from Radian Corporation. This is a valuable addition to the book, as users often confuse trademarks and product names with generic terms. The definitions range in length from one or two sentences to longer entries covering half a page. Diagrams and illustrations are included for selected definitions.

This is a well-produced, clearly written book which meets the stated intention "to clarify terms." The book more than lives up to its name. It is a sourcebook which can be used by anyone interested in information on all kinds of expert systems, programming systems, and sources of additional information. [R: Choice, Jan 87, pp. 742, 744]   Susan B. Ardis

Theoretical Issues

74. Brown, Frank M., ed. **The Frame Problem in Artificial Intelligence. Proceedings of the 1987 Workshop April 12-15, 1987 Lawrence, Kansas.** Los Altos, Calif., Morgan Kaufmann, 1987. 359p. illus. index. $24.95pa. LC 87-4140. ISBN 0-934613-32-X.

This series of papers was presented at a 1987 workshop sponsored by the American Association for Artificial Intelligence and several other groups. The body of literature on artificial intelligence grows apace as scientists extend the frontiers of teaching machines to reason and think. The "frame problem" seeks to describe in logical terms what properties persist and what properties change as actions are performed. Simply put, it asks, "what happens next?" Yet a precise definition is elusive. As one author puts it, "I can't tell you what the frame problem is, but I recognize it when I see it." But can the curious reader?

Well, it has to do with reasoning effectively about the future, or how to teach a machine to deal with probability in a world of uncertain outcomes. The frame problem touches such fields as statistics, physics, mechanics, mathematics, logic, and information science. Most of these papers (some article-length and some only one-hundred-word abstracts) are written for the specialist, and are so highly technical that only a specialist can follow, let alone understand them (check out some of these titles: "The Case for Domain-Specific Frame Axioms" and "Toward a Tense-Logic-Based Mitigation of the Frame Problem"). Daunting, aren't they? Familiar analogies to billiard balls and blocks in motion, television sets, and religious beliefs are made, but do little to clear matters up. The bottom line is *ramification*, or the equal importance of understanding all the things that *do not* change as a result of a specific action to understanding the things that do. Very technical, and far above the requirement level of most general students of automation and programming, this book is not a necessary purchase for most collections. For the specialist on the cutting edge of AI/expert systems, however, it is a valuable contribution.   Bruce A. Shuman

75. Brulé, James F. **Artificial Intelligence: Theory, Logic and Application.** Blue Ridge Summit, Pa., TAB Books, 1986. 178p. index. $18.95; $12.95pa. LC 86-5840. ISBN 0-8306-0371-9; 0-8306-0471-5pa.

Several years ago, after the Japanese decided to surpass current technology in problem solving with a fifth-generation computer, U.S. companies also intensified their research in expert systems and artificial intelligence (AI). Practical uses of AI in business and industry are now commonplace. As a "guide to the world of artificial intelligence and its application to the real world of business," this book first examines the theory behind AI, including an historical overview.

Logic, the second element of the book's subtitle, forms the basis for chapters on graph search, AI programming languages, problem solving, and pattern recognition. With its emphasis on classic puzzles, the chapter on problem solving presents as exercises two problems that are familiar to computer programmers: (1) The Traveling Salesman, in which the shortest route must be found for the salesperson to visit all of his or her accounts, and (2) The Tiles, in which scrambled tiles must be rearranged in a specific order.

The third major topic, applications, focuses on expert systems rather than AI. Although the distinction is often blurred, expert systems usually refer to the "software designed to deliver the expertise of a human expert." Among the applications discussed are systems used in aerospace, petroleum exploration, and medicine. Renee B. Horowitz

76. Genesereth, Michael, and Nils J. Nilsson. **Logical Foundations of Artificial Intelligence.** Los Altos, Calif., Morgan Kaufmann, 1987. 405p. bibliog. index. $36.95. LC 87-5461. ISBN 0-934613-31-1.

Written by well-known authors and key researchers in the field, this book presents a solid logical foundation for artificial intelligence (AI). The purpose of this book is not to present an overall tutorial of the general areas in AI, but rather to develop a basic framework for AI research based on the formal languages and mathematical techniques of logic. A variety of topics is discussed, including declarative knowledge, inference, resolution strategies, nonmonotonic reasoning, induction, reasoning with uncertain beliefs, knowledge and belief, metaknowledge and metareasoning, state and change, planning, and intelligent-agent architecture. Many of these topics are established areas in AI while the rest are subjects of current research efforts. The basic language used in the book is predicate calculus, which is briefly summarized at the beginning. Aimed for the graduate level courses, the material in this book requires a fair amount of mathematical sophistication. Knowledge in probability and set theory is helpful in understanding the text.

There are two outstanding features in this book. First, exercises at the end of each chapter are challenging and well chosen. Solutions to these problems are also provided at the back to facilitate learning and comprehension. Second, an extensive reference to existing works fosters the atmosphere of further research in current topics. This book is highly recommended to be used as a text for a graduate course in computer science or as a reference for upper division undergraduates and professionals.

John Y. Cheung

77. Hallam, John, and Chris Mellish, eds. **Advances in Artificial Intelligence. Proceedings of the 1987 AISB Conference, University of Edinburgh, 6-10 April 1987.** New York, John Wiley, 1987. 290p. illus. $49.95. ISBN 0-471-91549-1.

Hallam and Mellish observe that "most current practical applications of artificial intelligence are based on technical advances that were made more than ten years ago." The virtue of these papers, the editors assert, is that they are clear evidence that "healthy fundamental research" is continuing in artificial intelligence. Most of the work presented here is European-based, and as a result, is not "influenced by the 'parallel distributed processing' or 'connectionist' schools of thought so active in the USA." The twenty papers are arranged according to eight broad themes: philosophical issues, representing time, reasoning about the physical world, reasoning and formal systems, grammars and natural language, search control techniques, human problem solving and programming, and reasoning about belief.

Even though the contents are reproduced from the authors' original papers, the resolution of typefaces, equations, and graphs is high. Each paper contains an abstract and a bibliography. There is no index.

The materials presented in this volume are well edited and intelligently arranged. Most of them will be of interest only to specialists in the field. However, John Kelly's paper "Intelligent Machines: What Chance?" critically examines the likely development of intelligent machines and can be read profitably by anyone having even a tangential interest in the field.

Robert H. Burger

78. Hart, Anna. **Knowledge Acquisition for Expert Systems.** New York, McGraw-Hill, 1986. 180p. bibliog. index. $28.95. LC 86-14380. ISBN 0-07-026909-2.

The search for computers intelligent enough to perform as humans has, in certain very select areas, been quite successful. DENDRAL and MYCIN, which interpret spectrographs and diagnose meningitis, respectively, are two famous examples. These successes are in large part due to the fact that research in artificial intelligence has finally shifted from the exigencies of general problem-solving programs to the manipulation of lots of specific data, construed as knowledge. In fact, knowledge acquisition, or domain building, has been the key issue for researchers in the field. Unlike knowledge representation, however, the parameters of knowledge acquisition are still ill-defined, and its literature is sparse. Anna Hart's *Knowledge Acquisition for Expert Systems* is a welcome systematization of this material.

While hers is not the text for electronics engineers, it is an excellent book for domain experts, knowledge engineers, and project managers. In ten chapters, Hart covers the nature of expertise, expert programs, knowledge elicitation, probability theory, fuzzy reasoning, machine induction, and repertory grids. The early chapters, covering psychological and "commonsense" issues, are very insightfully constructed, frequently enhanced by "real-life" stories. The later, mathematical chapters are surprisingly transparent and well written. While discussing probability, though, Hart gives the general equation (p. 76) only after discussing the special equations (pp. 75-76), which is perplexing for nonmathematicians. The graphs are consistently appropriate and well chosen. Her short, classified and annotated bibliography compares well with a panoply of bibliographies in expert-system textbooks.

One small criticism: the glossary (pp. 169-75) might be expanded to include even more basic terms, such as *fuzzy sets* or *domain knowledge*, as well as antonyms for such terms as *rule-based programs* and *structured English*. All in all, though, a four-star effort. Would that all computing experts could write so well.

Judith M. Brugger

79.   Huhns, Michael N., ed. **Distributed Artificial Intelligence.** Los Altos, Calif., Morgan Kaufmann, 1987. 390p. (Research Notes in Artificial Intelligence). $26.95pa. LC 86-33259. ISBN 0-934613-38-9.

The central theme of this collection of twelve essays is the state of research in distributed artificial intelligence (DAI). The main concern of DAI is the cooperative solution of problems by a wide range of decentralized groups of agents. The key issue in this endeavor is the mutual sharing of information which has wide geographical distribution. The papers included in this first text on DAI describe architectures and languages for achieving cooperative problem solving in a distributed environment and include several successful applications of DAI in manufacturing, information retrieval, and distributed sensing. The papers on theoretical issues representing contemporary trends in DAI are of special interest to researchers, while system developers would benefit from the possibilities for utilizing DAI

delineated in the section on applications. An annotated bibliography of DAI is the last essay of the collection. Like the other issues of the same series, Research Notes in Artificial Intelligence, this book is indispensable for those academic libraries which support any of the vast array of programs in information technology, and for those special libraries and individuals involved in pure and industrial research in all aspects of artificial intelligence.

Antonio Rodriguez-Buckingham

80.   Langley, Pat, ed. **Proceedings of the Fourth International Workshop on Machine Learning June 22-25, 1987 University of California, Irvine.** Los Altos, Calif., Morgan Kaufmann, 1987. 403p. illus. index. $24.95pa. LC 87-3803. ISBN 0-934613-41-9.

Learning takes place, essentially, when an intelligence acts or behaves in a certain way, surveys the results, and modifies its behavior to gain improved results. This, at least, is the ideal path toward learning, which in humans frequently falls well short of the optimum. Still, the loose process known as problem solving ideally permits us to learn from observations and experience and to improve our behavior. Machines learn in the same way. A machine is programmed or "taught" to learn from "rules," from its own behavior, or from data it receives through various forms of input which assist it to improve its behavior, based on comparing its memory to experience.

These thirty-nine invited papers from a 1987 conference at the University of California, Irvine, bear on the thorny problem of machine learning, and concern teaching machines to improve their behavior or function based on experiences, input, or cases which lead to generalization. Some of these papers are highly technical and complicated; others, refreshingly, are not, rendered more readable through familiar analogies and conversational, readable prose. Most are accounts of experiments, successful or otherwise, in machine learning and artificial intelligence, with suggestions as to how one might improve (if never perfect) such systems and processes. It is reassuring that scientists are constantly at work on the problems and opportunities of this rapidly developing field, and that the eventual result should be progress. The papers in this volume are worth reading by anyone with enough background in mathematics and logic to be able to follow their sometimes abstruse reasoning. Computer science libraries will therefore want to own it; others must decide whether it is going to be over the heads of their readership.

Bruce A. Shuman

81. Lawler, Robert W., and Masoud Yazdani, eds. **Artificial Intelligence and Education. Volume One: Learning Environments and Tutoring Systems.** Norwood, N.J., Ablex Publishing, 1987. 439p. illus. index. $49.50; $19.95 pa. LC 87-956. ISBN 0-89391-438-X; 0-89391-439-8pa.

The computer has a role in education, and twenty-five expert authors of the eighteen chapters present an international perspective on the status of research on the subject. This is a realistic reflection of many computer uses in education, and the authors recognize the difficulties in delivering useful insights into how the computer will be integrated with education in math, physics, reading, writing, etc., presuming that the approaches discussed are adopted by educators. The classroom revolution expected from computers has yet to occur, but efforts like those discussed in this book will form the basis for it. The chapters are replete with jargon, the print of the camera-ready text is often small, and some typographical errors are present. The teacher interested in current thinking among researchers on progress and problems in developing the computer in education will find this a useful reference. The researcher in the area will find this a good overview.

Marvin K. Harris

82. Michalski, Ryszard S., Jaime G. Carbonell, and Tom M. Mitchell, eds. **Machine Learning: An Artificial Intelligence Approach. Volume II.** Los Altos, Calif., Morgan Kaufmann, 1986. 738p. bibliog. index. $39.95. LC 82-10654. ISBN 0-934613-00-1.

The intent of this book is to present overviews and selected articles representing the state of the art in machine learning. The goal was to make this a readable work, and therefore, accessible to a wide audience including researchers in artificial intelligence, knowledge engineers, computer scientists, linguists, and philosophers. While both volumes 1 and 2 cover the same general area, they were not designed to be used as a set.

Among the topics covered are cognitive aspects of learning, learning by analogy, and learning by observation and discovery. Each signed article includes work locations for the authors and a list of references. These references are specific to the article and are generally not included in the book's bibliography. The bibliography consists of 351 citations, primarily from conferences. Each bibliographic citation is categorized "along three dimensions: learning strategy; domain of application; and research methodology." Both recent and landmark con-

tributions are included. A glossary of selected terms is also included.

Artificial intelligence (AI) is experiencing extraordinary growth. This is an excellent one-volume overview and introduction to this fast-moving, exciting field. It should serve as an introduction for readers interested in learning about the basic aspects of the field and as a tutorial for those interested in learning specific techniques used by practitioners in AI.

Susan B. Ardis

83. Phelps, Bob, ed. **Interactions in Artificial Intelligence and Statistical Methods.** Brookfield, Vt., with Unicom Seminars by Gower Publishing, 1987. 187p. (Technical Press — Unicom Applied Information Technology Report Series). $83.50pa. ISBN 0-291-39743-3.

This collection of thirteen papers deals with a special research area common to both artificial intelligence (AI) and statistical methods. As suggested by the title, this collection of pioneer works may form the basis for further development through cross-fertilization of ideas and examples that are of interest to both research groups. Four major topics are covered. These include five papers in automating statistical methods, three papers in integrating AI to stochestic modeling, three papers in AI approaches to learning from data, and two papers in statistical methods in AI. An interpretative annotation on each paper is also given at the beginning of the manuscript. Though based on a technical conference, most of the papers are tutorial in nature and serve as introductions to recent technical development in the respective areas. This manuscript is an excellent addition to the Applied Information Technology Reports Series of the Technical Press — Unicom. This book is recommended for acquisition as a reference in college libraries.

John Y. Cheung

84. **Reasoning about Actions and Plans. Proceedings of the 1986 Workshop, June 30-July 2, 1986, Timberline, Oregon.** Michael P. Georgeff and Amy L. Lansky, eds. Los Altos, Calif., Morgan Kaufmann, 1987. 425p. index. $24.95 pa. LC 86-27748. ISBN 0-934613-30-3.

This volume of proceedings contains a collection of papers presented in the 1986 Workshop on Reasoning about Actions and Plans which was sponsored by the American Association for Artificial Intelligence and the Center for the Study of Language and Information. The main emphasis of the conference was to explore various approaches to developing intelligent machines that would deal effectively with the real world, that would reason about the effects of their actions, and that would subsequently form reasonable plans of action to achieve a given goal. These are important issues to be addressed in current artificial intelligence research. Investigators on the frontier of this research area provided many papers dealing with the various approaches. The purpose of collecting these papers into the present proceedings is to form a foundation for further research. This is a valuable reference tool for investigators in the area of artificial intelligence. Though the collected papers are somewhat technical in nature, this collection of papers is highly recommended for an academic library.   John Y. Cheung

85. Rich, Charles, and Richard C. Waters, eds. **Readings in Artificial Intelligence and Software Engineering.** Los Altos, Calif., Morgan Kaufmann, 1986. 602p. illus. bibliog. index. $26.95pa. LC 86-18627. ISBN 0-934613-12-5.

With an introduction that clearly presents the premise behind the application of artificial intelligence (AI) to software engineering, these readings look at different aspects of the problem and approaches for solving it. As the editors point out, automatic programming is the "ultimate goal of artificial intelligence applied to software engineering." Although programmers cannot yet indicate what software is required and have the program produced automatically, they can use AI techniques to modify existing programs. To examine the problem of fully automatic programming, Rich and Waters break it into manageable segments. They consider transformational approaches to be "the most active area in automatic programming research" and include six readings in this area. Another approach, theorem-proving techniques, deals with the problem by means of deductive program synthesis and program verification. This collection also reprints articles on specification techniques, very high level languages, programming by example, intelligent assistants, and knowledge representation. Each of these groupings begins with an introductory survey of the particular approach. Researchers and programmers will find the extensive bibliography particularly useful.

Renee B. Horowitz

86. Shwartz, Steven P. **Applied Natural Language Processing.** Princeton, N.J., Petrocelli Books, 1987. 293p. bibliog. index. $24.95 pa. LC 86-25330. ISBN 0-89433-260-0.

This is another book in the Petrocelli series on applied artificial intelligence. With special emphasis on the business aspect, this book presents the basics of natural language under-standing, a subfield in artificial intelligence (AI). More specifically, the material covers the different aspects of the application of an expert system in natural language understanding. The first part of this book begins with an overview of natural language understanding by people and by computers, followed by a brief note on AI in the commercial world. The second part presents a more in-depth look at the database and the language interface aspects specifically as applied to natural language understanding. The text concludes with a discussion on the commercial impact of the technology, particularly in terms of its future in the corporate and consumer marketplace. This book is not written for the academic reader. The primary goal is to present the business aspect and to analyze the commercial impact of this emerging field. As such, the material is written in a tutorial format, with many examples drawn from practical business problems. It would be of benefit to business managers or the general public who would like to keep up with this new area in computer science.   John Y. Cheung

AUTOMATION IN LIBRARIES
General Works

87. Barnett, Patricia J., and Amy E. Lucker, eds. **Procedural Guide to Automating an Art Library.** Tucson, Ariz., Art Libraries Society of North America, 1987. 40p. bibliog. (Occasional Papers, No. 7). $15.00pa. ISBN 0-942740-06-8.

This practical guide concentrates on bibliographical control, ignoring the problems associated with automating acquisitions and circulation. The five main essays are more or less equal in length and impact. The first two discussions review the concerns associated with retrospective conversion and implementation of an online catalog. The third essay, on linked authorities and authority control, is an excellent review of this most important topic and serves to make this publication of interest to a much larger readership. The essay has several sections, including discussions on theory, syndetic structuring, practical application, and standards. The essayist Patricia J. Barnett concludes with a sentence serving to summarize the importance of authority control: "With linked authority control our contribution—not service—to art research, will be realized." The two final essays cover linked bibliographic systems and suggest an organizational model for an integrated art information system. The guide concludes with a helpful glossary of terms used and an excellent annotated bibliography. Not all references given in endnotes appear in the bibliography, but those that further the discussion are selected for inclusion. Another good feature of the guide is the listing and brief description of projects and systems of interest to art librarians. This listing helps identify projects such as an inventory of American paintings executed prior to 1914, works of fine art and architecture in West Germany, and SCIPIO, a database for bibliographic control of auction catalogs.

Milton H. Crouch

88. Cortez, Edwin M. **Proposals and Contracts for Library Automation: Guidelines for Preparing RFPs.** Studio City, Calif., Pacific Information, and Chicago, American Library Association, 1987. 225p. index. $29.00pa. LC 86-30664. ISBN 0-8389-2043-8.

Every library director who has automation as part of short- or long-term plans will want a copy of this title in the office. It will also be a valuable text for an advanced computer/information technology class in a library school. Cortez provides a step-by-step and detailed description of the "how to's" of drafting and evaluating RFPs for library automation and negotiating with library automation vendors. "Perspectives for Library Automation," "The Procurement Process," "Preparing the RFP," "Final Selection and Implementation," and "Writing and Negotiating the Contract" are the titles of the five chapters, and each thoroughly and clearly covers those areas. Each chapter lists in italics under the chapter heading the subtopics to be covered. For example, in chapter 3, "Preparing the RFP," seven topics are covered, including staff and consultant responsibilities, drafting the RFP, the introductory section, the informational section, the special requirements section, and the contract section. Each of these includes very specific information, often in outline or table form. In a few chapters the examples are given in italics. In the introductory section of chapter 3, actual examples of background information on medium-sized public and large academic libraries and medium- and small-sized special libraries, which would be included in this section of a RFP, are set forth.

Technical vocabulary is clearly defined and twelve graphs and charts are included: a calendar of events, a PERT chart, a Grantt Chart, Candidate Selection Matrix, Table of Contents for Typical RFP, Equipment List Form, Price Quotation Form, Vendor Requirement Matrix, Cost/Performance Ratios, Log for System Reliability Test, Log for Functional Validity Test, and a Log for Full-Load Performance Test. There are also five valuable appendices: a list of thirty turnkey vendors and separate and extended examples of functional, technical, contract, and miscellaneous specifications. Finally, there is an ever-valuable index.

The guidelines presented here will remain constant even amidst the continuing changes in automation. The author has prepared a straightforward and practical text that will benefit library administrators and those involved in the intricate paper process and negotiation with vendors.   Marcia L. Atilano

89. Hewitt, Joe A., ed. **Advances in Library Automation and Networking: A Research Annual. Volume 1: 1987.** Greenwich, Conn., JAI Press, 1987. 232p. illus. $28.25; $56.50 (institutions). ISBN 0-89232-385-X.

Essays from some excellent names in the field including Ruth M. Katz, Larry Learn, and Michael Gorman have been collected on an important and timely topic for a new annual. Lengthier than periodical articles, these are written with the novice in mind as well as the advanced reader who is trying to broaden a perspective. Topics for the current volume include the Linked Systems Project, telecommunications, classification in an online catalog, bibliographic accessibility of computer files, online systems and the management of collections, organization of academic libraries for automation, trends in state networking, and cooperative collection development among research libraries.

Recommended as an important source for students and particularly library directors and library automation personnel who want to increase their knowledge across the broad spectrum of automation issues.

David V. Loertscher

90. **Retrospective Conversion in ARL Libraries.** By Barbara von Wahlde. Washington, D.C., Association of Research Libraries, 1987. 115p. bibliog. $20.00pa.

This publication is based on information and documents gathered as part of an April 1986 ARL Recon Project Questionnaire, supplemented with additional interviews and materials gathered throughout the year. The total number of libraries responding to the original questionnaire was 103, and detailed data on retrospective conversion plans were tabulated from the responses of 44 libraries.

Followed by the analysis of the survey, the book is divided into three parts: (1) planning documents, (2) studies, and (3) completed projects. A bibliography is also included for further information.

The work covers a variety of ideas, methods, and solutions. The information available in this publication is of extreme interest and importance to library administrators and technical and public services librarians. While many libraries have completed retrospective conversion, few have evaluated projects in print. As more libraries become involved with recon, it would be helpful to have available data widely shared about successful and less successful examples in order to help those preparing projects. This "Kit," as it is called by the System and Procedures Exchange Center of the Office of Management Studies, Association of Research Libraries, answers the needs of many libraries. However, the usefulness of the publication would be further enhanced if more libraries with a "completed project" and their actual experiences could be included.

Betty L. Tsai

91.   Shaw, Debora, ed. **Human Aspects of Library Automation: Helping Staff and Patrons Cope.** Champaign, Ill., Graduate School of Library and Information Science, University of Illinois, 1986. 129p. index. $15.00. ISBN 0-87845-072-6; ISSN 0069-4789.

This book presents papers which were originally speeches given at the 22nd Annual Clinic on Library Applications of Data Processing, this time focusing on the human aspects — helping staff and patrons cope more effectively with technology — of library automation. The clinic was sponsored jointly by the University of Illinois Graduate School of Library and Information Science and by area chapters of the American Society for Information Science.

Nine papers and a panel discussion are presented, each dealing with a specific aspect of the staff or the user and the automated system. Topics represented include the interaction between the public and the system, ergonomic factors, planning and implementation, online catalogs, specific clienteles (children and youth, the handicapped), designing effective promotional and instructional brochures, and privacy.

Most of the papers address the various considerations and problems attendant upon resistance to automation, both on the part of the staff and of the users of the library. Such papers generally include advice for overcoming initial suspicion of and hostility to the new technology. While none of the papers is of sufficient length to treat its topic in-depth (these are reworked speeches, after all), each contains enough common sense and sound recommendations to warrant consideration or discussion. There are no profound or novel concepts here, yet the overall effect of reading these papers is that a library can do much to counteract the inevitable problems inherent in automating

processes and procedures formerly done in more traditional ways. A thorough index makes it easier to extract specific nuggets of information in these readable, timely essays. Recommended. [R: BL, 1 Oct 87, p. 215; JAL, July 87, p. 172; RQ, Fall 87, p. 152]

Bruce A. Shuman

92.   Tracy, Joan I. **Library Automation for Library Technicians: An Introduction.** Metuchen, N.J., Scarecrow, 1986. 163p. illus. bibliog. index. $16.00. LC 85-26233. ISBN 0-8108-1865-5.

If you need a book that provides the most basic information about computer use in libraries by support staff, this may be for you. In ten brief chapters the author outlines how computers operate, their role in the library, and their specific applications in acquisitions, cataloging, serials control, circulation, administrative use (word processing, database management, and spreadsheets), and user services (online searching, selective dissemination of information, online catalogs, media bookings, reserve room, ILL, and computers for patrons). No section is very long; total text length is 153 pages and many of these pages are full of illustrations. Review questions at the end of each chapter suggest that the intended use of the book is in a classroom setting, which would explain some of the lack of details. The twenty full-page flowcharts could be reduced to half size with no loss of information and allow for more details in the text. Several of the black-and-white photographs add little or nothing to the content (for example, the page devoted to two pictures, one of children at a story hour and one of a person using a microform reader). There are no glaring errors, but the depth of coverage is so shallow that you will need backup material for the staff or students. The author provides a seven-item bibliography, three of which are general books for library technicians.

G. Edward Evans

Essays and Proceedings

93.   **European Conference on Library Automation: 11-12 September 1986, Harrogate, England. Proceedings of the Conference Organised and Sponsored Jointly by The Library Association and CLSI.** London, Library Association; distr., Chicago, American Library Association, 1987. 84p. (LA Conference Proceedings Series in Library Automation, No. 5). $15.00pa. ISBN 0-85365-508-01.

The editors of these proceedings indicate that this conference took shape in response to a demand by European librarians to outline developments in library automation in Europe to date. Interestingly, those consulted felt that keeping up-to-date with library automation developments in North America was easier than learning about events occurring not nearly as far away in the rest of Europe.

The intention of the conference's sponsors was not to provide an exhaustive description of automation projects in Europe. Instead, a number of representative countries were selected whose delegates could identify common problems and issues which might benefit from greater European cooperation in the future. Papers by authors describing library automation activities in the United Kingdom, France, the Netherlands, Scandinavia, and Southern Europe (Greece, Italy, Portugal, Spain, and Turkey) are included. The last two papers focus on European cooperation in library automation and identify a number of concerns regarding automation and the potential for networking capabilities. These papers grow out of the activities of the Commission of the European Communities. The Commission has been instituting a number of studies in order to analyze European library cooperation. According to this volume's preface, many issues were raised by the ensuing discussion. Unfortunately, they are not included in these proceedings.

There is little in the U.S. library literature that discusses the automation concerns of European countries. Several reasons can be pointed to for this lack: articles are written in languages other than English; many European countries are not as advanced in their automation developments as in the United States; and frequently, United States readers have some ambivalent feelings about projects that may not have a bearing on their own activities. For those who do have an interest in library automation projects beyond their front doors (and we should), the proceedings of this conference are most informative. Automation has made the library world a much smaller place, one in which the sharing of information, related concepts, and ideas becomes very important. As is implied in one of the last essays, cooperation cannot be mandated. Encouraging cooperation and networking through automation are common goals regardless of country. These proceedings point up the value of opening the channels of discussion at the very least.

Marjorie E. Bloss

94. Guidelines for Library and Media Automated Systems. By the League for Innovation Task Force on Automated Library Systems with Control Data Corporation and IBM Corporation. Laguna Hills, Calif., League for Innova-

tion in the Community College, 1986. 35p. bibliog. $10.00pa.

This slender volume may deceive the unwary, making them think that its attenuated size has something to do with the simplicity of the task. But if readers will study carefully this treatise's contents, they should come away with enough ammunition to begin an assault on the formidable task facing them as librarians and other information specialists.

The volume represents only one part of the work of the League for Innovation in the Community College. This volume was farmed out to its Task Force on Automated Library Systems. The Task Force is made up of directors, "information brokers," media specialists, computer experts, and educational media center leaders. Cathye J. Bunch, Director of Technical Services at the St. Louis Community College, was chair of the Task Force, and spearheaded the volume's production. Others on the Task Force included W. William Beuther of Cuyahoga Community College, Marilyn McDonald of Foothill College, Clifford Dawdy of Lane Community College, and Robert Vogt of IBM Corporation. Vogt and one other individual of the Control Data Corporation represent the computer business interest, both companies coproducing this volume with the League. One wishes, however, that there had been either fewer librarians, and thus a more representative body from other companies, or simply an "advisory" board of computer experts upon whom the Task Force could rely for matters outside its ken.

The animating spirit of this volume is to present for the user the whole nine yards of library service that can be automated, from acquisitions to reference. Under each heading, the Task Force has defined the area, outlined its purpose in the library or media center, posed policy questions, reviewed the production of the unit (i.e., what that unit "outputs"), and then summed up the data elements to be considered when automating that unit. Closing out the book are "chapters" (really one-page summaries) on equipment considerations, equipment maintenance, hardware considerations, and general systems requirements. A final chapter summarizes the discussions and makes recommendations.

It should come as no surprise to readers that the recommendations of the Task Force are that community libraries that cannot afford the so-called national systems now in place adopt a policy of buying prepackaged software offerings as opposed to in-house considerations. One wonders if the recommendations turned on any lights in the minds of the Control Data or IBM representatives. Be that as it may, the recommendation is probably a sound one, given the time, monetary, and human resources considerations that community colleges have at their disposal.

Mark Y. Herring

95. **Proceedings of the Nitobe-Ohira Memorial Conference on Japanese Studies: The University of British Columbia, May 23-25, 1984. Panel 8: Japanese Library Resources and Automation.** Tauneharu Gonnami, ed. Vancouver, B.C., Committee for the Nitobe-Ohira Memorial Conference on Japanese Studies, University of British Columbia, 1986. 118p. $5.00pa. ISBN 0-88865-334-4.

The complex title should warn against great expectations. This is a volume of proceedings, with the problems which that suggests, including an opening paper summarizing the five substantive papers. The papers were presented in May 1984 (published in August 1986) and are seriously dated. Of the five, two papers (by librarians at Stanford and Columbia) focus on access to Japanese materials in America with RLIN-CJK (in operation only eight months when presented), two focus on Japanese online information capabilities (by Japanese contributors), and the last cover general technological developments with a focus on Japan (by a British Columbia computer scientist). This latter offers interesting perspectives on Japanese characters in computing, but, despite admitting an unfamiliarity with library science, forecasts that the semilegendary Japanese Fifth Generation Project will greatly change the role and operations of libraries. The two most interesting papers, on Japanese information services, hardly seem to support this prognostication. The online services paper discusses some available Japanese resources, such as Japan Information Center of Science and Technology (JICST), but reveals an emphasis on access to foreign information. The other paper is a *plan* for an OCLC-like system linking academic libraries (more akin to the OCLC of Ohio College Library Center origins than the Online Computer Library Center of today) with the diagrams, flow charts, and details usual in descriptions of systems yet to be developed. The overall impression is that Japanese libraries have yet to reflect the technological innovations to which the Japanese corporate world has contributed. When the conference was held, the information here was probably timely. Now it is largely passé and mainly of historical interest.

K. Mulliner

96. Varlejs, Jana, ed. **Information Seeking: Basing Services on Users' Behaviors. Proceedings of the Twenty-Fourth Annual Symposium of the Graduate Alumni and Faculty of the Rutgers School of Communication, Information and Library Studies....** Jefferson, N.C., McFarland, 1987. 84p. $9.95pa. LC 87-42524. ISBN 0-89950-254-7.

This book is the fifth in a series which began in 1981 and which publishes the proceedings of the symposium cited in its title. It contains five papers on the topic of information seeking, defined here as the behavior of users and intermediaries in information retrieval.

The papers are "User/Intermediary Interaction Analysis: A Foundation for Designing Intelligent Information Systems," by Nicholas Belkin; "Cognitive Patterns in Online Searching," by Tefko Saracevic; "Stages in Child and Adolescent Development and Implications for Library Instructional Programs," by Carol Kuhlthau; "Using Reader Response Theory to Influence Collection Development and Program Planning for Children and Youth," by Kay E. Vandergrift; and "Information Seeking: Changing Perspectives," by Jana Varlejs.

The first four papers report empirical research on how users approach information systems, how users vary in their types and levels of needs, and users' understanding of those needs. Belkin and Saracevic also report on the behavior of searchers and the varying nature of search strategies. Vandergrift reports on how children and youth can have widely differing experiences with what they read. Varlejs relates the user-oriented approach to information seeking to some of the relevant literature.

The papers are all useful and, as transcribed speeches go, they read well. Each has bibliographic references but there is no index.

All in all, this book is most suited to library and information science collections. [R: JAL, Nov 87, p. 310]

James Rice

Databases and Software

97. Beiser, Karl. **Essential Guide to dBase III+ in Libraries.** Westport, Conn., Meckler Publishing, 1987. 276p. index. $19.95pa. LC 86-23877. ISBN 0-88736-064-5.

Over the last two decades, many libraries have been experimenting with computers. The old approach was to install a large system, primarily to handle circulation records. The new approach is to purchase one or more microcomputers and then try out a number of ideas on them. Word processing software can take the beginning librarian-informatician a long way in handling mailing lists, bibliographies, and small data files. It is usually easier to learn than database software, and is also cheaper. However, for larger applications or those that require greater automation or flexibility, database software is preferable. dBASE III + is a very popular software package that greatly extends the possibilities for database handling on micros over what one can do with a word processor. For example, it allows several related files to be used together, allows selection of records on combinations of conditions, and permits the automatic sorting of a set of records according to any field of each data record.

This book can assist the librarian-programmer who is already accustomed to the IBM PC (or compatible) in learning about and developing library-oriented applications using dBASE III +. The book is written as a tutorial organized according to case studies. A few of the cases treated are mailing-list management, bibliographies, newspaper indexing, abstracts, reference archive, acquisitions, serials control, catalog card production, overdues, circulation, and statistics. A large portion of the text consists of program examples. [R: BL, 1 Apr 87, p. 1175]

Steven L. Tanimoto

98. Hall, James L. **Online Bibliographic Databases: A Directory and Sourcebook.** 4th ed. London, Aslib; distr., Detroit, Gale, 1986. 509p. illus. bibliog. index. $105.00. ISBN 0-8103-2080-0.

This treatise, directory, bibliography, and index to bibliographic databases places particular emphasis on those databases which serve broad interests and which are likely to have a stable future. The work was produced in England and has an international scope. This fourth edition (for a review of the third edition, see *ARBA* 84, entry 90) increases the number of databases covered from 179 to 250. The opening expository sections describe in general what a database is and compare typical records among several different vendors. "Search templates" are provided for nine of the most popular vendors: these serve as a quick reminder of log-in, command, and output formats.

The main section is an alphabetical listing of databases, including information on the producer, the general subject areas covered, the number of records included and the years covered, the printed version (if any), a printout of a typical citation, the suppliers (vendors) who carry the database, and the costs of access as of 1986. Each listing also provides references to citations included in the 1,011-item bibliography which discuss the specific database in some capacity.

The appendices and indexes are actually a battery of finding aids which simplify access to the sections described above. These include a cross-reference list of database producers to their databases, a directory of vendors, a modified keyword listing of databases (including implied subject words), and a broad subject grouping of databases. One hundred fifty databases which are not included in the main section are instead described in the general index to the directory and bibliography. The compiler reminds one that even though these databases are not as popular, they are still important. Their subject, size, time frame, and producer and suppliers are noted here. In the front of the book, a handy table cross-references the 250 databases to the main vendors who handle them.

This sourcebook will be useful anywhere online searching is done to any great extent, and can serve as an adjunct reference text for those examining the range of database services available on an international basis.

Gary R. Cocozzoli

99. Rasmussen, Jens, and Pranas Zunde, eds. **Empirical Foundations of Information and Software Science III.** New York, Plenum, 1987. 272p. index. $52.50. LC 87-12275. ISBN 0-306-42585-8.

This book is a collection of papers as presented at a symposium of the same title. The purpose of the symposium was to provide a cross-disciplinary forum on the value of lexical aids, online help enhancements, and related topics that affect the human-computer relationship. The ultimate goal of all of these papers is to provide insight into the human interaction problem with the intent of improving the software designs. A wide variety of topics is discussed, from the trite to the esoteric.

The emphasis of the topics is in the realm of database management systems and management information systems, and this is not readily apparent to the user from the title. Empirical studies that shed light on the user's needs and human behavior are the bulk of the topics discussed. The use of graphics is sparse and a few typographical errors (e.g., *support* in the introduction, *measurement* on page 13) mar the text. The use of jargon remains a tedious necessity in this rapidly changing field with its myriad concepts, details, and software packages.

The strength of this book is in the variety of topics discussed and the viewpoints presented. Seldom are so many concepts and potential directions presented in one place. There are twenty papers in this book, and with the exception of two papers discussing text retrieval systems, overlap is minor. The best chapter is on early size estimation for software packages, since this has immediate application to software project management.

A few authors' viewpoints are definitely arguable. I take exception to the first author's assertions that research databases are small and that research scientists are relatively computer illiterate. This text clearly points out the difficulty of understanding human nature, and the necessity of understanding the user's needs before software design. Perhaps the major theme that runs throughout this text is that software design remains more of an art than a science.

Two important topics, graphics and knowledge-based systems, are largely ignored in these papers. Admittedly, graphics has not become an integral part of database software, but the advantages of this interface are now well recognized (if not understood) by modern software developers. The brief mention of knowledge-based systems (or expert systems) can only be attributed to the timing of the symposium. The same book today would emphasize knowledge-based systems as the tool of choice to fulfill the needs of education and ease of use of the new user. Natural language interfaces and decision support systems seem to be considered only sparingly and also deserve more space in this text. John A. Jackman

---

Library Information Networks and Systems

100. Ashby, Margaret. **HERTIS: The Development of a Library Network.** Hatfield, England, HERTIS, 1986. 141p. illus. bibliog. index. £5.00pa. ISBN 0-85267-159-8.

This detailed history of HERTIS, a college library network serving further and higher education and industry in Hertfordshire, England, is probably more interesting to North American librarians as a study in comparative librarianship than it is as an example of current practice in a library network. It is also illuminating in that it reveals the complex nature of the system of further and higher education in this country. Programs of cooperation among the approximately fifteen college libraries began in the 1950s, and most of the volume focuses on personalities and programs prior to the 1980s. The personal and professional commitment of individuals involved is a dominant theme as is the development of the concept and practice of "tutor-librarianship." The programs in the cooperating institutions emphasized the instruction and library usage, particularly for the teenage students in their colleges. Predating the eras

of instructional and computer technology, the network's main concerns were and seem to remain collection development and coordination and service to patrons. In this country the term *network*, since the 1970s, has been thought of increasingly as synonymous with shared computer-based systems. Although individual libraries in this network make use of computers for library operations, as of 1984 (when it appears that the text was completed) the network did not share computer capabilities, although a 1983 policy statement suggested that a shared system be developed. Much of what is written about networks in this country could be characterized as depersonalized. This provides a refreshing balance but little interest to those interested in network systems and services. [R: LAR, Mar 87, p. 149] JoAnn V. Rogers

101. **Automated Systems for Access to Multilingual and Multiscript Library Materials: Problems and Solutions. Papers from the Pre-Conference Held at Nihon Daigaku Kaikan Tokyo, Japan August 21-22, 1986.** Christine Boßmeyer and Stephen W. Massil, eds. Munich, New York, K. G. Saur, 1987. 225p. (IFLA Publications, 38). $34.00. ISBN 3-598-21768-4.

The papers in this volume are reproduced as they were presented at the IFLA Pre-Conference Seminar of the same title. The focus of the seminar was on Asian scripts, with one paper each on Arabic and Greek. The editors acknowledge these gaps in the coverage of the material, which resulted from the unavailability of speakers on the problems of Hebrew, Cyrillic, and Indian languages. There is no general bibliography or index, but most of the individual papers include references. The publication also includes lists of contributors and sponsors. All of the papers are in English, although the majority of the contributors are Asian.

A wide range of topics is covered, from the historical overview of problems in cataloging non-Roman languages to specific computer applications in the field. Particular attention is paid to the problems of transliteration of Chinese, Japanese, and Korean, and the absence of standard character sets for many languages.

While any addition to the small amount of literature in this area is helpful, this volume is unusual in presenting the topic from a non-Western viewpoint. The speakers emphasize that "solutions to problems of automating Roman language databases are not always applicable to automating other languages" (p. 185). Although this book would be most useful to those with some experience in library automation and multiscript cataloging, the range of problems mentioned makes it a handy introduction to the topic. This volume should be acquired by collections specializing in library automation and foreign-language cataloging.

Jean L. Cooper

102.　Hensinger, James Speed. **Printers for Use with OCLC Workstations.** Westport, Conn., Meckler Publishing, 1987. 161p. index. $29.95. LC 87-12259. ISBN 0-88736-180-3.

Hensinger, Manager of Micro Systems and Service for the Bibliographic Center for Research (BCR), has created an extremely helpful handbook for selecting and starting up printers to be used with OCLC terminals. The introduction claims that it will help the user prepare for buying, integrating, and using printers with OCLC's terminals and work stations. Chapter 1 addresses two different transmission technologies, parallel and serial, reviewing the technologies associated with both. Also included are explanations of baud rates, the advantages of buffers, and the use of data cables. There is a chapter devoted to how to change the baud rate of your terminal. It includes OCLC policies that might result in financial punishments to the library if not followed. How to modify cables is also addressed, and a chapter on why things do not work addresses problems associated with printers not matching OCLC character sets. There is a list of OCLC records that can be used to test printer configurations, and helpful suggestions are given for creating homemade printer stands and sound shields to suppress noise. How to avoid problems associated with label feeding and snarled cables or poor paper stock is also featured. An extremely helpful checklist and outline on how to buy a printer is based upon analyzing what it is you intend to print. One chapter is devoted strictly to instructions on printing information from DOS, while another lists the OCLC documentation that addresses issues relating to printers. An outstanding glossary is appended, as are the findings of a survey answered by 150 libraries that are serviced by BCR, along with the survey instrument. An additional helpful analytical tool is a table of service cost, frequency, and repair time. User satisfaction levels along with remarks by the respondents organized by printer model are invaluable aids for any library contemplating printer purchases. A useful index and a statement about the author establishing his credibility complete this must purchase technical service tool.

Ann Allan

103.　Inskip, Robin. **The Marigold System: A Case Study of Community Planning Networks and Community Development.** Halifax, N.S., School of Library and Information Studies,

Dalhousie University, 1987. 117p. bibliog. (Occasional Papers Series, No. 41). $14.50pa. ISBN 0-7703-9712-3.

This work is an exploratory case study of the 1978-1981 development of the Marigold Library System, the first regional public library system in Alberta. The specific research questions addressed were: Was increased provincial funding for regional libraries the most important factor in the development of Marigold? and Was the presence of a professional community developer important in that process? In addition, the author relates the Marigold case history to various models of diffusion of innovations, community development, and community planning and governance. The geographic area involved is predominantly rural, so the work is a contribution to the field of library services to rural populations, an area greatly in need of research.

Inskip provides a brief overview of literature on rural librarianship, an elementary introduction to the concepts of models to be employed (e.g., interactive community planning, the domain concept, network agents), a detailed account of events in the development of Marigold, and an analysis of the case in terms of the models. Increased financial support was found not to be the critical factor in the development of Marigold; the influence of the full-time community developer was found to be profound. Inskip also found that the Marigold case illustrates and lends tentative support to several models of community development. This work should be of interest to those concerned with library services to rural areas, to community developers and planners, and researchers interested in case study methodologies.

Joe A. Hewitt

104.　**International Transfers of National MARC Records: Guidelines for Agreements Relating to the Transfer of National MARC Records between National Bibliographic Agencies.** London, IFLA UBCIM Programme, 1987. 48p. bibliog. $32.00pa. ISBN 0-903043-45-9.

This slim publication "provides guidelines for agreements relating to the transfer of national MARC (machine readable cataloging) records between national bibliographic agencies." The guidelines were created under the direction and auspices of the International MARC Network Advisory Committee. This committee advises both the Conference of Directors of National Libraries and the International MARC Programme of the International Federation of Library Associations and Institutions (IFLA).

The expected result of use of the guidelines is greater commonality and completeness in agreements between national bibliographic agencies, recognizing the existence of different objectives and circumstances. The guidelines consist of a set of four recommended steps: (1) clearly identify the objectives of the agreement, (2) determine the number and type of agreements to be drawn up, (3) use the proposed checklist to determine the main sections of the agreement, and (4) prepare the text of the agreement with the assistance of a supplied glossary and checklist.

The publication is organized into five parts. The first provides an overview and background based on a review of related studies and patterns of international transfers of national MARC records. The second part summarizes the steps of the guidelines and their use. Part three includes lists of common objectives of agreements between national bibliographic agencies, a checklist of potential agreement sections, and a glossary. The fourth part offers "illustrative" or model agreements. The fifth part concludes with a reading list and references.

This booklet can be treated as a highly specialized reference tool for a selected audience within librarianship or among students of international policy. This is not a documentary; no text of existing agreements is included. However, detailed comprehensive illustrations and clearly stated step-by-step instructions offer both direction for creating such documents as well as attention to relevant concerns such as copyright, ownership, etc. The benefits of using these guidelines, as presented in this publication, are the faster and simpler preparation of agreements which in turn are easier to understand and interpret.   Danuta A. Nitecki

105. Kemper, Marlyn. **Networking: Choosing a LAN Path to Interconnection.** Metuchen, N.J., Scarecrow, 1987. 279p. illus. bibliog. index. $37.50. LC 87-12907. ISBN 0-8108-2031-5.

The LAN path referred to in the title of this book is that in the planning stage intended to connect the members of the South East Florida Library Information Network (SEFLIN), a multitype consortium including the Broward Community College Library system, the Broward County Libraries Division, Florida Atlantic University Library, Florida International University Library, Miami-Dade Community College Library, the Miami-Dade Public Library, the University of Miami Library, and the State Library of Florida. As the author indicates, the term *local area network* remains "ill-defined." The author's use of the term is broader than the reader might assume. It

actually refers to an "extended" LAN or wide area network linking disparate systems for multiple purposes. The HYPERbus network developed by Network Systems Corp. currently links the Broward County Main Library with other governmental agencies in the local area. This text looks at HYPERbus in terms of its use in linking initially two and eventually all of the SEFLIN members.

As the detailed table of contents demonstrates, however, the book goes well beyond examination of one situation. It includes much background information on communication concepts, network architecture and topology, and emerging standards summarized with the nonspecialist reader in mind. It emphasizes planning, design, and implementation intended to be used as a model for network development. In the background chapters, there are references to existing installations in university settings and to literature discussing LANs in a library and information setting. Each chapter includes a bibliography of references from library and information science as well as computer science and some engineering. There are a selected bibliography and a glossary with simple definitions. There are some problems with organization, causing unnecessary repetition of information and a scattering of information about the proposed library application. Also, the reader should expect only generalized goals and objectives for library functions and applications. Based on a case study for a dissertation in information science, this work has limited use as a text on the subject of LANs. It is a readable book for the practitioner and student without a technical background.

JoAnn V. Rogers

106. King, David. **Unmet Needs of ILLINET Users.** Springfield, Ill., Illinois State Library, 1987. 50p. bibliog. (Illinois Library Statistical Report, No. 23). free pa.

This work reports the results of an empirical study which profiles the characteristics of unfilled interlibrary loan requests in the Illinois Library and Information Network (ILLINET). A sample of 2,798 canceled interlibrary loan requests was taken over a one-year period from the eighteen ILLINET systems. Factors examined include provenance of the requests, the age level of the patron, the age level of the material requested, the subject of the requested material, the publication date, scope of the interlibrary loan search, reason for cancellation, bibliographic sources searched in the search process, and source of verification. Analysis includes numerous cross tabulations among these factors.

Among the more notable findings is that inaccessibility of recently published and high demand items is a principal reason for cancellation of requests, with one-third of canceled items being published during the two years immediately preceding the study. The study revealed a propensity to rely almost entirely on OCLC as a tool for identifying potential lenders outside of Illinois. Some 25 percent of items searched in OCLC that were not found by library staff were located in OCLC by the researchers, indicating a need for improved training of ILL staffs. Searches for older material in *Pre-56 Imprints* were conducted very infrequently, yet the researchers found that locations could be found in that source for up to half of the canceled requests for older materials.

This study succeeds in focusing attention on some of the causes of unmet needs of ILLINET users and concludes with suggestions for improvement in ILL services. Although these results are of limited generalizability to other networks, they may be provocative for anyone interested in ILL performance. The methodology may also be of interest to others doing similar studies.

Joe A. Hewitt

107. LaCroix, Michael J. **MINITEX and ILLINET: Two Library Networks.** Champaign, Ill., Graduate School of Library and Information Science, University of Illinois, 1987. 38p. maps. bibliog. (Occasional Papers, No. 178). $3.00pa. ISSN 0276-1769.

This short descriptive summary of the history, administration or governance, and programs of two statewide networks, the Minnesota Interlibrary Telecommunications Exchange and the Illinois Library and Information Network, focuses on 1985-1986 data, most of which were gleaned from official reports and publications of the networks involved. Following about ten pages of description of each, the author offers several paragraphs of "observations" about each. About five pages of comments and comparisons conclude the paper. Although the author uses primary source material, including telephone conversations with several network administrators, he seldom goes beyond very basic description and provides almost no evaluative information or comments. Much of the information presented here is available in the Association of Specialized and Cooperative Library Agencies's *Report on Library Cooperation 1986* (6th ed. American Library Association, 1987), which gives an overview of networks and services in most of the states.

JoAnn V. Rogers

108. **The North American Online Directory 1987: A Directory of Online Information Products & Services with Names & Numbers.** New York, R. R. Bowker, 1987. 379p. $85.00pa. ISBN 0-8352-2311-6; ISSN 0000-0841.

This directory is designed to serve as a quick reference tool describing online information products, services, and producers in the United States and Canada. The 1987 edition is greatly expanded over the previous edition, reflecting a growth in databases during 1986 of 65 percent and an increase in the number of producers from 785 to 1,076. Some 23,270 databases are included.

Arranged in broad categories of information production, information distribution, support services, conferences and courses, and information sources, the directory lists and profiles databases, databases classified by subject, database producers, database producers classified by services, online vendors and gateways, telecommunications networks, library networks and consortia, information collection and analysis centers, information brokers, information retailing classified by subject, information retailing classified by services, consultants, consultants classified by services, associations, online user groups, calendar of conferences, list of courses, reference books, and periodicals and newsletters. Information provided for each database includes producer, type of database, first year of coverage, updating schedule, description of contents, vendors, and user charges or subscription arrangements. The subject arrangements represent a notable improvement over previous editions. An acronym glossary and listing of names and numbers in the information industry are highly useful addenda.

Due to the broad scope of this work and its useful and well-designed arrangement, *The North American Online Directory* should be viewed as a basic reference source for any library or organization which makes use of online products and services. This tool comes close to matching the publisher's claim of being "the map to the 'global village.' "

Joe A. Hewitt

109. Westlake, Duncan R., and John E. Clarke. **Geac: A Guide for Librarians and Systems Managers.** Brookfield, Vt., Gower Publishing, 1987. 307p. bibliog. index. $79.95. LC 86-22904. ISBN 0-566-05215-6.

The authors of this book, a librarian and a systems manager from the London Borough of Hillingdon, have firsthand experience with the Geac Library Information System. They have written a thorough analysis of Geac and its library products. The book is divided into four major sections: an introduction to the company, an explanation of the hardware and its operation, a comprehensive description of the applications software, and a discussion of customer support. The appendices include a list of Geac library customers worldwide, a glossary, and an annotated bibliography. It is not necessary to read or understand the technical details in the hardware section in order to understand other sections of the book. A European slant is evident in some of the technical jargon and in descriptions of products that are not in general use in North America. The authors note some differences with North American applications.

The applications software section includes one chapter on each of the following functions: circulation, cataloging and the OPAC, acquisitions and serials control, backup systems and portable terminals, local information module, management information, and external communications. Circulation receives the most attention despite the fact that other modules now form the core of the Geac integrated system. The description of the acquisitions module is somewhat meager, given its complexity and capability.

This book was written for current users of Geac products, for prospective customers, and for researchers of library automation. Both technical specifications and general evaluative comments are included. The Geac system is too complex for all aspects of every module to be described and it changes too rapidly for an account of this nature to be completely current and accurate. Nonetheless, this book offers information of interest, even to persons who consider themselves well-versed with Geac library products. Lynn Morgan

Online Catalogs

110. Crawford, Walt. **Patron Access: Issues for Online Catalogs.** Boston, G. K. Hall, 1987. 259p. bibliog. index. $36.50; $28.50pa. LC 86-20861. ISBN 0-8161-1850-7; 0-8161-1852-3pa.

Focusing on issues to consider when dealing with patron access to an online catalog, this book covers processes the user can initiate along with protection issues in one chapter. The "database engine," or computers and software supporting patron access, are discussed in another chapter. The final ten chapters deal with presentation issues of the online catalog, including clarity, terminals, printers and workstations, commands, feedback, retrieval and browsing, searching, display issues, and specific displays.

Crawford does not make any final assertions and admits that no online system can offer each feature discussed; hence he does not advocate a particular system. The book presents considerations applicable for any size and any type of library; the assumption behind them is that the catalog which best suits the patrons' needs is the most valuable one.

The text has a healthy seventy-seven figures, but the chapters would benefit from concluding summary statements, helpful to the librarian at the beginning stages of automation. Some chapters contain unrelated topics; for example, "User Profiles" is in the chapter covering system clarity, while chapter 5, "Terminals: Input and Display," and chapter 11, "Display Issues," overlap on some points. The glossary is easy to read, and the index is comprehensive; however, the annotated bibliography of over one hundred entries is only one-third annotated.

The book is an excellent source of issues for a library considering desirable public access features when choosing an online catalog. It could also be used by a library with an existing online catalog when considering refinements and improvements of public access. [R: JAL, Sept 87, p. 245; LJ, 1 Oct 87, p. 70; WLB, Nov 87, pp. 75-76] Amey L. Kirkbride

111. Foulkes, John, ed. **Downloading Bibliographic Records. Proceedings of a One-Day Seminar Sponsored by the MARC Users' Group.** Brookfield, Vt., Gower Publishing, 1986. 72p. index. $21.00pa. LC 86-27122. ISBN 0-566-05014-5.

The purpose of this collection of papers is "to cover all issues relating to downloading." Topics covered include reasons for downloading, legal aspects, database owners' viewpoints, problems faced by library systems suppliers, and end users' needs. The eleven contributors represent the owners, suppliers, and users of downloaded information, but unfortunately for American readers, they are all British. Although the problems and issues are basically the same on both sides of the ocean, American readers unfamiliar with the British information environment are likely to be distracted by unexplained abbreviations and references to things that are common knowledge to British readers only.

Allen Foster's paper is the most useful and the one that is least affected by the British perspective. Foster defines downloading, outlines the technological developments that have made it possible, describes the types and purposes of downloading, discusses some of the problems involved, and provides a brief list of references. The remaining papers discuss the experiences of British suppliers and users of databases and are of less interest to American readers. A few of them include a very short list of references, and there is an index at the end.

This book provides a good introduction to the issues involved in downloading, but readers seeking an in-depth understanding and an American perspective will need to look elsewhere. It is not worth the price for most American libraries. [R: CLJ, Aug 87, p. 257; JAL, July 87, pp. 188-89]   Mark E. Schott

112. Lazinger, Susan S., and Peretz Shoval. **Prototyping a Microcomputer-Based Online Library Catalog.** Champaign, Ill., Graduate School of Library and Information Science, University of Illinois, 1986. 48p. bibliog. (Occasional Papers, No. 177). $3.00pa. ISSN 0276-1769.

Prototyping has emerged as an alternative to traditional "life cycle" concepts of systems analysis during the past decade. Based on new software development techniques which support rapid implementation of prototypes through applications generators, prototyping provides users with tangible models with which to interact early in the system development process. Thus the traditional approach involving exhaustive requirements analysis, specification, and design is replaced by a process of quickly providing the user with a working model of a proposed system, followed by iterative refinement of the original design. The prototyping approach to systems development offers many advantages in certain systems development situations, including some which obtain in libraries.

In *Prototyping a Microcomputer-Based Online Library Catalog*, Lazinger and Shoval define and describe prototyping, summarize the literature on prototyping in the context of systems analysis and library systems development, and demonstrate the use of the technique in the development of a microcomputer-based online catalog for the library of the Graduate Library School of Hebrew University. This is a useful work explicating and promoting the adoption of an approach to systems development which, when properly used in the appropriate context, can result in quicker development of library systems which more nearly meet the needs of users.   Joe A. Hewitt

113. Markey, Karen, ed. **Public Access Online Catalogs.** Champaign, Ill., Graduate School of Library and Information Science, University of Illinois, 1987. 1v. (various paging). index. (*Library Trends*, Vol. 35, No. 4). $10.00pa. ISSN 0024-2594.

Much research during this decade on the use of online catalogs has been stimulated by studies supported by the Council on Library Resources (CLR). The contributors to this issue of *Library Trends* are among those who have built on the reported findings of such research and who have initiated new efforts to confirm or extend previous conclusions.

The volume consists of eight articles which address issues about online catalog design, implementation, user training, user evaluation, and system improvement. The first two papers describe improvements of integrated library systems in the libraries of the University of Guelph (by Beckman) and the Ohio State University (by Logan). The next two articles reflect some of the thoughts presented during two CLR-sponsored conferences; Matthews offers guidelines for online catalog screen layouts and displays of bibliographic information, while Neilsen summarizes results of his CLR-sponsored research project investigating different teaching approaches and objectives to train users of online catalogs. Kalin promotes consideration of the invisible or remote users of online catalogs and recommends assistance for them which differs from that given to users who access online catalogs within the library. Significant findings are reported by Lipetz and Paulson from their 1984 CLR-supported study comparing searching by users at the New York State Library before and after introduction of subject search capabilities in the online catalog. Kinsella and Bryant summarize the main research areas to be given priority for support from the British Library Research and Development Department. In the last paper, Hildreth describes the functionality within his categorized three generations of online catalogs and offers suggestions for how system designers can enhance online catalogs with capabilities more responsive to users' searching.

Collectively, the references cited at the end of each article offer an excellent bibliography of current research on the use of online catalogs. The index (prepared by Burger) covers all of volume 35 of *Library Trends*, which includes this issue as well as three preceding ones.

This readable collection brings together usable findings from current research. Offering direction for technical development as well as insights for staff assisting users, the issue is recommended for professionals and students interested in the uses and developments of online catalogs. [R: JAL, Nov 87, p. 312]

Danuta A. Nitecki

114. Markey, Karen, and Anh N. Demeyer. **Dewey Decimal Classification Online Project:**

Evaluation of a Library Schedule and Index Integrated into the Subject Searching Capabilities of an Online Catalog. Final Report to the Council on Library Resources. Dublin, Ohio, Office of Research, OCLC Online Computer Library Center, 1986. 382p. bibliog. index. (Research Report, No. OCLC/OPR/RR-86/1). $25.00 spiralbound.

This research project used the nineteenth edition of the Dewey Decimal Classification Schedules as an online searching tool in the catalogs of four libraries. The project asked if the DDC online would improve subject searches so that patrons preferred a catalog with DDC online compared to one without DDC online. Patrons doing research preferred the catalog with online DDC, patrons doing general searching preferred the catalog without the DDC enhancement, and staff were equally divided in their preference between the two catalogs. The researchers found that the DDC can be used to provide subject access to searchers by providing new strategies for searching and browsing. The project also allowed a glimpse into online searching problems and was the first use of a classification scheme as an online searching tool of patrons.

The report is divided into nine chapters with seventeen appendices, a bibliography, and a comprehensive index. The text includes seventy-two illustrations and eighty-four tables. The research is comprehensive, thorough, and extensive. The report is excellent for its analysis of patron searching strategies and could be a useful source for projects studying the use of online classification schedules as searching aids in public catalogs.

Amey L. Kirkbride

115.   Matthews, Joseph R., ed. **The Impact of Online Catalogs.** New York, Neal-Schuman, 1986. 146p. index. $29.95pa. LC 85-32014. ISBN 0-918212-84-7.

In 1981, when the first online public access catalogs had been installed, the Council on Library Resources funded a large and important study of how OPAC catalogs were being used and accepted by library patrons. The project findings were summarized in *Using Online Catalogs* by J. R. Matthews, G. S. Lawrence, and D. K. Ferguson (Neal-Schuman, 1983). In 1983, at the Los Angeles ALA conference, the principal researchers spoke on the practical implications of their findings. This volume reproduces these presentations which are all clear, cogent, and nontechnical. They deal with the implications for system designers (Lawrence), technical services (Matthews), reference service (Ferguson), subject access (K. Markey), library

managers (R. Anderson), and evaluative data collection (L. Colaianni). The most significant of the CLR findings is related to subject searching in the online catalog and Markey—who subsequently published an important book on this topic (*Subject Searching in Library Catalogs* [OCLC, 1984])—contributes a particularly fine chapter. The volume concludes with a report, summarizing the findings of a 1983-1984 study that investigated patron utilization and acceptance of NYU's Geac catalog, Bobcat. By the time this review appears over five years will have passed since the CLR study was completed. This landmark study has had a tremendous impact on OPAC design and on the direction of library research. This little volume remains a useful introduction to the project and its findings. [R: CLJ, Aug 87, pp. 257-58; JAL, Mar 87, p. 35; JAL, July 87, p. 186; Online, Mar 87, pp. 102-03; RQ, Spring 87, p. 388]

Joseph W. Palmer

CAREERS

116.   Burrington, Gillian. **Equal Opportunities in Librarianship? Gender and Career Aspirations.** London, Library Association; distr., Chicago, American Library Association, 1987. 191p. bibliog. index. (Library Association Research Publication, No. 24). $24.00pa. ISBN 0-85365-877-3.

Gillian Burrington conducted a survey in the United Kingdom about the role of women in librarianship through the examination of a series of articles and studies from the late nineteenth century to the early part of the 1980s. The author provides an historical overview and a comprehensive study on one of the most critical issues of our profession: is this a career for women? Burrington's survey shows evidence of bias against women librarians in the United Kingdom. In general she found that women believe it necessary to work harder than men in order to be able to compete in their careers. It is also believed that women and men have different commitments and career aspirations. In publishing, power seems to be in the hands of male editors of British library journals, especially those with wide circulation and high status. One remarkable factor is that women seem to be more passive and relatively invisible and inaudible in their network, while men are definitely more aggressive. Assumptions about differences between men and women at work in libraries lead to unconscious discrimination in career paths. Bias in librarianship is not a unique factor; it reflects society at large and this complex view is difficult to change. Burrington foresees behavior that could influence women to counteract negative perceptions in libraries and in society. This comprehensive survey provides essential information for librarians of the future interested in the status of women. The sample is taken from a population based in the United Kingdom and is open to challenge, but this book will have broad implications for librarians, library educators, administrators, and women in the library profession all over the world because of its amplitude and its quality.

Camille Côté

117. Collard, Betsy A. **The High-Tech Career Book: Finding Your Place in Today's Job Market.** Los Altos, Calif., Crisp/William Kaufmann, 1986. 273p. illus. index. $12.95pa. LC 85-23086. ISBN 0-931961-32-7.

Collard, a career counselor in California's Silicon Valley, specializes in employment counseling for women. Her book is intended for all with levels of education from high school on up, to help them find jobs in high-tech companies and plan careers in related industries. The cover contains such appealing promises as "finding your place in today's job market," and "how to break in and move up." Sections cover (1) the organization of high-tech companies; (2) careers in functional areas; (3) careers in writing, training, graphics, and public relations; (4) "indispensable information," curiously, placed just past the middle of the book (shouldn't such information come either first or last?); and (5) trends in specific industries and career fields.

Coverage includes job requirements and responsibilities, career paths, corporate structure(s), pros and cons of different jobs, and job-seeking behavior and strategy which will maximize one's potential employability. Black-and-white illustrations are liberally scattered throughout and are generally effective. Appendices include organization charts, job descriptions, industry terms, professional associations, and a list of helpful publications. Attractively formatted, illustrated, and priced, this book is a useful tool for exploiting opportunities available to both technical and nontechnical job seekers. It is written for the layperson, and does its level best to cut through the jargon and technical verbiage which so often accompany job notices.

This title was published in January 1986, which makes it almost two years old at the time of reviewing, a circumstance, in such a volatile and fast-growing area, which diminishes somewhat the work's usefulness. New (possibly annual) editions will surely be welcome.

Bruce A. Shuman

118. Dewey, Barbara I. **Library Jobs: How to Fill Them, How to Find Them.** Phoenix, Ariz., Oryx Press, 1987. 171p. bibliog. index. $26.50 pa. LC 87-5642. ISBN 0-89774-300-8.

The profession of librarianship has changed tremendously during the last few years. It is becoming difficult for many librarians to find the right type of position for various reasons. Barbara I. Dewey has done a yoman service to the profession by writing an excellent book on how to fill and find library jobs.

The book is divided into eight chapters. Each chapter deals with various aspects of positions, including the process for developing job descriptions, writing resumes and cover letters, interview guidelines, job offers including salary and fringe benefits, job satisfaction and motivation, career assessment, and advancement in the profession. Each chapter has been written clearly with good examples and figures followed by a bibliography at the end of the chapter and a general selected bibliography at the end of the book for further research.

This is certainly a well-written book, based on the practical experience of the author as the placement director at one of the well-known library schools in the country. It is certainly a good guide for libraries to prepare their hiring process. On the other hand, it is an excellent guide for librarians who are seeking employment, especially at the entry or middle management levels. The book is recommended for all types of libraries and librarians. It is certainly a good addition to the library literature.

Ravindra Nath Sharma

119. Heim, Kathleen, and Peggy Sullivan. **Opportunities in Library and Information Science.** Lincolnwood, Ill., VGM Career Horizons/National Textbook, 1986. 150p. illus. bibliog. $9.95. LC 86-060149. ISBN 0-8442-6145-9.

The information provided here about careers in library and information science should be available in all high school and college counseling offices, libraries which have career information, and library education programs. Students engaged in general career exploration as well as those already enrolled in a program for library technical personnel, professional librarians, or information scientists will benefit from this multifaceted exploration of opportunities in information professions.

The chapter on career opportunities is written in a manner which will engage the reader with short vignettes as well as description by function and by agency type. The following chapter on education describes technical, undergraduate, and graduate programs. Although the section on undergraduate education for school library media specialists points out the limitations of nongraduate education for future career development, it does not make clear that some graduate programs offer the in-depth specialized courses and field experience opportunities depicted. Subsequent chapters deal with placement, general aspects of the employment process, and the future of the information professions. Appendices list references, associations, and American Library Association accredited programs.

The authors, both authorities in the field, write clearly and concisely and provide valuable insight into the multiplicity of opportunities for careers in library and information science. Highly recommended. Eliza T. Dresang

120. Herrup, Steven. **Exploring Careers in Research and Information Retrieval.** New York, Rosen Publishing, 1986. 140p. bibliog. index. (Exploring Careers). $9.97. LC 85-14262. ISBN 0-8239-0650-7.

Advising high school students, Herrup examines careers in research in business, law, and science. Educational preparation and possible specialties are discussed. One appendix lists sources for scholarships and another includes suggestions for further reading. There is also a subject index. In describing academic preparation, Herrup fails to mention information science itself as a course of graduate study after which students may apply research methodologies learned to various disciplines. Herrup ignores the innovations in libraries made possible by computer technology. Overall, his advice has a pedantic tone which high school students could find tiresome. The scholarship listing in this book will be useful but educators should look elsewhere for career guidance in information science. Margaret McKinley

121. Norback, Judith. **The Complete Computer Career Guide.** Blue Ridge Summit, Pa., TAB Books, 1987. 246p. illus. index. $18.95; $12.95pa. LC 86-5726. ISBN 0-8306-9554-0; 0-8306-2654-9pa.

This book claims to provide "common-sense guidelines on 25 major computer careers ... a current and comprehensive perspective, from job descriptions to the experience, training, and personality required ... where to find the perfect job ... instructions for writing your resume ... and helpful information on technical schools." Actually, the volume falls far short of these ambitious objectives.

It is not very well written. Many sentences in the book are poorly structured, wordy, or

vague. The book is not carefully put together. For example, one of the items in the table of contents, "Office Automation Specialist," refers readers to a page which contains a cross-reference to two other sections of the book, neither of which provides significant information about office automation specialists.

The book is sketchy throughout. For example, the section on resume writing is about one-half of a page and is on the one hand rigidly prescriptive, and on the other hand, unclear. There is no sample provided. The descriptions of the careers are not very useful. Most of what is not vague is common sense. One would do better to consult the Government Printing Office's *Occupational Outlook Handbook* (1986).

There are a few useful features, such as a fairly good description of certification (chapter 3) with a list of societies. There are six directories: institutions offering associate degree programs, placement services, trade and technical schools, accredited home study schools, associations, and publications. The latter are not in proper citation form, information such as author and date is not provided, and magazines are not distinguished from reference books.

A more useful source for job hunting in this area would be *Engineering, Science, and Computer Jobs*, ninth edition (1988) put out by the Peterson's Guide Series, especially when used in conjunction with the *Occupational Outlook Handbook*. James Rice

122. Warner, Alice Sizer. **Mind Your Own Business: A Guide for the Information Entrepreneur.** New York, Neal-Schuman, 1987. 165p. index. $24.95pa. LC 86-23641. ISBN 1-555-70014-4.

Based on the author's experience developing Warner-Eddison in the 1970s, her current sole proprietorship of The Information Guild, and a survey of over 250 self-employed information entrepreneurs, this is a readable, basic, down-to-earth guide to developing a small information business. Practical and detailed, its chapters cover analysis of personal goals, style, and temperament; development of business plans, finances; sales and marketing; and management issues. Most chapters are clear, succinct, and laden with handy examples and good references to more meaty information sources. An overview of financial planning and analysis is helpful, but as the author suggests, an accountant or other financial planner's advice is warranted. The chapter on sales and marketing especially needs to be augmented by reference to authorities in the fields. This is a good first introduction for any information professional considering entrepreneurship as a career option.

[R: BL, 1 Oct 87, p. 216; JAL, July 87, p. 182; JAL, Sept 87, pp. 230, 232; RQ, Fall 87, p. 156]

Esther R. Dyer

CATALOGING AND CLASSIFICATION

General Works

123. Foster, Donald L. **Managing the Catalog Department.** 3d ed. Metuchen, N.J., Scarecrow, 1987. 264p. bibliog. index. $20.00. LC 86-33884. ISBN 0-8108-1973-2.

The purpose of this book is to provide information on management routines and responsibilities in catalog departments. The information is given in separate chapters: functions of a catalog department; responsibilities of the department head; current issues (e.g., AACR2 and closing the card catalog); staffing; orientation, training, and evaluation; staff relationships; research and development; organizational growth; department communications; oral communications; and department tools and the computer. The book places great emphasis on manual routines. The amount of information varies according to the topic and some topics are only briefly described.

In its third edition, this book has been expanded and improved in several ways. It now includes a more detailed description and discussion of some issues relating to library automation. It also includes new sections on career development, performance standards, problem solving, time management, attitude surveys, and workshop training.

Previous reviews have been concerned about the brief and somewhat inadequate discussion of the challenge technological advances have posed for catalog department heads. This reduces the book's utility for managers who are responsible for large cataloging operations. While card catalogs still overwhelmingly predominate in libraries, many libraries use automation in some manner in their day-to-day operation. Additional in-depth descriptions of computer technology and how the computer affects cataloging operations and management would indeed be desirable. The "select bibliography" has been expanded to include some new publications but it still is limited to books.

These shortcomings should not obscure the fact that this volume provides a useful overview of the principles and practices of managing catalog departments. The librarian who has received his or her first management assignment will find this book a helpful source of background information. [R: JAL, Nov 87, p. 318]

Samson Soong

124. **Managing Copy Cataloging in ARL Libraries.** By Sharon E. Clark. Washington, D.C., Association of Research Libraries, 1987. 122p. bibliog. (SPEC Kit, No. 136). $20.00pa.

This book presents a series of reports on the copy cataloging procedures used by different academic libraries. These presentations are short and clear, and several are accompanied by documentation, diagrams, flow charts, and organization charts. Also indicated are the number and levels of staff involved: professional librarians, paraprofessionals, technicians, and clerical staff. The different tasks are listed along with who does them: searching, authority work, choice of subjects and call number, etc. Other topics discussed include who makes the decision whether to do original cataloging or to put the item in the backlog, and how long it remains there before it is searched again; handling priority items; differences in procedures for monographs and serials; and minimal versus full cataloging for particular items. Searching includes looking in both printed sources and online databases for bibliographic description and the name and subject access points.

These papers give useful guidelines for the reader, but there is no synthesis or comparison of the procedures which would help the reader set up a system in his or her own library. The reader is left to make an independent analysis of the advantages and disadvantages of each variation presented. A short reading list is found at the end of the work. The text is reproduced from the original submissions from the participating libraries, so there is a variety of typefaces; however, they are all sharp and clearly legible. The illustrations are also reproduced clearly.

Barbara E. Brown

125. Rowley, Jennifer E. **Organising Knowledge: An Introduction to Information Retrieval.** Brookfield, Vt., Gower Publishing, 1987. 454p. index. $53.95; $23.95pa. ISBN 0-566-03574-X; 0-566-03486-7pa.

Jennifer Rowley's book is "an introductory text on information retrieval and the organisation of knowledge." As such it covers cataloging, classification, and indexing techniques. The work consists of twenty-three chapters arranged in five parts: records, authors and titles, subjects, systems, and user perspectives. One topic, evaluation, was purposely omitted "in order to restrict the length of the text." There is an excellent subject index.

Rowley's work rests on the assumption that many information retrieval systems have "common elements and they differ from one another in the ways in which they select from the range of possible formats and fields." Although the assumption is a valid one theoretically, it is very difficult to write a book that fleshes out this principle satisfactorily. The author concentrates heavily on cataloging within the confines of AACR2 and classification. Less attention is given to such topics as back-of-the-book indexing. Even within her obvious area of expertise, cataloging, Rowley, who is British, fails to give adequate attention to the role of authority control in cataloging and the mechanisms used to achieve that control. Her presentation of subject analysis and classification is good, and will serve to enlighten the beginning student. Her chapters on systems tend to be more descriptive than analytical, nonetheless serving as a cogent presentation of existing systems, with an emphasis on those in the United Kingdom.

Overall, this is an important book. It raises the right questions and would be useful in general courses for the library student. Professionals would also benefit from a close reading of the text.   Robert H. Burger

Cataloging-in-Publication

126. Recommended Standards for Cataloguing-in-Publication: The CIP Data Sheet and the CIP Record in the Book. By International Federation of Library Associations and Institutions. London, IFLA UBCIM Programme, 1986. 30p. $26.00pa. ISBN 0-903043-43-2.

As its title suggests, this publication sets out an international standard for the selection, organization, and presentation of cataloging data. CIP (cataloging-in-publication) programs are carried out through agreements between national cataloging agencies (such as the Library of Congress, the British Library, and the National Library of Canada) and book publishers. Such programs facilitate the availability of cataloging data to libraries at the time that a book is published. These data are disseminated in two ways: through publication of the data in the book itself and through the inclusion of CIP catalog records in national bibliographies and on MARC (machine-readable cataloging) tapes.

As presented here, these standards were prepared and approved under the sponsorship of the Standing Committee on Cataloguing of IFLA. They draw on previously existing national standards and, insofar as possible, are a prescription for consistency in the selection,

organization, and level of bibliographic detail of CIP data across national boundaries.

The standards are in two parts. Part 1 prescribes a data sheet for selecting and recording CIP data. Part 2 specifies the content and format for presenting CIP data in publications. The standards themselves are clearly set out. Definitions are included to support the text and introductions and notes describe the background and rationale for the standards. Another important feature is the inclusion of a copy of the standard CIP data sheet to be used in selecting the appropriate bibliographic elements. There are examples of CIP records as they should appear in books in Canada, the United Kingdom, the United States, and West Germany as well.

This publication is one more important addition to an illustrious family of cataloging standards which includes ISBD, AACR2, and the MARC record. Another milestone in international cataloging, this publication and its contents have important implications for cataloging and catalogers throughout the world and the continued improvement in the efficient exchange of bibliographic and catalog records.

Nancy J. Williamson

Classification and Classification Schemes

127. Caster, Lillie D. **The Classifier's Guide to LC Class H: Subdivision Techniques for the Social Sciences.** New York, Neal-Schuman, 1986. 143p. bibliog. index. $29.95pa. LC 85-28459. ISBN 0-918212-99-5.

The introduction to this slim desk manual cites three inducements for its production: (1) the extensive tables associated with, and contributing to, the difficulties of *LC Class H*; (2) the changed format and significant revisions of the fourth (1980-1981) edition of that class; and (3) the paucity of instructions within the schedule itself for applying subdivision techniques. We are also reminded that, largely because of its variety of tables, *Class H* is often used as a paradigmatic text for library school training in the LC Classification. Part 1 offers seven chapters covering alphabetic/nonalphabetic order, dedicated and successive Cutter numbers, "subarranged like" notes, internal tables, "general special" sequences, and the two principles (alphabetic and classified) of geographical organization. Part 2, comprising nearly one-half of the total volume, expands on "Chapter 7 — Geographical Order" by region, by country or nationality, by constituent states of various countries, by local areas or governments, and by other geographical divisions, where pertinent. All chapters offer numerous examples. A useful bibliography and a three-page index of classification features complete this competent instructional aid.

Jeanne Osborn

128. Dershem, Larry D., comp. **Library of Congress Classification Class K Subclass KE. Law of Canada Cumulative Schedule and Index.** Littleton, Colo., Fred B. Rothman, 1987. 460p. index. (AALL Publications Series, No. 27). $75.00 looseleaf with binder. LC 87-24147. ISBN 0-8377-0126-0.

Law librarians welcomed with open arms Dershem's cumulative edition of the Library of Congress's schedule for classifying U.S. legal materials when it came out several years ago. They will want to add this volume to their reference collections as well.

As with the U.S. edition, Dershem has entered the Canadian schedule into an "updatable" database that allows him to merge revisions to the schedule and its index as soon as they appear. Law catalogers need to consult only one volume to have current and detailed information on changes to class KE, Law of Canada. Replacement pages for the looseleaf volume appear quarterly and are keyed to the issue numbers of LC's *Additions and Changes List*, which is also a quarterly publication.

The chief advantage here is that changes to the schedule and the index are cumulated into the original tables rather than appended. Catalogers do not need to page through years of material supplementing a schedule originally published in 1976 in order to have changes reflecting new laws, new court decisions, and new social concerns. As an added convenience, the volume has tab dividers for key subdivisions of KE, such as KEO for Ontario and KEQ for Quebec.

Berniece M. Owen

129. **Economics: H-HJ.** James Larrabee, ed. Albany, Calif., Livia Press, 1986. 1v. (various paging). index. (LC Cumulative Classification Series). $90.00 with looseleaf binder. ISBN 0-933949-19-7.

130. **Library of Congress Classification Schedules: A Cumulation of Additions and Changes through 1986. Class a: General Works.** Helen Savage, Kathleen D. Droste, and Rita Runchock, eds. Detroit, Gale, 1987. 20p. index. $2,275.00pa./set. LC 73-8530. ISBN 0-8103-2651-5.

131. **Library of Congress Classification Schedules: A Cumulation of Additions and Changes through 1986. Class c: Auxiliary Sciences of History.** Helen Savage, Kathleen D. Droste, and Rita Runchock, eds. Detroit, Gale, 1987. 37p. index. $2,275.00pa./set. LC 75-619090. ISBN 0-8103-2655-8.

132. **Library of Congress Classification Schedules: A Cumulation of Additions and Changes through 1986. Class h: Social Sciences: Subclasses HM-HX: Sociology.** Helen Savage, Kathleen D. Droste, and Rita Runchock, eds. Detroit, Gale, 1987. 56p. index. $2,275.00pa./set. LC 80-607033. ISBN 0-8103-2660-4.

133. **Library of Congress Classification Schedules: A Cumulation of Additions and Changes through 1986. Class u: Military Science.** Helen Savage, Kathleen D. Droste, and Rita Runchock, eds. Detroit, Gale, 1987. 27p. index. $2,275.00pa./set. LC 74-12064. ISBN 0-8103-2687-6.

134. **Library of Congress Classification Schedules: A Cumulation of Additions and Changes through 1986. Class v: Naval Science.** Helen Savage, Kathleen D. Droste, and Rita Runchock, eds. Detroit, Gale, 1987. 21p. index. $2,175.00pa./set. LC 74-12087. ISBN 0-8103-2688-4.

135. **Library of Congress Classification Schedules Combined with Additions and Changes through 1986. Class A: General Works.** Helen Savage, Kathleen D. Droste, and Rita Runchock, eds. Detroit, Gale, 1987. 66p. index. $4,500.00pa./set. LC 73-8530. ISBN 0-8103-2601-9.

136. **Library of Congress Classification Schedules Combined with Additions and Changes through 1986. Class C: Auxiliary Sciences of History.** Helen Savage, Kathleen D. Droste, and Rita Runchock, eds. Detroit, Gale, 1987. 190p. index. $4,500.00pa./set. LC 75-619090. ISBN 0-8103-2605-1.

137. **Library of Congress Classification Schedules Combined with Additions and Changes through 1986. Class H: Social Sciences: Subclasses HM-HX: Sociology.** Helen Savage, Kathleen D. Droste, and Rita Runchock, eds. Detroit, Gale, 1987. 255p. index. $4,500.00pa./set. LC 80-607033. ISBN 0-8103-2610-8.

138. **Library of Congress Classification Schedules Combined with Additions and Changes**

through 1986. **Class U: Military Science.** Helen Savage, Kathleen D. Droste, and Rita Runchock, eds. Detroit, Gale, 1987. 126p. index. $4,500.00pa./set. LC 74-12064. ISBN 0-8103-2637-X.

139. **Library of Congress Classification Schedules Combined with Additions and Changes through 1986. Class V: Naval Science.** Helen Savage, Kathleen D. Droste, and Rita Runchock, eds. Detroit, Gale, 1987. 148p. index. $4,500.00pa./set. LC 74-12087. ISBN 0-8103-2638-8.

140. **Sociology: HM-HX.** James Larrabee, ed. Albany, Calif., Livia Press, 1986. 1v. (various paging). index. (LC Cumulative Classification Series). $50.00 with looseleaf binder. ISBN 0-933949-21-9.

For years, catalogers and cataloging students had to struggle with the LC classification schedules that were infrequently published but had frequent additions and changes printed in brief bulletins. Knowing the latest LC number was a time-consuming searching problem. Now, there are three major sources which can be consulted to save time. The choice, however, must be carefully made because the tools are expensive.

Gale has published cumulated changes and additions for a number of years. By cumulating changes, the cataloger consulted the original schedule and a single Gale volume eliminating the necessity of looking through many individual bulletins. Each cumulation is published until LC replaces the schedule.

A better, but more expensive, solution is the Livia Press compilations in looseleaf format and the Gale classification schedules. Both publications reprint the schedules and keep them up to date. The Livia titles are updated quarterly and the Gale publications annually. Both require the cataloger to look in a single source for current numbers. The Livia Press volumes are updated more frequently and are cheaper than the Gale volumes. The quality of both is equally fine. Gale republishes almost all the schedules annually, but Livia Press is issuing only selected schedules as the editor is able to produce them.

All three tools are valuable additions to the cataloging department and to the quality of original classification that must be done. Whether the library can afford any of them is a major problem to be addressed.

David V. Loertscher

141. **Guidelines on Subject Access to Microcomputer Software.** By Resources and Technical Services Division, American Library Asso-

ciation. Chicago, American Library Association, 1986. 27p. bibliog. $4.50pa. LC 86-3402. ISBN 0-8389-0452-1.

The purpose of this slim volume is to provide assistance in subject analysis to individuals who assign subject headings and classification numbers to microcomputer software. These *Guidelines on Subject Access* were developed by an ad hoc subcommittee of the Resources and Technical Services Division (ALA), Cataloging and Classification Section. In the document the committee stresses that subject catalogers should mainstream software into the regular collection in their subject analysis and classification, using all available tools. They also propose the adoption of a form subdivision "Software" to better identify the home, game, and personal software packages libraries are now acquiring. A final recommendation is to avoid assigning individual subject headings for specific computer makes, models, and operating systems.

The guidelines are contained on the first eight pages. Following page eight are four appendices: (1) a listing of subject headings applicable to microcomputer software, (2) recommended sources for subject heading creation, (3) applicable Library of Congress and Dewey Decimal Classification numbers, and (4) three examples of MARC records. Most of the subject headings included in appendix 1 are Library of Congress. The ones which are not (such as those from the Hennepin County Library *Authority List*) the committee is suggesting for possible adoption and use.

As a whole the guidelines with appendices as presented should be helpful to those using Library of Congress Classification and subject headings. A consensus on the application of classification numbers and subject heading selection should lead to greater standardization in an area which is still being interpreted variously at the local level. One note of caution is for Dewey users. They may be disappointed in the brief coverage of Dewey Classification numbers.

Marilyn L. Shontz

142. Intner, Sheila S., and Richard P. Smiraglia, eds. **Policy and Practice in Bibliographic Control of Nonbook Media.** Chicago, American Library Association, 1987. 197p. index. $24.95pa. LC 87-1849. ISBN 0-8389-0468-8.

Traditionally, libraries' acquisitions have focused on print materials. Then, slowly, the importance of microforms, primarily for the purpose of preservation, became more accepted. Most other nonbook materials (with perhaps the exception of phonorecords) were relegated to the children's sections of public libraries. Recently, however, the newer products such as video technologies and computer software have emphasized the importance of nonbook materials in collections of all types.

The essays in this volume are compiled from the regional institutes on nonbook materials sponsored by the American Library Association Resources and Technical Services Division and the RTSD Council on Regional Groups. Some of the objectives for those attending the workshops included "to gain an understanding of the process of acquisitions, organizations, and access to nonbook materials, to learn about standards for bibliographic control for nonbook materials …, to gain an insight into the impact of cooperative networking, to explore the future of nonbook materials in libraries" (editors' introduction, p. vii).

The contributors to this work are all well-known experts in the field of nonprint materials: Lizbeth Bishoff, Leigh Estabrook, Sheila Intner, Nancy Olson, Arlene Taylor, and Jean Weihs. As a result, the essays are of the highest quality both in terms of writing and what is said. The organization of the chapters takes the reader through the background, theory, and management concerns of nonbook materials to the cataloging of individual media. The objectives of the workshops and this volume are fully realized. While much of the material found here has its parallels in Carolyn Frost's *Cataloging Nonbook Materials: Problems in Theory and Practice* (Libraries Unlimited, 1983), this volume updates and expands on the information there. Both works are essential for all libraries cataloging and purchasing nonbook materials. [R: JAL, Nov 87, p. 316; LJ, 1 Nov 87, p. 71]

Marjorie E. Bloss

143.   Kaula, P. N. **A Treatise on Colon Classification.** New Delhi, Sterling Publishers; distr., New York, Apt Books, 1985. 314p. bibliog. index. (Kaula Series in Library Science, No. 8). $40.00.

Since the Colon Classification has been an important influence on the theory and development of modern library classification in particular, and of modern indexing languages in general, any new publication which enables students of classification to understand this system better is a welcome addition to the literature. The principle of faceting, which has its roots in Colon, is fundamental to the logical and systematic development of library classification systems and to sound thesaurus construction.

Kaula, who is well qualified to explain Colon, has set forth a comprehensive discussion of theory and practice including an explanation of procedures and an analysis of each of the main

classes. However, despite the author's attempt to provide a treatise suitable for various levels of professionals, library and information professionals in the Western Hemisphere will not find this work easy to comprehend and digest. The topic is specialized, the system is complex, and the terminology is often foreign. Nevertheless, this is an important addition to the literature for library educators and students of classification theory. Important features of the work are the extensive bibliography, the definitions of terminology, and the correlation of the text with the seventh and latest edition of the Colon system. One of its weaknesses is the lack of an index.

Nancy J. Williamson

144.   Muller, Karen, ed. **Authority Control Symposium. Papers Presented during the 14th Annual ARLIS/NA Conference, New York, N.Y. February 10, 1986.** Tucson, Ariz., Art Libraries Society of North America, 1987. 138p. bibliog. (Occasional Papers, No. 6). $20.00pa. ISBN 0-942740-05-X.

This book contains the papers presented at a symposium on all aspects of authority control. Starting with an analysis and definition, it goes on to discuss different types of authorities and the problems encountered. Some of the papers deal with authorities for access points generally, without being limited to names, titles, or subjects. Also brought up are problems such as automatic searching for related words (e.g., the plural form of the single word being searched). Subject headings are studied in some detail. The choice of heading, the relationship to broader and narrower terms, and the use of cross-references are discussed in one of the papers. The problem of phrasing the search term to get the optimum result from the file being searched is also discussed in detail.

There is a very good bibliography at the end, and copious bibliographic footnotes are found throughout the text. Figures at the end of the text reproduce the printouts from several authority systems and show different aspects of authority files. Flowcharts and tables accompany the text. The lack of an index may be a slight drawback, but a useful index would have been very difficult to create because of the narrow subject. The typeface is clear and easy to read, and the layout is very good.

This book is highly recommended for catalogers, subject specialists, public service librarians, and others interested in authority control.

Barbara E. Brown

145.   **PRECIS: Recent Applications.** Mary Dykstra, ed. Halifax, N.S., School of Library Service, Dalhousie University, 1986. 130p.

bibliog. (Occasional Papers Series, No. 39). $14.50pa. ISBN 0-7703-0182-7. (Also available from Metuchen, N.J., Scarecrow, 1987. $18.50 pa. LC 87-17617. ISBN 0-8168-2060-9.)

This publication describes a spectrum of diverse practical applications of the PRECIS indexing system. Selective, rather than exhaustive, of "representative pockets of activity" in the use of PRECIS, there are five papers in all. Three of the papers assume the use of mainframe computers and have their origins in the Canadian bibliographical utility UTLAS International. "PRECIS at UTLAS" describes PRECIS software developed by UTLAS as an extension of its automated authority system, and available for use by UTLAS clients. A second paper discusses the application of this linguistically based system to the Chinese language. As such it contributes to research on PRECIS in the multilingual context. The third paper in this group, written by the editor, describes FORMAT, the system developed for the National Film Board of Canada for use in its computerized audiovisual information system and in the production of the index to its *Film Catalogue*. Two other papers discuss prevalent types of applications of the system. One application, in the field of education, addresses the computer aspects of PRECIS with particular reference to microcomputers, while the other deals with subject access to art slides.

All of the papers are succinct and well written. Explanations are clear and complete and well supported with examples and diagrams. Useful bibliographical data are included. Students of PRECIS and interested library and information professionals will welcome this addition to the literature of the subject.

Nancy J. Williamson

Descriptive Cataloging

146.   **Canadian MARC Communication Format: Minimal Level.** Ottawa, National Library of Canada, 1987. 1v. (various paging). $43.50; $52.20 (U.S.) looseleaf with binder. ISBN 0-660-12324-X. (Available by mail from Canadian Government Publishing Centre, Supply and Services Canada, Ottawa, ONT K1A 0S9, Canada.)

This document specifies the data elements for monographs and serials (recommended by the Canadian Committee on Cataloguing and their content designations recommended by the Canadian Committee on MARC) to be used in the creation of minimum-level catalog records. An addition not found in the now superseded *Canadian MARC Communication Format: Mini-MARC* is the requirements for reporting machine-readable accession records to the *Canadian Union Catalogue*. The content of this document adheres to the *Anglo-American Cataloguing Rules*, second edition, and other international standards, such as those published by the International Standards Organization.

Libraries may wish to use minimum-level records where staff is not available to provide full cataloging or where the use and/or nature of an item does not warrant the cost of full cataloging. However, optional elements have been included for libraries wanting somewhat fuller records for some or all of their collections.

Because this minimum-level format consists of tables, it should be used with *Canadian MARC Communication Format: Monographs* and *Canadian MARC Communication Format: Serials*. These full MARC formats provide the detailed descriptions of data elements and explanations of usage missing from this document.

This is a practical tool for Canadian libraries involved in automated cataloging, and an essential tool for those participating, or intending to participate, in the *Canadian Union Catalogue*. Jean Weihs

147.   **Corporate Author Authority List: A Dictionary of More Than 40,000 Verified Main Entries for Documents Cataloged by the National Technical Information Service.** 2d ed. Asta V. Kane, ed. Detroit, Gale, 1987. 2v. $180.00/set. LC 83-647075. ISBN 0-8103-2106-8; ISSN 0741-3270.

This print format of the National Technical Information Service's Corporate Author Authority database contains entries for the corporate authors of all U.S. government-sponsored research reports; technical reports; and analyses from U.S. and foreign government agencies, their contractors, or grant recipients.

Cataloging guidelines used are those of COSATI (Committee on Scientific and Technical Information), which employs the following sequence of information in the entry: (1) parent organization corporation, research center, committee, etc.; (2) location (city and state); and (3) smallest appropriate suborganization (e.g., department, lab, etc.). This information appears in boldface print, and it is immediately followed by the AACR2 entry, if it is known, which is indented and in italics. In addition, a nine-digit NTIS code number is included, as are any other agency codes for the current corporate author name; former name(s), if any; and their corresponding code numbers; and AACR2 entries and associated other agency codes, when known. Former names are included in the alphabetical listing. They do not appear in boldface type and are followed by a cross-reference to the current name.

Arrangement is alphabetical by corporate author. Volume 1 covers names beginning with A-I; volume 2 covers names beginning with J-Z, plus a brief one-page section where any corporate author name that begins with a number, whether current or former, is listed. Prefatory material carefully explains the arrangement and use of information in the authority list, as well as each component in a sample entry.

Because of the importance of consistency and accuracy in use of corporate authors for identifying and cataloging scientific and technical literature, this authority list will be a great boon to catalogers of scientific and technical government publications and as an aid for retrieval of corporate entries in a machine-readable system. In spite of going to a two-volume publication to accommodate the ever-expanding size of the NTIS database, the price of this second edition has increased very modestly from that of the first edition (prepared and published solely by the National Technical Information Service, U.S. Department of Commerce) which sold for $175.00 in 1983.   Lois Buttlar

148.   Hallam, Adele. **Cataloging Rules for the Description of Looseleaf Publications: With Special Emphasis on Legal Materials.** Washington, D.C., Cataloging Distribution Service, Library of Congress, 1986. 60p. $15.00pa. LC 86-600167.

Perhaps one of the more puzzling items for a cataloger to work with is the looseleaf publication which is periodically updated. Neither the principles applied to monographs nor those to serials seem to work very well. Catalogers, in particular law catalogers, who must deal with this kind of publication will welcome this handbook from the Library of Congress. Some points to note. The work is concerned only with the kind of looseleaf publication in which pages are periodically removed and replaced. Further, these publications are considered neither monographs nor serials, but a category all their own; however, a monographic record format is used to record information. This handbook is meant to act as a supplement to *AACR2*, and the rules are keyed to that publication. A short glossary concludes.

Philip A. Metzger

149.   Hopkins, Judith, and John A. Edens, eds. **Research Libraries and Their Implementation of AACR2.** Greenwich, Conn., JAI Press, 1986. 341p. bibliog. index. (Foundations in Library and Information Science, Vol. 22). $49.50. LC 85-23825. ISBN 0-89232-641-7.

There are two ways that one can approach *Research Libraries and Their Implementation of AACR2*: from a practical, "how-to-do-it" approach, or from an historical perspective. Since the vast majority of libraries who planned to adopt AACR2 did so in early 1981, it is a fairly safe bet to say that most librarians will not read this volume before an AACR2 conversion. The historical perspective, therefore, seems to provide the greater reason for purchase. Furthermore, as the editors point out that "while there was much written about AACR2 and strategies for coping with it prior to the time that libraries began to use it, little had appeared after the Library of Congress and other libraries started implementing it in January 1981" (preface). The essays in this work go beyond the plans for implementation to implementation itself. Finally, that a number of libraries closed their card catalogs or planned to close them in conjunction with adopting AACR2, an activity that many of us are now only beginning to experience, gives this volume additional depth.

Regarding the content of the book, the editors chose fourteen Association of Research Libraries (ARL) members that would provide a representative view of various strategies. (Selection was based on a survey sent to the 104 academic members of ARL.) Of the fourteen libraries, ten integrated AACR2 cataloging into existing catalogs while four began new catalogs (including COM and online) for *AACR2* records. An introductory essay by the editors provides an informative overview of the effects of the major rules found in AACR2 as well as an analysis of their implementation of those rules in the fourteen libraries. Understandably, there is some duplication of material in the essays— of decisions made, of techniques used. These repetitions, however, are much less annoying than in other works of topical collected essays because they are an integral part of the decision-making process and activities of implementation within each library. All essays are extremely well conceived and thought provoking. None is superficially written. An appendix provides the outline used by the libraries when describing their experiences. The volume concludes with a bibliography consisting of works having some bearing on code implementation, and an index.

To paraphrase, those who ignore history are doomed to repeat it. While the majority of libraries planning to adopt AACR2 have already done so, *Research Libraries and Their Implementation of AACR2* is not a book to be dismissed as passé. It provides us with a sense of history of some major concerns in our recent professional past. In addition, it will, as the editors state, "provide some light the next time libraries are faced with a major code revision" (introduction). This volume is strongly recommended for any library concerned with the important issues of library and information science. [R: JAL, July 87, p. 189]

Marjorie E. Bloss

150. LC Rule Interpretations of AACR2 1978-1986. First Update: Covers Cataloging Service Bulletins No. 28 (Spring 1985)—No. 33 (Summer 1986); Includes Rule Index to CSB. 2d cum. ed. Sally C. Tseng, comp. Metuchen, N.J., Scarecrow, 1987. 1v. (various paging). $32.50 looseleaf. LC 85-14527. ISBN 0-8108-1991-0.

It must be emphasized that this publication is an update. It contains pages that are intended to be incorporated into the base volume either as new or substitute pages. Filing instructions are provided to help the user insert the pages correctly. A new title page and rule index are supplied so that the base volume with updates will be properly titled and indexed. In response to users' requests, headings, keywords, and phrases have been added to the rule index to assist in locating a particular rule.

This update adds to the value of a very useful work and is recommended for all technical services departments that use Library of Congress copy. There is one caveat. The Library of Congress sometimes publishes rule revisions before the final wording has been approved by the Joint Steering Committee for Revision of AACR. Rule changes should always be checked in official publications; that is, packages of rule revisions published from time to time by the American Library Association, the Canadian Library Association, and the Library Association, or in the *Anglo-American Cataloguing Rules*, second edition consolidation, due to be published in mid-1988.   Jean Weihs

151. UNIMARC Manual. Brian P. Holt, Sally H. McCallum, and A. B. Long, eds. London, IFLA UBCIM Programme, 1987. 482p. bibliog. index. $39.00pa. ISBN 0-903043-44-0.

UNIMARC (*UNI*versal *MA*chine-Readable *C*ataloguing), a format sponsored by the International Federation of Library Associations and Institutions, is intended "to facilitate the international exchange of bibliographic data between national bibliographic agencies." It assigns specific tags, indicators, and subfields to bibliographic records in machine-readable form, and includes monographs, serials, music, sound recordings, graphics projected, and video materials with provisional fields for computer files.

The *UNIMARC Format* (1980) was first published in 1977. These publications were followed in 1983 by an interpretative guide, the *UNIMARC Handbook*.

The purpose of this document is "to provide a definitive statement of the UNIMARC format itself, combining and augmenting the *UNIMARC Format* and the *UNIMARC Handbook*" and to provide also "a model for the development of new machine-readable formats." Thus, it is "both a definitive statement of the format and a guide to its use," superseding the previous published works.

The ninety-eight pages of appendices include various types of codes, character sets, complete examples, a bibliography, and useful addresses followed by an index.

UNIMARC is used by national libraries that provide records for international exchange both in their national MARC and in the UNIMARC formats. It is the national MARC format (e.g., USMARC, CANMARC, UKMARC) that is used in local libraries and networks. Therefore, for most libraries UNIMARC is only of academic interest, and this work is a purchase of low priority.   Jean Weihs

Nonprint Materials

152. *Anglo-American Cataloguing Rules*. Second Edition. Chapter 9: Computer Files. Draft Revision. Michael Gorman, ed. London, Library Association, Ottawa, Canadian Library Association, and Chicago, American Library Association, 1987. 30p. $4.00pa. LC 87-1052. ISBN 0-8389-3339-4.

When *AACR2* was published in 1980, the microcomputer revolution was barely two years old. Characteristic of their plodding style, cataloging committees of ALA barely took notice until the avalanche of computer software and a lack of ways to catalog it became a major problem for every member of the cataloging committees. One would have wished these rules to have been drafted five years ago.

The current draft edition of rules to handle computer software precedes the publication of a consolidated edition of *AACR2* due to be published in 1988. As such, these rules take into account many of the cataloging problems faced by libraries and media centers. Improvements include using "Computer file" as the general material designation, recognition of versions as edition statements, a more realistic physical description, and more sensible samples for notes.

In the press for consistency, the rules require the cataloger to use the first screen of a microcomputer program as the official "title" page. Such a policy requires the cataloger to mechanically start the program in order to catalog it, a practice which may be quite impossible in many organizations.

The appendix to this publication is a draft revision of the main AACR2 rule for accompanying material. No mention of this generic rule is given in the introduction, but it is a major improvement on a very weak section of the main code. There are many problems concerning microcomputer software not covered in chapter 9. Classification, subject analysis, storage, and retrieval problems await attention by book and pamphlet writers rather than committees of the association.   David V. Loertscher

153.   Rogers, JoAnn V., with Jerry D. Saye. **Nonprint Cataloging for Multimedia Collections: A Guide Based on AACR 2.** 2d ed. Littleton, Colo., Libraries Unlimited, 1987. 301p. index. $23.50. LC 87-22589. ISBN 0-87287-523-7.

This second edition written with a collaborator is approximately one hundred pages larger than the first edition published in 1982. It is updated with the *Anglo-American Cataloguing Rules*, second edition (*AACR2*) rule revisions published in 1982, 1983, and 1985. Rules for the cataloging of computer files have been added. The five appendices containing various bibliographies have been replaced by one bibliography, which does not cover the field as extensively, and a section dealing with "characteristics of the rules and resulting bibliographic records using AACR2 [compared] with methods for cataloging nonprint used prior to its publication" has been omitted.

Most of the book is devoted to a study of the rules from *AACR2* chapters 3 and 6-11, and those from chapter 1 pertaining to nonprint materials. There is one chapter on pertinent rules for access points. Library of Congress rule interpretations are discussed where applicable. Most rules are exemplified, and full catalog records are given at the end of each chapter.

The authors have intended this book for "experienced catalogers, those responsible for policy decisions about the cataloging of nonprint in multimedia collections, and the serious student interested in gaining an understanding of the context of current cataloging practices as well as of the application of the rules." It will be particularly useful to those working in institutions that derive their cataloging from LC MARC records.

It should be noted that this useful work will be out-of-date when the consolidated revision of *AACR2* is published in the latter half of 1988.

New or revised rules in this consolidated revision will make parts of this book obsolete.
                                          Jean Weihs

154.   Smiraglia, Richard P. **Cataloging Music: A Manual for Use with AACR2.** 2d ed. Lake Crystal, Minn., Soldier Creek Press, 1986. 181p. illus. index. $35.00pa. LC 86-31615. ISBN 0-936996-19-6.

The scope of this work is both narrower and broader than is apparent from the title: narrower, because it covers only descriptive cataloging, not subject cataloging, classification, or shelflisting; broader, because it covers not only scores but also musical sound recordings in all currently available formats (including compact discs).

There are two main sections. The first consists of the relevant sections of AACR2 and their applicable Library of Congress rule interpretations and LC Music Cataloging Division decisions, arranged in a logical sequence (often not that in AACR2 itself), with interpretive comments by the author. The second presents a series of facsimiles of scores and recordings with a matching cataloging record, and brief explanations of how the record was created; while it was not possible to provide an example of everything a music cataloger might encounter, certainly all the more common aspects of music cataloging are illustrated. A good bibliography, a very brief glossary, a concordance of rules and rule interpretations, and a somewhat sketchy index are appended.

This work will be most useful to persons learning the basics of music cataloging, in a classroom or on the job, but even experienced music catalogers will want to have it on hand for the convenience of having both the rules and the interpretations in one place, well organized for easy consultation. Any library acquiring and cataloging scores and/or sound recordings will find it a worthwhile acquisition. [R: LJ, July 87, p. 56]   Paul B. Cors

155.   Zinkham, Helena, and Elisabeth Betz Parker, comps. and eds. **Descriptive Terms for Graphic Materials: Genre and Physical Characteristic Headings.** Washington, D.C., Cataloging Distribution Service, Library of Congress, 1986. 135p. bibliog. $20.00pa. LC 86-20017.

Prepared by Zinkham and Parker of the Prints and Photographs Division of the Library of Congress, this volume presents 513 descriptive terms for use by catalogers and researchers in their work with graphic materials. The standardized vocabulary for genre and physical characteristics are for use in MARC record fields 655 and 755—the addition of both fields having been authorized in 1984. Genre headings identify materials by categories such as pictorial type, method of projection/vantage point, intended purpose, creator characteristics, or method of representation. Physical characteristic headings distinguish graphic materials by production process/technique, production stage/version, instrument employed, size/shape, and markings.

The major portion of the book consists of the alphabetical display of authorized terms and cross-references. Public Notes (PN) and Cataloger's Notes (CN) are used frequently to assist users in correct interpretation and assignment. Both a "Classified Display" (p. 113) and a "Hierarchical Display for Photography and Print Terms" (p. 131) appear at the end of the alphabetical list. Especially helpful to the cataloger is a section of "Cataloging Applications" included in the introduction. The cataloging guidelines and examples "reflect practices developed in the Library of Congress Prints and Photographs Division which may be helpful for other pictorial collections" (p. xiii).

Traditionally, access to graphic materials has been by subject content and names of creators. The addition of fields for genre and physical characteristics along with the publication of this standardized vocabulary for use in those fields can greatly increase user access to graphic materials. Wide acceptance and use by catalogers and indexers of the controlled vocabulary contained in this publication will both improve retrieval and simplify the cataloging process.

Marilyn L. Shontz

CHILDREN'S AND YOUNG ADULT SERVICES

Reference Works

156. **Bookwaves: A Compilation of Reviews of Books for Teenagers, 1984 & 1985.** San Francisco, Calif., Bay Area Young Adult Librarians, 1986. 154p. index. $8.50 spiralbound. (May be ordered from Diane Walts [BAYA], 90 Normandy Lane, Walnut Creek, CA 94598.)

The Bay Area Young Adult Librarians (BAYA) is an organization of public and school librarians in northern California. Members review and discuss new books for young adults at their bimonthly meetings. *Bookwaves 1984 & 1985* is a compilation of more than six hundred titles reviewed by members of the group over the two-year period. *Bookwaves 1986* was expected to be available during the summer of 1987.

All reviews are brief; most are under two hundred words in length. Reviews are both critical and descriptive. They attempt to describe the book's interest for, appeal to, and uses with young adults as well as provide a plot summary. When applicable, the title is compared with similar books. Recommended, marginal, and rejected titles are included. Both fiction and nonfiction books are reviewed. Fiction is subdivided into the categories of general fiction, mystery, science fiction and fantasy, series, and short stories. Nonfiction categories include art and photography; beauty and health; biography; comics and humor; computers; jobs; military science; movies; music, dance, and drama; nature; oddments; poetry; reference; science and technology; sex and sexuality; social science; and sports and recreation. Books suitable for younger readers (junior high school) and mature readers (higher reading level and/or more sophisticated content) are marked "Y" and "M" respectively. There are author and title indexes.

Bookwaves would be a useful retrospective collection development aid. The more timely publication of the 1986 edition will make it a bit more useful than this edition for collection development, however. Students and young adult library patrons could use this publication to choose books they might be interested in reading. This use would also apply to individuals in young adult literature classes.

Carol J. Veitch

157. Broderick, Dorothy M., and Mary K. Chelton. **Librarians' Guide: Young Adult Paperbacks.** 3d ed. New York, New American Library, 1986. 48p. bibliog. free pa.

The third edition of *Librarians' Guide* again is produced by Dorothy Broderick and Mary Chelton. The sections "Reading Preferences of Young Adults," "Paperbacks and Your Library," "Promoting Paperbacks," "The Future," "Paperbacks for Young Adults," and "Bibliography/Addresses" remain as they were established in the second edition. Informally written and interesting to read, the guide is a quick and useful introduction to young adult paperbacks for school and public librarians.

Although there were significant revisions between the original 1977 publication and the 1982 edition, only minor changes have been made in the text of the 1986 version. Sections reflecting the greatest revision are science fiction (p. 13ff.), college and career choices (p. 11), bookfairs and censorship (p. 36), and the Reading Is Fundamental program (p. 37).

The total number of titles cited in the section "Paperbacks for Young Adults" is similar to the 1982 edition total. About one-half of both the "New American Library" and the "Other Publishers" entries are new to the lists—but not necessarily all are newly published. In the bibliography one new entry has been added and several addresses updated. Otherwise the forty-item list remains unchanged.

Although the text revision is limited, the well-selected and substantially new title listing makes the edition worth having and using with young adults.   Marilyn L. Shontz

Children's Services

158. Burke, Ellen M. **Early Childhood Literature: For Love of Child and Book.** Newton, Mass., Allyn and Bacon, 1986. 277p. index. $18.67. LC 85-9095. ISBN 0-205-08596-2.

Burke begins with the physical and cognitive development of young children ages three to eight and moves on to literature that meets the needs and interest levels of these children. Emphasis is on the literature: selecting appropriate titles and ways to share books and stories with children. Chapters include storytelling, book design and illustration, song and poetry, humorous stories, traditional literature, contemporary realistic fiction and fantasy, informational books, and the literature-rich curriculum.

Extensive bibliographies of professional reading and children's books follow each chapter. Discussion activities lead readers into literature experiences and experiments of their own. Almost every chapter has a checklist or chart providing developmental or evaluative criteria and examples of books which meet the needs or fit the criteria. The format of the book makes for easy reading and browsing. Appendices include an article on storytelling by Gwendolyn Jones, a list of Caldecott Medal books, and a bibliography of materials of special value to parents of young children. The book is indexed.

Preschool and primary grade teachers, school and public librarians, and parents of young children will find this a valuable resource. Students in early childhood or elementary education and library school students who are planning to work with children will find this a useful tool. Recommended.   Carol J. Veitch

159. England, Claire, and Adele M. Fasick. **ChildView: Evaluating and Reviewing Materials for Children.** Littleton, Colo., Libraries Unlimited, 1987. 207p. index. $19.50. LC 87-2635. ISBN 0-87287-519-9.

England and Fasick believe that evaluating and reviewing materials for children is more difficult than for adults since an adult reviewer's perspective is different from the child user's. The reviewer of children's books must, then, work from the dual perspective of adult and child. *ChildView* attempts to address the multitude of issues faced by reviewers of children's materials.

Part 1, "Establishing the Environment," provides background information on the considerations in reviewing materials for children. Chapter 1 deals with adult expectations for children's books and standards (popularity versus quality, conflicting values, etc.). Chapter 2 provides an overview of child development. The next two chapters discuss the importance of reviewing, major reviewing journals, types of books reviewed, contents of reviews, and the craft of writing a good review.

Part 2, "Focusing on the Genre," discusses specific literary elements and issues in reviewing materials for early childhood (picture books), traditional materials, fiction, poetry, biography and history, informational materials, dictionaries and encyclopedias, and nonprint materials. Checklists of selection criteria are included with each chapter. Some of these chapters, especially the one on nonprint materials, are superficial and need to be supplemented with other collection development tools.

In spite of its weaknesses, *ChildView* is a readable, useful work for librarians and teachers who have to review children's books or nonprint materials. It would make useful collateral reading for children's literature or materials selection courses. [R: EL, Sept/Oct 87, pp. 39-40; SLJ, Aug 87, p. 41; WLB, Sept 87, p. 82]   Carol J. Veitch

160. Irving, Jan, and Robin Currie. **Glad Rags: Stories and Activities Featuring Clothes for Children.** Littleton, Colo., Libraries Unlimited, 1987. 276p. illus. index. $20.00pa. LC 87-16921. ISBN 0-87287-562-8.

Glad Rags is a sequel to *Mudluscious* (Libraries Unlimited, 1986). Like its predecessor, it is a storytelling and literature activity book for adults who work with preschool and primary school age children. As the title implies, the theme of all the programs in *Glad Rags* is clothes. Clothing, according to the authors, identifies people's activities, roles, and work.

Each of the book's eight chapters begins with an introduction presenting the overall theme. Initiating activities are followed by annotated bibliographies of relevant picture books, related literature activities, games, crafts, and display suggestions. Chapter titles are provocative: "All by Myself"; "Shopping Bags and Laundry Tags"; "Umbrellas, Boots, and Swimming Suits"; "Long Ago and Far Away"; "Fairytale, Fantasy, and Just Pretend"; "Hats and More Hats"; "Sneakers, Socks, and Happy Feet"; and "Pockets and Paraphernalia." The work concludes with a resource bibliography, skills list, breakdown of activities by skills area, alphabetical listing of activities showing associated skills, and a literature index.

This is a valuable resource for anyone planning literature programs with young children. The variety of activities and books included allows for great individual flexibility. Stories, poems, and songs are included in the text, too, so the user does not need to rely entirely on the limitations of any library collection. The illustrations are clear and helpful. Highly recommended.   Carol J. Veitch

161.   Israel, Callie. **Budgeting for Children's Services.** Ottawa, Canadian Library Association, 1987. 12p. illus. bibliog. (Library Service to Children, 2). $5.00pa. ISBN 0-88802-222-0.

162.   Pearse, Linda. **Audio Visual Media for Children in the Public Library.** Ottawa, Canadian Library Association, 1987. 22p. illus. bibliog. (Library Service to Children, 8). $5.00pa. ISBN 0-88802-228-X.

163.   Roberts, Ken. **Pre-School Storytimes.** Ottawa, Canadian Library Association, 1987. 15p. illus. bibliog. (Library Service to Children, 5). $5.00pa. ISBN 0-88802-225-5.

164.   Van Vliet, Virginia. **Time for Tots: Library Service to Toddlers.** Ottawa, Canadian Library Association, 1987. 20p. illus. bibliog. (Library Service to Children, 4). $5.00pa. ISBN 0-88802-224-7.

The most useful of these booklets is *Time for Tots*, a how-to-do program for two-year-olds. It has a narrower focus, more specific examples, and covers less-charted ground. A strong feature is the in-depth description of the developmental characteristics of the average two-year-old. The least useful booklet is that on budgeting. The topic is too broad to be covered in twelve pages, and terms which take whole books to explain (e.g., PPBS) are given one paragraph. It is unclear what the budgeting examples are intended to illustrate. A person knowing little about budgeting would learn little from this booklet. The other two books, on audiovisual media and preschool storytimes (three-to-five-year-olds), are of slightly more value. Neither, however, provides new information. The audiovisual guide mentions the video/

film controversy but seems less emphatic than reality indicates that videos are rapidly replacing films; no mention is made of computers. The drawings in the preschool storyhour booklet depict boys and girls in the most stereotypic of roles. Bibliographies in all the booklets contain materials which are mostly five or more years old; newer and better resources exist on all topics. The series is aimed at the novice, and even the novice will find most of this information readily available in other more general publications.

Eliza T. Dresang

165.   Olsen, Mary Lou. **Creative Connections: Literature and the Reading Program Grades 1-3.** Littleton, Colo., Libraries Unlimited, 1987. 250p. illus. bibliog. index. $20.00pa. LC 87-29665. ISBN 0-87287-651-9.

Noting that reading "should not be taught in isolation," this practical, innovative source extends the typical basal reading program to include "learning through an integrated literature program" connected to content areas. These activity-oriented literature units spent two years in development and field testing among five hundred children in the Fullerton (California) School District, and focus upon multisensory thinking skills linked to Bloom's Taxonomy. They are keyed to the 1982 Ginn Reading Program, the 1983 HBJ Bookmark Program, and the 1987 Scott Foresman Reading Program: An American Tradition. Within each grade, the following information is provided: book citation, suggested grade level, format (e.g., poetry, folktale), theme, expected student outcomes, book synopsis; bio-bibliographical information on the author-illustrator, model lesson plans approximately twenty minutes in length, connections to the library media center, suggestions for computer software, related books, correlations with content areas, independent or guided reading enhancement, and parental support. It is obvious that much time, imagination, and energy contributed to the development of this book. Teachers will delight in its creative approaches and time-saving suggestions, and librarians will enthusiastically embrace the notion of extending literature across the curriculum. Most important, children will benefit by this sensible approach to integrated learning which links the language arts to math, science, social studies, art, and music—and makes learning fun!   Ilene F. Rockman

166.   Weeks, Ann Carlson, ed. **Current Trends in Public Library Services for Children.** Champaign, Ill., Graduate School of Library and Information Science, University of Illinois, 1987.

1v. (various paging). (*Library Trends*, Vol. 35, No. 3). $8.00pa. ISSN 0024-2594.

As Ann Carlson Weeks points out in her introduction to this timely collection, it has been almost twenty-five years since *Library Trends* devoted an issue to services to children in public libraries. Those twenty-five years have seen dramatic changes both in the social climate in which libraries function and in the materials and services in libraries themselves. The articles in this collection touch on many of the major issues in children's services. Jill L. Locke and Margaret Mary Kimmel set the stage by discussing the demographic and social changes which have affected children of the "Information Age." Other articles cover a wide range of topics, including an analysis of the trends in children's literature, a discussion of the changing views taken by library administrators toward children's services, and a discussion of the attempt to expand services to meet the needs of all children including members of minorities and the disabled. Barbara A. Ivy tackles the question of how children's librarians can develop managerial skills and raises the possibly contentious issue of the librarian's responsibility to satisfy adults who may object to some services provided for children. Linda Ward-Callaghan discusses the effect of emerging technologies on children's library services. Mary K. Chelton offers practical advice on how services to children can be evaluated without an inordinate expense of time or money. But it is difficult to single out particular articles as being valuable. All of the topics covered are of critical importance to youth librarians at this time, which makes this collection required reading for anyone determined to offer quality service to the public. Adele M. Fasick

Young Adult Services

167. Pilla, Marianne Laino. **Resources for Middle-Grade Reluctant Readers: A Guide for Librarians.** Littleton, Colo., Libraries Unlimited, 1987. 122p. bibliog. index. $18.50. LC 87-3736. ISBN 0-87287-547-4.

Marianne Pilla's book covers a topic on which little material is available. A computer-assisted search of *Books in Print* produced little. Spache's 1969 and 1974 titles, a 1981 International Reading Association title, and a 1982 title, Christine Cassell's *Teaching Poor Readers in the Secondary School* (Croom Helm), were the most promising, so Pilla had an open field. Her book covers upper elementary reluctant readers, how to understand them and their problems, guidelines for selecting materials and determining readability, program ideas, use of com-

puters, and bibliographies for students and for the professionals who work with them. There is also a title index for the children's titles.

The focus on meeting children where their interests and needs are is right on target, as is the emphasis on the importance of recreational or leisure reading. Acknowledgment of the expanding role of computers in checking student needs and interests and as a reading tool is timely. The graph and instruction for use of the Fry readability index is helpful. The professional bibliography is extensive.

The author emphasizes the need for cooperation between schools and public libraries and between school and public librarians. However, it is not clear when a public library children's specialist was meant, when a school library media specialist was meant, and when both were being included. This is confusing to the reader. A good approach would have been to explain how terms were to be used and to pick distinctive terms for the different specialists and for the generic librarian.

Under "Professional Cooperation," the author notes that "the librarian, who has no formal reading coursework, must compensate for this by working with the reading specialist or teacher" (p. 4). If she means public librarian, where is the school library media specialist who should certainly be in this planning group? If she means school librarian, she needs to be aware that in many states school librarians are required to have the same training as teachers and that many such specialists have actually been teachers, so to imply that they usually have no formal reading coursework is not accurate.

The author advocates "Classroom Libraries" (p. 14). While she emphasizes small size and frequent replenishment, that does not go far enough for the reviewer and thousands of school library media specialists who disagree with the idea of permanent classroom collections and favor frequently changed displays of materials from the school library or other sources.

The titles in the bibliography of children's books were fairly current. Nearly one-fourth were published within the last five years and two-thirds within the last ten. The inclusion of names and publishers of pertinent series was also helpful. Annotations regarding the overall range of quality of the series would have been beneficial. While any list for reluctant readers, especially of this grade level, will probably be well received, a list of only about 120 books over fourteen categories is extremely limiting. The author notes that "the listing is by no means complete" (p. 64), and the reviewer agrees.

More detail in the introductory chapters would have been appreciated. For example, "Cooperation between Public Libraries and Schools" is an important-looking heading in the chapter on program ideas (p. 49), with only two short paragraphs. More examples, plus a printed form, for interest inventories would have been another welcome expansion.

Despite imperfections this book helps plug an important gap and will be useful to public librarians, school library media specialists, and teachers working with middle-grade reluctant readers. [R: BL, 1 Oct 87, p. 327; BR, Nov/Dec 87, pp. 48-49; EL, Nov/Dec 87, p. 39]

Betty Jo Buckingham

168. Ravenger, Judith, and Ristiina Wigg, eds. **Libraries Serving Youth: Directions for Service in the 1990s. Proceedings of a New York State Conference, April 16-18, 1986, Mohonk Mountain House, New Paltz, New York.** New York, Youth Services Section, New York Library Association, 1987. 80p. $10.00pa. ISBN 0-931658-12-8.

Libraries Serving Youth is a reprint of a state conference held in April 1986 sponsored by two sections of the New York Library Association. The 160 attendees discussed the "future direction of our library service for youth and formulated a vision for the next decade along with strategies for the vision's implementation." The organization of the conference included nationally known speakers, reactor panels, and small discussion groups which developed action plans. This conference was the first step in implementing a plan of action that includes a variety of specific activities. The purpose of this publication is to share these proceedings with other states and library organizations.

This conference review is an interesting report that should prove to be helpful to other states. Not only can the information and the plan of action be helpful, but also the process which was used seems to be effective and can serve as an excellent model.

Marie Zuk

CHILDREN'S LITERATURE

General Works

169. Moss, Elaine. **Part of the Pattern: A Personal Journey through the World of Children's Books, 1960-1985.** New York, Greenwillow Books/William Morrow, 1986. 223p. index. $11.75. LC 85-30211. ISBN 0-688-04559-6.

Elaine Moss began reviewing books for children in the early 1960s after several years as a teacher and a librarian. Her practical background in working with children as well as her knowledge of and enthusiasm for children's books are revealed in this collection of essays and reviews. The book is divided into three sections: the first covers freelance work done during 1960-1970; the second includes contributions to *Signal* from 1970 to 1980; and the third includes talks given to various audiences between 1980 and 1985. Some of the early reviews have a quaint air—it is difficult to remember when *Where the Wild Things Are* had to be defended—but the essay "The Sixties: A Perspective" captures the essence of the decade in children's publishing. Interviews with Rumer Godden, Richard Scarry, and Raymond Briggs are highlights of the middle section of the book, as is the 1978 essay on information books. But it is in the final section that Elaine Moss's voice is heard most clearly and her contribution is strongest. "The Dream and the Reality," the 1980 Sidney Robbins Memorial Lecture which was originally published in *Signal*, comes to grips with the gulf between publishers and reviewers concerned with books as literary creations and teachers trying to bring children and books together. Moss's lively account of her stint as a school librarian gives each side its due and shows how real children and real books can form an enriching mixture. Although the emphasis is British, many American librarians and students of children's literature will find this book of value. [R: SLJ, May 87, p. 40]

Adele M. Fasick

Bibliographies

170. Brians, Paul. **Nuclear Holocausts: Atomic War in Fiction, 1895-1984.** Kent, Ohio, Kent State University Press, 1987. 398p. bibliog. index. $29.50. LC 86-10685. ISBN 0-87338-335-4.

This unique scholarly study is the "only compilation of its kind to deal exclusively with nuclear war in fiction." The author begins with a ninety-four-page background and analysis of the subject, treating it in five well-developed sections: "The History of the Holocaust," "The Causes of Nuclear War," "The Short-Term Effects of Nuclear War," "The Long-Term Consequences of Nuclear War," and "Avoiding the Holocaust." Prior to introducing the 249-page bibliography, Brians includes a helpful explanation and evaluation of the sources he consulted.

The fully annotated, alphabetically arranged bibliography, almost a publication in its own right, treats novels, short stories, and plays written in or translated into English between 1895 and 1984. Various editions of novels are listed, and each short-story entry identifies the collection(s) in which the story appears. The commentaries are thorough enough to help the reader decide whether the entry is worth pursuing. For the most part, they emphasize thematic content rather than literary quality. Excluded are those works in which an atomic war is averted or in which a civilization is blighted by a catastrophic nuclear accident unrelated to war. In addition to title and subject indexes, there is a "timeline" appendix, in which the stories and novels are listed under the date of first appearance. Supplementary checklists are provided as suggestions for further study on themes which are closely related to nuclear war: "Near-War Narratives"; "Doubtful Cases," where it is uncertain whether a war or some vague holocaust has occurred; and "Nuclear Testing," in which the source of disaster has been atomic bomb testing.

Most academic, public, and larger school libraries will find this specialized, modestly priced volume an attractive addition for their collections. [R: Choice, Dec 87, p. 596]

Charles R. Andrews

171. **Discoveries: Fiction for Elementary School Readers.** Washington, D.C., National Library Service for the Blind and Physically Handicapped, 1986. 93p. index. free pa. LC 86-600075. ISBN 0-8444-0530-2.

172. **Discoveries: Fiction for Intermediate School Years.** Washington, D.C., National Library Service for the Blind and Physically Handicapped, 1986. 90p. index. free pa. LC 86-600076. ISBN 0-8444-1531-0.

173. **Discoveries: Fiction for Young Teens.** Washington, D.C., National Library Service for the Blind and Physically Handicapped, 1986. 108p. index. free pa. LC 86-600078. ISBN 0-8444-0532-9.

These are bibliographies of selected fiction books that are available on disk, cassette, or in braille from network libraries and are provided by the National Library Service for the Blind and Physically Handicapped.

Arrangement is by topic (e.g., tales and mystery, historical fiction, family life), then by format (disk, cassette, braille). There are separate author/title indexes for each format and each bibliography is produced in clear, large print. *Elementary School Readers* covers grades kindergarten through six; *Intermediate*, grades four through seven; and *Young Teens*, grades four through nine and senior high school. Each entry is given an estimated grade level.

An order form is included but the lack of a list of cooperating libraries makes it impossible to know where to send it. A statement on the inside back cover describes the Free Reading Program and provides an address where one can obtain more information and specific eligibility requirements.

Nancy Courtney

174. **Fiction, Folklore, Fantasy & Poetry for Children, 1876-1985.** New York, R. R. Bowker, 1986. 2v. $499.95/set. LC 84-20474. ISBN 0-8352-1831-7.

This massive, two-volume bibliography contains a wealth of information which will be useful to librarians, teachers, literary scholars, and publishers. Volume 1 provides informative introductory information about children's books and about the history of the Bowker company as well as the separate author and illustrator indexes; volume 2 has an index by title and includes a section on book awards. Entries are full and include author/illustrator dates and pseudonyms as well as complete publishing information. At last the familiar questions from parents and grandparents about books remembered from childhood can be answered and precise information about author, title, and publisher located. The format and typography are similar to the familiar *Books in Print*, so the book is legible and easy to use. Unfortunately, the awards section seems less carefully edited than the other listings. The Newbery and Caldecott awards are the ones which are likely to be consulted most often, yet these are listed in a confusing way. The dates used are the publication dates of the books rather than the year in which the award was given, making this list incompatible with others. Also, the award winners and honor books are listed together in alphabetical order with no indication of which book won the medal. Even worse, the winners of the first Newbery (1922) and the first Caldecott (1937) medals are inexplicably missing, and to add to the librarian's woes, Newbery is misspelled in the heading. Despite the weaknesses of this section, the bibliography as a whole will be a welcome addition to libraries which take children's literature seriously. [R: Choice, May 87, p. 1376; JOYS, Fall 87, p. 108; RBB, 15 May 87, p. 1427]

Adele M. Fasick

175. Field, Carolyn W., and Jaqueline Shachter Weiss. **Values in Selected Children's Books of Fiction and Fantasy.** Hamden, Conn., Library Professional Publications/Shoe String Press, 1987. 298p. index. $27.50. LC 87-3874. ISBN 0-208-02100-0.

Children learn values not only at home and in school, but also from the books they read, especially if they enjoy the story and do not feel "preached at" by the author. This particular book annotates in great detail, and with quotations from the 713 books covered, fiction and fantasy published between 1930 and 1984. These are books that children from preschool level through eighth grade read and enjoy, without realizing that they are also learning.

Each of the chapters centers on a specific value, seen as the most important one stressed in the book, and is arranged by age level. The values included are cooperation, courage, friendship and love of animals, friendship and love of people, humaneness, ingenuity, loyalty, maturing, responsibility, and self-respect. Often there is a blending of values in a given book, though one has been picked as predominant.

While this particular book is intended as a reference tool in book selection for librarians in public and school libraries (and would also be extremely useful in church and synagogue libraries!), it is also a book to be read and enjoyed for itself. Any librarian who works with children, and is familiar with many children's books, will enjoy the annotations as a reunion with old friends.

This book should be strongly recommended not only to all librarians who deal with children, but also to teachers of children. [R: BL, July 87, p. 1684]

Judith E. H. Odiorne

176.   Jones, Dolores B., comp. **Bibliography of the Little Golden Books.** Westport, Conn., Greenwood Press, 1987. 172p. index. (Bibliographies and Indexes in American Literature, No. 7). $35.00. LC 86-27090. ISBN 0-313-25025-1.

The introduction of this bibliography relates a rather detailed story of the inception and development of Little Golden Books, including the people who created the series, the plan for marketing, and the spinoffs of the series, and comments on their literary value. A list of seventeen references follows.

This book is arranged in four parts. The first contains a "comprehensive list of all the Little Golden Book titles issued by Simon & Schuster (later Golden Press and Western) from the series inception in 1942 through 1985." The ninety-six-page title list is arranged alphabetically, with each reference containing an entry number, which is the publisher-assigned issue number. All of the titles are numbered chronologically, and there are 831 of them. With some variance, each reference contains complete title, author(s), illustrator(s), place of publication, publisher, and date. Library of Congress card number, copyright registration number and date, copyright renewal registration number and date, and series title are also included. When a

series number was used for more than one title, an X was added to the series number of the second. The reference may also include an abbreviation for format type (e.g., B for a braille book). A list of these and other abbreviations is found in the front matter.

The series list is the second part, and it provides all of the series and subseries issued. They are listed alphabetically by the series title and include a brief annotation. The titles within the series are arranged alphabetically or by numbers if the series had its own numbering system. Each title is followed by the title list entry number, which provides a cross-reference.

There is also a name index, arranged by the author, illustrator, narrator, songwriter, or producer. Pseudonyms or other variant forms are included in parentheses.

Finally, the format index is arranged by the format (braille, cassette, filmstrip, motion picture, recording, and videocassette) in which the titles were originally issued. Again, a cross-reference to the title index is provided by the entry number.

As with Jones's *Children's Literature Awards and Winners* (see *ARBA* 84, entry 1123), this title is comprehensive, and the indexes provide many points of access for users. It is reasonably priced and could find its way easily onto the shelves of college, university, and public libraries. [R: RBB, 1 June 87, pp. 1499-1500]

Marcia L. Atilano

177.   Kies, Cosette. **Supernatural Fiction for Teens: 500 Good Paperbacks to Read for Wonderment, Fear, and Fun.** Littleton, Colo., Libraries Unlimited, 1987. 127p. index. $16.50pa. LC 87-3228. ISBN 0-87287-602-0.

The best feature of this fine little bibliography is the *subject* access, admittedly limited in scope, that it offers to a popular genre where very little help of that sort is available. Compiled for use by teachers, librarians, booksellers, and of course young adults, it presents five hundred books from the vast field of supernatural fiction selected on the basis of their suitability for teens and the likelihood of their being currently available in paperback. The bibliography's selections are also limited to those that fall within one of three broad aspects of the supernatural: parapsychology and psychic phenomena, tales and legends with strong magical or occult elements, and horror. It does not cover overlapping genres of science fiction or pure fantasy unless these have mythic/occult themes or mutually common subjects such as lost worlds, time travel, or science gone wrong.

Arranged alphabetically by author, entries give full bibliographical information plus succinct annotations, a code indicating reading maturity level (i.e., whether the book is appropriate for teens, younger teens, adults, or is a classic), brief notes on movie versions, and a term or two in brackets specifying principal subjects. Appendices provide lists of books included in the bibliography that form series, a title list of all films cited, a directory of paperback publishers, and an index to the subject fields. These fields cover approximately seventy terms ranging from abominable snowman through zombies, and cut across alchemy, Arthurian legends, astrology, ghosts, lost worlds, reincarnation, time travel, unicorns, werewolves, etc.

Let us hope that Libraries Unlimited will continue to publish selective bibliographies like this one that, cumulatively, will substantially expand the topical access currently available not only to the supernatural but to the interrelated genres of fantasy and science fiction as well. [R: RBB, 1 Oct 87, p. 256; VOYA, Oct 87, p. 191]

Mary Jo Walker

178.   Knudson, Richard L. **The Whole Spy Catalogue: An Espionage Lover's Guide.** New York, St. Martin's Press, 1986. 182p. illus. $10.95pa. LC 86-15443. ISBN 0-312-87069-8.

This paperback is aimed at the aficionado of espionage fiction and film, or, as the book states, "for anyone who has ever dreamed of going undercover." It is formatted and illustrated for the popular market. An introductory chapter entitled "The Second-Oldest Profession" gives a brief overview of the history of espionage. Chapter 2 presents the major spy novelists of the English-speaking world in alphabetical order, with a brief description of their fictional characters and a list of their novels. Titles, publishers, and dates for both U.S. and British editions are given. Chapter 3 is a descriptive listing of the chief spies portrayed in motion pictures and on television. Chapter 4, "The Gadgetry of Spying," gives information on such topics as lockpicks, swordcanes, electronic bugs, other "electronic essentials," firearms, spy planes, etc. There is a brief chapter on cryptography and a final chapter on a few of the most famous real-life spies of recent years. There is a brief glossary but no bibliography in the book.

Although the work is so popularly oriented, it does pull together the major novelists in the genre with a listing of their novels. Other bibliographies, such as J. M. Reilly's *Twentieth Century Crime and Mystery Writers*, second edition (see *ARBA* 86, entry 1123), are more comprehensive and scholarly, but the present work has value in that it focuses on the spy novelist.

Necia A. Musser

179.   Morrison, Faye Brown, and Kathryn Cusick. **Golden Poppies: California History and Contemporary Life in Books and Other Media for Young Readers: An Annotated Bibliography.** Hamden, Conn., Library Professional Publications/Shoe String Press, 1987. 280p. index. $29.50; $18.50pa. LC 86-19993. ISBN 0-208-02139-6; 0-208-02099-3pa.

Providing information on approximately five hundred print and nonprint items related to California life and history, *Golden Poppies* is a work that should be welcomed by educators, parents, librarians, and others who work with or teach children and young adults. A revised edition of *Golden Poppies: An Annotated Bibliography of California Historical Fiction and Nonfiction for Young Readers* (California History Center, De Anza College, 1979) by Dorothy Pritchard Wright, Morrison and Cusick's version retains many of the original entries (often revised and rewritten) and supplements them with recent additions to the literature in a variety of formats, including books, filmstrips, posters, audio cassettes, puzzles, worksheets, spirit masters, slides, coloring books, workbooks, study guides, software, program planners, and songbooks. Materials considered appropriate for various age levels (elementary through senior high school and adult) are included.

The material is divided into three major sections—"Historical Fiction and Nonfiction," "Contemporary Life," and "Nonbook Media," and entries are arranged alphabetically by author within each. Appendices are provided for "Selected Media Distributors and Suppliers" and "Selected Publishers and Book Suppliers," and the work is concluded by separate author, title, and subject indexes.

Each entry provides complete bibliographic information, a descriptive "Content" annotation, a critically helpful "Comment" annotation, and a type/format and very general reading/grade level notation (e.g., "Non-fiction: junior high—adult," "Sound filmstrip: primary—intermediate").

Providing access to a wide variety of specific information that has often proved difficult to locate, this unique source would be a useful addition to the reference sections of academic libraries supporting education programs, school library media and curriculum centers, and public libraries, particularly those located in California or serving a clientele interested in California history. [R: BL, 1 Jan 87, p. 713]

Kristin Ramsdell

180.   Olderr, Steven. **Mystery Index: Subjects, Settings, and Sleuths of 10,000 Titles.** Chicago, American Library Association, 1987. 492p. $29.95. LC 87-1294. ISBN 0-8389-0461-0.

Mystery fans will greatly appreciate this fine new guide. On the one hand, they will find Olderr's thorough treatment and concept of arrangement admirable; on the other, they will lament the camera-ready copy, the omission of top-of-the-page name or letter guides, and the lack of boldface author entries. Even had the publisher raised the price to correct these minor, yet annoying, shortcomings, the finished product would have been worth it. This important compilation will, after all, be in many libraries for a long time to come.

The text is alphabetically arranged in four parts: a main entry section, a title index, a subject-and-setting index, and a character index. A main entry includes the author; the dates of birth and death (not consistently, however); U.S. title and UK title (if different from U.S.), as well as date(s) of publication; and—*mirabile dictu!*—the novel's primary character and the order of his or her appearance in a series. If the user knows a title or a character name, he or she should search those indexes first for a referral to the main entry. The subject-and-setting index will be extremely helpful for the reader who might wish to focus upon mysteries with a Long Island (36) or a New York City (674) locale, or those set in the Christmas season (27), or those dealing with libraries and librarians (29).

Olderr, a librarian himself, has limited his inclusions to twentieth-century hardbound titles "that the user has a reasonable expectation of retrieving from a library or through interlibrary loan." Although no cut-off date for entries is identified, a little detective work establishes (almost) beyond a reasonable doubt that it is 1985 (but if so, my dear Watson, where then is Robert B. Parker's Spenser novel, *A Catskill Eagle*?). [R: WLB, Dec 87, pp. 94-95]

Charles R. Andrews

181.   Pronzini, Bill, and Marcia Muller. **1001 Midnights: The Aficionado's Guide to Mystery and Detective Fiction.** New York, Arbor House, 1986. 879p. bibliog. $39.95. LC 85-30817. ISBN 0-87795-622-7.

The purpose of this guide to mystery and detective fiction is to provide "aficionados, students, and collectors, as well as casual and new readers, with a reference guide to one thousand and one individual titles; to additional works by their authors; and to books of a similar type (whodunit, thriller, police procedural, etc.) by other writers. Every major author in the field, beginning with Edgar Allan

Poe, and every major work up to and including books published in 1985 are covered in these pages" (p. 1). The guide is arranged alphabetically by author. Entries average about one-half page in length, are broadly classified as to type, and are "signed" by the reviewer.

The authors indicate that "because *1001 Midnights* is intended as a celebration of the genre, all but a small percentage of the reviews are favorable in nature" (p. 3). A perusal of the entries corroborates this statement. Unfortunately, the "negative" reviews can lead to an impression of inconsistent or contradictory reviewing. For example, an enthusiastically negative review of Robert Parker's Spenser novels has the tone of a diatribe: "There are those who find Parker's novels underplotted, pretentiously literary, excessively (and sometimes gratuitously) violent, fundamentally immoral, and populated by an array of unpleasant characters" (pp. 616-17). The entries on Mickey Spillane, in contrast, are characterized by an apparent admiration for the same elements: "There is violence galore, too, and a lot of voyeuristic sex.... None of this affects the story adversely, however. Typically, Spillane pulls it off" (p. 746). It should be noted that the reviews of Parker and Spillane were provided by different contributors. Nevertheless, the clash in tone of these reviews (one seemingly critical of gratuitous violence, the other condoning it) is a minor irritant.

A more serious limitation is the work's lack of indexes. Although relatively easy to use in its present format, particularly by those familiar with the genre, a title index and a name index of series characters would increase the book's utility as a reference work. These limitations notwithstanding, *1001 Midnights* generally achieves its primary purpose. It is an introduction to this fascinating genre that is not only useful but fun to use.

Larry G. Chrisman

182.   Ramsdell, Kristin. **Happily Ever After: A Guide to Reading Interests in Romance Fiction.** Littleton, Colo., Libraries Unlimited, 1987. 302p. index. $27.50. LC 87-22588. ISBN 0-87287-479-6.

Although librarians are indicated as the primary audience, with the avowed purpose of helping them to advise their patrons, this guide does not seem to fulfill its aim. The categories of romance fiction are too broadly defined and wide-ranging to be useful. Ramsdell tries to overcome this problem by advising readers of the difficulties in matching romance patrons with their preferences in romantic fiction.

For each romance category, this book provides definitions, specific appeal, readers' advisory pointers, a brief history, and a selected bibliography with some annotated entries. "Selected," is the key word here. Many contemporary romance writers are prolific in the extreme, but Ramsdell chooses books that are "typical, unusual, particularly good, interesting, or important examples of the genre." Despite these criteria, the reader puzzles over omissions; for example, why the only listing for Olive Higgins Prouty is *Stella Dallas* (source of the radio soap opera), with no mention of *Now Voyager* (basis for the Bette Davis film classic). One wonders also whether librarians should or would advise the Jane Austen reader to read Barbara Cartland, both included under "Regency Romances."

Another designated audience is the researcher. Research aids include information on history and criticism of romantic fiction, biographies of romance writers, periodicals and organizations devoted to romantic fiction, awards, collections, publishers' series, and indexes by name/title and subject.

Renee B. Horowitz

183. Schon, Isabel. **Books in Spanish for Children and Young Adults: An Annotated Guide. Series IV. Libros Infantiles y Juveniles en Español: Una Guía Anotada. Serie No. IV.** Metuchen, N.J., Scarecrow, 1987. 301p. index. $29.50. LC 87-9785. ISBN 0-8108-2004-8.

Isabel Schon is the outstanding expert in the United States on literature in Spanish intended for children and young adults. This volume updates three previous volumes with the same title and deals with books published since 1984 in thirteen Spanish-speaking areas (this includes Puerto Rico), the United States, and Sweden. The author continues to indicate whether she considers a title to be outstanding, marginal, or not recommended.

This bibliography is first arranged by country and then by type (e.g., fiction, folklore, poetry, science and technology) within each country. A brief plot summary is provided for a work of fiction and other evaluative comments are included on other types of material.

One is struck by the low quality of works that Schon describes and evaluates. Of the ten books listed from Cuba, six are not recommended and four are classified as marginal. Of the twenty-three titles from Costa Rica, eleven are not recommended, four are outstanding, and eight are marginal. The largest group of outstanding works was published in Spain. Some of these Spanish publications are translations from English and other languages.

It is noticeable that some outstanding contemporary writers for adults are not equally suc-

cessful, according to Schon, as are writers for children and young adults. She does not recommend the volume listed by Concha Zardoya, even though Zardoya is an outstanding poet and literary critic.

The Spanish titles are translated into English; grade level and prices are provided as well as list of reliable dealers. There are indexes of authors and titles. This volume, like the earlier ones, should be extremely useful to librarians who need information on the content and quality of books in Spanish for children and young adults.

Hensley C. Woodbridge

184. **Science Fiction, Fantasy, & Horror: 1986: A Comprehensive Bibliography of Books and Short Fiction Published in the English Language.** By Charles N. Brown and William G. Contento. Oakland, Calif., Locus Press, 1987. 347p. $35.00. ISBN 0-9616629-3-X.

This is the second volume in a series begun last year under the title *Science Fiction in Print, 1985.* It is also preceded by work formerly done separately by editors Brown and Contento: Brown through the magazine *Locus*, which he edits, and Contento through his *Index to Science Fiction Anthologies and Collections* (see *ARBA* 79, entry 1203). The result, as the title indicates, is a combination of books in print lists, magazine/anthology/collection indexes, and bibliographical essays.

Beginning with "1986: The S F Year in Review," the volume goes on to provide author and title lists of new books and reprints in the field (an astounding total of 1,502 titles, up 13 percent from last year, produced by 146 publishers, up 18 percent); a separate list of 1986 original publications; author and title indexes to stories in 1986 magazines and anthologies/collections; an issue-by-issue magazine contents list; reviews of films and magazines; a list of recommended reading; a necrology (1986 saw the demise of many greats); a compendium of small press publishers with their addresses; and a so-called subject index which is really a useful relisting of books under hard-to-separate categories such as science fiction novels, fantasy novels, art books, anthologies, reference books, and so forth.

Despite the lack of a real subject-analytical index, which may be an impossibility in such an immense (and immensely popular) genre, this volume represents one of the most comprehensive and useful reference sources yet to appear in the field.

Mary Jo Walker

185. Wilms, Denise, and Ilene Cooper, eds. **A Guide to Non-Sexist Children's Books. Volume II: 1976-1985.** Chicago, Academy

Chicago, 1987. 240p. illus. index. $17.95; $8.95 pa. LC 86-32262. ISBN 0-89733-161-3; 0-89733-162-1pa.

A new series has been created with the release of volume 2 (the 1976 book [see *ARBA* 77, entry 1142] is now known as volume 1, and volume 3 is slated for publication in 1990). Volume 2 is the same compact size as the earlier volume, has different editors, and contains 685 role-free titles representing preschool-grade 12 picture books, novels, poetry, folktales, and nonfiction. Entries are arranged by grade categories, are annotated (primarily descriptive) in one to four sentences, note if the title is an award winner, and provide full bibliographic information including grade level. No indication of format (paperback, library binding, etc.) is provided. Unlike the first volume, two detailed fiction and nonfiction subject indexes are available. Other helpful sections are a directory of small press publishers, an age-grade comparison chart, and the inclusion of black-and-white illustrations to break up the monotony of the text.

What is disappointing, however, is the lack of explanation about the criteria for title selection, and why some pre-1976 books overlooked in the 1976 volume are now included despite the subtitle "Volume II: 1976-1985" (one finds the 1972 *Dinky Hocker Shoots Smack*, the 1974 *M. C. Higgins the Great*, and the 1973 *Summer of My German Soldier*, for example).

The intent of providing an annotated guide to contemporary, role-free children's literature is noteworthy. One hopes that volume 3 will contain a detailed introduction of the title selection process, and a cumulative author, title, and subject index to the earlier volumes. [R: LJ, 1 Sept 87, p. 175]   Ilene F. Rockman

Handbooks

186. Estes, Glenn E., ed. **American Writers for Children since 1960: Poets, Illustrators, and Nonfiction Authors.** Detroit, Gale, 1987. 430p. illus. bibliog. index. (Dictionary of Literary Biography, Vol. 61). $92.00. LC 87-14352. ISBN 0-8103-1739-7.

Containing thirty-two biographies of illustrators, poets, and nonfiction writers for children, this volume complements the DLB volume *American Writers for Children since 1960: Fiction* (see *ARBA* 87, entry 1091). Illustrators are the focus of most of the four- to fifteen-page biographies, which relate the subjects' backgrounds and describe many of their works in some detail. Each contains a bibliography of the subject's works and most include a short list of references for further information. There are many illustrations which reproduce the dust jackets of the various books in black-and-white, facsimile reproductions of pages from the authors' original typescripts, and a photograph of each author or illustrator.

The table of contents reads like a children's literature hall of fame. Included are biographies of such noted children's writers and illustrators as Tomie de Paola, Eve Merriam, Maurice Sendak, Steven Kellogg, Marcia Brown, Chris Van Allsburg, and Nancy Larrick.

An appendix lists the winners of fifteen awards and prizes given for children's books, including the Caldecott and Newbery medals. There is a "Checklist of Further Readings" for more information about children's literature in general. Finally, the volume includes the usual cumulative index to DLB volumes 1-61, as well as the *DLB Yearbook* volumes for 1980-1986, and the *Documentary Series* volumes 1-4.

Nancy Courtney

187. Kingman, Lee, ed. **Newbery and Caldecott Medal Books 1976-1985.** Boston, Horn Book, 1986. 358p. illus. (part col.). index. $24.95. LC 86-15223. ISBN 0-87675-004-8.

Like its predecessors, this volume is a valuable guide to both the books and the authors and illustrators who have won the awards for the decade 1976-1985. Each book listed includes a summary of the plot, the official acceptance speech by the author at the Newbery Caldecott Awards Dinner, and a biographical sketch of the author or illustrator. All of this material has appeared in the *Horn Book* previously, but is brought together in a convenient form here. In addition to the reprinted information, original essays have been written for the volume which provide some critical perspective on the winners and the period of children's publishing. Essays are by Barbara Bader, Zena Sutherland, and Ethel L. Heins, all experts in the field. Recommended as a convenient one-stop place for the award-winner information and as an authoritative guide to the authors and their works.

Information in this volume can be supplemented with works such as *Something about the Author* and a whole host of other books whose purpose is to provide activities centered around these titles for use with children and young people. [R: BL, July 87, p. 1685]

David V. Loertscher

Indexes

188. **Children's Authors and Illustrators: An Index to Biographical Dictionaries.** 4th ed. Joyce Nakamura, ed. Detroit, Gale, 1987. 799p.

(Gale Biographical Index Series, No. 2). $140.00. LC 86-27035. ISBN 0-8103-2525-X.

Although the fourth edition of *Children's Authors and Illustrators* (*CA&I*) has a new editor, its primary purpose remains the same: to be as comprehensive as possible, including all known writers and illustrators of children's books whose work is accessible in English. Of the twenty-five thousand persons listed, five thousand are new entries, and of the 450 sources indexed, 175 have been added to those in the third edition; all information in the third edition is retained. A number of the new references indexed focus on women or ethnic groups, indicating that coverage is expanded in these areas. The fullest form of a person's real name is established with nicknames and variants at the end of the entry as well as references to entries under any pseudonyms.

Biographical references are chosen without attention to their content or point of view. Except for periodicals in *Biography Index*, all journals, magazines, and newspapers have been excluded as sources of biographies. Authors writing specifically for children as well as those whose works have been adopted by children or are frequently assigned to children are included. The term *children* is not defined, but an examination of the persons included indicates coverage through at least the early teenage years (Victoria Holt and Robert Cormier are included; Kurt Vonnegut is not).

A unique reference source, *CA&I* is useful to all persons with an interest in children's literature and illustration, and the new edition is updated enough to warrant its purchase by all such individuals and institutions. [R: EL, May/June 87, pp. 36-37; JOYS, Fall 87, pp. 109-10; RBB, 15 May 87, p. 1422]

Eliza T. Dresang

CIRCULATION

189. Intner, Sheila S. **Circulation Policy in Academic, Public, and School Libraries.** Westport, Conn., Greenwood Press, 1987. 228p. bibliog. index. (New Directions in Information Management, No. 13). $35.00. LC 86-14952. ISBN 0-313-23990-8.

This comparative survey of the circulation policies and procedures of twenty-two academic, twenty-two public, and eighteen school libraries of varying size, focus, and U.S. geographic location was conducted by a library school educator at Simmons College in 1983-1984. A questionnaire (reprinted in appendix 1) and a request for relevant documentation were sent to a representative sampling of libraries in each category. School libraries were the most

difficult group from which to obtain information. Libraries which answered the questionnaire and sent documentation, samples of which are interspersed throughout the text, are listed in appendix 2. Others responded only to the questionnaire and asked that their comments remain anonymous.

An introductory chapter provides background information. Alternate chapters first detail and discuss how various libraries in each of the three categories formulate and revise their circulation policies, and include plans for future changes, then analyze various libraries' borrowing privileges, discussing overdue procedures and problems, kinds of materials loaned, and who may borrow them. Data gathered are arranged in the same order in respective chapters to facilitate comparison. Similarities and differences within the particular types of libraries are delineated, with comparisons among the three categories summarized in a final chapter. Although computerized circulation systems are more prevalent in public libraries than academic or school libraries, more academic libraries than other types of libraries are planning future automation. Automation seemed to be valued as a means for better and more efficient control of circulation procedures rather than for its potential to expand services to library clients. Most school libraries used manual circulation systems and appeared to be satisfied with the limitations of the status quo.

The survey contains a wealth of detailed information which should prove useful to library personnel, their clients and governing boards, and library school students. There is a selective, partially annotated bibliography of sources which contains citations to earlier, classic library circulation studies. [R: BL, 1 Apr 87, p. 1175; JAL, July 87, p. 184; LJ, 1 May 87, p. 52; RQ, Winter 87, p. 289]

Virginia E. Yagello

COLLECTION DEVELOPMENT

190. Arthur, A. J. **Collection Development: A Report to the Swinburne Librarian.** Hawthorn, Australia, Swinburne, c1985, 1986. 2v. $50.00 pa./set. ISBN 0-85590-581-6.

If you are going to start a new academic library or thinking about making a major shift in your present collection development program, you will find many good ideas in this two-volume set from Australia. There is nothing new as such, but A. J. Arthur's sixteen-month "consultancy" was probably one of the most comprehensive collection development projects undertaken in an academic library. His objectives were to establish "1. a basis of assessing current collection adequacy; 2. a continuing basis for assessing collection adequacy; 3. appropriate selection policies—a) on a subject area basis, b) on a direct curricular and curriculum support basis, c) on proportions of materials by form within subject areas; 4. politics regarding discard and relocation of materials; 5. policies regarding the funding basis appropriate to the needs of each teaching area; 6. a basis for making comment on course support, especially for new courses, course amendments, and post-graduate studies; 7. a basis of library/staff liaison in selection of materials on a subject area basis; and 8. the job specification for the continuing position of Collection Development Librarian for 1985." The only major area of collection development not covered in the objectives is preservation. In essence this set is the consultant's report with all the details (data collecting methods, forms used, raw data), not just the recommendations. Volume 1 contains the recommendations and discussions of how the recommendations were generated and volume 2 contains the data collecting forms and raw data. Although not intended to be a "how-to" publication, it would serve as a good starting point; where else can you get a consultant for just $50.00? The material is neither new nor exciting but it does present a sound, workable approach, in easy to follow language, to establishing each of the objectives listed above. [R: JAL, Jan 87, pp. 400-401]   G. Edward Evans

191. Collection Development Organization and Staffing in ARL Libraries. Washington, D.C., Association of Research Libraries, 1987. 121p. (SPEC Flyer, No. 131). $20.00pa.

The SPEC Kits published by the Association of Research Libraries, Office of Management Studies, of which this is number 131, have for fifteen years provided a source of informative, unedited primary source documents related to the management and operation of large academic and research libraries.

In this kit, an introductory section reports on the results of a survey of collection development functions in ARL libraries suggesting that "there may be no other unit that currently shows as much diversity in composition and reporting relationships." Three basic trends appear from the responses and materials submitted by fifty-three academic libraries: "1) Continuing changes in the organization and staffing of collection development; 2) increasing emphasis on formal training and liaison with teaching faculty; and 3) growing interest in the development and execution of studies on the cost, performance, and

analysis of the collection development/management function." Organizational charts, position descriptions, vacancy announcements, orientation and training aids, and studies and reports of collection development functions follow, enabling librarians and administrators to study the documents other libraries have produced to address the issues and problems of organizing and administering their collection development functions.

Like others in the series, this kit will be useful to librarians wishing to keep up with recent trends, wanting to review or compare and contrast their approaches with others, or writing their own collection development documents.

Blaine H. Hall

192. Ellison, John W., and Patricia Ann Coty, eds. **Nonbook Media: Collection Management and User Services.** Chicago, American Library Association, 1987. 388p. bibliog. $35.00 pa. LC 87-1340. ISBN 0-8389-0479-3.

Ellison and Coty have assembled twenty-two different types of media, which are treated in structured essays by knowledgeable persons. Topics range from pamphlets to videodiscs and all discuss the medium, selection practices, maintenance and management concerns, and provide a bibliography of additional reading. While CD-ROM and compact disks are noticeably missing, the balance of the works provides, as the introduction states, a concise source for nonbook information. Each essay is factual and reasonably current and provides a one-stop source for students and librarians who are considering the addition of new formats to library collections. Recommended.

David V. Loertscher

193. Evans, G. Edward. **Developing Library and Information Center Collections.** 2d ed. Littleton, Colo., Libraries Unlimited, 1987. 443p. index. (Library Science Text Series). $29.50; $22.50pa. LC 87-3224. ISBN 0-87287-463-X; 0-87287-546-6pa.

This second edition of Evans's well-known textbook on collection development may be regarded as almost a model of what a new edition should be. Here is no superficial updating and revision but rather a substantially enlarged and rewritten presentation, well worth acquiring even by those libraries which already have the first edition (1979).

The main change in general approach is that Evans, recognizing the growing capacity of the computer to provide alternatives to books and periodicals, now places more emphasis on the broader concepts of information transfer and less on the forms in which the information is "packaged." With respect to specific contents, the main change is that chapters have been added on serials, government documents, fiscal management, automation, and preservation.

As a textbook, Evans's work must compete with and therefore be compared with the many other texts on collection development (at least five have been published in the last seven years). Stylistically, the comparison is not in Evans's favor—his writing is rather dense and will not win him high marks for readability or clarity. Substantively, however, Evans fares better: the range of topics covered is very broad; the "practical information" is accurate and up-to-date; the documentation, suggested reading lists, and indexes are more than adequate. My guess is that the beginning library school students for whom this book is primarily intended will find it tough going, but it will serve them well. [R: JAL, Nov 87, p. 322]   Samuel Rothstein

194. Hastreiter, Jamie Webster, Larry Hardesty, and David Henderson, comps. **Periodicals in College Libraries.** Chicago, Association of College and Research Libraries, American Library Association, 1987. 116p. (CLIP Note, No. 8). $17.00pa. ISBN 0-8389-7143-1.

The College Library Information Packet (CLIP) Notes program of the College Libraries Section provides "college and small university libraries with state-of-the-art reviews and current documentation on library practices and procedures." This number reports the results of a survey of 118 institutions. The fifty-five questions in the survey cover all aspects of the handling of periodicals: selection, acquisition, budgeting, maintenance, deacquisition, and automation. The responses contain much interesting and useful information for librarians concerned with the management of periodicals, but even more useful perhaps are the sample forms from many of the respondents. There is a wide variety of these: periodical request and review forms; selection policy statements; ordering forms procedures; management policy guidelines; formulas for allocating the periodicals budget; evaluation methods; format policy statements, especially for microforms; and retention and weeding policies and procedures. These can be most instructive, and they make this publication a worthwhile addition for the library staff's working collection. [R: JAL, Nov 87, p. 323]   Evan Ira Farber

195. McPheron, William, ed., with others. **English and American Literature: Sources and Strategies for Collection Development.** Chicago, American Library Association, 1987.

217p. index. (ACRL Publications in Librarianship, No. 45). $29.95pa. LC 87-1329. ISBN 0-8389-0476-9.

Conceived by the English and American Literature Discussion Group of the Association of College and Research Libraries, this compilation of ten essays explores various aspects of collecting materials pertaining to English-language literatures. In some respects, it serves as an expansion of Susan J. Steinberg and Marcia Pankake's chapter "English and American Literature, with Notes on Some Commonwealth Literatures," published in *Selection of Library Materials in the Humanities, Social Sciences, and Sciences* (American Library Association, 1985). Contributors are experienced bibliographers representing a variety of academic institutions.

Although the primary emphasis is on English and American literature, most of the essays also address other literature written in English, such as Canadian, Australian, and South African. The first chapter provides an overview of collection development activities in these fields. Other chapters focus on such topics as acquisitions procedures and methods; selecting current literary scholarship, serials, retrospective materials, and contemporary literature; textual studies and their relationship to choosing specific editions of a literary work; developing nonprint media resources; and selecting materials for reference and special collections.

Essays cover the practical aspects of selecting and acquiring materials (such as dealing with vendors and establishing approval plans) as well as the more philosophical concepts on which collection development decisions are based. Since the essays were prepared independently, some of them overlap, and several reflect significant methodological differences among the contributors. The perceived merit of a particular essay may depend on how well the reader's philosophy of collection development coincides with that of the author of the essay. For example, librarians who are concerned with developing "quality" collections may be disconcerted by Charles W. Brownson's "representative" approach to collecting current fiction and poetry. However, the diverse selection methodologies and collection development principles espoused in this volume enhance its value, since they are certain to provoke careful thinking and reassessment of one's own assumptions, policies, and procedures.

An especially valuable feature of this work is the provision in most of the essays of annotated bibliographies or bibliographic essays on pertinent selection sources. In addition, some chapters include bibliographies which can be useful for collection evaluation. Robert Hauptman's chapter on serials, for example, lists recommended core journals in English and American literature grouped into categories for small, medium-sized, and large academic libraries. A useful index provides access to titles of selection tools discussed and to topics covered.

Although one could quibble over the omission of certain selection tools or topics from specific essays (the aforementioned Brownson essay, for example, makes no mention of contemporary drama), this work should become an invaluable resource for academic librarians who are responsible for collection development in the areas of English and American literature. Neophytes will find it indispensable as an introduction and guide to the intricacies of selecting in this field, while experienced bibliographers will welcome the opportunity to learn new approaches to their work.

Marie Ellis

196. Nichols, Margaret Irby. **Selecting and Using a Core-Reference Collection.** Austin, Tex., Library Development Division, Texas State Library, 1986. 68p. index. free pa.

For some time, authorities on reference service have conceded the impossibility of constructing a core reference collection which will be universally acceptable to all people in all situations. It is therefore both refreshing and unnerving to encounter this annotated list of seventy-nine titles, plus an additional fifty mentioned in notes, without there being any indication of why they were chosen except that these works "should constitute the main reference holdings in a small library or a desk (ready-reference) collection in a larger library." Most of the titles are well-known factual reference sources—except for one periodical index, *Abridged Readers' Guide*—familiar to unilingual English-speaking graduates of a U.S. library school. No foreign-language titles appear, and except for a few British titles no non-American titles. On the other hand, there are many titles which deal exclusively with Texas.

For libraries and students outside Texas, the most valuable part of this book will be its priority ratings of sources in order of estimated value and its reference works exercises. Answers are not provided for the exercises. The work is indexed.

Peter F. McNally

197. Shapiro, Beth J., and John Whaley, eds. **Selection of Library Materials in Applied and Interdisciplinary Fields.** Chicago, American Library Association, 1987. 287p. index. $42.00. LC 86-32101. ISBN 0-8389-0466-1.

Like its predecessor, *Selection of Library Materials in the Humanities, Social Sciences and Sciences* (American Library Association, 1985), this volume is intended to aid the novice selector. The contributors, eighteen in all, did an excellent job preparing their chapters and even an experienced selector may find a few pieces of new information. Anyone given a new collection development assignment in a field such as agriculture, business, or race and ethnic studies would only need to consult this book in order to identify the basic issues, methods, sources, and major publishers. In addition to the three fields mentioned there are chapters on communication arts and sciences, criminal justice, education, engineering, environmental studies, geography and maps, health sciences, home economics, law, public administration and policy sciences, the radical Left and Right, social work, sports and recreation, urban planning, and women's studies. Naturally there is a certain amount of overlap due to the common aspects of collection building regardless of discipline. Many of the chapters address the issues of database and audiovisual acquisition, as well as "nontraditional" materials such as marketing reports, specifications and standards, environmental impact studies, and test instruments (questionnaires). All of the contributors have solid backgrounds in the fields they wrote about, and the editors did an excellent job of keeping repetition between chapters to an absolute minimum. A must purchase item for library schools, and very appropriate for large academic libraries and those special libraries dealing with one or more of the topics covered. [R: LJ, 15 June 87, p. 58]

G. Edward Evans

COLLEGE AND RESEARCH LIBRARIES

198. Carpenter, Kenneth E. **The First 350 Years of the Harvard University Library: Description of an Exhibition.** Cambridge, Mass., Harvard University Library, 1986. 216p. illus. (part col.). index. $20.00.

The Harvard University Library is the nation's premiere academic library, a resource of great breadth and unsurpassed quality. This volume captures the library's complex and continuing evolution over 350 years by reprinting a richly illustrated and gracefully written exhibition catalog. Manuscripts, documents, and photographs illuminate the history of the Harvard University Library from John Harvard's initial bequest to its current status as the country's largest university library, with eleven million volumes.

Harvard's massive, decentralized library has required pioneering solutions to many challenges such as remote storage and the undergraduate library. The evolution from donations to active collection development, the contributions of scholars and librarians, and the struggles of each generation of librarians to balance preservation with scholarly use are ably presented. Evolution of the card catalog, storage of materials, and early automation projects are treated in some depth. Collections and services of the many specialized libraries (more than one hundred) are given prominence.

The exhibition was planned and annotated by Kenneth E. Carpenter, University Library Assistant Director for Research Resources. The 216-page catalog includes a foreword by President Derek Bok and a preface by Sidney Verba, Director of the University Library. This exceptional catalog should stimulate preparation of a comprehensive history befitting the subject. [R: WLB, May 87, pp. 59-60]

Arthur P. Young

199. Energies for Transition. Proceedings of the Fourth National Conference of the Association of College and Research Libraries. Baltimore, Maryland, April 9-12, 1986. Danuta A. Nitecki, ed. Chicago, Association of College and Research Libraries, American Library Association, 1986. 248p. index. $30.00pa. ISBN 0-8389-6976-3.

This volume includes the sixty short contributed papers accepted by referees and presented at the 1986 ACRL national conference. There are research reports (seven), position papers (forty-four), and idea briefs (nine)—categories determined by the authors. The volume was distributed at the conference, printed from the authors' camera-ready copy, rather than as the papers were delivered. The volume does not include papers from the six theme sessions or descriptions of other conference activities; thus the title is misleading. The papers do not necessarily relate to the overall theme but focus on the speakers' immediate interests. The editor has arranged the papers in eight subject sections—ranging from bibliographic control, collection management, and library automation through service to readers and bibliographic instruction to general concerns on personnel, library administration, and academic and research librarianship. Papers on disparate subjects in a volume like this are easily lost in terms of bibliographic control. Happily, *Library Literature* has indexed all, except for the idea briefs. (Some of the papers have also appeared in *College & Research Libraries*.) Like all such volumes, this is a mixed bag, but with a

general level of quality assured through the referees' judgments. Even though the papers were separately prepared, the volume has a good uniform appearance and, given current prices, is a real bargain.

Richard D. Johnson

200. Hyatt, James A., and Aurora A. Santiago. University Libraries in Transition. Washington, D.C., NACUBO, 1987. 112p. illus. $22.00. LC 86-12819. ISBN 0-915164-29-9.

This book provides a detailed analysis of library automation in four major research university libraries. The focus is on the overall fiscal impact on each institution. Hyatt and Santiago examine the management and planning of university libraries and the impact of technological changes on libraries' current and future operations. Since the study was based on actual fact-finding site visits, interviews, and documents for both public and independent sectors of higher education, the work provides useful information to a broad range of institutions, even though each case under review has its own unique set of environmental and institutional peculiarities, thus resulting in different planning processes and individualized automated systems.

Each case details concise key elements in planning, from background profiles, sources of funds, and levels of expenditures to each layer of management processes, including implementation and evaluation. The study seems to demonstrate that these major university libraries have proven that they have an ability to move toward the innovative use of technology to better meet the needs of library users. A major highlight of the volume is the overview of study findings describing project design and methodology, with tables of figures and practical questions such as "Is cost-benefit analysis of automation possible?" The quality of writing is rather fragmentary, since the content is mostly drawn from the task force's report.

Although some supplementary materials such as indexes and appendices are lacking, this book is useful for any library automation planning effort. Clearly, this volume will serve as a model for automation projects and can be especially helpful for library administrators and systems librarians. It also will be a good training guide for library students who are interested in the operational characteristics of systems such as LCS, FBR, BOBCAT terminals, and MARVEL. It is recommended for all university librarians. [R: JAL, July 87, p. 183; JAL, Nov 87, p. 296]

(Christina) Young Hyun Allen

201. Kusack, James M. **Unions for Academic Library Support Staff: Impact on Workers and the Workplace.** Westport, Conn., Greenwood Press, 1986. 108p. bibliog. index. (New Directions in Information Management, No. 10). $25.00. LC 86-7709. ISBN 0-313-24991-1.

This book is based on the author's doctoral dissertation, "Support Staff Unions in University Libraries in the United States" (Indiana University, 1984). A perusal of the references revealed citations published after 1984. The book comprises five chapters, one of which describes the author's doctoral research. The questionnaire/testing instrument is included as an appendix, which is always helpful in evaluating research reports. There are references following each chapter and a "selected bibliography" following the questionnaire. There is also a two-page index which is somewhat superfluous.

The author provides an excellent overview of the history of library unions. There is also an extensive review of related research. The author concludes with suggestions for further research and a discussion relating to applications of library-related collective bargaining research.

The author observes that "while the literature on collective bargaining is extensive, only a small portion deals with white-collar employees in the American workplace. Still less centers on nonacademic employees at colleges and universities, and only a few researchers have looked at support staff unions in academic libraries" (p. 29). This volume provides research data on an aspect of library unions which has not been adequately studied. Because of this, as well as the excellent review of previous research, most readers will find *Unions for Academic Library Support Staff* to be an important contribution, and welcome addition, to the literature on collective bargaining in libraries. [R: JAL, July 87, p. 198; JAL, Sept 87, p. 229; RQ, Fall 87, p. 158; WLB, Mar 87, p. 64; WLB, June 87, p. 73]   Larry G. Chrisman

202. **Library-Scholar Communication in ARL Libraries.** Washington, D.C., Association of Research Libraries, 1987. 114p. illus. bibliog. (SPEC Flyer, No. 132). $20.00pa.

This ARL SPEC Kit differs from most publications in this series in that it contains a summary report of an independently conducted survey with complementary materials submitted by selected ARL libraries. The survey in question is the highly publicized Survey of Scholars conducted by the Office of Scholarly Communication and Technology of the American Council of Learned Societies. A report, "Librarians and Scholars: The Need for Channels of Communication," prepared by Ann J. Price, staff associate with the Council, focuses on the library related data obtained by the survey. This report is followed by in-house documents from ten university libraries which describe various programs for communicating with faculty both in terms of library-wide programs and the individual roles and responsibilities of teaching faculty. Finally, there is a report of an ARL survey on printed communication with faculty and examples of fact sheets, newsletters, etc. The result of this combination is a highly useful compilation of material related to the vital question of library/faculty communication in a time of technological change in scholarly communication.   Joe A. Hewitt

203. **Organization Charts in ARL Libraries.** Washington, D.C., Association of Research Libraries, 1986. 104p. (SPEC Flyer, No. 129). $20.00pa.

A straightforward collection of organization charts from sixty-one members of the Association of Research Libraries, this volume will be of interest to library directors and others in management and supervisory positions. The charts are reproduced from originals supplied by ARL members, with no editorial comments or interpretation, although a few include notes added by the contributors. Because of the direct reproduction, quality and format vary considerably. While this lack of consistency can be confusing, it also gives the reader an appreciation for the differing approaches taken by various institutions and the evolving nature of library organization. The collection also includes a two-page introduction summarizing changes made since the two earlier editions appeared (SPEC Kit No. 1, 1973, and the updated edition, 1977) and analyzing trends since 1973.   Susan D. Herring

204. Rudolph, Janell, and Rebecca Argall. **Academic Libraries: Concepts and Practice.** Dubuque, Iowa, Kendall/Hunt Publishing, 1985. 122p. $8.95 spiralbound. ISBN 0-8403-3698-5.

Designed to be used in library instruction courses, this work presents a solid conceptual overview of information sources and search strategies in the academic library setting. The authors have arranged concepts in a somewhat logical manner, moving from books to periodicals to selected parts of books to fact sources to other sources of information to library search strategy.

Each section opens with an "Information Menu," a high-tech outline of the contents of that section, and tear-out worksheets are presented at the end of each section, providing reinforcement through structured exercises. Fortunately, the authors provide only the format of the exercise, leaving decisions regarding content to the individual instructor. Examples of completed worksheets are gathered together in a final section.

As a whole, the work is written in a clear, concise style, and in a language that should be easily understood by most first-year college students. As always, however, the concepts included will need reinforcement through interpretation and explication on the part of an instructor. In places, conceptual discussions and definitions are over-simplified (e.g., "A bibliography lists information sources on a subject or lists works by an author," p. 45). Many a bibliographer or librarian would disagree with this limited definition. Similarly, the explanation of dictionaries is too succinct. A discussion of nonprint media is much too brief, and lacks citation to pertinent bibliographic tools.

The authors might have included a "Suggestions for Further Reading" section, to amplify concepts introduced in the text. Recommended with reservations for entry-level orientation only. [R: JAL, Mar 87, p. 44]

Edmund F. SantaVicca

205. Thompson, Ronelle K. H., comp. **Friends of College Libraries.** Chicago, Association of College and Research Libraries, American Library Association, 1987. 134p. illus. bibliog. (CLIP Note, No. 9). $17.00pa. ISBN 0-8389-7171-7.

CLIP (College Library Information Packet) number 9 reports the results of a survey of 187 small college and university libraries to obtain data on friends of libraries groups: their history, constitutions, by-laws, brochures, programs, newsletters and other publications. The compiler is director of Augustana College's library, which received the 1987 Academic Friends Award given by Friends of Libraries U.S.A.

Library friends programs, one way to retain and develop alumni and other groups' interests in libraries, constitute an effective method to raise funds to supplement regular budgets. Nevertheless, only 33 of the 136 responding libraries (24 percent) have friends groups. The findings provide the following information—that the existence of a friends group is not tied to the size of an institution, founding dates range from 1937 to 1987, most groups have a governing board, and alumni and community members represent the largest percentage of membership.

Groups or individuals considering forming a friends of libraries group will find the examples of constitutions, publications, projects, etc., helpful and existing groups may pick up some new and useful ideas.

Helen Howard

COMPARATIVE AND INTERNATIONAL LIBRARIANSHIP

General Works

206. Harvey, John F., and Frances Laverne Carroll. **Internationalizing Library and Information Science Education: A Handbook of Policies and Procedures in Administration and Curriculum.** Westport, Conn., Greenwood Press, 1987. 391p. index. $49.95. LC 86-9946. ISBN 0-313-23728-X.

Despite its innocuous title, this book is a manifesto. The very first sentence is a ringing assertion: "As far as librarianship is concerned, nationalism is dead and internationalism has replaced it" (p. ix). The rest of the book is a collection of twenty-five papers which seek to justify the above statement and to indicate how schools of library and information science should and could implement internationalism in their administrative services and curriculum. The formal term which the book uses for such implementation is *internationalization*, and clearly internationalization means much more than offering an elective course in international librarianship. In fact, the authors want nothing less than to change "the management and courses of all schools" to the point where the students' most basic attitudes and competencies will fully reflect the international perspective.

This is an ambitious goal indeed, and I do not believe that the book achieves it. The key paper, Frances Carroll's "Case for Internationalization," does a very good job of indicating ideals and rationales, but it does not convincingly enough deal with and dispose of the major obstacle to internationalism: the fact that the great majority of library school graduates work in their own countries and can easily get by without caring or knowing much about libraries abroad. The same criticism applies, more or less, to all the papers which show the specifics of how internationalization is to be achieved in this or that course. Usually the authors' hopes tend to outstrip probabilities and thus even the most highly detailed blueprints are not persuasive.

Even so, this is a most welcome book. Most library school instructors recognize the need for expanding the horizons of their courses and students. Harvey, Carroll, and their twenty-six able collaborators will offer them welcome encouragement and often very useful specific guidance in meeting that need. [R: JAL, July 87, p. 179; LJ, Aug 87, p. 100; WLB, Sept 87, p. 81]

Samuel Rothstein

207. Haycock, Ken. **Annual Proceedings of the International Association of School Librarianship: An Author and Subject Index to Contributed Papers, 1972-1984.** Kalamazoo, Mich., International Association of School Librarianship, 1986. 1v. (various paging). price not reported.

This small index (thirty-two pages) lists in four columns to a page the authors, titles, subjects, and conference numbers/pages of the contributed papers, part of the *Annual Proceedings of the International Association of School Librarianship* from 1972 to 1984. It is divided into two sections: a subject index and an author index. There is no introductory or explanatory material included, which would have improved the index's usefulness. The binding is a spiral type, with clear though small print. The four-column approach does not allow the complete title to be included on the page; abbreviations and acronyms are used in the title, as well as in the subject headings. For libraries or librarians possessing copies of the *Annual Proceedings* and the contributed papers (1972-1984) this index may be helpful.

Susan J. Freiband

208. **IFLA Annual 1986. Proceedings of the 52nd General Conference: Tokyo, 1986 Annual Reports.** Willem R. H. Koops and Carol K. Henry, eds. Munich, New York, K. G. Saur, 1987. 234p. illus. $37.00pa. ISBN 3-598-20667-4.

Reading this volume is not nearly the same as having been in Tokyo at the annual meeting of IFLA, but it is a moderately good approximation of it—and as close as many of us will ever get. As such, it is a useful resource for keeping up with the wider world of librarianship, a world of surprising diversity and varying concerns. The editors and the IFLA Executive Board are to be commended for continuing to publish this series on a regular basis.

The work is organized in four major sections: plenary session papers; annual reports of officers and major program managers; annual reports and abstracts of program papers presented at sections, divisions, and roundtable meetings; and separate alphabetical listings of participants and speakers. The first section is interesting and gives a good overview of IFLA

activities, themes, new programs, etc., but the annual reports and abstracts of papers sections are the core of the volume. Because of IFLA's multitude of divisions, sections, and roundtables and also because this is where the real work of IFLA is done, these reports are the essence of IFLA and the profession worldwide. Here, one can find the most recent summary of IFLA (as well as related organizations such as UNESCO and FID) work on a wide variety of topics and problems. The abstracts of papers presented are particularly interesting but also somewhat frustrating because of the desire to have immediately available the entire paper. Fortunately, the annual does provide the last two sections to further identify the authors of papers and annual reports so that they can be contacted. Many papers are also submitted to the ERIC system and may be obtained in that manner.

Abstracts of most papers are presented in English but some do appear in the author's native language. While a number of abstracts of papers, as well as reports of sections, divisions, and roundtables are missing from the volume (not having been submitted by the required deadline), most do appear here. One hopes that IFLA will become more insistent on submission of reports so that the record of all areas will be complete.

Overall, the work is a good representation and summary of the worldwide state—and plans—of the library profession. The text is clear and readable and the paperback work is well constructed and presented by the publisher.

Robert V. Williams

209. Plumbe, Wilfred J. **Tropical Librarianship.** Metuchen, N.J., Scarecrow, 1987. 318p. index. $29.50. LC 87-19984. ISBN 0-8108-2057-9.

The book contains a collection of articles, speeches, papers, reports, and editorials previously published by the author while working, visiting, or consulting on library matters in countries in Africa, Asia, and South America. Plumbe's writings span three decades with most of his contributions published in the 1960s and only one published in the early 1980s. The articles were originally written "with the intent at the time of their publications to make tropical libraries better known to the rest of the world" (p. vii). The reader would have been better served if the author had provided a rationale for wanting to have old contributions republished almost two decades later. Furthermore, it would have been most useful for potential readers if the author had provided a comprehensive chapter describing contemporary issues in librarianship in the countries under discussion and established a relationship between the past and the present. The article on medieval Islamic libraries is a summary of what has been published before by scholars of Islamic history and culture and in *E. J. Brill's First Encyclopaedia of Islam, 1913-1936* (E. J. Brill, 1987). A good part of the information on Southeast Asia and Malaysia can be found in greater detail in *The Barefoot Librarian*, by D. E. K. Wijasuriya and others (Linnet Books & Clive Bingley, 1975). This book has very limited value—its contents lack depth, and it does not add new information to international librarianship or to librarianship in Asia, Africa, or South America.

Mohammed M. Aman

Asia

210. Handbook of Libraries, Archives & Information Centres in India. Volume 2: Libraries & Archives. B. M. Gupta and others, eds. New Delhi, Information Industry Publications; distr., Columbia, Mo., South Asia Books, 1986. 509p. index. $44.00.

211. Handbook of Libraries, Archives & Information Centres in India. Volume 3: Information Policy, Systems and Networks. B. M. Gupta and others, eds. New Delhi, Information Industry Publications; distr., Columbia, Mo., South Asia Books, 1986. 255p. index. $44.00.

Volumes 2 and 3 of the proposed seven volumes of *Handbook of Libraries, Archives & Information Centers in India* deal with libraries and archives and information policy systems and networks respectively. Volume 2 is divided into eight sections dealing with topics such as archives resources and administration; books, journals, and copyrights; public library service and library legislation in India; library literature in India; library management; related areas of library and information science; translation activities; and promotional bodies. Each section has many articles dealing with various aspects of the leading topic of the section written by well-known professionals. Many articles included in these volumes have been reprinted from other journals. Only a few of the reprinted articles were updated. Some of the articles on UNESCO and its activities do not fit very well in this volume.

Volume 3 is devoted to information policy and systems and networks. It is divided into two sections. There are only two articles on information policy in India in section one. The second section has fifteen articles on various aspects of national information networks and systems. All the well-written articles are by experts and have excellent up-to-date information on the topic.

The editors have certainly worked hard to prepare both volumes. One objection: the quality of the paper used for printing the volumes is not very good. In spite of this problem the material included in the volumes will be very useful to all libraries, librarians, library educators, and researchers interested in Indian librarianship.

Ravindra Nath Sharma

212. Kabir, Abulfazal M. Fazle. The Libraries of Bengal 1700-1947. London, Mansell; distr., Bronx, N.Y., H. W. Wilson, 1987. 181p. bibliog. index. $35.00pa. ISBN 0-7201-1839-5.

This is the first book of its kind on the history and development of the libraries of Bengal, an eastern part of British India, covering the period from 1700 to 1947. The book is divided into six chapters dealing with the early period of the history of British Bengal, including social and educational background and the beginning of libraries under British rule. Chapter 2 deals with the academic and research libraries. The author has dealt with the development of school, college, university, and other educational libraries such as the Asiatic Society Library. Kabir is of the view that "academic libraries passed through several phases of development but could never become entirely complementary to college education" though university libraries enjoyed better status in Bengal. In his view school libraries had a "painful existence."

Chapter 3 deals with the development of public libraries. John Andrew is regarded as the founder of circulating libraries in 1770, which led to the other types of libraries such as reading rooms and the community libraries outside Calcutta. The Calcutta Public Library was founded on 21 March 1836 and certainly had a very successful growth, including collections, services, circulation, and an increase in the number of patrons. Chapter 4 deals with other types of libraries called "special libraries," such as military, railway, prison, society, and church libraries. Chapter 5 throws light on library developments in the twentieth century, with emphasis on the Imperial (National) Library which was founded in 1902. It also deals with the library education training given by the Imperial Library and the contributions of the Bengal Library Association founded in 1925 to the development of libraries in the United Bengal. According to the author, 1920-1940 was the golden period for the growth of libraries in that region. He has linked the development of libraries with "the expansion and influence of the English" in India in general and Bengal in particular. Though the development was slow compared to Western standards, it must be noted that a firm foundation was laid during the period for future development.

A selected bibliography will lead scholars to further research. This is certainly a well-written book, with an overview of the growth and development of all types of libraries in the United Bengal before the partition of India in 1947, which divided the library resources of Bengal into two nations, India and East Pakistan (now the independent nation of Bangladesh). This book is recommended for all library school collections and others interested in the history of libraries in South Asia.

Ravindra Nath Sharma

213.   Sharma, Jagdish Saran. **Library Movement in India and Abroad.** New Delhi, Ess Ess Publications; distr., Columbia, Mo., South Asia Books, 1986. 224p. index. $28.00. ISBN 81-7000-016-5.

This is not, as the title appears to suggest, a comprehensive history of the library movement in India and abroad. It is a personal and professional autobiography of an eminent Indian librarian, library educator, and author of novels, works on library science, and bibliographies. As a graduate student in history at the University of Delhi, Sharma was so impressed with S. R. Ranganathan that he decided to become a librarian. In an extremely personal style, he gives an interesting account of his studies, first at Delhi, then at the University of Michigan, where he received both a master's degree and a doctorate in library science, and of his nearly forty years of service as librarian and library school director at several Indian universities as well as librarian and research officer for the All India Congress Committee. He describes in detail his struggle to reunite and to develop the Panjab University Library, which had been split between several cities after the partition of India. In a frank and candid manner, he discusses the development of India's national and regional library associations, evaluating their contributions and lamenting the factionalism that is rife in the Indian Library Association. He also presents his philosophy of librarianship, library education, automation, and library cooperation, and compares library education in several countries. The American reader should be aware that the book is written in the English of India. There are, unfortunately, a number of typographical errors. However, Sharma's intimate involvement with Indian librarianship makes this work a primary source of information and insight not available elsewhere, and, therefore, a very worthwhile addition to subject collections.

Shirley L. Hopkinson

214.   Sharma, Ravindra Nath. **Indian Academic Libraries and Dr. S. R. Ranganathan: A Critical Study.** New Delhi, Sterling Publishers; distr., Columbia, Mo., South Asia Books, 1986. 268p. bibliog. index. $28.50. ISBN 81-207-0153-4.

Among professional librarians worldwide there are at least two names that most are likely to recognize: Melvil Dewey and S. R. Ranganathan. Previous studies of these two librarians have shown that there are a number of remarkable similarities between these two giants of the profession. This volume is a study of Ranganathan's influence on Indian academic libraries and librarianship. It is an interesting study and well done in a number of areas but unfortunately it is not, as the subtitle indicates, a *critical* study of the role and influence of Ranganathan.

The work was originally a doctoral dissertation. The author is a native of India but is currently a director of an academic library in the United States. The study has five fairly distinct sections: purpose and methodology of study; brief overview of Indian academic libraries in ancient and medieval times; development of academic libraries under British rule (ending in 1947) and from independence to about 1980; analysis of the work and influence of Ranganathan on academic libraries; and consideration of the current problems facing Indian academic libraries and specific recommendations for overcoming them. Extensive footnotes follow each of the seven chapters and a selective bibliography and adequate index are provided.

The basic methodology employed in this study is an historical approach. In general, the process works well and the result is an interesting story told in some detail over the several different periods of library development. The author makes good use of secondary and primary sources, including some oral history interviews with Indian librarians. A number of different issues affecting the libraries over time are treated in some detail. These include trends in Indian higher education, governmental programs (particularly the role of the University Grants Commission) and studies, foreign assistance, library education and training, and the development of the library profession in the country.

Unfortunately, all these various parts do not make a good whole. The author set a variety of goals that do not match analytically, and none of them are satisfactorily answered. Five specific questions are posed: (1) Why did academic libraries develop as they did and play an important role in Indian higher education before 1924? (2) What was Dr. Ranganathan's influence on academic libraries and why did he emerge into such a unique position? (3) Has the progress of academic libraries since independence been adequate, and how can we measure it? (4) Are the college and university libraries meeting the 1959 standards? (5) Are Indian academic libraries still the weakest link in higher education, and what are their problems today?

The focal point of the attempt to deal with these objectives, however, is clearly Ranganathan. Approximately 70 of the 250 pages are devoted to the career and influence of Ranganathan. The author clearly and convincingly makes the point that "Ranganathan dominated Indian library science from 1924 to 1972 and created a new school of thought" (p. 131), but is not successful in telling us what this school of thought actually is and the impacts which it and Ranganathan himself had on academic library development. According to the author, academic libraries had an unimportant role prior to Ranganathan and are still the weakest link in Indian higher education. What is well documented is Ranganathan's role and influence in specific situations at specific times and, particularly, the universal importance of his ideas on classification. The author is not able, however, to get beyond near idol worship of Ranganathan and to probe both his ideas and his influence analytically. For example, the author reports distinctly critical comments about Ranganathan from Indian librarians only as quaint carping by the disaffected, and does not pursue them in any depth. Similarly, there is no analysis of the reasons for the rapid decline in Indian libraries of use of the Colon classification system developed by Ranganathan. And, without even the slightest doubt, the author continues to promote Ranganathan's "Five Laws of Library Science" as scientific empirical laws rather than a philosophy of librarianship.

This is a book worth reading and using because it provides good (and well-documented) details on the development of academic libraries in India and on the career of one of the world's most famous librarians. Analysis of the reasons for the failure of academic libraries as a vital link in Indian higher education and critical attention to Ranganathan's role and influence on Indian and world librarianship, however, are only hinted at here. Admittedly, the author is not alone in neglecting this kind of analysis; it is difficult work and has been done in only a few instances anywhere, and not at all for Indian librarianship. Robert V. Williams

215. Thuraisingham, Ajita, ed. **The New Information Professionals. Proceedings of the Singapore-Malaysia Congress of Librarian and Information Scientists: Singapore 4-6 September 1986.** Brookfield, Vt., Gower Publishing, 1987. 356p. illus. $77.95. ISBN 0-566-05519-8.

To promote modern librarianship and library cooperation in Southeast Asia, two well-respected regional conferences have been held at regular intervals since the 1970s. These are the Congress of Southeast Asian Librarians (CONSAL), held in rotation every two to three years among the five ASEAN countries (Indonesia, Malaysia, the Philippines, Singapore, and Thailand) and the Singapore-Malaysia Congress of Librarians, held every two years under the joint sponsorship of the library associations of both countries. Though regional in nature, both congresses attract many participants from countries outside the regions, and the proceedings have been distributed worldwide as important information sources on library development in the region.

The special focus of the 1986 Singapore-Malaysia Congress was "The New Information Professionals." In addition to the keynote address by a British university librarian, the proceedings contain twenty-five pages grouped under the following eight headings: "The Librarian and the Information Scientist"; "Technology and the Book Trade"; "The Information Media Professionals"; "Information and Library Consultancy"; "Computerized Information — Planning and Networking"; "Information Technology"; "Human Resources Planning and Development for Information Services"; and "Country Papers."

Although most papers concentrate on the experience of Malaysia and Singapore, three of the five country papers deal with Australia, New Zealand, and the United Kingdom. Six other papers are written by people from outside the region, mostly from Britain.

Similar to most conference proceedings, the papers vary in quality and relevance. There is an inconsistency in the placement of charts, diagrams, tables, etc. Some are retained in the text, while others are gathered together in an appendices section at the end of the proceedings with incomplete pagination. Probably the most serious problem with this proceeding is not its content but its pricing, which reflects the unreasonable pricing policies of many British publishers. The exorbitant price makes this otherwise valuable publication unaffordable for readers whom it might serve. Hwa-Wei Lee

Europe

216. Harrold, Ann, ed. **Libraries in Colleges of Further and Higher Education in the UK.** London, Library Association; distr., Chicago,

American Library Association, 1987. 87p. index. $17.50pa. ISBN 0-85365-717-3.

A work of limited scope which serves as a complement to *Libraries in the United Kingdom and the Republic of Ireland*, this volume aims to serve as a directory of academic libraries other than those located in universities and polytechnics (information encompassed by the above title). As such, it attempts to include colleges with broad-based curricula, as well as specialist colleges in such areas as drama, music, and agriculture. Arranged alphabetically by town, the main listing is supplemented by an index listing institutions by type or by broad subject specialization.

Information encompassed in individual entries includes the name of the institution, name of library, address, name of librarian, indication of site libraries, local authority (as applicable), and telephone number. Concise and compact, this directory will prove useful to fellow professionals in the United Kingdom. Usefulness beyond this audience will likely be limited. Edmund F. SantaVicca

217. Sciberras, Lillian. **A Marketing Tool for the Information Industry: Malta and Its National Bibliography.** Bradford, England, MCB University Press, 1986. 40p. maps. (Library Management, Vol. 7, No. 3). price not reported. ISBN 0-86176-292-4.

Here is a fascinating booklet with not the best of titles. It contains a great deal of information about the little-known country of Malta in the Mediterranean Sea.

This work is an excellent analysis of the development of a national bibliography in terms of demand factors within the book trade and within the library/education sectors. It also shows the important contributions of bibliographic control to national development and to the management of information industries.

In doing all of the above, the work provides the following information: a chronology of major library and bibliographic developments in Malta from 1555 to 1986, descriptive chapters on the social and cultural climate of Malta, a history of library development, a current survey of the book trade and the bibliographic habitats, and an examination of the background leading to the compilation of the pilot edition for 1983 of the *Malta National Bibliography*. There are informative charts showing data from the *MNB* and about the Public Library System and the University Library System in Malta.

This report was part of a submission for a master's degree at London University. The author is Deputy Librarian of the University of Malta. [R: LAR, Apr 87, p. 196]

George S. Bobinski

218. Stone, Sue. **A Review of User Related Research in Humanities Information.** Sheffield, England, Consultancy and Research Unit, Department of Information Studies, University of Sheffield, 1985. 51p. bibliog. (CRUS Working Paper, No. 1). £4.50. ISBN 0-906-088-224-18.

This report presents the results of a two-month study by the Centre for Research on User Studies (Department of Information Studies, University of Sheffield) on humanities scholars' information needs and uses. The project was supported by the British Library Research and Development Department. The aims were "to conduct a review of user-related research and development in humanities information, to find out, collate and consolidate what is known about the humanities user, and to identify possible areas for further research" (p. 1). The methodology involved extending an earlier literature review, paying particular attention to user interface with new technology, and use of abstracts, indexes, guides to resources, and other bibliographic guides. Qualitative interviews with a small number of scholars and librarians were also part of the project. The report includes nine short chapters presenting results of the interviews and analysis of the literature. Two of the chapters include concerns of the British Library Lending Division and Reference Division. One chapter focuses on questions raised by the project and areas for further investigation. An appendix lists some organizations and individuals mentioned in the literature. There is also a bibliography (unfortunately unannotated) which includes both British and U.S. publications, books, and journal articles. The report contains interesting and useful material for discussion and further research. It would be of primary interest to library and information science faculty, researchers, and students. Even though the context is British, the report would be an appropriate and valuable addition to library and information science collections in schools of library and information science.

Susan J. Freiband

COMPUTERS

General Works

PHILOSOPHY AND THEORY

219. Bishop, Peter. **Fifth Generation Computers: Concepts, Implementations and Uses.** Chichester, England, Ellis Horwood; distr., New York, Halsted Press/John Wiley, 1986. 166p. index. (Ellis Horwood Series in Computers and Their Applications). $31.95. LC 85-27337. ISBN 0-470-20269-6.

In spite of the enormous amount of publicity surrounding fifth generation computers, books on the subject tend to divide into popularized summaries or in-depth treatments of specific aspects. Bishop's book is aimed at giving persons who have some knowledge about computing and information technology an overview of each of the areas involved in fifth generation computing: artificial intelligence with special attention to knowledge-based systems and intelligent user interfaces, parallel processing and other hardware developments, and software engineering including a look at relevant procedural and nonprocedural languages. The major fifth generation initiatives in Japan, Europe, England, and the United States are surveyed, as are the potential commercial, military, educational, and other applications of the new technology. Most chapters have a dozen or so references and there is a glossary of approximately one hundred terms. Specialists will correctly complain that the author's chapters are too brief, but readers who are merely computer literate will find this a well-written overview of a significant subject.

Robert Skinner

220. Bjorn-Andersen, Niels, Ken Eason, and Daniel Robey. **Managing Computer Impact: An International Study of Management and Organizations.** Norwood, N.J., Ablex Publishing, 1986. 248p. bibliog. index. (Computer-based Information Systems in Organizations). $39.50. LC 85-30754. ISBN 0-89391-358-8.

This book is the result of a research project undertaken by Austrian, Danish, British, American, and German social scientists. Research was conducted at "eight very different organizations in five different countries" (p. 1). The report is technical, employing many tables and assuming knowledge of sociological terminology. I would definitely put this title in the circulating rather than the reference collection, and would recommend it for colleges or very large institutions only. The companies studied are decidedly not small businesses, including, among others, the third largest airline in the world, a hospital with a staff of thirty-five hundred, the second largest mail-order firm in Germany, and a food and household goods wholesaler with a staff of 270, the smallest firm surveyed. Topics of concern are the ways in which tasks were changed, how well the computer fit the manager's perceived needs, perception of the quality of training and support, the impact on leadership style and on organizational power systems, influence of different user types, and any actual changes in the formal organization structure. The implications for managers seeking to control computer impact are concluded to be major enough to include in the initial systems planning. As one would expect in a scholarly work, there are a detailed description of research methodology, a bibliography, and indexing by author and subject.

Susan V. McKimm

221. Capron, H. L. **Computers: Tools for an Information Age.** Menlo Park, Calif., Benjamin/Cummings Publishing, 1987. 654p. illus. (part col.). index. $29.95. LC 86-26420. ISBN 0-8053-2249-3.

This volume was designed as a textbook for an introductory course in electronic computing. A number of supplemental packages are also available from the publisher. These packages, listed in the book, consist of an instructor's guide, a student study guide, test banks, transparencies, and a variety of software-related documentation. The volume itself is an informative and tutorial introduction to computers, with particular emphasis on microcomputing. Each of nineteen chapters ends with a summary and list of key terms, as well as review and discussion questions. Two appendices provide an overview of BASIC programming and numbering systems used in computing. A glossary and index complete the volume. Full-color illustrations are provided throughout. The book is clearly written, logically arranged, and easily understood by the novice. The only thing lacking is a good bibliography, although some information sources are provided.

A number of textbooks of this type are available, but this has to be one of the most up-to-date and comprehensive overviews of the hardware and software field. The volume begins with an interesting overview of computers, including an excellent history. Subsequent chapters develop more specific aspects of computing for a variety of configurations and architectures, as well as an informative chapter of communications and networking. Software aspects focus on programming languages, database management systems, word processing, and spreadsheets. A buyer's guide is provided for personal computers. Chapters on related topics include information management systems, security, privacy, ethics, computer literacy, and systems analysis.

This first of what appears to be many editions is certainly worth considering as a textbook or for personal reading. At the price, it is a best buy.

Andrew G. Torok

222. Danziger, James N., and Kenneth L. Kraemer. **People and Computers: The Impact of Computing on End Users in Organizations.** New York, Columbia University Press, 1986. 268p. bibliog. index. (CORPS [Computing, Organizations, Policy, and Society] Series). $32.50. LC 85-29989. ISBN 0-231-06178-1.

Everything has its down side, even the new technology which makes it possible for the individual worker to do in seconds what previously took days or weeks. This research, funded by the National Science Foundation, examined over twenty-five hundred workers in public organizations (mostly local government) to discern the effects of automation on individual productivity, efficiency, and general morale.

Danziger and Kraemer are professors and research scientists at the University of California at Irvine. Their study asks whether the effects of computers on workers have been generally favorable or unfavorable, and discovers, not surprisingly, a mixed bag of results. Workers using a computer to do tasks once done manually may bless or damn automation, or may have mixed feelings (or no feelings) about it. Still, the general trend of all these responses is favorable and this book tries to discern something in all the data which will help the employee or company cope better with problems that come with computerization of tasks. It is the individual worker who is the focus of this study, which is refreshing after all the studies which assess the effects of automation on large companies. The end-user's interaction with machines, in dealing with information-related tasks, generally leads to enhanced productivity, but individual cases vary. A few cautionary notes are sounded in the conclusions about the clash of technology with people but, hey, we already knew that, right? A full bibliography follows the study, which is indexed and well arranged. Nothing surprising emerges from this report, but it contains generally sound, useful, and optimistic conclusions. What about libraries? In fact, they are hardly mentioned, but libraries with employees

who do not seem to accept automation may take heart from these general findings.

Bruce A. Shuman

223.   Fischler, Martin A., and Oscar Firschein, eds. **Readings in Computer Vision: Issues, Problems, Principles, and Paradigms.** Los Altos, Calif., Morgan Kaufmann, 1987. 800p. illus. bibliog. index. $28.95pa. LC 86-27692. ISBN 0-934613-33-8.

Computer vision is an emerging field that employs techniques from such diverse disciplines as physics, computer science, mapping, art, industrial technology, mathematics, education, and psychology. Basically, it deals with the way in which machines and sensors derive images similar to those perceived by the human eye. Important topics considered by the computer vision scientist are the way in which three-dimensional images are recovered from two-dimensional data, image segmentation, image addressing, and space/time imaging techniques. More basic research in the field looks at the way in which machines and humans store and trace visual images.

This volume is a collection of reprints of major research papers from journals, public and proprietary technical reports, and books in the field. The collection is arranged in seven segments or topics covering the basic problems in the field as outlined above. The work begins with an introductory 1982 review paper by Azriel Rosenfeld that surveys image analysis techniques up to that time. The bulk of the papers presented are from 1984, 1985, and 1986, although a few are earlier. As the papers are reproduced from camera-ready copy, they appear in a variety of formats. This results in text that appears sideways in the book, in double and single columns, and in a wide variety of typefaces. There are two appendices, covering key ideas and assumptions and parallel computer architectures in computer vision, an excellent glossary, and a good bibliography, covering from 1950 until 1987. The papers are indexed by the editors which adds immensely to the usefulness of the work. The volume is a rather large paperback book with an attractive cover. It is perfectbound, which may cause problems with preservation in the future. The material presented is at the cutting edge of information processing technology, and as such is rather advanced in thought and presentation. Libraries with patrons interested in computer vision, mapping, or artificial intelligence will want to own this volume.   Ralph L. Scott

224.   Novelli, Luca. **My First Book about Computers.** Redmond, Wash., Microsoft Press;

distr., New York, Harper & Row, 1986. 63p. illus. (col.). index. $9.95. LC 86-12831. ISBN 0-914845-85-3.

This is one of a series of three books published by Microsoft Press for children in the eight to ten age group. Originally published by Mondadori in Italy and translated into English by Laura Parma-Viegel, the series features amusing full-color cartoon illustrations. Children learn about computers as they follow the adventures of Wendy and Bill, their dog Field, and Andy, "a very personal computer." The book details the history of computers, from the advent of the Chinese abacus to today's high-tech Silicon Valley microchips, explaining such concepts as binary systems, computer languages, and memory, and defining terms such as *ROM, RAM, CPU,* and *BUS* along the way. Also explored are the current and future applications of computers in science, medicine, engineering, telecommunications, and architecture, and the uses of modems and data banks. The text concludes with a ten-point summary of the preceding chapters and an index.

In a day when children are introduced to computers in schools in kindergarten and first grade, one may question the appeal to sixth graders of a title beginning "My First Book ..." as well as the cartoon format. The interspersion of handwritten and typeset text is somewhat disconcerting and the writing is uneven. However, the text is informative, concepts are presented in a logical manner, and the eye-catching format should entice younger readers to explore the world of computers.

Micaela Marie Ready

225.   Radlow, James. **Computers and the Information Society.** New York, McGraw-Hill, 1986. 456p. illus. (part col.). bibliog. index. $28.95pa. LC 85-23057. ISBN 0-07-003901-1.

This book has lived up to its stated objective, "to be used for the introductory course about computers, their applications, and their societal impact" (p. xv). It is not a textbook for computer science majors, but for students in the liberal arts, business, or social sciences. Students in library and information science will also find the book very useful in their introductory courses.

The book covers many topics in its fourteen chapters and 441 pages. Among the topics covered are the impact of computers on individuals and on society as a whole, how computers work, historical and futurist looks at the computer, computer architecture, programming, artificial intelligence, computer networks, robotics, databases, word processing, networks, and graphics. The book closes with two chap-

ters, one on simulation and another on the problems and promises of the computer age. In all chapters, the subjects are treated in non-computerese, plain English language. The color pictures and graphics enhance the text just as the summary and questions for review and discussion at the end of each chapter serve to enhance the quality of presentation. The list of readings, glossary, and index constitute equally valuable contributions to the book.

A must-read for every beginner in library and information science programs and a valuable addition to every college and public library.

Mohammed M. Aman

226.   Yourdon, Edward. **Nations at Risk: The Impact of the Computer Revolution.** New York, Yourdon Press, 1986. 616p. illus. index. $19.95. LC 85-22618. ISBN 0-917072-04-9.

The author's thesis is that "because of the existence of computer technology, the country is at risk." In surveying the impact of the computer revolution, he presents an overview of computers and society in which issues such as the effect of computers on what and how children learn and the changing nature of the workplace are explored. Governmental use of computing and its role in supporting research are reviewed, as are issues of personal privacy in a world in which the individual is part of numerous databases used by many individuals for different purposes. The role of computing in business and its progress in assimilating computer technology are criticized because of the lack of planning which would result in integrated systems within companies. These and related issues are explored in varying depths, and predictions are made about probable directions that will be taken. Consequences of these directions are suggested. On this base the author discusses the computer industry and its projected growth, the current and projected development of hardware and software, and the relation of these developments to business, society, and government. References at the end of each chapter indicate that the author reads widely and has a good grasp of the issues discussed.

There is a danger in being both author and a publisher of a work in that one does not have the benefit of an editor whose role is to clarify and to cut. Despite its verbosity, its many opinionated statements, over-long explanations, and sermonizing, sufficient information and insights are present to make this a book worth reading. With good editing one would have had a much smaller but more readable presentation.

Ann E. Prentice

Reference Works

BIBLIOGRAPHIES

227. Kilpatrick, Thomas L. **Microcomputers and Libraries: A Bibliographic Sourcebook.** Metuchen, N.J., Scarecrow, 1987. 726p. index. $49.50. LC 86-31341. ISBN 0-8108-1977-5.

This annotated bibliography of nearly thirty-seven hundred entries of books and articles covers microcomputers in all types of libraries. The entries are divided into sixty-two specific categories listed in the table of contents. An index is also included.

The bibliography includes literature concerning the use of microcomputers for management and application purposes in academic, school, public, and special libraries. Although sixty-one journals, standard information science indexes, and online searches were scanned regularly, the author admits that he cannot claim comprehensiveness. However, this resource is an excellent, close-to-comprehensive bibliography of the literature on this topic published from the late 1970s to January 1986.

Microcomputers and Libraries is an excellent addition to any reference collection that is used for research. It is well organized and fairly complete through 1985. Though it will quickly become out-of-date, it will continue to be a valuable bibliography of the literature for research purposes. The cost is prohibitive for small libraries and school libraries, but the book should be considered for purchase by academic and public libraries.   Marie Zuk

BIOGRAPHIES

228. Cortada, James W. **Historical Dictionary of Data Processing: Biographies.** Westport, Conn., Greenwood Press, 1987. 321p. index. $49.95. LC 86-31805. ISBN 0-313-25651-9.

This volume is one of a trilogy; the other two volumes are subtitled "Technology" (see entry 230) and "Organizations" (see entry 229). Topics and people in the three volumes are tied together by a notational system: a single asterisk indicates that the topic is treated in the technology volume; two asterisks, elsewhere in the present (biography) volume; and a dagger, in the organization volume.

More than 150 individuals whom the author has identified as being key figures in the history of data processing are dealt with in some detail. Each article has bibliographical references appended. While one might quibble with a few of the selections (e.g., Fourier, the mathematician, and A. B. Dick, the mimeograph entrepreneur), most are indeed appropriate selections. The volume is exhaustively indexed, and two appendices list the biographees by birth date and profession.

This volume stands alone; the other two volumes, while perhaps useful, are not required to justify this handy compilation of brief biographical information about key figures in the history of computing and data processing. It is likely to find frequent use in most public libraries and in many academic libraries. [R: WLB, Nov 87, pp. 93-94]   Edwin D. Posey

DICTIONARIES

229. Cortada, James W. **Historical Dictionary of Data Processing: Organizations.** Westport, Conn., Greenwood Press, 1987. 309p. index. $45.00. LC 86-19394. ISBN 0-313-23309-9.

This book, the first of a three-volume set (the other two are subtitled "Biographies" [see entry 228] and "Technology" [see entry 230]), is intended to meet the real need for a reference work succinctly defining the history of computerized data processing. Rather than a "dictionary," as the title implies, it is an historical introduction followed by brief articles on more than eighty "organizations" central to the subject.

Unfortunately, the work is flawed by misleading language and factual errors. In the preface, for instance, it is stated that "in 1960 less than 10% of all workers used computers"; however, in the same paragraph, "in 1984 five out of a hundred (5%) had one (a computer terminal)." This declining percentage is quoted in support of the general theme of the paragraph, an increase of some 10 to 15 percent per year.

A glaring error is the attribution of the development of COBOL, an important high-level language, to the Digital Equipment Corporation, while it is a matter of record that the language was developed by the Codasyl committee of the Conference on Data Systems Languages in 1959. This committee comprised government and industry representatives. The historical introduction is also badly flawed—on page 2, for instance, we are told about "movable printing presses" (it is assumed that he refers to movable *type*).

To summarize, there are enough difficulties such as these to preclude a general recommendation in favor of the book. This is particularly unfortunate because there is a need for such a work delineating the relationships between the people, organizations, and technological innovations. The serious researcher will be better advised, however, to seek out more lucid treatments, such as the excellent book by Michael Williams, *A History of Computing*

Technology (Prentice-Hall, 1985). [R: WLB, Nov 87, pp. 93-94]   Edwin D. Posey

230.   Cortada, James W. **Historical Dictionary of Data Processing: Technology.** Westport, Conn., Greenwood Press, 1987. 415p. bibliog. $55.00. LC 86-22751. ISBN 0-313-25652-7.

This is the third of a three-volume set of dictionaries presenting historically relevant data for the study of data processing. (Other volumes are subtitled "Biographies" [see entry 228] and "Organizations" [see entry 229].) The author is senior marketing program administrator for the IBM Corporation and has to his credit a number of books and articles on the history and management of data processing.

Arranged in dictionary format, entries range from brief five-hundred-word essays to discussions several pages in length (e.g., artificial intelligence). Each entry ends with bibliographic references for further reading or investigation. No claim is made that this work is the definitive history of data processing; rather, it presents key issues in a wide range of topics including computer development, programming languages, narrative histories of individual computers, software, peripherals, applications, and so forth.

This volume is appended with an index and a chronology of the development of data processing, beginning with the abacus in ca.3000 B.C. and ending with the 1985 announcement of IBM's 3090 MYS/XA computers.

While the work is useful primarily to the nonspecialist, technical features of individual computers are elucidated through tables as well. This work is recommended for those secondary school libraries with substantive collections, as well as for public and academic libraries that wish to provide material for the generalist.
Cynthia A. Steinke

231.   Meadows, A. J., and others. **Dictionary of Computing & Information Technology.** 3d ed. New York, Nichols Publishing, 1987. 281p. illus. $33.50. LC 87-5468. ISBN 0-89397-273-8.

This latest edition contains several hundred new definitions and alterations to those previously used. Major topics are treated at length, with italicized references to subtopics. The definitions tend toward the succinct, and illustrations are used where deemed appropriate.

The fact that three editions have appeared in five years is testimony to the volatility of the field. This reviewer attempted to find several jargon terms just encountered, such as *compunications* (computer communications), and was successful in most cases.

The choice of companies and brand names seems rather arbitrary—IBM, of course, is included, but DEC (Digital Equipment) and other key players are omitted. Spot checking definitions for accuracy turned up only one that might be questioned—*virtual memory* is a considerably more complicated concept than externally linked storage.

This is a competently produced reference work covering a field of interest and importance to a large potential clientele, and should be acquired by most academic and public libraries. It is highly recommended.   Edwin D. Posey

232.   Rosenberg, Jerry M. **Dictionary of Computers, Information Processing, and Telecommunications.** 2d ed. New York, John Wiley, 1987. 734p. $34.95; $18.95pa. LC 83-12359. ISBN 0-471-85558-8; 0-471-85559-6pa.

The first edition of Jerry Rosenberg's dictionary of computer terms was deservedly well received and the second edition adds some two thousand new terms, bringing the total number of definitions to over twelve thousand. As compared to similar dictionaries, Rosenberg seems to be more current than most and to have better coverage. Definitions, where appropriate, are based on identified sources, such as the International Standards Organization's *Vocabulary of Data Processing*. I found no major omissions (minor ones include the computer languages Smalltalk and Modula-2) and definitions are accurate within the limits imposed by conciseness (which can sometimes alter meaning: does one really think of the BASIC language as used primarily for numerical applications?). The only large category of terms missing relate to specific computer or cpu models: that is, you will find no entries for VAX or the 80386 microprocessor chip. This is a justifiable omission, and one welcomes the inclusion of a considerable number of entries on telecommunications. As with the first edition, there is an international glossary of Spanish and French terms on the subject. Highly recommended.
Robert Skinner

DIRECTORIES

233.   **The Computer Phone Book: Directory of Online Systems.** By Mike Cane. New York, New American Library, 1986. 685p. $18.95pa. LC 85-15233. ISBN 0-452-25652-6.

The first edition of *The Computer Phone Book* was published in 1983 in a single volume. *The Computer Phone Book: Directory of Online Systems* is the second half of the second edition. The first half carries the title *The Computer Phone Book: Guide to Using Online*

Systems, and is a necessary companion to the directory volume for novice users. The directory volume alone is sufficient for the user already familiar with telecommunications and the protocols of bulletin board systems.

Included in this directory are listings for thirty national and fifteen local systems, chapters on how users should conduct themselves in using systems, advice to system operators, and a survey of new technology that will change the online landscape. The core of the work, however, is the listings and descriptions of over six hundred bulletin board systems in the United States and Canada. Each listing includes CPB number, telephone number, system name, bps rate(s), location, protocol, access requirements, software, features, special interests, message bases, downloads, fees, FTC, Sysop, and comments. The comments are informative, often entertaining, and sometimes contain hard-nosed evaluations. This work is indispensable for anyone with a computer, a modem, and curiosity about what is happening in the playful, often weird, and sometimes serious world of online bulletin boards.   Joe A. Hewitt

234.   **Computers and Computing Information Resources Directory: A Descriptive Guide to Approximately 6,000 Live and Print Sources of Information on General and Specific Applications of Computers and Data Processing....** Martin Connors, John Krol, and Janice A. DeMaggio, eds. Detroit, Gale, 1987. 1271p. $160.00. LC 86-27130. ISBN 0-8103-2141-6.

Users of Gale's valuable *Encyclopedia of Associations* will recognize the format of this work. While "print sources" in the subtitle are self-explanatory, "live" refers to people, singly and in groups, who can provide expertise, technical assistance, consulting, and advice. Arranged by type of information source, the work provides names, telephone numbers, and descriptions for over four thousand resource associations, user groups, and a few individuals who have (and will share or vend) important substantial information on computers and, generally, on automation.

Massive and impressive, this first edition of what promises to be an ongoing annual provides comprehensive coverage of the eight major types of sources of information about computers and computing (numbers approximate): 650 trade and professional associations and user groups; 1,450 consultants and consulting organizations; 900 research organizations and university computing facilities; 1,000 special libraries and information centers; 400 trade shows, professional exhibits and association conventions; 240 online services and teleprocessing net-

works; 1,300 journals and newsletters; and 250 directories.

With Gale's characteristic thoroughness, the volume is indexed in three different ways: by master name and keyword index, geographically, and by personal names, with entry number. A truly useful work, this should become standard for libraries and companies seeking expertise and know-how for their automation requirements. Highly recommended for all academic reference collections and for larger public libraries, as well. [R: Choice, June 87, p. 1528; JAL, July 87, p. 192; LJ, Aug 87, p. 115; RBB, 15 June 87, p. 1576; SBF, Nov/Dec 87, p. 67]   Bruce A. Shuman

235.   Dewey, Patrick R. **101 Software Packages to Use in Your Library: Descriptions, Evaluations, and Practical Advice.** Chicago, American Library Association, 1987. 160p. index. $17.95pa. LC 86-22310. ISBN 0-8389-0455-6.

As the author notes, this book "is the only low-cost library-related software directory in existence ... which tells very much about the software it inventories." All software in this directory is recommended and is related to library activities. The author, a public librarian with over ten years' experience in library computing, examined each software described here himself. The inclusions were selected after the author read many microcomputer and industry periodicals and software directories. The Apple II series and IBM PC were the primary microcomputers used in the review process, although where applicable, other versions of software are noted in the entries.

Each of the slightly more than 101 review entries includes information on the title, vendor, price, hardware requirements, uses in the library, grade level (when appropriate), capacity (when appropriate), description, nature and quality of documentation, similar or related programs, and additional sources of information. Entries are grouped by function of the software's application into the following chapters: acquisitions, bibliography, cataloging, children's services/library skills, circulation, communications and online database systems, database management, integrated software, interlibrary loan, miscellaneous programs, public relations, serials control, spreadsheets and statistics, training programs, utilities, and word processing. Each chapter begins with background comments and selection guidelines for the category of software described. Two indexes and several useful appendices conclude the volume, including a directory of library user groups, a vendor list, a hardware-software cross-reference, and a glossary. In all, software data are accessible by title, microcomputer vendor, and application. The introductory chapter also has short, helpful guidelines for selecting software, for selecting hardware, on "good work habits for good computing," and on basic computer care.

This is clearly a reference tool of many uses to librarians in all types of libraries, as well as to anyone looking for software to help organize and retrieve information files or create public relations materials. The valuable information is excellently presented in a readable and highly usable manner. Our colleague should be commended not only for giving us such a timely resource, but also for providing an exemplary specimen of a practical reference tool. [R: BL, 1 Jan 87, p. 682; JAL, 1 June 87, p. 88]

Danuta A. Nitecki

HANDBOOKS AND YEARBOOKS

236. **Computer Annual: Introduction to Information Systems 1987-1988.** By Robert H. Blissmer. New York, John Wiley, 1987. 503p. illus. index. (Wiley Series in Computers and Information Processing Systems in Business). $24.00pa. LC 84-649824. ISBN 0-471-83795-4.

This is the second edition of what is advertised as a computer annual, the first having appeared for the period 1984-1985. As the subtitle, "Introduction to Information Systems," indicates, the book covers the technological spectrum from history of computing devices through end-user systems and computers in society. The volume is divided into four sections containing fourteen chapters, covering getting started, using personal computers, computers and society, input, output, processors and memories, mass storage, systems analysis, software development, hardware development, communications, database management systems, trends in office automation, and artificial intelligence and robotics. A fifth section contains appendices on the evolution of computer systems, computers and careers, shopping for a personal computer system, and number systems. A glossary and a brief index complete the volume.

The book is intended for use as a textbook, with objectives, outlines, review questions, exercises, and annotated bibliographies provided, although the bibliographies taper off at 1985. Supplements such as an instructor's manual, transparencies, slides, and a test bank are also available. The structure of the volume is quite similar to *Computers: Tools for an Information Age*, by H. L. Capron (see entry 221). Both volumes are slick, well-produced publications containing numerous black-and-white and color photographs and illustrations. Blissmer's book

contains approximately 150 fewer pages and has more blank sections. Some sections are more elementary, although both volumes target introductory classes in computing at the high school or undergraduate college level. For the money, Capron's book offers more pages, but either book is a good value.

Andrew G. Torok

237. **Computer Buying Guide, 1987.** By John Fry, Sally Hughes, and Ron Mansfield. Skokie, Ill., Consumer Guide Books, 1986. 288p. $4.95pa. ISBN 0-451-14583-6.

Consumer Guide has published another in its series of helpful, clear handbooks designed to guide the consumer through the huge variety of products available in the marketplace.

This guide, encompassing computers, peripherals, and software, is intended for novice, experienced, and expert users. Computers included are priced up to the $5,000.00 range; peripherals, in general, must work with several popular systems; and software is mainly for IBM compatible or the Macintosh/Apple II series.

An introduction to the book also defines a computer system's components, and discusses the relative merits of buying from a department or computer store. Evaluations of products in the three major categories follow, which are further divided into types of products—computers by price range; peripherals into seven categories; and software into eleven categories, such as communications or entertainment software. A glossary of computer jargon, a guide to major electronic information services, and a directory of manufacturers complete the volume.

A brief description of each category precedes individual reviews, which attempt to give the reader a "hands-on" feel for the product. Reviews include the name, price, evaluation, and ratings. Although it is emphasized that all items listed are excellent buys, ratings cover the product's overall value, performance, ease of use, and documentation available.

Computer Buying Guide saves the consumer both time and money by doing preliminary comparison shopping in the formidable field of computers, peripherals, and software programs. As this field is also characterized by frequent change, currentness is essential, and regular updates would enhance the usefulness of this guide. [R: RBB, 1 Jan 87, p. 692]

Anita Zutis

Access Control

238.   Baker, Richard H. **The Computer Security Handbook.** Blue Ridge Summit, Pa., TAB Books, 1985. 281p. index. $25.00. LC 85-14750. ISBN 0-8306-0308-5.

This is not a scholarly work: there is no bibliography, the few citations are incomplete, numerous references are to newspapers and other secondary sources, and more detailed, less sensational information is widely available elsewhere. The author exploits an irrational fear that everyday computers will likely be broken into. Even his own statistics show the incredible improbability of that. Most of the book is obvious checklists, many "borrowed" from other sources. With better literature on the subject readily available, this book is not necessary.
Stan Rifkin

239.   Lobel, Jerome. **Foiling the System Breakers: Computer Security and Access Control.** New York, McGraw-Hill, 1986. 292p. bibliog. index. $34.95. LC 85-24161. ISBN 0-07-038357-X.

Remember the movie *War Games*? Chilling, right? Well, this book is for all concerned with what can be done to protect the integrity and security of computer systems, data, and programs, against a devious and shadowy enemy—unauthorized access. Alarmingly, however one attempts to protect data, hackers are out there, diligently chipping away at one's access codes and seeking illegal entry into one's data. Why? For profit, maybe, but sometimes for the challenge, or just for the fun of it, wreaking wholesale havoc in the data. Even more shocking, perhaps, is how often such computer crime is an inside job!

Lobel knows whereof he speaks: he's spent over sixteen years dealing with computer security problems on almost a daily basis. He writes in a refreshing, direct, and hard-hitting style, not only to inform but to persuade. Computer hackers, even teenaged computer hackers, he says, are not pranksters bent only on a little youthful mischief, nor are they Robin Hoods, ripping off villainous multinationals, who can well afford (and may even deserve) a little electronic sabotage. Hacking (security code breaking) causes harm, sometimes calamity, and must be prevented, or at least defended against.

In readable, nontechnical chapters, Lobel provides good, sound, and timely advice on how to identify potential weaknesses in one's computer security, how better to control access, how to create a clearance and classification system based on need-to-know, and, finally, some state-of-the-art security tools for maintaining

acceptable levels of information control. For effective countermeasures against intrusion on private and confidential computer-stored information, or for those just wanting a good read on a timely topic, this book is highly recommended; not in reference, though. Let it circulate.
Bruce A. Shuman

Databases

THEORETICAL ISSUES

240.   Alagić, Suad. **Relational Database Technology.** New York, Springer-Verlag, 1986. 259p. bibliog. index. (Texts and Monographs in Computer Science). $33.00. LC 85-32108. ISBN 0-387-96276-X.

In this college-level text, Alagić describes concepts which form the foundation of any relational database. He presents tools and techniques for analyzing and designing data models and for restructuring these models into abstractions or views to meet specified user requirements. Alagić instructs the reader in the use of the relational language SQL (Structured Query Language) by means of which data may be extracted from a relational database. All of the logical concepts and techniques presented are translated into mathematical formulas. Each concept and technique is accompanied by an easily understood example relevant to a real world situation such as lecture schedules in universities, or lists of employees or students. Some background in algebra and set theory is helpful to a good understanding of this text but, because of the numerous examples, not essential. Readers who are interested in the theoretical structure behind their favorite database management system, or in a more complete understanding of information systems in general, will be well rewarded for the rigorous intellectual exercise which a careful study of this text demands.
Margaret McKinley

241.   Ariav, Gad, and James Clifford, eds. **New Directions for Database Systems.** Norwood, N.J., Ablex Publishing, 1986. 269p. bibliog. index. (Computer-based Information Systems in Organizations). $39.50. LC 85-30785. ISBN 0-89391-344-8.

This anthology contains the revised version of papers presented at the 1984 GNAW symposium on New Directions for Database Systems. According to the preface (p. vii), the intended audience of this book is "researchers, practitioners and members of the business community interested in the shape of data management and database systems in the years to come." The fourteen chapters in the book live up to the title and are organized along four major themes which cover the major thrusts of contemporary study of database systems. The authors of the chapters focus on the key issues of data management in the future. Examples of these key issues are presented in part 1 and include the ongoing changes in the shape of database management systems, the role of databases as components of larger systems, areas where databases technology is being applied, new data models which will underline future attempts to manage data, contemporary issues in database research and applications, future database machine architectures, and Prolog as a database language. Part 2 brings together chapters on databases as system components. Richard Pick highlights some of the building blocks and capabilities that have been included in the design of a database management system that accomplished the goals of real-time query and had the ability to have updates performed by more than one user at the same time. The result was the PICK Open Architecture, providing easily used computing power for commercial applications. Chapter 6 describes building blocks for decision support systems, with particular emphasis on KnowledgeMan, which is an implementation of the notion of a generalized problem processing system (GPPS). Part 3 describes application areas and database techniques that could apply to data management problems. The three chapters in part 4 deal with new data models, including semantic models, which are collections of constructs to structure and access databases in a way that reflects the meaning "semantics" of the data. Clifford and Ariav of New York University survey "some theoretical and practical efforts which have been aimed at the problem of developing more powerful databases that address the fundamental organizing concept of time" (p. 184). The articles are clearly written and very informative. Most, but not all, chapters conclude with a statement on further research issues, a feature which many researchers as well as practitioners may find useful.   Mohammed M. Aman

242. Furtado, Antonio L., and Erich J. Neuhold. **Formal Techniques for Data Base Design.** New York, Springer-Verlag, 1986. 114p. bibliog. index. $24.00. LC 85-12633. ISBN 0-387-15601-1.

Discussion of formal techniques for designing or specifying the database components of information systems is the stated purpose of this book. The topic is presented from two approaches. One approach is "to specify data base applications subjected to integrity constraints," considered in a conceptual design framework. A second approach is "to specify features of data models to be used for adopting data base applications to computing environments."

The book's organization into two major parts reflects these two approaches. Part A adopts an "application-oriented approach" and distinguishes three levels of specification which are informally outlined and then examined in-depth in separate chapters. These include (1) the information level, using logical formalisms; (2) the functions level, using algebraic formalisms; and (3) the representation level, using a programming language formalism. The different approach used in part B involves "semantic data models," known as information models, which are oriented toward real-world phenomena. The following three models are discussed in separate chapters to illustrate widely used approaches to semantic modeling of information systems: (1) logical database model, (2) entity-relationship model, and (3) temporal hierarchic model. The authors note that "none of these approaches are able to handle information systems which deal with texts, pictures, voice and dimensional descriptions as they appear in text processing, graphics, audiovisual systems ... for example" (p. 48). The reader is often referred to appropriate literature consisting mostly of reported research, which is cited in a list of references at the end of the book. A subject index concludes the volume.

The treatment of the subject is formal and requires an ability to follow mathematical notations, to interpret model illustrations, and to understand basic programming principles. Theoretical foundations, clear definitions, and simplistic examples are used to develop the presented subject matter. Although the book might be used as a reference by those familiar with the concepts presented, it is intended to be a textbook for graduate courses on information systems and on databases. The main audience is advanced, technical students rather than interested generalists or reference librarians involved in service applications.

Danuta A. Nitecki

243. Ghosh, Sakti P., Yahiko Kambayashi, and Katsumi Tanaka, eds. **Foundations of Data Organization.** New York, Plenum, 1987. 638p. index. $97.50. LC 87-2440. ISBN 0-306-42567-X.

Data organization, a branch of computer science, is a relatively new field that includes database applications, models, and machines as well as traditional file organization. "In the last five years, data base processing has expanded from logical processing of information to the field of artificial intelligence, statistical processing of information and distributed data bases" (p. vii). The papers of the International Conference on Foundations of Data Organization held in Japan in 1985 provide a status report of major advances worldwide. The fifty-five papers divided into twelve subject areas were revised for publication in 1987.

Those presenting papers are representative of the worldwide community of computing and computer science. They are also representative of industry and the university. The level of presentation is for the researcher and the skilled practitioner. It is not for the beginner or the individual who wishes to have a quick overview of the latest developments in such areas as file organization or aspects of relational databases. For the informed individual with time and interest to read the papers and follow up on the generous references that accompany most papers, this is a useful presentation. Given that the papers were presented initially in 1985 and that the field is moving rapidly, they may already be archival.   Ann E. Prentice

244. Jones, J. A. **Databases in Theory and Practice.** Blue Ridge Summit, Pa., TAB Books, 1987. 324p. index. $28.95. ISBN 0-8306-2600-X.

First, a word about what this excellent book is and is not. It is concerned with large-scale databases as they are developed on large, mainframe computers. It does not deal with microcomputer database management systems nor with bibliographic databases of the kind supplied by DIALOG or BRS. The example used throughout is of a large bank with many branches providing a multitude of services and storing its information in a central computer. The author assumes some knowledge of data processing, data storage and access methods (although there is a short appendix covering this topic), and COBOL.

The book is in three sections. Part 1 examines the principal features of a database system, historical background, definitions, and data manipulation languages. Part 2 focuses on database administration and includes database design, security, privacy, recovery, backup, and maintenance. Part 3 describes various existing database systems such as CODASYL (the network approach), IMS (hierarchical approach), DMSII (a mixture), and relational databases. A brief appendix lists database software and the machines on which they run and there is a dictionary of about one hundred terms.

The writing style is terse and humorless but the author provides an extraordinarily good balance between theory and practice. The

theoretical material, which can be a bit difficult, is clarified with illustrations and practical examples from the bank model. It should be noted that the book was first published in Great Britain. This should make little difference to American readers, except for a few spellings and peculiarities of the British banking system. All in all, this is an excellent book for anyone wishing to learn more about how to develop large databases.   A. Neil Yerkey

245. Kim, Won, David S. Reiner, and Don S. Batory, eds. **Query Processing in Database Systems.** New York, Springer-Verlag, 1985. 365p. index. (Topics in Information Systems). $32.50. LC 84-20274. ISBN 0-387-13831-5.

This is an anthology of reported research and development in database query processing. It is the second book of the Topics in Information Systems series which intends "to report significant contributions on the integration of concepts, techniques, and tools that advance new technologies for information system construction." Specifically, the volume deals with database and programming language concepts, artificial intelligence and database techniques, and database system tools.

During the past decade, research in query processing has extended in several directions, which are reflected in this book's articles. The eighteen contributed articles are organized into eight sections, beginning with an introductory survey of research results in query processing. Section 2, "Query Processing in Distributed Database Management Systems" (DBMS), contains three papers, including an overview of the R* distributed relational DBMS. Section 3 contains two papers on multimodel query optimization. One paper makes up section 4 on view update. The next section consists of three papers which describe data access problems imposed by different special applications (e.g., for engineering, knowledge-based, and statistical databases). Section 6 presents three papers examining techniques for optimizing the processing of multiple queries. Two database machines are discussed in the two papers of section 7. Finally, section 8, on physical database design, comprises three papers. Lists of references and authors and a subject index conclude the volume.

The articles are technical discussions, requiring a fairly high level of sophistication in understanding systems design and varied technological environments. The papers are presented in individualized camera-ready copy form, with abstracts and with collectively cited references. The international list of authors represents academic departments of electrical engineering, computer science, and business administration, as well as commercial research corporations, including several laboratories of IBM Research.

The target audience for this volume definitely is composed of the author's peers, advanced students, and researchers. This is not a general reference tool, except perhaps for the supportive collection of highly specialized, technical engineering research or systems design activities. Danuta A. Nitecki

246. Oxborrow, Elizabeth. **Databases and Database Systems: Concepts and Issues.** Bromley, England, Chartwell Bratt, 1986. 254p. index. bibliog. £8.25pa. ISBN 0-86238-091-X.

Elizabeth Oxborrow, associated with the Computing Laboratory of the University of Kent, Canterbury, has written this textbook for computer science students as part of the publisher's student text series. The volume is a comprehensive, but basic, introduction to the field of databases and database systems. It is relevant to library science because it covers the theoretical aspects of database conceptualization and implementation which are now so much a part of day-to-day library work. Furthermore it uses an automated library system as the major example to illustrate the ideas presented. (An approach used by at least two other authors of database introductions, Goldstein and Howe.) The author has successfully presented the basic concepts and mentions current research and areas of controversy. Coverage includes database systems, concepts and architecture, data modeling, database design, database query languages, database management systems, distributed systems, and new directions. While the writing is on the whole clear, the text suffers from two stylistic problems. It overuses the technique of foretelling about the contents of the chapter or next section. Furthermore, in the course of discussing a topic, terms or ideas are mentioned but detailed discussion is postponed until later in the text. As a result, space is wasted and the writing is stilted. A good bibliography of recent books and important review articles is included. Stronger editing before publication of a second edition is called for, and with questions or problems at the end of each chapter this would be a more competitive textbook. Thomas G. Kirk

247. Soergel, Dagobert. **Organizing Information: Principles of Data Base and Retrieval Systems.** Orlando, Fla., Academic Press, 1985. 450p. bibliog. index. (Library and Information Science). $55.50; $28.00pa. LC 83-15741. ISBN 0-12-654260-0; 0-12-654261-9pa.

As noted in the preface, "this book gives a theoretical base and a perspective for the analysis, design and operation of information systems, particularly their information storage and retrieval (ISAR) component, whether mechanized or manual." The principles discussed apply to the design of new systems and to the evaluation and upgrade of existing ones. These principles can support the efforts of managers, researchers, and engineers; inform the public; and provide a base for an artificial intelligence program.

The book is organized into five parts. Part 1 describes, from the systems approach, what the nature and structure of information and information systems are. Part 2 considers the objectives of ISAR systems in light of assessed user problems and needs. Part 3 deals with necessary rules in an ISAR system (data schemas and structures), with the logical representation of data and with structures for providing access to data. Part 4 examines index language functions and structures in terms of their concepts and database organization, and brings attention to subject retrieval in the process. Part 5 discusses the operation design and evaluation of indexing and searching systems.

The bibliography is exhaustive and is organized into two parts. Part 1 cites textbooks, readers, handbooks, and journals by topic. Part 2 offers a selected list of further readings for each chapter in the book. Reviews known to the author are referenced and several brief annotations are included. An author index and subject index (for the text as well as the bibliography) conclude the volume.

Written by a professor of library and information services, the book evolved from lectures and is intended primarily as a textbook in an introductory course on organizing and retrieving information. It also will be of interest to practitioners looking for more theoretical background for work in information science. The text is well organized and supported by clear examples, and specific concepts are clearly defined. Although its primary purpose is that of a textbook, the book may serve as a reference tool with easy access to explanations and definitions through the classified index offered by the table of contents and the cross-referenced subject index. The readership outside librarians and information scientists may include graduate level students, researchers, or managers in related fields such as business or journalism.

Danuta A. Nitecki

248. Speirs, Neil. **The Search Preserve Us: A Guide for Australian Database Builders.**

Hawthorn, Australia, Australian Database Development Association, 1986. 54p. $37.50pa. ISBN 0-9590967-1-X.

As one of the few guides to the perils of attempting to construct a database, this informative and entertaining Australian guide to that subject deserves a wide audience. It is by no means limited to constructing a database in Australia, although it naturally gives due recognition to the peculiar problems of building one in that particular country especially in light of its relatively small population and potential user base. Instead, this slender volume offers some excellent and direct commonsense advice to all who would contemplate such a venture. After making sure that the basic question of why one might build a database is satisfactorily answered, Speirs carefully examines questions of design, the gathering of material, equipment, data preparation and entry, distribution, support and care, and marketing. His good humor and sharp wit highlight some of the particular problems of such endeavors neatly. In considering why one might build a database, for example, he offers an analysis based on motives that include empire building, sheer altruism, blind enthusiasm for the subject, profit, and status in the profession. Always taking a cautious, conservative approach, without at the same time unduly dissuading the would-be entrepreneur, Speirs almost ensures that those foolhardy enough to construct a database will do a reasonably good job if only they follow his words of wisdom. This is the most practical guide to the most complex subject that one could imagine.   Norman D. Stevens

249. Tay, Y. C. **Locking Performance in Centralized Databases.** Orlando, Fla., Academic Press, 1987. 126p. bibliog. index. (Perspectives in Computing, Vol. 14). $19.95. LC 86-47916. ISBN 0-12-684400-3.

This is a technical research monograph in the Perspectives in Computing series from Academic Press. This monograph deals with performance issues in centralized database design. Though most of the materials have already been published elsewhere, the collection of these topics together in the present form further strengthens the interdependency of the subject matter. The primary topic covered in this monograph is the performance of concurrency control in the no-waiting case and the waiting case. In the present form, the author is able to present more fully the model used, the derivation of the analytic equations, and the simulation results. This monograph is highly technical in nature and is of interest to professionals involved in the design of centralized databases.

It is also useful as a technical reference for graduate studies.   John Y. Cheung

APPLICATIONS

250. Judge, Peter, and Brenda Gerrie, eds. **Small Scale Bibliographic Databases.** Orlando, Fla., Academic Press, 1986. 198p. index. (Library and Information Science). $29.95. LC 85-73034. ISBN 0-12-391970-3.

This source examines principles and asks specific questions which readers may wish to ask themselves when considering whether to develop a database. The eleven chapters are written by experts in database development and management from Australia and the United Kingdom. No specific hardware or software is used to develop the basic concepts of this book; the authors hope it will be both timely and timeless. The specific areas covered are (1) the small-scale database; (2) a general overview of a database system; (3) software options; (4) hardware options; (5) management, control, and cost benefit; (6) staffing and other management questions; (7) management with a DBMS; (8) input processing and editorial responsibilities; (9) subject control; (10) document acquisition and selection criteria; and (11) the future.

There are excellent charts and graphs located throughout the book. It concludes with a simple but accurate index. At the end of each chapter there are bibliographies and recommended readings, which are generally up-to-date. There were few entries from 1984-1985, but this might be because of the emphasis on 1978-1983 regarding database concept development.   Thomas L. Hart

251. Killen, Diana, ed. **Directory of Australian Databases.** 2d ed. Hawthorn, Australia, Australian Database Development Association, 1986. 238p. index. $40.00pa. ISBN 0-9590967-2-8; ISSN 0817-3214.

Since Americans, in our usual parochial fashion, tend to think of databases as our own invention and our preserve, it is startling to see and realize the extent to which substantial database development is occurring in other countries. The second edition of the *Directory of Australian Databases* is an excellent case in point. It lists and describes some 182 online databases, of which 160 are currently publicly available. That is a 130 percent increase over the figures reported in the first edition of this directory in late 1984, and an impressive array. For each database is provided name, producer, host, access, type, data source, descriptors, time span, size, update frequency, associated publication, staffing, cost, and characteristics. The available databases cover almost every imaginable subject from legal information, indexing and abstracting services in several fields, national bibliographic data, and census data to tourism. Comparatively speaking the coverage represents a major start to a comprehensive online national information system. In addition to the guide itself, this volume contains useful information about Australian database development, major Australian database vendors, and the Australian Database Development Association. It demonstrates the need for and utility of the companion volume, *The Search Preserve Us* (see entry 248), also issued by the Australian Database Development Association. Although direct online access to these databases from the United States is obviously limited for most potential users, it is useful to know the kinds and sources of online information that are available from Australia. [R: JAL, July 87, p. 186]

Norman D. Stevens

252. Popovich, Charles J. **Business and Economics Databases Online: Environmental Scanning with a Personal Computer.** Littleton, Colo., Libraries Unlimited, 1987. 276p. index. (Advanced Online Searching Series). $35.00pa. LC 87-2672. ISBN 0-87287-454-0.

The curious subtitle may be misleading. It refers to the social, technological, economic, and political environments in which an organization operates, with "scanning" used to describe the online method of exploring these factors. This manual is designed for the beginning or less experienced searcher who needs to be guided step-by-step from log-on to log-off in databases with business or economic interest. The work limits itself to those bibliographic business databases supplied by DIALOG and the economic and statistical databases available from I. P. Sharp, a Canadian vendor. Communication software such as SMARTCOM II and MAGIC, which are used to access these databases is also described. The work is concerned not only with bibliographic databases, but also with numeric databases, and the charting and graphing of these data are shown using LOTUS 1-2-3. This section in particular should hold the interest of the advanced searcher who is experienced beyond the scope of the early chapters but needs more practice with LOTUS and data manipulation. The appendices pinpoint and describe the specific business databases for both vendors, and there is also an index. This work is not a "reference" book; it is more useful as a textbook or manual to train searchers. Much of the information herein can be found in various sources most likely already owned by libraries which presently offer data-

base searching, but this source may be more convenient for the user. [R: RQ, Fall 87, p. 149]

Gary R. Cocozzoli

Microcomputers

253. Bodner, Michael Simon. **Micro to Mainframe Data Interchange.** Blue Ridge Summit, Pa., TAB Books, 1987. 273p. index. $24.95. LC 87-18006. ISBN 0-8306-2940-8.

This book deals with the problem of transferring (importing/exporting) data between programs or computers with differing data format requirements. The choices may be to retype the data, use packages like dBASE III (registered trademark of Ashton-Tate) or LOTUS 1-2-3 (registered trademark of Lotus Development Corp.) which have built-in import/export utilities, purchase a program especially written to convert data, or write a custom program. Using examples from business, the author leads the reader through each of these choices. Although the primary focus is on micro/mainframe interchange, much of the information applies also to micro/micro interchanges. The first chapters provide a cursory review of the basic concepts of information processing and an extensive treatment of the concepts of data communication. This is followed by descriptions of import/export utilities in existing microcomputer software and commercial stand-alone conversion programs. There is a chapter on data security and integrity which seems a bit out of place here. The last chapters describe a set of programs written by the author (in BASIC and dBASE III) to effect interchange. The complete set of nine programs, including a user manual, is included.

The descriptions of existing commercial programs and utilities will quickly become outdated, although the concepts which they illustrate may not. A more serious problem is that the final chapters are so much tied to the author's own programs that one wonders if the book is not being used to market his consulting service. Although he invites readers to use the programs freely, one is put off by the prospect of having to type seventy pages of BASIC code. Fragments from these programs are used as illustration, but they are very complex and more confusing than helpful. Still, the book provides a wealth of information on data interchange and is well worth the time it takes to study it carefully.

As this book gives only the briefest treatment of physical linkages and hardware requirements, it will need to be supplemented by others. Two recent books which concentrate on hardware and management aspects of establishing micro/mainframe networks are Ronald

Kopeck's *Micro to Mainframe Links* (McGraw-Hill, 1986) and Mathias Jarke's *Managers, Micros and Mainframes: Integrating Systems for End Users* (Wiley, 1986). Jeff Walden's *File Formats for Popular PC Software* (Wiley, 1986), which focuses on micro/micro interchange, would be a useful companion to this one.   A. Neil Yerkey

254. Bodner, Michael Simon, and Pamela Kay Hutchins. **Microcomputer Applications Development: Techniques for Evaluation and Implementation.** Blue Ridge Summit, Pa., TAB Books, 1987. 239p. index. $24.95. LC 86-30008. ISBN 0-8306-2840-1.

The microcomputer revolution has placed sophisticated yet inexpensive hardware and software within the reach of virtually every employee. This has occurred within the past decade, and very few of the potential users or their employers have the expertise to purchase an appropriate system, let alone use it effectively. This book is written for computer consultants who aspire to bring the revolution to the masses by identifying for the user what is available and how it can be used, at what price. The reader is presumed to be competent in computer science and emphasis is placed on the business, legal, marketing, and personnel aspects of consulting while providing a current (as of 1986) review of products and configurations that can be used in computerizing an operation.

No typographical errors were found, but computer dictionaries that proof text are presently incapable of editing unintended but validly spelled words—"please" should be "place" on page 54. The three-page project agreement contract example is repeated virtually verbatim in the case study chapter. Flow charts, common to mainframe codewriters, are deemed unnecessary for micros, and extensive documentation of code is mandated to allow team projects and easy revision.

The book is interesting and informative. The authors are convinced that there is a market for entrepreneurs capable of bringing computing to the masses, and this book provides a useful guide to anyone possessing the skills and optimism needed to function in that capacity. The media have touted the low cost and user friendly features of computing, but there are formidable problems for the uninitiated, and this book will help the computer tyro make the hype a reality.   Marvin K. Harris

255. Burton, Paul F. **Microcomputers in Library and Information Services: An Annotated Bibliography.** Brookfield, Vt., Gower

Publishing, 1986. 1v. (various paging). index. $35.50pa. LC 86-14913. ISBN 0-566-03540-5.

This bibliography of six hundred English-language references is drawn from library literature. Materials are included through October 1985 and comprise books, journal articles, and proceedings. These citations are categorized into twenty-four sections. The first eight sections deal with general information such as guides to the selection of microcomputers, hardware, and software; public use of micros; school library use; and computer literacy. The remaining sections consider specific applications such as acquisitions, information retrieval, circulation, and serials control. The annotations are descriptive and nonevaluative, and usually run between one and three sentences in length. Both subject and author indexes are provided.

The one weakness is a minor distraction concerning the style of the citations. There is no use of underlining, capitalization, quotation marks, or boldface print to differentiate among articles, journal titles, and book titles. The date of issue of a magazine is never included, just the volume, issue number, and year. This could make retrieval difficult for those items which are not paged continuously. Despite this fault, the bibliography is a worthwhile acquisition for librarians using or contemplating using microcomputers in their libraries.

Gary R. Cocozzoli

256. **Cahners/Bowker MMP 1987: Microcomputer Market Place.** New York, R. R. Bowker, 1987. 1115p. $95.00pa. ISBN 0-8352-2267-5; ISSN 0000-0884.

This directory is devoted to those companies which produce, distribute, or service microcomputer hardware, software, or peripherals, including CD-ROM. The work follows a pattern: an alphabetical list of companies is followed by an index or rearrangement by product rendered. There are no names of actual software packages or specific products, only general interest areas such as accounting or dot-matrix printers.

The 4,179 companies in the first list are software firms. In addition to the usual directory elements, information is provided on the number of software products published; general areas which these cover; operating systems which are supported; and whether or not outside authors may submit software, including contact person and guidelines, if any. This section is indexed by which company supports which microcomputer system (brand name, such as Radio Shack, Kaypro), operating system (AppleDOS, Unix), business or professional applications, educational applications, and consumer applications. The next major section provides profiles on 1,379 distributors, wholesalers, and mail-order houses, with information on the number of employees; annual sales; product categories; numbers of companies and software products represented; numbers of suppliers, microcomputer systems, and peripherals; and the number of sales representatives. This section is indexed by state.

Listings of microcomputer manufacturers, CD-ROM manufacturers, peripheral manufacturers, and supplies for computers are next, with the latter two indexed by the type of product made (e.g., joysticks, modems). Two sections which may also prove particularly useful are the lists of computer magazines, with price, frequency, circulation, and description of scope and area of interest, and the list of computer associations representing educational, nonprofit, and trade groups. The officers, number of members, site, and date of upcoming conventions, and a description of group interests, are included. The lists of CD-ROM special services are given by type of service, name of company, and by activity (e.g., consultants, market research). Companies which provide maintenance, software support, or consulting are listed next. The final list is a month-by-month survey of conferences, meetings, and exhibits planned in 1987.

The final section is a "telephone book" of twenty-three thousand organizations and personnel which includes address and telephone numbers (including toll-free where available). Names are coded with the area or areas of interest or specialization of the company or person.

This compilation is a massive undertaking and will find its use in larger libraries, and in those collections supporting promoting sales and business aspects rather than home and consumer aspects of computing. [R: RBB, 1 Jan 87, p. 694]   Gary R. Cocozzoli

257. Crawford, Walt. **Common Sense Personal Computing: A Handbook for Professionals.** Ann Arbor, Mich., Pierian Press, 1986. 204p. bibliog. index. (Common Sense Computing Series, No. 1). $24.50pa. LC 86-15074. ISBN 0-87650-218-4.

This collection of essays is an outgrowth of a series of articles from *Library Hi Tech* magazine. Some articles have already appeared there and in *Information Technology and Libraries.* With these articles, the author pleads with potential computer users to use common sense about any computer purchase. He warns that pragmatism and skepticism must take precedence over sales pitch.

The two introductory chapters explain concepts and ask readers to assess what, if any, their needs may be that would truly require or be improved by owning a computer. Some thoughts on what being "computer literate" means, or should mean, are included. The rest of the essays are grouped into three main sections: hardware, software, and aspects of buying and using a personal computer. The internal workings and external attributes of computers, printers, and other elements are described and put into perspective in the hardware chapters. The software section includes tips on selecting word processing, file management, telecommunications, and public domain and utility programs. The last section includes a purchaser's checklist, an assessment of microcomputer magazines, and consideration of the value of user groups. The glossary of computer terms is more lucid than many, and contains a great number of words that those new to computing will need to know. There are an index and a short bibliography.

The style and subject matter make this collection enjoyable to read for beginners as well as for advanced users. The word *professionals* in the title may be misleading for some readers: it merely indicates that the essays will not include information on games and educational programs, but on using the computer as a tool for task accomplishment.

The honest, practical approach of the author is as refreshing as it is informative. This collection can be recommended for most libraries where there is an interest in computing.
                    Gary R. Cocozzoli

258. Curtis, Howard, ed. **Public Access Microcomputers in Academic Libraries: The Mann Library Model at Cornell University.** Chicago, American Library Association, 1987. 211p. index. $14.95pa. LC 86-22315. ISBN 0-8389-0464-5.

The increasing importance of microcomputers on university campuses has led several academic libraries to provide computing resources for patrons. In this book, the staff of Cornell's Mann Library discusses their experiences in starting and maintaining a public access microcomputer center. The authors attempt to generalize from their experience and to focus on matters which are of common interest to any library considering opening a similar center, but the emphasis is almost exclusively on the Mann Library.

A good selection of topics is covered. The book stresses the importance of planning, policy, and staffing; the practical problems of collecting and organizing software; and the opportunities for user education. Despite the emphasis on practical details, some additional information regarding the physical facility would be helpful, such as the square footage allocated for each student workstation, the area needed for staff, and the total size of the center. Sections on software selection and user instruction are much more extensive and useful than the section covering hardware and facilities. Policy questions are considered in detail, and the discussion of copyright is both practical and thought provoking. Unfortunately, the scanty notes and lack of a bibliography weaken the book's usefulness.

This is valuable as a case study of one library's experience and will be very helpful for those considering initiating a public access microcomputer center; however, it cannot serve as a primary resource for most readers. [R: JAL, Sept 87, p. 232]   Susan D. Herring

259. Emmett, Arielle, and David Gabel. **Direct Connections: Making Your Personal Computers Communicate.** New York, New American Library, 1986. 316p. illus. bibliog. $22.95pa. LC 86-5258. ISBN 0-452-25649-6.

The subtitle of this "how-to" volume indicates the practical nature of the contents. In fourteen chapters, the authors present methods which allow different kinds of personal computers to communicate. Following the easy to read instructions, computer users can transfer data between systems regardless of the hardware configuration. The first seven chapters discuss computer basics, how computers differ, and the role of modems. Chapter 8, on modern connections, is the essential guide which allows the user to apply various case studies to connect modems (e.g., IBM PC to Apple IIe or Kaypro to Apple IIe). Chapter 11 details direct connections (e.g., Apple Macintosh to Radio Shack TRS-80 Model 100). Other chapters are brief comments on file compatibility, networks, and linking micros to the mainframe. The eight appendices are also practical guides, including an ASCII code chart and a brief directory of communications software vendors.

The volume is not written for the novice, but individuals familiar with personal computers will find it a useful guide. Written in a straightforward style, *Direct Connections* is designed for varied computer applications where the case studies apply. Expensive for a paperback.   Boyd Childress

260. **Essential Guide to Apple Computers in Libraries. Volume 1: Public Technology: The Library Public Access Computer.** By Jean Armour Polly. Westport, Conn., Meckler, 1986.

169p. illus. index. $19.95 spiralbound. LC 86-17929. ISBN 0-88736-049-1.

This guide is packed with useful information written in an easy to read, enjoyable style. The work grew out of the practical experience the author accumulated in the process of building a free computer usage program for patrons in a public library. This experience included a survey of access to computers in one hundred public libraries. The survey is used as a basis for much of the information presented throughout the guide. Although the guide discusses only Apple computers, much of the information is valuable to any library planning to offer computer services, regardless of the kind of hardware used.

The contents include hardware set-up and maintenance, acquisitioning and technical processing of computer programs, management of services, training library personnel to deliver services, and user policies. The illustrations are appropriate and make the text clearer. The practical nature of the guide is illustrated by the number of programs recommended in the chapter on collecting computer programs. The guide provides a list of titles that would provide a good beginning collection for any public library. In conclusion, the guide provides excellent information helpful to any public library planning to offer free access to computers.

William E. Hug

261. **Essential Guide to Apple Computers in Libraries. Volume 2: Hardware: Set-up and Expansion.** By Jean Armour Polly, Larry Polly, and Rick Fensterer. Westport, Conn., Meckler, 1987. 224p. illus. index. $24.95 spiralbound. LC 86-17929. ISBN 0-88736-075-0.

The Apple II family (II+, IIe, and IIgs) plus a Macintosh are commonplace in many libraries as mix and match machines; however, each has its own unique setup procedures, transferability potential, and quirks. This publication does what individual manuals for each of the machines does not—it compares the basic principles of hardware configuration and operation for all the machines.

The authors of this volume have managed to include a wealth of information on the disk operating system, monitors, printers, modems, the AppleTalk Network, interfacing, and troubleshooting, and they have done so in a succinct, readable manner. The text is packed with illustrations, examples, and specific problems that can occur in any computer set-up. Both Apple and third-party hardware are covered up to 1987. The authors provide sensible advice and lead the user through the maze of competing commercial products as only experienced users can do.

David V. Loertscher

262. Essential Guide to the Library IBM PC. Volume 4: Data Communications: Going Online. By Robert F. Jack. Westport, Conn., Meckler, 1987. 245p. bibliog. index. $24.95 spiralbound. LC 85-10535. ISBN 0-88736-036-X.

Jack has written a very informative first guide to the online world for the librarian. In six interestingly written chapters, he covers data communication, hardware and software consideration, going online, searching, postprocessing, and "everything else." Six appendices provide an excellent reference tool for the beginner for access telephone numbers, communications software, reference sources, and other helpful information.

This book is a good introductory manual, providing a basic review for the person who is now doing online searches, but does not understand what really happens in a technological sense. There are a number of excellent books on the market which describe the online world in general, but Jack orients his writing to the library online world, making this manual a good introduction to others. Highly recommended.

David V. Loertscher

263. Essential Guide to the Library IBM PC. Volume 6: Spreadsheets for the IBM: A Librarian's Guide. By Patricia Johnson Swersey. Westport, Conn., Meckler, 1987. 211p. index. $24.95 spiralbound. LC 85-10535. ISBN 0-88736-047-5.

Swersey provides a simple and understandable guide to three spreadsheet programs for the IBM or compatible computer: SuperCalc, Multiplan, and LOTUS 1-2-3. The comb-bound manual is divided into four sections: an introduction to spreadsheets, the basics of spreadsheets, organization of spreadsheet models, and effective use of spreadsheet programs.

While advertised as a librarian's guide, Swersey does not provide enough examples to make the manual worthwhile. As each major command is given, a paragraph for each of the three programs describes specific keys to use. For the person trying to use one of the programs, descriptions of the other programs get in the way. While the manual is helpful as an overview, librarians would do better with a good manual for the program that they would like to learn, even though they would have to put up with examples from the business world.

David V. Loertscher

264. Jarke, Matthias, ed. Managers, Micros and Mainframes: Integrating Systems for End-Users. New York, John Wiley, 1986. 302p. bibliog. index. (John Wiley Information Systems Series). $29.95. LC 85-31490. ISBN 0-471-90988-2.

The influx of microcomputers into business organizations is causing a management dilemma. Organizations recognize the potential of end-user computing but they also fear loss of control over data processing activities and information resources. Advances in network technology are now allowing an integration of microcomputers with centralized mainframe processing. This book contains seventeen papers from a symposium on micro-mainframe integration held in 1985 by the Graduate School of Business, New York University. Although the first five chapters provide an overview of technology, the book was written for managers, not technicians. The papers discuss managerial issues such as efficiency, costs, risks, planning, and training. Several chapters report the result of research into company experiences of end-user computing, including some which have failed to make the transition. A particularly interesting chapter gives guidelines for exploiting information technologies to design more effective organizations. As is the case with most collected symposium papers, some chapters are more to the point and better written than others, but all are scholarly and require diligence on the part of the reader. There is an extensive bibliography. Readers interested in a more popularly written overview should consult Ronald Kopeck's *Micro to Mainframe Links* (see entry 265).

A. Neil Yerkey

265. Kopeck, Ronald F. Micro to Mainframe Links. Berkeley, Calif., Osborne/McGraw-Hill, 1986. 286p. illus. index. $18.95pa. ISBN 0-07-881228-3.

The widespread use of microcomputers in today's information processing environment is changing the way computer activities are managed, and the issue of integrating and linking PCs to mainframes has become a hot topic. This book was written for managers and planners responsible for selecting and implementing micro-mainframe links. With a minimum of technical detail it covers how file servers, local area networks, gateways, and bridges are integrated into a network.

The writing style is informal, nontechnical, and personal. It uses clear, helpful line drawings and tables to illustrate concepts. Although there are listings of link and network vendors, the book does not describe or evaluate different products. Its strength is in its coverage of planning and management aspects: needs assessment, problems of security, data transfer options, use of existing networks, testing and evaluation of networks, and the real and hidden costs involved in the various alternatives. It will provide adequate understanding for managers and others who want only an introduction, but as one gets closer to the implementation of a system, more technical detail certainly will be required.   A. Neil Yerkey

Online Searching

266. Alberico, Ralph. **Microcomputers for the Online Searcher.** Westport, Conn., Meckler, 1987. 299p. illus. index. $24.95pa. LC 86-23847. ISBN 0-88736-093-9.

This book is intended for those people who are in the field of online database searching, such as librarians and professional searchers. It is not intended for the novice.

It is divided into three parts: "Hardware Medium," "Software Tools," and "People and Machines." The author discusses advantages of personal computing technology, telecommunications, database searching in general, value-added online searching, downloading, gateway softwares, etc. Prices are given to allow readers to do "comparative shopping" if desired. A list of software vendors and a glossary that defines terms related to micro-based searching are included. A list of references/recommended readings has been included at the end of each chapter.

The book is readable, sometimes humorous. Unlike many computer books, the use of jargon has been kept to a minimum. Because timely information is important in this field, readers are advised to consult the trade literature and manufacturers for the latest products and up-to-date prices. With the increasingly important role of microcomputers in the online community, this book will be a basic reference in using them for the online searching.

The book requires stronger binding from the publisher. This reviewer finds her copy falling apart after a thorough reading in a correct manner. [R: BL, 1 Oct 87, p. 214; JAL, July 87, p. 185; RQ, Winter 87, pp. 292-93]

                              Betty L. Tsai

267. Bysouth, Peter, ed. **The Economics of Online.** London, Taylor Graham, 1987. 229p. (Foundations of Information Science, Vol. 2). £20.00pa. ISBN 0-947568-14-X.

Edited with commentary by Peter Bysouth, this book brings together twenty-six different reprinted journal articles of both British and American origin. The purpose of the book is "to provide a survey of the multi-faceted nature of the costs involved in providing an online search service whether in an industrial, academic, or public environment" (p. 2). The subject is divided into five major topics: choosing manual versus online, estimating costs, assessing benefits, charging for services, and future trends. It was published as volume 2 in Taylor Graham's Foundation of Information Science series, edited by Blaise Cronin. All of the reprints included were photoreproduced from the original, with the result being a wide variation in size, type, and quality of printing. There is no index.

Several comparisons of the readings reveal more of the nature of the contents. Of the readings selected for inclusion, two-thirds have copyright dates from 1980 to 1984, while the rest were originally published from 1976 to 1979. One-half are reprinted from one of four journals: *Journal of Library Automation, Journal of Chemical Information and Computer Sciences, Aslib Proceedings,* and *Online Review.* The others were scattered in thirteen different journals. Ten of those included are reports of the results of a survey or research project; the others are essays, guidelines, or models. In addition, it should be noted that several articles mentioned in the commentary for section 3 on assessing benefits are actually reprinted with those on estimating costs in section 2.

A closer look at one of the five sections gives a perspective on how Bysouth intended to achieve his purpose. Section 4, on charging for online services, includes the results of a 1974-1976 DIALIB project offering free online searching services in four San Francisco area public libraries; a 1982 summary of the pros and cons of charging, from a library administrators' point of view; a 1982 report of the implementation of a dual fee/free charging system at an American college library; and a 1983 summary of arguments for and against charging for online searches in British academic libraries.

Although the original publication dates of the readings included in this volume are three to ten years old, it does serve the purpose of bringing together in one source a number of useful articles which may not be readily available, especially in smaller libraries. Readers should also be aware that the introduction and five commentaries include references to an additional seventy-two journal articles on the topic of online economics. The variable quality of the photoreproduction and the lack of an index certainly remain disadvantages. [R: LAR, Dec 87, pp. 667-68]

                              Marilyn L. Shontz

268. Dorrington, Linda, ed. **Online Information Retrieval in Practice: Proceedings of the 2nd UK Online User Group State of the Art Conference, Bristol, 1986.** London, Taylor Graham, 1987. 158p. £18.00pa. ISBN 0-947568-23-9.

The fifteen papers collected here are from the second conference of this group, which concentrated on the state-of-the-art, that is, current research relevant to the day-to-day provision of online services, not futuristic ideas or advanced research. They are organized around four topics: end-user searching, education and training for online searching, developments in hardware and software, and document delivery. The papers range in length from four to thirteen pages. Some have good bibliographies, others have none. There is no index.

In general, the authors, both users and providers of service, provide mostly practical, useful information with little or no theory. One of the more theoretical papers is by David Ellis and others. It concerns the "best match" method of information retrieval, as opposed to the more usual Boolean method. Only a few of the papers are so British or European specific as not to be of some interest to those outside this setting (e.g., the one surveying developments in the teaching of online in UK schools of librarianship and information science). The final paper, by Verina Horsnell of The Library Association, reviews some of the current problems and issues facing online users. The distinction between problems and issues is that whereas both have to do with areas "where everyone agrees that all is not right" (p. 151), the former have solutions for which there is general agreement, the latter do not. Many of the current issues for the profession revolve around the question of control of information; the author cites downloading, data protection, "fee or free," freedom of access, and transborder data flow. It was disappointing that none of the papers at this conference dealt with these issues. Perhaps future conferences will.

Anna L. DeMiller

269. Glossbrenner, Alfred. **How to Look It Up Online: Get the Information Edge with Your Personal Computer.** New York, St. Martin's Press, 1987. 486p. index. $24.95; $14.95pa. LC 86-27945. ISBN 0-312-00133-9; 0-312-00132-0pa.

Alfred Glossbrenner is known for writing wide-ranging, in-depth books on personal computers and software in an easy to read, conversational style. *How to Look It Up Online* is true to form. The author covers the world of online information sources from the viewpoint of the information seeker. The emphasis is always on the user, with the assumption that the person accessing information is (or should be) the end-user. Like any book on any computer topic, this one is, inevitably, dated, but the author readily admits this and encourages readers to acquire current information from database vendors and producers. Almost every discussion ends with the name, address, and telephone numbers of appropriate contacts, information which by itself makes the book invaluable.

The work begins with a section introducing online databases — their organization, access, costs, vendors, and search techniques. Part II profiles and compares the major vendors: DIALOG and BRS (and their subsidiary services), NEXIS, ORBIT, Dow Jones News/Retrieval Service, VU/TEXT, NewsNet, and WILSONLINE, fortunely without any attempt to teach readers how to use them. The final section, which may be the most valuable for the person with online search experience, focuses on brief summaries of specific databases. These are arranged by the type of information included — books, articles, news and wire services, people and organizations, investment and industry information, sales and marketing, political information, and government publications. Weak points include numerous proofreading errors and an appendix on importing downloaded information into various programs which is beyond the comprehension of the novice. Overall, this is an important and valuable book for anyone who wants to tap into the world of online information, regardless of level of experience. [R: Choice, June 87, p. 1532; LJ, 1 Apr 87, p. 139]   Susan D. Herring

270. Palmer, Roger C. **Online Reference and Information Retrieval.** 2d ed. Littleton, Colo., Libraries Unlimited, 1987. 189p. index. (Library Science Text Series). $25.00pa. LC 87-29713. ISBN 0-87287-536-9.

Updating the 1983 edition (see *ARBA* 84, entry 247), this basic textbook focuses on bibliographic databases and now provides a more detailed table of contents. Included are new material on search strategy development, microcomputer telecommunications, keyword searching, controlled vocabulary, end-users and end-user systems (Dow Jones, CompuServe, The Source, WESTLAW); a historical development of online services; new developments (e.g., gateways, laser discs); and teaching suggestions. Retained are the chapters on database producers, database indexing, and the client interview. The emphasis of the book remains on the transference of knowledge from system to system and "teaching by example," helpful approaches for both the classroom-based student and the experienced professional needing independent study.

Chapters are well illustrated and include appended bibliographies for further reading. Comparative search strategies are provided for the four major vendors (DIALOG, BRS, ORBIT, and WILSONLINE), and clear examples are included for teaching Boolean logic.

It is unfortunate that the text was probably completed too soon to include a full discussion of the explosion of CD-ROM technology and the emergence of both Silver Platter and OCLC as competitors to DIALOG in this area. Also missing are mention of graphics databases (e.g., Trademarkscan), patent searching, and the Pergamon International Information Corporation.

However, as a beginner's guide to the fundamentals of database searching, this source is more broad in scope than *Easy Access to DIALOG, ORBIT, and BRS* (Marcel Dekker, 1984) and more suited to the needs of the student than *Online Searching* (Libraries Unlimited, 1984).   Ilene F. Rockman

271.   Pasqualini, Bernard F., ed. **Dollars and Sense: Implications of the New Online Technology for Managing the Library. Proceedings of a Conference Program Held in New York City, June 29, 1986.** Chicago, American Library Association, 1987. 118p. $10.00pa. ISBN 0-8389-3338-6.

Ever since online information sources became available, libraries have been struggling with formidable practical and philosophical issues. If money were no object, libraries could do everything, but burgeoning information technology has coincided with fiscal hard times. As bibliographic and full-text databases, end-user devices, and optical disk systems proliferate, machine-assisted reference services are becoming an absolute necessity for all kinds of libraries. To pay for these new services, libraries may have to drastically revise their priorities.

This collection of papers from a conference sponsored by the Reference and Adult Services Division of ALA addresses these issues. It puts the problems in focus and offers some helpful, practical suggestions to boot. Each of the contributors has something thought provoking and worthwhile to say. Standouts include Barbara Quint on "Setting Our Priorities," Martin Kesselman's advice on ways to save money on online searches, Rebecca Kroll's observations on the "Ripple Effect" and how online services will have an impact upon every aspect of library functioning, Joseph T. King's comments on financial considerations related to front ends and gateways, and Delores Meglio's analysis of the economic realities of full-text online delivery

services. Other papers offer commonsense advice on costs and pricing strategies, contract options, and statistics gathering, or report on research studies and trends related to the free or fee controversy. Two appendices—"Online Reference Services—Funding Methods" and "Online Reference Services—Costs and Budgets"—provide useful topical outlines and bibliographies. [R: BL, 1 Apr 87, p. 1175; JAL, Sept 87, p. 228; RQ, Fall 87, pp. 149-50]

Joseph W. Palmer

272.   Rowlands, Ian, ed. **Text Retrieval: An Introduction.** London, Taylor Graham, 1987. 80p. £15.00pa. ISBN 0-947568-24-7.

Text retrieval (TR) is British for what Americans call full-text database searching. These technical chapters are contributions made to a course (of the same title) organized and developed by the Institute of Information Scientists in the United Kingdom in October 1986. Unlike bibliographic searching, which principally focuses on citations and other forms of document surrogation, TR involves the retrieval of full text of articles and other documents, using coordinate indexing, keywords, Boolean search logic, and the like. TR also involves the acquisition of software packages, and this book is intended as a sort of consumer's buying guide to what is available. A chapter enumerates applications of TR: administrative, financial, legal, manufacturing, marketing, personnel, and in science and engineering.

In a series of essentially no-nonsense papers, throwing brand names around, the authors deal with command languages, Boolean terminology, search refinement, and other tricks of the trade, in prose liberally salted with jargon, acronyms, and initialisms. Problems (e.g., standardization) of the emerging technology of TR are dealt with summarily and, at times, superficially. Also covered are expert systems and gateway software, optical disk technology, upgrading, security, downloading, multilingual versions, printers, and telecommunications packages. References are supplied but there is no index, which would have made finding specifics much easier. The best feature is a comparison chart, near the end of the book, which presents various software packages in tabular form; also commendable is the careful definition of terminology. For audiences in Britain, this book will serve as a useful buying guide to interactive software in the full-text area. Stateside audiences, however, can probably give it a miss.

Bruce A. Shuman

Software

273. Andriole, Stephen J., ed. **Software Validation, Verification, Testing, and Documentation.** Princeton, N.J., Petrocelli Books; distr., Blue Ridge Summit, Pa., TAB Books, 1986. 389p. bibliog. $49.50. LC 85-29750. ISBN 0-89433-269-4.

This sourcebook on software is edited down from five separate reports published by the U.S. Department of Commerce, National Bureau of Standards. The whole idea is that the development and refinement of standards is an idea long overdue. Heretofore, manufacturers put out their own equipment according to their own criteria. Now there is a growing push for standardization, but the usual thorny questions of by-whose-foot-the-measure continue to arise.

The writing is highly technical, and the illustrations do not clear up a whole lot for the nontechnical reader. There are sections on planning for software validation, verification, and testing (VVT), an overview of software development, a framework for VVT, thirty techniques and tools for software VVT, and applications of VVT. A three-page index and a four-page bibliography are found in the middle of the volume.

There is a problem of structure and sequence—the parts do not seem to flow together logically, due to the five-fold, bound-together nature of the book. The introduction promises a practical approach, oriented toward the development of easy to use systems, but even the chapter on limiting the complexity of programs seems unnecessarily complicated. We concede that such a comment may well say more about the reviewer's competence in this subject area than it does about the structure, content, or writing of the book. What it *is* safe to say is that this is highly technical material, and, despite illustrations, hard to follow for the nonprogrammer. Technical collections in computer science will want to have it. Libraries catering to general audiences, amateur micro freaks, and weekend programmers may safely forego this volume.   Bruce A. Shuman

274. Breslin, Jud. **Selecting and Installing Software Packages: New Methodology for Corporate Implementation.** Westport, Conn., Quorum Books/Greenwood Press, 1986. 242p. index. $39.95. LC 86-12403. ISBN 0-89930-158-4.

The goal of systems analysis and design is the clear articulation of the information needs of an organization and the successful implementation of a modified or new system to meet those needs. Breslin argues in general terms, without specifics, that the implementation of existing software packages is preferable to in-house development. Therefore, this book is about a modified analysis and design process which focuses on the selection, purchase, and adaptation of off-the-shelf software to meet local needs. While this approach has held sway in the library automation field for a number of years, it is still not the norm in the business world. The book has done a thorough job but for one serious omission. Like so much of systems analysis and design practice today, the book focuses on technical and financial issues. There is little discussion of the role of employees in the process either as partners in the decision-making process or as users of the system. Implementation of a new system is not rightly viewed as the organizational change process which it is. The book is short on citations to relevant literature. Not recommended as a reference source for librarians looking for additional guidance in the purchase of software since a number of specific works are available. Despite the lack of focus on people in the process, however, the book is a thorough exploration of the technical and financial issues which business people might find useful.   Thomas G. Kirk

275. da Cruz, Frank. **KERMIT: A File Transfer Protocol.** Bedford, Mass., Digital Press, 1987. 379p. illus. bibliog. index. $25.00pa. LC 86-16696. ISBN 0-932376-88-6.

More than just a software user guide, this comprehensive software reference is perfect for a first-time programmer or initial user of KERMIT and invaluable for the advanced or professional programmer.

KERMIT is a free software protocol for transferring files between various types of computers. It is used internationally and is available for over two hundred different machines and operating systems. That makes this book an invaluable addition to any library that carries software reference.

Thirteen chapters are grouped into four thematic parts. Part 1 gives an easy to read introduction to KERMIT and its uses. Part 2 is a technically sound and comprehensible primer explaining important and pertinent facts about computers in general, files, and data communication. Part 3 is a user guide to KERMIT. Included are short sample sessions with user commands printed in green. Part 4 provides all the information needed by programmers to create their own KERMIT program and gives cautions and advice on distribution. A contact address is also provided.

Numerous helpful tables and figures appear throughout the chapters. Humorous illustrations and examples get important points across. Appendices include a command and packet summary for easy reference; the ASCII character set; arithmetic processes for binary, octal, decimal, and hexidecimal numbers; references and trademarks; and an extensive glossary. Indexed.   Andreas E. Mueller

276.   Lecarme, Olivier, and Mireille Pellissier Gart. **Software Portability.** New York, McGraw-Hill, 1986. 219p. bibliog. index. $29.95. LC 85-23656. ISBN 0-07-036948-8.

In talking about software portability, Lecarme and Gart consider the two parts of a software program's environment: (1) the material environment, or that of the computer and its devices; and (2) the software environment, consisting of the operating system with its various programming languages. The portability of a program would then depend "upon the ease with which it can be transferred and made useful, without modification of its properties in a new environment" (p. 10).

The purpose of this book is threefold: (1) use as a self-study guide by interested computer users; (2) use as a complementary textbook for a general undergraduate computer science course in software engineering; and (3) serving as a basis for a specialized course, seminar, or workshop on software portability. The work is arranged in two major parts and is followed by a 361-item bibliography of references and an index.

Part 1, "The Bases of Portability," comprises five chapters, including an introduction to the subject in chapter 1, which attempts to explain the diversity of concepts, from legal to technical, associated with software portability. Chapter 2 describes the major problems encountered in the design, construction, distribution, and use of portable software, covering the environment, numeric software, data, property rights, and protection, while chapters 3-5 discuss possible and actual solutions to these problems (software tools, linguistic means, and implementation methods).

Part 2, "Case Studies," has as its objective demonstration of how elementary techniques can be combined and applied. In chapter 6 case studies deal with language processors; in chapter 7 operating and programming systems are covered.

In light of the fact that software programs are increasingly more expensive as hardware costs decline, this volume should be of timely interest to designers, users, and evaluators of software products. The authors explain how to develop a program that can be transported from one system to another and how to increase cost effectiveness (decreasing development costs while increasing program efficiency, range of applicability, and life span). While much of the content of this work requires some background in computer science, computer users who are unsophisticated in program design and development, as well as librarians and others who find themselves in the position of selecting and evaluating software materials, will be able to profit from the information included in this work.
                    Lois Buttlar

277.   **The Software Encyclopedia 1986/87.** New York, R. R. Bowker, 1986. 2v. index. $125.00/ set. ISBN 0-8352-2090-7.

This is a comprehensive listing of personal computer programs. This year's edition makes significant improvements over last year's. In particular, programs are indexed by twenty-two microcomputer operating systems. There are descriptions of twenty-seven thousand programs by four thousand providers. The programs are listed alphabetically and described in a few paragraphs in one of the volumes, and the other volume contains descriptions by index category. It took a little practice to use the index, which is by computer/operating system, then application area, then an alphabetical list of programs and their descriptions. The index is well done and is a very useful finding aid. The audience for this is anyone who needs personal computer software. The only reservation I have is that Macintosh programs seem not to be well covered, particularly those from Apple; Realia COBOL is missing. The value-for-price ratio is competitive with other sources; I recommend this set.
                    Stan Rifkin

Systems

278.   Bank, Adrianne, and Richard C. Williams, eds. **Information Systems and School Improvement: Inventing the Future.** New York, Teachers College Press, 1987. 252p. index. (Computers and Education Series). $25.95. LC 86-30148. ISBN 0-8077-2842-X.

This work is a series of twenty-one essays concerning the melding of the computer's capacity to store and analyze masses of data with the need of educators to more effectively manage instruction for a diverse and mobile student population. The papers were first presented at a two-day conference held at UCLA in 1985, supported by a grant from the National Institute of Education to UCLA's Center for the Study of Evaluation. The contributors primarily came from California and the far West. The conference and this book promote the concept that computers can manage instruction and improve on existing instructional management systems.

Some contributors present optimistic views on increased productivity, increased individualization, and increased student achievement. Other authors are cautious, presenting an analysis of work in progress, struggles, and achievements in breaking new ground for computerized instructional management.

The book concludes with an appendix of information about the twenty-one contributors and a useful index. As with most books with contributors there is an unevenness of presentation, but there still is evidence of a single idea providing an overall framework for the book. Highly recommended for examination by all principals and superintendents making decisions about computer management applications.

Thomas L. Hart

279.   **Computers System Designers & Consultants: 1987 Directory.** Omaha, Neb., American Business Directories, 1987. 1v. (various paging). $105.00 spiralbound.

What would you have if you pulled together all the names, addresses, and telephone numbers of companies listed under "Computer System Designers and Consultants" in the nation's forty-eight hundred "yellow pages?" If you took the time to track down all the zip codes, too, you would have the 7,378 listings found in this slim, spiralbound directory.

The companies are arranged alphabetically by state, then by city. Each entry includes the business's name, address, city, state, zip code, and telephone number. The entries also indicate whether or not the business is a franchise (and if so, which one), the size of the company's "yellow pages" advertisement, and the year of the advertisement's first appearance (starting with 1985). The data are presented in very tightly spaced, apparently computer-generated columns. The 60 pages of listings are preceded by a "how-to-use-this-book" section and followed by 63 pages of information on other services available.

American Business Directories has compiled similar information for more than seven hundred industries, and boasts a database of some fourteen million business entities. The publisher's clientele is companies marketing nationwide to specific industries. Keeping in mind the various marketing techniques available, the information is also available online, on mailing labels, as prospect lists, on 3-by-5-inch cards, and on magnetic tape or diskette. According to the publisher, the information "reflects market condition(s) that existed nine to twelve months prior to publication," and is about as reliable and comprehensive as your local "yellow pages" directory.

Although public libraries would have no need to purchase such a narrowly focused resource, especially given its high price, this directory would nevertheless be a valuable business tool for those who need it. All business libraries should be aware of these directories, as should all business librarians in public and academic libraries.

G. Kim Dority

280.   FitzGerald, Jerry, and Ardra F. FitzGerald. **Fundamentals of Systems Analysis: Using Structured Analysis and Design Techniques.** 3d ed. New York, John Wiley, 1987. 1v. (various paging). index. (Wiley Series in Computers and Information Processing Systems for Business). $33.95. LC 86-7831. ISBN 0-471-88597-5.

The third edition of the FitzGeralds' book has been changed extensively. "It now contains a comprehensive and thorough explanation of structured analysis and design techniques, a workbook-style cumulative case that requires the students to perform case tasks using structured techniques, and a matrix approach to designing controls when using structured analysis and design." The book's primary purpose is to teach systems thinking. It is divided into three parts. Part 1 (chapters 1-2) contains a general introduction to systems analysis and structured analysis and design techniques. A ten-step system development life cycle (SDLC) is presented. The various techniques are integrated into this ten-step structure. Part 2 (chapters 3-12) is devoted to a detailed examination of the ten SDLC steps and their associated techniques. Part 3 (chapters 13-19) covers other systems analysis tools not covered in previous chapters. At the end of each chapter are questions and student tasks as well as situation cases to be analyzed. These are in addition to the cumulative case that extends throughout the book. A glossary and an index provide good access to the book's contents. This work, aimed primarily at business students, would also be applicable to any organization's systems problems. It is logically structured, clearly written, and well seasoned with illustrative examples. The authors' objectives have clearly been met, and exceeded.

Robert H. Burger

281.   Gallegos, Frederick, Dana R. (Rick) Richardson, and A. Faye Borthick. **Audit and Control of Information Systems.** Cincinnati, Ohio, South-Western Publishing, 1987. 716p. bibliog. index. $39.95. LC 84-50213. ISBN 0-538-10940-8.

Computer auditing involves the evaluation of computer information systems, practices, and operations to assure the integrity of the information. Because computer auditing is related to financial reporting and auditing, the intended audience for this book is quite broad and includes students and professionals in business management, computer information systems and accounting, auditing, and finance. In fact, the book is aimed at anyone who will need a working knowledge of the principles and techniques of computer auditing.

The book consists of four basic parts. Part 1 covers the conceptual framework of computer auditing and includes examples of computer fraud and abuse. In part 2 the authors cover concerns and objectives with particular emphasis on defining the mission of computer auditors in the areas of prevention, detection, correction, and implementation of control functions. Part 3 focuses on performing computer audits and includes typical audit patterns. Part 4 consists of discussions of management concerns, including privacy, risk assessment, and cost/benefit analysis.

The appendices include a glossary of terms; a bibliography of selected standards, books, and articles; and five case studies. The book is designed to serve primarily as a learning experience rather than as a "how-to" manual for performing audits. It gives good coverage to the steps of an audit, the purpose of the audit, and what managers should do with the results of an audit. The book should be of interest primarily to auditors, future auditors, and managers of auditors. — Susan B. Ardis

282. Ishikawa, Akira. **Future Computer and Information Systems: The Uses of the Next Generation Computer and Information Systems.** New York, Praeger/Greenwood Press, 1986. 138p. illus. bibliog. index. $32.95. LC 86-519. ISBN 0-275-92091-7.

The Fifth or Next Generation computer project is a long-term project supported financially by the government in Japan. This rather short book, written by Akira Ishikawa of the Rutgers Graduate School of Management, is an overview of the project and a review of its implications for managers and computer users.

Starting with a general overview of computer and information science development through time, Ishikawa goes on to describe and compare the Fifth or Next Generation systems with those of earlier generations. Japanese project goals and development aims are contrasted with the U.S. project version, being developed by the Microelectronics and Computer Technology Corporation. Another section in the work

covers the application areas of these new computers. Ishikawa's work has a three-page bibliography, the latest item of which is dated 1984. Appendices include a thirty-page project overview prepared for a November 1984 International Conference on Fifth Generation Computer Systems, and a Report on the Fifth Generation Computers, by Kazukiyo Kawanobe of the Institute for New Generation Computer Technology, Tokyo. The report states: "This prototype is to be completed within fiscal 1984," which leads the reviewer to believe that the "current status report" was in fact written at some undisclosed time in 1984. No other dating information was found in the "current status" report. There is an index of sorts, but it only covers up to page 67, and thus does not include about half of the book. There is also a rather extensive glowing vita of the author at the end of the book.

It is hard to gauge the exact measure of this book. On the one hand it is a rather high price to pay ($32.95) for "current information" dated 1984. Material presented is rather general and nebulous (e.g., "Finally, as more integrative knowledge systems are built, people must also classify and solidify moral and ethical foundations," p. 68). On the other hand, it is a fair treatment of a topic which the Japanese have been understandably rather reticent about releasing information on. There are other books that cover the subject in more depth. It is hard to recommend this work without the above caveats. If, however, you need general information on Fifth Generation systems from the Japanese viewpoint, this work will have some insights for you. Business and computer collections desiring a comprehensive collection on this topic will want to acquire this work. Others will be better served by more recent and substantial treatments of the topic.

— Ralph L. Scott

283. Laudon, Kenneth C. **Dossier Society: Value Choices in the Design of National Information Systems.** New York, Columbia University Press, 1986. 421p. bibliog. index. $45.00. LC 85-29154. ISBN 0-231-06188-9.

This is a compelling book. Although we are all aware in a general sense of the importance of information systems in our lives, very few of us are really aware of the extent to which these systems affect us—beyond merely being the sources of information about our credit ratings and our status, as motorists, with local law enforcement.

This well-written, well-indexed, well-documented, and informative book explores the impact of automated information systems in the area of law enforcement, or "computerized criminal history (CCH)." The insights which Laudon shares with the reader are quite thought-provoking and thoroughly thought-*promoting*. For instance, in one of the many excerpts from interviews found throughout the book, an Oakland police officer candidly observes that the "younger kids" (newer police officers) are spending too much time punching the computers in their squad cars and not enough time pounding the beat and meeting the people that populate the area for which they are responsible. The author makes the observation that not only does this point out that the newer "high tech-oriented" officers are losing touch with the community by not making themselves personally known in the community, but also that there has been a shift in the role of law enforcement officers, that of the "arrest agent." Information systems have provided police officers with a tool of strategy with which they can quickly identify automobiles that are stolen, drivers with outstanding warrants, stolen property, etc., thus shifting emphasis from *prevention* to *apprehension*.

But there is much more to the book than simply the making of observations. There is a detailed analysis of the history and development of the "De Facto National Data Centers," in the form of the huge information systems of the Social Security Administration, the Internal Revenue Service, and the FBI's National CCH. While the emphasis is on CCH, the book uses observations from that system to make more general comments about the others. The author also has plans for two additional books, one on the IRS system and the other on the SSA. But the book is not just about systems, it is about how these systems affect organizations that use them and, consequently, how they affect us, the citizens whose vital and not-so-vital statistics fill these information systems.

Richard A. Leiter

284. Leeves, Juliet. **Library Systems: A Buyer's Guide.** Brookfield, Vt., Gower Publishing, 1987. 274p. $71.50. ISBN 0-566-03553-7.

This guide compiles information on commercially available, stand-alone library systems to assist buyers of library systems in the selection process. The guide was compiled under the auspices of the Centre for Catalogue Research, University of Bath, in collaboration with the Library Technology Centre at the Polytechnic of Central London. Microbased systems are included if they are both multifunctional and multiaccess. The guide also provides information on suppliers of services to support a stand-alone system, such as bibliographic and author-

ity data and retrospective conversion services. Only systems and services marketed in the United Kingdom are covered.

An especially useful feature of this work is the fact that only systems functions and features actually observed in operation by the author are described, thus avoiding the pitfalls of guides based exclusively on unverified vendor reports. Systems descriptions are presented in a moderate level of detail and in a logical and well-organized format. An introductory "Overview of Stand-alone Systems" synthesizes the data collected and serves as an excellent state-of-the-art review of systems available in the United Kingdom. The text is clearly written and suitable for the administrator and nonspecialist in library systems. In spite of the British orientation, there is sufficient overlap with the U.S. market to render the guide useful to U.S. librarians. It is especially recommended for its high quality and data accuracy. [R: CLJ, Dec 87, p. 434; JAL, July 87, pp. 190-91]

Joe A. Hewitt

285. Nickerson, Raymond S. **Using Computers: The Human Factors of Information Systems.** Cambridge, Mass., MIT Press, 1986. 434p. illus. bibliog. index. $22.50. LC 85-24163. ISBN 0-262-14040-3.

The stated purposes of this book are "to provide an overview of where information technology is and where it appears to be headed, to review some of the human-factors research that has been done on computer-based systems to date, and to identify some of the issues and questions that are especially worthy of further research." The author has the depth of experience and qualifications to meet these objectives and has accomplished them in large part.

The book is very well written and well organized. The clear, smooth writing style should make the book enjoyable and understandable to a broad audience. It has a thorough name index and a sketchy but adequate subject index. A very strong aspect of the book is the bibliographic coverage. There are fifty-six pages of up-to-date references from a wide variety of fields. Although some major researchers and authors from this reviewer's field were included, some were not. But as a survey with near encyclopedic depth in covering this vast topic, the book stands firmly as a contribution in its field.

This reviewer could identify two areas within this topic that were not adequately covered. One is the information retrieval industry and library automation. The use of online information systems, bibliographic utilities, and library catalogs is not discussed except indirectly within a brief section entitled "Consumer Information Services." Another area of omission is the effects of computers on children and their development: socialization, concentration skills, receptiveness to human interaction and teaching, psychological adjustment, and so forth. But one can hardly fault the book for omissions such as this considering the perspective of the author and the size of the field being covered.

All in all, this is a fine contribution to the literature which provides within one useful volume a great deal of information and ideas. It is recommended for academic libraries, larger public libraries, and those special collections that could benefit from survey books dealing with the effects of technology on life in general. [R: SBF, Mar/Apr 87, p. 209]

James Rice

286.   Peterson, W. Wesley, and Art Lew. **File Design and Programming.** New York, John Wiley, 1986. 381p. bibliog. index. $30.95. LC 85-22666. ISBN 0-471-82311-2.

Developed from course notes for a one-semester class taught at the University of Hawaii, this text-type book provides basic information on the role of files in computer systems and on their structure, design, maintenance, and programming. It is well organized. Readers can select specific topics of interest from a detailed table of contents or index, choose to read just one of the two major parts into which the book is divided, explore thoroughly programming examples in their language of choice (COBOL, PL/I, or FORTRAN), or read the book from cover to cover.

Not all librarians will find *File Design and Programming* of use or interest. A writing knowledge of at least one programming language or a reasonable grounding in data structure analysis and design are assumed. However, interested readers for whom neither of these assumptions holds true should not hesitate to examine Peterson and Lew's clearly and systematically presented discussion. A wealth of introductory and definitional information, as well as suggestions for further reading on topics such as database systems, programming languages, magnetic tape, or operating systems, can orient the little experienced, and point the uninitiated in the right direction.

This book would make an excellent addition to computer science collections, and to library science collections that emphasize computer literacy.   Connie Miller

287.   Warren, Kenneth S., ed. **Selectivity in Information Systems: Survival of the Fittest.** New York, Praeger/Greenwood Press, 1985. 176p. index. $34.95. LC 84-11607. ISBN 0-03-069749-2.

This collection of ten essays explores various facets of information transfer, based on a mathematical model of an ecological system. It is written by researchers of, or practitioners in, communication systems and information dissemination from the fields of medicine, mathematics, librarianship, sociology, and psychology.

Warren begins the collection with a description of the ecosystem of scientific communication. Larkin discusses, from a psychological viewpoint, the human limitations of handling information overload and what is needed of computers to help us use information more effectively. The two ends of the research system are critically examined first, by the Coles, in an insightful review of the grants application process, and then by Bailar and Patterson in their revealing study of peer review for journal publications. Small considers the survival over time of the intellectual life of scientific papers. Mosteller writes of factors contributing to reading strategies appropriate to selection of papers by quality of design, analysis, and reporting. Goffman applies a two-stage information retrieval process to the problem of literature selection of both journals and papers. Bruer reports on diagnostic tests for quality in one subject literature. Bleich describes *Paper Chase*, a self-service computer system for retrieval of titles of articles. Stam's concluding essay notes that a high degree of selectivity functions at all levels of the ecosystem, and adds attention to the physical preservation issues as well.

The tone of nearly all the papers is that of well-constructed research reporting. Bibliographic notes to further readings and a good index also encourage reference use of the book. Offering thought-provoking insights and empirically substantiated models, this is a book more for professional reading than reference work, although it can provide valuable research data and secondary source material for the student of information systems.   Danuta A. Nitecki

CONSERVATION AND PRESERVATION

288.   **Brittle Books: Reports of the Committee on Preservation and Access.** Washington, D.C., Council on Library Resources, 1986. 31p. free. LC 86-8913.

The rapid deterioration of the paper which has been used to print books since 1850 has, in recent years, become a major concern of all those interested in preserving our written heritage. This booklet outlines a major national effort to deal with the problem.

In 1982 a group of librarians, faculty, and university and foundation officers was asked to consider the changing character of research libraries and the future needs of their users. One of the major topics that emerged at this meeting, called Forum I, was that of the preservation of library material. At a second forum, held in 1983, the discussion focused on preservation and the group assembled asked the Council on Library Resources to undertake the establishment of a national program on preservation. The Council appointed a Committee on Preservation, later renamed the Committee on Preservation and Access, which began its work in June 1984 under the leadership of Billy E. Frye, Vice President for Academic Affairs and Provost of the University of Michigan. This booklet reports on the work of that Committee.

The Committee was asked to devise a management structure, outline a funding plan, and set the characteristics of and conditions for a national preservation program. The first document in this booklet is the report of the Committee which defines the problem, makes some general observations, and then addresses the three basic charges of the Council.

In 1986 Forum III was convened by the Committee, and its report was made to representatives of organizations with an interest in preservation. The "Summary Report" from Forum III, containing the recommendations of the participants, is the second document in the booklet. The publication is rounded out by an Interim Report of the Committee, a summary of background studies carried out by the Committee, and lists of the Committee members and the participants in Forum III.

Dean H. Keller

289. Darling, Pamela W., comp. **Preservation Planning Program Resource Notebook.** Revised edition by Wesley L. Boomgaarden. Washington, D.C., Association of Research Libraries, 1987. 675p. bibliog. $35.00 looseleaf.

This publication is a monumental anthology of recent publications, in-house guides and forms, and other difficult to locate documents on the subject of the preservation of library and archival material. Originally compiled in 1982 by Pamela W. Darling, this new edition was prepared by Wesley L. Boomgaarden from material available in late 1986 and early 1987. It contains reproductions of over one hundred articles and documents and references to over two hundred other items of significance.

The resource notebook is issued looseleaf and is divided into eleven main sections, all preceded by a bibliography which is organized to conform to the sections of the notebook. For each section the items which are reproduced are listed first, followed by citations for additional reading, and each group is listed in alphabetical order by author, or by title when the author is not given. Those items which are recommended to be read first are printed in boldface type.

The sections, and subsections, into which the resource notebook is divided are: (1) "Introductory Readings"; (2) "The Physical Environment," subdivided into "Environmental Conditions," "Insects," "Light," and "Monitoring"; (3) "Protection of Library Materials," subdivided into "Storage and Handling," "Exhibits," "Educating Patrons about Preservation," and "Security"; (4) "Surveying Collection Conditions," subdivided into "Survey Techniques" and "Sampling Methodology"; (5) "Preservation Organization and Administration," subdivided into "Policy and Planning," "Descriptions of Library Preservation Programs," "Organizational Documents," and "Collection Management and Development Issues"; (6) "Disaster Prevention and Preparedness"; (7) "Preservation Microfilming"; (8) "Cooperative Preservation Activities"; (9) "Preservation Supplies"; (10) "Education and Training for Preservation"; and (11) "Library Materials: Physical Nature and Treatment," subdivided into "Repairing Library Materials," "Documenting Treatment," "Paper," "Binding," "Leather," "Photographs," "Moving Images," "Recordings," and "Machine-Readable Records."

The 1982 version of this resource notebook proved to be very useful and certainly this revised and up-to-date edition will be equally welcome. [R: JAL, Nov 87, p. 325]

Dean H. Keller

290. Gwinn, Nancy E., ed. **Preservation Microfilming: A Guide for Librarians and Archivists.** Chicago, American Library Association, 1987. 207p. illus. index. $40.00pa. LC 87-10020. ISBN 0-8389-0481-5.

Here, in one convenient book, are detailed and authoritative discussions of all aspects of preservation microfilming. After the introduction, which presents the historical background, there are six chapters that treat various aspects of the subject. Chapter 1, "An Overview of Administrative Decisions," may be looked upon as an abstract of the remainder of the book and provides a good working base for what is to follow. The difficult questions that must be considered when decisions are made about what parts of the collection should be microfilmed are dealt with in chapter 2, which is called "Selection of Materials for Microfilming." Suggestions for organizing material for microfilming, and the steps in that process, are considered in chapter 3, "Production Planning and Preparation of Materials," and "Microfilming Practices and Standards" are discussed in chapter 4. This chapter is especially valuable as a guide through the published standards and specifications which are available in terms a nontechnician can understand. Once preservation microfilming has been accomplished, it is important that the film be properly cataloged and the fact that preservation quality film exists must be shared with others. Chapter 5, "Preservation Microfilming and Bibliographic Control," describes cataloging practice in some detail. Costs for equipment, supplies, labor (including preparation, filming, cataloging, and inspection), storage, contract services, etc., are examined in chapter 6, "Cost Controls." Each chapter concludes with a "List of Suggested Readings."

Among the important features of the book are four appendices: (1) "Preservation Microfilming: Standards, Specifications, and Guidelines"; (2) "Sample Preservation Microfilming Contract"; (3) "Glossary"; (4) "Organization and Institutions Involved in Preservation Microfilming." The book contains a number of useful illustrations, charts, tables, and forms, and there is an index.   Dean H. Keller

291. Mount, Ellis, ed. **Preservation and Conservation of Sci-Tech Materials.** New York, Haworth Press, 1987. 171p. (*Science and Technology Libraries*, Vol. 7, No. 3). $22.95. LC 86-33540. ISBN 0-86656-650-3.

This monograph (published simultaneously as *Science and Technology Libraries* 7, no. 3, Spring 1987) consists of six signed essays on problems inherent in the conservation and preservation of science/technology materials and examples of projects and studies undertaken to cope with these problems. The first paper presents some of the current preservation activities for certain types of materials: architectural drawings, archival materials, electronic information systems, photographs, sound recordings, etc. The second essay describes both accomplishments since the early 1970s and future goals and financial/administrative concerns connected with conservation of the research library collections at the American Museum of Natural History. In the third paper the programs of the American Institute of Physics's Center for History of Physics in preserving valuable historical source materials

are discussed. The preservation efforts of the health sciences library, University of Puerto Rico (the fourth essay) make it clear that in a tropical climate preservation problems are intensified because of excessive heat, high humidity, and insects. The fifth paper traces the development of preservation as an integral part of collection management within the MIT Libraries, including creation in 1985 of a position of Preservation and Collections Librarian. The value of a grant for preservation planning at the Brooklyn Botanic Garden Library is recounted in the sixth paper.

The remainder of this work—the larger portion—consists of the regular departments of *Science and Technology Libraries*: "Special Paper," "Sci-Tech Collections," "New Reference Works in Science and Technology," "Sci-Tech Online," and "Sci-Tech in Review." To be specific, the special paper describes a cooperative effort between the University of Miami School of Medicine's Library and two corporate members benefiting from a fee-for-service network which offered the library's services to non-university individuals and organizations. The "Sci-Tech Collections" department is a paper, "Fiber Optics: A Survey of Current Literature Sources." Libraries with subscriptions to *Science and Technology Libraries* may not need the monograph as well.   Wiley J. Williams

292. **Preservation Guidelines in ARL Libraries.** Washington, D.C., Association of Research Libraries, 1987. 110p. bibliog. (SPEC Kit, No. 137). $20.00pa.

This SPEC Kit completely updates the SPEC Kit on the same subject issued as number 70 in 1981. Developments in the preservation of library material have been rapid and far-reaching, and the ARL has been in the forefront of these preservation efforts. The SPEC Kit begins with the "Guidelines for Minimum Preservation Efforts in ARL Libraries," approved by the ARL membership in 1984, and continues with "Preservation Policies and Priorities," "Decision Making," "Brittle Books Programs," and a seven-item selected reading list. As is usual with the SPEC Kits, the contents of these sections are made up of documents from ARL libraries. Documents from the University of Cincinnati, Emory University, Columbia University, the National Library of Medicine, and Northwestern University are reproduced in the first section, while "Decision Making" documents from the University of Wisconsin, the University of California at Berkeley, the University of Washington, the University of Michigan, Johns Hopkins University, the Library of Congress, Yale University, The Ohio State University, and the University of Connecticut make up the contents of the second. Documents describing brittle books programs at Berkeley, Stanford, the Library of Congress, Michigan, and Pittsburgh make up the concluding section. There is much to learn from the statements, documents, and forms generously provided by these major research libraries in this timely publication. [R: LJ, Dec 87, p. 84]   Dean H. Keller

293. Preservation Planning Program: An Assisted Self-Study Manual for Libraries. 1987 ed. By Pamela W. Darling with Duane E. Webster. Washington, D.C., Association of Research Libraries, 1987. 117p. $15.00pa.

This manual provides the framework for carrying out a preservation planning effort in most library situations. Information, examples, ideas, and suggestions are provided on all phases of preservation planning. Used in conjunction with the *Preservation Planning Program Resource Notebook*, which was issued by the OMS, the manual can lead to informed decisions and appropriate action. The original edition of the manual contained ten chapters, the first two providing introductory material, rationale and background, a discussion of the decision to do preservation planning and how it is made, and an overview of the framework of the study. The remaining chapters describe the phases of the study. Chapters 3 and 4 consider Phase I, "Establishing the Study Framework"; chapters 5-9 describe Phase II, which is the work of five Task Forces on environmental conditions, physical condition of the collections, organization, disaster control, and preservation resources. Phase III, described in chapter 10, is called "Planning for Preservation," and discusses how the information, ideas, and recommendations of the Task Forces are analyzed and synthesized and brought together in a final report.

This manual was published originally in 1982, but a supplemental grant from the National Endowment for the Humanities enabled the Office of Management Studies to produce two additional chapters, the occasion for this "expanded edition." These chapters establish two additional task forces under Phase II: "Staff and User Education" and "Interinstitutional Cooperation." [R: JAL, Nov 87, p. 325]
                            Dean H. Keller

294. Watson, Aldren A. Hand Bookbinding: A Manual of Instruction. New York, Macmillan, 1986. 160p. illus. index. $19.95. LC 86-16261. ISBN 0-02-624430-6.

The tools, techniques, and procedures needed to bind and repair books using tradi-

tional hand tools and methods are spelled out with great clarity and detail in this excellent manual. Step-by-step instructions lead the reader through the stages of traditional hand bookbinding from the cutting and folding of the paper through the manufacture and attachment of covers. Other chapters provide instructions for such special projects as the making of dust jackets, the production of single signature paper-covered and multi-signature hard-covered books, the binding of manuscripts and music, the rebinding of an old book, the making of a slipcase, and the designing of labels. The final chapter gives instructions for inexpensively manufacturing one's own bookbinding tools and equipment. What makes this book particularly effective is that it is so well illustrated. Two hundred and seventy-three large, well-labeled drawings describe in pictorial terms all the important concepts discussed by the text. [R: JAL, July 87, p. 190; JAL, Sept 87, p. 229]
                         Joseph W. Palmer

COPYRIGHT

295. Helm, Virginia M. What Educators Should Know about Copyright. Bloomington, Ind., Phi Delta Kappa Educational Foundation, 1986. 50p. bibliog. $0.90. LC 85-63688. ISBN 0-87367-233-X.

This reviewer has a long-standing bias against little pamphlets about the copyright law. They frequently mislead readers by oversimplifying complex legal matters. This is a splendid exception to the rule. It is divided into six major chapters. The first chapter provides a readable summary of the underlying theory of fair use. The remaining chapters treat specific issues: photocopying, computer software, audiovisual materials, videotaping off the air, and performances.

The chapter on photocopying seems unduly conservative by its failure to identify the congressional fair-use guidelines as minimum standards. It creates the impression that any copying in excess of the guidelines is an infringement, which does not appear to be true. The chapters on audiovisual materials, videotaping off the air, and live and transmitted performances are sound and readable. The chapter on computer software is outstanding; the author's special competence in this field is conspicuous in her lucid presentation of the vague and contradictory facts.

The pamphlet closes with a brief bibliography of court decisions and books. The books seem well chosen. A serious omission is a pamphlet by Beda Johnson, *How to Acquire Legal Copies of Video Programs*, which is available for $11.00 from Video Resources (P.O. Box 191218, San Diego, CA 92119).

This pamphlet belongs in every library that serves educators. Highly recommended.

Jerome K. Miller

296. Reed, Mary Hutchings. **The Copyright Primer for Librarians and Educators.** Washington, D.C., National Education Association, and Chicago, American Library Association, 1987. 60p. bibliog. index. $7.95pa. LC 87-1014. ISBN 0-8389-0472-6.

A practical guide to the new developments in copyright interpretation using the question and answer approach: background to copyright, fair use, library copying under Section 108, classroom photocopying, college and university photocopying and library reserve room copying, music, sheet music, videotapes (home use, classroom use, and library use), video guidelines, off-air taping, computer software (library and classroom lending, library and classroom use, software guidelines), infringement liability and remedies, and how to obtain permission. Each section opens a discussion of the law with background and explanatory information, then closes with realistic questions and answers. Reed's explanations are clear and concise. They will help librarians and teachers to understand the intent of the law, so they can make more intelligent decisions.

Mary Hutchings Reed is the legal counsel for the American Library Association and is a partner in the law firm of Sidley and Austin in Chicago. It is obvious that she is extremely knowledgeable about copyright laws and is able to simplify a complex area of librarianship and education.

The booklet concludes with a listing of copyright sources used in the text, example cases, and other sources of copyright information. The index prepared by Gene Heller is easy to use and accurate. [R: BR, Nov/Dec 87, p. 49]

Thomas L. Hart

297. Vlcek, Charles W. **Copyright Policy Development: A Resource Book for Educators.** Friday Harbor, Wash., Copyright Information Services, 1987. 164p. bibliog. index. (Copyright Information Bulletin, No. 2). $17.95. ISBN 0-91413-08-5.

Although the title indicates a single use for this book (i.e., as an aid to development of a copyright policy), in reality it has another utility, as a comprehensive source of the information as it exists in mid-1987 on the use of satellite programming in educational institutions. An entire chapter, as well as appendix information, is devoted to the satellite question. Only the first

fourteen pages of the book contain author comments on why and how a copyright policy should be developed. The initial chapter contains extremely persuasive, lucid, and otherwise hard-to-find statements about why a policy is needed. A distinction is made between a policy statement and a manual; more attention is devoted to content and organization of the former. Further guidance on the latter would have enhanced the book. Appendices, which include seven sample copyright policies from various parts of the country, account for 138 pages of the book. The author notes that some information in the policies is contradictory, so the policies should be used as examples of form and language rather than as a source of definitive information on copyright. One of the policies included, from the Madison Metropolitan School District, is nearly a decade old and is in the process of revision. More recent policies focus on newer technologies. Recommended as a supplementary resource for institutions writing copyright policies and for those dealing with satellite use.

Eliza T. Dresang

DATA COMMUNICATION

General Works

298. Sauvant, Karl P. **International Transactions in Services: The Politics of Transborder Data Flows.** Boulder, Colo., Westview Press, 1986. 372p. (Atwater Series on The World Information Economy, No. 1). $38.50pa. LC 85-31522. ISBN 0-8133-0310-9.

The subtitle of this volume reveals its contents, for the "services" emphasized are data services. It is the first in a series from the Atwater Institute, itself subtitled, "The World Information Economy Centre," as described in a foreword by its officers. Preceded by an author's preface and an introduction and summary, the analysis is presented in five chapters: "Services," "Data Services and Their Impact," "The Interest Constellation," "The International Policy Discussion: Bilateral and Regional Fora," and "The International Policy Discussion: International Fora," all with copious notations. Following a conclusion chapter are nine "annexes" presenting official statements by national, regional, and international actors germane to the author's themes. The final two pages contain an essential list of acronyms. Most of the pages have at least one acronym and many have a half-dozen or more, such as GATT (General Agreement on Tariffs and Trade), FDI (foreign direct investment), and EFT (electronic funds transfer). This characteristic makes an already dense argument almost unreadable, except that the theme, that "data industries, ... especially data services, are the pole around which economic development is being restructured," is important. A major value of the volume is the data, which it compiles in seventy-two tables and sixteen figures as well as the "annexes." Given the pervasiveness of the subject matter, it will serve researchers in international relations, telecommunications, economics, business, information science, and many other areas.   K. Mulliner

299. Turpin, John, and Ray Sarch, eds. **Data Communications: Beyond the Basics.** New York, McGraw-Hill, 1986. 305p. illus. maps. index. (Data Communications Book Series). $28.95pa. LC 86-2892. ISBN 0-07-606950-8.

The world of library and information science has changed dramatically in the last decade and gives every indication of continuing to do so. Librarians who were totally unfamiliar with simple "computerese" are now necessarily becoming more comfortable with the fluid spectrum of data communications and telecommunications in order to keep pace with developing technology. Professionals in numerous other fields have been struggling with similar developmental concerns. In order to facilitate the increasing need to understand heretofore uncharted areas of knowledge, a volume entitled _Basic Guide to Data Communications_ was published in 1985 as a part of the Data Communications series. One year later, _Beyond the Basics_ appears as a supplement to that earlier volume.

Beyond the Basics is an apt title, as this work contains intermediate and advanced level articles which originally appeared in _Data Communications_ in 1984-1985. As a compilation of articles, the content areas range widely and are loosely arranged into five major categories: planning and design, technology, application, management, and futures.

This text is definitely not for the uninitiated, who should begin with the earlier volume. However, for those conversant with the topic area and interested in "a sampling of today's and tomorrow's data communications technology in many of its varied aspects," this text should prove most useful. This sampling includes such topics as data compression, digital transmission, transport protocols, artificial intelligence, and projected network architectures. Numerous illustrations add clarity to the text.

At the existing rate of technological development, this reference work will rapidly become historical documentation. Meanwhile, it can provide a window into a complex technology and should be considered for purchase by libraries collecting in this area.

Darlene E. Weingand

Networking and Networks

300. Archer, Rowland. **The Practical Guide to Local Area Networks.** Berkeley, Calif., Osborne/McGraw-Hill, 1986. 283p. illus. index. $21.95pa. ISBN 0-07-881190-2.

This is one of several recently published practical guides to the acquisition of a local area network (LAN). Of all of them it must be said that they are only starting points. The field is moving too quickly for a book on LANs to be fully up-to-date. Archer's guide focuses in the first half on the issues that should be taken into account in the selection of a system. The discussion assumes a background in microcomputers and telecommunications, and therefore this volume is not for the novice. After posing and answering the questions "What is a LAN?" and "Should you buy a LAN?" (better stated as "How do I decide if I need a LAN?"), the author walks the reader through the processes of planning, selection, and use of a LAN. In the second half of the book, five networks currently available for IBM PCs are discussed (IBM PC Network, 3COM EtherSeries, Corvus Omninet, Novell Network, and Orchid PCnet). This is an evaluative section in which standardized technical and performance information is provided for each network. Evaluative information, both positive and negative, is provided in a balanced presentation. Compared with others, such as James Harry Green's _Local Area Networks_ (Scott, Foresman, 1985) and Richard G. Lefkon's _Selecting a Local Area Network_ (American Management Association, 1986), Archer provides less background material for the novice in deference to the extensive reviews of the individual LAN systems. Therefore, as a general reference on LANs, Green or Lefkon, for example, are preferable, while those planning the acquisition of a LAN based on the IBM PC will find Archer a good place to start.

Thomas G. Kirk

301. Bridges, Stephen P. M. **Low Cost Local Area Networks.** Wihnslow, England, Sigma Press; distr., New York, Halsted Press/John Wiley, 1986. 182p. bibliog. index. $24.95. ISBN 0-470-20758-2.

This work is a basic, highly practical treatment of local area networks (LANs) oriented to the user or organization considering the implementation of LAN technology. The author's objectives are to explain LANs, to describe the underlying technology, to indicate what LANs can and cannot do, to describe the status of LANs in the computer marketplace, and to provide a comprehensive account of currently available systems. These objectives are accomplished with as little esoteric language as possible.

Among the topics covered are network topologies, access methods, transmission media, standards, specifying user requirements and purchasing LANs, practical installation, related systems (e.g., PABX65, intelligent terminal switches, wide area telephone networks), research networks, proprietary networks, and future trends. "Low cost" is a relative term and no specific cut-off point in terms of cost is used. However, the work does concentrate on bottom-end LAN technologies and all systems examined in detail are in the low cost range. *Low Cost Local Area Networks* is an extremely useful introductory treatment of an exciting new technology and is highly recommended to anyone considering the installation of a LAN at the lowest possible cost.

Joe A. Hewitt

302.   Gofton, Peter W. **Mastering Serial Communications.** Berkeley, Calif., SYBEX, 1986. 289p. illus. bibliog. index. $19.95pa. LC 86-61481. ISBN 0-89588-180-2.

If you have ever faced the prospect of plugging in all the cables to your microcomputer, or wonder why your modem does not work, then this book is for you! Serial communications is a complex subject involving the methods through which your computer can talk with other data equipment that is not physically located in your computer's cabinet. Examples of serial devices are modems, printers, plotters, black boxes, and other computers. Major aspects of serial communications include connecting the parts together physically (called hardware interfacing), programming standards (called software protocols), and modems (devices that convert signals on the twenty-five-wire computer cables to a two-wire telephone line system).

Topics covered by Gofton in the book include hardware interfacing; data transmission; handshaking/buffers; modems and their protocols, file transfer (XMODEM, KERMIT); UART programming (writing your own modem software); IBM PC Communications (DOS and BIOS); interrupt routines; and serial programming in BASIC, C, and Assembler. Appendices include common pin connection diagrams, a nice glossary, and a very brief unannotated bibliography.

This work is well done and written in a style that both the novice and the expert can understand. Other books cover an aspect of serial communications (such as the RS232C standard),

but this volume is the most comprehensive. Gofton has a master's degree from Oxford and writes well. The work has an attractive page layout and typographic design. Libraries with any clients interested in microcomputers cannot afford to miss this $19.95 gold mine. Recommended as the best and most comprehensive book on the topic of serial communications.

Ralph L. Scott

303.   Held, Gilbert. **Data Communications Networking Devices: Characteristics, Operation, Applications.** New York, John Wiley, 1986. 372p. index. $29.95. LC 85-27139. ISBN 0-471-90947-5.

Few librarians have an engineering background, and yet we are increasingly called upon to make decisions about the application of data communications technology to library operations. This book, written for the nonspecialist on a level appropriate for graduate study, fulfills a need for practitioner and student alike to understand "how communication devices operate, where they can be employed in networks, and the cost and performance parameters which should be considered in selecting such equipment." The wealth of information which it contains is presented in a lucid, intelligible manner organized to demonstrate interrelationships of various devices which constitute a system. The first chapter of about seventy pages presents an excellent overview of fundamental concepts, including such things as transmission modes, techniques, rates, and codes. It covers link terminology from several disciplines, and concludes with a short description of the Open System Interconnection Reference Model on which the Linked Systems Project is based.

The remaining six chapters cover data transmission and concentration equipment, redundancy and reliability aids, automated assistance devices, and other specialized devices such as security devices for communication systems. The final chapter covers integrating components in a data communication system pointing out the need for regularized ongoing evaluation of all system components in terms of developments in the field and economics of the industries involved. Although much of the detailed technical information related to characteristics and specifications of devices is not relevant to those merely interested in use of a system in place, anyone interested in understanding how systems work and with a need to make decisions about choice of systems to perform any number of operations in a library setting will find the information invaluable. Although reference to specific applications in libraries is not the focus of this text, it will greatly aid the librarian in understanding and communicating with data communication specialists and consultants whom we increasingly call upon. It is highly recommended as both a reference source and a text.   JoAnn V. Rogers

304. Hordeski, Michael F. **Microcomputer LANs: Network Design and Implementation.** Blue Ridge Summit, Pa., TAB Books, 1987. 340p. illus. bibliog. index. $26.95. LC 87-10012. ISBN 0-8306-2888-6.

This book presents a broad introduction to local area networks (LANs) from a system standpoint for managers and supervisors. It provides readers with basic knowledge of the different hardware and software components of LANs and the skill to design and evaluate a proper LAN using the available resources. Topics covered include data communications, network design, protocols, packet/message switching, network testing/maintainability, LAN planning, and implementation. The presentation is tutorial and fundamental. A mathematical background is not required. Some knowledge of computers is helpful but not necessary. Much emphasis is placed on explaining commonly used industrial terminology and giving exact definitions of the related standards. A review of a number of popular networks is also enlightening. A special, extremely useful feature is the forty-one-page glossary. This book is highly recommended for acquisition as reference material by management personnel and consultants.   John Y. Cheung

305. **The Local Area Networking Sourcebook.** 4th ed. Dana M. Richens and Mark R. Kimmel, eds. Potomac, Md., Phillips Publishing, 1987. 328p. illus. index. $167.00/yr. ISBN 0-934960-32-1.

Formerly published under the title *The Local Area Networking Directory*, this book lists by company name over one hundred local area networks in the private sector, providing for each entry the company's address; telephone, telex (LAN), and FAX numbers; names and titles of key personnel; year founded; number of employees; branch offices; and a description of the network, including technical characteristics and standards or protocols supported. Separate chapters contain alphabetically arranged entries for manufacturers and distributors of local area networking hardware products, suppliers of LAN software packages, and vendors of LAN-related business and technical services. Local area networking standards and standards groups are described in another chapter. All reported information was furnished by the organizations listed, without verification by the editors. Articles providing an overview of local area networking, an appendix of forecasts for the LAN industry through 1990, a glossary, and a company index complete this volume, which is amply illustrated with numerous figures and tables. Only business libraries specializing in telecommunications require this expensive paperbound directory.   Leonard Grundt

306. **The Local Network Handbook.** 2d ed. Colin B. Ungaro, ed. New York, McGraw-Hill, 1986. 389p. illus. index. (Data Communications Book Series). $30.95pa. LC 86-2891. ISBN 0-07-606949-4.

This handbook is actually a collection of articles on the topic of local area networks. The second edition is revised significantly from the first edition in 1982. It retains only eight of the original chapters and incorporates fifty new chapters which come (as did those in the first edition) from *Data Communications* magazine. The resulting fifty-eight articles are arranged into six topical sections: technology, network design, implementation, planning and management, software, and applications. It provides as up-to-date coverage as possible given the time lag from publication in the magazine to assimilation in this monograph.

The articles deal with a wide range of issues in local area networks, such as international standards, the products and advancements of front-running research and development, and related topics such as private branch exchange. The chapters are illustrated with numerous charts, tables, graphs, and photographs. As collections go, these contributions are well written for the most part, and are indexed by brand names and general subjects at the end of the volume.

This handbook is recommended for academic libraries that would like the compilation of these articles or for those libraries that do not have *Data Communications* magazine.

James Rice

307. Pickholtz, Raymond L., ed. **Local Area & Multiple Access Networks.** Rockville, Md., Computer Science Press, 1986. 291p. index. (Advances in Telecommunications Networks). $50.00. LC 86-4218. ISBN 0-88175-143-X.

Technologies related to Local Area Networks (LANs) have emerged as one of the more significant developments in telecommunications in recent years. As the editor of this volume points out, the LAN represents a highly volatile technology which promises to affect the entire telecommunications environment in a substantial way. The methods and techniques of LAN design are being applied to Metropolitan Area

Networks and in interfacing LANs with private branch exchanges (PBXs). The purpose of this collection is to bring together a group of self-contained, original papers which, taken together, accurately reflect the current state-of-the-art of the LAN and address the major issues related to LAN technology.

This work contains thirteen technical papers by recognized experts. Examples of chapters are "A Tutorial on the IEEE 802 Local Network Standard," by William Stallings; Leonard Kleinrock's "Channel Efficiency for LANs"; "A Programmable VLSI Controller for Standard and Prioritized Ethernet Local Networks," by Imrich Chlamtac; A. A. Nilsson, K. W. Hanson, and W. Chou on "Performance Evaluation of a Metropolitan Area Network"; and "Collison Detection in Radio Channels," by Raphael Rom. The articles display a combination of conceptual, mathematical, experimental, and descriptive/applied treatments.

The editor expresses the hope that this volume "will stand as a milestone in the further progress that lies ahead" in the convergence of LAN and other telecommunications technologies and in the development and expansion of LAN technology generally. He has substantially succeeded in that ambitious goal. This work is essential for computer science and telecommunication collections and highly recommended for major collections in information and library science.

Joe A. Hewitt

308.   Yakubaitis, Eduard A. **Local-Area Networks and Their Architectures.** New York, Allerton Press, 1986. 338p. bibliog. index. $58.50. LC 86-70929. ISBN 0-89864-018-0.

This is a translation of a 1985 Russian-language book. It contains the usual information about standards and technology, and in addition there is considerable information about European (only) standards promulgated by the European Computer Manufacturers Association (ECMA). There is also a thorough description of the author's own system, the Experimental Computer Network (ECN), that interconnects five institutes of the Academy of Sciences of the Latvian SSR. Although it may be of some interest to the advanced professional who collects LAN books, this work has little that has not already been explained, perhaps more clearly, in such standard references as Andrew Tannenbaum's *Computer Networks* (Prentice-Hall, 1981). [R: Choice, Jan 87, p. 785]

Stan Rifkin

EDUCATION AND TRAINING

309.   Boaz, Martha. **Librarian/Library Educator: An Autobiography and Planning for the Future.** Metuchen, N.J., Scarecrow, 1987. 314p. bibliog. index. $27.50. LC 87-4349. ISBN 0-8108-1988-0.

Part 1 of this volume—the autobiographical section—consists of twenty-nine chapters largely dealing with "the library profession, and with library education, and with the School of Library Science at the University of Southern California, in particular." This portion is especially strong in recounting Boaz's varied activities while dean of the USC library school (1955-1979) and since 1979: problems of administration, goals and programs of a library school, fund raising, curriculum revision, professional associations, honors and awards, etc. It concludes with notes and additional sources for part 1 and a bibliography of Dean Boaz's works.

Part 2, "Planning for the Future," opens by noting that 1987 was the centennial year of library education, then addresses (in thirteen chapters) the writer's major theme: "the urgent need to examine the library education profession and focus on improvement, new directions, perhaps drastic changes." Topics discussed include new instructional media and information technology, administrative and faculty responsibilities and student recruitment, research, accreditation, funding, and international education. Along the way some of the giants of library/information science education, past and present—Melvil Dewey, C. C. Williamson, Leon Carnovsky, Samuel Rothstein, Herbert S. White, Jesse Shera, Kathleen Heim, etc.—are cited. The volume concludes with a bibliography and an index, principally of personal names.

All in all, Boaz's work should be of considerable interest to library/information science educators and students.   Wiley J. Williams

310.   Carter, Ruth C., ed. **Education and Training for Catalogers and Classifiers.** New York, Haworth Press, 1987. 195p. illus. (*Cataloging & Classification Quarterly*, Vol. 7, No. 4). $32.95. LC 87-8535. ISBN 0-86656-660-0.

The efficacy of formal education for library staff and the value of practice versus theory have been topics much discussed at conferences and in the library press. This book, first published as the Summer 1987 issue of *Cataloging & Classification Quarterly*, brings together five professors, three administrators of cataloging departments, three practicing catalogers, and two people whose jobs combine administration and cataloging to present their views of the skills needed in a cataloging department and the methodology to be used in gaining those skills.

Several of the professors describe the teaching of a particular aspect of cataloging in their faculties of library science (e.g., descriptive cataloging at the University of Washington) or what should be the content of a particular course (e.g., the subject control of information). The library staff detail on-the-job training programs in their institutions: Pennsylvania State University, New York State University, Albany, the Library of Congress. Two serials catalogers give a personal history of their education and training. An interesting article tells about the training of public service librarians at the University of Illinois at Urbana-Champaign to undertake the cataloging of monographs.

This book presents a well-rounded picture of the education and training of librarians as catalogers. There is less information about the training, and none about the education, of paraprofessional staff. An article about the formal training in cataloging given in library technician programs would have completed the picture of the total available pool of skills.

Employers; administrators; those who participate in, or are planning to inaugurate, in-house training programs; and those who are interested in the educational process will find useful information in these articles.

Jean Weihs

311. Creth, Sheila D. **Effective On-the-Job Training: Developing Library Human Resources.** Chicago, American Library Association, 1986. 121p. index. $15.95pa. LC 86-14187. ISBN 0-8389-0441-6.

This book is a guide to developing training programs and procedures for library staff. It begins with a discussion of the need for systematic training and retraining in libraries, proceeds through the planning stages and actual execution of such programs, and ends with their ultimate evaluation. Interspersed are exercises or assignments through which the reader/supervisor may relate the discussion to his or her own work situation. The appendices reprint sample job training plans for clerical, technical, and professional levels; there is also a very handy orientation checklist for new employees.

The book was developed from the author's workshops on job training held during the last few years. Staff needs for, and fear of, training and retraining for automation are mentioned

frequently. From its detail one can readily see how helpful the program would be for clerical and technical assistants, but the sample plans in appendix A for professional librarians struck me as appropriate course syllabi for library schools. I am surprised that employing libraries need to spend such large quantities of time teaching professionals on the job. Orientation, even for experienced individuals, is essential in any new job situation. Training for new skills, such as the various aspects of automation now common to the library scene, is quite appropriate and could well be handled by following this guide's suggestions. [R: CLJ, Oct 87, pp. 353-54; JAL, July 87, p. 169; LAR, 9 Sept 87, p. 475; WLB, Mar 87, p. 59]

Carol June Bradley

312. **Financial Assistance for Library Education: Academic Year 1987-88.** Chicago, American Library Association, 1986. 52p. index. free pa. ($1.00 postage and handling). ISBN 0-8389-7095-8.

An annually revised guide to financial assistance for library education, this booklet includes awards from state library agencies, national and state library associations, local libraries, and academic institutions offering undergraduate or graduate programs. National associations, foundations, and other agencies known to grant financial assistance for library education are also listed. The introduction includes suggestions about the availability of grants from fifteen other sources.

Each entry includes source of award, program level, type of assistance, number available, amount of award, academic requirements, application deadline, and where to apply. The work concludes with an address list of the graduate library education programs accredited by the American Library Association, a brief but useful index, and a key to abbreviations. An up-to-date and valuable resource, printing of which was made possible by a grant from the H. W. Wilson Foundation, Inc.

Thomas L. Hart

313. Gardner, Richard K., ed. **Education of Library and Information Professionals: Present and Future Prospects.** Littleton, Colo., Libraries Unlimited, 1987. 154p. bibliog. index. $27.50. LC 87-16809. ISBN 0-87287-564-4.

A festschrift that is not really a festschrift is the best characterization of this collection of essays prepared in honor of Martha Boaz. Why isn't this a festschrift? One reason is that most of the contributors really only know Boaz from her publications and some contact through professional associations; none were former colleagues. A second reason, as the editor points out, is that the authors are from a younger generation, not members of Boaz's own generation. The book, while assessing the present and future for library and information science education, is directed toward the profession at large, not library educators. All but one of the nine essays were written for this book. "Librarianship and Information Paradigm" by Richard Apostle and Boris Raymond, first appeared in the *Canadian Library Journal* in 1986. The paper is interesting, but this complex topic requires greater depth of treatment than is possible in a short essay. Only one essay, the first, by Peggy Sullivan, focuses on Martha Boaz and her contributions to the profession and her deanship at the University of Southern California. Beverly Lynch's paper, "The Role of the Profession in the Education of Its Members," is the only one prepared by a "practitioner." As might be expected, it presents a somewhat, but not radically, different perception of accredited degree programs, the question of certification, continuing education, and practical experience. Miriam Tees's essay goes into greater depth on the questions surrounding accreditation and certification. The following essays explore and describe issues and areas of curriculum development (Evelyn Daniel, Guy Garrison, and Thomas Martin). The importance and role of research in library education is described in Jean Tague's contribution. Dean Richard Gardner's essay provides the unifying theme for the essays, in that he reviews, in general terms, the current status of library education, and what the future may hold. All the essays reflect careful thought and preparation; Gardner's editing is excellent. It is doubtful that library educators will find the book of great interest, except as a source of readings for a foundations course. Practitioners who do not closely follow developments in library education may be surprised by some of the content.	G. Edward Evans

314.	Griffiths, Jose-Marie, and Donald W. King. **New Directions in Library and Information Science Education.** Westport, Conn., Greenwood Press, 1986. 465p. bibliog. $45.00 spiralbound. LC 85-23107. ISBN 0-313-25779-5.

This is many studies in one, each of which merits individual treatment. The purpose of this federally funded project was to describe the information environment, its information needs, its providers, and its technology, and within this context to identify and describe the competencies required at several levels and in several areas of professional specialization. More than fifty recent research studies were reviewed and served

as the base to describe the environment within which information professionals work. Through interviews, journal articles, and reports, twenty-two functions in twelve work settings and eighty-eight hundred individual competency statements were identified, described, and validated. From this broad-based study, recommendations are made for education of information professionals. There are also papers on competency issues, an overview of supply and demand in various work settings, a listing of certification requirements by state, an extensive bibliography, an annotated bibliography focused on education, competencies and certification, and much, much more. The study is not easy to read, largely because it follows a research report format and because it is packed with information. It is useful as a guide for those who educate information professionals, those who employ them, and those who contemplate entering the world of information work. It is most useful as a reference resource for many aspects of information personnel activity.

Ann E. Prentice

315.	**Professional Education and Training for Library and Information Work: A Review by The Library and Information Services Council.** London, Library Association; distr., Chicago, American Library Association, 1986. 177p. bibliog. $17.50pa. ISBN 0-85365-707-6.

This book presents a series of papers developed by The Library and Information Services Council (LISC) of Great Britain in 1981 and 1982. It is the final report, prepared under the auspices of the Office of Arts and Libraries, of a Working Party set up by LISC in response to recommendations made in *The Future Development of Libraries and Information Services* (HMSO, 1982). The keynote paper identifies significant changes in the economic, political, social, technological, and educational environment which affect the scope and organization of library and information services, as well as the manpower, education, and training requirements for librarians. This paper is followed by three specialized papers on basic education, training, and continuing education which make specific recommendations for action. The follow-up papers are set in the same context as the keynote paper, and respond to issues and problems previously identified. Part 4 of the book is a brief listing of recommendations in each of the three specialized areas. It is followed by nine short appendices. The first three present analyses of comments received from organizations and institutions who were sent the three specialized papers. The other appendices include an analysis of job titles, a survey of short courses in library and information work (in Great Britain), information on regional management centers (in England and Wales), and on the Centre for the Study of Management Learning (Lancaster University), a glossary of acronyms and code names, and a short unannotated bibliography of "useful publications." The scope of the book is broad, providing an outline and guide to the topics covered, but lacking much detail or substantial information. Since the situation in Great Britain with respect to library development, education, and training differs significantly from that in the United States, the usefulness of the book to U.S. librarians is decidedly limited. The fact that the papers are now over five years old is another important limitation. However, the book still represents a useful contribution to the literature of comparative/international librarianship and library education. It is most appropriate for library science collections supporting schools of library and information science, especially those with special interests in these areas and/or with doctoral programs. The papers are of most interest and relevance to library educators, library school faculty, and students.

Susan J. Freiband

316. Prytherch, Ray, ed. **Handbook of Library Training Practice.** Brookfield, Vt., Gower Publishing, 1986. 444p. index. $68.95. LC 85-27121. ISBN 0-566-03543-X.

Intended as a "blueprint of good training practice," this source serves as a complement to the earlier *Staff Training in Libraries: The British Experience*, and presents a definite British perspective. The thirteen signed chapters are practical in nature and are divided into three sections—"Pervasive Training Techniques," "Relationships with Users," and "Training for Specific Skills" (such as automation or conservation). The authors are academic librarians, public library administrators, or library school professors hand-picked by the editor. Integrated within the text are reproductions of training documents, role playing exercises, performance appraisal forms, and training questionnaires, all meant to be modified to meet local needs.

Once the American reader gets past phrases such as "induction training" for new employees and "stock management" for inventory control, some of the chapters can be made applicable to U.S. conditions. However, besides the checklists and charts, most practicing librarians responsible for staff development or training, will be better served by Sheila Creth's *Effective On-the-Job Training* (American Library Association, 1986) which is also less expensive. It

also includes exercises, is intended for an American audience, and is easier to read.

Prytherch's work will appeal to students of comparative librarianship, library school professors, and those interested in overseas staff exchanges. Its rather steep price will warrant careful purchase by only those comprehensive library science collections. [R: JAL, May 87, p. 107; JAL, July 87, p. 190]

Ilene F. Rockman

317. Rehman, Sajjad ur. **Management Theory and Library Education.** Westport, Conn., Greenwood Press, 1987. 150p. bibliog. index. (New Directions in Information Management, No. 14). $29.95. LC 86-22736. ISBN 0-313-25288-2.

David Kaser's foreword sets forth the purpose of Rehman's study as follows: "Until now ... no one has known—except by chance—just who [the] instructors in the field of library administration really are, what their personal profiles entail, what their educational preparation and library experience have been, what their aims are, or even what in terms of theoretical content they are teaching in their courses. This is what Dr. Rehman [sought] to determine."

The first chapter traces the evolution of management education in library schools as represented by the divergent views of respected library educators, practitioners, and administrators. In the second chapter, management education in selected professional and vocational-technical areas (e.g., business schools, programs in health care, physical education, and pharmacy education) is reviewed in order to provide a comparative framework by which to examine library management education. Chapter 3 opens with an overview of management education in the library schools of the United Kingdom, followed by a description of management courses in North American library schools and identification of needed managerial competencies, observed deficiencies, and library education programs. These three chapters provide the framework for the remaining three chapters ("Research Framework and Methodology," "Findings," and "Findings and Interpretations")—the in-depth analysis of (1) the contents of the basic management course; (2) the instructors' perceptions of course goals and teaching preferences for different management theories and topics (classical, behavioral, and systems schools, personnel management, organizational design, etc.); and (3) a profile of instructors in terms of the variables of education, experience, publications, and age. The appendix reproduces the questionnaire sent to all instructors of the basic management course. The bibliography concluding the book includes very few nonlibrary or information science articles and books. It does not include many of the titles (also mainly from the library and information science literature) in the notes appended to each chapter (except chapter 5).

This overview of management education in the library curriculum is, nevertheless, a valuable contribution for library school faculty, administrators, and researchers. [R: JAL, Sept 87, p. 239; LJ, 1 Nov 87, p. 71; WLB, Sept 87, p. 81]   Wiley J. Williams

318.   Reid, William H. **Four Indications of Current North American Library and Information Doctoral Degree Programs.** Champaign, Ill., Graduate School of Library and Information Science, University of Illinois, 1987. 83p. bibliog. (Occasional Papers, No. 176). $3.00pa.

The series of Occasional Papers published by the University of Illinois Graduate School of Library and Information Science since July 1949 typically includes "papers which are too long or too detailed for publication in a library periodical or which are of specialized or temporary interest" (editorial guideline published in each issue). Given these criteria for selection, the significance of the individual papers varies widely. For example, Michael Winter's analysis of *The Professionalization of Librarianship* (reviewed in *Library Science Annual* 85, entry 128) is considered timely, well written, and documented. Unfortunately, the paper under review here does not meet those same standards.

Reid's work on North American doctoral degree programs in library and information science is described by the author as "an early product of my curiosity about this subject.... The four perspectives of interest were provided by (1) a survey of faculty publications over the five-year-period 1978-1982, (2) brief summaries of the programs' curricula drawn from catalogs and related materials disseminated by the programs to prospective students, (3) a survey of dissertations completed during the five-year-period, and (4) an opinion questionnaire that drew responses from students at 13 of the 17 programs" (p. 3) that Reid had identified from an October 1982 *Library Quarterly* article by Jonathan S. Tryon.

The results of Reid's research are of dubious value in all areas although selected data may be of interest to individuals who are looking for a single source of information about doctoral programs that existed during the 1978-1982 time frame. Reid did examine the catalogs of the seventeen schools identified (sixteen in

the United States, one in Canada) and the program descriptions of the degrees are accurate as based on the material reviewed. Also his data, reproduced in table and narrative format, on the number and types of faculty publications provide information impossible to locate without redoing his literature search of *Library Literature, Library and Information Science Abstracts,* and *Information Science Abstracts.* Further, his attempt to categorize the subjects of the faculty publications and the dissertation topics might be useful to the researcher who wished to draw conclusions about the relationship between doctoral program emphases, faculty publication areas (specializations?), and dissertation topics. At the same time, the data are so broadly sketched that there can be little reliable interpretation, and Reid attempts none. Moreover, two of the schools have since closed, and even during the period studied, faculty and programs changed. In particular, his approach to student evaluation of the respective programs is so poorly executed that the data are meaningless for any purpose.

It is reasonably clear that Reid was aware of the problems in his data collection. What is not clear is who will find this work of even "temporary interest" given its admitted limitations in methodology and presentation. [R: JAL, July 87, p. 179]

Laurel Grotzinger

INDEXING AND ABSTRACTING

319.   Heeks, Richard. **Personal Bibliographic Indexes and Their Computerisation.** London, Taylor Graham, 1986. 189p. bibliog. $28.50pa. ISBN 0-947568-11-5.

The growing importance of personal bibliographic indexes to academic researchers prompted this study, funded by British Library Research and Development. Data were gathered by a mixture of questionnaire, case study, and interview. Telephone interviews were conducted with computing representatives of the biochemistry, economics, and English departments at five British universities and one polytechnic, though researchers at Leicester University, mostly doctoral students, comprised the majority of those questioned. Aims of the project included surveying current indexing practices, comparing time costs and expediency of manual and computerized versions, and assessing attitudes toward computerization.

An executive summary introduces the project's methodology and definitions. The following text examines alternative methods, index programs, and computer possibilities, and a summary offers conclusions and recommendations for future programs. Seven appendices, with additional information on personal bibliographic indexes, and a bibliography complete this volume.

The author concludes that, while manual versions are currently more widespread, developing technologies are increasing the possibilities of constructing computerized ones, and also that the advisability of using either type is largely determined by the researcher's own needs and variables.

The study, while limited to Great Britain, and to a select locale and population of users, is detailed, thorough, and helpful in deciding whether or not to computerize. Many of the study's findings will be applicable to researchers in other areas, as well, and the arguments presented will be valid in assisting the researcher in choosing between manual indexes and the array of computerized personal bibliographic indexes available.   Anita Zutis

320. Pratt, Allan D. **INDEXIT: A Microcomputer Indexing Program and Manual.** New Haven, Conn., Graham Conley Press, 1986. 56p. index. $49.95 looseleaf with binder (with disk). ISBN 0-912087-01-3.

This modestly priced, IBM PC-based command-driven software program has all the capabilities needed for compiling a basic index, including merging, editing, and moving of text. It accommodates both hard and floppy disk systems, comes with a clearly written manual in a three-ring binder, and is specifically designed for indexing a book, newspaper, or archival collection.

Data entry begins by accessing the "add" option, which permits entries as long as the disk capacity. The system can file letter-by-letter or word-by-word, and has the ability to ignore user-defined stop words in the filing sequence. The "merge" option sorts duplicate entries into a single alphabetical sequence, the "reform" option permits data to be attractively reformatted, and the "print" option allows use of the "reform" file to create a single- or double-spaced product. Advanced functions include cross-references and subindexing.

For first-time indexers, a helpful chapter on basic principles and general guidelines establishes the fundamentals. Appendices present filing tips, a quick reference table of keys and commands, and a subject index keyed to page numbers.

Although no tutorial disk is included, the "starting up" portion of the manual takes the user through a sample exercise and various options. However, it is difficult to escape or

get help in the middle of an option, and if (by chance) the printer is not turned on during the "print" option, it is difficult to escape or continue.

Yet, this program is flexible and easy to run. It is hoped that as upgrades or enhancements are made available, they will be as affordable as this version 1.1 of the initial program. [R: JAL, Mar 87, p. 55]   Ilene F. Rockman

321. Strickland-Hodge, Barry. **How to Use Index Medicus and Excerpta Medica.** Brookfield, Vt., Gower Publishing, 1986. 60p. index. $31.50 spiralbound. ISBN 0-566-03532-4.

As the title indicates, this manual is aimed at improving search techniques in the two most heavily used English-language health science indexes in the world. Written from the British viewpoint (e.g., with respect to spelling variants), the manual presents examples from the indexes and various index aids such as thesauri and permuted indexes. Aside from a brief historical review the volume does not intend to cover the use of online equivalents of the indexes, something that will be treated in a forthcoming volume in the series.

The manual is well organized and indexed, with numerous excellent examples. The typography is excellent although the spiralbound format may not last long under normal use. The real quarrels with this volume are with the price and extent of coverage. Considering that much of what is presented is distilled from existing guides and user aids one might expect more for the price. Analytics on overlap between the indexes and relationship to other information sources might have made a more original contribution. One is paying more for the packaging than the information. Considering the cost, the quantity, and the British slant, American users will benefit as much from less expensive or free user aids.   Andrew G. Torok

INFORMATION MANAGEMENT

322. Awani, Alfred O. **Data Processing Project Management.** Princeton, N.J., Petrocelli Books; distr., Blue Ridge Summit, Pa., TAB Books, 1986. 308p. bibliog. index. $29.95. LC 86-22507. ISBN 0-89433-234-1.

Awani's book has two objectives: first, to give persons responsible for data management projects an introduction to the broader field of project management, and second, to provide methods for applying these concepts to all types of data processing projects, particularly those in which the reader has no previous experience.

The author begins by surveying the basics of data processing management (e.g., system development life cycle and a breakdown of a typical data processing project). The next third of the book discusses project management with particular emphasis on network techniques, such as Critical Path Method (CPM) and Program Evaluation and Review Technique (PERT). The following chapters cover project costs, scheduling using linear programming, control of individual projects and integrating multiprojects, software maintenance, and system evaluation. The final chapter discusses microcomputer projects. Awani's writing is clear and the use of mathematics is kept to a minimum. There are short bibliographies after most chapters, although no citation is later than 1983 (and most of these are to Awani's own *Project Management Techniques*, also published by Petrocelli Books). Persons responsible for data processing projects, especially those with little experience, should find this work a useful overview.   Robert Skinner

323.   Brophy, Peter. **Management Information and Decision Support Systems in Libraries.** Brookfield, Vt., Gower Publishing, 1986. 158p. bibliog. index. $39.00. ISBN 0-566-03551-0.

Brophy describes management information systems in three major sections: theoretical foundations, in which management information concepts are analyzed and related to actual organizations; the development of library applications including automated systems; and future developments. In each section, there are thorough reviews of the current literature. This is a conceptual, rather than a practical, text oriented towards libraries in England. American library managers interested in developing management information systems or modifying existing systems will, however, find this a useful background text. Its readability is enhanced by Brophy's awareness of human capriciousness, which leavens his complex topic. [R: JAL, July 87, p. 195]   Margaret McKinley

324.   Burton, Paul F., and J. Howard Petrie. **The Librarian's Guide to Microcomputers for Information Management.** New York, Van Nostrand Reinhold, 1986. 271p. illus. bibliog. index. $41.95. LC 86-19072. ISBN 0-442-31770-0.

An update of the 1984 *Introducing Microcomputers: A Guide for Librarians*, this 1986 version continues the practice of offering brief, but clear, information on the use of micros in the information world. This edition will be particularly useful for its first section, "Electronics for Macrocomputers and Microcomputers: The

Building Blocks." These chapters contain, among other topics, a discussion of making microprocessors and good explanations of CD-ROM, videodiscs, and digital optical disks. Later chapters may prove less useful in part because of the decided British focus of the examples, but also because of the specific hardware and software recommendations that might best be handled by suggestions for consulting directories, reviews, catalogs, and periodicals for current information. I also fail to understand why authors of books about computers feel compelled to include photographs of hardware components, but many do, and unfortunately Petrie and Burton are no exception. I doubt if it is possible "to provide a single source of information on the process of automation with a microcomputer" as the authors suggest, but this book is certainly worthy of purchase for the quantity of useful information it does contain.

Elisabeth Logan

325.   Burwasser, Suzanne M. **File Management Handbook for Managers and Librarians.** Studio City, Calif., Pacific Information, 1986. 165p. index. (Professional Skills Series). $24.50pa. LC 86-25345. ISBN 0-913203-15-7.

Librarians are formally trained in library school to catalog all types of materials: books, audiocassettes, kits, films, and videocassettes. But what about correspondence, reports, checks, ledgers, etc.? How do we catalog them? *File Management Handbook for Managers and Librarians* will serve as a sourcebook on developing filing systems of all kinds for librarians, record managers, and general managers.

Chapters include "The Document Life Cycle," "Developing a Records Retention Schedule," "Long-term Storage," "File Equipment Analysis," "Filing Systems," "Categories of Filing Systems," "Setting up Filing Systems," "Staff Responsibilities," "File Maintenance," "Departmental Files Management Program," "Developing a Filing Classification System," and "File Maintenance Program."

This work provides information on how to determine the life cycle of a document (i.e., ask the important question "Why would anyone refer to this again?"). Helpful examples and illustrations of record inventory forms, work flow plans, and sample floor plans for storage assist the reader. Numerous types of filing systems and coding categories are described.

Records management is a necessity, painful though it is. *File Management Handbook* will help ease the pain considerably for even the novice.

Janet R. Ivey

326. Collier, Mel, ed. **Microcomputer Software for Information Management: Case Studies.** Brookfield, Vt., Gower Publishing, 1986. 166p. illus. index. $33.50. LC 86-7704. ISBN 0-566-03555-3.

Mel Collier has collected case studies of six English public, academic, and medical libraries' experiences with specific applications of microcomputers to library management, acquisitions and fund accounting, online catalogs, circulation systems, and preparation of specialized bibliographies. The software discussed in the case studies and the systems they run on includes dBase II (IBM), Compsoft DMS Diamond (Commodore), Data Machine TDM (Apple II), PICK (Altos), MICROCAIRS (Apricot), and Condor (Apple II). Several of these are implemented on networked or multi-user systems. This book is of value first for the descriptions of several software packages (and computer hardware and operating systems) largely unfamiliar to readers on this side of the Atlantic, and second, for the methodologies used to choose and implement the information systems. While individual parts of the case studies are outdated, there is a good introduction to the software chapter written by Paul Burton, which discusses videodiscs and surveys a number of additional programs currently in use in England. There are some illustrations and references for each study. The book seems adequately edited and proofread, except that the page numbers in the table of contents and index are off by one beginning with page 95. [R: LAR, May 87, p. 244]   Robert Skinner

327. Feeney, Mary, ed. **New Methods and Techniques for Information Management.** London, Taylor Graham, 1986. 364p. $43.50pa. ISBN 0-947568-12-3.

The introduction states that "information management is now recognized as a discipline" but concedes it "is somewhat difficult to pin down 'tending' to mean different things to different organizations and in different contexts." The eclectic nature of this "discipline" is evident in the section titles: "Hardware and Software"; "Text Capture and Handling"; "Information Storage"; "Information Retrieval"; "Online Databases"; "Menu-driven Systems"; "Expert Systems"; "Text Transfer Systems"; "Communications"; "Telecommunications"; and "Some Legal and Regulatory Issues." Each section is subdivided, with an introduction and subsections the authors considered pertinent; each subsection consists of a summary followed by subdivisions of the topic and ending with conclusions and references for further reading. Cross-referencing is accomplished with

asterisks. No index is provided. The format used places the text on the righthand two-thirds of the page and uses the wide margin for subdivision heads of typically one to three words in length. This seems wasteful.

Presumably, the primary audience for this book is the information manager. Topics are covered by reviewing past UK and U.S. activities on the subject and plans for further efforts and cost, or short descriptions of processes. Accessing and following up on this information would have been enhanced by an index and a centralized system of referencing. Organizations and prices are liberally identified in the text in a general way; one is left to one's own devices for obtaining specific information. An example from page 64 illustrates this: typewriters can be linked to Wordnet @ 500 UK $/machine; Wang Laboratories has a system for printing text of an Arabic/English document in the same operation—who makes Wordnet or the linkage machine is not identified, and Wang was not identified further. Those who can best use and understand this book do not need it and those who need to learn and use the information can find better resources on this subject.

Marvin K. Harris

328. Harris, Colin, ed. **Management Information Systems in Libraries and Information Services: Proceedings of a Conference Held at the University of Salford, July 1986.** London, Taylor Graham, 1987. 164p. £18.00pa. ISBN 0-947568-18-2.

This work contains proceedings of a conference held at the University of Salford (England) in July 1986. The introductory address, by John Ashworth, vice-chancellor of the host institution, is a gem, literate, witty, and to-the-point. He begins by stating that "librarians have always been notoriously weak in their use of management information," and that the conference is intended to remedy that deplorable condition.

The central theme is that increasing pressure for financial accountability and increasingly complicated needs conspire to cause librarians to feel threatened, sometimes overwhelmed, by the need to corral and disseminate vital information to their constituents. Librarians must borrow liberally from the private sector of business and apply private-sector profit-and-loss concepts to their enterprises. Management Information Systems (MIS) has much to offer, especially some of its performance measures and evaluation techniques, and packaged statistical databases are designed and built to achieve that end. Statistics is an area only dimly understood, if at all, by librarians, say these authors. We need accurate, plentiful information to run our concerns more effectively, and we need sophisticated programs and databases to use statistics. One of these authors warns, however, that we must be ever alert to change, "lest we measure things in a certain manner, "only to find that the chaps have moved off into another part of the ballpark." These papers are not all as witty or amusing as Ashworth's, but most are informative, dealing with the role of MIS in such important areas as library and information systems, research, and education, and there is much that American librarians can learn and adapt from their British counterparts. Recommended.   Bruce A. Shuman

329. **Information Management.** P. M. Griffiths, ed. Elmsford, N.Y., Pergamon Press, 1986. 362p. bibliog. index. (State of the Art Report 14:7). $545.00. ISBN 0-08-034096-2.

Information Management is a complexly structured work designed "to provide a balanced and comprehensive view of the latest developments in information management." The report is divided into three parts. Part 1 consists of fifteen invited papers that examine various aspects of information management, such as "Information for Strategic Advantage," "Using Communications for Competitive Advantage," and "The Information Factory." Part 2 is an analysis of information management trends written by the editor of the report, P. M. Griffiths. Her section is divided into five parts: (1) "Introduction—Linking Information Systems (IS)/Information Technology (IT) with Business," (2) "Information Planning," (3) "Organisational Aspects," (4) "Information Management," and (5) "Competitive Performance." Part 3 of the report is a 250-item annotated bibliography on the role of information management in competitive success. A subject and contributor index is provided.

The emphasis of the book is on business use of information systems and information technology for competitive advantage. The invited papers are well written and are primarily by British authors. The analysis is equally valuable and integrates insights of the various papers with the editor's own wisdom and experience. It would be very useful for any manager interested in learning how to conduct business in the Information Era.   Robert H. Burger

330. **Information Management Sourcebook: The AIIM Buying Guide and Membership Directory 1987.** Stephen A. Saft, ed. Silver Spring, Md., Association for Information and Image Management, 1987. 430p. $40.00pa.

This big blue paperback is the premier (1987) edition of what will be an annual from now on. It's not a new publication, however, as it carries on the five-year-old tradition of the former *AIIM Buying Guide*, which it now supersedes. In addition to established sections on such topics as retrieval devices, cameras, processors, COM recorders, consultants, and the like, there are new divisions on areas such as bar code technology, document/records management software, and networking. This book, by the way, does not purport to represent the entire information management industry. A free listing in the *Sourcebook* (the editor informs us) is a privilege granted AIIM trade members. First-timers may get freebies also, as a one-time inducement to join. All others pay cash, based on an unpublished fee structure.

The work is designed to be an all-in-one, as it provides extensive lists of people, places, and things in one convenient publication, as well as a cross-reference section for products and suppliers. The last 150 (blue) pages constitute a 1987 AIIM membership directory, and its alphabetically arranged entries are barebones, consisting of names, addresses, telephone numbers, and (sometimes) corporate contacts. Advertising, some in color, is sprinkled throughout, a practice which is either disconcerting or helpful, according to one's motivations and preferences. For information managers and those concerned with information management, this is not only a useful publication, it's likely to be the only game in town. Generalist libraries and smaller public ones can probably get along without it.

Bruce A. Shuman

331. Kazlauskas, Edward John, and Pamela Cibbarelli, eds. **Directory of Information Management Software, 1987/1988: For Libraries, Information Centers, Records Centers.** Studio City, Calif., Pacific Information, 1987. 301p. index. $49.00pa. ISBN 0-913203-18-1.

The current update of the directory is a decided improvement over the past edition. It is larger, more detailed, and more easily read. As in the previous editions, criteria for inclusion are clearly stated in the introduction and each entry contains a consistent set of descriptive information. Entries for items such as hardware, system requirements, availability, documentation, maximum record and file size, etc., facilitate comparisons between software options. There are separate indexes for vendor name, hardware, and applications as well as a general index to all entries. The main body of the directory is divided into two parts: part 1 contains detailed information on 110 different software packages, and part 2 provides brief information on 64 additional packages. The major problem with the directory, aside from the ever-present problem of timeliness, is the lack of page numbers associated with index entries. Entries in parts 1 and 2 are alphabetical, so that entries *can* be found, but the arrangement is awkward and can be confusing. For instance, under OCLC in the vendor index are listed ALIS II and LS 2000. Information about LS 2000 can be found in part 1, but the reader must look in part 2 for ALIS II. Page numbers would eliminate this type of double searching. In spite of this limitation, the directory is a useful, if somewhat expensive, tool for anyone considering software purchases for library and information center applications. I hope we can look forward to continued expansion and enhancement in future editions.   Elisabeth Logan

332. Marchand, Donald A., and Forrest W. Horton, Jr. **Infotrends: Profiting from Your Information Resources.** New York, John Wiley, 1986. 324p. bibliog. index. $24.95. LC 85-29438. ISBN 0-471-81680-9.

The primary purpose of *Infotrends* is "to address the business issues and management concerns that arise in an information economy, and to point medium- and large-sized businesses in the proper direction, so that they can manage information resources and assets to their competitive advantage." In order to accomplish this task the authors have arranged their book in nine chapters: "The Information Economy," "The Information-Processing Industry," "Rethinking Your Business in the Information Economy," "New Strategies for Gaining Competitive Advantage," "Strategic Information Management," "New Structures and Functions for Corporate Information Management," "Managing and Planning for Information Productivity," "The Knowledge Worker," and "The Changing Role of Business in the Information Society." Each chapter contains charts, diagrams, and tables that illustrate the authors' ideas. The work also has a bibliography and an index.

Marchand and Horton's work is more than a popular guide to winning in the new information economy. In clear and lively writing they cite both the scholarly business and management literature, as well as actual recent case studies, in order to drive their points home. As a result the book should prove useful to managers and theoreticians alike.   Robert H. Burger

333. Senn, James A. **Information Systems in Management.** 3d ed. Belmont, Calif., Wads-

worth Publishing, 1987. 800p. illus. bibliog. index. $41.00. LC 86-19119. ISBN 0-534-07482-0.

In a modular text for information systems students, Senn first reviews management information and systems concepts, placing them in an organizational context. Next, in the computer systems module he discusses hardware for personal computers and mainframes and provides an overview of software history and current technology. The transactions processing module includes discussions of files and file processing, database management techniques, and data communications methodologies. Transaction processing systems, management information systems, decision support, and expert systems are analyzed in the information systems module. Finally, the student is introduced to the management of information systems, including analysis and planning, system design and end-user input in development, and the impact of information systems on corporate strategy and the future of information systems. Each chapter includes minicases and application problems. Extended case studies appear in an appendix. Supplemental chapters cover number systems and arithmetic operations, the programming cycle, input validation techniques, cost/benefit analysis, and software development. Senn has gathered a formidable amount of material together in a coherent and logical fashion. He also makes the most difficult concepts understandable. His many case studies emphasize the difficulties of installing or managing information systems in the real world. Senn dismisses the capabilities of libraries as sources of management information. This is, however, a minor flaw in a text that could be used for independent study by librarians or other information specialists seeking to improve their knowledge of this field of study.

Margaret McKinley

334. Singh, Indu B., and Vic M. Mishra, eds. **Dynamics of Information Management: Concepts and Issues.** Norwood, N.J., Ablex Publishing, 1987. 257p. index. $34.50. LC 87-978. ISBN 0-89391-404-5.

This book discusses the relationship of information technology (computing and telecommunications) to government and other institutions. It is a diverse collection of articles on information management in schools, the educational process, U.S. manufacturing, politics, business, health care, Third World development, international trade, and banking. Each of the fifteen articles was written by a different author (or pair of co-authors); the style and perspective vary greatly throughout the book.

Some articles are relatively technical (e.g., dealing with videoconferencing) while others are like guides and others read more like sociology papers. The article by Pipe, "International Information Policy," gives a good analysis of national policy issues related to computerization, and it cites the work of the OECD (Organization for Economic Cooperation and Development) and countries like Sweden. This paper discusses the concept of "transborder data flow," which the author shows to be a useful approach to analyzing a country's relationships with others. Some of the papers have significant lists of references given, while others do not. The typesetting, illustrations, and binding are uninspired but acceptable.

Steven L. Tanimoto

335. Smith, Allen N., and Donald B. Medley. **Information Resource Management.** Cincinnati, Ohio, South-Western Publishing, 1987. 304p. illus. index. $32.93. LC 85-61784. ISBN 0-538-10180-6.

The major justification for this book is that information is a valuable business asset that is growing rapidly. Information resource management (IRM) requires expertise in managing technology for handling information and familiarity with procedures designed to meet business needs. The emphasis is on generic management and not on the acquisition, manipulation, or application of particular information. The twelve chapters concern four major areas of IRM: a history of management and development, principles, processes, and directions. The authors are businesspersons and their pragmatism permeates the production-oriented text. Line diagrams, tabular illustrations, and flowcharts complement the text. The possibilities for managing information have exploded from penciling data in a pocket notebook to electronically logging purchases, sales, and employee records, and almost infinite manipulation capabilities for everything. Placing this information in the right hands at the right time and simultaneously safeguarding it is a complex problem that successful businesses must solve. The authors recognize the emerging nature of this problem and have provided a state-of-the-art book for understanding why IRM is needed and how management can be organized and conducted, as well as laying the groundwork for future changes that are certain to occur. This book is well written and well organized and has a useful index. It will make a fine text for courses in IRM.

Marvin K. Harris

336. Smith, Milburn D., III. **Information and Records Management: A Decision-Maker's Guide to Systems Planning and Implementation.** Westport, Conn., Quorum Books/Greenwood Press, 1986. 285p. index. $39.95. LC 86-638. ISBN 0-89930-111-8.

The author believes this book to be the "first to encompass the interrelated functions of information and records management." He states that the book offers "complete instructions on how to assess an organization's system's requirements, plan and develop an information and records management system, select vendors and equipment, set the system in motion and use it effectively." The guide, in reality, brings together and simplifies information already available in library science textbooks, secretarial handbooks, library or office equipment catalogs, and popular computer magazines.

The coverage is cursory, with the emphasis on definitions and stating basic truisms. A good example of this type of coverage is found in the chapter "Conducting an Inventory," which makes the following points: "it can be surprising how quickly records are inventoried once a methodology is developed" and "overwhelming volume is probably a sign that records retention policies are law." Neither is followed by recommendations, suggested techniques, methodologies, or strategies. Another similar example of cursory or simplistic treatment of complex topics is found in the chapter "Managing Users." This chapter consists of ten pages subdivided into the following categories: "Impact of Office Systems on Human Networks," "Computer Use in the 1980's," "Managing Resistance," "Facilities Planning," "The Record Manual," "Who Will Read the Manual," "The Manual's Content," "Updating the Manual," "Training," "Secretarial Training," "Professional Training," and "Corporate Computer Literacy." Several of these topics deserve more than a page. For example, "Facilities Planning" consists of five paragraphs and makes statements such as "the records manager can ease the transition to an automated system by making certain that the new environment fits human as well as technological needs." This is a truism which does not then lead into discussions of how to plan a facility or determine human and machine requirements.

This book seems to be an enlarged dictionary, whose primary audience would be supervisors of libraries or records management systems who need a basic overview of the topic. It would not help users who want more detailed instructions on filing systems, cost analysis, inventorying, etc. More detailed information on basic record keeping functions can be found in several modern secretarial handbooks.

Susan B. Ardis

337. Synnott, William R. **The Information Weapon: Winning Customers and Markets with Technology.** New York, John Wiley, 1987. 334p. index. $29.95. LC 86-32393. ISBN 0-471-84557-4.

This book reminds me of the technocrats of the 1930s, who thought technology was the cure for all our social ills. Synnott feels that the application of information technology to management is a "competitive force — an information weapon — that is opening up new ways of doing things, better, faster, and cheaper. The firms that are able to grasp and exploit these new information technologies will excel and lead the competition as we move into the 1990's." The author goes on to discuss the myriad information resources available today. Other topics presented are strategic planning methodologies for information use, the architectural framework for information flow in a decentralized environment, and techniques for effective change management.

Synnott's analysis of the impact of information technologies is thought provoking. The book for the most part makes excellent reading for those interested in management strategies. Some of what the author suggests needs re-examination and critiquing. For instance, it remains to be seen if the frequently cited General Motors decentralized information-based technology actually results in a "better, faster, and cheaper" product. Some suggestions given by the author, such as putting terminals in your customers' offices, may in time violate antitrust legislation.

The typography and layout of the book are pleasing. The quote by Nicholas Murray Butler on page 315 is cited as "publication unknown"; it would be nice to know where the author found the quote in the first place (or has it passed into our folklore?). On balance the price/value relationship for this book is a fair one. You get a lot of useful information for your $29.95. Just remember that information, like technology, is not the answer to all problems. Just ask the NASA administrator who, when bombarded with information, managed to launch a manned space vehicle with a major structural flaw. Another example can be found in American automobiles of the late 1970s, such as the Aspen: Chrysler had the information available to make good, long-lasting cars in the 1960s (witness the legendary Darts and Valiants of the period), but why bother? Synnott however, has many good ideas and most libraries with clients interested in management will find ready patrons for this work.

Ralph L. Scott

INFORMATION TECHNOLOGY

338. Adams, Roy J. **Information Technology & Libraries: A Future for Academic Libraries.** Dover, N.H., Croom Helm; distr., New York, Methuen, 1986. 188p. bibliog. index. (Croom Helm Information Technology Series). $34.00. LC 86-6298. ISBN 0-7099-0577-7.

In this typescript book, Adams, a self-assured prognosticator, describes the academic library of the future both in the United States and in Europe (including the United Kingdom). Drawing upon a number of other writer's views of the present and the future, Adams notes that the academic library must get into the business of information transfer as opposed to information storage and retrieval. He warns that traditional organizational patterns and the present service structure are likely to kill the academic library because in a world of electronic information and pressure from other agencies to service information needs, the academic library will evolve into a useless and antiquated organization. If, however, the library becomes the information broker and pushes the information consultant role, while at the same time enhancing relationships with students and faculty, the future is bright.

While Adams's tone of certainty about the future is annoying, he does present both the current issues and some possible future avenues for thinking and planning. There are many articles about the problems Adams discusses, but his view of academic libraries, covering more than just the United States, is valuable. For library administrators wanting to discuss futurism with their staffs, Adams should be used as a checklist of issues.

David V. Loertscher

339. Behan, Kate, and Diana Holmes. **Understanding Information Technology: Text, Readings, and Cases.** Englewood Cliffs, N.J., Prentice-Hall, 1986. 493p. illus. index. $20.75 pa. ISBN 0-13-935917-6.

This introductory text emphasizes the role of information technology (IT) in business applications using the computer and associated devices. The fourteen chapters discuss the need for information; computers; information output, information input, information storage, information management, programming computers, communications systems, converting to a computer system, computer packages, developing IT systems, how growth and diversity affect IT, IT and society, and practical case studies. The organization is logical and each chapter is relatively independent, allowing flexibility in assignments. Study questions at the end of each chapter provide a review and a self-check on comprehending the material. Liberal use of pertinent articles by other authors provides additional perspectives in each chapter. The actual form of implementing the information provided by the text into laboratory exercises is left to the reader (or teacher) and an instructor's guide (not reviewed) is available for use. This text is a thoughtful, comprehensive, and informative work on IT. I highly recommend it.   Marvin K. Harris

340.   Beniger, James R. **The Control Revolution: Technological and Economic Origins of the Information Society.** Cambridge, Mass., Harvard University Press, 1986. 493p. illus. bibliog. index. $25.00. LC 85-31743. ISBN 0-674-16985-9.

Beniger begins "desir[ing] to understand the new centrality of information" (p. v) and, revealing the grandeur of his ambition, concludes that the "rise of the Information society itself ... has exposed the centrality of information processing, communication, and control to all aspects of human society and social behavior" (p. 436). The central theme is summarized in the subtitle of the concluding chapter: "Control as Engine of the Information Society." Although the book focuses on the "crisis of control" in the nineteenth century, the theoretical basis is far wider. In the first of three sections, "Living Systems, Technology and the Evolution of Control," the author draws on thermodynamics, information theory, computer programming, decision analysis, and DNA research to assert that control is a characteristic of living systems. In the second section, "Industrialization, Processing Speed, and the Crisis of Control," it is argued, using commercial evidence and technological variables, that processing speeds in the Industrial Revolution outpaced control functions until tamed by innovations in communications and information processing. The third section, "Toward an Information Society: From Control Crisis to Control Revolution," identifies mass production and distribution, mass consumption, and data processing and bureaucracy as results. The thirty-eight-page bibliography has some curious omissions, most notably Jeremy Rifkin's *Entropy: A New World View* (Viking Press, 1980), which offered an opposing analysis of systems. The seventeen-page index is useful, as would have been a list of the numerous tables and figures. The overall argument suffers from an Anglo-American bias in its evidence and tiring, selective commercial histories, but the timeline tables, ranging from social transformation theories to transportation crises, and the argument itself are stimulating

and provocative although not convincing. One need be chary of assuming that "nothing like us ever was" (Carl Sandburg, "Four Preludes on Playthings of the Wind").   K. Mulliner

341.   Blackler, Frank, and David Oborne, eds. **Information Technology & People: Designing for the Future.** Letchworth, England, British Psychological Society; distr., Cambridge, Mass., MIT Press, 1987. 262p. index. $30.00. LC 86-20119. ISBN 0-262-02260-5.

The rapid development in information technologies has had an inevitable impact on our society and our workplace and in our homes. Such changes are necessary for the economic growth of industrial nations. Yet the impact of these innovations has not been pervasive. The authors note that resistance is due largely to the generally low level of usability, applicability, and acceptability of information systems and products. The main theme of this collection of twelve articles is that human factors relating to the operation and use of these new technologies should be incorporated in their design and implementation. Well-designed technologies should be logical so that they can be easily understood and easily mastered with a minimum of effort. Their use should be transparent, with low probability of error. At the present, the field of psychology has accumulated much knowledge on the limits of human attention, human memory, problem-solving strategies, visual search paths, manual skills, perception and recognition, learning, and instruction. Psychologists could contribute towards the prediction and understanding of users' behaviors in relation to information technologies. They are, however, underutilized. In other words, not enough attention has been directed to the ergonomic and user-friendly aspects of systems design. Behavioral issues are important for the success or failure of technological changes.

This book is published by the British Psychological Society. The primary objective is to survey existing relevant research in human factors with respect to information technology, and to consider how such knowledge could be put to use. Technology is examined with respect to organizations, health and education, and society. Examples are drawn from factory automation, office automation, medical expert systems, application to the disabled and the classroom, and teleshopping in the home.

The concern of people in the design of information technology is a vast area. Its characteristics vary widely depending on the types of technology. The authors noted that ergonomic considerations in the United Kingdom have lagged behind those in the United States. Although advances in some areas such as screen design and office automation have been made, other problems in the use of expert systems are not yet solved. Somehow, these concerns of the "individual" user instead of the generic "user" coincide with the current interest of the information user as an individual in the information science community. Although there is a heavy British emphasis in the works cited, the arguments are valid. In particular, the article by Neil Frude on "the promises as yet unrealized" sketched a realistic scenario of what is soon to come. It is unavoidable that better information products and services will follow. Although the content of the book is not particularly profound, this publication will be of some interest to our field.   Miranda Lee Pao

342. Edmunds, Robert A. **The Prentice-Hall Encyclopedia of Information Technology.** Englewood Cliffs, N.J., Prentice-Hall, 1987. 590p. illus. index. $67.50. LC 86-17038. ISBN 0-13-695214-3.

This one-volume encyclopedia features over 150 cross-referenced topics covering broad areas in the field of information technology. Through a comprehensive index at the end of the book, users can find references to terms found within the alphabetically listed topical articles. The index is essential to locate the embedded terms within the broad topics. The general topic "Chip technology" can be used as an example. The reader is advised to see also the related topics "Computer architecture," "Fifth generation technology," "Microprocessors," and "Microcomputers and microcomputer systems." The article itself includes such subtopics as "types of chips" (by number of components, by function, and by design). The terms found in these sections (e.g., *MOS, Microprocessors, VLSI,* etc.) are also listed in the index, but nowhere else in the volume.

As the preface states, "this is not a technical 'bits and bytes' book." It is written in nontechnical terminology, providing the reader with a basic understanding of the subjects. In places, the author tries so hard to be readable that his style becomes ungrammatical. This is especially true in the case of subject/verb agreement. ("Data *is* ..."; "The design and manufacture of chips *is*....") Errors of this type, plus cross-references instructing one to *see* rather than *see also* a particular topic, detract somewhat from the work. Still, this encyclopedia's topical approach, the nontechnical explanations, and the overall readability of articles make this work a valuable, basic introduction to the subject of information technology. [R: Choice, Mar 87, p. 1028; RBB, 1 May 87, pp. 1346, 1348]
      Marjorie E. Bloss

343. Ennals, Richard, Rhys Gwyn, and Levcho Zdravchev, eds. **Information Technology and Education: The Changing School.** Chichester, England, Ellis Horwood; distr., New York, Halsted Press/John Wiley, 1987. 235p. index. $29.95. ISBN 0-470-20757-4.

This book addresses emerging issues, national perspectives, and classroom responses in information technology (IT) and education in fourteen chapters by sixteen competent authors. The five chapters on emerging issues are sometimes informative, provocative, radical, unrealistic, and naive, but always interesting. The six on national perspectives are often pedestrian, litanical, and collectively repetitive, as might be expected from a discipline (IT) less than twenty years old. The three on classroom responses tended to the mundane, consistent with the state of the art of IT currently available for general use by students. Gwyn suggests the computer will relieve burdens from our brains to an extent comparable to what the Industrial Revolution did for our backs, and Sendov advocates a reassessment of what we teach, with most authors mentioning that learning how to learn is well suited to using the computer in education, especially since the computer can be relied on for retaining and representing facts on command. Presumably students that learn how to learn using the computer will adapt better to the changing world, be more employable and serve as catalysts to make IT in education a reality. But if weak backs accrue from sedentary existence (also due to the Industrial Revolution), the blessing of IT may have a darker side. Not to worry. Hager notes that changing a school system requires more than seven years, while computer technology has revolutionary innovations every two years. Modern education has grown accustomed to being a generation behind the information cycle but appears to be overwhelmed by the technological capabilities currently emerging. The premature headlong rush of education to IT echoes in every chapter, but ideas must precede actions and much good will yet come from it, as glimpses provided by examples given for special education with the handicapped attest. This is a good book although typographical errors abound (e.g., "grammer," page 122) and some writing is weak and needed stronger editing. [R: Choice, Mar 87, pp. 1122, 1124]

      Marvin K. Harris

344. ESPRIT '86: Results and Achievements. Edited by Directorate General XII, Telecommunications, Information Industries & Innovation. New York, Elsevier Science Publishing, 1987. 953p. index. $89.00. ISBN 0-444-70160-5.

ESPRIT '86 contains the proceedings of the third ESPRIT Conference held in Brussels, 29 September-1 October 1986. ESPRIT's (European Strategic Programme for Research in Information Technology) objectives are "to foster industrial cooperation, to build the technology base needed for the early 1990's, and to pave the way for international standards." ESPRIT is the European Community's response to U.S. and Japanese hegemony in information technology research and its applications. Most of the papers deal with hardware and software (e.g., advanced microelectronics, software technology, and computer-integrated manufacture), but there are also sessions devoted to human factors and management (e.g., office system science and human factors). All the papers arose from a concerted European Community research effort that was highly selective in awarding funding.

All the papers are in English, offering access to American IT researchers, most of whom are monolingual. They are, for the most part, clearly written, and are well illustrated. Other than the table of contents, arranged by the session's topic, the only other access is through an author index. This cooperative program in general deserves attention by U.S. firms, not only because of the research advances presented, but also for the apparently successful cooperative effort that promises to benefit the entire EEC.   Robert H. Burger

345. Goldfield, Randy J. Office Information Technology: A Decision-Maker's Guide to Systems Planning and Implementation. Westport, Conn., Quorum Books/Greenwood Press, 1986. 226p. index. $35.00. LC 86-614. ISBN 0-89930-108-8.

The purpose of *Office Information Technology* is "to equip the reader with tools to create and implement an office automation (OA) strategy." The author's focus on the office is based on both experience and projected trends. Goldfield, who is president of The Omni Group, has come to see the office as a "nerve center" of today's business. Indeed, the author asserts: "Much more than a physical entity, the office houses and facilitates a set of business relationships centered on the generation and exchange of information." Moreover, the importance of the office is growing. If projections by the Bureau of Labor Statistics are correct, by 1990 more than half of the American workforce will be occupied within the office.

The book begins with a general introduction to office automation and is then followed by chapters specifically devoted to quantifying white collar productivity, information processing, hardware technology, software, telecommunications, records management, office ergonomics, relations with vendors, staffing, and training. The work ends with a summary chapter on establishing an integrated office automation strategy, in which Goldfield clearly and succinctly outlines procedures to be followed. An appendix contains nine illustrative case studies. The discussion throughout the book focuses on central office automation issues, assuming a practitioner's knowledge of management practices. A glossary of terms and an index are also provided.

Goldfield's book is clearly written and uses examples well to give body to managerial prescriptions. Goldfield does not, however, use a cookbook approach. Instead, she wisely and logically sets out principles applicable to the automation of all types of offices.

Robert H. Burger

346. Gordon, M., A. Singleton, and C. Rickards. **Dictionary of New Information Technology Acronyms.** 2d ed. London, Kogan Page; distr., Detroit, Gale, 1986. 243p. $56.00. ISBN 1-8103-4315-0.

The field of library and information science is perhaps the "worst" offender in terms of developing a language of jargon which contains an extensive number of acronyms. This dictionary is an attempt to make some sense out of this chaos.

Concentrating on the United Kingdom and the United States, its 243 pages are devoted to an alphabetically arranged listing of approximately twelve thousand acronyms which occur with any frequency in the field. It is to be expected that this is not an all-inclusive listing; becoming a super-sleuth with the aspiration of tracking down each and every acronym seems a superhuman task. Some notable acronyms not found include: ALISE (Association for Library and Information Science Education) and its corresponding journal *JELIS* (*Journal of Education for Library and Information Science*); of ALA divisions, ACRL, AASL, and LITA are listed but PLA, LAMA, ALSC, ALTA, ASCLA, RASD, RTSD, and YASD are not. Rather than a condemnation, this mention of omissions serves to highlight that this volume must not be viewed as comprehensive.

Another caveat to be observed is that no volume of acronyms can possibly claim to be current, since the field is changing so rapidly. However, as an attempt to get a handle on this monumental jargonistic confusion, this work would be a useful addition to any reference collection.   Darlene E. Weingand

347.   Madnick, Stuart E., ed. **The Strategic Use of Information Technology.** New York, Oxford University Press, 1987. 206p. index. (Executive Bookshelf). $18.95. LC 87-1606. ISBN 0-19-505048-7.

As with other volumes in the series Executive Bookshelf, this book is a selection of articles from the prestigious *Sloan Management Review*. Edited by an authority in business and large-scale information systems, this volume consists of an introduction written by the editor on the effectiveness and impact of information technology and twelve articles organized into three parts. Part 1 deals with integrating information technology into corporate strategy. Discussions center on the means by which an organization may identify strategic opportunities and on explanations of how to move the organization to take full advantage of those opportunities. Part 2 discusses changes in the roles of the information systems organization itself and of the chief information officer; part 3 examines the responsibilities of the corporation in relation to information systems, mainly in the areas of computer security and employee privacy. The articles, each preceded by an abstract, are authoritative and scholarly, yet written in easy to read, nontechnical language. The book is highly recommended for managers in general and considered indispensable for academic libraries, libraries supporting business or management programs, and special business-management libraries.

Antonio Rodriguez-Buckingham

348.   Piercy, Nigel, ed. **Management Information Systems: The Technology Challenge.** New York, Nichols Publishing, 1987. 323p. index. $39.50. LC 86-18112. ISBN 0-89397-260-6.

The book contains thirteen original studies on the impact of new information technology on the management information systems in different types of business operations and in the various functional areas of management. The chapters are grouped in three parts. Part 1 emphasizes the social and organizational impact of information systems and new technology. Part 2 deals with applications in theory. Part 3 brings together two studies on applications in practice, and part 4 includes three studies on strategic implications. The authors, who represent the university and industry, attempt to address postgraduate students of management, and especially the practitioner in the field of management information systems. The studies are supported

by a number of figures and supplemented by bibliographies of select items. The book provides informative and interesting reading on MIS and how it is affected by the latest technology, as well as how information technology is affecting society.

Mohammed M. Aman

349.   Poppel, Harvey L., and Bernard Goldstein. **Information Technology: The Trillion-Dollar Opportunity.** New York, McGraw-Hill, 1987. 207p. index. $19.95. LC 86-27782. ISBN 0-07-050511-X.

This book, primarily addressed to managers in the information technology (IT) industry, was written by two partners at Broadview Associates, an IT mergers, acquisitions, and venture capital firm. The work's purpose is to help "readers anticipate and capitalize on information technology (IT) developments. Therefore it posits a 'unifying theory' of the IT industry that spotlights, links, and interprets the pivotal market forces, technologies, and impacts."

The book is divided into three parts. Part 1 documents and interprets five "infotrends" that are, in the authors' view, changing the fundamental nature of the IT industry. These factors are content (substance of IT), interoperability (standardization), disintermediation (restructuring of the industry), globalization (expansion to worldwide markets), and convergence (cross substituting of products and services). Part 2 describes how these trends are affecting each of the "clusters" of the IT industry—communications services, information services, entertainment services, consumer electronics, office equipment, and business operation equipment. The final part identifies "critical success attributes" and demonstrates how they are measured and managed across the entire range of IT suppliers.

Although this work does not entirely avoid either the hype or the jargonistic and turgid prose common to the genre, it does offer insights into the way IT is changing business enterprises of all kinds. The authors' perceptions and analyses will be helpful to IT industry managers and useful to anyone attempting to understand the effect information technology is having on our culture.   Robert H. Burger

350.   Slater, Don. **Information Technology.** New York, Franklin Watts, 1986. 32p. illus. (col.). index. (Modern Technology). $10.40. LC 86-50031. ISBN 0-531-10198-3.

This latest volume in the Modern Technology series is an attractive picture book description of some of the more obvious aspects of information technology. Home shopping, CAD/CAM, electronic publishing, electronic offices, etc., are discussed in illustrated, one- or two-page spreads.

Although the descriptions are simplified, the book gives basically accurate information and specifically emphasizes the relationships between telecommunications and the computer.

Photographs, full-color diagrams, and brief descriptions in large print make this book appropriate for the elementary or middle school library media center. For the novice looking for an introduction to information technology the book may serve as a useful quick reference guide to some terminology and basic concepts. [R: SBF, Mar/Apr 87, p. 229]

Elisabeth Logan

351. Zorkoczy, P. I., ed. **Oxford Surveys in Information Technology. Volume 3: 1986.** New York, Oxford University Press, 1986. 324p. index. $67.50. ISBN 0-19-859018-0.

This volume offers nine surveys of aspects of information technology. The book also provides brief biographies of the contributors, an inaccurate index of authors cited in the surveys (page numbers for the first three authors I looked up were incorrect), and content lists for volume 1 (1984) and volume 2 (1985).

The first survey looks at Japan's software industry and its efforts to improve software development by an order of magnitude. Another article considers rapid prototyping, which brings users into the software development process.

Surveys that concentrate on telecommunications management and development review the influence of government policies on information services and the managing of intelligent networks. An examination of the limitations of digital optical-fiber communications concludes that this area requires more research.

The last group of surveys is application-oriented. Subjects include international trends in the electronic information industry, text retrieval systems, and use of electronic technology to work at home (telecommuting). The final article surveys innovative applications of information technology from a global perspective.

Unfortunately, the editor makes no attempt to analyze the material or explain why individual pieces were included. The surveys all provide extensive reference lists, perhaps the most useful aspect of this work.

Renee B. Horowitz

INTELLECTUAL FREEDOM AND CENSORSHIP

352. Bosmajian, Haig A., ed. **Freedom of Religion.** New York, Neal-Schuman, 1987. 163p. index. (First Amendment in the Classroom Series, No. 2). $24.95. LC 86-33317. ISBN 1-55570-002-0.

Second in a series of books of legal sources relating to the First Amendment, this volume provides the text of twenty-one court-related decisions concerning the First Amendment to the U.S. Constitution and the schools. Twelve concern rulings on formal prayers or periods of time for prayer, or meditation (one supported a minute for meditation, the others opposed prayer or time for prayer or meditation). Two relate to scriptures being read or posted, and four relate to formal instruction, teaching of evolution, and provision of meeting space for religious programs. All ruled against such activities. One case supported a student's conscientious objection to required participation in ROTC, and one supported a school's policy relating to religious holidays and teaching about religion.

Five cases are from the U.S. Supreme Court, seven are from various circuits of the U.S. Court of Appeals, seven are from U.S. District Courts, one is from a state supreme court case, and one is the opinion of a state supreme court in response to a legislative request.

The book was designed to meet "the need for teachers, students, parents, and school board members to become more aware of how First Amendment rights apply to the classrooms of a free society" (p. v). The editor provides a clear overall summary of the cases in his introduction and equally clear, brief summaries for each individual case. In addition, he has provided detailed notes for most cases giving further examples and explanations.

The reviewer discussed Bosmajian's book with a lawyer who is a consultant in education law. She found the collection of cases in this area very useful, and the explanations helpful. It appears that nonlawyers will find the book and the series even more useful since they will have less access to other sources of case law and less practice in reading it.

Betty Jo Buckingham

353. Franklin, Justin D., and Robert F. Bouchard, comps. and eds. **Guidebook to the**

Freedom of Information and Privacy Acts. 2d ed. New York, Clark Boardman, 1986. 1v. (various paging). index. $75.00 looseleaf with binder. LC 86-6161. ISBN 0-87632-500-2.

This guidebook contains a wide array of materials on the topics of the Freedom of Information Act and the Privacy Act, the laws which govern the public's ability to gain access to records held by the federal government. The book also contains a state-by-state compilation of the laws which govern public access to records held by state governments. A number of essays that have been prepared by the federal government are in the guidebook, including "Short Guide to the Freedom of Information Act," prepared by the Department of Justice. Legislative histories are also presented, as well as lists of the regulations issued by each federal agency under the Freedom of Information and Privacy acts, and lists of people to contact at each agency for matters pertaining to these laws.

The 1985 supplement to an earlier version of this book was reviewed by me in *Library Science Annual* 86 (see entry 170). At that time I pointed out that virtually all of the materials in the guidebook are in the public domain, and are readily available to those who know where to look. The value of the guidebook, then, is in the compilation of a wide variety of reference materials that are otherwise scattered. Taken on its own terms, the book remains valuable for its convenience as a one-stop reference source. Those seeking more, such as a detailed analysis or an original viewpoint, would do well to look elsewhere.   Michael Rogers Rubin

354. Freedman, Warren. **The Right of Privacy in the Computer Age.** Westport, Conn., Quorum Books/Greenwood Press, 1987. 163p. index. $35.00. LC 86-9362. ISBN 0-89930-187-8.

The legal protections for personal privacy in the United States are described in this book. In various chapters, the author deals with different aspects of personal privacy. Thus, the second chapter addresses the protection of personal dignity from such threats as appropriation of a person's name or likeness, the public disclosure of private facts, and so on. The third chapter discusses constitutional protections for personal privacy, including not only the Fourth Amendment protections against governmental searches, but also the Supreme Court decisions that have laid out a narrow constitutional right to privacy. Legal protections against technological methods of surveillance are discussed in the fourth chapter, and the last chapters discuss legal remedies for the invasion of privacy, and the international aspects of privacy protection.

This book contains a terse description of the law in this country as it pertains to the protection of personal privacy. It contains no analysis of those laws to determine their adequacy to serve their stated purpose, and makes no suggestions for changes that might be necessary to improve the laws. The book is simply a legal reference tool, and a good one.
                                       Michael Rogers Rubin

355. **Government Information: An Endangered Resource of the Electronic Age. Papers Presented at the First Annual State-of-the-Art Institute, October 19-22, 1986, Washington, D.C.** Washington, D.C., Special Libraries Association, 1986. 277p. $21.75 spiralbound. ISBN 0-87111-322-8.

Fifteen papers presented at the First Annual State-of-the-Art Institute have been edited and brought together as a compendium of thought about the necessity of becoming involved in and concerned with government information. Most papers read well; material omitted, according to the editor, consisted chiefly of spontaneous remarks expanding upon the statements in the papers. A complete transcription of the institute is in the Special Library Association (SLA) Archives.

Speakers at the conference were from the executive branch of the government (three), the legislative branch (two), universities (three), a public library (one), and private consulting firms and businesses (six). All have appropriate positions from which to address their topics.

Six general themes emerging from the conference are identified by David Bender in the introduction: technology is affecting the workplace; it is moving faster than the legislation to control it; government information policies are shifting; information has a worldwide impact; public/private sector partnerships provide accessibility to government information; and the misuse of information bringing on charges of malpractice is a growing concern to information professionals.

This nonindexed collection of papers is not for ready-reference but is appropriate for obtaining background knowledge and informed opinion on some complex and important issues relating to government in our information age. [R: LJ, 1 June 87, p. 88]

                                         Eliza T. Dresang

356. Hernon, Peter, and Charles R. McClure. **Federal Information Policies in the 1980's: Conflicts and Issues.** Norwood, N.J., Ablex Publishing, 1987. 467p. bibliog. index. $35.00;

$54.50 (institutions). LC 86-22292. ISBN 0-89391-382-0.

This volume updates, reorganizes, and greatly expands upon a contract report prepared in 1984 for the U.S. Congress, Office of Technology Assessment as part of its investigation into government provision of public information. A chapter on federal information policy under the Reagan administration has been added, as well as two chapters by experts in their field: "Public Access through the Freedom of Information and Privacy Acts," by Harold C. Relyea, Congressional Research Service, and "Federal Science and Technology Information Policies," by Steve Ballard, University of Oklahoma. The authors examine conflicting interests among various stakeholders in the development of information policy (such as the Joint Committee on Printing and Office of Management and Budget); review and analyze existing legislation and regulations on federal information policy, such as Title 44, U.S. Code and OMB Circular A-130; analyze the impacts of federal information policies on public access to government information (including the federal depository library program); analyze the impact of new information technologies on access to government information; and offer sound recommendations for developing more effective information policies. In treating the underlying issues, the authors do an outstanding job in objectively identifying and discussing conflicts, contradictions, ambiguities, and gaps in the interpretation and implementation of administrative and statutory laws with regard to all aspects of information policy—not just that published information distributed by the Government Printing Office to depository libraries. The authors provide excellent historical background as a basis for analysis of current issues. The appendix includes suggested topics for further research including brief description and analysis, and research objectives.

LeRoy C. Schwarzkopf

357.   How to Use the Freedom of Information Act. Washington, D.C., Washington Researchers, 1986. 52p. (Briefcase Series, Vol. 2). $30.00 pa. ISBN 0-934940-41-X.

As the title suggests, this book is a "hands-on" guide to requesting information from the federal government using the Freedom of Information Act. The book contains a variety of materials that would be useful to anyone preparing to actually make a request for information under the act. A copy of the act is included, along with a readable and accurate explanation of the act and its exemptions. Also included are form letters that the reader may use in making

requests, as well as a list of addresses where requests should be sent under the act for each federal agency. Every contingency is covered, since the book even includes form letters that the reader may use to appeal initial decisions of an agency to refuse a request for information.

This book is accurate and technically correct in its description of the Freedom of Information Act, and in its explanation of the uses of the act.

Michael Rogers Rubin

358.   Ingelhart, Louis Edward. Press Freedoms: A Descriptive Calendar of Concepts, Interpretations, Events and Court Actions, from 4000 B.C. to the Present. Westport, Conn., Greenwood Press, 1987. 430p. bibliog. index. $45.00. LC 86-31834. ISBN 0-313-25636-5.

With a marker focus on the development of freedom of the press in the United States and Great Britain, this volume should interest many in the fields of journalism, history, law, political science, and the media. Arranged in forty-four chronological subdivisions, the work attempts to highlight and discuss major events, concepts, and interpretations relevant to press and intellectual freedom. Each division has a particular temporal and geographic scope, encompassing prehistory to the mid-1980s, with projections into the next century.

An overview of the topic, its relevance to contemporary culture and society, and cultural perspectives on the notion of press freedom are explored in a preface and introductory sections. A representative bibliography and comprehensive index supplement the main text. Treatment of the various events and concepts appears to be uneven in places; a major shortcoming of the work is the lack of complete bibliographic references to quotations appearing in the text. However, the volume will prove useful to a wide audience, not the least of whom will be students in need of a quick synopsis of historical developments relating to freedom of the press. This work will likely be useful in libraries ranging from high school to university. Recommended as a supplement to historical guides on the topic.

Edmund F. SantaVicca

359.   Less Access to Less Information by and about the U.S. Government: 2: A 1985-86 Chronology: January 1985-December 1986. Washington, D.C., Washington Office, American Library Association, 1986 [1987]. 33p. $3.00pa.

Regrettably, this has become a serial publication, since the flow of U.S. government information continues to be restricted. Indeed, the problem may be getting worse, since the 1986 listings in this compilation require six more pages than the 1985 listings.

A one-page introduction summarizes the issues and the American Library Association's policies in this area; the rest of the work is devoted to a chronological listing of events from January 1985 through December 1986. Individual entries are brief, usually a single paragraph; most are abstracts of more extended reports first published elsewhere, and include a bibliographic citation to the original publication. Sources used include federal documents, newspaper and journal articles, and news releases.

Anyone concerned with freedom of access to government information in the United States will find this a convenient, if sometimes discouraging, summary of current trends. An index would have been useful, but its lack is not critical. Some readers may have a problem with the small typeface used to print the work.

Paul B. Cors

360. Nordquist, Joan, comp. **Pornography and Censorship.** Santa Cruz, Calif., Reference and Research Services Press, 1987. 64p. (Contemporary Social Issues: A Bibliographic Series, No. 7). $15.00pa. ISBN 0-937855-13-8.

This handy little pamphlet fills an important need. It provides quick access to current literature on the pornography debate, one of the important social issues of the 1980s.

The bibliography contains 633 entries, without annotations, mostly since 1980, under twelve categories: "Background" (15), "Pornography" (175), "The Meese Commission" (18), "The Research" (90), "The Law" (78), "Pornography and the Mass Media" (74), "The Feminist Debate on Pornography" (35), "Gays, Lesbians and Pornography" (19), "Child Pornography" (54), "Censorship" (48), "Bibliographies" (14), and "Organizations" (13).

The beauty of the work is that you can easily get a "starter set" range of responses to such things as the Meese Commission, child pornography, feminist legislation, research on the link between violence and pornography, cable porn, dial-a-porn, *Not a Love Story*, active advocacy groups, and so forth.

There are, however, two weaknesses. The "Feminist Debate" section is small and does not contain such people as Andrea Dworkin, and ideally there should have been a separate section on religious responses to pornography. Perhaps "Background" entries and especially entries from the large and unfocused "Pornography" section could have been better allocated in these two areas.

Edward J. Gallagher

361. **The Plain Rapper.** By the New Hampshire Educational Media Association. Keene, N.H., Drew Library, Keene High School, 1985, 1986. 115p. bibliog. $4.00 spiralbound.

Why a deadly serious manual directed to school administrators and library media professionals would be put under a title that would suit a seminar on censorship titillation for the downside of a state education convention is puzzling. This is in reality a typical manual prepared by a committee assigned to address censorship issues for a state association. It brings together relevant documents from the state and national groups such as the American Library Association and the American Civil Liberties Union. It provides a sample selection policy and a long section on legal precedents drawn from various sources, with about two-thirds of the space going into a very detailed account of the *Pico vs. Island Trees Union Free School Board* case. There is an extensive bibliography, but its relevance to drawing up selection policies or molifying an irate citizens' group is at best to be considered slipshod (e.g., Jackson, Holbrook, *The Fear of Books*, London, Soncino Press, 1932). The bibliographic entries are inconsistent in form and occasionally seem to lack needed details such as a source. For comprehensive collections only. (The work can be obtained from Drew Library, Keene High School, 43 Archer St., Keene, NH 03431.)

Gerald R. Shields

INTERLIBRARY LOANS

362. Exon, F. C. A. **A Preliminary Survey of Australian Inter-Library Lending: A Report to the Australian Commonwealth Tertiary Education Commission.** South Bentley, Australia, published for the Commonwealth Tertiary Education Commission by the Library, Western Australian Institute of Technology, 1986. 109p. bibliog. $10.00pa. ISBN 0-908155-21-2.

This is not a study of interlibrary loan. It is an early (1985) step in that study in which prior research is identified briefly, appropriate questions to ask about interlibrary loan in Australia are determined, and the sample to be studied is described. An outline of prior studies in document supply provides the context for the proposed study. The presentation is replete with charts, tables, and definitions to support the study under discussion. The several appendices include copies of documents related to the study such as correspondence with the contracting agency, a budget for early stages of the study, questionnaires, interview timetables, and preliminary findings.

The body of the book appears to be organized as a log or stream of consciousness of decision making leading up to a study. The appendices, which constitute nearly half of the book, include everything from letters authorizing the study to preliminary results. There is no general summary of decisions made or activities undertaken. It would be much more useful to read the survey if and when it is completed than to work one's way through this most preliminary collection of data and decisions. [R: JAL, Mar 87, p. 49]   Ann E. Prentice

363. Kohl, David F. **Circulation, Interlibrary Loan, Patron Use, and Collection Maintenance: A Handbook for Library Management.** Santa Barbara, Calif., ABC-Clio, 1986. 362p. bibliog. index. (Handbooks for Library Management, Vol. 5). $35.00. LC 85-15798. ISBN 0-87436-435-3.

According to the dictionary, a handbook is a short treatise or guide book in any occupation or area of study. This handbook is a reference book for library managers. In the foreword, Alford asserts that "this book brings together knowledgeable and important data from both the public and private sectors to address the critical issues surrounding collection development and patron use." The handbook is part of a series designed for library decision makers who regularly need information. It presents the readers with summaries of original research findings on very specific aspects of circulation, interlibrary loan, patron use, and collection maintenance. It also provides excellent bibliographic citations for further consultation. Like any handbook, the style is very concise and the information is in a capsule format more or less like that of a statistical compendium rather than a textbook. One very important and interesting feature of this book is the pages devoted to demographics. We seldom encounter this kind of attention to demographics in the library world. Other appreciated features are a very detailed table of contents that almost serves as an index and an extensive bibliography covering North American periodical literature from 1960 to 1983, to which there are footnoted references in the text.

This quick reference tool can lead the reader to the best research findings on the many aspects of technical services in a library. The wealth of information contained here is amazing and can be extremely useful to library decision makers who do not have time to perform extensive literature searches and for whom data are of the utmost importance. The reader will find data on almost anything pertaining to technical services. It is hoped this handbook will find a

place on every reference shelf of our libraries. If the other five volumes in this series of Handbooks for Library Management are of the same high quality as this one, they will be essential not only in libraries but on the personal shelves of most librarians.   Camille Côté

364. **Local Initiatives in Business Information Provision: A Report on the Second Stage of a Study on Local Library and Information Cooperatives....** Stamford, England, Capital Planning Information, 1985. 103p. £10.00. ISBN 0-906011-31-0.

This study, identified as British Library RDD Report 5868, is a follow-up of the Stage I report, *Local Library Co-operatives: Their Role with Special Reference to Inter-lending*, published in 1984 (BLRDD Report 5824). Both reports were commissioned by the British Library Research and Development Department and prepared by Capital Planning Information. The earlier report traced the development of British local library cooperative schemes from their beginning in 1932 to the present. A 1984 seminar at Loughborough University on that report urged BLRDD "to commission additional research ... to determine if the establishment of a co-operative actually improves the provision of information to commerce and industry in its areas" (p. 11). It was further suggested that comparisons were needed with areas where no cooperative exists.

The present report chose for detailed study three major cooperatives from as many geographical areas: Hampshire Technical Research Information Commercial Service (HATRICS), Liverpool and District Scientific Industrial and Research Library Advisory Council (LADSIR-LAC), and Calderdale and District Information Service for Business and Industry (CALDIS). The two control areas selected (in which a central public reference library provided information to local firms) were Bristol and Cambridge. A user survey collected data on a variety of aspects of patron services and satisfaction; in addition, telephone and personal interviews were carried out with a sample of users. Issues considered included clarity and achievability of service objectives, local availability of materials and information, marketing and promotion of services, costs, impact of new technologies, and staff commitment and awareness. The report concludes that "in general the range and depth of contacts between information providers and users is more substantial in the areas with co-operatives than in those without" (p. iii). It also reiterates the importance of personal attitudes toward cooperation, outlines guidelines for a model cooperative, makes recommendations for further research, and appends the survey questionnaire.   Wiley J. Williams

365. White, Brenda. **Interlending in the United Kingdom 1985: A Survey of Interlibrary Document Transactions.** London, British Library; distr., Wolfeboro, N.H., Longwood Publishing Group, 1986. 86p. (Library and Information Research Report, No. 44). $22.50pa. ISBN 0-7123-3068-2.

In 1985, the British Library Lending Division, on behalf of the National Committee on Regional Library Cooperation, conducted a survey on the nature of interlibrary loan in the United Kingdom. The survey was a follow-up to a survey conducted in 1977. This document is a report of the 1985 survey results. In addition, it provides a comparison of those results with the 1977 survey results. The bulk of the work is devoted to presenting statistics that were derived from the survey. Nine of the twelve chapters in the report cover the variables measured: volume of traffic by type of library and region of the United Kingdom, type of material requested, length of time for supply of materials, types of location tools used, means of transmission of requests, methods of delivery of materials, channels used for requests, source of eventual supply of material, and whether the material is loaned or supplied for retention. Each of these categories is thoroughly graphed and charted. Appendices include the data collection forms for both the 1977 and 1985 surveys, the additional explanatory material supplied to participants in the 1985 survey, and six tables of the actual figures and percentages in several of the categories listed above. Finally, an annotated list of related titles in the report series is supplied.

The 1985 survey found little change in the patterns of interlibrary loan from those determined in the 1977 survey. A significant exception was in delivery time for materials requested. Despite the availability of new technologies for interlibrary loan activities, this important factor has deteriorated in the eight years between the surveys. In general, the 1985 survey found that the availability of new technologies had not affected interlibrary lending patterns. Not surprisingly, in the United Kingdom the majority of requests are fulfilled by or channeled through the British Library Lending Division. This report is an appropriate addition to a collection supporting a library science program. It has a dual value as a well-constructed statistical report of interlibrary loan within the unique lending atmosphere of the United Kingdom and as an excellent example of

developing a survey to obtain appropriate statistics.   Kay Vyhnanek

LIBRARY FACILITIES

Architecture

366. Harrison, K. C., ed. **Public Library Buildings 1975-1983.** London, Library Services, 1987. 228p. illus. index. £29.50. ISBN 1-870144-00-7.

Harrison and his several associates, including an architect, continue a series of volumes originally sponsored by the Library Association itself; this edition, covering nine full years of British projects, is under the aegis of the London and Home Counties Branch of the association. The major difference is that this edition is devoted to public libraries only. No less than 581 projects from 129 authorities are listed in the tables; the majority are new buildings. On the basis of site visits by members of the editorial team, one hundred were selected for presentation with detailed data, plans, photographs, and critical appraisal.

Arrangement is by authority, then by city/town/village. References to publications about individual libraries are included. Building sizes range from village branches to large central libraries. Many are interesting conversions, such as a town hall (Camelford); a market house (Stamford); two corn exchanges (Hexham and Winchester); a cinema (Droitwich); and a great house turned school, then library and museum, now restored to fifteenth- and sixteenth-century appearance and specifications, with a brand-new addition in the old schoolyard (Shrewsbury Castlegates). Styles of the new buildings range from the dull public facility to the elegant and the innovative; some resemble the best (and not so good) recent American libraries. Critical comments are based on a study of goals, problems in attaining them, original and maintenance costs, community reactions, and effectiveness. Now that British building is approaching Northern European and American building, this is a useful addition to the planner's shelf.
                                        Walter C. Allen

367. **Libraries: A Briefing and Design Guide.** New York, Van Nostrand Reinhold, 1986. 182p. illus. bibliog. $35.95. ISBN 0-442-24631-5.

Libraries is the first in a series of briefing and design guides for a number of major building types. The editor of the series, Allan Konya, a British architect and lecturer, appears also to be the author of the present volume. While its terminology and most of the references are British, the work is sufficiently general to be useful for planners in other nations. There is a general introduction, followed by "Inception and the Preliminary Brief," largely devoted to architectural practice and the relationship with clients. The heart of the book consists of a further introduction (to libraries), followed by "Inception and Initial Brief," "Feasibility," "Detailed Brief," "Outline Proposals/Scheme Design," and a number of useful appendices on such topics as "References and Sources of Information," site surveys, illustrations (almost all British), consultants, and "Briefing and Design Methods." There are many models, diagrams, flowcharts, and other general and detailed visual aids. The impression is one of good organization, a considerable amount of detail, and many useful measurements (e.g., the relationship between structural grids and the spacing of stack ranges). British terminology and metric measurements may put off some American librarians and architects, but serious planners will find the book useful.

Walter C. Allen

Space Utilization

368. Boss, Richard W. **Information Technologies and Space Planning for Libraries and Information Centers.** Boston, G. K. Hall, 1987. 121p. bibliog. index. $36.50; $28.50pa. LC 87-19798. ISBN 0-8161-1859-0; 0-8161-1870-1pa.

Having written this book "in response to the lack of information about the impact of information technology on space planning," Boss first presents a brief overview of libraries and information technologies, including bibliographic utilities, other commercial services, and various types of networks. Next, in a chapter on automated library systems, he addresses space, electrical/telecommunications, and environmental requirements for a midsized minicomputer with thirty to sixty terminals. In other chapters, he describes the newest technological advances in compact storage, microforms, optical media, and telefacsimile transmission. In his penultimate chapter, Boss summarizes space planning standards developed by a few representative state or educational planning bodies. Finally, and most usefully, Boss lists space planning recommendations which take into account the new technologies. While one might quibble with Boss's predictions for the future or with some details in his suggestions for placement of equipment intended for public use, his general space planning recommendations are eminently sensible.

Margaret McKinley

LIBRARY HISTORY

369. Brichford, Maynard, and Anne Gilliland. **Guide to the American Library Association Archives.** 2d ed. Chicago, American Library Association, 1987. 11p. with 3 microfiche. $5.00 pa. LC 87-14533. ISBN 0-8389-2048-9.

The vast collection of original records pertaining to the American Library Association, located at the University of Illinois Library, are classified according to archival principles and accessible to scholars through this microfiche edition. An introductory section explains how to use the guide, provides background on the growth and organization of the project, covers onsite visits to the archives, refers the researcher to other relevant repositories, and outlines the PARADIGM system employed by the University of Illinois Archives. Finally, a selective bibliography of works relating to the history of ALA and its divisions is appended.

The guide consists of three microfiches. Fiche 1 is a 117-page classification guide which includes a list of record groups and an extensive treatment of administrative histories of major ALA units. Fiche 2 is a 171-page record series description listing. Fiche 3 is a 159-page subject index to record series, an alphabetical list of subject descriptors followed by numbers of records series containing information on each subject. The microfiche set is logically organized, professionally executed, and particularly useful. This guide should be consulted along with Brichford's *National Catalog of Sources for the History of Librarianship* (1982), a union list of archival holdings and manuscripts relating to librarianship in other collections. Few professional associations have been the recipient of such extended archival care as that rendered by Maynard Brichford and his talented staff. We are all in their debt.

Arthur P. Young

370. Keeling, Denis F., ed. **British Library History: Bibliography. 1981-1984.** London, Library Association; distr., Chicago, American Library Association, 1987. 190p. index. $25.00 pa. ISBN 0-85365-837-4.

The appearance of the fourth supplement to *British Library History: Bibliography* covering the years 1981-1984 is a welcome event. This well-organized and comprehensive compilation follows the same format as previous volumes in the series. A short introduction discusses the highlights among the library history publications appearing during the years covered in this volume. It is followed by a bibliography of 761 individually numbered items. Entries are arranged under five general headings: librarians, librarianship, libraries (further subdivided into ten types of libraries), reading, and the study of library history. All types of relevant materials are listed in the bibliography, including pamphlets and obituaries as well as books and journal articles. An item will be listed if the compilers feel that it contains a sufficient amount of material relating to library history, even if another subject is its primary focus (e.g., there is an entry for a recent biography of Lewis Carroll). The compilers have also written brief twenty- to sixty-word descriptive annotations for each item, and if it is a book they list several library journals that have reviewed it along with the reviewers' names. Cross-referencing is extensive, and when used in combination with the author index and the subject index, it is almost inconceivable that a careful person would miss something of interest using this bibliography. The American Library Association is to be commended for deciding to distribute this publication in the United States. [R: LAR, June 87, p. 292]   Ronald H. Fritze

371.   Norton, Aloysius A. A History of the United States Military Academy Library. Wayne, N.J., Avery Publishing, 1986. 40p. illus. $6.95. LC 86-7930. ISBN 0-89529-352-8.

This is an interesting little book. The question one asks is, "interesting to whom?" The book might find readership among library school collections, military history buffs, and graduates of the Military Academy, but beyond that, its appeal appears quite limited. While it appears, too, that Norton has done extensive research on the topic, he mingles that research with other points about the Academy that do not appear germane to the library itself. The style of writing is loose, and many of the paragraphs are interminably long for comfortable reading. Conjecture seems to be mixed in with fact, and some points about the library's physical existence are not quite stated, leaving the reader to wonder where the library was at "such-and-such a time."

Conjecture about the library profession's basic definitions also is found; does Norton present well the library's automation achievements and the terminology used in library automation? It does not seem so. Pictures of the library "today" are actually quite out-of-date. The length of the work is just enough for very casual interest, but not in-depth enough for a library scholar. The typeface is clear, although several typographical errors remain. The old photographs and drawings are interesting to the history buff.   Robert D. Adamshick

LIBRARY INSTRUCTION

372.   Berge, Patricia, and Carol Lee Saffioti. Basic College Research. New York, Neal-Schuman, 1987. 155p. index. $24.95pa. LC 86-33287. ISBN 0-55570-018-7.

This workbook is designed with the intent of teaching college students to do library research independently. It covers topics ranging from choosing a topic through library resources to the final paper. Each of the twenty chapters concludes with an assignment. Appended are a guide for citing sources and a sample paper. The book is indexed, but has no bibliography.

As a textbook, it will be most useful in introductory library courses, and not in conjunction with English composition or other courses which have a library component, because of the detailed and sometimes lengthy assignments. Instructors may well be put off by the surprising price of $24.95 for a paperbound workbook. Basic and selective, the book provides a walk-through approach to the research paper, and consequently the library. It would have benefited from a bibliography of standard sources making possible the leap from "assignment" to subsequent research strategy. In addition, a preferable alternative to providing sample citations in appendix 1 would have been a list of style manuals from which the student could choose.

Librarians and instructors who do not favor the workbook approach to the library will be better served by Thomas Mann's *A Guide to Library Research Methods* (Oxford University Press, 1987), which is, incidentally, cheaper. Not a comprehensive guide to the research process, *Basic College Research* will be more useful to instructors of introductory library courses and to novice library users than librarians and instructors in nonlibrary college courses.

Jean Parker

373.   Cook, Sybilla Avery. Instructional Design for Libraries: An Annotated Bibliography. New York, Garland, 1986. 274p. index. (Garland Reference Library of Social Science, Vol. 345). $27.00. LC 86-14591. ISBN 0-8240-8575-2.

This work selectively covers the elementary, secondary, and college levels concerning the design of library and information science skills. Books, journal articles, and ERIC documents spanning the years 1970-1985 have been compiled from text and online searches of the *Current Index to Journals in Education, Education Index, Library Literature,* and *Resources in Education* for a total of 667 descriptively annotated entries.

The author, an elementary library media specialist, has chosen to arrange the work in a unique way, according to eight unconventional chapters: history and purpose of library instruction, types of programs, state requirements, learning styles, group instruction, individualized instruction, evaluation, and future implications. Each chapter has a brief introduction. The work concludes with separate indexes for author, title, and broad subject; a listing of journal titles and ERIC document numbers cited; and a directory of state media services and departments of education.

Although much energy has been expended to produce this work, there are typographical errors, and a gap in the literature has not really been filled. Those libraries with a special interest in bridging library skills from level to level may find the source helpful. Others may be able to forego purchase by relying upon the excellent bibliography by Deborah Lockwood, *Library Instruction* (Greenwood, 1979) supplemented by articles published in journals such as *Research Strategies* and *Reference Services Review*, as well as the American Library Association/Library Instruction Roundtable newsletter.

Ilene F. Rockman

374. Grassian, Esther, ed. **Directory of Library Instruction Programs in California Academic Libraries 1986.** Los Angeles, Calif., CLA California Clearinghouse on Library Instruction, 1986. 127p. $12.50.

The third edition of this popular work updates the 1983 edition, and includes 47 more entries, for a grand total of 217 public and private, two- and four-year California libraries.

The introduction reports on the results of the survey questionnaire used to gather the data. It discusses the prevalent forms of instructional programs and materials, the range of paraprofessional help, the amount of time spent on instruction by librarians, methods of evaluation and publicity, and a glossary of terms.

The bulk of the work is a directory alphabetically arranged by institution, with only two entries per page for ease in reading. Information provided includes the name, address, and telephone number of the library, with a code indicating the type of institution; the population served (e.g., students, faculty, staff); modes of instruction; if a credit course is offered and its description; materials used; how the program is administered, evaluated, and publicized; and the name of a contact person. The work concludes with a subject index, a copy of the questionnaire, and fourteen tables of analyzed data; a list of the CCLI officers; and an unannotated

bibliography of textbooks used in formal courses.

Although information is printed on only one side of each page and includes various types of computer-generated type fonts, this source is valuable since it contains unique information not found elsewhere. It will be most useful to California academic librarians since it updates and enlarges the previous edition, but can serve as a useful guide and model for other states' library directories.   Ilene F. Rockman

375. Hauer, Mary G., and others. **Books, Libraries, and Research.** 3d ed. Dubuque, Iowa, Kendall/Hunt Publishing, 1987. 266p. illus. index. $15.95pa. LC 87-80154. ISBN 0-8403-4294-2.

This volume is designed as a textbook for an undergraduate course in library use. Ten chapters cover such traditional topics as development of writing, books, and libraries; classification; the library catalog; reference books; indexes; online databases; government publications; and the research paper. The text is supplemented with illustrations and/or bibliographies of library materials. The authors have been thorough in covering all of the basic concepts and major search tool categories which a college student should have learned about in high school or should master in the first two years of college. Chapters conclude with review questions which could be used as class assignments. If a librarian/teacher has chosen a separate course approach to teaching the use of the library to college students, this is a text which should be considered. It has several features to commend it: attention to modern technology in the library, use of flowcharts to show identification and location processes, and use of well-chosen sample pages from reference tools. I only wish there were more of the latter. On the other hand there are some faults: the annotations are inconsistent in length and type of information provided, search strategy is inadequately addressed, too much space is given to listing reference sources and not enough attention is given to using guides to reference sources, not enough attention is given to the role of the reference librarian, and the topic of primary/secondary sources is handled from a limited social science/history perspective. Perhaps the most critical fault is the lack of an integrating mechanism. Unless the teacher provides such integration, until the last chapter on search strategy students will find only a series of library search tools and manipulation techniques without any sense of when they are to be used and for what purposes.   Thomas G. Kirk

376. Kirkendall, Carolyn A., ed. **Marketing Instructional Services: Applying Private Sector Techniques to Plan and Promote Bibliographic Instruction. Papers Presented at the Thirteenth Library Instruction Conference Held at Eastern Michigan University....** Ann Arbor, Mich., Pierian Press, 1986. 157p. illus. $19.50. LC 86-60025. ISBN 0-87650-201-X.

This book, edited by the director of the LOEX Clearinghouse at Eastern Michigan University, contains papers presented by seven speakers on various aspects of marketing libraries and instructional services. The introductory paper is an excellent overview by a business librarian of marketing which relates its usefulness to libraries. It is followed by a thought-provoking presentation which questions whether libraries should be marketed at all. A librarian and a faculty member discuss the successful marketing of bibliographic instruction in a large university from the "buyer's" and the "seller's" viewpoints. With a different outlook, a British librarian examines the reasons for the lack of marketing academic libraries in the United Kingdom. The "holistic" approach to marketing and the importance of public relations are discussed. The volume includes seven Poster Session abstracts and an extensive bibliography on marketing libraries and information services. It also provides an annotated bibliography of 1983 publications on library orientation and instruction, facsimiles of handouts for public relations and marketing, and the names and addresses of conference participants.

Since the early 1970s, a great deal has been written on marketing libraries and information services, but little has been published about marketing bibliographic instruction prior to this compilation. Despite two years having elapsed since the conference and two papers being omitted, this book will supply librarians involved in library instruction with helpful information and techniques which will be useful in marketing and promoting their programs.   O. Gene Norman

377. Mann, Thomas. **A Guide to Library Research Methods.** New York, Oxford University Press, 1987. 199p. index. $16.95. LC 87-1565. ISBN 0-19-504943-8.

Thomas Mann, general reference librarian at the Library of Congress, has written an interesting and useful guide to the use of libraries. The book aims to assist readers with the basics of library research and methods for effective searching in libraries. The book covers basic information (encyclopedias, the catalog, classification systems, indexes), more specialized resources (citation indexes, computer searching, review articles, government publications), and

additional research ideas (union lists, interviews, *librarians*). Not intended solely for the library illiterate, Mann's book will be of interest to all levels of library users, including bibliographic instruction librarians searching for new ways to say seemingly old things. The book is written in a clear, easy-to-read style, and includes many interesting examples culled from reference desk inquiries. An attractive feature of the book is the extensive descriptions of many of the sources recommended by Mann. This is a readable book which should assist novice users as well as veterans.   Jean Parker

378. McDonough, Kristin, and Eleanor Langstaff. **Access Information: Research in Social Sciences and Humanities.** Dubuque, Iowa, Kendall/Hunt Publishing, 1987. 291p. illus. index. price not reported. LC 87-80123. ISBN 0-8403-4298-5pa.

This collection of library instruction materials, compiled over a twelve-year period at Baruch College for use in a library class, contains actual copies of handouts (some of which are difficult to read) illustrating the use of such tools as citation indexes, encyclopedias, and Boolean logic.

The book, no doubt a reflection of the course, moves from the general to the specific. After discussing the role of information and libraries in society, McDonough and Langstaff describe the literature search, detailing the use of books, journals, government publications, statistical and biographical sources, and (in a way which misleadingly segments online searching into a format category of its own) computer-based search services.

A whole section is devoted to "Shaping the Research Report," and a model paper complete with bibliography and note cards demonstrates that suggestions for conducting research can be transformed into actual products. Finally, disciplines in the humanities and social sciences receive brief but individual treatment in the form of lists of major reference sources. An index, which the table of contents fails to list, identifies subjects not named by chapter headings. As they design their own classes and programs, instruction librarians will find the handouts and other practical materials in *Access Information* very useful. Junior or senior students doing research papers could benefit from using the advice-filled book on their own.

Some potential purchasers may be discouraged by the fact that this practical research manual suffers from the problem that plagues all librarians responsible for presentations: poor-quality copies.

Connie Miller

379. Mellon, Constance A., ed. **Bibliographic Instruction: The Second Generation.** Littleton, Colo., Libraries Unlimited, 1987. 204p. index. $27.50. LC 87-4049. ISBN 0-87287-563-6.

The genesis and conceptual framework of this volume evolved from the "Think Tank on Bibliographic Instruction," a preconference activity held in conjunction with the 1981 conference of the Association of College and Research Libraries. The volume is intended to serve as a forum for the first generation of instruction librarians to communicate the issues and theory underlying the field to the second generation of educators and practitioners. Part 1 is an overview of the Think Tank and its influence on bibliographic instruction; part 2 reviews the characteristics of bibliographic instruction over the past decade; and part 3 offers reflections on the future. The fifteen chapters were written by twenty-two individuals, and cover such areas as learning theory, curriculum specialization, technology, and professional models.

Many of the authors convey the message that bibliographic instruction has passed from the stage of special pleading and "glad tidings" to a higher ground characterized by increasing acceptance and theoretical integration with other disciplines and technologies. Challenges awaiting solution include the appropriateness and extent of end-user training, assessment of the effectiveness of information literacy training, and realignment of library staff responsibilities. The online juggernaut raises a host of issues related to the delivery, content, and evaluation of bibliographic instruction. Donald Kenney confidently asserts that "librarians who do not educate their patrons are doomed to do their work for them," an observation that will not be universally embraced.

Works of multiple authorship are invariably uneven, and this volume is no exception. Nominations for best essays go to Bobbie Collins, Constance Mellon, and Sally Young for chapter 6, "The Needs and Feelings of Beginning Researchers," and to David King and Betsy Baker for chapter 7, "Human Aspects to Library Technology." Omission of a chapter on the research literature of bibliographic instruction is regrettable. Overall, editor Mellon and the others have ably summarized the field and identified agendas for the future.

Arthur P. Young

380. Reichel, Mary, and Mary Ann Ramey, eds. **Conceptual Frameworks for Bibliographic Education: Theory into Practice.** Littleton, Colo., Libraries Unlimited, 1987. 212p. index. $25.00. LC 87-22587. ISBN 0-87287-552-0.

This is not for beginning BI librarians or those who give only basic instruction. The book does not deal with basics; rather, it assumes an ongoing program, and provides for librarians in such programs ideas and methods that could make instruction more interesting and more effective. Those ideas and methods are based on the use of conceptual frameworks: "general principles drawn from a field of study and used to organize the content of an instructional presentation." Such conceptual frameworks can vary considerably, and in eleven of the book's sixteen chapters, each author shows how he or she applies that approach to a separate discipline in the social sciences, humanities, or sciences. The first three chapters provide background and general remarks on the approach, and the last two discuss conceptual instruction for database searching and for OPAC use, respectively.

The book is well edited. With sixteen different authors, one expects some repetition and inconsistencies, but they are few. All chapters are well written and substantive, a commendable combination of theory and practical suggestions. Several have examples of presentations which, while not to be adopted as given, can be used as models.

This reviewer would have liked one chapter—coming after those on the disciplines—that reflected on the similarities and differences for giving BI in those disciplines. But that's a minor criticism.

All serious BI librarians ought to know the book. It is provocative and sensible and could well serve as a basis for BI staff discussion and development.

Evan Ira Farber

381. **Tools for Learning: Information Skills and Learning to Learn in Secondary Schools.** Sharon Markless and Paul Lincoln, eds. London, British Library; distr., Slough, England, INSIS Project, NFER, 1986. 124p. (British Library R&D Report, No. 5892). £4.50 spiralbound. ISBN 0-7123-3085-2.

The focus of this work, clearly stated in the introduction, is on the tools of learning with which the authors feel secondary school students should be familiar. In meeting its objective the work presents a systematic approach to solving a learning problem. It is to the learner what instructional design is to the teacher. The user is presented with a framework of skills consisting of seven basic units: thinking forward (realistic goals), thinking about finding information, thinking about using resources, thinking about recording information, thinking about using information, thinking about communicating information, and thinking back (what has been achieved). Each unit contains a section stressing decisions that need to be made and a section citing skills useful in identifying, locating, selecting, interpreting, and evaluating information.

This British publication can be helpful to American library media specialists and teachers seeking help in developing their own framework of learning skills. In doing so, they should be aware of the guiding principles set forth by the authors: purposeful and effective use of a skill must overshadow verbal abstraction, learning is a continuing activity, the content of learning and the skills of learning should be coordinated, the teaching of skills should be integrated into the curriculum, and development of a ritual in using skills should be avoided. The work is a British Library R&D Report, well illustrated with both diagrams and examples. Its basic use lies in its stated purpose: as a training package for teachers, librarians, and others.

Anthony C. Schulzetenberg

LIBRARY SECURITY

382. Lincoln, Alan Jay, and Carol Zall Lincoln. **Library Crime and Security: An International Perspective.** New York, Haworth Press, 1987. 163p. bibliog. index. $24.95. LC 87-12059. ISBN 0-86656-480-2.

This is a separate hardcover edition of a study originally published as volume 8, numbers 1 and 2 of the periodical *Library and Archival Security* (Spring/Summer 1986). The work is based on a detailed questionnaire sent to hundreds of public libraries in Canada, the United Kingdom, and the United States. A reading of the text and the many tables indicates the nature of the questionnaire, but including the actual questionnaire as an appendix would have been a good idea. It is also annoying not to be told the exact date of the study—1982? The chapters concerned with the results of the questionnaire review the types of crimes committed in public libraries, possible patterns, costs, and a summary of the major findings. Both the discussion and tabulated results of the questionnaire are interesting. For example, in the early 1980s U.S. libraries had more problems with drug users and indecent exposure, Canadian libraries had more problems with damage to books, while British libraries had more problems with vandalism outside the building, arson, and assault against staff. Some of the finds are rather obvious to librarians: inner city libraries have more problems than small town libraries; the larger the circulation of a library, the more mutilation of library materials. Some findings are frightening: assaults on library staff and arson are growing

problems. A checklist of security considerations is given in the final chapter and deserves the careful attention of government officials and library administrators.

The book introduces most of the security problems faced by libraries. However, the security issues presented by computers within the library are not covered. A new questionnaire should be sent to public libraries to glean information on computer crime. For libraries, this would include information on copyright infringement, outright theft of educational software, and mutilation of the machines themselves.

Milton H. Crouch

MANAGEMENT

General Works

383. Blasingame, Ralph, and Robert L. Goldberg. **Planning, Another View.** Philadelphia, College of Information Studies, Drexel University, 1987. 131p. (*Drexel Library Quarterly*, Vol. 21, No. 4). $10.00pa. LC 65-9911. ISSN 0012-6160.

Planning for library services has become increasingly important in recent decades as an attempt to ensure a rational future. The editors have placed three representative case studies of planning activities in the context of planning efforts in the United States in the past century, a review of traditional planning methods in libraries, and the description of a library planning model with commentary on how it was envisioned and implemented and what resulted.

Silver's description of "America's Planning Legacy" places planning in the context of American historical trends with roots in the nineteenth century. Planning is a vehicle for social reform, a means of government intervention and an application of scientific management to the workplace. We are a planning and are becoming a planned society made up of many fragmented and often local plans, of which planning for library service is an element. Summers identifies and describes briefly the important library surveys since 1876, charts the shift toward and then away from national surveys, and makes some critical but deserved comments about the quality of survey research used in many of these studies. Palmour's review of planning strategies with a critical review of *Planning Process for Public Libraries* (American Library Association, 1980) is brief and to the point. These articles are followed by case studies of planning in very small libraries (under five thousand population), a very large library (New York Public Library), and publishing (H. W. Wilson). The product is an excellent overview of planning: how it came to be, what it is, and how it is used. It will be most appreciated by those who have had experience with planning for libraries. For those new to planning, it provides context and valuable information to assist in avoiding pitfalls.

Ann E. Prentice

384. Jennings, Margaret S., and others. **Library Management in Review. Volume II.** Washington, D.C., Special Libraries Association, 1987. 165p. $13.75pa. ISBN 0-87111-329-5.

This volume is a reader made up of twenty-six articles previously published in *Library Management Bulletin* between 1981 and 1986. According to the preface, "they are intended to reflect up-to-date responses to the rapid changes in economic conditions, technology, and user needs that determine the direction modern libraries must take." The articles are grouped under eight headings: improving library visibility and use, financial management, human resource management, records management, writing skills for library managers, library automation, career advancement strategies, and alternative careers for librarians. The articles are in general brief, ranging from two to twelve pages in length, with an average of about five. Almost half the articles provide no references to other literature. The most recent reference is one in 1984. This volume does not reflect "up-to-date responses" and adds no new material beyond that originally published. Its publication does not bode well for the continuation of the series begun in 1981.   Helen Howard

385. Lomas, Tim, ed. **Management Issues in Academic Libraries: Proceedings of the Joint Annual Study Conference of the Colleges of Further and Higher Education Group and the Education Librarians Group of the Library Association, Chester, 1-4 April 1985.** London, Rossendale, 1986. 84p. $19.50pa. ISBN 0-946138-08-7.

This slight volume contains the texts of six short papers delivered at the conference. The first two, describing some general developments in British higher education and the role of the Audit Commission in evaluation, are meaningful only to those familiar with the structure and terminology of public higher education in Britain. The third paper summarizes methods and objectives of evaluating academic library services. The fourth is titled "The Evaluation of Services: A Series of Case Studies," but the case studies are fairly typical of those in library personnel management. The final two papers are on library management techniques—one on

planning, the other on staff development. Both are basic, practical introductions.

Much of the information is limited to current British experience. Even more critical, though, is the fact that the papers were prepared as a basis for discussions, and since the discussions are not included, what remains is only rather basic material, neither attractively nor interestingly presented. Unless one is interested in looking at everything published on library management, American librarians need not spend any time on this volume. [R: JAL, July 87, p. 183]   Evan Ira Farber

386. Nasri, William Z., ed. **Legal Issues for Library and Information Managers.** New York, Haworth Press, 1987. 145p. bibliog. (*Journal of Library Administration*, Vol. 7, No. 4). $24.95. LC 87-4. ISBN 0-86656-591-4.

This collection of essays grew out of a course on legal issues and information handling at the University of Pittsburgh School of Library and Information Science. Editor Nasri has a law degree as well as a background in libraries. The articles cover an important range of topics which should be very useful to most library administrators. The contributors share an interesting mix of legal, library, and human relationship management expertise.

Articles include discussion of such traditional library topics as privacy of circulation files and copyright. Some essays on personnel administration mention libraries only in passing to note that recommendations apply equally to library managers as to other employers. On the other hand, there are many examples of library versus employee cases in the discussion of collective bargaining, and the author talks about ALA's policy statement on collective bargaining as well.

Another author describes successful and not-so-successful contracts for acquiring computer systems, a topic of immediate importance to many library administrators. Still another outlines the history of proposed legislation to compensate authors for library use of their copyrighted works—a question with serious implications for library managers.

This book is unique in drawing together the legal elements of many important library questions and supporting the discussion with case notes and court decisions. [R: BL, 1 Oct 87, p. 215]

Berniece M. Owen

387. St. Clair, Guy, and Joan Williamson. **Managing the One-Person Library.** Stoneham, Mass., Butterworths, 1986. 178p. index. $19.95. LC 85-30965. ISBN 0-408-01511-X.

The authors, one from the United States and the other from the United Kingdom, aim to cover the problems and opportunities in one-person libraries of all types in such a way as to provide the person in charge (often not a professional librarian) with a sense of order and direction. Their integration of American and British perspectives should broaden the horizons of readers on both sides of the Atlantic. A wide range of topics is covered, including the isolation of the person in charge of the one-person library, the position of the library within the parent organization, self-management, time management, collection development, technical services, budgeting, personnel, library services, automation, and public relations. The book closes with a chapter entitled "Afterword: Why Work in a One-Person Library?" Some chapters are given more extensive treatment than others; all provide references to other sources of information. The abundance of practical advice should be of considerable assistance to the neophyte and comparison of American and British practices has the potential for stimulating experienced staff members to assess their practices. [R: LAR, Feb 87, p. 85; WLB, Mar 87, p. 58]　　　Helen Howard

388. Stueart, Robert D., and Barbara B. Moran. **Library Management.** 3d ed. Littleton, Colo., Libraries Unlimited, 1987. 376p. index. (Library Science Text Series). $35.00; $23.50pa. LC 87-3044. ISBN 0-87287-550-4; 0-87287-549-0pa.

Barbara B. Moran replaces John Taylor Eastlick as Robert D. Stueart's co-author for this third edition, which incorporates new information and examples beyond those in the second (1981). The basic organization is the same—a general historical chapter on management development, followed by a series of chapters following a modified POSDCORB outline: planning, organization, staffing, directing, and control (which incorporates elements from coordinating, reporting, and budgeting). A final chapter, as in the second edition, treats of change and its impact on library management. Lengthy appendices incorporate sample documents, many of which are new or updated from the second edition. A list of readings at the end of chapter 1 gives a basic bibliography on management, and endnotes in each chapter perform a similar bibliographical function. Numerous charts and tables help explain the written text, and there is an index. In view of its comprehensive treatment of library administration in all kinds of libraries (but stronger for public and academic), its revisions, new data, and the recent literature cited, this third edition merits

a place in all library science collections next to the earlier editions. It will also serve as a useful text in library schools.

Richard D. Johnson

Budgeting

389. **Performance Contracting: Negotiating Your Systems Contract.** Cincinnati, Ohio, William Nieman Consulting, 1986. 106p. $19.50 spiralbound.

As a public librarian, my first impression of this book is that the spiral binding and paper covers will not hold up under the careless handling library books often receive, and some libraries might want to have this rebound at once. Also, the title and author appear nowhere on the cover, a seemingly minor point, but one that can cause the book to stagnate on the shelf.

These quibbles aside, the actual contents of the work appear useful and concrete, getting into specific contract provisions that need consideration, and avoiding the Pollyanna-ish prose so common in how-to-do-it business books. Major topics covered include "General Negotiation Concerns," "Contract Categories," "Negotiation Realities and Vendor Ploys," "Planning Acquisition and Negotiation Relationships," "Contract Provisions," "Payments and Costs," and "Additional Provisions of Importance." The explanations are concise, and do not substitute for the services of a lawyer or accountant. The primary advantage of this work seems to me to be the invaluable help in seeing that all bases are covered by the negotiators. Also, I consider this to be as much a circulating as a reference title. An increasing number of systems professionals are deciding to strike out on their own, and there should be a fairly high demand for this title in any major urban library.

Susan V. McKimm

390. Prentice, Ann E., ed. **Budgeting and Accounting.** Philadelphia, College of Information Studies, Drexel University, 1987. 115p. bibliog. (*Drexel Library Quarterly*, Vol. 21, No. 3). $10.00pa. LC 65-9911. ISSN 0012-6160.

As the bibliographies for each of the papers in this *Budgeting and Accounting* issue of the *Drexel Library Quarterly* would indicate, this is a topic much considered and written about in the library literature. Within this brief presentation Ann Prentice has brought together papers on various elements of the process which both update and guide the reader. The result is reasoned and effective without being particularly innovative or flashy.

Lauren Kelly's paper discusses the critical importance of the budget process for nonprofit organizations. It is fair to say that while there is a bias toward research libraries in these papers, many generalities can serve budget officers in a variety of library types. In fact, Koenig and Alperin conducted a survey of academic, special, and public libraries to illustrate the fact that zero-based budgeting and PPBS were not being utilized despite the considerable publicity devoted to them some years ago. The authors do indicate that along with the drawbacks of these techniques, there are some definite strengths which should be considered and incorporated into a new system. Other papers explore the value of information and the costing and pricing of it, use of the spreadsheet model to aid accounting, and a report on the types of financial reporting which can be done. Software which can aid in this process is reviewed.

This work represents a state-of-the-art look at processes which are essential to the functioning of the nonprofit organization.

Patricia A. Steele

Personnel

391.   Academic and Public Librarians: Data by Race, Ethnicity, and Sex. Chicago, Office for Library Personnel Resources, American Library Association, 1986. 34p. bibliog. $4.00pa. ISBN 0-8389-7061-3.

A compilation of a survey conducted to obtain national statistics on the library profession, this study serves as an update to the 1981 American Library Association (ALA) Office for Library Personnel Resources (OPLR) publication, *The Racial, Ethnic, and Sexual Composition of Library Staff in Academic and Public Libraries.*

The statistics, taken from questionnaires sent to a random sample of academic and public libraries in the United States, include the number of librarians who were members of the racial and ethnic minorities and the number of librarians who were male and female. The racial and ethnic definitions are those established by the Equal Employment Opportunity Commission: American Indian or Alaskan native, Asian or Pacific Islander, black, Hispanic, and white. Because *ALA Survey of Librarian Salaries* (American Library Association, Office for Research and Office for Library Personnel Resources) is published biennially, salary information has been omitted from this study. The statistics are based on work force data as of 1 September 1985.

Fifteen tables make up this survey: (1) librarians by racial and ethnic group in academic and public libraries; (2) male and female librarians in academic and public libraries; (3) dis-

tribution of total work force by racial/ethnic/ sexual group for librarians in academic and public libraries; (4) sexual distribution of each racial/ethnic group for librarians in academic and public libraries; (5) racial/ethnic distribution of each sexual group for librarians in academic and public libraries; (6) distribution of directors, deputy, associate and assistant directors by racial/ethnic/sexual group in academic and public libraries; (7) sexual distribution of each racial/ethnic group for directors, deputy, associate and assistant directors in academic and public libraries; (8) racial/ethnic distribution of each sexual group for directors, deputy, associate and assistant directors in academic and public libraries; (9) distribution of branch and department heads by racial/ethnic/sexual group in academic and public libraries; (10) sexual distribution of each racial/ethnic group for branch and department heads in academic and public libraries; (11) racial/ethnic distribution in each sexual group for branch and department heads in academic and public libraries; (12) distribution of entry level librarians by racial/ ethnic/sexual group in academic and public libraries; (13) sexual distribution of each racial/ ethnic group for entry level librarians in academic and public libraries; (14) racial/ethnic distribution of each sexual group for entry level librarians in academic and public libraries; and (15) racial and ethnic composition of undergraduate degree holders compared with graduates of master's programs in library/information science and librarians in academic and public libraries.

This is not just a book of tables. Throughout, summaries of what the tables reveal, as well as comparisons to the 1980 survey, are included.

Janet R. Ivey

392.   Job Analysis in ARL Libraries. Washington, D.C., Association of Research Libraries, 1987. 95p. bibliog. (SPEC Kit, No. 135). $20.00 pa. ISSN 0160-3582.

This SPEC Kit (Systems & Procedures Exchange Center) is typical of the long-running series designed to provide timely information and materials on the management and operations of large academic and research libraries. As part of a survey by the ARL Office of Management Studies on the use of task analysis for determining what job elements or tasks are professional, and what ones are not, relevant documents were collected. Thirty-nine libraries were interviewed for this SPEC Flyer and Kit.

The flyer is a one-page narrative summary of the survey results and includes discussion of changing staff roles, the use of job analysis, job analysis projects in libraries, and future considerations. The kit consists of unedited, direct reproduction of documents from eleven identified libraries. They include five examples of information gathering tools (questionnaires), ten program descriptions, five position classification descriptions, and a brief selected bibliography. One program description discusses the application of job analysis to develop a compensation program, while another is a detailed list of clerical and professional reference tasks. The majority of the documents deal with professional librarian positions. This material provides a starting place for any library investigating the use of job analysis or rewriting job descriptions. As with earlier kits, *Personnel Classification Systems* and *Staff Development, Job Analysis* does not provide a finished plan, but acts as a point of departure for a library's planning efforts and as a stimulant to innovative approaches to problem solving.

Judith M. Pask

393. Jones, Noragh, and Peter Jordan. **Staff Management in Library and Information Work.** 2d ed. Brookfield, Vt., Gower Publishing, 1987. 315p. bibliog. index. $50.50. LC 86-22865. ISBN 0-566-03563-4.

The first edition of this work was published in 1982. During the intervening five years there has been considerable change in the library world as a result of computerization. This volume focuses primarily on anticipated manpower needs in the library and information field through the end of this century. The bulk of this work concentrates on such topics as job description and personnel specifications, recruitment and selection of staff, staff appraisal, staff training and development, and staff supervision and interpersonal skills training. One of the early chapters gives a good summary of management theory, tracing its developments from Scientific Management theory to the Human Relations School of Management (e.g., Mayo and Maslow) and beyond McGregor's Theory X and Theory Y. Theories regarding job satisfaction and staff motivation are also discussed.

The authors' intended audience for this volume is students who would use this as a classroom text (exercises are included), or library managers and supervisors. The slant of this work is obviously British, as can be seen in the numerous examples. Some of these do not "translate" very well for readers outside the United Kingdom. Even so, this reviewer was interested in the treatment of similar managerial concerns in the two countries and found the book valuable when viewed in this light.

The changes in libraries brought about by automation have caused a ripple effect in the

ways in which information is accessed and the creation of networks formed for the purpose of sharing data. The book's first chapter acknowledges these environmental changes and, of course, automation is the underlying force when describing the changes in library staff management through the end of the century. More emphasis could have been placed on tracing the impact of automation on already existing positions, not to mention the changing relationships of staff both inside and outside their own institutions.

All in all, this volume works very successfully as a classroom text or as a basic management tool for the beginning manager or supervisor. It is somewhat disappointing for more advanced managers who look for detailed discussions of the intricate managerial problems confronting them in the next thirteen years.

Marjorie E. Bloss

394. Kathman, Michael D., and Jane McGurn Kathman, comps. **Managing Student Workers in College Libraries.** Chicago, Association of College and Research Libraries, American Library Association, 1986. 182p. bibliog. (CLIP Note, #7). $17.00pa. ISBN 0-8389-7097-4.

This issue in the CLIP Note series sponsored by the CLIP Notes Committee of ACRL is intended to provide small university and college libraries with basic data and sample documents regarding management practice with student employees. For their survey the authors sent a questionnaire to a sample of 150 libraries whose library directors had previously agreed to a CLIP Note survey. Responses were received from 102, for a response rate of 67 percent. The data and their analysis are presented in twelve pages, while the rest of the volume contains sample documents and a two-page bibliography. The survey results include the following: student worker employment represents between 12 and 13 percent of library personnel budgets, and there are at least twice as many student employees as regular library staff; about 72 percent of the responding libraries have written policies and procedures in addition to those of their parent institutions; application forms are used by 50 percent, and the information sought varies considerably; about 61 percent provide a general orientation for student employees but only 50 percent include statements of library goals and objectives; and 63 percent carry out performance evaluation. The authors suggest that more attention be directed toward federal work study library student employees. Sample documents are provided for job descriptions, applications and interviews, general orientation and training, quizzes and tests, evaluations, and "miscellaneous." This volume, while lacking in aesthetic appeal, meets the authors' objectives and provides practical assistance for the effective management of the student employee segment of a college and small university library work force.   Helen Howard

395. Revill, Don H., ed. **Personnel Management in Polytechnic Libraries.** Brookfield, Vt., Gower Publishing, 1987. 234p. index. $37.50. LC 86-31813. ISBN 0-566-05268-7.

This collection of ten readings covers three areas of personnel management, defined by the editor as structure and staffing, mergers and retrenchment, and examination of four significant staff roles common to academic libraries.

Although geared to polytechnical librarians and administrators in Great Britain, issues discussed, including staff training and effectiveness, recruitment, and communication, will be of interest to other library professionals as well. Somewhat unique to this collection is detailed consideration of "staffing in contraction" and "staff in mergers." Bibliographies at the end of each section will be useful to researchers.

This book offers supplementary material for classes in personnel management or comparative librarianship. The British orientation to some degree limits application to American libraries; however, it affords the advantage of a fresh perspective on matters of continuing interest.   Ahmad Gamaluddin

396. Russell, N. J. **The Job Satisfaction of Non-Professional Library Staff.** Leeds, England, School of Library and Information Studies, Leeds Polytechnic, 1986. 171p. bibliog. (Research Report, No. 20). £10.00pa. ISBN 0-9007-38-38-3.

This research report fulfills the requirements for the degree of Master of Philosophy from Leeds Polytechnic, School of Library and Information Studies. The thesis, which was completed in January 1984 and published as a report in October 1986, does not seem to have been edited for publication. As a result, the reader must plod through a mass of detail to determine the key elements of the research design, data analysis, and findings. The purpose of the study is to assess the job satisfaction of nonprofessional library staff. Such staff are defined as those, both full-time and part-time, filling nonprofessional positions. The sample was drawn from staff in six libraries, three in Northern Ireland, three in the north of England. A total of 571 subjects were identified, 323 in Northern Ireland, 248 in England. Of these, 135 were in academic libraries and 436 in public libraries. Data were collected by a mailed modi-

fication of the Minnesota Satisfaction Questionnaire. The response rate was 60 percent. The results of this study of self-selected subjects cannot be generalized, and somewhat different results were obtained depending upon the specific measurement used. The responses to direct questions indicated that 85 percent of the respondents were satisfied or very satisfied with their jobs, while the responses to indirect questions indicate a figure somewhere between 60 and 70 percent. Finally, 73 percent of the scores on the rating scales fell below the theoretical mean for general satisfaction. The greatest dissatisfaction arose from library policies, promotion and career prospects, treatment by library management, and relationship with professional staff. Other conclusions were that respondents in academic libraries were less satisfied than those in public libraries, as were those engaged mainly in technical services duties when compared with those in public service. This study is of an exploratory nature and could be a useful starting point for future research. [R: CLJ, Aug 87, pp. 255-56]

Helen Howard

397. **University of Waterloo Library Staff Manual.** Waterloo, Ont., University of Waterloo Library, 1987. 80p. (UW Library Technical Paper, No. 3). $22.00pa. ISBN 0-920834-05-1.

This third edition of the *Staff Manual* has been prepared as a paperback in response to requests from outside the University of Waterloo. The manual has four goals: (1) to introduce new staff members to the library, (2) to summarize and refer to the most pertinent personnel policies of the parent institution, (3) to provide samples of forms, and (4) to introduce staff to other pertinent library documents. Underlying these goals is the University Librarian's belief in consultative management and the need for staff to be aware of the library's history, organization, and goals and objectives. The volume is divided into five sections and three appendices. The first three sections cover the library's history, organization, and goals and objectives; section 4 lists standing committees, and section 5, in forty-one subsections, presents specific policies and procedures. The appendices consist of organization charts, sample forms, and other library documents. In some instances, as for example, "Flextime Regulations," the full text is reprinted, while in others, such as "Emergency Procedures Manual and Disaster Plan," only the title page and contents are reproduced. This manual meets its goals and could serve as a model for other libraries. Ease of use could be enhanced, however, by including in the contents a breakdown of the contents of the appendices.

Helen Howard

Public Relations

398. Cullen, Patsy, and John Kirby. **Design and Production of Media Presentations for Libraries.** Brookfield, Vt., Gower Publishing, 1986. 83p. bibliog. index. $42.00. LC 86-4750. ISBN 0-566-03548-0.

This volume purports to be a comprehensive description of the production of media presentations for libraries. The authors draw from their personal experiences to explain the process. However, there are several weaknesses in the work which will greatly limit its use. First, it is a British work and liberally sprinkled with typical British terminology and spelling (e.g., *dustbinmen, programme*). Second, the level of reader is difficult to determine. A basic background in media production is assumed since no definitions of terms, such as *story-boarding*, are included. In this country persons having that basic background will be familiar with the techniques described and have no need for the book. Beginners would need a more detailed explanation of technical terms and techniques with more useful diagrams. Third, only three types of presentations are described: video, tape/slide, and interactive video, excluding the whole area of audio and print media.

The volume would be much more valuable if the authors had included specific instances; for example, examples of interesting beginnings as opposed to uninteresting ones would be much more useful than merely a statement.

The illustrations are overly large; a whole page is devoted to diagrams of two small slides to show how to mark them for projection.

The overall concept that media presentations are of value to librarians for publicity, user education, staff training, and community access is a good one. It is regrettable that the authors did not give us a more practical "how to" guide which a librarian could use to learn script-writing and evaluation of programs, etc., rather than a superficial rendering of information found elsewhere. Not recommended. [R: LAR, June 87, p. 295]   Sara R. Mack

399. Dodd, Debbie. **Show Your Stuff: Creating Imaginative Library Displays.** Oregon City, Oreg., EllehCar Press, 1986. 166p. illus. index. $12.95 spiralbound.

This small, spiralbound book is a collection of easy display ideas, organized monthly according to Chases's Calendar of Annual Events. Each month has suggested themes followed by several pages of potential display ideas. For example, "September means: Back to school, shorter days, cooler nights, new fall wardrobes," etc. September is also "Be Kind to Editors and Writers Month." The display "Write Right," featuring books about writing, is one of the suggested themes. For November, ideas range from "Incredible Edibles," celebrating Good Nutrition Month to "Head for the Hills," commemorating Daniel Boone's birthday. Access to topics is also provided through an index.

Contrary to the author's assertion that these displays will appeal to users of all ages, the suggested themes are primarily suited to children and young adults. Many of the titles are clever and would catch a youngster's eye; display content, style, and ideas are inappropriate for older teenagers and adult users. Understaffed and overworked young adult, children's, and school librarians may find this a handy resource to give to volunteers, aides, and clerks who could quickly assemble a display on their own. In addition, many of these themes could be used in an elementary classroom by teachers with their pupils, or in daycare centers. Simple sketches illustrate various points. Opposite each monthly calendar of events is a page headed "Notes," which may present a problem if the book is to be placed in circulation.

Currently Adult Services Coordinator of the Oregon City Public Library, the author is a member of the Publicity and Marketing Committee of the Cooperative Library Network of Clackamas County. This book began as a committee project and much of the text was serialized in the network's newsletter. It is recommended for purchase by elementary and children's librarians who do not want to purchase Chases's Calendar of Annual Events and develop the displays themselves.

Esther R. Dyer

400. Heath, Alan. **Off the Wall: The Art of Book Display.** Littleton, Colo., Libraries Unlimited, 1987. 153p. illus. bibliog. index. $19.50pa. LC 86-33792. ISBN 0-87287-578-4.

This softbound volume offers a lively approach to book display, complete with detailed instructions and simple "how-to" instructions. Part 1 offers tips on "Preparing Your Display," which range from basic instruction on lettering techniques and the seven "classic" design shapes, to the use of cardboard tubes, photographs, mobiles, puppets, and even audio-cassettes in book display.

This author brings a touch of both humor and appealing whimsy to the creation of attractive displays, as he details ways to mount displays from ceiling, floor, chair leg, and table.

Even potted plants hold small signs and complain "Shhhh, can't you see I'm reading?"

Part 2 of the volume describes specific display themes, most of which are best suited for school libraries, or the children's department of public libraries. Approximately fifty different displays are discussed throughout the text, which winds up with part 3, "Expanding the Book Display Concept." This section briefly discusses such topics as "activity centers" and "displays to make with children."

Anyone involved in display work could probably pick up a few useful tidbits from this volume, although it focuses heavily on displays for children and young adults. It ends with a bibliography, an index, and a list of "periodicals with creative layouts" to browse for ideas. [R: BL, 1 Oct 87, p. 215; JAL, July 87, p. 184]

Mary Ardeth Gaylord

401. Kies, Cosette. **Marketing and Public Relations for Libraries.** Metuchen, N.J., Scarecrow, 1987. 202p. bibliog. index. (Library Administration Series, No. 10). $14.50. LC 86-20219. ISBN 0-8108-1925-2.

Marketing and Public Relations for Libraries is an important volume in a series of ten. The public relations and marketing functions of the library's administrative process are placed by Kies in a theoretical framework that is conceptually clear and practical. The text is composed of concise, readable chapters on the definitions of marketing and public relations.

Marketing is presented as the broader, more inclusive concept, whereas public relations, communications, merchandising, and related topics are treated as components of the larger marketing function. The author views the marketing function as integral to the administrative process as a means of maintaining communication with constituencies and users: effectively planning for services, maximizing resources, and evaluating performance.

The historical development, principles, and concepts of marketing and public relations, the practice of library marketing, library promotional techniques, analysis, evaluation and marketing research, designing a plan, national efforts, and current trends are covered effectively. References are provided at the end of each chapter.

The topics apply to all types of libraries, including academic, public, school, and special. The blend of practical information and theoretical concepts makes this volume extremely useful to library planners, managers, trustees, and practicing professionals.

The appendix includes the results of the 1980 survey of the public relations section of the Library Administration and Management Association of the American Library Association. A bibliography of monographs is included. [R: BL, 1 Apr 87, p. 1175; EL, Sept/Oct 87, p. 39; RQ, Fall 87, p. 155; WLB, June 87, p. 74]

Margaret E. Chisholm

402. **Library Systems in Alberta: Guidelines for Development. Vol. II.** Edmonton, Alta., Library Services, Alberta Culture, 1986. 31p. illus. maps. bibliog. free. ISBN 0-919411-41-X.

Volumes 1 and 2 of *Library Systems in Alberta* have been published to encourage the development of library systems in Alberta. Volume 1 introduced the concept of library systems, how a group of interested citizens could work with the Library Systems Branch of Alberta Culture, the establishment of a steering committee, and the tasks of a project development team. Volume 2 carries the planning process forward until the time the proposed library system has been established but is not yet operational. The phases are described succinctly and clearly. What could have been dull reading is actually lively and illustrated with meaningful photographs, tables, and diagrams. For example, the section on financial planning illustrates the differences between a line and a program budget. There are three appendices, consisting of maps of existing library systems and projects in Alberta, and pertinent sections from the Province's Libraries Regulations. Although the guidelines are written specifically for use in Alberta, this volume is worthy of a wider audience not only because of its content but also as an example of good public relations material.

Helen Howard

403. Tuggle, Ann Montgomery, and Dawn Hansen Heller. **Grand Schemes and Nitty-Gritty Details: Library PR That Works.** Littleton, Colo., Libraries Unlimited, 1987. 237p. illus. index. $19.50pa. LC 87-21171. ISBN 0-87287-565-2.

Chosen from the John Cotton Dana Library Public Relations contest over the last decade, the first part of this book includes nine "grand schemes" or public relations principles that have worked in a variety of libraries. The second part comprises five sections that address the practical aspects or "nitty-gritty details," ranging from planning a public relations program to using print and audiovisual media effectively.

Practical examples abound and the text is accompanied with helpful illustrations of appropriate points. There are some good ideas here, but little new information. The text is geared to the novice in public relations and written for an audience with little or no background in public relations planning. The grand schemes are easy to adapt and the nitty-gritty details are axiomatic in nature. The text is general in nature and should not be used as a guide for specific subjects. In particular, the sections on audiovisual materials are simplistic at best. Many subjects, such as slide/tape presentations and photography, are deserving of a book in and of themselves.

The authors assume that anyone can develop and effectively promote public relations programs and publicity. The art of publicity, placing appropriate copy in targeted media, merits a book in and of itself. Good public relations programs are not simple. They proceed from a research base to a campaign designed expressly for a particular library and its community. Very often this requires the help of an outside public relations agency or advertising firm. What's missing here is how to identify, appropriately use, and evaluate such agencies.

Esther R. Dyer

NEW TECHNOLOGIES
General Works

404. Johnston, Ann, and Albert Sasson, eds. **New Technologies and Development: Science and Technology as Factors of Change....** Paris, UNESCO; distr., Lanham, Md., UNIPUB, 1986. 281p. bibliog. $16.75pa. ISBN 92-3-102454-X.

The issues involving new technologies and their applications in information, agricultural biotechnologies, health, energy, and education are presented from a perspective of developing countries. Authorship of six chapters is encoded in the acknowledgments section, noting twenty-four participants in the colloquium held in December 1984 at UNESCO headquarters in Paris. The preface notes that coverage is sometimes uneven, with overlapping themes and generic treatment of subject matter rather than detailed case studies. The discussion of the benefits and challenges these new technologies offer the developing world is relatively unhampered by these self-admitted deficiencies. A major theme permeating each chapter is that new technologies must be deliberately integrated into the individual political, cultural, social, and economic fabric of each developing nation. Participation in conception, development, and production of new technologies must be tailored to resources and aspirations of each developing country and typically involves substituting labor for capital, unlike developed countries. High-tech often is a solution in search of a problem

and planners are well advised to devise pragmatic approaches that fit national needs rather than using scarce resources in pursuit of prestige. Tables and figures complement the text. This reference provides a sound descriptive overview of the promises and pitfalls involved in pursuing new technologies in developing countries and will be of use to national planners everywhere in comprehending the challenges.

Marvin K. Harris

405. Kratz, Charles E., and others, eds. **Training Issues in Changing Technology.** Chicago, Library Administration and Management Association, American Library Association, 1986. 91p. $16.00pa.

This is a slender, paperbound volume consisting of introduction, preface, and the transcriptions of eight papers presented at the 1984 ALA Conference in Dallas. The training focused on in this volume centers on the human-human interactions of automated library systems. The editors encourage readers to envision their libraries in the year 2000, and to try pegging their current efforts in training to a continuum that moves smoothly towards the needs of the future.

Part 1 is devoted to a general theoretical overview of training issues in the library environment. "Personal human frailty" is a quality discussed in the article by Ruth Person (Catholic University). Dorothy Anderson (UCLA) provides a helpful list of do's and don'ts for designing training programs. S. Michael Malinconico (New York Public Library) is the compiler of a bibliography on organizations in transition.

Part 2 consists of papers on four topics of practical significance. First, R. Bruce Miller (Indiana University) considers safety and ergonometric guidelines for the use of video-display terminals. Janet Schroeder (Duluth Public Library) discusses training proposals aimed at flattening administrative structures. William Garrison (Northwestern University) writes about migrating from one automated environment to another. Kathy J. Coster and Lynne E. Bradley (of Baltimore's Library Video Network) extol the virtues of video training formats. And last, Ruth J. Patrick (University of Montana) presents a case study of her staff's introduction to Apple micros.

Most of the articles make the worthwhile suggestion that the whole staff be consulted in decisions which affect them.

Judith M. Brugger

CD-ROM

406. Buddine, Laura, and Elizabeth Young. **The Brady Guide to CD-ROM.** New York, Prentice Hall Press, 1987. 476p. illus. index. $21.95pa. LC 87-12788. ISBN 0-13-080631-5.

This moderately priced, clearly written, and well-organized practical manual about how to develop and produce a CD-ROM application will be extremely useful to librarians interested in and anxious to keep up with developments in compact disk technology. The book consists of two major sections. "A Guide to CD-ROM" includes overviews of optical storage and technology; discussions of appropriate and cost-effective CD-ROM applications; examinations and comparisons of retrieval software; and an introduction to premastering, mastering, and manufacturing. "Technology and Standards" explains compact disk technology and its audio, read-only-memory, and interactive applications in detail. It also reviews the High Sierra Standard and discusses the specifics of data structures. Appendices provide a list of service bureaus and annotated descriptions of CD-ROM products.

The particular value of a book like *The Brady Guide* lies with its integrated approach. Many publications on optical technology, particularly those aimed at librarians, have been collections of papers, with each paper highlighting a specific topic, development, or application. While such collections offer wide arrays of information all in one place, they tend to leave readers with fragmented views of a complex, evolving technology. By focusing on a central theme—the actual production of CD-ROM applications—*The Brady Guide* allows librarians to move beyond the limited view of compact disks only as alternatives to the expensive, connect-hour restrictions of online searching.

Buddine and Young have done an excellent job of making a complicated technology accessible to a broad range of readers. *The Brady Guide to CD-ROM* is highly recommended as a book to be read cover to cover or as a technical and informational reference.   Connie Miller

407. Hendley, Tony. **CD-ROM and Optical Publishing Systems: An Assessment of the Impact of Optical Read-Only Memory Systems on the Information Industry and a Comparison between Them and Traditional Paper, Microfilm, and Online Publishing Systems.** Westport, Conn., Meckler Publishing, 1987. 150p. $39.50 pa. ISBN 0-88736-192-7.

Although this book presents valuable information about compact disk read-only memory (CD-ROM) and other optical publishing sys-tems, the author discusses CD-ROM as a potential system for electronic storage of information. Since this system is now available, the book is particularly useful in its assessment of the applications of CD-ROM as a bibliographic database.

A CD-ROM disk holds twenty-five times as much information (thousands of pages) as a hard disk, thus allowing complete reference works to be stored on one disk. The author believes that "CD-ROM could begin to challenge microfilm and paper as a generic publishing medium for distributing a wide range of information from technical manuals and directories to encyclopedias and dictionaries." The recent appearance of the first mass-market CD-ROM material, a reference library appropriately called Bookshelf, supports this prediction.

As a guide to the processes involved, standards needed, applications, and benefits of CD-ROM and other optical publishing systems, this report succeeds in its purpose. It also compares these systems to other methods of information storage and retrieval. However, the list of potential suppliers of optical publishing services, hardware, and software will be outdated almost immediately, a fact that the author acknowledges in introducing these lists.

                                        Renee B. Horowitz

408. Lambert, Steve, and Suzanne Ropiequet, eds. **CD ROM: The New Papyrus: The Current and Future State of the Art.** Redmond, Wash., Microsoft Press; distr., New York, Harper & Row, 1986. 619p. illus. index. $34.95; $21.95pa. LC 86-2369. ISBN 0-914845-75-6; 0-914845-74-8pa.

409. Ropiequet, Suzanne, with John Einberger and Bill Zoellick, eds. **CD ROM: Volume Two: Optical Publishing: A Practical Approach to Developing CD ROM Applications.** Redmond, Wash., Microsoft Press; distr., New York, Harper & Row, 1987. 358p. index. $22.95 pa. LC 86-2369. ISBN 1-555615-000-8.

CD-ROM stands for compact disk read-only memory. The audio hi-fi technology of the compact disk can, with minor modifications, be made to provide a mass-memory capability for computers. The little pits on the reflective surface of the compact disk can store data and programs as well as music. The capacity of a single compact disk is astounding: six hundred megabytes, or equivalently, six hundred books of about five hundred pages each.

CD ROM: The New Papyrus is a general introduction to this new technology and its possibilities. It is a compendium of forty-four articles by various technologists, corporate executives, and futurists. Beginning with Vannevar Bush's "As We May Think," reprinted from the July 1945 issue of the *Atlantic Monthly*, the book covers the roles of books and computers in our information society, the basic principles of CD technology, the information codes employed in the Philips and Sony standards, manufacturing methods, and possible uses of the CD-ROM medium for education, entertainment, and business.

CD ROM: Volume Two: Optical Publishing is a shorter compendium of articles (sixteen) that are more closely coordinated than those in the large volume. Here each article is a chapter, and the book is organized as a tutorial on how to publish material (data, programs, audio and video for computer-based presentation) on compact disks. Some of the chapter titles are: "Changing the Publishing Paradigm," "CD ROM Characteristics," "Preparing Text," "Full Text Retrieval and Indexing," "Displaying Images," "Using Audio," "Premastering and Mastering," "Updating CD ROM Databases," "The First CD ROM Publication," and "A Clinical Medical Information System on CD ROM."

Both these books make excellent reference material, not only for patrons, but also for librarians. One word of caution is appropriate, however. These books are published by an organization that has a clear interest in the success of the CD-ROM technology. In all fairness to readers, we should mention that there are some difficulties with CD-ROM that might not be apparent from these books. The main problems with the CD-ROM medium for software publishers are (1) that it will be a limited market for a while—there aren't enough people with the equipment around yet, and the price of CD-ROM readers (which attach to a personal computer) needs to come down to the $300.00 range (it's $800.00 or so, now); and (2) unlike publishing a book, the startup production costs for a CD are very high, and one should not enter into a CD publishing venture lightly. Thus, there is a lot of potential for CD-ROM, but the action for the time being will be mostly for markets that can bear the high prices.

Steven L. Tanimoto

410. Myers, Patti. **Publishing with CD-ROM: A Guide to Compact Disc Optical Storage Technologies for Providers of Publishing Services.** Westport, Conn., published in association with National Composition Association by Meckler Publishing, 1986. 98p. illus. $19.95pa. ISBN 0-88736-181-1.

In spite of how much we hear about CD-ROM these days, there is still not that much on the market yet, either software or hardware. Because of this, many individuals and companies are interested in the potentials of optical storage media, and Myers's book is intended to orient prospective developers to producing publications for CD-ROM. Her book discusses the various types of optical disks, how an optical disk publication is produced and indexed, and what types of playback (delivery) system are required. There are a number of specific examples of optical disk publications available as of 1986 and a useful appendix of CD-ROM publishers which indicates areas of specialization. Myers writes well and makes the material comparatively easy to understand. There is a surprising amount of material covered in this small publication, which makes the lack of an index something of a problem.

Unfortunately for all of its worth, Myers's book is in competition with the second volume in the Microsoft Press CD-ROM series, entitled *CD ROM: Optical Publishing: A Practical Approach to Developing CD ROM Applications* (see entry 409). *Optical Publishing* is over three times as long as the Myers's book but costs only $3.00 more, and covers all of her topics in more depth. While no small portion of this length is devoted to background material (such as a discussion of the basics of computer graphics), prospective publishers (and librarians!) will need to become familiar with these subjects, too. *Optical Publishing* also deals in considerable detail with the very important High Sierra standardized format, which receives little coverage in *Publishing with CD-ROM*. In Myers's favor, she offers a somewhat less technical approach and a more digestible format. [R: LJ, 15 Feb 87, p. 146]   Robert Skinner

411. Rasdall, Mark, ed. **The International Directory of Information Products on CD-ROM 1986/87.** London, Alan Armstrong, 1986. 125p. index. £17.50pa. ISBN 0-946291-16-0.

Defining a new technology and informing potential users is a difficult task. The directory is a first step in identifying sources of information about CD-ROM and in identifying CD-ROM products currently on the market. A brief overview of CD-ROM and the current state of the market is followed by listings of information products, hardware and software services, information providers, books and journals, and conferences and exhibitions where CD-ROM is discussed and/or displayed. Each entry is on a separate page. The section on information products includes product title, vendor, information provider, type of information, update, general configuration, hardware and software needs, and price. Most CD-ROMs listed offer catalog information or bibliographic databases. Business and financial information is available on CD-ROM, as is the Electronic Encyclopedia from Grolier. With the information provided, one can quickly compare content, cost, and other information. Those who provide hardware and software services are identified and their U.S. and UK addresses are given. Information providers and other sources of information about CD-ROM are described. The publisher's name is given, but no address. As many publishers in this area are difficult to locate, it is hoped that the second edition will include addresses. A master index ties each of the sections together so that one can search all by publisher, product, subject, or other element. This is a good beginning, and as the editors move to the next editions, they will be able to increase the comprehensiveness of this useful directory. [R: LAR, Oct 87, p. 537; WLB, May 87, p. 66]   Ann E. Prentice

Robotics

412. Ardayfio, David D. **Fundamentals of Robotics.** New York, Marcel Dekker, 1987. 430p. illus. index. (Mechanical Engineering, 57). $79.95. LC 87-6850. ISBN 0-8247-7440-X.

This book covers the fundamental design principles of robotics as it is applied especially to robot arms or manipulators. Written primarily for college seniors in mechanical engineering, the material covers all aspects of robot designs and applications. Topics presented in these twelve chapters include the basic components of robot arms, the sensors, the controllers, programming, vision systems, and various related analytical concepts. The text is amply illustrated with pictures of functioning robot manipulators with particular emphasis on robot application in the automotive industry. Extensive references for further reading at the end of each chapter and a detailed index are special features of this book. Since most of the mathematical formulations are presented only in the last four chapters, the bulk of the material is easy to read and understand. This book is recommended for acquisition as a reference in college and general libraries.

John Y. Cheung

413. Blume, Christian, and Wilfried Jakob. **Programming Languages for Industrial Robots.** New York, Springer-Verlag, c1983, 1986. 376p. index. $50.00. LC 86-26000. ISBN 0-387-16319-0.

The German edition of this book was first published in 1983 under the title *Programmiersprachen für Industrieroboter.* During the translation process the text was enlarged and revised to include the languages SRL, PASRO, and AML, as well as the IRDATA software interface. Elements of the individual languages are used as examples in the discussion of general concepts. As a result the book does not attempt to aid in learning any of the languages introduced; rather the intent is to give a better understanding of the problems and techniques involved in robot programming.

The presentation of computer science problems takes up more space than the basic robot technology, primarily because it is more complex and less understood. However, basic robot movements and terminology are covered.

The appendices make up nearly one-third of the text and cover the main elements of each language. Of special interest is appendix L, which consists of a table of language comparisons. A list of references is provided. This is a highly specialized tool for individuals with access to robots.   Susan B. Ardis

414. Fu, K. S., R. C. Gonzalez, and C. S. G. Lee. **Robotics: Control, Sensing, Vision, and Intelligence.** New York, McGraw-Hill, 1987. 580p. illus. bibliog. index. $34.95. LC 86-7156. ISBN 0-07-022625-3.

Intended primarily as a text for students of robotics, this book is also a valuable reference work. It brings together material from mechanical engineering, electrical engineering, mathematics, and artificial intelligence, all relevant to the design, operation, and analysis of factory robotic systems.

The book begins with an overview and brief history of robotics, then delves into robot-arm kinematics, dynamics, planning manipulator trajectories, control of manipulators, sensing, low-level vision, higher-level vision, robot programming languages, robot intelligence, and task planning. Full comprehension of the book requires the reader to have a good mathematical background, including linear algebra, geometry, trigonometry, differential equations, and mathematical logic. However, readers interested only in particular sections need not have all this background; in this respect the book functions well as a reference tool.

The writing is generally clear and the mathematics explicit and unmysterious. The vision section includes not only helpful diagrams but a number of photographs that further clarify the problems and techniques for robot vision. While the vision coverage is not as extensive as that in *Computer Vision*, by D. Ballard and C. Brown (Prentice-Hall, 1982), it is broader than that in *Robot Vision*, by B. Horn (McGraw-Hill, 1986). Written by three distinguished professors of engineering, including the late King-Sun Fu (sometimes called the father of automatic pattern recognition), this book must be considered authoritative. The typesetting, figures, and other production aspects are all excellent. Altogether, this book is a unique and useful compilation of information for the design of industrial robots. Steven L. Tanimoto

415. Staugaard, Andrew C., Jr. **Robotics and AI: An Introduction to Applied Machine Intelligence.** Englewood Cliffs, N.J., Prentice-Hall, 1987. 373p. illus. bibliog. index. $34.95. LC 86-25140. ISBN 0-13-782269-3.

The book is intended as an elementary text on robotics and artificial intelligence to be used at the undergraduate level in a one-semester engineering, computer science, or technology course. Written in a conversational mode, and often in the first person, it is a readable text complete with problem sections and answers. The book is divided into eight chapters covering intelligent robotics, basic concepts of artificial intelligence, elements of knowledge representation, speech synthesis, speech recognition and understanding, vision, range finding and navigation, and tactile sensing. A bibliography of thirty-five items, the most current of which is dated 1984, is also provided. A brief subject index completes the volume. Illustrations appear throughout the book.

The volume is well organized and quite interesting to read. Some sections require a basic understanding of electrical devices, Boolean algebra, and elementary linguistics. The book should serve well for a basic course (as it is intended to) provided the instructor provides more current information to bring the student up-to-date. For more detailed presentations or a broader knowledge base, other sources such as the Ellis Horwood Series in Artificial Intelligence (Wiley) should be consulted. [R: Choice, May 87, p. 1434] Andrew G. Torok

Other Technologies

416. Braggins, Don, and Jack Hollingum. **The Machine Vision Sourcebook.** New York, Springer-Verlag, 1986. 358p. illus. bibliog. $144.00pa. ISBN 0-387-16355-7.

Recent technological developments in the use of machine vision (most simply stated, a television camera is linked to a computer) and image processing have led to many new applications of its use, particularly in industry, pharmaceuticals, medicine, automobile engineering, aerospace, and defense. Now tasks that formerly required the eyesight of humans can be carried out repeatedly, reliably, sometimes faster,

more safely, and without being subject to the errors associated with human fatigue and lack of concentration.

This sourcebook attempts to update and expand, with a more international perspective, the information provided in an earlier treatment of the subject, *Machine Vision—The Eyes of Automation,* by Jack Hollingum (IFS Publications, 1984), which emphasized the machine vision industry in Great Britain. This new sourcebook is divided into six parts. Part 1, "Introducing Machine Vision," borrows heavily from Hollingum's earlier work. It clearly defines what machine vision is, how it is used, and how potential users can identify suppliers to help solve specific problems via machine vision, as well as future trends in the field.

Part 2 is a totally new section of sources of products, information, and services on an international basis. The first and largest section, "Manufacturers and Builders of Vision Systems," contains a narrative discussion followed by pages of tables listing details about each company, product name, areas of application, input, process speed, and cost. Other sections identify component part suppliers; local sources (secondary distributors and sales and service offices); and research and information sources.

Part 3, "Company Profiles," is the largest section of the book and consists of statements submitted by the organizations to comprise descriptive company portraits. Case studies of selected organizations depict practical applications of machine vision in part 4. Many of these also describe generic applications for industrial settings. A brief bibliography of books, reviews/bibliographies/reports, conference proceedings, and periodicals follow in part 5, and a glossary is in part 6. The questionnaire used to solicit information for the sourcebook is appended.

The newcomer to robotics operations and machine vision technology will find a wealth of information in this reference work and, of course, valuable sources available in the field.

Lois Buttlar

417. **Essential Guide to the Library IBM PC. Volume 8: Library Applications of Optical Disk and CD-ROM Technology.** By Nancy Melin Nelson. Westport, Conn., Meckler, 1987. 252p. illus. index. $24.95 spiralbound. LC 85-10535. ISBN 0-88736-052-1.

418. Nelson, Nancy Melin, comp. **CD-ROMs in Print 1987.** Westport, Conn., Meckler Publishing, 1987. 102p. index. $29.95pa. ISBN 0-88736-179-X; ISSN 0891-8198.

CD-ROM, which has been called "the new papyrus," has captured the attention of librarians as a major new technology. Nelson has compiled two sources which serve as a first in-print listing. *CD-ROMs in Print* lists close to two hundred sources; *Library Applications* lists about half that many. *CD-ROMs in Print* begins with an informative essay by Nelson concerning CD-ROM as a technology; it gives a brief history, notes the major products available, and discusses the acceptance of this medium by libraries to date. The second part is the product directory or in-print list, arranged alphabetically by title. Each product listed includes product name, version, type of product, demo availability, price, system requirements, search software available, address of vendor, and supplier telephone number. The directory is followed by an excellent glossary of terms. The final sections include a list of five out-of-print titles, a supplier index, and a title index.

Library Applications covers only about half of the sources, but does so in depth. Descriptions are fuller and include not only the items of the in-print version, but samples from screens, producers' comments, and longer hardware statements.

The puzzling factor is why Meckler has issued both titles. As a user, this reviewer would prefer a comprehensive *Library Applications* publication since the descriptive comments are more helpful than the in-print listing. At this early stage of CD-ROM, such in-depth treatment is possible while keeping the publication a reasonable size.

Libraries are advised to purchase *CD-ROMs in Print* rather than *Library Applications*, since the former is more comprehensive.

David V. Loertscher

419. Hardy, Joe. **Introduction to Micrographics.** Silver Spring, Md., Association for Information and Image Management, 1986. 36p. illus. bibliog. $18.00pa. LC 86-26582. ISBN 0-89258-098-4.

Micrographics is defined herein as the science, art, and technology by which information in another form can be converted to microfilm, readily stored, and quickly retrieved. The field actually dates from 1839, and became a widespread technology in the banking industry in the 1930s. Its development, therefore, both preceded and paralleled that of the computer. The term *micrographics* covers roll film, aperture cards, fiche, and ultrafiche. Hardy, the author, works with (or for) the Association for Information and Image Management.

Micrographics, a competitive technology to computerization, is one in which the principals

learned that when you can't fight 'em, join 'em, leading to the development of computer output microform (COM). Hardy's drift, perhaps a bit defensively, is that micrographics have not been replaced or outmoded by computer technology but rather have been able to keep pace, using related and complementary technology. COM has supplanted paper output for numerous important publications, and will always be an inexpensive alternative to online searching in libraries.

The book contains brief illustrated sections on photographic and microfilm imaging, different microform formats, image quality, cameras, film processing, duplicators, viewers and viewer-printers, COM, and a good glossary. Finally, there are applications, including those for libraries and education, and a look into the future. For a quick understanding of the diversity, accomplishments, and problems of micrographics, and discussion of some of the applications common to libraries and educational institutions, this book (actually a booklet) is recommended for its clarity, illustrations, and definitions.

Bruce A. Shuman

420. Kuecken, John A. **Fiberoptics: A Revolution in Communications.** 2d ed. Blue Ridge Summit, Pa., TAB Books, 1987. 346p. illus. index. $28.95. LC 87-10185. ISBN 0-8306-0986-5.

Covering both the history and the latest developments in fiberoptics, Kuecken offers a basic resource book on the uses of these tiny and flexible glass fibers as conductors of light for communication. An inventor himself, Kuecken concentrates on the practical applications of the technology. He uses concrete examples such as fiber-guide systems in military aircraft and in local area computer networks to illustrate the importance of the technology.

Pictures and sound travel through light-weight fibers with the speed of light, and Kuecken gives engineers, physicists, computer scientists, technicians, students, and electronics hobbyists solid facts on how to make the connections between the optical fibers and the end devices.

Using a good mixture of photographs, diagrams, mathematical formulas, and plain-language text to describe concepts and suggest experiments, Kuecken includes chapters on the nature of light, polarization and wave interference, photodetectors, noise degradation, and AT&T's transatlantic fiberoptic cable, to list only a sample. He includes a short index, but no bibliographic references or glossary. The book will not be easy for nonscientists, but it will not be incomprehensible either.

Berniece M. Owen

421. Lambert, Steve, and Jane Sallis, eds. **CD-I and Interactive Videodisc Technology.** Indianapolis, Ind., Howard W. Sams, 1987. 206p. index. $24.95pa. LC 86-62443. ISBN 0-672-22513-1.

This reasonably priced and graphically attractive introduction to the world of CD-I and videodisc technology is a bargain in light of its contents. It is intended to examine the similarities and differences between interactive videodisc (IVD) and compact disc-interactive (CD-I) as forms of information delivery and entertainment, and succeeds quite well.

Eight chapters, written by "recognized experts in their field" and preceded by brief biographical sketches of the authors, can be read individually or collectively. They range in subject matter from the technical aspects of CD-I and authoring systems to their educational uses. Information is accurate as of August 1986. The source concludes with a glossary of terms, a directory of hardware and software producers (called "resources"), and a subject index. One regrets the lack of a bibliography or references for further reading.

With CD-I and laser-videodisc technology permeating the business, health, military, and educational sectors of society, this source should be welcomed by programmers, interactive media producers, librarians, researchers, and potential users. It was scheduled for online access in late 1987 or 1988 according to the Seattle-based editors, and it is hoped that it will be expanded and updated in this rapidly changing world of computer and video technology.

Ilene F. Rockman

422. McQueen, Judy, and Richard W. Boss. **Videodisc and Optical Digital Disk Technologies and Their Applications in Libraries, 1986 Update.** Chicago, American Library Association, 1986. 155p. $25.00pa. LC 86-17400. ISBN 0-8389-7041-9.

This excellent examination of videodisc and optical digital disk technology is updated from a previous volume published in March 1985. This updates the information to February 1986. At the time of writing of each, the term *CD-ROM* was not as familiar as it is today. As a result, the focus is on potential impact of the technology and emerging trends. It accomplishes this very well with an overview, a comparison of CD with videodiscs (both laser and CED), a discussion of optical digital technology, and the applications the library and information science communities may make with them. Also included is a near-exhaustive compilation of the current commercial products available and the ongoing research in the area.

Throughout the text are clear, concise examples and definitions of the various technologies. Products and companies/organizations are mentioned by name, and only the lack of a comprehensive name and address listing is unfortunate. For better or worse, marketing issues are not discussed. This is due in part to the somewhat pessimistic views of the authors about the possibility of these technologies gaining wider acceptance in libraries in the near future.

A brief appendix details the method of converting text, graphics, and audio to digital form, including OCR (Optical Character Recognition) and image scanning.

McQueen and Boss have done a nice job, via their grant from the Council on Library Resources, of chronicling the videodisc and optical digital disk field thus far. It can only be hoped that they continue this in the coming years as this technology begins to emerge as the major source of information storage and retrieval in the field of library and information science.

Daniel F. Phelan

423. **Optical Discs for Storage and Access in ARL Libraries.** By Ralph Holibaugh. Washington, D.C., Association of Research Libraries, 1987. 111p. bibliog. (SPEC Kit, No. 133). $20.00pa.

Practicality characterizes the Association of Research Libraries, Office of Management Studies System and Procedures Exchange Center (SPEC) Kits. The kits provide unedited primary source documents from a variety of libraries that offer "a wide range of approaches to specific issues." They are intended to be put to use by administrators and decision makers, committees and task forces, and individual library staff members in reviewing current practices, instituting new policies or services, or keeping current with trends in the field.

This is an excellent example of a SPEC Kit. Its selection of proposals, pilot and demonstration projects, evaluations, and planning documents will serve as valuable guidelines for libraries planning to or already implementing optical disk programs. A variety of applications is described, including the Smithsonian Institution Libraries' use of optical digital disks for archival storage, University of Illinois/River Bend Library System's and Massachusetts Institute of Technology's use of CD-ROM for online catalogs, Library of Congress's optical disk nonprint project, and Brown University's Infotrac experiment. Two of the more interesting sections of the SPEC Kit are selected pages from Massachusetts Institute of Technology's "Proposal to project Athena for a videodisc resource system" and University of Michigan's "BIBLIO: A library-based academic's workbench."

As with all monographic materials published on the rapidly changing area of optical technology, *Optical Discs for Storage and Access* cannot be expected to describe the latest developments. Its usefulness to libraries and librarians as a planning and implementation tool, however, makes it well worth the $20.00 price. [R: JAL, Sept 87, p. 248]

Connie Miller

424.   **Optical Information Systems '86. [Conference Proceedings].** Judith Paris Roth, comp. Westport, Conn., Meckler Publishing, 1986. 299p. index. $30.00pa. ISBN 0-88736-113-7.

Optical Information Systems conferences are not only one of the major forums for the dispersion of technological and applications developments, they are also very expensive. The publication of these proceedings, therefore, allows more librarians to benefit from the range of valuable conference presentations that cover everything from lasercards and videodisc authoring systems to the uses of compact disk technology in medical records management.

Because it includes only copies of handouts or transparencies, the "Preconference Workshops" section is the least useful. By contrast, the appendices are very useful. A list of conference speakers, moderators, and participants and an index to papers by session and title offer a bird's-eye view of the conference, and allow readers to choose readings like attendees chose presentations. Appendix 3 provides the initial prospectus, presented by the Interactive Video Consortium and the Smithsonian Institution, for a National Demonstration Laboratory for Interactive Educational Technologies. Knowledge of such a facility is crucial to librarians involved in educational planning on academic campuses.

Between the preconference workshop handouts and the appendices are the conference presentations. Those who use the "Index to Papers by Session and Title" will be disappointed in the number of presentations that could not be included in the conference proceedings (e.g., Robert Hayes's paper, "Working Towards an Integrated Information Delivery Workstation: A Multimedia Approach"). Among the thirty-two papers that were included, however, readers at varying levels of knowledge and sophistication will locate topics of interest. Librarians may find Young and Cohen's cost comparison of paper, online, and CD-ROM as storage media and Bezanson's discussion of integrating

CD-ROM with printed and online services of particular relevance.

The characteristics common to most conference proceedings—poor format and irregular quality of papers—also distinguish *OIS '86*. In spite of its limitations, the information-filled volume is worth its $30.00 price.

Connie Miller

425.   Pentland, Alex P., ed. **From Pixels to Predicates: Recent Advances in Computational and Robotic Vision.** Norwood, N.J., Ablex Publishing, 1986. 398p. illus. index. (Ablex Series in Artificial Intelligence). $55.00. LC 85-13413. ISBN 0-89391-237-9.

Most information available to humans derives first from a two-dimensional visual perception that is processed and analyzed, in context and from experience, to describe the world around us. This capability is innate. The complexity of this process becomes especially apparent when machines are pressed into our service to interpret two-dimensional visual data. This book discusses "models of image formation, process and part models, and specialized models" in three sections and sixteen chapters. Each chapter provides a useful overview before partitioning the specific subject into the small components the researcher requires for state-of-the-art investigation. The status of the technology expressed in terms of human development is at least preschool if not prenatal regarding predicating meaning from pixels. Each chapter forcefully demonstrates that our machines "see" better, by many orders of magnitude, than they can interpret and act. This field is in its infancy and the limited capabilities presently available are of recent development. Possibilities for application of visually sentient machines are boundless, thereby justifying intensive investigation of this intractable problem. The book provides a fine entry into the field for the serious student and researchers on the periphery, but is not for the layperson. References are by chapter and the author and subject indexes are useful.

Marvin K. Harris

426.   Saffady, William. **Optical Disks for Data and Documents Storage.** Westport, Conn., Meckler Publishing, 1986. 94p. illus. bibliog. index. $29.95pa. LC 86-12501. ISBN 0-88736-065-3.

The technology of information storage and retrieval is progressing. This report summarizes the current state of the art of optical disk storage technology, describing recent products, issues, and applications. Emphasizing optical videodisks and CD-ROM, the author clarifies the relationship of this technology to the publishing industry and online information services. An extensive bibliography is included. The book, while short, is well written, and it is enlightening to readers interested in how the information explosion might be managed at the level of recorded media. [R: BL, 1 Jan 87, pp. 682-83]   Steven L. Tanimoto

427. **Trends in Optical and Video Disk.** Silver Spring, Md., Association for Information and Image Management, 1987. 157p. illus. bibliog. (Special Interest Package, No. 23). $25.00pa.

This compilation of articles on optical disc technology provides information on optical disc types, applications, standards, and trends. Photocopied from their original sources, articles and graphics are uneven in appearance. A cover page for each article provides helpful information, including an abstract.

Although the point is made that rapid development of optical storage technology makes it "difficult to keep informed of new products and services," this special interest package attempts to surmount the problem by examining trends in read-only and read-write technology. Thus, an "Executive Summary" from a study commissioned by the Association for Information and Image Management stresses that optical digital mass storage technology is one aspect of the revolution in information management. As such, its impact will be considerable over the next decade because rapid growth and increased complexity in electronic processing and storage of information will affect the entire information and image management industry.

A survey of micrographic users reports their views of trends in information storage technology. Another article predicts that microfilm storage will coexist with optical disc storage, with competition leading to new micrographic methods and materials. This emphasis on 1990s trends makes the book valuable for those who expect to process and store large amounts of information in the future.

Renee B. Horowitz

PUBLIC LIBRARIES

General Works

428. Bakewell, K. G. B. **Business Information and the Public Library.** Brookfield, Vt., Gower Publishing, 1987. 309p. illus. bibliog. index. $47.50. LC 86-14901. ISBN 0-566-03537-5.

This is a basic textbook on public library service to the business community from a decidedly British slant. Written by a distinguished library science faculty member at Liverpool Polytechnic, the book is divided into three parts, with part 1 ("Business Information") exploring the nature of business information and how to assess business users' needs for information, and part 2 ("The Public Library's Role") discussing organization of services to businesses by public libraries and means of promoting that service, while part 3 ("Some Major Sources") is a topically arranged bibliography that is British in scope.

Extensive use is made in the first two sections of research gathered in a major survey of public library use by businesses, sponsored by the British Library Research and Development Department (The Bakewell/Roper Report), and other recent research on public library service to business. Use of this material throughout gives credibility and immediacy to the author's observations. Additionally, many illustrations, especially of actual promotional material used in British public libraries, are an effective device. When used in conjunction with such titles as *Business Information Sources*, by Lorna Daniels (University of California, Berkeley, 1985) to get at American business titles, this book can be a welcome addition to the literature on specialized public library services. Recommended for all library science collections and larger public libraries; but in consideration of its price, it would be better suited as a purchase for systems headquarters and state library professional collections than for small and medium-sized public libraries.   Chris Albertson

429. Dixon, John, ed. **Fiction in Libraries.** London, Library Association; distr., Chicago, American Library Association, 1986. 218p. index. (Handbooks on Library Practice). $25.00 pa. ISBN 0-85365-505-7.

This British imprint, the sixth in the Library Association's Handbooks on Library Practice series, is a good introduction to the subject of fiction in public libraries. Although grounded in practice in Great Britain, it should prove useful to American librarians as well. Six chapters cover, respectively, a survey of size and type of fiction holdings and provision of fiction in British libraries; a discussion of genres; fiction in talking book format; censorship, selection, and reviews; organization and promotion of fiction; and fiction as a subject in education for librarianship. Editor John Dixon concludes with a three-page chapter suggesting topics for future research. While E. J. Carrier's *Fiction in Public Libraries 1876-1900* (Scarecrow Press, 1965) and *Fiction in Public Libraries 1900-1950* (Libraries Unlimited, 1985) would provide an accompanying historical view of American practice with regard to fiction as well as useful bibliographies on the subject, this title is recommended as a lively and thorough text for all library school and professional collections. [R: LAR, Dec 87, p. 661]

Chris Albertson

430. Foss, Sam Walter. *The Library Alcove and Other Library Writings.* Selected and edited by Norman D. Stevens. Jefferson, N.C., McFarland, 1987. 166p. bibliog. index. $25.00. LC 87-42522. ISBN 0-89950-256-3.

Sam Walter Foss was librarian of the Somerville (Massachusetts) Public Library from 1898 until his death in 1911 at the age of fifty-three. Foss came to librarianship late, without library training and after establishing a career as editor, author, and lecturer. He was nationally known as a writer of humorous verse. Librarians today may know him as the author of the "Song of the Library Staff" which appeared in 1906 in *Library Journal* and has often been reprinted.

At Somerville Public, Foss quickly established his philosophy of librarianship, which, simply stated, was to "get the books to the people" by starting an art collection, opening a children's room, fostering cooperation with the schools, expanding agency and branch libraries, offering home delivery of books for a fee, purchasing multiple copies of popular works, opening the library on Sunday, and providing open stacks. All of these ideas, and even more important, his ideas on the value of books and reading in the lives of people, he presented with style and humor in the library and public press.

This book assembles all of his "library" poems; an excellent selection of his articles on library matters; two important but unpublished addresses, "The Use of the Library" and "The Usefulness of Books"; and extracts from his annual reports for the Somerville Public Library. Among his most important writings, and, except perhaps for the poems, those that reached the widest public, were the columns he wrote for *The Christian Science Monitor* from 1909 to 1911 under the title "The Library Alcove." Nearly all of these pieces are included in this collection.

The book also contains a brief biography of Foss, his obituary from *Library Journal* (by Charles K. Bolton), a list of writings by and about him, and an index. There is much to admire in this book, and much to be learned from this enthusiastic, innovative, and committed librarian.

Dean H. Keller

431. **Illinois Library Statistical Report No. 24.** Springfield, Ill., Illinois State Library, 1987. 105p. free pa.

This is a collection of unrelated studies from the Library Research Center of the Graduate School of Library and Information Science at the University of Illinois at Champaign/Urbana, prepared under the aegis of Herbert Goldhor on behalf of the Illinois State Library. Included are a discussion of the relationship between the length of loan period and circulation in public libraries; a survey of the head librarians of thirty outstanding Illinois public libraries; an investigation of the use of weeding and displays as methods to increase the stock turnover rate in small public libraries, and several additional short studies. Reports of these projects include methodology, summary data, statistical analysis, and detailed discussion. While the head librarian study is a fairly brief summary, the stock turnover and loan period reports are extremely detailed.

Goldhor finds that circulation is little affected by the change in the loan period. With the current emphasis on output measures, stock turnover rate has become of greater interest to more libraries. While this may not have been the researchers' intention, this study points out how difficult it may actually be to substantially increase this factor. Several shorter studies as well as an index to previous statistical reports conclude the volume.

Suzanne K. Gray

432. **Libraries — Public: 1987 Directory.** Omaha, Neb., American Business Directories, 1987. 1v. (various paging). $135.00 spiralbound.

American Business Directories compiles its information from the yellow pages of "all the cities and towns in the United States." Therefore, they make no claim as to completeness or currency, but the lists are based on directories used daily by millions of people.

This public library list contains 10,622 listings. Arrangement is alphabetical by state and by town or city within the state. Pertinent information includes name, complete address, telephone number, and year of first appearance in the directory. The *American Library Directory 1987-88* contains far more information, including budget, personnel, and special collections.

Comparing one state's listing to that compiled from the *American Library Directory*, this reviewer found that listings of branch libraries in the American Business Directories' publication were quite incomplete, and certain other libraries classified as "public" in the *American Library Directory* were missing.

It would seem that yellow pages listings for governmental agencies such as public libraries are not an adequate source of information; for profit-oriented businesses, the result promises to be far better.

For the convenience of the business seeking a mailing list, these listings are available in almost any format as well as the printed, spiral-bound directory: Cheshire or pressure-sensitive labels, magnetic tapes, and diskettes. Online access is also available. All information is protected and, as with most mailing lists, seeded to detect unauthorized use.   Shirley Lambert

433. Output Measures for Public Libraries: A Manual of Standardized Procedures. 2d ed. Prepared for the Public Library Development Project by Nancy A. Van House and others. Chicago, American Library Association, 1987. 99p. illus. index. $12.50pa. LC 87-11479. ISBN 0-8389-3340-8.

This new edition relates much more closely to the planning process document (now *Planning & Role Setting for Public Libraries*; see entry 434) than did the earlier edition. That integration emphasizes the commitment made by the PLA's Public Library Development Program to a complete and easily implemented approach to public library planning.

The use of output measures to evaluate public library services is the focus of this handbook. Evaluation is the "feedback loop" of the planning process and must be tied closely to every step from role selection to activity design. Twelve output measures are described in easily followed detail. Simplification of approach and analysis are stressed. The new edition has a new format and has been rewritten to lead planners painlessly through the process. Even a cursory comparison of the two editions illustrates the success revisors have had in addressing some of the difficulties of the earlier manual. Libraries are asked to switch to the procedures detailed in the new edition and are assured that existing data will be comparable. Larger sample sizes are encouraged also to provide more accurate data.

The refinements in approach and explanation seen in this new edition will help make an already valuable and innovative instrument more significant to public libraries as they approach the quantitative aspects of the vital planning process. More appropriate and credible planning efforts should result. [R: LJ, 1 Sept 87, p. 160; RQ, Winter 87, pp. 293-94]
Patricia A. Steele

434. Planning and Role Setting for Public Libraries: A Manual of Options and Procedures. Prepared for the Public Library Development Project by Charles R. McClure and others.

Chicago, American Library Association, 1987. 117p. illus. index. $14.00pa. LC 87-11445. ISBN 0-8389-3341-6.

The development of this volume, which builds upon while not revising *A Planning Process for Public Libraries*, represents a continued commitment by the PLA to planning, measurement, and evaluation in the nation's public libraries. The commitment signals a movement away from the creation of national standards as such. This manual is one of three products of the Public Library Development Project (PLDP), the others being a revised edition of *Output Measures for Public Libraries* (see entry 433) and a Public Library Data Service (PLDS) which has a planned implementation date of 1988. The PLDS will collect and make accessible data from libraries across the United States to provide comparative data to enhance planning efforts. These tools should increase the planning efforts in public libraries and assure their effectiveness.

The format of this manual invites its use. Photographs, tables, and a summary list break up the text and add to overall attractiveness. Sample public library roles are delineated and explorations of role implications are included. Levels of planning effort are defined for the various elements of the process. There are selective bibliographies to facilitate further exploration of elements in the process, and appendices include workforms and a good summary of measures from the output measures handbook.

This book provides the definition, process, and resources to improve and individualize public library management and evaluative processes. Its simple and adaptable concepts invite its application and represent a significant step in helping public libraries achieve excellence. [R: LJ, 1 Sept 87, p. 160; RQ, Winter 87, pp. 293-94]
Patricia A. Steele

435. Prucha, Isabel D. **Your Library: A Friend: An English-Vietnamese Bilingual Guide. Thu Viện: Một Người Bạn.** Santa Ana, Calif., Golden Palm Press, 1986. 76p. illus. $10.95pa. ISBN 0-937319-00-7.

The author has succeeded in writing an easy to understand handbook for Vietnamese-Americans on how to use public and academic libraries. Translated into Vietnamese by Hoang Chu Duy, the book provides a guided tour of libraries in a style that is amiable and concise. It covers services provided by libraries, arrangement of materials, library membership, and types of libraries. Information on the usage of card catalogs and computer catalogs is included. The author's ability to include essential and interesting information about libraries for first-time users while avoiding verbosity is admirable.

The format of this paperback is very plain. The black-and-white photographs and line drawings nicely complement the text. It is an essential book for library staff working with Vietnamese users. I highly recommend it to any librarian involved in providing library tours or library skills classes to any group of new users.

Susan E. Kotarba

436.   Shuman, Bruce A. **River Bend in Transition: Managing Change in Public Libraries.** Phoenix, Ariz., Oryx Press, 1987. 167p. index. $27.50pa. LC 87-14025. ISBN 0-89774-320-2.

This is the third volume in a series of case study texts by Shuman. Whereas *The River Bend Casebook* (Oryx Press, 1981) was a general collection of public library management cases, this third title continues the narrowing of scope begun in *River Bend Revisited* (Oryx Press, 1984), which emphasized the "problem patron." *River Bend in Transition*, however, takes for its theme situations that provoke change, especially in relation to automation and new technology. The thirty-six case topics include such issues as consultants, space planning, and public relations, all in regard to an automation project, but broaden to address employee strikes, homework, and the homeless as well. Although authentic in setting and thorough in detail, the cases are moderate in length, and by dealing with a specific problem, allow for a focused analysis by the reader. Each ends with a set of questions to be pondered and several pertinent citations, while an indexed list of subjects refers back to individual cases.

Seasoned managers and library students will both be challenged by this work, and it is recommended for supplementary use in any public library management course or continuing education program where case study material is desired. Similar resources would include the Scarecrow Press series by the late Mildred H. Lowell (*Management of Libraries and Information Centers*, vols. 1-3, 1968, and vol. 4, 1971; *Library Management Cases*, 1975) and the Bowker Series in Problem-Centered Approaches to Librarianship (e.g., *Case Studies in Library Computer Systems*, by R. P. Palmer, 1973; *Problems in Intellectual Freedom and Censorship*, by A. J. Anderson, 1974). [R: LJ, Dec 87, p. 84; WLB, Nov 87, p. 74]

Chris Albertson

437.   Turock, Betty J., ed. **The Public Library in the Bibliographic Network.** New York, Haworth Press, 1986. 89p. (*Resource Sharing and Information Networks*, Vol. 3, No. 2).

$24.95. LC 86-14915. ISBN 0-86656-595-7.

Very few public library administrators of the 1980s have not questioned the feasibility of their participation in bibliographic networks. Most have not had access to information as valuable as that presented in the work under review.

The seven articles—"Costs and Benefits of OCLC Use in Small and Medium Size Public Libraries," "The Kewanee Public Library Votes Yes on OCLC," "We'll Wait and See," "A WLN Dilemma," "Linking CLSI and UTLAS to Meet Local Needs," "Present and Future Network Base for New Mexico's Public Libraries," and "Networking at the Principal Public Library in Rhode Island"—provide insight into the benefits and costs of networking by libraries of varying sizes and geographic locations.

The contributors explain in detail why they did, or did not, join bibliographic networks, the network costs (including the initial and ongoing expenses), and staffing needs.

This volume was the direct result of the Public Library Association's Task Force on Network Relations, established in 1982-1983, and was published simultaneously as the journal *Resource Sharing and Information Networks* (volume 3, number 2).

Recommended for all public libraries considering bibliographic networking. [R: BL, 1 Oct 87, p. 216; RQ, Winter 87, pp. 294-95; WLB, June 87, p. 73]

Janet R. Ivey

Adult Education

438.   Johnson, Debra Wilcox, with Jennifer A. Soule. **Libraries and Literacy: A Planning Manual.** Chicago, American Library Association, 1987. 38p. $12.50pa. LC 87-1305. ISBN 0-8389-0478-5.

This is nothing new; discussion of the library's role in stemming illiteracy can be found throughout library literature. What makes this manual noteworthy is that a body of writing on the subject has been condensed into its simplest form. Now it is the perfect vehicle for a quick read through whenever needed. Because of its incisiveness library planners will refer to it often in lieu of having to scan many more pages of scattered text. Of the thirteen brief chapters, "Materials Selection" is the longest (five pages), "Resources" will be the first turned to (how to pay for a literacy program), and "Making the Decision" the shortest but the most consequential (one-half page before crossing the Rubicon). Several of the chapters have at the end a further reading section. The appendices include a selected list of publishers of adult education materials and a planning checklist. The authors are both experienced in this area: Johnson is project coordinator of the Libraries and Literacy Education Project at the University of Wisconsin, and Soule is project director of the Wisconsin Alliance to Promote Programs for Literacy among the Elderly. Since this is a manual and not a full-fledged text its brevity is welcome. The information given is sufficient and avoids redundancy, though a couple of case studies would have rendered the whole plea more meaningful. Trying to visualize just how a library might find illiterates, convince them to participate in a literacy program (not to mention convincing overworked librarians), and make a success of the venture when money is tight, is difficult. Recommended especially for public libraries whose mission statement should incorporate such planning. [R: LJ, July 87, p. 56]

Bill Bailey

439. Weingand, Darlene E., ed. **Adult Education, Literacy, and Libraries.** Champaign, Ill., Graduate School of Library and Information Science, University of Illinois, 1986. 345p. (*Library Trends*, Vol. 35, No. 2). $8.00pa. ISSN 0024-2594.

This collection focuses on the importance and potential of libraries in relation to U.S. adult education and literacy. It includes a thoughtful array of the problems and possibilities of the "library-learner dynamic." Philosophical and theoretical approaches at the beginning and end offer useful perspectives. Weingand sets the tone for the contributions by describing the library in relation to the overall U.S. educational system. Concluding the volume, David Carr's perceptive review of the adult independent library learning project offers a classic study of the implications of that brave venture into library possibilities. Carr challenges librarians to "a different way of knowing" and a difference in what libraries provide learners.

The issue of literacy is woven throughout, accenting the growing awareness of its importance and the role of libraries in an age of information. Monroe, in particular, analyzes library involvement with literacy and asks for expansion to address the present-day literacy challenge.

Adult education and literacy involvements of the American Library Association are detailed and broad-scoped treatments of federal and state government efforts described. Volunteer efforts of the Literacy Volunteers of America, now actively involved in libraries nationwide, reveal many projects. Strong studies support the importance of libraries to enable learning efforts of the learning disabled adult and groups with special needs, especially those faced

with the need for career choice/change information and skills.

This collection serves as a survey of past and current efforts as well as a catalog of the challenges to be addressed.

Barbara Conroy

Branch Libraries

440. **Profiling the Community: A Practical Guide for Librarians. Vol. 1: Handbook on Community Profiling.** Sunderland, England, Borough of Sunderland, Department of Recreation and Libraries, 1986. 63p. bibliog. £10.00 pa. ISBN 0-905108-03-5.

This handbook was originally compiled for branch and divisional librarians in the Borough of Sunderland, England. It aimed to serve as a guide for community profiling, one of the responsibilities of these librarians. It was developed in conjunction with the statistical information from the 1981 census data provided to each library in Sunderland. The guidelines included in the handbook aimed to help librarians interpret the data provided by the census printouts. After a brief introduction, chapters cover people, environment, services, politics and religion, and summary and conclusions. Each includes several sections which describe how to present the data and interpret the relevant statistics. Two appendices present sources of population statistics for Great Britain and performance ratios of branch libraries. There is also a short, unannotated bibliography of primarily British references. The handbook was developed for a specific purpose and a specific clientele. Its applicability outside this context is limited. The British terminology and point of view presented in the handbook differ from those of the United States. Public librarianship in the two countries is markedly different. However, this handbook may serve as a useful model for community survey research with public libraries. It would be of interest primarily to library science students and faculty. [R: JAL, Jan 87, p. 387]

Susan J. Freiband

Budgeting

441. Ballard, Thomas H. **The Failure of Resource Sharing in Public Libraries and Alternative Strategies for Service.** Chicago, American Library Association, 1986. 289p. index. $20.00pa. LC 86-22318. ISBN 0-8389-0460-2.

Ballard's book is probably the most controversial and thought-provoking work on public librarianship in years. Readers will either enthusiastically endorse or vigorously denounce his ideas, but no one will be able to stay neutral.

Ballard questions many of the goals and services of modern public libraries, then provides a clearly articulated, carefully supported argument for his positions. Resource sharing, networking, and programming are among the public library functions which Ballard considers too expensive for the costs involved. Improved collection strategies to meet the immediate needs of patrons would be more cost effective and beneficial to patrons than the resource sharing currently endorsed. He also argues for conveniently accessible collections which lend themselves to patron browsing. Other sections discuss branch library theory, library architecture, automation, and the value of reference services in the public library.

An important volume for public library professionals, library trustees, and others who are concerned about public librarianship into the next century. Highly recommended. [R: JAL, July 87, p. 180; LAR, Oct 87, p. 535; WLB, Mar 87, p. 58]   Carol J. Veitch

442.   Campbell, William D. **A Budgeting Manual for Small Public Libraries.** Clarion, Pa., Center for the Study of Rural Librarianship and the Small Library Development Center, College of Library Science, University of Pennsylvania, 1987. 54p. bibliog. $6.95pa.

Budget preparation is a major and persistent headache for new and inexperienced directors of small public libraries, who must often serve as financial officers as well as administrators. Consequently, a book which gives clear advice on ways to prepare such a document for the novice manager of a small public library is welcome. Campbell, a professor of business administration at Clarion University, treats his material in a dry manner, eschewing humor and hominess to stress helpful advice for the first-timer.

The format is simple: plain, typed P/C pages, and no artwork. Tables called "exhibits" are provided as checklists, to help the budget preparer in following a step-by-step path. While three types of budgets are discussed (line-item, functional, and capital) only the first one is explored in any depth, presumably because the preponderance of small public libraries employ line-item operating budgets.

One of the "exhibits" consists of a list of the major steps in budgeting for new libraries, setting this book apart from others of its type which dwell primarily on ways in which one presents a budget for an existing institution. Another useful feature: a list of ways in which one forecasts revenues. There are even "worksheets," but these are, alas, filled in with figures to be used as examples. It would have been more

helpful had another set of blank-form worksheets been furnished, permitting the librarian to plug in specific values.

The book makes no attempt to allay the fears of the novice, getting right into its lists of what to do, and when to do it. While nothing is particularly innovative, there are sound recommendations which can be used in preparing a budget, especially where one wishes to determine if anything important has been disregarded or left out. Recommended. [R: WLB, Mar 87, p. 66]   Bruce A. Shuman

Trustees

443.   Williams, Lorraine. **The Ontario Library Trustee's Handbook.** Toronto, Ontario Library Trustees' Association, Ontario Library Association, 1986. 58p. illus. bibliog. (OLTA Trustee's Kit, No. 1). $15.00pa.; $12.00pa. (U.S.). ISBN 0-88969-025-1.

This manual is valuable to all public librarians as a model handbook for trustees. It serves as a model not only for the information it contains, but also for its layout. Information is brief, easily found, arranged logically, and provides a clear statement of areas of concern for trustees. Topics include legal statements, roles of the library board, roles of the library, relationships with the community, responsibilities of librarians and services, cooperation with other libraries, and many common terms that trustees need to know. Highly recommended.
          David V. Loertscher

User Studies

444.   Allen, Janice, and Jenny Potter. **Evaluating the Performance of Public Library Outreach Services: A Consumer View.** London, British Library; distr., Wolfeboro, N.H., Longwood Publishing, 1986. 36p. (British Library Research Paper, Vol. 8). $7.50pa. ISBN 0-7123-3098-4.

This report is an outgrowth of an earlier study of British local government services, including library services, entitled *Measuring Up, Consumer Assessment of Local Authority Services: A Guideline Study* (1986). This report reviews the main conclusions of the earlier report, describes the aims of the additional study of library outreach services to disadvantaged clients, and proposes a framework for performance measurement of these library programs. The report offers practical suggestions for defining target groups to be served, isolates the questions to ask about performance, and suggests indicators to be used in evaluating the success or effectiveness of the service in meeting its stated objectives and providing its intended benefits to clients. For each indicator, the report suggests the kind of input and output data library authorities will need to collect to answer the questions. The study and the suggested assessment model rely heavily on client surveys in an effort to keep the focus on user perceptions of the usefulness and quality of the outreach programs provided them. The report also suggests five crucial determiners of effectiveness librarians should concentrate on in evaluating performance: (1) the extent to which services reach the target group, (2) the availability of special materials for that group, (3) data on actual use of the services, (4) awareness of service by the target group, and (5) the frequency/extent of contact between staff and clients. This is a useful case study for librarians developing a performance measurement program of library services to users. Blaine H. Hall

445. Kim, Choong Han, and Robert David Little. **Public Library Users and Uses: A Market Research Handbook.** Metuchen, N.J., Scarecrow, 1987. 370p. index. $29.50. LC 87-13126. ISBN 0-8108-2021-8.

Choong Han Kim and Robert David Little developed a conceptual frame and measures to interpret data from an LSCA-funded study called the Indiana Community Analysis Project (ICAP). The results are presented in this handbook. It establishes an empirical frame for "community needs assessment"—a highly useful process in the public library world. The authors' principal hypothesis was that there is a positive correlation between one's occupation and the ways one uses the local public library. According to the authors, this hypothesis is confirmed, and it is further asserted that public libraries will be a necessity to most employed people in the future.

The study sought to (1) describe and explain how people use public libraries in their communities, (2) provide library professionals with methodologies for assessing their communities' information needs, (3) provide comparative data for local planning efforts, (4) help librarians create and maintain local user databases, and (5) improve the assessment/information process. Very detailed analysis of the surveys of over seventy-six hundred respondents in seven Indiana public libraries provides some specific data as well as a methodology librarians can follow.

In his foreword, Herbert Goldhor invites tests in other libraries of the basic hypothesis of the Kim-Little study. Such an expansion of this work, which is based on library users' own perceptions, could be a positive contribution

toward the development of valid output measures. Reading of *Public Library Users and Uses* is probably an imperative for practitioners and researchers in public librarianship. It is not, however, for the casual reader; its interesting insights will require time and attention on the part of those who would benefit from this research.
Patricia A. Steele

446. Prabha, Chandra, John Bunge, and Duane Rice. **How Public Library Patrons Use Nonfiction Books.** Dublin, Ohio, Office of Research, OCLC Online Computer Library Center, 1987. 68p. illus. bibliog. (Research Report Series). $11.00 spiralbound.

Research efforts undertaken for the purpose of developing an electronic information system that is more effective than conventional or traditional means of obtaining information include this study, which examined information-seeking behavior associated with the use of nonfiction books in an electronic mode. Two premises of the study were (1) that nonfiction books (nonreference type circulating books) are consulted for specific information, and (2) that they are consulted in parts, rather than read in entirety. The study was designed to test these premises (the term *hypothesis* is not used in this report) and also to study the search techniques used by patrons in locating a book.

The methodology of data collection selected for this study was that of personal interview. Patrons at five of the twenty branch sites of the Public Library of Columbus and Franklin County (representing different types of neighborhoods) served as subjects, using a random stratified sample. The interviewer followed the same script of twenty-nine questions with each of the 347 subjects after it had been subjected to several pretests and revisions and was refined for final use.

Findings indicated that almost 85 percent of the subjects found the information they sought in nonfiction books. For reading lengthy texts, book format might be preferred to the electronic mode, while short sections of texts read for short durations might lend themselves better to retrieval via electronic medium. Additional findings indicated that in two-thirds of the cases, only parts of nonfiction books were read by borrowers. Interview responses allowed categorization of patrons into groups of known-item users, catalog users, and browsers, with browsers accounting for over 55 percent of the library patrons in the study. Data collected also permitted path analysis for identifying the series of options used for finding specific information. The researchers concluded that certain features would be required of electronic information systems using complete texts of nonfiction books. They recommend that (1) systems must accommodate a subject approach to searching; (2) they should also permit known-item searching; (3) features for displaying or emphasizing new acquisitions are needed; (4) browsing and display features for scanning text, tables of contents, book indexes, and illustrations should be incorporated into the system; and (5) users should be allowed to skip and scan at individual (variable) paces.

Suggestions for further research are numerous, and the researchers explain the stratified sampling techniques and its limitations, as well as the weighting scheme used to adjust for library size, in a statistical notes section. Data are reported in over forty tables in this study, providing such information as profiles of participating libraries, gender distribution of eligible and noneligible participants, patrons' reasons for reading just parts of nonfiction books, features patrons used for finding specific information, responses by three groups of users, browsers' methods for selecting a book, and topics on which patrons sought information. While some of these topics are of interest to the design of the study, others have long-range implications for future design of electronic information service systems. The data provided in this OCLC Research Report provide answers to many questions (and suggest others) for researchers in the field of library and information science who are interested in or concerned with design and development of electronic information systems.   Lois Buttlar

447. **Review 1984-1986—Developing Public Library Services in Ottawa.** Ottawa, Ottawa Public Library, 1986. 44p. bibliog. free spiral-bound. ISBN 0-919603-08-4.

During 1984 and 1985, the Ottawa Public Library in Ontario, Canada, designed and conducted five surveys of various groups: 800 library users over the age of ten; 125 children under fourteen; 100 bookmobile users; 50 users of visiting services, and 500 Ottawa residents fifteen years or older who were telephoned. The findings of these surveys as well as relevant demographic and library statistics are presented in this brief bilingual report. Those who have read similar reports will not be surprised by the findings: most of the respondents in the library users survey were frequent library users who lived fifteen minutes away or less from the library, the most popular fiction area was mystery, and the most popular nonfiction was biography. Of the five hundred respondents in the telephone survey, 46 percent did not use the library. The reasons given for nonuse were lack

of time, use of another library, or no particular reason (which could cover a multitude of causes from inability to read to antagonism toward librarians). For the most part the nonusers were aware of the location and services of the library, so their choice not to use the resource was a deliberate one. Also included in the report are the board decisions taken over the period of the review. The twenty-four pages of appendices include statistics about the library's resources and services as well as some comparisons with other libraries of similar size in Ontario. Public libraries which, like the Ottawa library, serve a population of approximately 300,000, may find this report of interest for comparative purposes. It will also be useful in research collections, especially in library schools.

Adele M. Fasick

448. Rubin, Richard. **In-House Use of Materials in Public Libraries.** Champaign, Ill., Graduate School of Library and Information Science, University of Illinois, 1986. 213p. bibliog. (Monograph, 18). $15.00.

The Coalition for Public Library Research, a project of the Library Research Center at the University of Illinois Graduate School of Library and Information Science, conducted this study in six of its member libraries located in Illinois, Iowa, Minnesota, North Carolina, Pennsylvania, and Texas. In-house use was investigated in a total of twelve agencies of different sizes serving a variety of communities. Methods employed included counts of materials left on tables, questionnaires, face-to-face interviews, unobtrusive observation of patrons, and marking of materials left on tables. The primary finding was that public libraries probably underrepresent their in-house use by a significant amount when they simply count materials left on tables. The questionnaire was found to be the best method for measuring the in-house use of library materials. Five appendices provide summary and analysis tables and samples of forms used in the study. This report is an excellent example of well-planned, well-executed library research.   Leonard Grundt

449. Ryder, Julie, ed. **Library Services to Housebound People.** London, Library Association; distr., Chicago, American Library Association, 1987. 221p. illus. bibliog. index. $28.00. ISBN 0-85365-667-3.

This is a comprehensive, up-to-date guide to current services in Great Britain for library authorities to use in evaluating their services. The fifteen chapters deal with the readers, staffing, book selection, nonbook materials, and services to mentally and visually handicapped and extension activities. Although the volume contains valuable information, this reviewer found the British terminology and descriptions distracting. [R: LAR, Dec 87, p. 668]

Janet R. Ivey

PUBLISHING

Reference Works

450. Gillespie, John T. **Publishers and Distributors of Paperback Books for Young People.** 3d ed. Chicago, American Library Association, 1987. 190p. index. $15.00pa. LC 86-32260. ISBN 0-8389-0471-8.

This book is an expanded and updated version of the second edition of *Paperback Books for Young People* (American Library Association, 1977). It serves as a supplement, buying guide, and method of updating the author's three-volume set, *The Elementary School Paperback Collection* (American Library Association, 1985), *The Junior High School Paperback Collection* (American Library Association, 1985), and *The Senior High School Paperback Collection* (American Library Association, 1986). It is divided into two parts: an introduction and directory of the leading publishers of paperbacks and their imprints, and a listing of paperback distributors and their services. Three appendices include a brief discussion and annotated listing of selection aids for paperback books, the questionnaire sent to paperback distributors, and the names and addresses of the members of the Educational Paperback Association. The book also includes a brief subject index to paperback publishers, intended "to highlight major areas of specialization in paperback book publishing" (p. 183). This is a particularly useful feature. The directories of paperback publishers and distributors are divided into separate sections for the United States and Canada. About three hundred publishers were selected for inclusion. Publishers of religiously oriented materials, educational (textbooks and aids for classroom use) materials, and foreign language materials were omitted. Information for each entry includes in addition to name and address, kinds of paperback books published, typical authors and titles, series for young people, special services, price ranges, and ordering information. Many cross-references facilitate use. Information about paperback distributors includes number of suitable titles in stock, minimum order per out-of-stock title, types of paperbacks, and promotional aids supplied. The usefulness of this directory as an acquisitions tool is clearly evident. It is an important addition and supplement to the basic paperback

collection guides previously mentioned, and would be a valuable addition to professional collections in all types of school media centers, as well as in public libraries. [R: JOYS, Fall 87, p. 111; VOYA, Oct 87, p. 190]

Susan J. Freiband

Desktop Publishing

451. Bove, Tony, Cheryl Rhodes, and Wes Thomas. **Art of Desktop Publishing.** New York, Bantam Books, 1987. 296p. bibliog. index. $19.95pa. ISBN 0-553-34441-2.

Purporting to provide enough information to enable you to "learn how to start an 'instant' electronic publishing house right at your desk," *Art of Desktop Publishing* covers the basics of creating newsletters, brochures, catalogs, reports, books, and more, using a Macintosh or an IBM PC computer system and software. Major areas covered include how to do your own typesetting, design and layout, computer art using "paint" programs and computer clip art, selecting laser printers and printer software, type fonts, and looking to the future with new technological developments such as CD-ROM and optical disks.

Using a step-by-step approach, this book is designed so that those with no knowledge of computers or publishing can "get their feet wet," beginning with an overview of desktop publishing, how to create and organize text, using printers and typesetters, creating graphics, page makeup techniques and programs, design and production methods, discussion of professional composition and typesetting, and more. Also included are a glossary, appendices (companies, products, bibliography), and an index.

Specific instructions for processes using desktop software and hardware are often buried in descriptive text and are difficult to locate for any particular use: "When typing text into your PC Paint window, press Return...." This material is preceded by a paragraph on font sizes and prices for PC Paint and Paint Plus, and followed by a paragraph on the screen area of PC Paint (p. 131). Critical instructions can easily be overlooked when buried in surrounding text, such as on page 167: "When using MacWrite for preparing text ... keep in mind that the text should begin at the 1-inch mark ... if you started the text at the default ... the text would then appear on the PageMaker page 0.25 inches indented." There is simply no way to access this type of instruction and use it for actual applications unless you are reading every word on every page. The instruction portion of the text would have been easier to use if it were set out in a step-by-step manner *after* the discussion of the many elements involved.

There is no question that books of this type are invaluable in assisting anyone to better use the new technology. While aimed at the novice, many of the discussions are quite technical. This effort can be compared to *Desktop Publishing from A to Z* (see entry 452) and *Desktop Publishing with Your IBM PC & Compatible* (see entry 455) in its overall presentation. The bulk of the illustrations here are reproductions of screens with the actual material being discussed displayed on them. Considering how involved some procedures are, the screen images can be very useful, essential in fact for full understanding of the text. The eight-page list of companies standing by to assist you, and the product list, two pages of trade name items with the company that owns them, are pluses. The index to products, companies, hardware, software, accessories, technical terms, procedures, etc., is a vital part of the book, and provides access to the wide-ranging information to your fingertips.

The entire book was written, edited, and typeset in a span of three months using an Apple Macintosh computer. The layout is easy to read, and boldface heads and subheads help to lead the reader through the various processes from basic level to more advanced discussions. Among the spate of books offered by Bantam Computer Books of related interest, this one is a winner. Within a few months there will be a veritable deluge of projects like this one, honing in on specific systems and capabilities. This can be counted among the leaders at this time and it is highly recommended for anyone considering, or already involved in, the desktop publishing revolution. Judy Gay Matthews

452. Grout, Bill, Irene Athanasopoulos, and Rebecca Kutlin. **Desktop Publishing from A to Z.** Berkeley, Calif., Osborne/McGraw-Hill, 1986. 219p. index. $17.95pa. ISBN 0-07-881212-7.

Closely paralleling other entries in the flood of materials on desktop publishing, this effort maintains that with a desktop publishing system, page layout software, and a printer, you can write, edit, insert graphics, and create pages effortlessly, and goes on to provide an introduction to the basic publishing process from conceiving, planning, and producing the project. Also covered are budgeting, tracing expenses and profit, and ways to distribute and market the finished product.

Eight chapters (200 pages) cover "What Is Desktop Publishing?" "First Decisions" (business decisions, editorial direction, copyright, and ISBN), "Profiles in Profit" (budgeting, income from advertising), "Desktop Publishing Equipment," "Designing Pages for Publication," "Preparing for the Print Shop" (fundamentals of pasteup), "Getting the Word Out: Distribution," and "Publicity and Promotion." A four-page list of trademarks and an index are included.

This book is for beginners and introduces but does not teach the skills and standards necessary for professional publishing. It is a fairly exhaustive effort to provide enough information to enable beginners to "perform most of the work of publishing a document yourself.... Write and edit text with ease.... Produce effective, well-produced publications less expensively than commercial publishers can." Well, maybe, but it will take a lot of work to master this text and the software that is discussed.

Most examples of desktop publishing equipment and software highlighted are associated with the Apple Macintosh. Apple supports desktop publishing as a developing market full of potential, and while there are programs available for the IBM PC, they are mainly for the professional publishing market. One book that explores the potential of desktop publishing with the IBM PC and compatibles is *Desktop Publishing with Your IBM PC & Compatible* (see entry 455). Chapters in both books outline the industry from description of the field, recommended hardware and software, fundamentals of typography, design and layout, and creating graphics, but *Desktop Publishing from A to Z* goes one step further and emphasizes ways to distribute the finished product using direct mail to retailers and electronic distribution.

The authors have succeeded in developing a very readable and informative book that will help this fast-growing area to expand in an orderly fashion. This work and others like it will be essential as this new area develops. If you produce documents, newsletters, business reports, office publications, or just about anything, this book can be a tremendous help in getting started. Timely and straightforward, it will find a wide audience among writers, students, researchers, and professionals of all types who will appreciate the careful explanations, ideas, and examples. The expanded line spacing and clear crisp typeface are easy on the eyes and at $17.95 it is priced right to join other titles that cover this fast-changing field.

Definitely aimed at do-it-yourselfers with little or no experience in the field, this book provides advice and encouragement, but strongly states that only through lots of practice and additional study is it possible to produce a quality product; the basics you need are here, but the real work is up to you.   Judy Gay Matthews

453. Lang, Kathy. **The Writer's Guide to Desktop Publishing.** Orlando, Fla., Academic Press, 1987. 184p. index. $19.95pa. ISBN 0-12-436275-3.

Lang's guide to desktop publishing appears to be the first in the field to go through the various activities involved in this growing area of publishing in a simple manner aimed at the amateur. The benefits and drawbacks of desktop publishing are outlined, followed by an explanation of basic requirements. Equipment needed is also discussed. The author then moves on to the "how-to" of planning and preparing text and illustrations, providing general instructions in two separate parts of the book (these might more logically have been grouped closer together). Various aspects of layout are covered in several chapters. A brief discussion of "document handling" is followed by very general material on printers and typesetters and publication methods. The glossary is full of useful definitions of terms peculiar to the publishing field, but the index is quite brief.

The author makes a genuine and generally successful effort to include both British and U.S. information in this volume (the book is British), though of course any costs given can only be used for a general sense of the expensiveness of materials.

Overall, this should be a useful guide for the amateur audience that seems to be its primary target; it is doubtful that professional publishers seeking to make use of desktop publishing techniques would turn to this book for assistance.

A few comments on this book as a product of the technology it espouses: The layout and design of this book are not particularly attractive, and while they would be fine for in-house documents and little "how-to" guides like this one, this book itself should not be taken as the best example of what the technology discussed can produce. Also, the repeated summaries and lists of contents of each chapter in the book are really overkill. The book's users will be amateurs, but that does not necessarily mean they will be unable to follow the reasonably logical organization of this book without extra help.

Recommended for those individuals interested in a general introduction to the practical side of this growing field.

Sharon Kincaide

454. Westerfield, Wiley. **Desktop Publishing/Teletypesetting: A Resource Guide to Electronic**

Publishing. San Diego, Calif., Westerfield Enterprises, 1987. 154p. $16.95pa. LC 87-90075. ISBN 0-942259-00-9.

This small volume bills itself as the "definitive" work on the subject. Desktop publishing is one of the fastest moving areas of computer applications, and the notion that any guide to the field could be "definitive" for more than a short time is risible. A disclaimer at the beginning points out that there may be errors and omissions, sometimes of important information. In short, the disclaimer explicitly denies what the rest of the book claims—definitiveness. The use of the word is pure hype. The guide's purpose is to provide information to persons seeking hardware and software to set up desktop publishing programs. Information is arranged by name of manufacturer, with an index to product names. Each manufacturer's section carries a list of numeric codes reflecting the categories of products offered. The result is that information about various kinds of software and hardware is jumbled together. There is no way, for instance, of finding the names of all the printers listed other than going through the entire book, page by page. The descriptions of each item are barebones: barely enough to identify their purpose or function. Some of them sound a bit like sales pitches, and to read them is to find that no product has any drawbacks or deficiencies. A helpful glossary ends the book, and may be the most useful part. Rather ironically, the text has been prepared using a dot matrix printer with a rather unattractive type style, in no way reflecting the sophistication of the subject matter being treated.

Philip A. Metzger

455. Willis, Jerry, with others. **Desktop Publishing with Your IBM PC & Compatible.** Tucson, Ariz., Knight-Ridder Press/HP Books, 1987. 310p. illus. index. $15.95pa. LC 87-3697. ISBN 0-89586-586-6.

The heart of desktop publishing is a good word processor and a laser printer capable of high-quality output that is graphically a huge step ahead of dot matrix and daisy wheel. The success of this book lies in its ability to take the reader through the crucial steps of learning to use word processors, hardware and software necessary and an explanation of the skills required to use them; basics of typography, layout, and design; publishing on a budget; getting the right laser printer for your application; various types of software; and creation and use of graphics. Also provided are answers to questions about how desktop may fit into your plans, advantages and disadvantages of laser printers, steps in selecting a system, name brands versus no-name clones, disk drive options, and much more.

Fundamentals of design and layout are covered in thirty-nine pages packed with information on "the grid," designing for text-only pages, selecting typefaces, parts of a book, methods of binding books, and how to communicate with a printing firm. Two chapters getting extensive coverage are "Laser Printers" and "The Software Side of Desktop Publishing." Discussed in detail (twenty-five pages) are laser printers, criteria for selection of a printer, speed, options, type fonts available, compatibility with other software, software support, and hardware and accessories. Prices, limitations of memory or downloading features, compatibility with other software, graphics ability, documentation, and page or document composition language information is given specifically for HP LaserJet, LaserJet Plus, Apple LaserWriter, Laser Writer Plus, and Cordata Laser printers.

"Creating Graphics" and "Integrating Text and Graphics" can be wedded together to form a basic discussion of how desktop graphics help eliminate both expensive and time-consuming graphics often secured from outside sources. Included in this chapter are how to plan the space for graphics, types of graphics (line art, photographs), creating electronic artwork, drawing programs and computer-assisted design software, input devices for graphics programs, using a light pen, and some legal issues regarding copyright (don't miss this discussion!).

Sources of additional information are changing constantly and the books, magazines, and publishing associations listed are invaluable. Some seventy-five names, addresses, and telephone numbers are provided to lend support when answers are needed for questions that are not covered in this useful book. An essential five-page index is included.

Every chapter has numerous illustrations: technical examples of typeface design; photographs; charts; laser printed examples of illustrations; how to lay out newspapers and announcements; special effects such as cross-hatching, stippling, and line art with screens; and how to manipulate photographs for various special effects.

This is a good, clean effort that appears to have been produced on desktop equipment. Unfortunately the typeface chosen appears pinched and the line spacing could have been expanded to lessen eye strain. Less density on some pages would have made the text more readable and easier to comprehend, but these three-hundred-plus pages really deliver the goods and provide a ready-reference tool which covers very well a general discussion of desktop publishing as well as providing application-specific terminology and illustrations to illuminate all areas of the text.   Judy Gay Matthews

REFERENCE SERVICES

General Works

456.   Benham, Frances, and Ronald R. Powell. **Success in Answering Reference Questions: Two Studies.** Metuchen, N.J., Scarecrow, 1987. 311p. index. $29.50. LC 86-14629. ISBN 0-8108-1940-6.

Two research investigations into the accuracy of information provided by reference librarians are reported in this volume. The purpose of the first study, by Frances Benham, was to determine if typical graduate library science admissions requirements (undergraduate grade point average and Graduate Record Examination scores) and performance (grade point average) in an ALA-accredited library school would predict accuracy in reference information provided by librarians. The second study, by Ronald R. Powell, investigated the relationship between reference collection size and success in answering reference questions. Both studies were originally conducted as doctoral dissertations, and both used obtrusive methods, in that subjects were aware that they were being tested. Previous studies reported in the literature used unobtrusive telephone calls where the librarians were not aware that reference answers were being evaluated.

The significance of the problem, hypotheses, review of related literature, research methodology, analysis of data, findings, and conclusions are presented in each case. Benham used correlation coefficients and regression analysis in the first study, and her findings corroborated other studies in library science and other fields in that admissions requirement scores and graduate program grade point averages have too narrow a range for purposes of prediction. Scores on the quantitative section of the GRE were the only ones from among the hypothesis variables capable of predicting accuracy in answering reference questions. Benham concluded that library educators should place greater emphasis on learning specific sources and on practicing adequate use of them, as the ability to name a correct source was predictive of providing an accurate answer. Another finding of the study is that about 50 percent of factual questions are answered incorrectly in public and academic libraries, with no differences in the response accuracy of public and academic librarians. Attitudinal factors influence reference service accuracy, but collection size and reference collection size were not very important factors in this study.

On the other hand, Powell found that his major research hypothesis, which predicted a causal relationship between reference collection size and the percent of correctly answered questions, was supported. A nonlinear relationship indicated that increasing collection size beyond a certain point (approximately thirty-five hundred volumes) would not continue to result in an increased rate of staff performance. Factor analysis indicated that variables of wages and salaries, expenditures for reference materials, size of reference staff, total number of volumes held, and total operating expenditures were also related to the reference collection and/or service. Multiple regression analysis indicated other variables were related to reference performance, namely, weekly number of reference questions received, the level of education of participating librarians, and their perception of the adequacy of their reference collection.

These two studies not only provide valid information about variables determining successful reference service, but they serve as outstanding models of research in librarianship.

Lois Buttlar

457. Hawley, George S. **The Referral Process in Libraries: A Characterization and an Exploration of Related Factors.** Metuchen, N.J., Scarecrow, 1987. 188p. bibliog. index. $22.50. LC 87-9201. ISBN 0-8108-2010-2.

Although it is common for librarians to make referrals either to other libraries or to other resources within their own institutions, relatively little has been written on this aspect of reference service. George Hawley therefore made it the subject of his doctoral dissertation at Rutgers University, on which this book is based. As might be expected, the theme is examined logically and exhaustively, seeking to determine why "librarians often will neither answer a question correctly nor furnish a referral." The plan of research involved interviews with reference librarians in academic and public libraries. Key personal factors (e.g., empathy, tact, and independence) were identified, as well as factors related to the referrer's library (interaction with coworkers, training, activity level, etc.), outside resources, and the users. A major variable emerged: equity, the concern that people should get the level of help they deserve. Examining the literature of social psychology on equity, Hawley then focused on three major theories: self-interest, idealism, and empathy. Relating these theories to his research findings,

Hawley determined that "the contributions rule motivated by self-interest predominates" in the referral process (p. 138). In other words, in this interaction various conditions and relationships between libraries affect the empathy and idealism of reference librarians, and "even apparent altruism is performed with the expectation of some repayment" (p. 157). Nonetheless, at least one of the librarians interviewed emerged as "the Exemplary Referrer." Rather than introducing his literature survey at the start of his study, Hawley includes it in an appendix, determining that other studies verify his own findings.

In his preface Hawley calls his book a "diffuse presentation ... following many separate concepts" (p. vii). Close examination of one aspect of the reference process and its relationship to social and psychological concepts has some value, but at times the findings seem to state the obvious (for example: "Achievement motivation, then, impels the librarian to perform well, and its absence can cause inadequacy in reference and referral service," p. 32). However, "Implications for Further Research and for Practice" offers, in the form of questions, specific concerns that emerged during the study. These could well provide libraries with a basis for an objective assessment of their referral practices and lead to substantial improvements.

Joan W. Jensen

458. Hernon, Peter, and Charles R. McClure. **Unobtrusive Testing and Library Reference Services.** Norwood, N.J., Ablex Publishing, 1987. 240p. bibliog. index. $35.00. LC 86-28736. ISBN 0-89391-383-9.

While the testing of reference services is nothing new, the attempt to gain a greater degree of objectivity through unobtrusive testing is a more recent innovation. Most notable among these efforts was the 1983 study *Improving the Quality of Reference Service for Government Documents*, published by the American Library Association. The study at hand complements the 1983 study by expanding the scope to general reference.

The appeal of unobtrusive studies is apparently that they will aid in administrative analysis of services, making planning more accurate and sophisticated. The idea is that this method reduces bias because it is "based on participant observation and assessment of responses to a predetermined set of questions" (p. 15). This volume attempts to determine the place of unobtrusive testing in reference service evaluation, to report the correct answer rate as a form of measure, to help library planners use this form of evaluation, and to point out additional areas for application of this sort of testing.

Reactions to the notion of unobtrusive testing have not been without controversy. The question of ethics has been raised which, while worth thinking about, might better be called professional manners. In addition, the notion that quality is better determined by professional consensus than by testing should not escape thoughtful planners. For those, however, who are sold on unobtrusive testing, this volume will be valuable. [R: JAL, Sept 87, p. 244]

Bonnie Collier

459. Jennerich, Elaine Zaremba, and Edward J. Jennerich. **The Reference Interview as a Creative Art.** Littleton, Colo., Libraries Unlimited, 1987. 107p. bibliog. index. $24.50. LC 87-3064. ISBN 0-87287-445-1.

The importance of communication skills in dealing with reference questions is a topic frequently addressed in the library journal literature. The Jennerichs have produced a short, basic text on using interpersonal communication techniques which should be very useful for the inexperienced reference librarian or one with little practice in one-on-one interview situations.

The techniques emphasized include both verbal and nonverbal communication skills generally recognized as necessary for effective reference interviews. Methods of teaching these skills are presented, including role-playing and videotaping both practice and actual interviews. In addition, the book briefly covers evaluation, use of paraprofessionals and students in reference work, the physical layout of the reference desk, and dealing with handicapped and non-English-speaking patrons.

Many of the concepts discussed are covered in Katz's two *Reference and Information Services* readers (Scarecrow, 1978 and 1982), but the authors of this work have succeeded in producing a helpful text with a good bibliography which will be worthwhile for library school students and for general collections in librarianship.   Susan D. Herring

460. Katz, Bill, comp. **Reference and Information Services: A Reader for Today.** Metuchen, N.J., Scarecrow, 1986. 425p. $32.50. LC 86-13122. ISBN 0-8108-1873-6.

In this third collection of articles on reference and information services (the first two having appeared in 1978 and 1982), Bill Katz has taken a fresh view of directions and priorities, suggesting that the new technology is perhaps not the only vital issue facing reference services; instead, the question of ethics and evaluation

are "even more important than the new technology." Consequently, he has devoted a section of this collection to "Ethics and Evaluation of Reference Service." Katz's own view of ethics in this context is narrowly confined to the matter of accuracy in reference answers, but one article in the collection stands out as a good example of the rich possibilities for research in the field of information science. Mary Lee Bundy, Amy Bridgman, and Laura Keltie conducted a study to see how public libraries handle "antiestablishment" information, information which "challenges government policy." Their conclusion was that it is difficult for the public to obtain information from the library about unpopular views. In addition, there was much misinformation on controversial issues. This article asks some deeply important questions which drive to the heart of reference work's reason for being. It was published, however, in *Public Library Quarterly*, a journal read by only one segment of the library community. It is only because of anthologies like this one that important pieces of work surface for the rest of us to read. Bill Katz is to be congratulated for compiling this collection and for urging us to turn our attention to some ethical questions of serious concern.

Other articles in other categories, such as "The Reference Process," "Access to Information," and "The Computer—and Beyond," are handily reprinted, with the unfortunate omission of an index.

All librarians should see this book. [R: BL, 1 Apr 87, p. 1176; JAL, Nov 87, pp. 297-98; LJ, 1 May 87, p. 52]   Bonnie Collier

461. Katz, William A. **Introduction to Reference Work.** 5th ed. New York, McGraw-Hill, 1987. 2v. index. $33.95/vol. LC 86-10247. ISBN 0-07-033537-0(v.1); 0-07-033538-9(v.2).

Bill Katz's two-volume opus remains the standard and best textbook on reference works in all types of libraries. All editions have been reviewed in *American Reference Books Annual* (e.g., see the review of the fourth edition in *ARBA 83* [entry 282]).

Volume 1, *Basic Information Sources*, follows the same organizational pattern as in the fourth edition with one exception. A brief "introductory" chapter on "Computerized Online Reference Service" has been added. More on this topic is provided in the second volume.

Most descriptions of reference sources and bibliographic citations have been updated to mid-1986. What else should one say? Cheney's more sophisticated treatment in *Fundamental Reference Sources* (see the review of the second edition in *ARBA 82*, entry 300) is now dated, but students still should consult it from time to time. Katz is no substitute for Cheney, but is more comprehensive, up to date, and very readable. Generally speaking, it is also quite accurate, and an overview of reference services in the second volume is well executed. There are helpful "suggested readings" in both volumes, which are updated in this new edition.

All in all, *Introduction to Reference Work* is an essential text to all library school students and a good refresher for a novice in the reference department.   Bohdan S. Wynar

462. Lewicki, Pawel. **Nonconscious Social Information Processing.** Orlando, Fla., Academic Press, 1986. 237p. illus. bibliog. index. $39.50; $22.95pa. LC 85-15618. ISBN 0-12-446120-4; 0-12-446121-2pa.

The major thesis of this book is that nonconscious acquisition and processing of information plays a major role in human social interaction. The writer goes on to postulate an internal processing algorithm (IPA) for nonconscious acquisition of information. These IPAs refer to the memory representation co-variation between two or more features or events that meet the following conditions: it is acquired nonconsciously, it nonconsciously influences behavior, and it cannot be controlled or examined directly. Lewicki goes on to describe a series of experiments involving adults and children that test various facets of IPA development, modification, and abandonment.

The author's thesis has some interesting applications for the reference interview. The fact that prior reference interview success plays a nonconscious role in future interaction outcome is perhaps a frequently observed, if little researched, phenomenon. Prior failure in reference success (perceived correct answer to a question) will influence the patron to nonconsciously seek out a different librarian the next time, according to the IPA thesis. The author also demonstrates that a change in the success perception can lead to a new IPA that determines the patron's attitude toward the reference librarian in the future. The old experience is still retained nonconsciously and can be added to future experiences. The author's thesis is demonstrated through a series of experiments covering various aspects of IPA generation and observation.

Lewicki's study has interesting implications for the reference interview and reference/bibliographic instruction. Most nonpsychologists will find the work tough going at times. The wealth of information presented amply rewards the librarian for any difficulties encountered. All those interested in the reference interaction will

want to read this work. Recommended for all psychology and library science collections.
                    Ralph L. Scott

463. Mann, Margaret. **Browsing: An Annotated Bibliography.** Loughborough, England, Library and Information Statistics Unit, Loughborough University, 1986. 41p. index. (Centre for Library and Information Management Report, No. 53). $6.50pa. ISBN 0-948848-01-4.

In this valuable annotated and classified bibliography of 137 items, Margaret Mann who is Research Fellow at Loughborough's Department of Library and Information Studies, provides access to an important concept in librarianship whose definition is ambiguous to the point of being contradictory. Moving from the least systematic to the most precise and technical, her introduction identifies the following usages of browsing: "the book man's browse," which is completely random; "general purposive browsing," which is more purposeful; and browsing in computer searching.

Her classification scheme identifies six major categories: general, browsing for pleasure, browsing and academic libraries, browsing and public libraries, nonbook materials, and computer browsing. Both the annotations and the introduction address various issues connected with the topic, such as the importance of browsing in the humanities, the attacks against it by people who consider that browsing reflects intellectual laziness, the desire of browsers for open access collections, and the development of "browsing rooms" and of "reader interest categories" instead of orthodox classification schemes as aids to browsers.

The annotations seem more detailed and evaluative in the earlier entries than the later ones. There is an author index. Researchers and professionals will be able to use this work for a variety of purposes.   Peter F. McNally

464. Mann, Peter H. **The Reality of Reference Work: A Study of the Leicester Information Centre.** Loughborough, England, Library and Information Statistics Unit, Loughborough University, 1986. 47p. bibliog. (Centre for Library and Information Management Report, No. 51). $6.50pa. ISBN 0-904924-76-9.

Beginning with the assumption that a reference service must be a place of first resort that provides sources of information permitting users to answer their own questions without necessarily referring them to a librarian, Mann has undertaken a very interesting case study of the Humanities and Commercial/Scientific/Technical Division of the Leicester Libraries Information Centre, which is distinct physically but not administratively from this British city's public lending libraries.

Employing both a questionnaire survey of users and an evaluation survey conducted by research-observers at the reference desk (of the question-answer process), the study provides statistics and insights that will be as valuable to North Americans as to Europeans. Among other things, the study concluded that the bulk of users were young, middle-class, reasonably well-educated males who used the reference center as their first source of information on questions dealing primarily with leisure and work. While happy with the assistance given, approximately 50 percent did not request staff assistance in answering their questions. The overwhelming majority of the questions were straightforward, requiring little information skill and only a few minutes of staff time, although more user time.

In conclusion, Mann emphasizes the importance of marketing reference services and of accepting that the need in a public library is to accept the right of ordinary people to have answered their mundane questions.

Peter F. McNally

465. Reichel, Rosemarie. **Improving Telephone Information and Reference Service in Public Libraries.** Hamden, Conn., Library Professional Publications/Shoe String Press, 1987. 123p. bibliog. index. $21.50; $16.00pa. LC 87-14998. ISBN 0-208-02156-6; 0-208-02157-4pa.

This manual aimed at bettering the telephone reference function in public libraries covers every aspect of the service. Reichel discusses administration, promotion, policy (how to handle ethical, legal, medical questions; trivia; homework assignments), statistics, collection development, clipping files, and online searches as they relate to telephone reference. The book is grounded in her own long experience in a busy telephone reference area. In addition, she walks the reader through fifty sample questions and their answers.

Any librarian or library assistant who has handled telephone inquiries will recognize the issues raised in the book (as well as some of the sample questions). While the issues may seem obvious and the point somewhat strained, library staff serving the public on the telephone will be reminded of the importance of the function, for the library as well as the patron. Most reference librarians will be familiar with the issues raised in the book, but novices and libraries instituting or expanding telephone reference will find much of interest in this small book.

Jean Parker

466. Ridgeway, Trish, Peggy Cover, and Carl Stone, eds. **Improving ref'·er·ence man'·age·ment: Papers Based upon a Conference Sponsored by the Southeastern Library Association and the Reference and Adult Services Division, American Library Association, May 10-12, 1984.** Chicago, American Library Association, 1986. 73p. $15.00 spiralbound. ISBN 0-8389-7046-X.

This pamphlet offers six papers on a most timely topic: reference management. Even though the papers are based on a 1984 workshop, they highlight a number of perennial topics, such as reference standards, performance evaluation, the use of paraprofessionals at the reference desk, librarian burnout, and creativity. All the papers include bibliographies, and a review of the contributor qualifications at the back of the volume reveals that there is substantial experience behind the research.

Most of the papers are well written, but they tend to deal with broad concepts rather than offer specific solutions. Some useful specifics can be found, however, such as a list of in-house training methods for paraprofessionals, or the research results reporting the work events most likely to make librarians "feel good or bad" about their jobs.

Other thought-provoking ideas are scattered throughout the volume; for example, one contributor notes in the introduction that some library staffs will soon be "80% public services, and 20% technical services." Another author points out that some administrators expect annual increases in reference statistics, ad infinitum, even though staffing levels are not increased.

This volume addresses a number of issues of interest to both reference managers and librarians, with perhaps some emphasis on the academic library environment. Other librarians and library science students may benefit from the descriptions of universal concerns, however, such as how to handle stress, or the descriptions of brainstorming and "brainwriting" activities.

Mary Ardeth Gaylord

467. Watson, Paula D., ed. **Reference Policy and Administrative Documents.** Chicago, American Library Association, 1985. 51p. $20.00 spiralbound. ISBN 0-8389-6933-X.

This apparent spinoff from a survey conducted by an ALA committee contains microfiche reproductions of reference documents collected from some forty research libraries. These documents include policies on reference service and procedure, online service and reference collection development, and reference department organization charts and internal job descriptions. This information is organized into a fifty-page introduction in pamphlet form, and ten negative microfiche containing 851 pages of actual documents.

The introductory pamphlet "attempted to highlight policy issues and to draw attention to areas of consensus and areas where accepted practices diverge." While this goal is accomplished, the narrative style employed is a stream of consciousness approach, which is interesting, but does not include succinct summaries of any research conclusions. Instead, a general "discussion" of "some issues," or of what "some reference departments" are doing, is offered, with a surprising attention to the "unique" or exceptional documents, rather than the norms.

While the documents themselves may indeed "serve as a source of ideas and potential models," other related collections have been published, including various ARL SPEC Kits. Both library science students and practicing academic librarians may find this large, reasonably priced collection of interest, however, particularly when looking for examples of how other libraries have handled tough reference policy or administrative decisions.

Mary Ardeth Gaylord

468. Watson, Paula D. **Reference Services in Academic Research Libraries.** Chicago, American Library Association, 1986. 82p. $15.00 spiralbound. ISBN 0-8389-7047-8.

In this report based upon a survey of members of the Large Research Libraries Discussion Group and the Medium-Sized Libraries Discussion Group of the Reference and Adult Services Division of the American Library Association, information is provided on "the reference departments of almost all the academic libraries which are members of the Association of Research Libraries as well as ... of the four largest predominantly black universities" in the United States. Information concerning a number of Canadian universities is also included.

Brief chapters summarize the information, elicited through a questionnaire, as follows: staffing of reference departments and services offered, provision of general reference services, productivity, related general services, bibliographic instruction, online search services, personnel, and general administration. The second half of the publication contains tables, figures, and summaries of the questionnaire results.

This study, which is an expanded version of a similar study conducted by the same group in 1977 (ERIC documents ED 142 184 and ED 149 775 by Paula D. Watson and Martha Landis) is "no more successful than the 1977 survey in arriving at norms for reference staff size or at isolating external factors which might influence staff size; [it also fails] to arrive at norms for reference librarian's productivity or for departmental levels of instructional activity."

The great value of this work lies in the enormous amount of information gathered which "underlines the diversities in organization and function of university library reference departments rather [than] the similarities." [R: JAL, July 87, p. 184; RQ, Spring 87, pp. 393-94]

Peter F. McNally

469. Whitehall, Tom, ed. **Practical Current Awareness Services from Libraries.** Brookfield, Vt., Gower Publishing, 1986. 109p. index. $39.95. LC 86-9889. ISBN 0-566-03519-7.

Most libraries that provide current awareness services (CAS) belong to corporate or government organizations. In compiling this book, Whitehall has drawn on the expertise of six information professionals from such organizations. As a result, the emphasis of this book is on the practical rather than the theoretical. Chapters 1 and 2 describe various approaches to providing CAS and different methods for choosing between them. Chapters 3-5 and chapter 7 provide case studies of CAS in different organizational environments. The primary focus of chapters 3-5 is on how new technology has affected management decisions regarding CAS, while chapter 7 provides a detailed discussion of various methods used to evaluate the cost, value to users, and effectiveness of a particular current awareness service.

Chapter 6 departs from the practical approach by describing the results of a 1985 survey of "industrial information units." This survey was part of the research conducted for Jane Rogers's master's thesis in library science. The survey was designed to discover several things: (1) the impact of computers and communications technology on CAS, (2) the impact of more accessible secondary bibliographic sources, (3) CAS's problems and opportunities as seen by management, and (4) how present attitudes and methods compare to both past current awareness services and to the ideal objectives of CAS.

The book provides an index and some chapter references. Since all the contributors are British, some of the terminology may be unfamiliar. Nevertheless, the book is recommended for library school students interested in special librarianship and for corporate librarians, especially those interested in evaluating or planning their own current awareness services.

Mark E. Schott

Reference Sources

470. Bryant, David. **Finding Information the Library Way: Guide to Reference Sources.** Hamden, Conn., Library Professional Publications/Shoe String Press, 1987. 148p. $22.50. LC 86-21288. ISBN 0-208-02132-9.

In *Finding Information the Library Way*, compiler David Bryant has attempted to list books which will provide "practical information weighted toward economic and business matters and the conduct of personal and professional affairs" (introduction). Appropriate books are listed under some 265 subject headings. The choice of these headings is inconsistent and hard to understand. Users are provided with the heading "Great Britain" but not "France" or "Germany," "Seed Catalogs" but not "Gardening," and "Television" but not "Motion Pictures" or "Theater." Under some of the headings Bryant chose to omit specific titles and only gives a general scope note. These notes seem to state the obvious, as under "Addresses" when users are told that "the right address can speed you to information that you need." When it comes to the core of this work, the specific books chosen for inclusion, Bryant's selection of titles is hard to defend. Under "Dictionaries" he lists the *Oxford English Dictionary* and Webster's *Third New International—Unabridged.* Certainly, those are standard titles, but for practical purposes it would have been helpful to suggest one or two of the excellent desk dictionaries. Under the heading "Reference Books" neither Sheehy's *Guide to Reference Books* nor *ARBA* is mentioned. Inadequate proofreading also mars this book. Under the heading "Facts," the compiler lists *Finding Facts Fast* as written by Alden Toddy, published in 1979, but under "Reference Books" the same title is given as written by Alden Todd, published in 1985. Because of its limited coverage and arbitrary choice of subjects and titles, this work can not be recommended. A somewhat better choice will be James Hillard's *Where to Find What* (Scarecrow, 1984). [R: JAL, July 87, p. 191; RBB, 1 May 87, p. 1342; WLB, Mar 87, p. 64]

Donald C. Dickinson

471. **Canadian Book Review Annual 1985.** Dean Tudor and Ann Tudor, eds. Toronto, Simon & Pierre, 1986. 480p. index. $69.95. ISBN 0-88924-182-1; ISSN 0383-770X.

Earlier reviews (see *ARBA* 77, entry 196 and *ARBA* 84, entry 2) have substantiated the contribution of *Canadian Book Review Annual* as a selection aid to recently or currently available Canadian items. *CBRA* is like *American Reference Books Annual* in its arrangement and approach, but with some important distinctions. As a "review" source, it is widened beyond reference materials to include poetry, novels, short stories, children's picture books and juvenile items, biography and memoirs. *CBRA* deals solely with Canadian English-language imprints, primarily those copyrighted in the preceding year, but also reprints of books published before 1975, when *CBRA* began. This aid is divided into reference materials, humanities and applied arts, literature and language, social science, and science and technology. It reflects hardback trade publishing but does include any federal government publications or educational titles that appeal to the general market. Now, with approximately five thousand short reviews, good indexes, and its appearance in July of each year, *CBRA* has established itself as an important survey of the publishing output of Canadian presses.   Claire England

472. Devine, C. Maury, Claudia M. Dissel, and Kim D. Parrish, eds. **The Harvard Guide to Influential Books: 113 Distinguished Harvard Professors Discuss the Books That Have Helped to Shape Their Thinking.** New York, Harper & Row, 1986. 300p. $18.95; $7.95pa. LC 86-45090. ISBN 0-06-055013-9; 0-06-096084-1pa.

In this volume 113 Harvard professors provide brief comments on books that have "shaped their thinking." Most of the books, but not all, were positive influences. Negative comments on certain "classics" are especially interesting. The participating scholars are listed alphabetically, as well as by their Harvard college or school affiliation. Biographical information on them is sketchy, which is understandable considering the volume's focus on books.

A twenty-eight page "Index of Works Cited" is very useful, as it includes the names of every person citing a particular title as being an influential book. Currently available paperback editions are listed if they are in-print, but prices are omitted. Some entries are less enlightening than others (e.g., the reasons why Joe DiMaggio's *Lucky to Be a Yankee* and the Book of Job [KJV] are important to anthropologist Stephen J. Gould are not provided). Overall, this is an interesting, but highly idiosyncratic, best books bibliography.   Gary D. Barber

473. **The Reader's Adviser: A Layman's Guide to Literature.** 13th ed. Fred Kaplan, ed. New York, R. R. Bowker, 1986. 3v. index. $195.00/set. LC 57-13277. ISBN 0-8352-2145-8(v.1); 0-8352-2146-6(v.2); 0-8352-2147-4(v.3); ISSN 0094-5943.

With the publication of this thirteenth edition, *The Reader's Adviser* continues to present "a reflection of the current state of the best available literature in print in the United States," with consideration given to "those books generally available to an intelligent reader through the facilities of the library system of a moderately-sized municipality." The intended audience, then, is not scholars, but nonspecialists such as librarians, booksellers, students, and general readers.

The book has been expanded again. The eleventh edition, published in 1968, grew from one to two volumes (see *ARBA* 71, entry 99), while the twelfth edition included one volume published in 1974 (see *ARBA* 75, entry 1314) and two more in 1977 (see *ARBA* 78, entries 2 and 1090). Now *The Reader's Adviser* consists of six volumes; the three forthcoming will cover the literature of philosophy and religion (volume 4); science, technology, and medicine (volume 5); and a cumulative index (volume 6). Volumes 1-3 follow basically the same format as the twelfth edition, though volume 3 now covers fewer subjects, because of the creation of volumes 4 and 5.

In addition to general expansion, some significant changes have been made within each volume. Volume 1, covering the literature of American and British fiction, poetry (subdivided by periods and genres), essays, literary biography, general bibliography, and literature reference, now includes a chapter on Commonwealth literature. This new chapter represents works and authors from Australia, Canada, and New Zealand. Also, the chapter "Essays and Criticism" has been revised and expanded. The subdivisions now used are much clearer and more definitive ("General Reading," "Collections," "Contemporary Criticism," and "Authors").

"The Best in American and British Drama and World Literature in English Translation" is still covered in volume 2, including nineteen different national literatures. More entries are included for British drama in this edition, and the section on Shakespeare has been revised and expanded. Also, volume 2 contains "completely revised introductions, biographies, bibliographies, and reference lists." The bibliography for drama, for instance, includes several new titles with copyrights from 1980 to 1985.

The third volume has enlarged sections on social science, history (ancient, U.S., Western Hemisphere, British, and world), and the arts and communications. The former chapter "The Lively Arts and Communications" has been developed into separate chapters: "Music and Dance," "Art and Architecture," and "The Mass Media."

The indexes in the new volumes have also undergone a change. The old author index has become a name index. In addition to providing the names of authors covered in each volume, this index also gives the names of authors and editors of the books listed in the bibliographies. Boldface print is used for the names of authors who are subjects, rather than sources. The new edition also provides separate subject and title indexes, while the twelfth edition used a combination subject/title index in each volume.

Other improvements in all three new volumes include larger, easier-to-read print, a chronology of the authors in each volume, and a more detailed contributors' list. Also, the list of authors in each section is now arranged alphabetically, as opposed to chronologically according to date of birth (as in the previous edition).

Quality of coverage in *The Reader's Adviser* remains about the same. In the section "Books about [Nathaniel] Hawthorne," for example, the new editor omits some very old titles which appeared in the twelfth edition and adds a few newer ones, but some important titles which should be included, such as *Hawthorne's Early Tales: A Critical Study*, by Frank Neal (Doubleday, 1972), *Hawthorne and the Modern Short Story*, by Mary Rohrberger (Mouton, 1966), and two other interesting works, *The Sins of the Fathers: Hawthorne's Psychological Themes*, by Frederick Crews (Oxford University Press, 1966), and *Nathaniel Hawthorne and the Truth of Dreams*, by Rita K. Gollin (Louisiana State University Press, 1979) are left out. Considering the subjectivity of the selection, the researcher would want to check other sources in addition to *The Reader's Adviser*.

Overall, *The Reader's Adviser* offers a very good reference source for its audience, and with the improvements included in this edition, is now much easier to use. [R: Choice, Oct 87, p. 288] Kari Sidles

474. **Recommended Reference Books for Small and Medium-sized Libraries and Media Centers 1987.** Bohdan S. Wynar, ed. Littleton, Colo., Libraries Unlimited, 1987. 282p. index. $32.50. LC 81-12394. ISBN 0-87287-597-0; ISSN 0277-5948.

This seventh edition of *Recommended Reference Books* reprints 577 of the 1,749 reviews published in the 1987 volume of *American Reference Books Annual*. Titles included were selected by the editor as "the most substantial titles in all subject areas suitable for small and medium-sized libraries and media centers" (p. xi). However, works dealing with individual artists or authors, genealogical materials, and regional botanical and zoological guides have been excluded.

The volume is divided into four major categories: general reference works, social sciences, humanities, and science and technology. These sections are further subdivided by subject and/or type of work. Letter codes preceding each review indicate whether the particular source is considered appropriate for smaller college libraries, public libraries, or school media centers. As in *ARBA*, references to additional reviews in ten library periodicals, such as *Choice* and *Wilson Library Bulletin*, are cited at the end of each review.

The index includes entries for titles, subjects, authors, compilers, and editors. For ease of access, subject references appear in boldface type.

A comparison of various sections of *Recommended Reference Books* with *ARBA* revealed the omission of several sources that would be valuable to medium-sized academic and public libraries, for example, *The Drama Scholars' Index to Plays and Filmscripts, Volume 3*. However, selecting only one-third of the titles from *ARBA* must be a difficult task, especially considering the range of libraries for which this work is intended.

For those libraries that cannot afford or do not need the more comprehensive coverage offered by *ARBA*, this annual selection tool is a useful alternative. [R: EL, Nov/Dec 87, pp. 40, 42]   Marie Ellis

475. Reference Books Bulletin 1985-1986: A Compilation of Evaluations Appearing in *Reference Books Bulletin*, September 1, 1985-August 1986. Sandy Whiteley, ed.; Penny Spokes, comp. Chicago, American Library Association, 1986. 140p. index. $22.50pa. LC 73-159565. ISBN 0-8389-3336-X; ISSN 8755-0962.

This is an annual cumulation of reviews appearing in *Reference Books Bulletin* (1 September 1985-August 1986). The eighteenth edition continues the long tradition of providing quality evaluations prepared by members (past and present) of the RBB Editorial Board. Included are selected English-language titles suitable for medium-sized libraries (public, academic, and school). At the beginning of this volume is an omnibus of bibliographic essays on topics believed to be of interest to reference librarians: career information sources; college directories; annuals, supplements, and yearbooks; quotation books; an encyclopedia roundup; and reference sources for the physically disabled.

The arrangement is alphabetical by title, and access is provided by means of a two-part index, by subject and type of material. After the main body of the work, some token space is devoted to databases, in which H. W. Wilson's WILSONLINE is discussed, and software, the focus of which is a computerized atlas by Software Concepts. More on databases and software would be helpful in future editions.

Dianne B. Catlett

476. Sable, Martin H. Research Guides to the Humanities, Social Sciences and Technology: An Annotated Bibliography of Guides to Library Resources and Usage, Arranged by Subject or Discipline of Coverage. Ann Arbor, Mich., Pierian Press, 1986. 181p. index. (Basic Reference Guides Series, No. 1). $24.50pa. LC 86-15049. ISBN 0-87650-214-1.

This annotated bibliography of 161 literature guides from all fields of study will prove useful to librarians, students, and specialists. The guides are organized by major branches of study beginning with the humanities, followed by the social sciences and then science and technology. Within each major branch, general guides are described, such as Rogers's *The Humanities: A Selective Guide to Information Sources* (2d ed.) followed by guides for the individual disciplines and applied fields arranged alphabetically. In the case of the humanities, there are nine disciplines from art to theater arts. There are twenty-one such divisions in the social sciences, from anthropology to women's studies, and fifteen in the science-technology area, ranging from agriculture to physics. Each guide listed is covered in-depth through description of its purpose, authority, arrangement, scope, indexes, and special features as well as a citation to an evaluative review in the literature. The guides listed are concerned primarily with the description of reference books in the field, although in most cases they include additional information on trends in the field, organizations, etc. Unique contributions or specialties are identified for each. The emphasis is on guides published after 1970 in the English language, and no guides are included which were published prior to 1950. Full bibliographic data are given for each. Title and author indexes provide access. The work is anticipated to be published on a periodic basis.   Ron Blazek

477. Walford's Guide to Reference Material. Volume 3: Generalia, Language & Literature, The Arts. 4th ed. A. J. Walford and L. J. Taylor, eds. London, Library Association; distr., Chicago, American Library Association,

1987. 872p. index. $80.00. ISBN 0-85365-836-6.

Albert John Walford's *Guide to Reference Materials* was first published in one volume in 1959. Its success led to the publication of a second edition, in three volumes, which began in 1966. The second edition was completed in 1970 and the third edition in 1977. The current three-volume set comprises volume 1, *Science & Technology*, fourth edition (see *ARBA* 81, entry 1362), volume 2, *Social & Historical Sciences, Philosophy & Religion*, fourth edition (1982) and volume 3, reviewed here. The goal of the work, as stated in the introduction (pp. vii-viii) to volume 3, is to "provide a signpost to reference books and bibliographies published in recent years." The fourth edition of this volume encompasses over seventy-three hundred main entries and twenty-two hundred subsumed entries. There is a wealth of new material on library and information science, music, video, and leisure activities. Reviews consist of brief annotations with occasional short quotations from leading review journals, frequent references to similar works, and descriptive rather than critical editorial comments. Bibliographic citations routinely contain Universal Decimal Classification (UDC) numbers and the price in British pounds. Volume 3 also incorporates a subject index and a cumulated author/title index for all three volumes.

Walford's is the British counterpart of Eugene P. Sheehy's *Guide to Reference Books* (see *ARBA* 87, entry 17). Both are general bibliographic guides to reference materials, with an international scope, which annotate the major titles used in reference service today. Their arrangement, however, differs considerably in approach as well as style. Walford uses the Universal Decimal Classification system to divide his work into three separate volumes. Together, the set reviews over seventeen thousand main entries and five thousand subsumed entries. Sheehy's guide has five main sections in a single volume which covers about fourteen thousand titles. Thus, Walford's combination of main and subsumed entries provides more in-depth coverage in this respect. Walford's work is strongest in the area of European and British titles, while Sheehy's concentrates on U.S. and Canadian titles.

In comparing Walford's table of contents with Sheehy's, the former was found to be sorely lacking in clarity and detail. Although both works begin with large subject headings and subdivide by smaller subjects and forms, Walford's brevity is astonishing considering the overall comprehensiveness of his work. Under the main subject heading "Literature," for ex-

ample, Walford lists only six general subheadings: "English," "Germanic," "Romance," "Classicial," "Slavonic," and "Oriental/African." A search for American literature would thereby necessitate a hunt through the index. In stark contrast, Sheehy lists eight general subheadings which break down into over a hundred smaller subheadings. Thus, under the subheading "English language literature" we find, among others, listings for "American," "Afro-American," "English," "Irish," "Scottish," "Welsh," and "Commonwealth" literature.

In a detailed examination of several sections of volume 3, frequent factual and typographical errors were found. Under *Reference Books in English* (pp. 110-13), for example, there was obsolete information for Sheehy's guide (i.e., 9th ed., 1976) and *ARBA* (volume 14, 1983). These texts have each been published in a more recent edition which should have been included in this volume. In addition, listings under the heading "American Literature/Steinbeck" were found to be incomplete. Missing works include *John Steinbeck: A Dictionary of His Fictional Characters*, edited by Tetsumaro Hayashi (Scarecrow, 1976) and *A Handbook for Steinbeck Collectors, Librarians and Scholars*, edited by Tetsumaro Hayashi (Steinbeck Society of America, Ball State University, 1981).

Overall, Walford provides more inclusive coverage of titles while Sheehy provides more accurate and up-to-date information on individual titles. The obsolescence factor in Walford's is due, in part, to the ten-year span between the third and fourth editions of this volume. This lengthy incubation period was recently addressed by Charles Ellis, Managing Director of LA Publishing, in *Library Association Record*: "I am sorry it [volume 3] is much later than scheduled—we ran into major production problems. The enforced delay gave us the opportunity to take stock of what we have done in the past and how we did it and what to do in the future. No one had taken a hard look at the *Guide* since the day it had gone into three volumes—over 20 years ago" (89 [March 1987]). Ellis reports that responses to a survey revealed that Walford users desire more frequent publication (e.g., one volume per year in a three-year cycle). Thus, the *Guide to Reference Material* is currently undergoing major revision and the publisher is working toward the goal of yearly publication by developing an electronically based production system.

In conclusion, although there is some overlap between Walford's and Sheehy's work, this standard in the reference field is highly recommended for public, academic, and research library collections around the world. A. J. Walford (who is eighty at this writing) and his assistant L. J. Taylor should be commended for their dedication to this monumental creative effort. We look forward with anticipation to the fifth edition of volume 3, earmarked for publication in 1990. [R: BL, Aug 87, p. 1732]

Micaela Marie Ready

RESEARCH

478. Current Research for the Information Profession 1986/87. Elliott Pirkko, ed. Chicago, American Library Association, 1987. 266p. index. $80.00. ISBN 0-85365-548-0; ISSN 0268-7372.

In this third annual cumulation of entries listed in the quarterly journal, *Current Research in Library and Information Science*, the Library Association, London, has indexed 1,239 projects from forty-six countries.

The entries are organized according to the classification scheme used in the quarterly and in *Library and Information Science Abstracts*, also published by the Library Association. They provide the projects' full title, name(s) of the researcher, institutional affiliation, duration of the project, its financial support, and a description of the project and its aims. In this volume, as in the previous two, the largest number of entries falls into the sections on reader services and subject indexing. In addition to a brief preface that attempts a very superficial analysis of the projects, there is a name index and a subject index.

While this directory is far from exhaustive even for the countries included, it does constitute an excellent starting point for anyone needing information on current research in library and information science.

The major question must be whether the cumulation is necessary for libraries subscribing to the quarterly as by definition the information dates so quickly. The major problem is the failure to include an outline of the classification scheme. [R: LJ, 15 Oct 87, p. 50]

Peter F. McNally

479. Fingerman, Joel, and Richard Lyders. **Applied Statistics for Libraries: A Primer in Statistical Techniques and Library Applications.** Stanford, Calif., Association of Academic Health Sciences Library Directors, 1986. 129p. index. $39.50pa. (with disk). ISBN 0-938505-00-9.

The preface clearly states the goal of the authors: "to enhance the use of data in the 'Annual Statistics of Medical School Libraries in the United States and Canada' " (p. ix). To aid the nonstatistically inclined or the occasional user

of statistics, the authors proceed systematically through data gathering, how to describe quantitative data visually with some helpful guidelines for displaying it, and statistical concepts. Starting with descriptive statistics for samples and populations, they explain measures of central tendency and dispersion, range, interfractile range, deviation from the mean, variance, standard deviation, skewness, and kurtosis. Then they move on to discuss normal distributions, small sample distributions, and statistical inference—type I and type II errors, one- and two-tailed tests, chi-square, analysis of variance, correlation, and regression. Although the concepts may sound forbidding to the nonstatistician, the authors' purpose is to give the reader a primer in statistical techniques using library applications. They do remarkably well, making a difficult topic easy to understand. The use of medical library data should help librarians see possible applications of statistics. A diskette is included, for use on an IBM PC/XT/AT or compatible, which contains the medical library data, and they can be used to replicate the applications described in the book. Because the data are in ASCII code they can be used with most statistical packages, but the examples in the book are from SPSS/PC + . [R: JAL, Jan 87, p. 404]

Nathan M. Smith

480. Thirty-First Annual Report/1987. By Council on Library Resources, Inc. Washington, D.C., Council on Library Resources, 1987. 65p. index. free pa. LC 58-915 rev. ISSN 0070-1181.

Contained herein is a brief history of the funding of CLR and a quick rundown, in "Polaroid" language, of the grants made for 1986-1987. Chiefly those grants have been in research, access, bibliographic services, preservation, and librarianship in general. Committee officers, members of the council, and the financial statements for the year are also included.

What is both astonishing and puzzling is the historical impact of CLR. Since 1978, CLR has spent over $11 million! Two areas alone account for more than 70 percent of the expenditure of funds: bibliographic services and professional education. The question lingers in the mind, however: What hath CLR wrought? Some years ago it was reported that the Ford Foundation, along with a number of other educationally minded philanthropic organizations, had spent more than $500 million on educational innovations, most of which had gone the way of all flesh. One wonders, but hopes against hope, that such is not the case here.

The CLR guidelines proclaim that CLR "supports work by individuals and organizations on matters pertinent to library service and information systems, with the primary objective of improving the quality of performance of academic and research libraries." Yet a scan of last year's institutional recipients leaves one with the impression that this granting business is *fait accompli*: Columbia University, Yale University, University of Chicago, Northwestern University, and the University of California, Berkeley, to name but a few. The overwhelming majority of the individual recipients of CLR's bounty are situated in the nation's most prominent institutions.

Libraries interested in having quick access to CLR's programs, guidelines, areas of interest, and committee members are encouraged to write CLR for this paperback.

Mark Y. Herring

SCHOOL LIBRARY MEDIA CENTERS

General Works

PHILOSOPHY AND THEORY

481. Gomberg, Karen Cornell. **Books Appeal: Get Teenagers into the School Library.** Jefferson, N.C., McFarland, 1987. 129p. index. $13.95pa. LC 86-43224. ISBN 0-89950-255-5.

Books Appeal is a collection of library activities to be used specifically with junior high school students, as specified by the author in the introduction. The activities are organized into seven categories: "Contests and Active Games, Banquets, Fairs, Parties and Programs"; "Bulletin Board Activities"; "Fun with Book Lists"; "Reference Books"; "Quiet Mental Games"; "Displays"; "Projects and Exhibits."

All 201 suggestions are basically short activities that can be used as individual activities, adapted easily as part of longer units, or used in planning learning centers. There is a great deal of flexibility offered by this resource for the junior high librarian. In addition, the descriptions are short but precise, making it extremely practical for the busy librarian.

The title of the book, however, is misleading. *Books Appeal: Get Teenagers into the School Library* gives the impression that the activities are geared for not only junior high but also high school students. The activities generally lack the sophistication needed for most teenagers, but are definitely appropriate for junior high. In fact, the elementary librarian may find this a useful resource to use with upper elementary students.

This slim volume is an excellent, practical addition to the professional library of any junior high school. The librarian or library class teacher will find it a welcome and valuable resource.

Marie Zuk

482. Kemp, Betty, ed. **School Library and Media Center Acquisitions Policies and Procedures.** 2d ed. Phoenix, Ariz., Oryx Press, 1986. 274p. index. $44.50. LC 86-42752. ISBN 0-89774-160-9.

The purpose of this volume is primarily to present the school librarian/media specialist with a good solid basis of information concerning the topic. The book is divided into four parts. The introduction includes a short review of literature, a discussion of the microcomputer and selection policies, and a review of the survey completed by 159 media specialists in 1985. In part 1, the editor has reprinted the full selection policy of fifteen school districts. Partial policies by specific category are reprinted in part 2, while part 3 includes specific procedures and forms. Finally, the appendices include a listing of resources and adopted statements that may be used as part of library policies.

Generally, this resource can serve as a valuable aid for school districts who are reviewing and updating their selection policies and procedures or for those who are in the process of developing a policy for the first time. It is well organized, complete, and includes useful examples of adopted policies.

This second edition includes selection and evaluation of computer hardware and software. However, in the listing of National Library Organizations, the Association for Educational Communications and Technology, specifically the Division of School Media Specialists, which deals with educational technology, is not included. Also, readers need to be aware of state and regional media computer organizations which also may help in determining selection policies and procedures.

Marie Zuk

483. Loertscher, David V., and May Lein Ho. **Computerized Collection Development for School Library Media Centers.** Littleton, Colo., Hi Willow Research and Publishing; distr., Littleton, Colo., Libraries Unlimited, 1986. 180p. (with 2 disks). (Excellence in School Library Media Programs, No. 2). $40.00 spiralbound.

This looseleaf volume has, according to Loertscher and Ho, two main purposes: (1) "to provide step-by-step instructions in creating an entire collection development system on an Apple computer using the program Apple-Works" and (2) "to provide a handbook for a workshop leader" (p. 2). The collection development system is divided into four phases. Phase I is the basic collection mapping instructions and examples; phase II is collection mapping indepth; phase III applies the results of collection mapping to include consideration files and computerized acquisitions; and phase IV instructs the user in the final collection evaluation stage. Each phase is progressively more involved, with a minimum of a two-year time period recommended for full implementation. The system was pilot tested by the authors in research projects in eighty different schools.

Accompanying the text are two 5¼-inch template disks to be copied and used with AppleWorks, which must be bought separately. Each of the four disk sides corresponds to phases I-IV and contains blank template programs as well as "Sample School" templates for use in workshop instruction. In addition there are six appendices specifically to aid the workshop organizer/presenter. The seventy-eight pages of "Teaching Aids" include transparency masters, blank and sample forms, and examples to accompany text instructions.

School library media professionals wishing to computerize some or all aspects of their collection development will find this a well-developed and thorough system and publication. However, it is not for the computer-timid or for the inexperienced. The authors recommend that users have a working knowledge of AppleWorks before beginning their collection development process. This reviewer concurs and would like to add an additional caution and a helpful hint. The process described in this publication assumes the existence of a good, well-weeded collection. It is not designed to help those whose major need is analysis of items in the collection by currency, use, condition, and age factors. Also, although chapter 2 is meant as an overview, browsing through the examples in the appendices provides a better initial overview of the various phases for the new user.

Marilyn L. Shontz

484. Prostano, Emanuel T., and Joyce S. Prostano. **The School Library Media Center.** 4th ed. Littleton, Colo., Libraries Unlimited, 1987. 257p. illus. index. (Library Science Text Series). $28.50; $21.50pa. LC 87-21174. ISBN 0-87287-568-7; 0-87287-569-5pa.

The fourth edition of the Prostanos' successful library school text differs from its predecessors of 1971, 1977, and 1982 in that it is the first edition to focus on the purpose, structure, and function of the school library media center *in the context of education* rather than viewing the center in terms of the individual

school or at the district level. The preface notes that "a wave of intense criticism has focused on the perceived failure of the educational system to prepare the nation to compete effectively with Japan and other nations in scientific and technological endeavors." Chapter 1 is an overview of the condition of education in light of the aforementioned criticism and proposals for correcting deficiencies—for example, such reports as *A Nation at Risk: The Imperative for Educational Reform* and *Schools of the Future.* The preface also affirms the authors' continuing emphasis on the LMC as a system, the improvement of management practices, and expanding developments in the field. These matters are the content of the remaining seven chapters: "The Library Media Center," "Management Activities," "Achievements," "Personnel," "Facilities and Furniture," "Media and Equipment," and "The Budget." Each chapter provides a list of learner objectives, suggested activities designed to reinforce textual concepts, well-chosen and well-placed charts, diagrams, lists, and notes and bibliography updated to late 1986.

Appendix material has been expanded to include a chart showing the scope and sequence, from K to 12, of teaching various concepts/skills in using the media center (e.g., location of materials, the card catalog) and media center materials (dictionaries, encyclopedias, indexes, etc.). The chart shows, for instance, that students are first introduced to the Dewey Decimal Classification system in grade 3 and to the Library of Congress scheme in grade 11. There is also a performance appraisal instrument for a media coordinator and a paper prepared by ALA legal counsel on library use of copyrighted videotapes and computer programs.

All in all, this edition of *The School Library Media Center* will provide students, practitioners, teachers, and school administrators with an up-to-date overview of today's LMC.

Wiley J. Williams

485. Yesner, Bernice L., and Hilda L. Jay. **The School Administrator's Guide to Evaluating Library Media Programs.** Hamden, Conn., Library Professional Publications/Shoe String Press, 1987. 244p. bibliog. index. $26.00; $19.50pa. LC 87-3118. ISBN 0-208-02147-7; 0-208-02148-5pa.

The purpose of this book is exactly as the title states: to help the principal, coordinator, supervisor, or other administrator evaluate and supervise library media programs. The authors first establish a "Context for Evaluation" by defining and discussing the roles of the management chain of command, followed by a discussion of the various roles of a library media specialist. The next section includes an "Evaluation Module" for each of sixty specific areas of concern. A module begins with a short discussion followed by specifics under these headings: "Recognizing Positive Elements," "Recognizing Negative Elements," "Identifying Missing Elements," and "Possible Solutions." The appendix includes reprints of sample evaluation forms, student evaluation questionnaires, sample job descriptions, and the Library Bill of Rights. An excellent glossary, annotated bibliography, and index complete the book.

The role of the school administrator in both evaluating the library media program and working with the library media specialist to improve the program is well defined by the authors. The book is easy to read, easy to use, and can serve as a valuable tool for any administrator. It is one that all supervisors will find interesting and helpful.   Marie Zuk

REFERENCE WORKS

486. El-Hi Textbooks and Serials in Print 1987. New York, R. R. Bowker, 1987. 914p. index. $75.00. LC 70-105104. ISBN 0-8352-2308-6; ISSN 0000-0825.

Claiming a longevity of 115 years, Bowker describes *El-Hi Textbooks and Serials in Print* as listing 34,514 works from 845 textbook publishers. The definition of a textbook is loosely understood to include actual textbooks K-12 (although some college texts are listed), auxiliary materials which accompany textbooks, and reference materials of value to teachers.

Entries are indexed under twenty-two main subject categories, such as art, business, literature, or microcomputers. Citations include author, grade, publication date, publisher, price, ISBN, and ordering information. Specific items can be found not only by subject, but by author, title, and series title.

As with *Books in Print*, Bowker relies on the publishers to report and keep the database for this publication current. Actual books are not examined for accuracy of information. Bowker is thus at the mercy of publishers who often do not report what is actually in-print and what is out-of-print. Publishers often report materials outside the scope of the publication, but these also are listed.

The weakest portion of the volume is the list of serials by subject and title. The coverage here is not comprehensive and is very uneven. For example, under "Library and Information Sciences," the following are listed: *ALSC Newsletter, Books for Secondary School Libraries, CHLA Quarterly, Directions, ERIC/IR, Edu-*

cation Libraries, Elementary School Library Collection, IASL Conference Proceedings, Interface, Iowa Media Message, Library Administrator's Digest, Ohio Media Spectrum, School Library Journal, School Library Media Quarterly, Science and Technology, and *Scientific Information Notes.* This list is not terribly relevant or comprehensive.

The user will need a magnifying glass to read the entries and will need $75.00 annually to keep this tool up-to-date, but despite these drawbacks, a library which must supply information about textual materials cannot afford to be without this tool. There is no other which covers the topic, and one wonders if anyone could do a better job.

David V. Loertscher

487. Magazines for School Libraries: For Elementary, Junior High School, and High School Libraries. By Bill Katz. New York, R. R. Bowker, 1987. 238p. index. $49.95. ISBN 0-8352-2316-7; ISSN 0000-0957.

The stated purpose of this publication is to select from among the seventy thousand now in circulation not only the best periodicals, but those most likely to appeal to and be read by children. Each entry consists of title, date founded, frequency, price, editor, publisher and address, presence of illustrations, index, advertising, circulation, whether the publisher will supply a sample issue, the date each volume ends, whether the publication is refereed, availability of a microform edition, where indexed, whether book reviews are contained, and the audience. Thirteen hundred titles have been selected from the larger *Magazines for Libraries* (see *ARBA* 87, entry 80). Therein lies the flaw. This reviewer looked in vain for annotations by any school librarians. Evidently some consultation with school librarians was done, but evidence abounds that not enough took place. For example, not all of the titles in *Abridged Readers' Guide to Periodical Literature* are reviewed.

Several sections of the guide were examined for appropriateness and completeness. The first section to be reviewed was computers. *Byte* is suggested for use, but not the important *InfoWorld. MacWorld* is recommended, but the more useful *MacUser* is not. *Apple Users Group Newsletter* and *CDC News* are indispensable but are not even mentioned. An unfamiliarity with schools is evident when *Classroom Computer Learning* is considered basic, but *Computers in Education* is not. The reviewer states that *Microzine* is for high schools, when actually it is targeted toward elementary students. Of periodicals of interest to the school librarian,

Library Literature is missing. So also are *School Library Media Activities Monthly, Ohio Media Spectrum*, and *Florida Media Quarterly*. These are glaring gaps in coverage.

In addition to these gaps in coverage, reviewers do not mention curricular uses of the titles selected, particularly those which are not indexed in *Readers' Guide*. School libraries can afford to select few titles not indexed in *Readers' Guide* because of minimal budgets. Titles must be exceptional in some curricular sense if they are to merit attention.

Finally, the high cost of the publication puts it out of reach of most school libraries. The cost of $50.00 for a magazine selection tool is much too much for a source which is created by academic librarians for school librarians. Selma K. Richardson's *Magazines for Children* (see *ARBA* 85, entry 562) and *Magazines for Young Adults* (see *ARBA* 85, entry 563), published by ALA for $22.00, while older, will suffice. Katz is recommended for large high school collections and district professional collections if the larger version of the title is not available. [R: BL, 1 Sept 87, p. 42; WLB, Sept 87, p. 96]

David V. Loertscher

488. **School Library Media Annual 1987. Volume 5.** Shirley L. Aaron and Pat R. Scales, eds. Littleton, Colo., Libraries Unlimited, 1987. 339p. index. $40.00. ISBN 0-87287-567-9; ISSN 0739-7712.

Like previous volumes, *School Library Media Annual 1987* has definitely achieved its purposes, which are to explore professional concerns of importance to school library media specialists; to describe events and influences which have had a major impact on the school media field in the past year; to evaluate materials, equipment, and collection development practices; to review and appraise important current issues and identify future trends; and to analyze program elements contributing to improved media services.

This volume is divided into three parts. Part 1 deals with contemporary events and issues; part 2 covers programs and collections; and part 3 discusses research and development.

School library media practitioners and researchers will find much valuable information in this well-organized guide, including basic advice on copyright and new technology, promoting and implementing school library media programs, and developing collections, as well as selected research studies about school library media programs, resources, and personnel.

This is indeed a fine reflection of the professional literature and the current status of school library media centers in the United States.   Isabel Schon

489. **Senior High School Library Catalog.** 13th ed. Ferne E. Hillegas and Juliette Yaakov, eds. Bronx, N.Y., H. W. Wilson, 1987. 1324p. index. (Standard Catalog Series). $96.00. LC 87-7377. ISBN 0-8242-0755-6.

The thirteenth edition of this standard selection tool presents a smaller core collection of reference and major works for the high school library than its last two editions (4,654 versus 5,056 and 5,281). Works are listed in Dewey Decimal Classification order with an extensive analytical index.

The percent of titles allocated to each main class of Dewey has remained very near constant over the past five editions of this tool. This, along with the affirmation of the stated purpose for the present edition, shows that very little change in focus has been made since 1962. Therein lies the major flaw. The problem is not what the list contains, it is what it does not contain which puts it out of touch with what the profession needs at this time. A few of these needs and a comparison against this tool are: (1) a multimedia core list is needed—*SHSLC* contains only books; (2) a solid core list would range from nine to ten thousand titles—*SHSLC* is half that size and getting smaller; (3) school librarians no longer need a core list which is also a cataloging tool, nor do they need an in-depth analytical index to the core list—*SHSLC* retains these features; and (4) school librarians need a core list which is targeted to every curricular area taught in the current high school curriculum—*SHSLC* retains its bias toward social studies and literature.

For these and many other reasons, it would behoove H. W. Wilson to rethink the function of *Senior High School Library Catalog*. While this tool used to be the Bible of the school library, it no longer serves that function. Even the idea of a printed catalog should be questioned.   David V. Loertscher

Reading and Curriculum Instruction

490. Allen, Adela Artola, ed. **Library Services for Hispanic Children.** Phoenix, Ariz., Oryx Press, 1987. 201p. bibliog. index. $30.00pa. LC 86-42788. ISBN 0-89774-371-7.

This book is divided into three sections: "Serving Hispanic Children: History and Approach," "Professional Issues Related to

Library Services for the Hispanic Child," and "Books, Nonprint Materials, Software and Resources." Part 1 provides a historical background of the development of library and educational services to Hispanic children, and discusses the influences of language and culture on cognitive styles, perceptions, and behavior. Exclusive of the index, part 2 constitutes half of the book. The examples of programs and activities suggested, such as booktalks and storytelling, are made distinctive by their emphasis on the needs of Spanish-speaking children. Especially useful are the chapters which include lists of terms and expressions in Spanish with their English equivalents. The chapters on guidelines for selection of materials could have been made more useful only by including publishers' addresses for the sample series of collections of published materials for Spanish-speaking children and youth. Part 3 does list publishers' addresses for the annotated best children's books in Spanish. A bibliography of educational software lists peripherals and hardware on which the programs will run.

This book is needed by teachers, librarians, and all who wish to provide library and educational services to America's fastest growing minority group. Tales and stories reflect the multicultured backgrounds of Hispanic-Americans, but would be of interest to all children. The editor and thirteen contributors have made a valuable addition to the literature. [R: BL, July 87, p. 1685; BL, 1 Sept 87, p. 42; RQ, Fall 87, pp. 153-54; SLJ, Oct 87, p. 42]

Robert M. Ballard

491. Benedict, Emma Lou, and Darla Shaw. **The Reading Consultant/Library Media Specialist Team: Building the Reading Habit.** Hamden, Conn., Library Professional Publications/Shoe String Press, 1987. 201p. index. $27.50; $19.50pa. LC 87-3947. ISBN 0-208-02102-7; 0-208-02103-5pa.

Benedict and Shaw, a library media specialist and a reading consultant, have compiled "a continuum of ideas, programs, plans, and strategies" (p. xiii) which they have used successfully in their Ridgefield, Connecticut, school over the past ten years. The suggestions included are interdisciplinary in nature and stress the integration of study and research skills into all segments of the school curriculum. Two specific program ideas are described in parts 1 and 2: an interdisciplinary program which addresses inquiry, search, thinking, and comprehending skills; and a literature and reading program. Parts 3 and 4 contain numerous reading motivational techniques and activities for community involvement with reading.

The Interdisciplinary Study and Research Skills program described in part 1 was developed first by the authors for the seventh grade reading, library, English, and social studies classes. Later expansion was to eighth grade students and math, science, music, and special education classes. The program includes lessons on retrieval of information, processing of information, and application of the processed information to a subject content research assignment. Materials required, a content outline, procedures, and helpful suggestions are given for each of the more than thirty-five specific lessons.

The literature and reading program in part 2 is one which uses trade books and study guides in place of the usual basal readers. It was designed for sixth grade students, to be taught by classroom teachers with the support of the reading consultant and the library media specialist. The authors characterize the roles of the library media specialist, the reading consultant, and the classroom teacher as well as book selection and book discussion/book sharing ideas.

The activities and suggestions in parts 3 and 4 have all been tried and found successful. Part 3 is a wealth of motivational strategies to be used with students, staff, and parents/families. Ideas for book fairs, booktalks, displays, contests, awards, and newsletters are just a few of those included. Part 4 describes a variety of programs for making reading a family and community affair. A community celebration of reading, a storytelling and family folklore project, a young adult authors' and readers' conference, and some staff continuing education programs are detailed.

Potential users of this volume who wish to develop programs in their own schools such as the interdisciplinary skills program or the reading program with trade books should take seriously the authors' cautions in the introduction. Development and implementation requires commitment by the school board, school district administration, principal, and classroom teachers. Cooperative planning and ample communication among the participants is essential. Those potential users who are looking primarily for new activities and ideas will find the thorough index, the bibliography at the end of part 2, and the appendices especially helpful. Overall, although the volume is limited to those activities that worked in one school district, it is a great source of reading program ideas.

Marilyn L. Shontz

492. Cullinan, Bernice E., ed. **Children's Literature in the Reading Program.** Newark, Del.,

International Reading Association, 1987. 171p. illus. index. $18.00pa. LC 86-27786. ISBN 0-87207-782-9.

This book is a timely and proactive contribution to the literature-based reading instruction movement which is attracting attention nationwide. This collection of fourteen short articles by well-known and respected individuals in the combined fields of children's literature and reading provides appropriate background and initiating strategies for teachers who wish to use "whole language" and literature either as the basis for instruction in reading or as a vehicle for expanding a child's reading experiences beyond the confines of basal text.

The authors hint at a theory of children's literature which is centered in the child reader—an "inside-out" view of the dynamics of readership and of the utility of literature for children. Though the articles address different aspects of use of the literature in the classroom, taken together they deliver a larger, implicit message. Overall, these authors suggest that the reader must *own* the reading experience and exercise that ownership for right and real reasons (inside-out reasons) in order for literary experience to be genuine. The teaching ideas suggested tend toward the staging or development of whole experiences with pieces of literature within the contexts of literary events, hence bringing reader, author, and text together inside of the definitive circumstances of a larger social context than that of direct subskill instruction. A number of these ideas seem designed to encourage the reader to "compose" not only meaning, but the function and form of the literary experience itself.

The collection reiterates those important lessons in language learning which much reading teaching has persistently failed to practice—lessons about keeping language whole; about trusting the inductive and natural operations of language acquisition as these apply to written language; about reading as the most effective means to learn to read; about reading the "real," the genuine stuff of written language transaction; and about presenting children with whole (top level) structures (e.g., "story") even at the earliest stages of encounter with written literature. Cullinan identifies the potential that traditional, isolated subskill focused reading instruction has to "ruin" literature and literary experience for children, particularly if teachers simply graft basal teaching approaches intact onto the children's literature. And Tomie de Paola provides testimony to certify that children know the difference between a real (desired) literacy event and a (less desirable) concoction intended to teach child readers *about* reading.

While this collection of articles does not provide a complete architecture for shifting the focus of reading instruction from the studying of the features of language and of basal stories to using a genuine literature in authentic literacy events, it does offer a substantial array of alternative (literature-based) approaches and experiences which make learning to read more of an implicit dimension of instruction. The likes of asking a child to find the word with the consonant digraph is a serious enough offense, and an operation of arguable necessity, even when applied to the contemporary basal story. But such methods become that much more damaging, as Cullinan makes clear, when they are enforced on such genuine works as Audrey Wood's *The Napping House*, Bill Martin's *Brown Bear, Brown Bear*, or heaven forbid, a piece with the craft and power of *The Velveteen Rabbit* (Marguerite Williams). The International Reading Association, with this collection of materials, has taken a step towards pointing literature-based reading instruction in a better and more legitimate direction, away from the deadly routines and entrapments of the bottom-up, isolated subskill applications which still drive much contemporary reading instruction.

Sandra A. Rietz

493. Toor, Ruth, and Hilda K. Weisburg. **Sharks, Ships, and Potato Chips: Curriculum Integrated Library Instruction.** Berkeley Heights, N.J., Library Learning Resources, 1986. 258p. illus. bibliog. $29.50 spiralbound. ISBN 0-931315-02-6.

This book contains library skills activities, bulletin board and publicity ideas, teaching units, and "Pencil Puzzler Pointers" for eight curriculum-based themes for grades K-8.

At least since Berner's *Integrating Library Instruction with Classroom Instruction at Plainview Junior High* (American Library Association, 1958) was published, advocates of integrated skills instruction have tended to identify skills, levels at which they should be taught, and how they should be integrated in the curriculum in various grades and subject areas, with teachers and library media specialists planning together preferably for the whole K-12 program. Both the preface and the subtitle of this publication point to the importance of "curriculum integrated library instruction," but the approach is markedly different from other integrated library instruction publications. There is no clearly identified table of skills and when they should be covered. Broad themes, such as trees, presumed to be familiar to students because of frequent coverage in classrooms, provide the foundation for reading and skills activities and teaching units. Each theme does include a brief section titled "Beyond the Basics" which makes some suggestions for involving subject area teachers. However, library media specialists and teachers seeking for curriculum-integrated library skills instruction will need to seek further.

The authors have provided attractive ideas for bulletin boards, bookmarks, and other publicity which would be useful to both school and public libraries. They have also provided a number of library skills activities which could be helpful for library media specialists who liked *66 Media Skills Puzzlers* (Library Learning Resources, 1984). [R: BL, 1 Jan 87, p. 714; EL, Mar/Apr 87, pp. 35-36]   Betty Jo Buckingham

494. Volz, Carol Brandenburg. **Keep It Simple: Bulletin Board Ideas for Grades 7-12.** Metuchen, N.J., Scarecrow, 1987. 133p. illus. $17.50pa. LC 86-31373. ISBN 0-8108-1969-4.

Volz and Mari Tru, illustrator, have created nineteen designs, especially for high school classrooms. Each one has patterns for tracing, which can also be (easily) enlarged. Patterns for the alphabet are also included. The bulletin boards themselves are imaginative and are aimed at various curricular areas (physics, math, etc.).

This is a much simpler book than the Creative Copycat series by Marian Canoles (Libraries Unlimited, 1982, 1985, and 1988), which is aimed specifically at libraries and contains many more ideas which are appropriate for both elementary and secondary students.

Keep It Simple also uses simple materials and specifies which materials and colors go where. A good blueprint for even the completely unartistic and uninspired!

Shirley Lambert

495. Wilson, Patricia J., and Ann C. Kimzey. **Happenings: Developing Successful Programs for School Libraries.** Littleton, Colo., Libraries Unlimited, 1987. 124p. illus. bibliog. index. $19.50. LC 87-3190. ISBN 0-87287-522-9.

Happenings is "designed to encourage school librarians at all levels to plan and execute library programs as part of their day-to-day library activities" (p. xiii). The authors explain their concept of library programming as part of the overall school library media program, and discuss planning, organization, and execution of such programming. Nine programs are detailed and a bibliography is provided. Sample report and evaluation forms are given, as is a sample library program plan.

Like the authors, the reviewer found books on the subject of library programs for school libraries or media centers to be basically missing. However, there is little in *Happenings* that has not been used by both school and public librarians. The value of this book is that it pulls a number of suggestions together for the new librarian. It provides a good, current bibliography (nearly 50 percent of the titles cited were published within the last five years and only 16 percent are ten years old or older). It encourages evaluation of individual programs, provides examples of evaluation forms, and recommends establishment of a community resource file. It emphasizes the use of quality storytellers and suggests a file of program ideas.

While the book discusses curriculum support, it does not address library skills instruction, the relation of such instruction and programming, and how the librarian finds time for both. It proposes the use of PTA parent volunteers without considering the dearth of such volunteers in many communities; nor do the authors mention the possibility of using retired people as volunteers. Another concern in working with volunteers is the amount of training time required and the relative lack of control the librarian has over their activities. Wilson and Kimzey merely refer to the need for "proper training" (p. 60), for not assigning "dull, unenjoyable tasks" (p. 62), and for emphasizing dependability (p. 62).

The experienced school library media specialist will probably not need *Happenings*. The new school library media specialist will find it helpful. Both may find the bibliography useful. [R: RBB, 1 Oct 87, p. 256; SLJ, Dec 87, p. 43; VOYA, Dec 87, p. 257]   Betty Jo Buckingham

SERVICES FOR THE AGING

496. Dee, Marianne, and Judith Bowen. **Library Services to Older People.** Wolfeboro, N.H., Longwood Publishing, 1986. 186p. (Library and Information Research Report, 37). $18.75pa. ISBN 0-7123-3056-9; ISSN 0263-1709.

This volume is a report of a study on library services to older people in England and Wales carried out in 1984. The authors attempted to answer four specific questions, relating to the needs of older people for library service, the cost of such service, the allocation of resources, and types of interagency cooperation engaged in to provide such service.

The first three chapters cover the purposes and methodology used in the study and provide a very thorough review of both British and American library services to older persons. The final four chapters include findings of the questionnaire survey and the case study interviews, conclusions and recommendations, and an extensive bibliography. The appendices contain copies of the questionnaire, the cover letter, and interview questions, with a summary of the survey findings. Evidence from the study revealed that librarians still hold a "medical model" of older people (i.e., that they are frail and have poor eyesight). There is little recognition of the younger group of active elders who could benefit from library service. It was found also that except for the purchase of special materials (notably large print books), few resources were set apart for elders. While the findings of the study are not different from what one might expect, it is useful not only for the information it provides, but also, for American libraries, for the well thought-out methodology is presents. In addition, it is an excellent overview of this increasingly important aspect of library service.   Lucille Whalen

SPECIAL LIBRARIES AND COLLECTIONS

General Works

PHILOSOPHY AND THEORY

497. Anderson, Beryl L. **Variables Affecting Services Offered by Canadian Special Libraries/Information Centres: Some Exploratory Observations.** Ottawa, Canadian Library Association, 1986. 55p. bibliog. $15.00 spiralbound. ISBN 0-88802-218-2.

Assuming that the distinguishing feature of a special library is the type of service it offers, Beryl Anderson, Head of the Library Documentation Centre at the National Library of Canada, surveyed by questionnaire (in 1985) Canadian bank libraries, company libraries (largely petroleum companies) in the city of Calgary, government libraries in the provinces of Alberta and Ontario, and hospital libraries across the country. The response to her survey was strong, with replies from more than three hundred libraries. Tabulation of the results shows that eight of the thirty-two services she listed are core services. Factors which influence the number of services provided are type of sponsoring body, subject specialization, user work orientation, and qualifications of staff. The report is clearly organized and Anderson's observations are candid and well informed. Her text is supported by figures, eighteen tables, and copies of the correspondence and questionnaire. This is a useful addition to the sparse literature

on special libraries and information centers in Canada.   Patricia Fleming

498. **Printing and Publishing Evidence: Thesauri for Use in Rare Book and Special Collections Cataloguing.** By the Standards Committee of the Rare Books and Manuscripts Sections. Chicago, Association of College and Research Libraries, American Library Association, 1986. 28p. $7.50pa. ISBN 0-8389-7108-3.

For a long time rare book and special collections librarians have kept files to highlight aspects of their collections which ordinary cataloging does not reflect. Computer cataloging has brought the opportunity to automate these files, and also the challenge of standardizing what had been purely local procedures. Recently the MARC format has added fields, specifically 655 and 755, to accommodate the tracing of physical aspects of items in a collection. The Standards Committee of the Rare Books and Manuscripts Section of ALA has responded with several useful thesauri of standardized terms, of which this one is the most recent, although probably not the last. It provides a list of headings for characteristics, sometimes copy specific, relating to printing or publishing operations. A few examples of terms included will suggest the type meant: cancel leaves, imposition errors, miniature books, stamped corrections. The terms, as well as various cross-references, are contained in one alphabetical list, followed by a hierarchical arrangement. This indispensable rare book and special collections cataloging aid is not for the neophyte: few terms are defined, and so one must already be familiar with their meaning.   Philip A. Metzger

499. Schram, A. M. **Managing Special Collections.** New York, Neal-Schuman, 1987. 201p. bibliog. index. $35.00pa. LC 86-16431. ISBN 0-918212-98-7.

This is a most useful guide for the neophyte curator to develop and apply some of the basic administrative policies essential to the management of special collections. It covers how to set up an acquisitions program with specific priorities and goals and how to select and implement budgetary systems best suited to a department's long- and short-term needs. In addition, it discusses classifying, cataloging, and automation techniques as well as public relations strategies, evaluating gifts and endowments, and preparing an annual report. The last two chapters include a list of organizations and libraries which the curator of special collections may wish to join or consult and a list of reference works to form the nucleus of a departmental reference section.

The author's easy to understand style, practical suggestions, interesting examples, and important reminders will definitely be valued by curators in the United States and abroad. Perhaps the only disappointment about this guide is that the author basically describes special collections as those housing the traditional rare and valuable works and ignores some important examples of modern special collections in libraries, such as miniature books or books in Spanish for children and young adults. [R: CLJ, Aug 87, pp. 259-60; JAL, July 87, pp. 169-70; LJ, 1 Apr 87, p. 50; RQ, Fall 87, pp. 154-55; WLB, June 87, p. 74]

Isabel Schon

REFERENCE WORKS

500. Directory of Special Information Resources in Utah. rev. ed. By Special Libraries Section, Utah Library Association. Salt Lake City, Utah, Utah State Library Association, 1987. 62p. $5.00pa.

This directory consists of listings for libraries in Utah that maintain some kind of special collections, though the scope and criteria for inclusion are not mentioned. The listings include special libraries, as well as branches and collections in public and academic libraries. A significant number of the entries describe libraries in state agencies and state branches of federal agencies.

Each entry gives the address, telephone number, contact person, and subject headings for the special resources of that library. Three queries with "yes/no" answers indicate whether there are access, loan, and copying privileges for the collection. Concluding the work are indexes by subject, personal name (for contacts), and library type (such as academic or church).

This directory may be useful to those needing regional information on Utah which can be found only within the state's libraries. Particularly noteworthy are local history, genealogy, natural resources, and technical business collections. Most of these are not contained in Lee Ash's *Subject Collections* (see *ARBA* 86, entry 35). However, many of the entries seem less useful, such as those of the main branches of academic libraries which offer subject information easily found in many other libraries. Also, several libraries offer neither access nor loan possibilities, leaving one wondering why they were included. The compilers would do a service to readers if, in a future edition, they would describe the scope of the work and reasons for including or excluding any collections.

Christopher W. Nolan

501. Directory of Special Libraries and Information Centers 1987: A Guide to More Than 18,000 Special Libraries, Research Libraries, Information Centers, Archives, and Data Centers.... 10th ed. Brigitte T. Darnay, Holly M. Leighton, and Carol Southward, eds. Detroit, Gale, 1987. 3v. (v.1, 2 pts.). index. $335.00/2 pts.(v.1); $275.00(v.2). LC 84-640165. ISBN 0-8103-1896-2(v.1); 0-8103-1897-0(v.2); 0-8103-0281-0(v.3); ISSN 0731-633X.

502. Subject Directory of Special Libraries and Information Centers 1987: A Subject Classified Edition of Material Taken from "Directory of Special Libraries and Information Centers," Tenth Edition.... Brigitte T. Darnay, Holly M. Leighton, and Carol Southward, eds. Detroit, Gale, 1987. 5v. index. $650.00/set. LC 85-645199. ISBN 0-8103-2118-1; ISSN 0732-927X.

The tenth edition of the *Directory of Special Libraries and Information Centers* comprises three volumes. The overall scope and format of the set are the same as those of earlier editions (see *ARBA* 83, entry 116). With over one thousand new entries and many updates since the ninth edition (1985), this edition contains about eighteen thousand listings covering special library collections in universities, public institutions, government libraries, and documentation centers, as well as in facilities maintained by business firms, nonprofit organizations, and educational foundations. Together, these specialized research libraries provide sources of information on more than three thousand topics.

Volume 1 (in two parts) uses an alphabetical approach to all U.S. and Canadian special libraries. A typical entry provides name of sponsoring institution, name of library, address and telephone number, name of person in charge, founding date, size of staff, subjects represented in the collection, size and composition of holdings, number of serial titles, services available, publications, special catalogs, and names and titles of professional supervisory staff. Seven appendices include information on networks and consortia, libraries for the blind and handicapped, patent depository libraries, UN depository libraries, etc. A subject index concludes this double volume. Volume 2 is a geographic-personnel index. The geographic section lists the institutions in volume 1 by state or province. The personnel section lists the names of all library personnel along with their professional title and affiliation. Volume 3 is a periodic supplement to volume 1.

The *Subject Directory of Special Libraries and Information Centers* contains the same information as that found in the *Directory*, arranged in five subject-oriented volumes: *Business and Law, Education and Information Science, Health Science, Social Sciences and Humanities,* and *Science and Technology.* For a review of the ninth edition, see *ARBA 86* (entry 600).

Both the *Directory* and the *Subject Directory* reflect high professional standards and provide comprehensive, up-to-date information. The former has long been a standard for all library collections; the latter is an especially useful tool for researchers and would be a welcome asset to any large reference department.　Micaela Marie Ready

503. Evinger, William R., ed. **Directory of Federal Libraries.** Phoenix, Ariz., Oryx Press, 1987. 271p. index. $65.00. LC 86-42744. ISBN 0-89774-244-3.

This comprehensive directory identifies more than twenty-four hundred libraries serving the federal government throughout the United States and overseas. The organizational arrangement generally follows the order found in the *United States Government Organization Manual 1986/87*; that is, legislative branch libraries first, followed by those of the judicial branch, executive branch, independent agencies, and other boards, committees, and commissions. Within the executive branch departments, departmental libraries are listed first followed by those of subordinate bureaus, offices, services, etc. Within an agency listing, libraries located in the continental United States, Hawaii, and Alaska precede entries for overseas libraries. The following information is provided for each library, if appropriate and available: name, address and telephone number (including FTS and AUTOVON number); name of head librarian or administrator in charge of the collection, plus the name of the person(s) in charge of acquisitions, reference, and interlibrary loan; type of library (categorized as presidential, national, academic, health and medicine, law, engineering and science, general, hospital [patient's], penal, training center and instructional [technical] school, special, and elementary/intermediate/secondary library); special subjects and special collections; depository library designations (primarily Title 44 Government Printing Office depositories); availability of online commercial databases; participation in shared cataloging network(s); membership in library networks and consortia; participation in any electronic mail network; and availability of circulation and reference services to other federal libraries, other libraries, and to the general public. Information is not provided on such matters as size of collections, number of staff, and budget/expenditures for operations, acquisitions, staff, hours, etc. Includes type of library and subject indexes. [R: BL, 1 Sept 87, pp. 36, 38; Choice, Sept 87, pp. 85-86; JAL, July 87, p. 192]

LeRoy C. Schwarzkopf

Archival

504. Cook, Michael. **Archives and the Computer.** 2d ed. Stoneham, Mass., Butterworths, 1986. 170p. bibliog. index. $49.95. LC 85-19533. ISBN 0-408-10882-7.

In the six years since the publication of the first edition of *Archives and the Computer* in 1980, many new systems have been developed, and indeed, the entire field has been revolutionized. In this updated text, Cook uses the same format and chapter headings as for the first edition, beginning with a chapter describing general computer principles and applications to archives. This is followed by chapters examining individual systems in use for records management and for archival description/retrieval/management in various institutions. Many of the systems described include detailed analyses of field structures, samples of output, and comments on any special characteristics of the system. Cook acknowledges in the preface that, because of the rapidly expanding field, the second edition limits its focus primarily to systems in use within Great Britain. The advantages, problems, and requirements of machine-readable archives are discussed in the fourth chapter. Appendices include a glossary of technical terms, a directory of archival systems, guidelines for selection of records for permanent preservation, and a select bibliography. Cook's compact book serves as an excellent introduction for archivists contemplating the automation of their collections and will be helpful to readers with varying levels of computer savvy.　Judy Dyki

505. Couture, Carol, and Jean-Yves Rousseau. **The Life of a Document: A Global Approach to Archives and Records Management.** Montreal, Que., Vehicule Press, 1987. 357p. bibliog. $40.00; $25.00pa. ISBN 0-919890-63-6; 0-919890-57-1pa.

This work originally appeared in Montreal in 1982 under the title *Les archives au XXième siècle,* and represents what must be a vital archival tradition in Quebec. Although some reference is made to legal conditions affecting archives in that province, geography is not an important limitation. The work constitutes a comprehensive manual of archival practice, with a strong records management orientation. It is concerned only with the management of institutional papers, from their creation to final disposition. Topics range from the theoretical to points of detailed practice, such as the layout of forms for particular purposes. Charts and diagrams are used well. The text is divided into three sections: archives and society, archives and administration, and archives and research. Each section contains both theoretical and practical chapters. The former material will remain current for a long time; the latter, including discussions of new technologies of preservation, will no doubt date relatively quickly. Indeed, the more broadly conceived chapters are the most valuable. Section 3, which contains a discussion of the philosophy of archival organization, should perhaps be read first, and then much of the other material in the text will be better understood. The work concludes with a lengthy glossary and a substantial bibliography. Regardless of the reader's views on the utility of certain practices, and there seems to be nothing eccentric in the book, he or she will be challenged and stimulated. [R: LJ, 1 Nov 87, p. 71]

Philip A. Metzger

506. **International Council on Archives: Proceedings of the 10th International Congress on Archives ... Conseil International des Archives: Actes du 10e Congrès international des Archives....** Munich, New York, K. G. Saur, 1986. 332p. index. (*Archivum*, Vol. 32). $37.00 pa. ISBN 3-598-21232-1; ISSN 0066-6793.

Traditionally archivists have been concerned with collecting and storing documents pertaining to the heritage of institutions or nations. The technological, social, and political changes now felt throughout the world have underscored a need to re-evaluate this traditional role. The 10th Congress of the International Council on Archives met in 1984 at Bonn, Federal Republic of Germany, to discuss the widening range of archival responsibilities. Appropriately, the theme chosen for the congress was "The Challenge to Archives: Growing Responsibilities and Limited Resources." Attended by over one thousand delegates of ninety-three countries, the meetings dealt with such timely subjects as the increasing social role of state archives, the impact of decentralization on archival administration, and the handling and preservation of information in nontraditional records. Of special importance are the sessions that dealt with archives and modern technology, the management of human resources, and international exchanges of archival

materials through reprography. This issue of *Archivum* is a must for medium-sized and large archives, and for university libraries.

Antonio Rodriguez-Buckingham

507. McCrank, Lawrence J., ed. **Archives and Library Administration: Divergent Traditions and Common Concerns.** New York, Haworth Press, 1986. 184p. index. (*Journal of Library Administration*, Vol. 7, Nos. 2/3). $24.95. LC 86-19405. ISBN 0-86656-590-6.

The ten essays which make up this volume focus on aspects of archival management from the point of view of the administrator. All of the contributors have demonstrated a deep commitment to archives and their experiences range from the practical to the administrative and theoretical.

The collection is arranged in four sections. The first section, "Archivist Perspectives on Library Administration of Archives," contains two essays which explore the pervasive dilemma of the archives under the administration of the library. Three authors present views on automated systems and networks in the second section, "Resource Sharing: Archival and Bibliographic Control."

"Cooperative Program Development at Institutional and National Levels," the third section, which also contains three essays, parallels a strong movement among research libraries which recognizes that individually libraries can no longer provide all that their users need and that cooperative efforts must be made. Finally, two authors look at "Education and Professional Development," a critical area if the archivist and librarian are to lead the academic community in the acquisition, arrangement, preservation, and access of primary resource material. At a time when issues are large and complex and technology changes rapidly, education and professional development are essential.

The book contains a list of abbreviations and acronyms, an introduction by Lawrence J. McCrank which effectively characterizes the content of each section in the volume, biographies of the contributors, and an index. [R: WLB, June 87, p. 74]

Dean H. Keller

Art Libraries

508. Baxter, Paula A. **International Bibliography of Art Librarianship: An Annotated Compilation.** Munich, New York, K. G. Saur, 1987. 94p. index. (IFLA Publications, No. 37). $22.00. ISBN 3-598-21767-6.

The unique nature of the materials found in art libraries and the surrounding issues have given rise to many specialized publications and associations. Baxter's work serves as a guide to this broad spectrum of activity. The bibliography was undertaken as a project of the IFLA Special Libraries Division, Section of Art Libraries, and outlines the major writings in the field for approximately the last seventy-five years (1908-1985). As the author states in the introduction, the emphasis is on post-1960 English-language materials—the most accessible and potentially the most useful. Publications are grouped in eight major categories: "Art Librarianship: Theory and Practice"; "Art Libraries"; "Art Library and Collection Management"; "Art Library Information Services"; "Art Library Technical Services"; "Special Services"; "Unique Materials"; and "Visual Resources." Books and periodicals both are included, and brief annotations accompany each entry. These chapters are preceded by two lists identifying the basic books and periodicals on art librarianship. The international scope of the bibliography provides a variety of perspectives and approaches, especially for the more theoretical topics. Baxter's work is the most comprehensive bibliography on art librarianship published to date and will prove to be a valuable source for students and practitioners alike. [R: LAR, Oct 87, p. 535]   Judy Dyki

Business Libraries

509. Industrial and Commercial Libraries: An Introductory Guide. By the Library Association Industrial Group. London, Library Association; distr., Chicago, American Library Association, 1986. 44p. bibliog. index. (Library Association Pamphlet, 39). $8.50pa. ISBN 0-85365-577-4.

This brief British pamphlet seeks to summarize the practical aspects of setting up and running a "commercial" library. The authors had a good idea when they decided to design a "checklist" to be used "in support of a case to management," and they have itemized a number of concepts relating to the staffing, funding, services, equipment, and space requirements of corporate libraries.

The checklist description implies somewhat more detail than is offered here, however; this volume is truly only introductory in nature. The writing style is articulate and concise, but librarians may not wish their management to read it in a vacuum, since authors seem to offer occasional advice on company politics (the "informal organization"), budget negotiation, and more.

One outstanding feature is the unique table illustrating a "service analysis"; an extremely handy tool of value to library managers in any

environment. A number of practical issues are also addressed throughout the volume, including library staff qualifications, potential services, and even library acoustics.

This guide should indeed prove useful to those corporate librarians who must establish or justify library needs. Library science students and others involved with special libraries may also learn from this volume. [R: JAL, July 87, p. 181; LAR, June 87, p. 295]

Mary Ardeth Gaylord

510. Vernon, Ken, ed. Library and Information Services of Management Development Institutions: A Practical Guide. Washington, D.C., International Labor Office, 1986. 122p. bibliog. (Management Development Series, No. 24). $15.75pa. ISBN 92-2-105593-0; ISSN 0074-6703.

Prepared and published by the International Labor Organization, this work is intended to provide a short, practical guide on the most immediate needs in developing a small business library. The foreword states that it is designed for librarians and information officers as well as managers of institutions responsible for information services. However, the information provided is for the most part rather basic, and any trained, experienced librarian or information specialist will benefit only marginally from its contents. Seven chapters are included on such topics as management literature and business information; using a library and information service; operating an effective small library; and planning, budgeting, and control in a library and information service.

Overall, this title is of limited usefulness except to nonlibrary and information science trained personnel seeking a starting point for beginning a small business library.

Frank Wm. Goudy

Government Publications

511. Directory of Government Document Collections and Librarians. 5th ed. Barbara Kile, ed. By Government Documents Round Table, American Library Association. Bethesda, Md., Congressional Information Service, 1987. 658p. index. $45.00. LC 74-10760. ISBN 0-912380-15-2.

This fifth edition of the directory continues to provide the most extensive listing available of government documents collections, institutions, agencies, organizations, and individuals concerned with documents librarianship. Based on a questionnaire, and therefore dependent upon response and dated by the information available at the time, this directory nonetheless is a valuable source of information.

It lists each library by state and city, assigning it a unique accession number, and includes the address and telephone number, personnel, whether the library is a depository library (and for which documents), subject specialties, and areas of acquisition. This information is indexed by library, document collection, special collections, and by names of documents librarians. There is also a directory of library school instructors teaching documents courses, state documents authorities (both agencies and individuals), and state data centers responsible for providing access to Bureau of the Census data.

Some libraries with specialized or limited collections who did not respond to the questionnaire for the past several editions of the directory have been excluded; others who did not respond, but who have large or important collections have been retained.

This is a thorough work and will find its place in any library needing access to documents collections, particularly those with highly specialized collections in the state, local, or international field.   Shirley Lambert

512. Lane, Margaret T. **Selecting and Organizing State Government Publications.** Chicago, American Library Association, 1987. 254p. bibliog. index. $35.00pa. LC 87-1341. ISBN 0-8389-0477-7.

Margaret Lane has prepared a useful and valuable guide on the topic of state government publications. It is not, however, a reference book; instead, the term *handbook* or *textbook* would seem appropriate. This is, therefore, a well-prepared book that lends itself to any course that would familiarize a student or concerned layperson with the selection and organization of state government publications.

The author provides a very good overview of the work and the topic in the introduction, discussing the range of publications, the role of libraries, working definitions, sources of information, and the scope of the work. The book is divided into eleven chapters and four appendices. There is a brief index. Chapter 3 provides a definition and description of state agencies; chapters 4, 5, and 6 are devoted to the distribution of state government publications, libraries, and the acquisition process. The author then discusses state checklists and bibliographies, information services, processing documents in a library, and cataloging and classification practices.

The various chapters include short discussions on background matters, issues or concerns specific to the subject matter, guides and printed sources of access devices to the literature pertinent to the topic, and practical advice on how to deal with government publications. The book is informative and very well researched, with important practical advice on working with state publications. There are no discernible biases in the preparation of this work, even though the author is a law librarian and might have been tempted to stress the legal areas and publications.

While not suited for a reference collection, this is an important new book that will be very useful for library science students interested in state publications, and librarians working in government documents sections or in acquisitions departments. It belongs in four-year academic libraries, large public libraries, and governmental libraries with responsibility for working with state government publications.

Roberto P. Haro

513. McClure, Charles R., Peter Hernon, and Gary R. Purcell. **Linking the U.S. National Technical Information Service with Academic and Public Libraries.** Norwood, N.J., Ablex Publishing, 1986. 268p. bibliog. index. $29.50; $47.50 (institutions). LC 86-8067. ISBN 0-89391-377-4.

This research study makes a valuable and unique contribution to the literature on government publications. The first chapter presents an excellent historical review of the development of the technical report, and the role of the National Technical Information Service (NTIS) and its predecessors. A critical review of the literature is also presented. The next two chapters provide an analysis of current NTIS information products and services, their implications for libraries, and NTIS sales and services related to academic and public libraries. The next three chapters describe methodology and results of original research which the authors conducted. This consisted of unobtrusive testing of six reference questions at three academic libraries and three metropolitan public libraries, and case studies pertaining to those libraries. The seventh chapter describes problems of bibliographic access to NTIS publications through the *Monthly Catalog of United States Government Publications* and the OCLC database, including original research on the extent of these problems. The final chapter provides summaries of major findings related to NTIS, and to library staff and clientele of academic and public libraries. Also included are a number of excellent recommendations to improve the current situation. The appendices have a useful collection of reference materials: extracts of orders and public laws which established NTIS, and set its authority and functions; complete list of SCRIM (Selected Research in Microfiche) categories; reprint of NTIS *User's Guide to NTIS*; reprint of NTIS's *How to Submit Your Information Items to NTIS: A Manual for Information Sources; NTIS 100 Best Seller List, 1974-September 1984*; and documents relating to the authors' research study, including questionnaire and interview guide. [R: JAL, Sept 87, pp. 229-30; WLB, June 87, pp. 73-74]

LeRoy C. Schwarzkopf

514. Robinson, Mary, comp. **Local Authority Information Sources: A Guide to Publications, Databases and Services.** Over, England, Standing Committee on Official Publications, 1986. 78p. index. £6.50. ISBN 0-9512011-0-7.

In Great Britain, local governments and their subdivisions produce about fifty thousand reports and documents a year. Few of these achieve wide distribution, yet many might be of interest and value to other agencies, organizations, and individuals. Recognizing the need for improved access to these publications and spurred on by the passage of the 1985 Local Government (Access to Information) Act, the Standing Committee on Official Publications of the Library Association has sponsored the production of this slim but informative directory of information sources (databases, information agencies, local government libraries) that could help the searcher find relevant local authority documents. The guide is divided into three sections. The first ("Databases, Networks, and Services") lists and provides basic information (provider, contact, subject, service/content, availability) for thirty-seven online databases and information agencies. Section 2 is a list of local government librarians and information officers in England, Wales, and Scotland. Finally, there is an index section which indexes the previous two sections by persons, organizations, and subjects. British librarians will certainly find this a valuable resource. On the other hand, it is difficult to estimate the publication's value elsewhere. It seems unlikely that there will be much demand for this kind of information in most North American libraries. [R: LAR, Mar 87, p. 147]

Joseph W. Palmer

515. Schwarzkopf, LeRoy C., comp. **Guide to Popular U.S. Government Publications.** Littleton, Colo., Libraries Unlimited, 1986. 432p. index. $29.50. LC 85-28444. ISBN 0-87287-452-4.

This work is the third in a series of guides published by Libraries Unlimited and a complete revision of the previous edition compiled by Walter L. Newsome, *New Guide to Popular Government Publications* (Libraries Unlimited, 1978). Schwarzkopf's guide covers U.S. government publications distributed to depository libraries in paper format. It contains information on twenty-nine hundred general-interest titles in over eighty wide-ranging subject categories, including agriculture and farming, clothing care and repair, minorities and ethnic studies, television and radio, and women. Schwarzkopf's work focuses on documents published since June 1978, the last date covered in the previous guide. Earlier U.S. documents are included if they are still available in-print and for sale by the Superintendent of Documents.

While following the same overall organizational format as the earlier guide, Schwarzkopf's work does contain some changes. Several subject categories (e.g., "Children") which were subtopics in the 1978 edition appear as main topics in this guide. Also, some earlier topics and appendices have been deleted and other topics added. Entries are arranged alphabetically within broad subject categories and subcategories. Each entry includes title, issuing agency, publication date, pagination, collation statement, series statement, publication number, stock number, price for sales publications, Superintendent of Documents Classification number, and a brief annotation.

Schwarzkopf's work is an excellent subject guide to the wide array of inexpensive government publications available on many different topics. One minor criticism is the guide's lack of currency; the most recent publications are dated 1985. However, many of the publications included are serials and the most recent editions can be located through the *Publications Reference File*. This work is an essential reference source for locating popular U.S. government publications in academic and public libraries and for ordering items directly from the Government Printing Office.

Louis Vyhnanek

516. Williams, Wiley J. **Subject Guide to Major United States Government Publications.** 2d ed. Chicago, American Library Association, 1987. 257p. index. $21.95. LC 87-1152. ISBN 0-8389-0475-0.

This guide is a revised and expanded edition of the 1968 work of the same title by Ellen Jackson. Like the earlier edition, it lists significant U.S. government publications of permanent value under more than 250 broad topics which reflect the wide range of federal government activity. Topics are arranged alphabetically and follow Library of Congress subject headings with some modifications. The guide includes about 60 percent new material. Each entry provides full title, issuing agency, personal authors or editors (if any), date of publication (for monographs), pagination, note of illustrations, series note (if applicable), and Superintendent of Documents (SuDocs) classification number. Most entries include brief annotations. Many of the significant titles listed are serials, in which case the author provides very useful publishing histories including changes in title, frequency, and SuDocs numbers. The selection of titles is excellent, and will be useful to the researcher as well as the reference librarian. The appendices include a selected list of guides, catalogs, and indexes, and directories to U.S. government publications or related information resources, and a list of Government Printing Office *Subject Bibliographies*, a series of more than 250 partially annotated bibliographies of publications sold by the Superintendent of Documents. There is a title index. [R: LJ, 15 Nov 87, p. 60]   LeRoy C. Schwarzkopf

History Libraries

517.   Dewe, Michael, ed. **A Manual of Local Studies Librarianship.** Brookfield, Vt., Gower Publishing, 1987. 419p. illus. index. $89.95. LC 86-31999. ISBN 0-566-03522-7.

Local history and its support by libraries in the United Kingdom is the subject of this excellent manual on local studies librarianship. Sixteen chapters contributed by local studies librarians and library school lecturers provide a "state of the art" review of the field, furnish practical advice on all major aspects of the specialization, and promote developing areas of local studies activities such as oral history and computerization of records. Local studies collections, long viewed as a public library specialty, are treated in the broader context of university, college, and polytechnic libraries. Work in other countries is also covered. Several themes are emphasized throughout the narrative: emergence of larger local authorities, automation, publication programs, oral history, and conservation.

"The World of Local History," chapter 2, outlines the growth of people's interest in their locality and the resources—museums, archive repositories, and libraries—which facilitate that commitment. Successive chapters delineate the development and structure of local studies in public libraries and academic libraries. Sound management is emphasized in the sections dealing with policy formation, finances, personnel, and housing. The acquisition, organization, and retrieval of materials is highlighted in separate chapters on collection development, bibliographic control, cataloging, and indexing. Concluding essays address the issues of user services

and extension activities, education, oral history, visual materials, and publications.

Local history collections are vital resources for the citizen and the scholar. This well written and perceptive volume should become the standard guide to local studies librarianship, an area which we neglect at the risk of losing our collective memory. The volume's price, however, is simply too high.   Arthur P. Young

Law Libraries

518.   Moys, Elizabeth M., ed. **Manual of Law Librarianship: The Use and Organization of Legal Literature.** 2d ed. Boston, G. K. Hall, 1987. 915p. index. $65.00. LC 86-18508. ISBN 0-8161-1854-X.

The *Manual of Law Librarianship* is a masterpiece if there ever was one written on such a topic. It is complete and extremely well done. As a cooperative effort by more than twenty contributors, overseen by editor Elizabeth M. Moys, that the book reads as well as it does and is so well focused on the topic is a credit to both the editor and the contributors.

Many manuals on large topics fail because they never are able to take command of the topic. They often contain a variety of formats and styles with no continuity among various sections, leaving the user with the feeling that there always is something lacking in the treatment of specific topics. Somehow substance often manages to rule over form, and the result is really not a "manual" at all; what you have is a cross between a dictionary and a series of explanations of related subjects which seem to have been written without reference to each other.

The *Manual* treats all topics in terms that leave the reader with confidence that he or she knows as much about a topic as is necessary to conduct useful research in the area. In addition, the reader knows exactly what has *not* been described in each section because, in all sections, mention is made of virtually all relevant materials even if the text does not treat every source in great detail. Since the book is British, written by and for British law librarians, one can gain unique and helpful insights into the structure and uses of U.S. legal materials by reading the appropriate sections. By the same token, it is the definitive reference work on the use and organization of British and Irish legal materials. (Indeed, it is definitive for many jurisdictions of the world.)

But the *Manual* is more than simply a book about legal bibliography. It also devotes over two hundred pages of text to law library administration. The information contained in these sections is both insightful and informative. Treatment of the various topics that fall under the heading of administration is brief, but somehow satisfactory.

The book, above all, is well written and well laid out. This is an excellent reference book which should be an essential part of any law library's reference collection, especially if the library contains materials from foreign jurisdictions. The treatments of British, European Communities, civil law, religious, and socialist legal systems are without peer. Each chapter contains a good bibliography of materials for further reading on each topic, and the book is very well indexed.   Richard A. Leiter

519.   Pennington, Catherine A. **Microcomputer Software Selection for the Law Library. Part One: General Business Software.** Dobbs Ferry, N.Y., Glanville, 1987. 135p. illus. index. (Law Library Information Reports, Vol. 9). $100.00 pa. ISBN 0-87802-087-X.

General Business Software is published as part of Glanville's Law Library Information Reports series. Each of the series' nine distinct titles addresses matters of law library administration. Although Pennington's work has a particular bent toward law library automation, it could also prove valuable to administrators of other types of libraries.

The chapters cover the following topics: word processing; spreadsheets, database management, and graphics; communications; educational software; project management and outline processing software; utilities; and future planning. Each chapter begins with a brief questionnaire designed to help readers identify their library's current needs. The readers are then referred to the specific part of the chapter that addresses the level of software sophistication of their institution. Illustrations are plentiful and generally very legible. A bibliography with brief annotations concludes each chapter.

Pennington offers practical advice based on her own extensive experience as a former law firm librarian and currently as Associate Law Librarian at St. John's University Law Library. She provides a framework for assessing a library's needs and identifies the features of software that meet those needs. Her straightforward recommendations suggest particular software that she has found effective. The casual, nonthreatening tone of the work does not obscure the fact that Pennington is very knowledgeable about library software. Even acknowledging the book's many merits, however, the $100.00 price tag is excessive, placing this work out of reach for most libraries. In view of the wealth of other literature available on

software selection for library applications, and because this work focuses on software selection for law libraries, this book is recommended only for law libraries. Librarians in other types of libraries would be better advised to spend their money on two or three other works with more general application.   James S. Heller

520.   **Private Law Librarians 1986.** New York, Practising Law Institute, 1986. 688p. (Commercial Law and Practice Course Handbook Series, No. 396). $45.00pa. LC 86-62275.

This latest handbook from a 1986 Practising Law Institute conference covers some valuable topics for law librarians: "Roberta's Rules of Reference," "Conducting, Evaluating and Presenting the Results of Interdisciplinary Online Searches," "Copyright," "Microcomputers in the Law Library: Hardware Selection," "Space Planning for Law Librarians," "Technical Services in Law Firms: Some Policy Considerations," "The Law Firm Library Budget: A Systematic Approach," "The One Person Law Library: An Optical Illusion," and appendices including position descriptions, task checklists, and performance standards. There is much practical information for beginning and experienced law librarians, but the format is poor. A few of the chapters are single-spaced or are in very small print, while others are double-spaced and have been prepared in outline format with graphs and sample forms. Many of the thirty-five articles contain bibliographies, and a list of the prestigious contributors is given at the end of the book.

The volume as a whole or each chapter at the least is in dire need of an index. This compact volume is not easily read because of the format, although it covers pertinent information that law librarians will want to have available.
          Marcia L. Atilano

Map Libraries

521.   Larsgaard, Mary Lynette. **Map Librarianship: An Introduction.** 2d ed. Littleton, Colo., Libraries Unlimited, 1987. 382p. illus. maps. bibliog. index. $43.50. LC 86-21381. ISBN 0-87287-537-7.

Like the first edition of *Map Librarianship*, this volume is intended for students preparing to enter the field of cartographic materials librarianship or librarians given responsibility for a collection of cartographic materials. As before, the emphasis is on "theory, techniques, and practice, and on the practical short-term and long-term aspects ...; thus the volume may be used as a classroom text, a working manual, and a reference source." The order of the chapters has for the most part been retained: selection and acquisition; classification; cataloging and computer applications; storage, care, and repair; reference services; public relations; and education. (In the 1978 edition reference services and public relations constituted one chapter, preceding a chapter on administration of a map library and one entitled "Map Librarianship: A Brief Overview" and including education for map librarianship.) Then follow a sixty-page bibliography of works (to early 1986) cited in the text and a variety of appendices (e.g., sample collection development policies, specialized bibliographies supplementing the bibliography, a list of general world atlases, addresses of publishers and distributors of globes and raised-relief maps, a list of equipment and supplies companies, and a sample course syllabus [new to the 1987 edition]) A subject index concludes the work.

While all chapters and the bibliography and the appendices have changed because of updating, the introduction notes that the chapters on collection development and cataloging have changed the most—because of the publication of AACR2 and the extent of cartographic materials cataloging provided by OCLC.

For these reasons, Larsgaard's revised edition of *Map Librarianship*, even more than the first, is the single most comprehensive text available for its intended audiences. Its nearest rival is probably Harold Nichols's *Map Librarianship* (2d ed., London, Clive Bingley, 1982), but the latter is far less comprehensive and is addressed primarily to British practicing map librarians rather than to both students and practitioners. [R: JAL, July 87, p. 181; JAL, Nov 87, pp. 296-97]   Wiley J. Williams

Medical Libraries

522. Jones, Margaret C. **Non-Book Teaching Materials in the Health Sciences: A Guide to Their Organization.** Brookfield, Vt., Gower Publishing, 1987. 159p. bibliog. index. $42.50. LC 87-356. ISBN 0-566-03560-X.

This handbook, according to its introduction, is intended to "serve as a self-instructional guide to establishing and running a collection of non-book materials, for use by people who have not undergone any formal courses of instruction in librarianship." Additionally, it is noted that the book may be of some interest to librarians and library school students desiring to become familiar with the handling of nonbook materials. It is divided into three major sections, each subdivided into chapters. The chapters in part 1, on the materials, provide a definition of nonbook materials, then discuss their selection

and evaluation, storage and maintenance, equipment, copyright, confidentiality, and obscenity. It is the province of part 2, on the collections, to address such matters as size of the collection, users, housing, cataloging and classification, circulation, techniques for evaluating the collection (e.g., questionnaires, statistics), and promoting its use. Part 3, on the people, briefly examines the role of the administrator of a nonbook collection, formal and informal means of educating users (tours, talks, handbooks, audiovisual aids, signs and instructions, etc.), the administrator as teacher of a course or courses of instruction on nonbook materials for users and staff, and continuing education/personal development opportunities for administrators. Each chapter concludes with "practical" rather than "theoretical" exercises and a selected bibliography. A few chapters include tables or other illustrations (e.g., a table summarizing storage requirements for various nonbook formats, a main-entry and a subject-entry catalog card).

This volume concludes with identification of the references within chapters, a bibliography of books, journal articles and journals, and a title/subject index. All titles are in English, and are predominantly British and American sources. The author, a freelance library/information consultant, is the audiovisual column editor for *Health Libraries Review*, the journal of the Library Association's Medical Health and Welfare Libraries Group. She is author of *International Guide to Locating Audio-Visual Materials in the Health Sciences* (Gower Publishing, 1986).

The title under review, with its emphasis on British spelling, literature, and practice, will probably be more useful as a self-instructional manual for a British rather than an American audience.   Wiley J. Williams

National Libraries

523. Hahn, Gerhard, and Hildebert Kirchner, eds. **Parlament und Bibliothek. Parliament and Library. Parlement et Bibliothèque: Internationale Festschrift für Wolfgang Dietz zum 65. Geburtstag.** Munich, New York, K. G. Saur, 1986. 452p. $50.00. ISBN 3-598-10634-3.

This is an important book, though its appeal will be limited. "Parliamentary librarianship" is the term most frequently employed in the world at large for what North American librarians call "legislative reference service." Parliamentary libraries often have notable holdings and they almost always offer the "maximum" in reference service. For these reasons and especially because the work of parliamentary libraries is directed to extremely important ends (helping legislators frame good laws and regulations), parliamentary librarianship is of major significance in our field even though only a very small percentage of librarians actually engage in such work.

Wolfgang Dietz, the Parliamentary Librarian of West Germany and an admired world leader in his calling, became sixty-five in 1986, and this occasion prompted the present festschrift collection of thirty-nine papers contributed by parliamentary librarians from nineteen countries (fourteen papers are in English). The papers fall into three main groups: analyses of the role of information services in the legislative process (three papers); detailed descriptions of individual parliamentary libraries (twenty-six papers); and the work of parliamentary librarians in the international arena, particularly IFLA (nine papers).

The papers, mostly written by the chief parliamentary librarians of their countries, together comprise a kind of scholarly handbook on parliamentary librarianship, with special emphasis on its international and comparative aspects. Understandably but perhaps unfortunately, the authors tend to aim their remarks at fellow parliamentary librarians, so most papers will be somewhat over the heads of nonspecialists. Even so, this book will stand as a major contribution: a comprehensive, cosmopolitan, and authoritative account of a most significant subject.   Samuel Rothstein

524. Thorin, Suzanne E., ed. **Automation at the Library of Congress: Inside Views.** Washington, D.C., Library of Congress Professional Association, 1986. 57p. $10.00pa. LC 86-600054.

Two questions come to mind while perusing this book. One is forensic, the other theoretical. The first has to do with the placement of this collection of essays on the efforts to automate various facets of the Library of Congress. After one has read an artist's laboriously metaphysical description of a piece of modern art, and then twisted and turned one's head in an owl-like fashion trying to give the artist the benefit of the doubt, one usually leaves with the question, "But is it art?" Likewise, after reading this fine collection of essays, absorbingly fascinating and genuinely informative, one must still ask the question, "But is it reference?" While not being too charitable, but nevertheless beneficent, the answer must be a guarded yes. The theoretical question will be postponed for now.

The authors of this inexpensively produced book take the reader on a tour through the good, the bad, and the ugly of automation at LC. Included in this volume are articles addressing the historical development of automation at LC, automated book paging, traveling books, LOCIS, the closing of LC's famed card catalog, optical disk pilot programs, computer-readable collections, and automation and copyright. Especially good in this collection are Charles Goodrum and Helen Dalrymple's twenty-year overview of automation at LC, Linda Arret's piece on retrospective conversion, Catherine Garland's essay on music automation, and Stanley Goldberg's apologia for the closing of the card catalog. Louis Drummond's visionary article on the new reference librarian also deserves mention here.

Of course such a work is of very limited use to patrons other than professional librarians. A general disclaimer on the copyright page makes it clear that this work is neither an official publication of LC, nor of the Library of Congress Professional Association, but of the authors themselves. They should be proud of their work, and the Association somewhat chagrined for not taking advantage of so many skilled writers.

This brings us, however, to the theoretical question. All of the innovations at LC from "eMail" to LOCIS are marvelous. But so is the three-legged horse, and the two-headed calf that made Ripley rich. After a fashion, we must ask ourselves if these useful machines will not eventually make us useless people. We must never lose sight of the fact that the Baconian idea of progress may turn out to be an ideal that can never make its way from an incautious imagination to a safe reality.

Mark Y. Herring

Newspaper Libraries

525. **Automating the Newspaper Clipping Files: A Practical Guide.** By Members of the Newspaper Division, Special Libraries Association. Washington, D.C., Special Libraries Association, 1987. 51p. $30.00pa. ISBN 0-87111-328-7.

In eight essays, members of SLA's Newspaper Division offer practical advice for librarians of newspaper libraries, that is, special libraries that serve the editorial staffs of specific newspapers. The authors offer suggestions for presentation of proposals to management and staff, analysis of manual systems, selection of an in-house system or service bureau, installation of the system selected, design of procedures and establishment of policies, and marketing of database products in-house and to specific user communities. A nonevaluative directory of commercially available systems is included. There is also a glossary of terms associated with computer hardware and software. These essays are full of sound advice for automating a specialized type of collection. The suggestions offered could be helpful, however, to librarians planning to automate other types of clipping files or current awareness files.

Margaret McKinley

Presidential Libraries

526. Veit, Fritz. **Presidential Libraries and Collections.** Westport, Conn., Greenwood Press, 1987. 152p. bibliog. index. $29.95. LC 86-25732. ISBN 0-313-24996-2.

Veit provides a historical overview of the treatment of presidential collections from the presidency of Washington to that of Carter. He identifies five distinct historical periods. Perhaps the most significant of these begins with the passage of the Presidential Libraries Act of 1955, which established presidential libraries as we know them today. Chapter five identifies and describes all official presidential libraries, the first being the FDR Presidential Library. The Hoover library was constructed and deeded to the federal government at a later date. The facilities are museums and collections of memorabilia as well as libraries. Chapter 6 discusses the papers and collections of the presidents preceding Hoover. Its relative compactness serves to underscore the point made by the author in an earlier chapter, that presidential papers were originally considered to be the private property of the presidents. The author indicates that it was a reaction against President Nixon's maintenance of that point of view which lead to the passing of the act in 1978 making those records federal property. Only six collections of papers of former presidents are described in chapter 6, although table 5 lists and describes depositories of information for others. Unfortunately, some materials have been dispersed privately, and others simply may no longer exist.

The first six chapters of this book are well documented. It includes much useful information on the financing and administration of presidential libraries. Much of the latter is included in chapter 2, which may have been better placed in the rear of the book and combined with chapter 7, a two-page discussion of the future of presidential libraries. The book is indexed and includes bibliographies and tables. A useful reference which could lead to other investigations. [R: Choice, July/Aug 87, p. 1681; JAL, July 87, pp. 173-74]   Robert M. Ballard

Prison Libraries

527. Coyle, William J. **Libraries in Prisons: A Blending of Institutions.** Westport, Conn., Greenwood Press, 1987. 141p. bibliog. index. (New Directions in Information Management, No. 15). $29.95. LC 86-25719. ISBN 0-313-24769-2.

Prison libraries have been in existence, in one form or another, for two centuries, but the question is, what are they for, and how can they best accomplish their purpose? These topics are addressed by a prison librarian in this well-written history containing his theories about institutional libraries today.

Five chapters discuss the early development of prison libraries to the present, a criticism of the use of the public library as a model, and a change-based model for correctional libraries. Appendices explore the topics of standards for adult correctional institutions, and agreements made in the states of Colorado, Washington, and Illinois. A bibliography presents material for additional reading, and includes a list of case law citations.

This very readable work is an important addition to the field of prison librarianship, and will be of interest to schools with criminal justice departments, as well as to library schools. [R: BL, 1 Oct 87, p. 214; JAL, July 87, p. 181; LJ, 15 June 87, p. 58]

Carol Willsey Bell

528. Hartz, Fred R., Michael B. Krimmel, and Emilie K. Hartz, comps. **Prison Librarianship: A Selective, Annotated, Classified Bibliography, 1945-1985.** Jefferson, N.C., McFarland, 1987. 115p. index. $19.95pa. LC 86-43080. ISBN 0-89950-258-X.

The titles listed in this annotated bibliography have been collected only after an extensive and diligent search by the authors, one of whom served as a prison librarian. The lack of an up-to-date guide to prison librarianship and its literature has been alleviated with this new publication.

Nineteen topics have been covered, including administration and planning of correctional libraries, background reading about prison life, censorship issues, rehabilitation, funding, history of correctional libraries, law libraries, services to prisoners, public library services, and guidelines for correctional libraries. Each of the 185 entries has been capsulized in the excellent annotations. The work is improved by the inclusion of subject and author indexes. The introduction sheds light upon the special problems faced by prison librarians.

This title will certainly be of interest to library schools, and should also be added to the collections of schools with criminal justice departments. [R: JAL, July 87, p. 181; LJ, Aug 87, p. 100]   Carol Willsey Bell

Rare Books

529. Cloonan, Michèle Valerie, ed. **Recent Trends in Rare Book Librarianship.** Champaign, Ill., Graduate School of Library and Information Science, University of Illinois, 1987. 256p. illus. (*Library Trends*, Vol. 36, No. 1). $10.00pa.

Rare book, or, as it is now often called, special collections librarianship has changed a great deal since the last *Library Trends* survey of the subject thirty years ago. This collection of fifteen articles by various hands is meant to examine aspects of the current state of the field, and all of them are successful to varying degrees. Topics range from the somber technicalities of the proton milliprobe to the sprightly generalities of Dan Traister on the profession of rare book librarianship. Indeed, the contrast of these two articles, one of breadth and one of narrowness, suggests the major flaw of the volume: a collection of very useful fragments does not add up to a coherent picture of the topic as a whole. Traister's article, along with others, contributes much more toward that picture than the proton milliprobe discussion, however useful that information may be. This flaw stems, I think, from a combination of two factors. It is possible that the increasing complexity of the field precludes the kind of comprehensive survey one might wish for. However, the impression is also that there was no overarching editorial plan to the volume, to which authors were invited to contribute their carefully conceived pieces. Nor does the introductory material assist much in bringing the topic together with any depth of thought. The result is that the profession has been sampled rather than surveyed, a useful, though not comprehensive, result.   Philip A. Metzger

Science and Technical Libraries

530. Mount, Ellis, ed. **Innovations in Planning Facilities for Sci-Tech Libraries.** New York, Haworth Press, 1986. 158p. illus. (*Science and Technology Libraries*, Vol. 7, No. 1). $22.95. LC 86-14849. ISBN 0-86656-592-2.

The contents of this volume were also published as *Science and Technology Libraries*, volume 7, number 1 (Fall 1986). Of the 158 pages, 65 are devoted to the description of five library and information facilities. The rest of the volume contains the periodical's regular features: a special paper on the impact of online search services on special libraries, a collection development paper on laser science and technology, coverage of new reference works and online information, and a short review section. The five facilities described are (1) Ayerst Laboratories Inc., Princeton, New Jersey; (2) Upjohn Company, Kalamazoo, Michigan; (3) the John Crerar Library on the University of Chicago campus; (4) College of Holy Cross, Worcester, Massachusetts; and (5) the Los Alamos National Laboratory, New Mexico.

Each description provides background about the parent organization, a floor plan and photograph, and a variety of data, usually including the gross area occupied, size of collection, number of staff, size of user population, date of completion, and a list of special equipment. The description of the planning process and the steps leading to the completion of each facility is interesting but does not warrant the reissue of this periodical issue as a hardbound monograph.   Helen Howard

531. Mount, Ellis, ed. **Role of Computers in Sci-Tech Libraries.** New York, Haworth Press, 1986. 145p. (*Science and Technology Libraries*, Vol. 6, No. 4). $24.95. LC 86-7619. ISBN 0-86656-577-9.

This hardbound monograph is one in a series simultaneously published as the journal *Science and Technology Libraries*. Computer applications are discussed in the following libraries: Molycorp, Inc., Science and Engineering Libraries at Purdue and the University of Rochester, Cornell University, and the Chemical Abstracts Service Library. Other libraries are mentioned in less detail. The applications include many of the technical and public services functions, with two articles focusing on collection and use of computer-based statistics and the impact of online searching on print collections. Two concluding articles focus on the impact of the Matheson-Cooper report on academic science and technology libraries. Regular sections include a review of new reference works in science and technology, new developments in online searching, and brief reviews of selected articles dealing with the use of science information.

The information presented in the volume is interesting, well written, and for the most part still relevant. An index would have made it more useful. At the same time, considering how quickly information technology changes and the value of companion volumes, most libraries might find it more cost-effective to subscribe to the journal format. Andrew G. Torok

532. Mount, Ellis, ed. **Sci-Tech Libraries Serving Societies and Institutes.** New York, Haworth Press, 1987. 149p. (*Science and Technology Libraries*, Vol. 7, No. 2). $22.95. LC 86-26969. ISBN 0-86656-618-X.

Published also as the journal *Science and Technology Libraries*, this hardbound volume presents brief descriptions of several scientific and technical libraries, including The Washington Chemical Society, American Institute of Aeronautics and Astronautics, Institute of Paper Chemistry, Institute of Textile Technology, Portland Cement Association, Society of Automotive Engineers, Society of Manufacturing Engineers, the science library at the University of Rochester, Space Telescopic Science Institute, and the American Petroleum Institute. Other entries include a brief (undated) survey of eighteen libraries serving scientific and technical societies and associations, a guide to burn care literature, and standard sections on new reference works in science and technology, sci-tech online, and sci-tech in review.

For the most part, the entries are well written and present data of interest to special librarians and library science students. As with other volumes in the series, an index would have been helpful. Considering the price, a subscription to the journal equivalent might be more desirable. Andrew G. Torok

533. Pruett, Nancy Jones. **Scientific and Technical Libraries.** Orlando, Fla., Academic Press, 1986. 2v. bibliog. index. (Library and Information Science). $45.00/vol. LC 86-10829. ISBN 0-12-566041-3(v.1); 0-12-566042-1(v.2).

The purpose of this two-volume set is to provide a current overview of all aspects of science and technology librarianship, omitting the area of medicine, primarily for librarians working in various types of science and technology libraries. Managers of large libraries of this type, library school students, and faculty teaching courses about this area of librarianship will also find it useful. It is the first broad survey of the field since the publication of the second edition of *Scientific and Technical Libraries: Their Organization and Administration* by Lucille J. Strauss, Irene M. Shreve, and Alberta L. Brown (Wiley-Becker-Hayes, 1972).

Volume 1 consists of twelve chapters in three parts. Part I is an introduction which includes a comparison of three earth science libraries illustrative of the impact of different environmental settings—university, corporate, and government agencies—on library services

and policies. In part II the major functions of science and technology libraries, defined as information retrieval, current awareness, collection development, collection control, and document delivery, are outlined, explained, and evaluated. Part III describes management, space planning, library automation, and provision of library equipment as secondary functions which support the primary function of getting information to the scientists and engineers who use the library.

Volume 2 is divided into two parts. Part I discusses thirteen special types and formats of science and technology materials: conference literature, dissertations and theses, government documents, in-house and proprietary information, journals and other serials, maps, microforms, numeric data, patents, software, standards and specifications, technical reports, and translations. Part II describes four science libraries: biology, chemistry, mathematics, and physics, and three applied science libraries: engineering, geoscience, and pharmaceutical research.

Coverage is more comprehensive of those topics for which little has been published and less complete in areas where already adequate sources of information exist. Well structured, authoritative, and easily readable, this two-volume set is informative and achieves its purpose, yet manages to convey the excitement of present-day librarianship. There are seven signed chapters and three signed essays on specific types of science and technology libraries and two signed chapters on document delivery and library automation by knowledgeable librarians in the specific areas, including two by the author. Both volumes not only incorporate valuable references to additional sources of information in the text but also append extensive, selective bibliographies of additional sources with emphasis on the current literature. Each volume also has an index for quick access to specific topics of interest.

Virginia E. Yagello

Serials

534. Chatterton, Leigh, and Mary Elizabeth Clack, eds. **Serial Connections: People, Information, Communication. Proceedings of the North American Serials Interest Group: 1st Annual Conference, June 22-25, 1986. Bryn Mawr College, Bryn Mawr, Pennsylvania.** New York, Haworth Press, 1987. 200p. index. (*Serials Librarian*, Vol. 11, Nos. 3/4). $34.95. LC 86-32021. ISBN 0-86656-654-6.

In 1985, a new organization called the North American Serials Interest Group (NASIG) was formed. Patterned after the United Kingdom Serials Group (USKG), NASIG's members include educators, librarians, serials publishers, subscription agents, bibliographers, and any other group interested in serials. Its purpose is to establish communication and education among these various constituencies by offering an open and equal forum for the discussion of mutual problems and concerns. Although it is not formally affiliated with other library, information service, or publishing organizations, cross-over membership is most apparent and encouraged.

As part of its emphasis on the sharing of ideas across a broad interrelated serials network, NASIG initiates annual conferences: intensive two-to-three day sessions devoted solely to serials. At this first conference, papers dealing with a wide range of serials concerns were presented: serials automation, standards, online public access catalogs and their relationships to serials, serials from the perspective of the publisher and vendor, and, of course, the "hot topic," serial pricing. In addition to these presentations, five workshops were held so that participants could discuss and interact with one another on such topics as the effects of serials cataloging in an automated environment, serials education for librarians, and serials binding. Summaries of these discussions are also included in this volume.

While some may view NASIG as a splinter group of the American Library Association, NASIG's membership is considerably broader. Those presenting papers at this conference are among the top in serials work: Richard Boss, Mary Ellen Clapper, Ronald Gardner, Charles Hamaker, Betty Landesman, and Marcia Tuttle, to name but a few.

This volume comes highly recommended to all serials librarians with a further recommendation that, if at all possible, they should try to attend future NASIG meetings. [R: JAL, Nov 87, p. 323]   Marjorie E. Bloss

---

Theological, Church, and Synagogue Libraries

535.   Pritchett, Jennifer. **Providing Reference Services in Church and Synagogue Libraries: With Bibliography.** Portland, Oreg., Church and Synagogue Library Association, 1987. 57p. illus. (CSLA Guide, No. 15). $6.95pa. LC 87-15776. ISBN 0-915324-26-1.

536.   Smith, Ruth S. **Cataloging Made Easy: How to Organize Your Congregation's Library.** rev. ed. Portland, Oreg., Church and Synagogue Library Association, 1987. 40p. illus.

index. (CSLA Guide, No. 5). $6.95pa. LC 86-30974. ISBN 0-915324-25-3.

Any church or synagogue that has even considered having a library would do well to acquire as many as possible of the guides put out by the Church and Synagogue Library Association. They are written with several valid assumptions: very little money is available, most work will be done by volunteers, and most volunteers will have more enthusiasm than library expertise.

Providing Reference Services in Church and Synagogue Libraries is not a guide on how to answer all kinds of religious reference questions, but rather on how to build and use a core collection of reference materials. It includes a well-chosen and annotated bibliography of books, as well as suggestions about encouraging the use of a reference section. It also includes a listing of publishers of religious reference works, with their addresses.

Cataloging Made Easy is a simple crash course in how to organize books so people will be able to have easy access to what they are looking for. "Consistent" is the operative word, rather than slavish devotion to AACR. Lots of examples are given, to help a nonprofessional librarian classify and organize books by means of a card catalog.

Strongly recommended for all churches and synagogue libraries.

Judith E. H. Odiorne

STATISTICS

537.   **ACRL University Library Statistics 1985-86 & 1986 "100 Libraries" Statistical Survey.** Robert E. Molyneux, comp. Chicago, Association of College and Research Libraries, American Library Association, 1987. 1v. (various paging). $30.00pa. ISBN 0-8389-7144-X.

This is the fourth volume in a continuing series of academic library statistics by the Association of College and Research Libraries (ACRL). The first volume appeared in 1980 and was prepared for the purpose of obtaining and publishing statistical data about the 103 university libraries that were not members of the Association of Research Libraries (ARL). Since that first volume of 1978/1979 data (which became known as the "100 Libraries" Statistical Survey), ACRL has continued to publish these statistics, with some variations in coverage and content, on a regular basis. The overall result has been an improvement in the availability of information on non-ARL university libraries and has improved the ability of the profession to make comparisons across institutions and over time.

In this volume, ACRL makes some significant departures from the earlier volumes in the series. First is the inclusion of two new sections of statistical data on "representative" college and junior college libraries in the United States and Canada. (This, according to ACRL, is the first step in the development of a large-scale academic libraries statistical database.) Second, ratio measures for comparison among the three groupings of libraries and with ARL libraries are used more extensively. Third is the use of a new survey form, developed by the Department of Education's Center for Education Statistics, for the collection of the data reported here.

The volume is divided into three major sections: university library data, college library data, and community/junior college data. Three appendices contain the original questionnaire used to collect the data, a methodology discussion by compiler Robert Molyneux, and a set of notes relevant to the data on certain institutions. Each of the three major sections follows the same basic format: data tables on each institution (done as foldout sheets), totals, analysis of selected variables, and selected ratios. The university libraries section has more extensive information than is given on college and community/junior college libraries in order to keep it parallel with previous years and to make comparisons with ARL university libraries. Rank order tables are given for seventeen different variables covering the most useful aspects of staff, collections, and expenditures. A summary table, by institution, of these seventeen rank order tables is provided for easy total comparisons on these variables and matches a similar table provided in the ARL statistics (*ARL Statistics, 1985/86*, 1986).

For the eighty-one university libraries reported here (apparently there were several nonrespondents of the total 103 non-ARL university libraries) superb comparative information is provided. Directors and staff of these libraries should have a field day comparing themselves with each other and with the ARL libraries. Librarians in the college and community/junior college libraries can also make useful comparisons but with far less satisfactory results. Indeed, one questions the merit of reporting these data because it is unclear just how representative they actually are of the two groups of libraries. No mention is made of how the individual libraries (forty-two college and twenty-six community/junior college libraries) reported here were selected; one simply must take the assurances of ACRL that they are "representative." A response rate of 85 percent is given, but with no indications of how the responses vary within the three groups. This

simply will not do, and reflects either an inadequate editing job or poor statistical reporting—and possibly both.

Fortunately, the methodology section by Molyneux on what was actually done with the data once they were collected is excellent. Formulas for calculations and indexes are given, notes are provided on interpretations made for issues that could cause problems in reliability (particularly the infamous problem of "not applicable"), and extensive notes are given on the nature of the data from a particular institution. It is unfortunate that equally careful technical attention was not given to the problem of the selection of the institutions shown in the college and community/junior college libraries sections so that one could know just how well they were truly representative of their groups.

Robert V. Williams

538. **ALISE Library and Information Science Education Statistical Report 1987.** Timothy W. Sineath, ed. State College, Pa., Association for Library and Information Science Education, 1987. 259p. $30.00pa. ISSN 0739-506X.

The eighth annual statistical report on library and information science education published by the Association for Library and Information Science Education (ALISE) follows the same format as those of previous editions. Although both ALA accredited and non-accredited schools are surveyed, the volume is primarily a report of accredited programs. Sections of the report include (1) faculty (Timothy W. Sineath, University of Kentucky), (2) students (C. Glenn Sparks, University of Texas), (3) curriculum (Daniel Barron, University of South Carolina), (4) income and expenditures (Fred W. Roper, University of South Carolina), (5) continuing education (Darlene E. Weingand, University of Wisconsin-Madison), and (6) summary and comparative analysis (Jane Robbins, University of Wisconsin-Madison). The report is an excellent source for statistical information about accredited library education programs, with 95 percent of accredited schools represented in the report. Information in the report about non-ALA schools is interesting but cannot be considered representative of such programs because only seven non-ALA schools responded to the survey.

Nathan M. Smith

539. **Australian and New Zealand Academic Library Statistics, Part A Tables, 1953-1983.** rev. ed. Alice Leong, ed. Bentley, Western Australia, Library, Western Australian Institute of Technology, 1986. 345p. bibliog. (Western

Library Studies, No. 6). $59.00. ISBN 0-908155-29-8.

Apart from practicing academic librarians in Australia and New Zealand, only the most dedicated library statistician and/or library historian will find this compendium of thirty-one years of academic library growth and development in those two countries to be of much interest. Unfortunately the categories of information collected, and specialized jargon ("vote") which remains unexplained in the introductory matter or the text, make it difficult even to use these figures for any comparison with American academic libraries or those in other countries. Those difficulties exist even though one appendix on the average prices of British and American publications for the period and another on exchange rates of foreign currencies for the period are provided. Arranged on a year-by-year basis, and reflecting many changes that have been made in the data collection process over time, these facts and figures provide basic information about university libraries and colleges of advanced education, as separate categories, derived from several basic sources including, in particular, the annual *Australian Academic and Research Libraries (AARL) Supplement*. This volume is, naturally, the source of such information.   Norman D. Stevens

540.   **Illinois Library Statistical Report 21.** Springfield, Ill., Illinois State Library, 1986. 121p. free pa.

Compilation of this statistical report was funded by a Library Services and Construction Act Grant. The research was performed at the Library Research Center at the Graduate School of Library and Information Science of the University of Illinois. The first topic of the report was an assessment of whether public libraries should be grouped by the size of the population served, by total operating expenditures, or by equalized assessed valuation. This was followed by a summary of selected analyses of data collected from annual reports of Illinois public libraries and from other sources. Three other studies in the report focused on personnel data on children's librarians, catalogers, reference librarians, and head librarians in Illinois libraries (1984-1985); a survey of children's librarians in Illinois public libraries; and a study of circulation per capita and the exploration of possible alternatives for increasing circulation statistics.

This statistical report is free to those who wish to request a copy from the Illinois State Library Publications Unit. The writing is clear and concise, but a rudimentary knowledge of statistics is necessary in order to clearly under-

stand all of the details of the report. The manual is recommended for institutions asking similar questions; for those people interested in the methodology used in compiling such a report; and for individuals or institutions interested in, or responsible for, the current state of affairs of Illinois libraries. The publication is also of (limited) interest to those seeking employment as librarians in the state of Illinois. Clearly, a great deal of time and research have been expended to compile such an informative and statistically detailed look at the current state of Illinois librarianship.   Barbara Sproat

541.   **Library Statistics of Colleges and Universities, 1985: National Summaries, State Summaries, Institutional Tables.** Chicago, Association of College and Research Libraries, American Library Association, 1987. 240p. $30.00pa. ISBN 0-8389-7147-4.

Thanks to some recent work by individual researchers, such as Robert Molyneux (*The Gerould Statistics, 1907/08-1961/62*, Association of Research Libraries, 1986), and the regular statistical publications of the Association of College and Research Libraries (ACRL) and the Association of Research Libraries (ARL), we are finally beginning to get a moderately good picture of the nation's academic libraries. This volume, thanks to the work of ACRL in getting it published, is a welcome addition to this growing body of information. It is unfortunate that the compilers did not go a little further and provide needed technical details that would help in making judgments on the reliability and validity of the data reported here.

The statistics reported here were collected as part of the U.S. Department of Education's Center for Education Statistics HEGIS XX, 1985 survey. The data are reported in fifteen basic tables grouped according to national summaries, state summaries, and institutional data. The national summary tables report selected variables (e.g., operating expenditures, number of books, staff, etc.) by type and size of institution. The state summaries contain similar variables with breakdowns by state. The institutional tables occupy the bulk of the volume and report, by state and individual school, data on approximately fifty different variables. There is wide variety in the variables reported for the institutions, and all major areas (expenditures, collections, staff, etc.) are represented in some detail. Indexes for some variables are also reported in several tables, and this is a useful addition that makes comparison at institutional, state, and national levels a simple matter.

Even though the data for all of the different levels are interesting, it is in making comparisons that this volume will be of greatest use and that use, one hopes, will be extensive. Administrators of academic libraries will find here enough data to formulate countless arguments to their presidents and hundreds of memos to their department heads for upgrading or changing priorities.

These comparisons and arguments for change, however, could be made on much more comfortable grounds if the compilers had given the reader the minimal technical details about the survey methodology, particularly the response rate on which the data are based. True, the survey was conducted by the CES, a group well noted for the quality of its work, but none of the technical details ordinarily found in their reports are provided here. Particularly needed were comments on the following: (1) Is this a universe survey? (it appears to be since all types, sizes, and geographical areas are well represented); (2) If a universe survey, then what was the response rate? (3) Were there problems from respondents on particular variables that raise reliability issues? and (4) What kinds, if any, of institutions of higher education were omitted? Minimal answers to these questions would make the user a little more comfortable in making comparisons and arguments—and would have strengthened what is already a good and useful work.　　　　　　　　　Robert V. Williams

542.　Lynch, Mary Jo. **Libraries in an Information Society: A Statistical Summary.** Chicago, American Library Association, 1987. 32p. $4.00pa. ISBN 0-8389-7145-8.

OCLC provided a grant to ALA that partially supported preparation and production of this volume. Its purpose is "to bring together in one place basic statistics about libraries in the United States that will help persons understand what libraries are and do, how they are used and by whom, what they contain, how they are financed and staffed, and how they spend their resources." This summary has been written for persons outside the library community who want to know more about libraries (e.g., city and county councils).

The summary chapters are: (1) "Resources for Information, Education, Culture"; (2) "Count of Libraries in the U.S."; (3) "People Served by Libraries"; (4) "Resources and Services Provided by Libraries"; (5) "Technology Used to Manage Libraries"; (6) "Library Finance"; (7) "Library Staff"; and (8) "Library Buildings."

Examples of graphics which illustrate the statistics gathered include (1) size of student population served by academic and public school libraries, (2) volumes held by public and academic libraries, (3) operating expenditures of public and academic libraries, and (4) academic and school library media library staffs.

It is hoped this volume will be updated on a regular basis.　　　　　　　　　Janet R. Ivey

543.　**Planning for Management Statistics in ARL Libraries.** Washington, D.C., Association of Research Libraries, 1987. 106p. bibliog. (SPEC Kit, No. 134). $20.00pa. ISSN 0160-3582.

This Office of Management Studies SPEC Kit focuses on statistics gathered by ARL libraries by including selected report forms along with definitions and planning reports from nine ARL libraries. Of importance to all management levels within academic libraries, the introduction stresses the need for statistics in order to describe library performance, evaluate and enhance effectiveness, and plan for the future. In gathering materials for this report it was found that fifty-six of the ninety-one libraries completing the survey used LOTUS 1-2-3 to manipulate statistical data. Also noted was that five general categories of statistics were measured: (1) activity and work load; (2) holdings; (3) facility (building) use; (4) resources generated and expended; and (5) others. It was found that the quantitative data collected were most often used to support budget requests and intralibrary reporting. Eighty-one percent of the respondents reported using statistical data to assist in basic management activities, 85 percent to compare their library with others. Statistics were most often collected for the following five areas in descending order: circulation, interlibrary loan, acquisitions, cataloging, and serials. A selected reading list reflects the publications that were referred to most often for help in collecting library statistics. The definitions supplied by Stanford University are comprehensive and of great value to other libraries revising or clarifying their own definitions. Among the planning papers, New York University and Duke focus on sampling public service statistics and reasons for obtaining such statistics. Included among the very helpful planning memos are recommended changes to public service statistics devised by Stanford University. Any university considering changes in a statistic gathering method should study this work closely.

　　　　　　　　　Ann Allan

STORYTELLING

544.　Baker, Augusta, and Ellin Greene. **Storytelling: Art and Technique.** 2d ed. New York, R. R. Bowker, 1987. 182p. illus. index. $24.95. LC 87-26539. ISBN 0-8352-2336-1.

The emphasis here is on storytelling as an oral art, and the intent is to encourage librarians and teachers to share stories with children regularly. The manual covers the selection, preparation, and presentation of stories, and includes sections on storytelling in special settings or to children with special needs, program planning, and administration. A lengthy bibliography suggests sources for the storyteller.

This second edition was written in response to requests for further information and updated bibliographies. It retains the detailed chapters on selection, preparation, and presentation of stories that reflect the authors' knowledge and experiences. Many concrete, practical points are covered, such as handling disruptions and what to do if you forget a story while telling it; there is even a detailed list of six suggestions on timing. There are new sections on storytelling to infants and toddlers, storytelling to the learning disabled, and on children and young adults as storytellers. While less detailed, the chapters on telling to special groups, planning, administration, and the appendix on planning workshops are valuable. These sections help to put storytelling in context and thus enhance the book, giving a balance other storytelling books do not always have. Also, their bibliographies readily lead the user to more detailed information about these subjects.

Overall, this manual is for public libraries, academic libraries, or school districts without the first edition, and very useful for those with the first needing the more current, updated information.   Carol A. Doll

545.   Livo, Norma J., and Sandra A. Rietz. **Storytelling Activities.** Littleton, Colo., Libraries Unlimited, 1987. 140p. illus. bibliog. $15.50 pa. LC 86-33727. ISBN 0-87287-566-0.

Storytelling Activities is designed for "group leaders, teachers, parents, and students" (p. xiii) and offers suggestions for finding, designing, and presenting stories to people of all ages. There are six chapters, each dealing with a particular aspect of the storytelling process and containing specific examples of activities such as using newspaper articles to develop a story. Each chapter concludes with a list of further references. A detailed table of contents breaks the chapters down into specific units (e.g., the chapter "Using Media in Storytelling" has sections on radio, murals, and television). Other activities involve physical movement, music, and fingerplays. Chapter 4, "Some Stories to Tell," contains the texts of a number of stories arranged by the following types: mythology, folklore, family history, and participation stories. Four appendices deal with evaluating story-

telling, keeping a storytelling journal, a matrix of educational skills and activities, and a bibliography of books about storytelling. The matrix is fairly complex and connects each activity described in the book to a list of thirty-eight educational skills from the National Council of Teachers of English; Bloom's Taxonomy levels; categories such as social, reading, or listening activities; educational level of the participants; and whether or not it is a group or individual activity.

Some activities require more information than is given in the book. For instance, the section on using sign language simply directs the reader to ask a librarian for help in finding books on sign language. However, *Storytelling Activities* contains many useful suggestions and serves adequately as an introductory text for prospective storytellers. [R: EL, Sept/Oct 87, p. 40]   Nancy Courtney

546.   Nichols, Judy. **Storytimes for Two-Year-Olds.** Chicago, American Library Association, 1987. 141p. illus. bibliog. index. $20.00pa. LC 86-32151. ISBN 0-8389-0451-3.

After explaining why libraries should sponsor toddler storytimes, the planning and programming elements necessary for success are considered. Next a sample program is outlined including what to do before the toddlers arrive, opening routine, body of the program, quiet time, and closing routine.

The author, a librarian and storyteller, presents thirty-three program themes which have been successful with two-year-olds. Sample themes include bears, boats, clothing, colors, farms, kittens, rain, sounds, vehicles, and winter. For each program idea suggestions are included for book titles, fingerplays, crafts, poetry, creative drama, and follow-up ideas for parents and children at home. Each suggested program concludes with program notes designed to assist the storyteller with the mechanics of the presentation. The appendices include directions for construction of storytime materials; suggestions for how to read a picture; and bibliographies of storytelling resources, parenting books, and titles used in the programs.

Librarians responsible for planning toddler storytimes and preschool teachers will find this book valuable and easy to use. Storytimes for two-year-olds have only recently gained widespread interest. This title will provide valuable information for librarians considering toddler programs.   Connie Champlin

547.   Sitarz, Paula Gaj. **Picture Book Story Hours: From Birthdays to Bears.** Littleton, Colo., Libraries Unlimited, 1987. 190p. illus.

bibliog. $18.50pa. LC 86-21439. ISBN 0-87287-556-3.

In an attractive, easy to use format, the authors have compiled twenty-two story hour program plans they have used successfully with preschoolers. Each plan is developed around a theme which will appeal to preschoolers, including "Yummers: Stories about Food," "Things That Go," and "Down on the Farm." The first chapter presents a guide to selecting, organizing, preparing, executing, and evaluating materials for story hours. Simple publicity ideas precede each program plan.

A clear step-by-step plan is presented for each program. Brief but adequate annotations accompany the ideas for introductions, read-aloud books, booktalks, and participation activities. Unannotated suggestions for alternative books and materials are included. The complete text for many of the fingerplays and action rhymes recommended is provided, a very useful feature of this title.

The comprehensive nature of this book will make it a valuable resource for new librarians who are responsible for planning preschool programs. More experienced librarians will find ideas and titles to supplement their existing programs.   Connie Champlin

TECHNICAL SERVICE

548.   Hahn, Harvey. **Technical Services in the Small Library.** Chicago, American Library Association, 1987. 10p. (LAMA Small Libraries Publications, No. 13). $1.95pa. LC 86-32118. ISBN 0-8389-5689-0.

This work is a basic introduction to technical services functions in small libraries. It is designed to meet the needs of both professional and nonprofessional staff in public libraries serving communities of ten thousand to fifteen thousand people, as well as school, small special libraries, and church and synagogue libraries.

Functions covered include acquisitions, cataloging and classification, processing, collection repair and maintenance, and file maintenance. Brief treatments of staffing and the application of new technologies are also included, along with a selected bibliography.

Technical Services in the Small Library is a simply written, straightforward work with a highly practical orientation. It could serve as a useful introduction to librarians and staff facing the challenges of technical services work in a small library for the first time.

Joe A. Hewitt

549.   Peet, Terry C., and Marta Stiefel Ayala. **A Guide to Spanish Correspondence for Acquisitions Librarians.** Madison, Wis., SALALM Secretariat, Memorial Library, University of Wisconsin, 1987. 127p. bibliog. index. (Bibliography and Reference Series, 18). $18.00pa. ISBN 0-917617-13-4.

Librarians involved with acquisitions from Spanish-speaking areas will be delighted with this useful and most comprehensive manual. Even though this manual assumes a solid knowledge of Spanish grammar and ease in reading the language, native and non-native Spanish speakers and readers will find helpful phrases, paragraphs, and letters which will expedite their correspondence in Spanish. It is organized by general broad categories of statements and ideas such as acknowledgments, proposals to exchange, request for publications, additions and deletions from mailing lists, blanket order language, and many others. Appendix A includes excellent samples of blanket order profiles. The only undesirable part of this manual is appendix B, "Sample Form Letters," which includes too many spelling, grammatical, and typographical mistakes in Spanish. Librarians would be wise to completely ignore this section.

Isabel Schon

Part III
REVIEWS OF
PERIODICALS

Reviews of Periodicals

NATIONAL

550. **Australian Academic & Research Libraries**, Vol. 1- , No. 1- . Bundoora, Australia, Borchardt Library, La Trobe University, 1970- . quarterly. $18.00/yr.; $20.00/yr. (institutions); $16.00/yr. (UCLS members). ISSN 0004-8623.

Founded in 1970 by D. H. Borchardt, and edited by him through 1984, *Australian Academic & Research Libraries* is a solid and valuable professional journal. Its scope and content are similar to that of the *Journal of Academic Librarianship*, which it predates, and the quality of its contents and its writing is as good as, and frequently better than, that of *JAL. AARL* deals with all aspects of libraries in institutions of higher education and research and specifically seeks to publish articles on librarianship, pure and applied bibliography, automation in libraries, and information science and related subjects. Published quarterly, each issue runs approximately forty to sixty pages and typically contains four or five lengthy articles, usually one or two letters to the editor, the occasional news notes, and five to ten brief book reviews. The annual library statistics for Australian and New Zealand academic and research libraries are published each year as a loose supplement. The articles, which are on such familiar themes as reader education (i.e., bibliographic instruction), collection management, and faculty status, are typically by Australian librarians although there are sometimes papers given by foreign librarians in Australia. Topics are generally approached from an Australian viewpoint, naturally, but they are usually topics of general interest to academic librarians throughout the world. The well-written and thoughtful articles often contain broadly useful information and insights. The books reviewed are published throughout the world, although special attention is given to books on Australian librarianship, and are evaluated in terms of their general value to academic librarians. Borchardt, one of the great names of contemporary Australian librarianship, is still a frequent contributor; his sprightly and insightful commentary on professional ethics in the March 1987 issue is an excellent example of the kind of piece that serves an international audience. Taking into account the small base of potential contributors and the relatively small readership, Australian academic librarians can be justly proud of their thinking and writing as set forth in *AARL*. The high-quality journal that Borchardt founded maintains that quality as it continues, under the able editorship of J. I. Horacek, to meet the purposes it has set for itself.

Norman D. Stevens

551. **The Australian Library Journal**, Vol. 1- , No. 1- . Ultimo, N.S.W., Australia, Library Association of Australia, 1951- . 4 issues/yr. $25.00/yr.; $7.00 (single issue). ISSN 0004-9670.

Since its founding in 1951 *The Australian Library Journal* has served as the journal of the Australian Library Association and the basic library journal in Australia. Published quarterly, and now edited by John Levett, this general journal specializes in short features (up to one thousand words in length) and longer articles (up to five thousand words in length) on topics primarily related to librarianship in Australia or of interest to Australian librarians. It also offers reviews of a range of domestic and foreign library publications, covering about a half dozen titles or so in each issue, and has a typical "letters to the editor" column. Except for a brief editorial in each issue, that's it. News, comment, columns, coverage of Australian literature, and other topical items are left to others.

Now published in a 6¾-by-9¾-inch format, with roughly between forty and sixty pages in each issue, this is, in every respect, a good solid journal. There are only a few articles in each issue, all devoted to a straightforward, serious discussion of a library topic. Since Australian librarianship takes an extremely broad view of its field of interest, articles on indexing and the book trade are found along with articles on retrospective conversion, service to the aged and minorities, and various aspects of library management. The articles, which are primarily written by Australian librarians with an occasional contribution from a foreign visitor, are generally well written and informative. Overall this is *the* primary source of ongoing information about librarianship in Australia, but it somehow seems too staid even for Australia. It is not a journal one is likely to look forward to receiving with enthusiasm, nor does it give any real sense of the breadth and depth of the many issues facing librarianship, one assumes even in Australia, today.

Norman D. Stevens

552. Bulletin of the American Society for Information Science, Vol. 1- , No. 1- . Washington, D.C., American Society for Information Science, 1974- . bimonthly. $50.00/yr. (United States, Canada, and Mexico); $60.00/yr. (other foreign countries); $11.00/yr. (included with membership); $9.00 (single issue). ISSN 0095-4403.

The American Society for Information Science (ASIS) issues two official publications. The *Journal of the American Society for Information Science* is cited as the official journal of the society. The articles in this publication are predominantly research-oriented—scholarly and technical papers contributed by information science professionals. With its emphasis on statistical analysis, the society's journal is not for the casual reader. The *Bulletin of the American Society for Information Science*, on the other hand, is described as "a news magazine that concentrates on issues affecting the information science field, pragmatic management reports, opinion, and the news of people and events in the information science community" (p. 2 of the cover). The *Bulletin*, therefore, will probably appeal more to the general reader as well as to the one wishing to acquire specific information on ASIS and information science activities as a whole.

The table of contents of the *Bulletin* is divided into three major sections: "Features," "Columns," and "Departments." The articles in "Features" are short and general; sometimes a number of articles focusing on one specific topic (e.g., health sciences), sometimes dealing with a variety of topics. The "Columns" section

includes information on areas predetermined by the editors to receive ongoing attention: education, policy, international, standards, etc. "Columns" are not included in every issue of the *Bulletin*. Obviously, they are written based on the availability and relevance of information. The "Departments" section is divided into four categories: "Inside ASIS," "Information Science News," "Information Science Products," and "Information Science Events." This section can be viewed as the news section of the publication. It focuses primarily on ASIS activities and its members as well as on products and affiliated groups and their activities as they relate to ASIS.

The publications in the library and information science field most similar to the *Bulletin of the American Society for Information Science* are *American Libraries* and *Library Journal*. The general type of news information, feature articles, and the length of those articles found in all three publications are conceptually the same. The *Bulletin* and *American Libraries*, however, can be viewed as house organs of specific organizations. As a result, news of those organizations is the focal point. The perspectives found in each publication can be different, and of course, certain news items are more relevant to one than the other. While the overall contents of *Library Journal* are similar to the *Bulletin* and *American Libraries*, it is not nearly as closely associated with an organization as are the latter two publications.

Based on the publisher's description of what is included and what its objectives are, the *Bulletin* succeeds admirably. Feature articles are well written and concise. Because of the frequency of the publication (bimonthly), there is an understandable time lag between the time that an event occurs and the time it is reported. Other publications make up for this lack. Evaluated on its own merits, the *Bulletin* is a valuable publication, providing needed information to its community.

A careful review of the audience served must be made if budgetary constraints come into play, and an "either/or" decision must be made among the four publications cited. The *Journal of the American Society for Information Science* is certainly the most scholarly and analytical publication of the four, appealing to a narrower audience than the others. The differences between the *Bulletin of the American Society for Information Science* and *American Libraries* and *Library Journal*, however, are not that wide in scope. A slightly different slant among these publications and the frequency of the news items are the major differences. As always, the adage "know your community" is the bottom line.

Marjorie E. Bloss

553. The Canadian Journal of Information Science, Vol. 1- , No. 1- . Ottawa, Canadian Association for Information Science, 1976- . quarterly. free with membership. ISSN 0380-9218.

Published for the express purpose of contributing "to the advancement of information science in Canada," this is the official journal of the Canadian Association for Information Science. Published annually since 1976, with volume 11 (1986) it has become a quarterly publication.

A refereed journal, it includes scholarly articles and with the change in frequency has begun to add book reviews and brief announcements. The articles are of high quality and the scope of the journal is broad, covering topics in both library science and information science. Emphasis is on research findings and many of the papers relate to research in Canada. However, the topics are of international interest and the policy is to include only articles which have not been published elsewhere. A sample of topics covered in past issues includes telecommunications, computer conferencing and education, cognition and expert systems, online searching, microcomputer software, and transborder data flow. With the change in frequency, the editors are seeking to broaden the scope of the journal to include more international contributions. They are also encouraging the submission of short papers on new findings and papers on the "design and application of information systems, user studies, managerial and economic analyses of information systems and services." The book reviews appear to be of good quality and are both critical and informative, although as yet, too few reviews have been published to make a general judgment possible.

The format of the journal is attractive. Page presentation is clear and aesthetically pleasing and headings and subheadings are prominently set out in boldface type. Some articles are in English, while others are in French, but regardless of the language of the text of the article, the titles and abstracts are in both languages. Access to the contents of the journal is enhanced by its coverage in six indexing services, including *Computer and Control Abstracts, Library and Information Science Abstracts, Library Literature,* and *Social Sciences Citation Index.*

This journal is the Canadian counterpart of the *Journal of the American Society for Information Science,* and as such makes a major contribution to the research literature of the field.

Nancy J. Williamson

554. College & Research Libraries News, Vol. 1- , No. 1- . Chicago, Association of College and Research Libraries, American Library Association, 1939- . 11 issues/yr. $15.00/yr.; $3.50 (single issue). ISSN 0099-0086.

In the almost twenty years since *C&RL News* first appeared, it has experienced many changes, most of them creating an ever more useful and polished publication. Editors such as Davis Kaser, Michael Herbison, Allan Dyson, John Crowly, and George Eberhart have expanded the publication into something closer to a small journal than a newsletter. Even during the early years the total number of pages was impressive (350 to 425 pages per year), but currently the average is closer to 700 pages. Slick covers, occasional color photographs, and increasingly longer "news" articles also create a journal-like appearance.

One of the major factors leading to establishment of *C&RL News* was a need to handle an increasing volume of articles and news items in *College & Research Libraries (C&RL).* The "first supplement" to *College & Research Libraries* was in May 1966. Authorization was "to begin publication, as soon as possible, of a series of monthly news supplements, thus separating the two types of information service: (1) a scholarly journal and (2) rapid news dissemination."[1] While a few individuals may question how scholarly *C&RL* may be, no one questions the success of *C&RL News* in meeting its stated purpose. About the only other library publication that is more rapid in news dissemination would be R. R. Bowker's *Library Hotline.* Given the differences in frequency, scope of coverage, and purpose, the two are just about equal.

Basic areas of coverage have remained fairly constant over the years. "News from the Field" has been present since the beginning, as has "Personnel" (now "People"). Over the years subsections of the veteran columns have been split off to form separate columns. For example, today's "Publications" and "Calendar" (formerly "Meetings") were part of "News from the Field." "Publications" provides brief annotations of items thought to be of interest to ACRL section members; frequently the items are of the type that book review editors would not select for review in a scholarly/professional journal. Entries always provide ordering information. "Calendar" lists meetings, workshops, conferences, and programs of potential interest by month. If you are seeking information about a meeting, you must check each issue, as this column's coverage is spotty and somewhat inconsistent. For example, the April 1987 issue listed programs for August and October, while the June 1987 issue made no mention of either month and there was no "Calendar" section in the July/August 1987 issue. "People" now has five subsections: "Profiles," which provides two- or three-paragraph biographies (with photograph) of selected individuals who are changing jobs; "People in the News," which contains single-paragraph announcements of special awards, honors, and activities of ACRL section members; "Appointments," which provides single-sentence announcements of recent job changes; and "Retirements," which is similar in format to "People in the News," as is "Deaths." "Washington Hotline" is now a regular feature, as is the classified ads section.

The "news" articles are of a very diverse character, ranging from "ACRL President's Report, 1986/87" to reports of programs in libraries, and covering such items as "think/opinion" pieces and preliminary reports on projects and research activities. Often drafts of standards or service statements are published, thus providing all members of the ACRL section with an opportunity to read and comment. For example, the April 1987 issue contained a draft position paper, from the Community and Junior College Libraries' Committee on Services to the Disadvantaged, on service to the academically disadvantaged. The article noted that an open hearing would be held in San Francisco and/or written comments could be sent to the committee chair. Approved standards, guidelines, and statements are usually first published in *C&RL News* and later are made available as separate ALA publications. In essence this is the basic method of communicating current news to all members of ACRL. It has, and continues to perform, this function effectively and efficiently.

Notes

1"ACRL Board of Directors—Brief Minutes," *College & Research Libraries* 27 (March 1966): 150.

G. Edward Evans

555. **The Horn Book Magazine**, Vol. 1- , No. 1- . Boston, Horn Book, 1924- . 6 issues/yr. $30.00/yr.; $33.00/yr. (foreign); $5.00 (single issue). ISSN 0018-5078.

The Horn Book Magazine began in 1924 as the vehicle of the Bookshop for Boys and Girls in Boston. Bertha Mahoney Miller, the proprietor, and Elinor Whitney Field wanted to share their enthusiasm, or as Miller stated at the beginning of the first issue, "to blow the horn for fine books for boys and girls" (untitled background information provided by the editor). Hence the title *Horn Book* and the horn-blowing huntsmen parading across the cover for years.

Reviews of books have always been an important feature of the *Horn Book* although its initial emphasis reflected the bookstore milieu. The magazine's editors have tried to respond to the time in which they wrote. For example, in the 1940s *Horn Book* articles addressed the effects on children of the war and celebrated the survivors. Its editors reacted calmly to the influx of controversial books led by J. D. Salinger's *Catcher in the Rye* (Little, Brown, 1951) (untitled, p. 10). Illustrators became more important after the war and were added to the stable of writers for the *Horn Book*. "The Horn Book League" gave children a sounding board within the magazine from 1949 to around the mid-1970s.

Jennie Lindquist assumed the editorship in 1951 and responded to the emphasis on series books such as Beginner Books and the Landmark series (untitled, p. 14). Ruth Hill Viguers became the editor in 1958. She continued the pattern of responding to trends by adding science reviewer Isaac Asimov, and by increasing the total number of reviews in light of expanded federal funding for school libraries and the resulting publishing boom. She also maintained the *Horn Book* tradition in support of "fine books." The reviewer still has a copy of Frances Clarke Sayers's attack on Walt Disney's "debasement of the traditional literature of childhood" (untitled, p. 19), which appeared while Viguers was editor. It continues to be a valid comment according to such authors as Jo Carr who urges "The Pursuit of Excellence in a Disney World" (*Top of the News*, Summer 1987, pp. 357-59).

Paul Heins became the first male editor of the *Horn Book* in time to add paperback coverage in the mid-1960s and to help mourn the curtailment of publishing of children's literature brought about by decreasing federal funds. The developing young adult fiction received mixed reviews in the pages of the *Horn Book* during Heins's editorship. He introduced a column about children's books in England and followed in Bertha Miller's footsteps in welcoming "diversity of opinion not only in [*Horn Book*'s] book reviews, but in its articles" (untitled, p. 24). His wife, Ethel Heins, became the editor in the mid-1970s. She introduced the "Second Look" at important older titles and began reviewing Spanish books.

In 1985, Anita Silvey became the editor. She reemphasized the magazine's beginnings by including a column called "Musings," by Bob Hale, founder of the New England Booksellers Association. Picture books, Books in the Classroom, and autobiographies of reviewers received attention. But always the editors sought, in the face of a wide range of materials, to review a few select titles.

A typical issue of *Horn Book* has thirty-eight pages of advertising, twelve articles or columns from two to seven pages long, and reviews for over fifty hardbacks with brief descriptive entries for a lesser number of paperbacks. Out-of-print and Spanish-language books also get a look. Articles tend to be by or about authors and illustrators. There are regular columns on bookstores, publishers, and the classroom and reading.

Many of the articles are acceptance speeches for children and young adult literature awards such as the Newbery and Caldecott Awards. Most of these speeches are available to the library user in such publications as *Top of the News* (the journal of the Association for Library Service to Children and the Young Adult Services Division units of the American Library Association).

The *Horn Book* reviews are much like those in *School Library Journal* and *Booklist*, although *Horn Book* reviews tend to be longer, more loosely knit, with more emphasis on literature and illustration. *School Library Journal* and *Booklist* reviews appear to say nearly as much but in fewer words and to put more emphasis on relation of materials to curriculum and other user needs. Probably the greatest difference in the reviews is in the number available. The *Horn Book* reviews around fifty to seventy hardbacks including fiction and nonfiction for preschool through young adult according to a sample of six issues. A sample of *School Library Journal* averaged over 200 hardback reviews while *Booklist* averaged over 125.

The *Horn Book* does include reissues and paperbacks, Spanish books, and special columns relating to specific areas. While *Booklist* does not cover Spanish books in each issue, it features books in such languages as Spanish, French, Creole, Korean, French Canadian, and Russian in different issues. "Paperback Reprints" appears to be a once-a-month feature in *Booklist*.

Both *School Library Journal* and *Booklist* offer reviews of audiovisual materials and computer software. These are important to school, children's, and young adult librarians. Apparently the closest *Horn Book* comes to reviewing

in the nonprint format is reviewing wordless picture books.

Both *Horn Book* and *School Library Journal* offer articles. But while most of *Horn Book*'s articles are by and about authors (nice but not essential for the librarian), a typical issue of *School Library Journal* might offer articles on art exhibits, teenage reading, a survey of high/low fiction, and how to preserve family history, in addition to a number of short articles on the news related to school and public library interests, reviews of professional books for librarians, and a checklist of free and inexpensive materials available. *Booklist* does not offer articles, but it does review adult fiction and nonfiction and gives detailed reviews of reference books.

The relative cost—*School Library Journal*, ten issues, $54.00; *Booklist*, twenty-two issues, $47.00; and the *Horn Book*, six issues, $30.00—seems to favor the *Horn Book* until one considers issue price. When one adds to that the other features, school and public libraries will no doubt continue to consider *Booklist* and/or *School Library Journal* essential selection tools. *School Library Journal* may also be considered an important source of library management information. *Horn Book*, with its well-done reviews "of a few select titles" and its literary articles will probably continue to be a "nice to have" magazine for libraries and others who are interested in reviews of many books. It may have a wider audience in or be a more frequent first choice of literature or reading teachers and bookstore managers who like information about authors and are not likely to be exposed to library-related periodicals such as *Top of the News*.   Betty Jo Buckingham

556. IFLA Journal: Official Quarterly Journal of the International Federation of Library Associations and Institutions, Vol. 1- , No. 1- . Munich, New York, K. G. Saur, 1975- . 4 issues/yr. $50.00/yr. ISSN 0340-0352.

IFLA Journal, the official quarterly journal of the International Federation of Library Associations and Institutions, was originally designed "as a means of communication between members of the library profession." The first issue appeared in 1975 under the direction of W. R. H. Koops with the assistance of an eight-member editorial committee. This editorial structure still exists, with Koops as current editor. The journal itself is a successor to *IFLA News* and the "IFLA Communications Section" of the journal *Libri*.

The contents, which cover all aspects of librarianship around the world, consist mainly of state-of-the-art reviews, surveys of IFLA activities, and IFLA statements. The news and reports section are always in English, whereas other material is either in French, German, or English. Abstracts of articles in all three languages follow the contents page. Occasionally an issue is devoted to special topics: volume 12, number 4 (1986) was devoted entirely to articles on IFLA's core programs; number 1 (1986) was partially devoted to preservation.

The journal itself has a neat, crisp appearance, using white and a handsome green to frame the contents on the cover of each issue. Illustrations, diagrams, and reproduced photographs appear when needed. Articles are well written and edited and informative. *Libri*, the *Unesco Bulletin for Libraries, International Library Review,* and the *IFLA Journal* cover the field of international librarianship in complementary ways. *IFLA Journal*, however, is necessary reading for those wishing to stay abreast of IFLA activities and projects worldwide.

Robert H. Burger

557. **Journal of Librarianship**, Vol. 1- , No. 1- . London, Library Association, 1969- . quarterly. $79.00/yr.; £35.00/yr. (United Kingdom); £42.00/yr. (other countries). ISSN 0022-2232.

In 1967 the British Library Association formulated a plan to establish a quarterly journal — not an official publication (which already existed in the form of their *Library Association Record*) — but rather a scholarly general journal designed to cover a broad range of interests. At that time, the Association's Publications Committee concluded that such a journal would not lack for material (the *Record* being inundated with articles, most of which had to be shortened in order to fit into that publication's format) and that recent developments in libraries and library research would be well served by a new forum.

Thus in January 1969, over the objections of some Association members who took issue with its subscription status, the *Journal of Librarianship* began. Patterned in some ways after the successful *Journal of Documentation*, the journal in its early days included three to four articles and one signed review per issue. From the beginning, the articles covered a broad range of topics: academic and public libraries, foreign libraries, library history, bibliographical issues, and technical services. Articles in the first volume included "Library Provision for the Indian and Pakistani Communities in Britain" and "University Libraries in English-speaking Central Africa." Early contributors included D. J. Foskett, B. C. Vickery, and Alec Ellis. And

from the beginning as well, authors were paid a fee for their manuscripts, which were tightly refereed. Even in its early stages, the journal was financially successful, breaking even its first year. Today its subscribers number fourteen hundred, two-thirds of whom are overseas.

The first editor of the journal, F. J. Cornell, presided over its publication for twelve years, until 1980. During that time, the journal established a well-deserved reputation for readability, a reputation that exceeded that of the *Journal of Documentation*, which tends to become highly technical. In 1976, under Cornell, the journal expanded its reviewing practices, and since that time the number of critical reviews in each issue has increased considerably. Anywhere from three to ten books might be reviewed in a single issue, with each review running between five hundred to one thousand words. At times, several similar books are covered in one review. Occasional review articles appear as well, in which the review is expanded into a discussion of pertinent literature and topics. These normally average between two thousand and three thousand words in length. Recent review articles have included "The Literature of Librarianship and Information Science," by R. T. Bottle and "Tackling the Big One: Cataloguing the Books of the Nineteenth Century," by Clive Hurst.

Material for publication is chosen by a nine-member editorial board, which includes the editor of the *Library Association Record* and the managing editor of the *Journal of Documentation*, as well as practicing librarians. In addition, the board calls upon the pooled talents of their twelve editorial consultants. Until recently this group comprised mostly librarians from the United Kingdom, but since 1984 membership has become increasingly international. Current consultants are from a variety of nations: Italy, the United States, India, Hong Kong, West Germany, Brazil, Nigeria, Norway, and Australia. Oddly, the number of articles devoted to comparative librarianship has remained much the same.

Since Cornell's term as editor ended in 1980, the journal has had four editors in rather quick succession: David Pratt (1980), Frances Toms (1983), Frances Moore (1985), and Susan Elders (1987). The change in editors has brought little change in format. The typical issue today still contains three to four articles running between four thousand and seven thousand words in length and three to ten book reviews. Examples of current articles include "Racially Segregated School Libraries in Kwazulu/Natal, South Africa," "Libraries and Humanistic Scholarship," "Rural Information Provision in

Leicestershire," "French Library and Information Careers," "Public Libraries and Technical Education 1850-1902," and "Evaluation of Technical Services Functions."

The change in editors has, however, brought about a change in design. The spare, elegant cover designed by Margaret Sweeney (a student of Eric Gill) was replaced with a more contemporary but less appealing cover designed by Mechanick Exercises in 1981; the same firm produced yet another cover in 1982, one that was equally modern but slightly more distinguished. That cover remains in use today. The typeface, too, went through several changes under the aegis of new editorships. The original Centaur, designed by Bruce Rogers, gave way to Helios and Garamond in 1981, only to be replaced by Helvetica and Garamond a year later. The resulting design in use today is sleek, modern, and dignified, somehow less bookish than the original but not unattractive.

Alix Thayer

558. **Journal of Youth Services in Libraries** (formerly *Top of the News*), Vol. 1- , No. 1- . Chicago, Association for Library Service to Children, American Library Association, 1987- . quarterly. $25.00/yr. (United States, Canada, Mexico, Spain, and other PUAS countries); $12.50 (included in membership dues); $35.00/yr. (other foreign countries); $8.00 (single issue). ISSN 0040-9286.

With the fall 1987 issue, *Top of the News* (which has been published since 1942) changed its name to *Journal of Youth Services in Libraries* (*JOYS*). *Journal of Youth Services in Libraries* is the quarterly journal of the Association for Library Service to Children (ALSC) and the Young Adult Services Division (YASD), both of which are divisions of the American Library Association. It "primarily serves as a vehicle for continuing education for librarians working with children and young adults, as a showcase for current practice in both specialties, and as a spotlight for significant activities and programs of both divisions" (title page). It is indexed in *Library Literature, Library and Information Science Abstracts, Current Index to Journals in Education,* and *Book Review Index.* The journal averages about nineteen pages of advertising from as many companies, nearly 90 percent of which are publishers, producers, or jobbers. Regular columns include "Top of the News," a potpourri of information about awards, association projects, program announcements, publicity materials, and professional publications, "Editor's Note," "Reviews" (of professional books), and "Focus on Research." Several issues

also offered a section on letters including typical "letters to the editor" for its offerings.

Many of the major articles relate to literature or association activities, such as award acceptance speeches, controversy in children's literature, and females in children's literature. However, topics like the history of public library service, education of librarians serving children and young people, the management of collections, and the importance of networking are also covered.

The journal has regularly reviewed professional books. The majority of reviews seem related to selection of material and presentation of books through storytelling or booktalks, but nearly a fourth dealt with library management or instruction, frequently for school libraries rather than children or youth departments in other libraries.

There are few journals which could be said to be like the *Journal of Youth Services in Libraries.* The *Horn Book,* for example, includes many of the same award speeches, but places more emphasis on reviews and gives no attention to library management. Perhaps the most nearly comparable journal would be the *School Library Media Quarterly* (*SLMQ*), published by the American Association of School Librarians (AASL), the other "youth division" of the American Library Association. *SLMQ* "is read by building level library media specialists, district supervisors, and others concerned with the selection and purchase of print and nonprint media and with the development of programs and services for preschool through high school libraries" (title page). It is indexed in most of the sources that index *JOYS,* plus several more. It has less but more diverse advertising. Both carry information about awards, conferences, and projects. Both include the ALSC and YASD "notable" books and audiovisual materials lists. Where *JOYS* provides the most news about ALSC and YASD, *SLMQ* offers more news about the AASL.

Both periodicals have a research column, but the approach is different. *JOYS* typically covers one research topic or examines related concerns such as how to find grants. *SLMQ* covers one research topic in-depth, discusses briefly a number of research-related ERIC publications, and occasionally notes dissertations in progress.

Both periodicals review professional materials, but *SLMQ* includes more titles relating to management, especially of school library media centers. Neither publication consistently reviews student books, but *SLMQ* regularly presents reviews of computer software of use to students, teachers, and library media specialists.

SLMQ articles stress management, planning for teaching of learning skills and other administrative concerns, although it does include topics such as "Books to Help Kids Deal with Difficult Times" (Spring 1987), and a regular column, "Book Sharing," by Lee Bennett Hopkins. *SLMQ* rounds out its offerings with an "Issues Alert" column edited by Eileen Cooke of the American Library Association's Washington Office, a "Readers' Queries" column which addresses questions raised by conference attendees or mailed to the journal by readers, and an "Idea Exchange" which provides a vehicle for members to share ideas that have worked for them.

For the school library media specialist who must limit the number of journals purchased, *School Library Media Quarterly* offers more about management, more ideas, plus reviews of computer software and the same "notable" lists that *Journal of Youth Services in Libraries* offers. For the children or young adult services librarian who is less concerned with management than with literature and needs management with a public library flavor, *JOYS* will be an important journal.

For the school library media specialist with a strong interest in literature, especially in the selection activities of the ALSC and YASD, *Journal of Youth Services in Libraries* will also be a major journal. In addition, the journal may be considered more informal, and, therefore more appealing, to some readers.

Betty Jo Buckingham

559. **Voice of Youth Advocates**, Vol. 1- , No. 1- . New Brunswick, N.J., Voice of Youth Advocates, 1978- . bimonthly. $27.00/yr.; (add $4.00 for foreign orders). ISSN 0160-4201.

Voice of Youth Advocates (*VOYA*) is a bimonthly, national professional journal for young adult librarians serving the middle school through senior high levels. Its major focus is on providing book reviews, although other media formats are also covered. Although articles and features seem directed at school library media specialists, this periodical would also be of interest to public librarians working with teens and preteens.

VOYA began publication in April 1978 under the editorship of Dorothy M. Broderick and Mary K. Chelton, two young adult librarians who felt that young adult services were often neglected, as they were so often lumped together with children's services. Broderick is now managing editor of *VOYA*; Chelton is senior consulting editor.

In an interview published in *Illinois Librarian* (65 [September 1983]: 445-46), Chelton explained how undertaking this publication was an attempt to counteract this bias towards YA services in the library press and to provide a wide range of perspectives in youth development. In her words, "we are really trying to advocate YA exposure to multiple points of view" (p. 446), and "to articulate the developmental and philosophical basis for a service to adolescents" (p. 445). So the journal was begun with the editors securing a small personal bank loan, purchasing some duplicating equipment, and producing the early issues from their homes. It is easy for the reader to see how, over the years, the initial homemade "offset" look gradually evolved into the present sophisticated, professionally produced publication. One of the first improvements was justification of the margins (perhaps using a microcomputer word processing package) in 1982, then a slick laminated-type cover in 1983, and in 1984 the addition of the stripe on the cover which adorns the current issues. Even from the very start the editors included a large number of reviews (over two hundred per issue) and the number of pages per issue has been fairly consistent (approximately fifty to fifty-five pages).

In a recent editorial column ("On My Mind," April 1987) Broderick, reflecting on the tenth year of publication of *VOYA*, stated: "First and foremost, VOYA exists to carry the message to adults working with adolescents that young people have a right to read, view, or listen to the materials that interest them." In perusing issues of the past year (1986), this philosophy is apparent as the books reviewed covered a large share of so-called controversial or alternative titles, dealing with a wide range of topics including adolescent prostitution, love and sexuality, homosexuality, teen pregnancy and parenthood, abortion, adoption and searching for birth parents, sex and the mentally retarded, bioethics, teenage suicide, rape, incest, and sexually transmitted diseases. The more standard adolescent fare is also well covered: biographies of rock music stars; romance; self-image; drug use and abuse; and other issues confronting young adults, such as racial prejudice, constitutional rights, stress, depression, and divorce. Reviews are arranged in the following categories: software; audiovisual; fiction; science fiction and fantasy; nonfiction; pamphlets, professional; reference; and reprints.

Reviews are well written and detailed enough for librarians and media specialists to find them very useful in making appropriate selections for their YA collections. Even those who would object to providing some of the titles for youngsters can, at least, know what is out there for them to read. A typical review is about

250 words in length, but some are twice that long or more. The reviews contain many critical and evaluative comments in a style that is direct and informal. Sometimes brief excerpts from the book are quoted; at other times comparisons are made from one title to others by the same author or to works that might have similar appeal to young people. Each review is assigned at least three codes, as each title is ranked for quality (Q), popularity (P), and grade level (M, J, or S). Even the terminology of excerpts from *VOYA*'s rating scale (Book Review Code) provides some of the editorial style and flavor of this refreshing periodical: "5Q Hard to imagine it being better written, 2Q Better editing or work by the author might have warranted a 3Q, 1Q Hard to understand how it got published, except in relation to its P rating (and not even then sometimes)" or "5P Every YA (who reads) was dying to read it yesterday ... 3P Will appeal with pushing, and 1P No YA will read unless forced to for assignments."

In addition to reviews, some regular features of *VOYA* include the editorials, news columns, articles by and about YA librarians (or special aspects of librarianship for adolescents and the school media centers that service them), extensive topical reading lists, and an index. Each issue is liberally interspersed with illustrated publishers' advertisements. Popular music is regularly reviewed in a section called "Rockingchair."

Emergency Librarian, a Canadian published periodical, provides some of the same services for school librarians as does *VOYA*. It includes a regular section reviewing magazines, but it does not begin to review as many books, or have the scope of coverage, as does *VOYA*. Nor are the style and tone as interesting, being somewhat more stilted. *Booklist* has sections devoted to young adult material and some articles about them, but reviews are briefer and YA coverage less extensive. While *School Library Journal* has lengthier reviews and provides more help in the way of computer software and audiovisual materials, for sheer volume of books reviewed *VOYA* is, again, ahead of the game. On the other hand, a young adult librarian who picks up a copy of *VOYA* is immediately totally immersed (visually and verbally) in YA interests and issues.

Most young adult librarians would find *VOYA* a very readable and relevant journal, as well as an excellent reviewing source and selection guide. *VOYA* is indexed in *Library Literature, Book Review Digest, Science Fiction Index, Book Review Index,* and by ERIC for *Current Journals in Education.*   Lois Buttlar

SUBJECT-ORIENTED

560. **Academic Library Book Review**, Vol. 1- , No. 1- . Lynbrook, N.Y., E.B.S., 1984- . 6 issues/yr. $36.00/yr.; $44.00/yr. (foreign); $7.50 (single issue).

As its title indicates, this publication provides reviews of books suitable for academic libraries. A few reference works are reviewed, but periodicals and nonprint materials are not. The reviews are arranged under some nineteen subject headings such as art and architecture, computers, engineering, history, law, literature, psychology, science and technology, and social science. There are an average of about 88 titles in each issue (based on the four issues examined by this reviewer) for a total of about 528 titles per year. Of the eighty-six titles in the June 1987 issue, fifty-nine had a publication date of 1987, twenty-four had a date of 1986, and two were included from 1985. Author, title, and publishers' indexes accompany each issue.

The bibliographic information includes author and/or editor, title, subtitle, edition, publisher, date, number of pages, LC number, ISBN, and price. The place of publication is not given. Information on whether the book also has such features as a bibliography, index, maps, charts, and illustrations is often, but not always, included. Unfortunately there are frequent errors in this information. In one issue authors' names are misspelled in two reviews; words are misspelled in three titles; and in one entry in addition to a co-author's name being mistakenly placed first, the ISBN is incorrect.

The reviews themselves vary in length from about seventy-five to three hundred words. They range from short, descriptive reviews to those that provide thorough, critical evaluations with recommendations for purchase. A few negative and mixed reviews can be found among the largely favorable or neutral ones. Comparisons to previous editions or similar works are not always made. For example, both the *Book of Days 1987* (Pierian Press, 1986) and *Directory of Research Grants* (Oryx Press, 1987) could have been compared to similar reference books, the latter to previous editions as well. Many errors in spelling and punctuation detract attention from the reviews themselves, as do awkward sentence constructions, words used in the wrong context, and pronouns with no antecedents.

Each review is signed. Short one- to four-line biographies are provided for reviewers in a list at the end of each issue. The reviewers come from a wide variety of backgrounds; a few are professors or librarians, but most are teachers or authors and hands-on people such as practicing attorneys, biologists, artists, dancers, social workers, and engineers.

Of the major book reviewing publications *Choice* is the only one that targets the same audience as *ALBR*; both concentrate on the undergraduate level of academic libraries. Though *Choice* reviews about ten times as many books per year as *ALBR*, a title by title check of one *ALBR* issue showed only eleven out of eighty-six titles were reviewed in both. Of these eleven titles the reviews for seven appeared first in *Choice*, three were in *ALBR* first, and one appeared in the same month. In contrast to the large number of hands-on reviewers for *ALBR*, the majority of *Choice* reviewers are professors and librarians. Reviews are signed in both. *Choice* reviews generally include a recommendation statement; *ALBR* only occasionally includes such a statement.

In spite of its limited coverage of the total number of academic books published each year, this publication might have been useful as a supplemental source of book reviews if not for the errors, omissions, and inconsistencies described above.

Anna L. DeMiller

561. Advanced Technology/Libraries, Vol. 1- , No. 1- . Boston, G. K. Hall, 1972- . monthly. $78.00/yr.; $7.50 (single issue). ISSN 0044-636X.

This monthly "green" newsletter has been published continuously since 1971. Published by Becker and Hayes in Los Angeles in 1971 and 1972 and by Knowledge Industry Publications in New York from 1973 to January 1978, it is currently being published by G. K. Hall in Boston. The format is strictly that of a newsletter, with no attempt to expand news items beyond three hundred to five hundred words. It offers the latest in newsworthy information from the world of information technology. A brief index on the front page facilitates scanning for news items of interest. Since it is restricted to timely news items, the publication's focus differs from its nearest competitors, *Library Hi Tech News* and *Library Systems Newsletter*, both of which include other features as well as offering limited coverage of short news items. Targeting some of the same readers as *Information Today* and *InfoWorld*, *Advanced Technology/Libraries* nevertheless maintains its unique position by offering a quick overview of the most current events in the fast-paced information world. Keeping up with the rapid changes in the information technology industry is difficult in any case; *Advanced Technology/Libraries* is well worth the price to make the task a little easier.

Elisabeth Logan

562. Art Documentation: Bulletin of the Art Libraries Society of North America, Vol. 1- , No. 1- . Tucson, Ariz., ARLIS/NA, 1982- . 4 issues/yr. free with membership; $35.00/yr. (foreign). ISSN 0730-7187.

Art Documentation replaces the former *ARLIS/NA Newsletter*, which ceased publication with volume 9, number 6, December 1981. The first two volumes of *AD* comprised five issues (six numbers, with one combined issue); since 1984, *AD* has been published quarterly. *AD* serves as a vehicle to communicate recent research, current news and views, calendars, and ARLIS/NA organizational information to its membership, the primary audience. The focus is on subjects pertinent to art and/or architecture, library and information science, and library collections and services.

Each issue includes approximately five researched and documented articles, written in a lucid, formal style. A sampling of articles from recent issues: "Who Are the Folk in Folk Art? Inside and Outside the Cultural Contexts," and "Bibliographic Databases for the Art Researcher" (Spring 1987); "Bibliographic Instruction for Museum Docents," and "Service in the Client-Centered Library" (Winter 1986); "Architecture without the Capital 'A': Documentation in a Postmodern Age," "Archives of American Art/ Smithsonian Institution," and "Artists' Video Collections: The Banff Experience" (Fall 1986). Variety and quality are evident in each issue.

In addition to articles, the following columns are regular features: "Reports of Conferences and Meetings"; "ARLIS/NA News Section," wherein special interest groups within the organization provide brief reports, news items, etc.; "Government Publications," "On Preservation," "Professional Literature," "Women and Art Documentation Group," "AAT Update," "Bibliographic Notes," "News and Notes"; and "The Review Section," containing professional reviews for the art/architecture selector. An average of fifteen reviews appears in each issue: these are signed reviews averaging five hundred words in length. Appended is a list of publications received, but not yet reviewed.

By providing a variety of columns and features, coupled with sound, well-researched, and well-written articles, *AD* makes a significant contribution to the professional development of librarians, curators, and other readers. Display advertising appears throughout — a well-planned visual diversion from the text. As a physical product, the bulletin has a clean, uncluttered appearance, reinforcing the orderly nature of the contents.

The editors are to be congratulated for producing a pertinent, quality publication. Recommended for relevant collections.

Edmund F. SantaVicca

563.   **Art Libraries Journal**, Vol. 1- , No. 1- . Preston, England, ARLIS/UK and Eire, 1976- . quarterly. £29.00/yr.; free with membership. ISSN 0307-4722.

This sophisticated periodical began publication in 1976. It is published by the British and Irish Art Libraries Society for the art library profession. From its inception, it has had as its goal the coverage of international developments in art librarianship.

Philip Pacey, who served as the original editor from 1976 to 1978, has returned to that post as of 1986. Pacey's affiliation with IFLA (International Federation of Library Associations) and his four years as Chair of the Art Libraries Section of that organization brought him in contact with art libraries and librarians throughout the world. With these many contacts, he has shaped a journal which features articles about collections and developments in many countries. Most of the articles are descriptive, informing readers of the history and development of various collections and organizational methods. Automation projects are of continuing interest. Each article has a brief boldface abstract at the beginning in English, although occasional articles are in another European language. Frequently references are cited, and there are occasional illustrations.

Each issue includes at least one book review or a bibliographic update. These are thoughtful, signed considerations of professional literature, or books of major interest to art librarians.

North American art librarians will find this a valuable resource. Its character is a bit more formal than the newsy and informative quarterly *Art Documentation* published by ARLIS/NA (Art Libraries Society of North America). However, the continuing focus on art libraries in other countries and depictions of unusual resources are most informative. It differs considerably from another scholarly international journal: *Visual Resources: An International Journal of Documentation* (quarterly), which is published by the Visual Resources Association. *Visual Resources* is more closely focused on pictorial, slide, and photograph collections, including matters of conservation and iconography.

This journal is highly recommended for all art libraries as well as for information and library science collections.

Sydney Starr Keaveney

564.   **Book Research Quarterly**, Vol. 1- , No. 1- . New Brunswick, N.J., Transaction Periodicals Consortium, 1985- . quarterly. $30.00pa./yr.; $50.00pa./yr. (institutions); (add $2.50 for foreign); $15.00pa. (single issue). ISSN 0741-6148.

BRQ first appeared in the spring of 1985, edited for a year by John G. Dessauer, long-time observer of the publishing scene, former statistician for the Association of American Publishers, and head of the Center for Book Research at Scranton. The present editor is Judith Appelbaum, a publishing consultant and editor/columnist/author. Intended for "professional scholars—writers, publishers, printers, binders, librarians, booksellers, critics, and observers—whose lives are devoted to books," the journal seeks to encourage and disseminate research into "the creation, publication, and distribution of books, past, present, and future" (editor's statement in the first issue). Each issue contains articles (often theme-oriented), some statistical notes, and book reviews. Among the issue themes: "The Book in the Electronic Age," "School Adoptions and Textbook Quality," "Culture and Concentration in the Book Industry," and "New Perspectives on Copyright." Volume 3, number 1 (Spring 1987) is typical. The theme is "The Book as a Mass Commodity," with articles by John Leonard, former editor of the *New York Times Book Review*, on the importance of the book; Elizabeth Long, a sociologist, on the audience for books; Leonard A. Wood, of the Gallup Organization, on demographics; and editor Appelbaum, setting the stage for four articles by publishers on 1,000,000 plus copy sellers. Outside the theme is an article on Louisa May Alcott's relations with her publishers, by Donald Shealy, an Alcott specialist at Clemson. There is a column on trends, followed by "Statistical Series," a regular feature with tables of book industry statistics and commentary; and "Reporting Book Prices," another regular column, this one entitled "Managing the Rising Cost of Materials" (in libraries); and ten book reviews, ranging from short notes to a couple of columns. The quality of the contributions ranges from adequate to distinguished; editing seems to be on target and consistent. There have been few illustrations so far. The general impression is that this is a solid contribution to librarians' knowledge of an industry upon which they rely heavily. Most issues have somewhat fewer reviews, the quality of which ranges from so-so to excellent; the coverage of out-of-the-way items is notable. The only other journal of comparable worth is *Scholarly Publishing*, which is devoted to research and commentary on university press and other scholarly publishing; they do not overlap.

Walter C. Allen

565. Canadian Association of Law Libraries Newsletter/Bulletin, Vol. 1- , No. 1- . Toronto, Canadian Association of Law Libraries, 1970- . 5 issues/yr. $45.00/yr.; free with CALL membership. ISSN 0319-5376.

In 1988 the Canadian Association of Law Libraries (CALL) *Newsletter* will be into its thirteenth volume. It is still published five times yearly. Each issue includes a listing of CALL offices, committee and special interest group chairs, editorial guidelines, letters to the editor, and information on application for membership.

The text of each issue consists, *inter alia*, of feature articles, book reviews, bibliographic descriptions of legal research books and periodicals, conference reports, lists of books wanted or available, and news and developments of interest to Canadian law libraries. This newsletter differs from the American Association of Law Libraries (AALL) newsletter in a number of respects. For example, the AALL newsletter does not include feature articles, and it does not include bibliographic descriptions of new publications. In a number of other respects both newsletters are similar in content, except that the AALL newsletter is published on a monthly basis with the exception of January and July.

The CALL newsletter encourages contributions from its members. Emphasis is placed on people, events, and developments in the field, and information on public documents and materials not widely publicized is encouraged.

James M. Murray

566. CD-ROM Librarian, Vol. 1- , No. 1- . Westport, Conn., Meckler Publishing, 1986- . 10 issues/yr. $65.00/yr.; (add $10.00 for foreign). ISSN 0893-9934.

CD-ROM Librarian used to be named *Optical Information Systems Update/Library and Information Center Applications*. The new name does, as the editor notes, better reflect the journal's content. It is also likely to attract more subscribers who will expect a publication with the shorter name to include the practical and applicable product reviews, bibliographies, standards information, and industry and optical news that fill each bimonthly issue.

The journal first appeared in January 1986, offering to "provide critical, unbiased, and informative analysis of products, services, and marketing developments and trends in the optics industry." There are more polished and less expensive publications available that focus on compact disks (e.g., *CD-ROM Review* that costs $19.97/yr. compared to $65.00/yr. for *CD-ROM Librarian*) but none will be more useful to library and information center personnel attempting to make informed decisions concerning a relatively new and rapidly changing technology. Technologically sophisticated readers may find some articles (e.g., "Installing a CD-ROM Drive: A First-Hand Account") too simplistic; those on the industrial cutting edge may be aware of products such as Online Computer Systems' four-drive units and OPTI-NET local area network products before *CD-ROM Librarian* points them out. Most librarians, however, will quickly learn to rely on what is subtitled "The Optical Media Review for Information Professionals" to keep up with trends and to make acquisitions decisions.

Other things besides the name have changed about *CD-ROM Librarian* since it was first published. Its format has improved somewhat, and its price has doubled. The journal's informal style and clear, readable tone are part and parcel of its practical, extremely useful intention; it would be a shame if escalating costs limit librarians' access to this functional tool.

Connie Miller

567. CM: A Reviewing Journal of Canadian Materials for Young People, Vol. 1- , No. 1- . Ottawa, Canadian Library Association, 1971- . 6 issues/yr. $30.00/yr.; $6.00 (single issue). ISSN 0821-1450.

Unpretentious in format and modestly titled, *CM* is a source of some of the sharpest reviewing in Canada: practical, informed evaluation by teachers, librarians, and academics of materials not just for children and young people, but also for adults and professionals. The broad scope includes research and museum publications, regional and small press materials, and films and serials.

Entries provide publisher, date, format, price, ISBN, series, address for small presses, and grade level. All reviews are signed with name and affiliation and there are references to reviews in earlier issues. There are also a column of news and announcements including paperback reprints and a topical article or bibliographic essay. In reviewer's parlance, it is worth the price and highly recommended.

Patricia Fleming

568. Communications of the ACM, Vol. 1- , No. 1- . New York, Association for Computing Machinery, 1958- . monthly. $90.00/yr.; free with membership; $12.00 (single issue); $6.00 (single issue/membership). ISSN 0001-0782.

In the first issue of *Communications of the ACM*, Alan J. Perlis, its editor-in-chief at the time, announced that the intention of the new periodical would be "for the rapid dissemination of information whose kind and quality will be of value to the membership of the Association." It was not to take the place of the *Journal of the ACM*, the first archival research publication in computer science, but instead would "provide space not elsewhere available for publishing worthwhile, but possibly fragmentary, developments in the use and understanding of computers." In 1958 this covered topics such as descriptions of computer programs, computer inspired techniques in numerical analysis, and educational efforts. Beyond that, and perhaps most important, it was to be a forum, at least with the "letters to the editor" department, "for nourishing controversies that illuminate informed differences of opinion." From these clearly stated goals a highly regarded journal has emerged that is now received by over seventy-five thousand members of the ACM worldwide.

Material now presented in the *Communications* appears in one of four sections: articles (or special features), computing practices, research contributions, and departments. Recent articles include such topics as electronic markets and electronic hierarchies, arithmetic coding for data compression, IBM 360-370 architecture, intelligent information sharing systems, and computer system reliability and nuclear war. The writing is very well edited. Because of this and the timely contents, the usefulness of the journal is undisputed, even for those whose primary interest is not the technical side of computing.

Robert H. Burger

569. **Computerworld**, Vol. 1- , No. 1- . Framingham, Mass., CW Communications, 1970- . weekly. $44.00/yr.; $110.00/yr. (Canada, Central & South America); $165.00/yr. (Europe); $245.00/yr. (all other countries); $2.00 (single issue). ISSN 0010-4841.

Computerworld celebrated its twentieth birthday in 1987, making it one of the longest-lived computer periodicals and one of the most important. An introductory issue appeared on 14 June 1967 (volume 1, number 0), and the regular numbering started with 21 June 1967. Although it is described in the masthead as "the newsweekly for the computer community," subscribers have always received more than fifty-two issues a year. A subscription in 1987 would bring fifty-one weekly issues and twelve monthly issues of *FOCUS*.

Computerworld's emphasis has changed over the years as the nature and use of computers have matured. Even in the late 1970s,

there was very little coverage of microcomputers; today micros and their applications easily compete with mainframe and minicomputers for equal space. The periodical emphasizes news and features of interest to persons responsible for management information systems, data processing, and office automation systems. Recent issues have averaged around 130 pages in length. The table of contents illustrates the type of coverage regularly provided: "News," "Software & Services," "Microcomputing," "Networking," "Systems & Peripherals," "Management," "Computer Industry," "Employment Today" (including personnel ads), "Executive Report," "In Depth," "Opinion & Analysis," and three departments. Interspersed are numerous ads, themselves often useful sources of information.

Computerworld supplements its news stories with more in-depth feature coverage in a variety of ways. Special internal supplements, "Spotlights," focus on a variety of topics ranging from the Macintosh market to manufacturing technology. There have been entire issues on special topics, such as "Forecast '87: Harnessing Forces of Change." The monthly *FOCUS* (1985-) issues are also on specific themes. Interestingly, there are no individual reviews of software although there are a few short book reviews in most issues.

Computerworld has a large staff liberally assisted by other writers, many of whom are in the industry. The Macintosh spotlight referred to above, for example, featured a number of established writers who regularly contribute to specialized Macintosh magazines. The quality of writing is good and readable, although a fairly high degree of computer sophistication is presumed. Recent issues have begun making use of color for other features besides advertisements and the periodical is well designed and laid out.

Many persons in the information industries consider *Computerworld* to be required reading. There are other periodicals which are of interest to MIS/DP professionals (for example, the bimonthly but more glossy *Datamation*), but *Computerworld* remains one of the best sources for keeping current on the computer hardware and software industries.

Robert Skinner

570. **Current Research in Library & Information Science**, Vol. 1- , No. 1- . London, Library Association, 1983- . quarterly. $195.00/yr.; £86.00/yr. (United Kingdom); £103.00/yr. (other countries). ISSN 0263-9254.

The successor to the *RADIALS Bulletin*, which ran from 1974 through 1982, this abstracting service lists and describes research projects from all countries, with some emphasis on the United Kingdom and the United States. " 'Research' is used ... in its widest sense, including investigations, studies, surveys, and evaluated innovations." This includes academic work at the doctoral, postdoctoral, or research staff level, as well as "in-house or action research from practising librarians, information workers, archivists and documentalists." In the main section, project descriptions are arranged by the Classification Research Group's scheme (the one used in *Library and Information Science Abstracts*); name and subject indexes are appended. (Beginning in 1986, the name index can be used to find entries by country.) The project descriptions are quite thorough, providing, first, the names of the research workers, expected duration of the work, funding and references, and, second, a description of the project, often in some detail, with the person to be contacted for further information. All information is in English. There is also a listing of "Sub-Doctoral Theses and Dissertations," though so far they have been pretty well confined to British, Canadian, and Australian institutions.

Current Research appears quarterly, with the fourth number a cumulative one. It is an important publication for schools of librarianship and information science, and for anyone interested in keeping abreast of research in those fields.   Evan Ira Farber

571. Documents to the People (DttP), Vol. 1- , No. 1- . Chicago, ALA/GODORT, 1972- . quarterly. $15.00/yr.; free with membership. ISSN 0091-2085.

Now in its fifteenth year, *Documents to the People (DttP)* began as and continues to be the official publication of the Government Documents Round Table (GODORT) of the American Library Association. The first issue of *DttP* appeared in 1972 and since then its frequency of publication has varied. It began as a quarterly publication, switched to a bimonthly, and for the last several years has resumed publication of four issues a year. Several documents librarians have served as editor of this excellent source of current information on government documents, the most distinguished being LeRoy Schwarzkopf, who served as editor from 1978 to 1982. The current editor, whose tenure began with the March 1987 issue, is Diane Garner from the Documents Department at Pennsylvania State University.

Over the years *DttP* has expanded from a fifteen to twenty-five page publication to one now averaging fifty to seventy pages per issue. It has improved its typography, layout, and cover design while at the same time sticking to its editorial goals of providing "current information

on government publications, technical reports, and maps at local, state, national, foreign and international levels; on related governmental activities; and documents libraries" (statement at beginning of each issue). Each issue is crammed full of useful information for documents librarians and those interested in the world of government information. Regular features include "Newsnotes," which covers current activities in documents librarianship; "New Publications," which lists recent documents sources and reference works; "Washington Report," which covers current federal government information activities; and a more recent column called "High Tech Docs," which explores the increasing role of electronic technology and government information.

DttP also contains regular bibliographies on state and local documents, international documents, documents librarianship and government information, as well as extensive reports on GODORT activities at the American Library Association's national and mid-winter meetings. This includes individual committee reports, reports of task forces, and the texts of individual conference programs involving documents. Each issue also contains several short articles on current topics in documents librarianship. In the most recent issues of *DttP* these have included extensive coverage of the Reagan administration's efforts to restrict access to government information.

DttP has become an indispensable source for remaining current on new developments in the fields of government information and documents librarianship, and for providing up-to-date information on GODORT activities. It is an essential periodical for every ALA-accredited library school and any library having even a small documents collection. Documents librarians find *DttP* particularly useful for the wealth of timely information on all areas of government documents contained in every issue.

Louis Vyhnanek

572. Electronic Publishing Business, Vol. 1- , No. 1- . Los Altos, Calif., Electronic Publishing Ventures, 1983- . 11 issues/yr. $95.00/yr.; $120.00/yr. (foreign); $10.00 (single issue); $15.00 (single issue/foreign). ISSN 0888-0848.

This sixteen- to thirty-two-page newsletter succeeded the *EPB Electronic Publishing and Bookselling*, published by Oryx, in May 1986 (no April issue appeared). *EPB* first appeared in May 1983 with three issues, grew to six issues in the second volume (1984), and in May 1985 to twelve. Previous editors Sandra K. Paul and Barbara E. Meyers are listed as associate publishers with the present publishing company.

The new publisher, Brett Butler, defined electronic publishing in the May 1986 issue as encompassing three distinct businesses: "Electronic production of traditional printed publications and non-published information, electronic distribution of information created in both print and electronic form, [and] true electronic publishing of information only in electronic media." The serial is attractively produced but with most graphics confined to advertising, and offers the usual fare of trade newsletters, including a calendar of events, short news features from press releases, conference reports, and editorials. The few book and software reviews in each issue are an excellent guide to the most important developments in the field. The newsletter is served by a knowledgeable editorial board, with Brian Aveney as editor, and a number of contributing editors in such areas as desktop publishing and optical developments. Each issue usually offers a few useful short articles. Examples of topics covered in articles in 1986 included optical storage (CD-ROM and others), bar coding by publishers, the Electronic Manuscript Standard of the Association of American Publishers, and computer use in publishing and marketing.

The high point of most issues is an interview with an exceptionally articulate, even if not necessarily well known, participant in the industry. These wide-ranging, thought-provoking conversations, treating such disparate subjects as a "software of the month" club, computerized type design, and archiving typesetting tapes as a future source for linguistic studies, are worth the pricey (although moderate by trade newsletter standards) subscription rate and deserve a wide audience in the publishing, writing, and library and information communities. For those seeking to monitor the direction and challenges of this dynamic and increasingly important information industry or just to have their thinking broadened and stimulated, it is invaluable. K. Mulliner

573. Information Retrieval & Library Automation, Vol. 1- , No. 1- . Mt. Airy, Md., Lomond Publications, 1965- . monthly. $48.00/yr. ISSN 0020-0220.

This newsletter, or digest as the editor calls it, has been published for twenty-two years under the editorship of Lowell H. Hattery. It began as *Information Retrieval Letter* while the editor was at American University. Its purpose is to serve as a current awareness tool to professionals working in information transfer, library and information networks, computers and systems, videotext, communications, copyright, indexing and the like. It contains terse reports of

new developments, research activities, and future trends. Each issue has a "cover story" of one to two pages in length describing some future trend such as fiber optic communications or CD-ROM. The rest of the issue is divided into three sections: a news section consisting of about five pages of short (one to five paragraphs) summaries of new services, issues, or business ventures; a meetings and seminars section including two or three meeting or seminar descriptions; and a literature section providing five to ten synopses (not really critical reviews) of books, reports, conference proceedings, special journal issues, and the like. A subject and author/title index is published in May.

The layout is very clear and easy to read. It uses a two-column format with capitalized, boldface heads. Boldface type is used throughout to highlight important topics and an occasional small photograph or graph accompanies some articles. The latest issues, of about twelve pages each, are on good quality, buff-colored paper with burgundy type. Although it may be a personal quirk, this reviewer prefers the previous black on white typography. Those issues seem to be easier to read and give a more professional appearance.

There are a number of other newsletters covering library and information systems, and it is difficult to define strengths and weaknesses, or even differences, among them. They all try to carve out their own niches, but there is a great deal of overlap. For example, *Advanced Technology/Libraries* (G. K. Hall, monthly) mostly covers library automation systems, including online searching. It is the poorest in terms of physical layout. It has no apparent organization, looks like a typewritten manuscript, uses no special typefaces other than italics, and is not divided into columns. *Information Hotline* (Science Associates International, monthly) is well presented in quality typeset with color headlines and boldface highlights. It places more emphasis on news items and includes a section on NSF grants. *LITA Newsletter* (American Library Association, quarterly) contains some submitted articles, but the news is mostly of the Library and Information Technology Association. *Library Systems Newsletter* (American Library Association, monthly) contains articles and news of library automation systems, exclusively. It is a spinoff of *Library Technology Reports*, published by ALA.

IRLA is more comprehensive in scope and provides good coverage of new developments. It is consistently well written in terse, but not telegraphic, language (some newsletters are nearly impossible to read because of their tendency to present information in a telegraphic style). Because of its coverage and excellent readability, this publication will go a long way toward helping librarians and other information professionals keep up with their rapidly changing fields.   A. Neil Yerkey

574. **International Cataloguing**, Vol. 1- , No. 1- . London, IFLA UBCIM Programme, 1972- . quarterly. $36.00/yr.; £20.00/yr. (other countries). ISSN 0047-0635.

From 1972 when the first issue was published until 1986 *International Cataloguing* was the official bulletin of the International Federation of Library Associations and Institutions' international program for universal bibliographic control. In 1987 the IFLA Universal Bibliographic Control and the International MARC Programme were merged, with the result that *International Cataloguing* became the "Quarterly Bulletin of the IFLA UBCIM Programme."

Each issue is divided into two main sections. The first section deals with IFLA and UBCIM news and activities. It gives full coverage to the IFLA Division of Bibliographic Control, such as its annual report, reports of international meetings and studies, and news about pertinent activities around the world. Of particular interest is information about part of UBCIM's mandate and the development and revision of the several volumes of the International Standard Bibliographic Description: ISBD(M), ISBD(CM), ISBD(NBM), etc. This section frequently includes notices about books published by IFLA and other publishers, sometimes accompanied by short, unsigned book reviews. More accomplished book reviews can be found in other periodicals. However, from time to time there is a useful notice or review of a book that has not appeared in better reviewing sources because it has been published outside the United States, Canada, or Great Britain, and has not found its way into the normal "reviewing stream."

The second section is devoted to articles on a wide range of topics in the field of national and international bibliographic control. This wide range is demonstrated in the following titles selected at random from volume 15 (1986): "Translating ISBD and AACR2 into Finnish," "The Trend of Classification in Japan," "The Library of Congress Classification: Problems and Prospects in Online Retrieval," and "The Bibliographic Control of United Nations Documents and Publications." Many of these articles are papers presented at the annual IFLA conference. Generally, one issue a year contains articles about bibliographic control in the country that will host the annual conference. The articles tend to be factual rather than philosophical

in content. The majority of articles are published in English, with a few in French. Some French-language articles are preceded by an abstract in English.

International Cataloguing is a slim journal, usually ranging in length from twelve to forty-eight pages, without illustrations, color, or advertising. There appears to have been little attempt to make it visually appealing. The writing in the first section is concise and factual, with few rhetorical embellishments. A knowledge of the vocabulary and acronyms associated with bibliographic control is assumed. Writing styles in the second section reflect the diversity of its contributors. However, the general style is scholarly.

A yearly index is supplied, and the journal itself is indexed in *Library Literature* and *Library and Information Science Abstracts*.

Because of its slight size and unattractive format, *International Cataloguing* could be easily overlooked. This would be a mistake. No other periodical focuses its attention on international bibliographic control to the degree found here. *International Cataloguing* is an essential acquisition for those catalogers or institutions wishing to keep abreast of bibliographic control in other countries, of international library standards, and/or of the activities of IFLA in these fields.   Jean Weihs

575. **International Leads**, Vol. 1- , No. 1- . Madison, Wis., International Relations Round Table, American Library Association, c/o University of Wisconsin, 1987- . quarterly. $12.00/yr.; free with membership. ISSN 0892-4546.

This journal, issued quarterly by the International Relations Round Table of the American Library Association, gives a good overview of what is happening in the IRRT and related issues. *International Leads* succeeds the publication that appeared in twenty-eight volumes, beginning October 1957, under the name *Leads*. A subscription to the journal is included with a membership in the round table.

In the beginning, *Leads* was a mere fact sheet of the IRRT. In 1983, W. L. Williamson (Professor Emeritus of the School of Library and Information Studies, University of Wisconsin, Madison) became editor of *Leads*. Under Williamson's dynamic leadership, the journal took shape, including new features while still providing many brief news stories and other noteworthy commentaries. The format changed from two to three columns in order to expand coverage of foreign library issues. Its balanced perspective and readable format make it especially relevant to nonmembers as well as IRRT members.

Although this publication concentrates on the national scene, its scope is worldwide, as it reports news of international library organizations and lists dates of scheduled meetings. It offers a wealth of materials including IRRT and IRC activities and news of other ALA committees concerned with international relations. There is a plethora of valuable information here, including news about the international work of ALA and other organizations, international activities, and people and publications in the field.

Also included is news about librarians working on projects overseas, foreign librarians visiting the United States, area chairpersons' reports and reviews, newly published materials, and educational travel tours, as well as articles on librarianship. In addition, the publication covers newsmakers, promotions, and job opportunities. Persons who wish to exchange positions outside their own countries are listed. According to Williamson, "there is no other publication that effectively duplicates *International Leads.*" It is a good source for those who are interested in the promotion and support of international library relations. It also can be a good mechanism to provide information which will further the international interests of all librarians.   (Christina) Young Hyun Allen

576. Journal of Systems Management, Vol. 1- , No. 1- . Cleveland, Ohio, Association for Systems Management, 1949- . monthly. $17.50/yr.; free with membership; $20.00/yr. (foreign); $2.00 (single issue). ISSN 0022-4839.

This monthly has been published for forty years by the Association for Systems Management, the professional society for systems and information resource management. The journal covers a broad range of issues of interest to the systems professional, primarily from a management rather than a technical perspective. Among topics treated in 1987 are controlling the project development cycle, work flow analysis, application software documentation, information system problems from the user's perspective, developing the project management manual, project accountability, forecasting, financial planning models, selecting computer vendors, DSS models, and computer-assisted PERT simulations.

The journal also includes papers on broader issues of interest to the systems professional, such as the general status of information management in business organizations, change and the systems professional, the impact of information technology on organizations, and the consultant-client relationship in the information service context. Authorship of published papers

is fairly evenly balanced between academics, usually associated with schools of business, management, information management, or computer science, and practitioners in the systems management field.

The audience of *Journal of Systems Management* is clearly the systems and information resource management practitioner. Although theoretical and research-based content is included, editorial treatment is aimed at the transfer of information from the research to the practice environment. Editorial quality is highly competent and consistent. Most papers in the journal are accessible to general managers and other professionals who might be described as informed nonspecialists in the field of systems management.

The *Journal of Systems Management* should be considered indispensable to collections which support programs of business, systems management, computer science, and information resource management. It is also a basic journal for special librarians working in the business environment and for systems specialists in other libraries. For that reason, the journal is highly recommended for collections in librarianship. Although the preponderance of material is oriented to business organizations, it treats many topics applicable to the management of libraries, particularly those heavily involved in library automation and information technology.
                                    Joe A. Hewitt

577. Library Acquisitions: Practice & Theory, Vol. 1- , No. 1- . Elmsford, N.Y., Pergamon Press, 1977- . quarterly. $75.00/yr. ISSN 0364-6408.

An editorial in the premier issue of *Library Acquisitions* stated that the journal was to be a forum for "exchange of knowledge, ideas and experience among library professionals and non-professionals in education, research and practice." Its first and only editor, Scott R. Bullard, intended to "bring together disparate subfields and persons within the area of library acquisitions" and to publish a journal which would cover the field of library acquisitions comprehensively. It would consider both practical and theoretical issues. The journal has, throughout its eleven-year history, faithfully adhered to this plan publishing research-oriented articles, practical advice ("Controlling Duplicate Orders or, Riding a Camel"), personal professional experiences ("The Acquisitions Allocation Formula at Ohio University"), and vigorously expressed opinion articles ("Harrassowitz: A Detailed Response to VCH"). Highlights of relevant ALA preconferences, discussion groups, committee meetings, and programs are regularly included, as are selected papers from conferences on library acquisitions. In most issues, there are one to four book reviews between one-half and two pages in length. Articles expressing varying viewpoints are often grouped in one or more themes in an issue. One theme, appearing in two issues, was "Collection Development and Acquisitions in a Distance Learning Environment." "Acquisitions Roundtable" provides an opportunity for authors to express their personal views. The writing in this journal has been consistently and uniformly excellent, with clear evidence of careful editing. Articles are frequently on the cutting edge of acquisitions librarianship in the United States and abroad. Illustrations are generally limited to line drawings, maps, and graphs. Typography and layout, as with all Pergamon Press journals, are excellent. Author, title, and subject indexes covering volumes 1-10 appeared in volume 11, number 1. Since no other journal is devoted exclusively to library acquisitions, *Library Acquisitions* offers the library community a unique communications tool. The journal itself reflects the vision of its editor, Scott R. Bullard, who deserves the applause of his colleagues for encouraging discussions of controversial topics and promoting an understanding of the acquisitions process in foreign libraries.

Margaret McKinley

578. **Library Administration & Management**, Vol. 1- , No. 1- . Chicago, Library Administration and Management Association, 1987- . quarterly. $25.00/yr.; $12.50/yr. (U.S., Canada, Mexico, and other PUAS countries); $30.00/yr. (other foreign countries); $7.50 (single issue). ISSN 0888-4463.

This is the official journal of the Library Administration and Management Association, a division of the American Library Association. Its expressed objective is "to support association objectives by bringing to the membership and other library and information professionals articles, news, and reviews that help them to understand and react appropriately to recent developments in the library management world and the Library Administration and Management Association."

The statement of purpose further indicates that contents are to include a focus on management issues or personalities; debates by leaders in the field; conference program information; a calendar of association events; a column on management techniques; news on research, new services, or products; legislative items; a president's message column; and more.

Articles in the first issue covered several topics. By the fourth issue a theme pattern

seemed to be emerging as the third issue concentrated on middle management and the fourth on library buildings. Each of the first four issues also contained an interview with a current library personality, including Marilyn Gell Mason, director of the Cleveland Public Library; John R. Rizzo, professor of management at Western Michigan University and author of books and articles on library administration; David Kaser, distinguished professor of library and information science at Indiana University and noted library building consultant; and Patrick O'Brien, director of the Dallas Public Library.

While not mentioned in the statement of purpose, a "staff development column" consisting of an annotated bibliography on specific elements of staff development also appeared in each of the first four issues. The publication is a general purpose journal which will appeal to a wide audience of librarians interested in current management topics. The articles have been timely, stimulating, well written, and carefully edited. An appealing ingredient of the publication is the cover graphics. They have consisted of a changing array of geometric figures set in a common square with a theme title placed below the square. The effect is very attractive. There have also been photographs of persons interviewed and of library buildings.

Library Administration & Management is definitely a worthy addition to the literature of the profession. The material is of good quality, the writing meets high standards, and the presentation is attractive.   P. Grady Morein

579. **The Small Press Book Review: A Review of Books from Independent and Smaller Presses**, Vol. 1- , No. 1- . Southport, Conn., Greenfield Press, 1985- . 6 issues/yr. $22.00/yr.; $4.00 (single issue). ISSN 8756-7202.

Specifically targeted for use by librarians and booksellers, this fifteen- to twenty-page bimonthly newsletter, begun in 1985, continues to address the growing popularity of small press titles recognized for promoting experimentation and creativity. *The Small Press Book Review* provides descriptive and critical evaluations of some twenty-five to thirty titles in each issue. Reviews are done by staff with broad backgrounds in the book trade and by recognized subject specialists. There is a concerted effort to review the most noteworthy titles of the expanding number produced by small press publishers. Order information and publisher's address are included for each title reviewed, and titles can be ordered through the *Review* if so desired. Titles reviewed include fiction and nonfiction, novels, poetry, children's literature, self-help or how-to books, cookbooks, and books on special subjects such as art and architecture. Titles reviewed range from those representative of the avant-garde to those tackling more traditional subjects.

In addition to the book reviews, each issue includes articles on the development of the small press publishing industry, a list of the bestselling small press books, and a "news notes" column reporting significant activities and events in the small press world. Beginning with the May/June 1988 issue, the last issue of each volume will carry an index of all reviews and articles in that volume. *The Small Press Book Review* will soon be indexed by *Book Review Index.*

Although *Publishers Weekly, Library Journal,* and *Choice* review a number of small press titles, *The Small Press Book Review,* the *Small Press Review* (Dustbooks, 1967-), and *Fine Print: The Review for the Art of the Book* (Kirshenbaum, 1975-) are significant additions to review sources which concentrate more heavily on mainstream publication titles for review. An ever-increasing number of literary and alternative periodicals are devoting attention to reviews of the small and fine arts press. Thus far, there is little duplication in reviews among these small and fine arts press reviewing sources, and most editors, like Henry Berry, are able to recognize the most meritorious and high-quality productions for review. The *Small Press Review,* edited by Len Fulton, will undoubtedly remain the leading contender, because of the "expert" reputation maintained in the small press publishing world, but *The Small Press Book Review* is certainly a worthwhile and valuable addition to the proliferating reviewing sources, and its inexpensive price, easy-to-read format, fine print quality, and heavy stock paper are more appealing than the *Small Press Review*'s messy newsprint quality. Maureen Pastine

580. Trends in Law Library Management and Technology, Vol. 1- , No. 1- . Littleton, Colo., Fred B. Rothman, 1987- . 10 issues/yr. $75.00/yr. ISSN 0893-6773.

A prominent academic law librarian, considered by many as among the leaders in legal information technology, recently asked a rhetorical question whether it is at all possible to keep up with the vast array of new developments in automation applicable to law libraries. *Trends* now attempts to accomplish this goal by providing an alternate means to sifting through the mountain of technical magazines, announcements, journals, and advertisements flooding the marketplace. This newsletter is published ten times each year. Contributors are encouraged to present information and their views

from all types of law libraries and legal information providers. The first issue, for example, contains articles on implementing a microcomputer center in a library, the changing role of the private law librarian, the manager's role in developing a good working relationship with the boss, and the latest in software for the library. Forthcoming issues will include articles on such matters as low-end cataloging software, spreadsheet templates for library management, space planning, executive workstations, techniques in records management, law firm networking, and legislative and judicial information systems. Law librarians considering or implementing automated practices or changes in their operations should find this brief but informative newsletter an easy to read and understandable resource for gaining insight into and knowledge about current developments in the field.

James M. Murray

REGIONAL

581. Alberta Association of College Librarians. Newsletter, Vol. 1- , No. 1- . Lethbridge, Alta., Alberta Association of College Librarians, 1978- . semiannual. $10.00/yr.

Published semiannually since January 1978, the *Newsletter* of the Alberta Association of College Librarians, formerly the Alberta Council of College Librarians, is the vehicle of communication of the Association and its Council predecessor.

As its title suggests, each issue of this periodical is a series of short announcements, news items, and reports of the activities and conferences of the Association as well as news of the community college libraries in Alberta. In addition, some issues include short articles on topics of interest to community college library staffs. Some, for example, "Tenure Criteria for Librarians," are related to professionalism, while others discuss policy making or are on general topics of current interest, for example, "What Is DOBIS?" Recent issues contain news from the various community college libraries, and there is an effort to share with other institutions annual reports, promotional brochures, and similar information.

There is no stated editorial policy, but most of the articles are signed. Moreover, there has been a concerted effort to save time and effort while making information available, at low cost. The *Newsletter* is printed on 8½-by-11-inch paper and is reproduced by photocopying. The copy is reproduced as submitted. Hence, the print quality is uneven because of the use of a variety of typewriters and word processors. Some inclusions are reproduced from other publications and there are illustrations in the form of cartoons. The issues vary in size, with most issues being twelve to sixteen pages long, but some are as much as thirty pages in length.

While this publication is neither elegant in format nor scholarly in content, it is an important vehicle of communication for community college librarians in the province of Alberta, Canada, where distances are great and the library community is thinly spread. At the same time, the *Newsletter* will also be of interest to professional and paraprofessional staff in libraries of similar institutions in other parts of Canada and the United States.

Nancy J. Williamson

582. BCLA Reporter: The Newsletter of the British Columbia Library Association, Vol. 1- , No. 1- . Vancouver, B.C., British Columbia Library Association, 1957- . 6 issues/yr. free with membership. ISSN 0005-2876.

The *BCLA Reporter* began in 1938 as *Bulletin* in a mimeographed state, originally published twice a year. By 1957 it was a quarterly and was split into two succeeding publications: the *BC Library Quarterly* for the articles and the book reviews, and the *BCLA Reporter* for news and announcements. In 1967 the *Quarterly* won the H. W. Wilson Periodical Award; it had developed into an excellent "literary" journal. But it was later suspended, in Spring 1975, for lack of funds. Articles and book reviews returned to the *Reporter*, but it was not the same. The articles are more—how should I put it?—"prosaic" and deal with nitty-gritty items. For instance, in 1987 the *Reporter* had long features on automation in British Columbia libraries (an article on each of school, public, special, and academic libraries in the province). It also had a feature on the personal, business, and political records of W. A. C. Bennett, a former premier of the province. There is an annual article on the employment situation and job market for recent graduates from the U.B.C. library school, the province's sole postgraduate school in information science. There are always in-depth profiles of individual libraries, as well as items on perennial concerns such as vendors and problem patrons.

The book review section is quite useful, since it concentrates solely on books dealing with British Columbia, published in British Columbia, or written by residents. It is a long-running forum, and the reviews are very cogent within their allotted 250 words or so. Of course, all reviews are signed.

As the "official newsletter of the BCLA," there are quite a few newsy items on people, budgets, local library boards, regional boards, and so forth, all funneled upwards through the volunteer system of regional and subject correspondents. They are rarely of interest for out-of-province readers, except when chasing down elusive ideas. I have found that most of what I have discovered through newsletters is based on serendipity anyway, and that is definitely the case here yet again. Regular reports recur, such as those on the annual conferences, the BC Newspapers Project, the BC Libraries Week, user surveys, fundraising and casino nights, JOBLINE issues, continuing education workshops, and the usefulness of the "grant" mechanism.   Dean Tudor

583. The Bookmark, Vol. 1- , No. 1- . Port Moody, B.C., British Columbia Teacher-Librarians' Association, 1939- . quarterly. free with membership. ISSN 0381-6028.

The British Columbia Teacher-Librarians' Association (BCTLA) is a Provincial Specialist Association of the British Columbia Teachers' Federation. As a membership benefit, *The Bookmark* aims to meet the information needs of practicing teacher-librarians in British Columbia.

BCTLA, formerly called the British Columbia School Librarians' Association, began in 1939. *The Bookmark* started as an irregular news sheet and in 1972 became a journal. In 1984 *BCTLA Reviews*, a separate reviewing publication, was incorporated as a regular feature of *The Bookmark*. Other publications of the BCTLA have included occasional papers and special monographs such as *Young Relationships, Periodicals for B.C. School Libraries,* and *Fuel for Change: Cooperative Planning and Teaching*. In 1986 a videokit entitled *Fuel for Change: Cooperative Planning and Teaching* was produced as a joint project by the BCTLA, University of British Columbia, and the Canadian School Library Association.

The Bookmark has a volunteer editorial board. Their energy, enthusiasm, and commitment are supported by contributions from many professionals throughout the province. Such involvement results in the production of a highly relevant and practical publication. The success of *The Bookmark* in large measure may be credited to the dedication of such teacher-librarians as Liz Austrom, Dianne Driscoll, Alan Knight, and Gerald Soon. In 1984-1985 Alan Knight served as senior editor, and he tripled the size of the journal, expanding the number of regular features and adopting a thematic approach to each issue. From 1985 to 1987 Gerald Soon as senior editor continued the development of the thematic issues and received the 1987 Canebsco School Library Media Periodical

Award for *The Bookmark*'s valuable contributions to the school library profession.

The greatest strength of this journal rests in the variety, timeliness, and usefulness of the articles, bibliographies, teaching units, notes, and news found in each issue. Articles are often reprinted from other educational and library journals. These add immeasurably to the quality of the journal's content. The looseleaf format is designed so that teacher-librarians may insert each issue into a three-ring binder. Elementary and secondary teacher-librarians find without fail articles worthy of circulation to teachers in their schools. Some of the themes which have been explored have included public relations, strategies for satisfying social studies, and art ovations. So much material is offered in a single issue that a quick perusal of the materials is not possible. Each issue must be read cover to cover and by so doing a plethora of practical ideas and resources is gleaned.

Regular features of *The Bookmark* are distinctive. Via "letters to the editor," through the "Point/Counterpoint," column, where controversial articles are printed in order to elicit comment and debate, and by means of the "Ask the Experts" column, the voice of teacher-librarians in British Columbia may be heard. "In Circulation" provides an opportunity for the president of the BCTLA to communicate directly with the membership. "Notes and News" highlights conferences, workshops, and courses of interest to teacher-librarians. "B.C. Government Documents" is an annotated select list of government publications considered suitable for school library collections. The "Portrait" column features British Columbia authors and publishers. Annually the results of a "Learning and Working Conditions Survey" are printed, providing invaluable statistical data about school library services in British Columbia. In the "BCTLA Reviews" section ten to fifteen reviews of Canadian learning resources appear. Each review is written by a teacher-librarian, and complete classification and cataloging information is given.

In order to keep the costs of producing the journal to a minimum, it is printed by the British Columbia Teachers' Federation. No assistance with typing or layout is provided. Print styles vary from one article to the next and this detracts from the clarity and visual attractiveness of the journal. More white space and greater uniformity in layout and design would do much to enhance the readability of each issue. A more detailed table of contents listing both the author(s) and the titles of the feature articles would make it easier to consult.

The Bookmark is by far one of the most superior regional school library association publications in Canada, surpassing such journals as *Medium, MSLAVA Journal,* and *Alberta Learning Resources Journal.* It prints an annual index, and is also indexed in the *Canadian Education Index. The Bookmark* admirably fulfills its mandate, and it is an essential tool for teacher-librarians in British Columbia. It is excellent value for the money and would also be of interest to teacher-librarians outside of the province. Through the leadership, participation, and dedication of the BCTLA membership, *The Bookmark* represents an outstanding example of an effective professional publication.

Jo-Anne Naslund

584. **Communicator**, Vol. 1- , No. 1- . Los Angeles, Calif., Librarians' Guild, AFSCME Local 2626, 1969- . monthly. $10.00/yr.; free to Guild members, the Los Angeles Public Library system, select government agencies, the media, and other unions.

Professionals below the level of division librarian at the Los Angeles Public Library (LAPL) formed a union, the Librarians' Guild, AFSCME Local 2626, in 1968. The *Communicator*, which began appearing on an irregular basis in 1969, is the official newsletter of that labor organization. It became a monthly in 1973, but it has been published on a bimonthly basis — and even less frequently — for the past few years. During 1986, only four issues (volume 19, numbers 1-2, January-February; numbers 3-6, March-June; numbers 7-10, July-October; and numbers 11-12, November-December) appeared. The current editor of the *Communicator*, Helene Mochedlover of LAPL's literature and fiction department, explains the failure to change the frequency note in the masthead by saying that a return to monthly publication is anticipated.

Typical issues of the 8½-by-11-inch *Communicator* vary in length from twenty-four to fifty-six pages each. Contents include short articles, most of which are signed, focusing on activities at LAPL's central library and branches, union business, political action, staff news, and other professional concerns. Some black-and-white drawings and photographs illustrate the text. Special issues have highlighted, among other things, pay equity, censorship, and the disastrous fire at LAPL's central library on 29 April 1986.

The *Communicator*, which has a circulation of over seven hundred, recently received an award from the Western Labor Press Association. Because it is not indexed, few librarians outside the Los Angeles area read it. Nevertheless, it would be useful to anyone interested in professional unions and large public libraries.

Leonard Grundt

585. **Dixson Library Report**, Vol. 1- , No. 1- . Armidale, Australia, Dixson Library, University of New England, 1981- . quarterly. free (within university). ISSN 0728-6481.

This slim, attractively printed report is available on a quarterly basis from the University of New England, Armidale, Australia. The journal is free to members and students of the university and available to others by writing to the university for order information. The purpose of the quarterly journal is to establish a network of communication between the university and Dixson Library; to "inform staff and students of library developments relevant to the University's teaching and research" (5, no. 2 [June 1986]).

Each quarterly edition contains four or five articles of topical interest to the university and library communities. These articles range from lists of recently acquired materials (a regular feature) to a beautifully illustrated article on an introduction to rare books in the Dixson Library. These journals are extremely valid for the immediate readership for which they are written, but of limited interest to a wider circle of people. Consequently, purchase would most likely be limited to institutions offering a wide range of foreign publications, foreign libraries and universities, and those library schools offering coursework in international librarianship.

Barbara Sproat

586. **Focus**, Vol. 1- , No. 1- . Toronto, Ontario Library Association, 1975- . 5 issues/yr. $35.00/yr.; free with membership. ISSN 0318-0247.

The Ontario Library Association, Canada's oldest library association, has published a variety of journals over the years. *Focus* was initiated in 1975 and was for several years a sixteen-page newsletter for the association. In 1982, a new, enlarged format was adopted, and with volume 9 in 1983 the journal began publishing longer articles in addition to news items about OLA and all of its divisions. At that time the divisional newsletters ceased publication. At the present time, each issue of *Focus* includes approximately forty pages of articles, book reviews, news items, booklists, and letters from readers. Although journalistic rather than scholarly, most of the articles are informative and topical. Many issues are built around a theme, and among those covered in recent issues have been copyright, public relations, and

collection building. Most of the articles are written by public librarians in Ontario or by faculty members at one of the province's two library schools. Although the Ontario Library Association includes members from all types of libraries, the emphasis on *Focus* seems to be heavily weighted with articles of interest to public libraries, especially the small libraries which form a high proportion of Ontario's more than five hundred library boards. The emphasis in articles is on the practical demands of running an effective library service rather than on research or theory. Many articles are accounts of services or methods which a library has found successful, others offer analyses of public policy or legislation and their relevance for libraries.

Readers who are familiar with *American Libraries* will find that the emphasis, as well as the mix of articles, news reports, and book reviews, are similar to that journal. The book reviews in *Focus* are brief, often no more than annotations which call attention to books of professional interest. Occasionally an issue contains a round-up of reviews of books in a specific area, such as collection development. The quality of writing throughout the journal is professional. It is clear that the editing is careful and few typographical errors or obvious mistakes appear. The format of the journal is attractive, with a good use of graphics and illustrations ranging from photographs of events to cartoons on library issues. Libraries in Ontario, particularly public libraries, will find *Focus* useful for its articles and as a record of OLA and provincial library events. Outside of the province it deserves a place in library science collections and large public libraries which want to stay abreast of library developments across Canada.

Adele M. Fasick

587. **The Georgia Librarian**, Vol. 1- , No. 1- . Tucker, Ga., Georgia Library Association, 1964- . quarterly. $12.50/yr. ISSN 0016-8319.

The Georgia Librarian began publication in March 1964, as a sixteen-page journal issued twice a year. Since then, the periodical has undergone a number of changes in format, content, and arrangement, with a major expansion occurring in 1979 when it became a quarterly and changed size to 8½-by-11-inches. In recent years, issues have averaged about twenty-eight pages in length.

As the official organ of the Georgia Library Association, the main emphasis of *The Georgia Librarian* has always been on communicating with GLA members. Initial issues were devoted primarily to news about GLA affairs and library activities throughout the state. Over the years, the ratio of articles to news has varied considerably. Current issues usually contain two or three articles, which are generally of an informative or descriptive nature. Examples of recent articles include a series describing special collections in five Georgia libraries (May 1987) and a guide to newsletters published by colleges and universities in Georgia (February 1987).

In addition to reports and announcements concerning GLA matters, regular features include a "Bulletin Board" section for noting upcoming events, awards, and other items of interest to Georgia librarians; sections for news from academic libraries, public libraries, and school media centers throughout the state; and a "People" column that highlights the accomplishments of individual librarians and announces personnel changes. An extremely useful section is "On the Shelf," which contains book reviews of literary works by Georgia authors as well as nonfiction works pertaining to all aspects of Georgia. This column generally reviews from seven to nine titles per issue. Contributed by Georgia librarians and teaching faculty, the reviews range in length from two- to three-hundred words.

Selectively indexed in *Library Literature,* *The Georgia Librarian* is an attractive, carefully edited magazine. The layout is pleasing, and graphics are stylish. Since 1984, the editor has been James Dorsey, whose regular columns are refreshing and informative.

The Georgia Librarian admirably fulfills its function as a state association journal by providing a vital link among the libraries and librarians of the state, whose diverse situations and concerns often overshadow their common goals and professional interests.   Marie Ellis

588.   **Letter of the L.A.A.**, Vol. 1- , No. 1- . Edmonton, Alta., Library Association of Alberta, 1977- . 6 issues/yr.; free with membership. ISSN 0705-4890.

The regional/provincial state publications of our professional associations, at their best, fulfill a number of missions. They publish news of the association, of members, and of professional developments in their geographic area. They often include columns of opinion/letters, questions, and of forthcoming events of possible professional interest. Less characteristically, they sometimes publish speeches, articles, and papers about research done by members. The format can be that of a newspaper, tabloid, stapled sheets, or booklet. The newsletter in hand is typical of its genre in that it publishes news items from Alberta and beyond, and includes columns of information for members. Its format is typed, stapled in booklet style, with simple graphics and photographs.

The *Letter* supersedes an earlier publication, *LAA-LAA-LAA*, which lasted for twenty-nine issues and replaced an even older, distinctively colored "centerfold" in the Association's *Bulletin*. The issues now range between twenty and thirty-five pages, and are aimed at library workers and trustees in the province of Alberta. The LAA's membership includes librarians from all types of libraries, as well as library technicians and trustees. Customarily, each issue contains several types of material. First, there is usually a message from the president of the LAA. There are often reports from the executive of the Association. Then there are short reports and news from libraries around the province. This can include notice of jobs available, news of awards made, new projects, etc. Fourth, the news and notes from around Canada bring information from beyond the province. This section may have news from the Canadian Library Association, calls for information, information notes, news of new appointments, job announcements, conference announcements, etc. There is, too, a letters column, which recently has featured letters from government agencies or directors of information centers, announcing changes or developments in policy. Interestingly, there are seldom letters from the grass roots membership. Finally, each issue closes with a listing of forthcoming events of interest to Alberta librarians, whether these events are to occur within the province, in other parts of Canada, or in the United States. There are also a few ads in each issue.

The *Letter* is a more interesting publication than its antecedents, and, with the more settled editorship in the last two years, should continue to fill a niche in western Canadian librarianship. It brings news of library happenings to a diverse and scattered (often isolated) population, and it keeps the membership informed about association intentions and news. The *Letter* does not attempt to publish articles of opinion or research, but defines its function more narrowly as an informational one. In this it succeeds well, and will be of use to libraries in Alberta, and to those interested in Albertan and Canadian librarianship.   Elizabeth Frick

589.   **Mississippi Libraries**, Vol. 1- , No. 1- . Clinton, Miss., Mississippi Library Association, 1936- . quarterly. $16.00/yr.; free with membership; $4.00 (single issue). ISSN 0026-6302.

Mississippi Libraries began in 1936 as *Library News*, a publication of the Mississippi Library Commission. For most of its existence, from 1954 until 1982, it was a joint product of the MLC and the Mississippi Library Association. From 1955 until 1978 it was known as the

Mississippi Library News, becoming *Mississippi Libraries* in 1979. Since 1983 it has been the quarterly journal of the Mississippi Library Association and the inheritor of an interesting tradition.

Library service in Mississippi was practically unknown outside the state's colleges and largest cities in 1936. Lacking a strong professional association, the fledgling Library Commission presided over the genesis of the journal. Today's publication evolved through struggle; Mississippi has been numbered among America's least progressive states.

A few dedicated individuals prevailed over an apathetic legislature to produce a strong state association and a better than average example of a mediocre genre, the state library journal. Typically, *Mississippi Libraries* has few feature articles. These vary in interest appeal and are nonscholarly. This weakness has prompted *Library Literature* to drop the title beginning in 1987. Book reviews vary from strong, critical reviews by scholars to the inevitably favorable reviews of local and regional works by practicing librarians (again a weakness of the format).

The raison d'être of the state library journal, exemplified in *Mississippi Libraries*, is as a forum and clearinghouse for ideas and as a bulletin board for activities and elections within the association. Inherent in the word *journal* is its function as a news bulletin.

The editorship of this journal has changed every other year or more often, compromising prospects for continued improvement. Only time will tell if the necessary continuity is achieved.

With the adoption of a slick, larger format in 1981, *Mississippi Libraries* compares favorably with its Southern counterparts. It inherits and is nurtured by a literary tradition that has produced two Faulkners, Welty, Hodding Carter, Sr., Willie Morris, Tennessee Williams, and others. This association is apparent in the generally high quality of the prose. As the library profession progresses into the new age of automation, it will be interesting to see if *Mississippi Libraries* evolves with the appropriate sense of mission.   T. P. Williams

590. **MO INFO**, Vol. 1- , No. 1- . Columbia, Mo., Missouri Library Association, 1970- . bimonthly. $6.00/yr.; free with membership; $10.00/yr. (foreign). ISSN 0884-2205.

MO INFO is a creditable, competently produced newsletter designed to bring information to the members of the Missouri Library Association. In its eight pages, members can find out about library-related legislation, continuing education information, MLA members "in the news," and current awareness items. The design quality is unexceptional, if not unique, and the ivory pages contain a multitude of short articles with few pictures or advertisements to provide variety. In a newsletter of this type, controversy and scholarship are equally avoided. Missouri librarians will be interested in the contents of *MO INFO*, but most library school collections will choose the slicker and more substantive *Show-Me Libraries* as their representative Missouri publication.   Stephanie C. Sigala

591. **MPLA Newsletter**, Vol. 1- , No. 1- . Vermillion, S.D., Broadcaster Press, 1976- . bimonthly. $17.00/yr. ISSN 0145-6180.

Initiated in 1956 under the title *Mountain-Plains Library Quarterly*, this regional publication became the *Mountain/Plains Library Association Quarterly* in 1974. In 1975 it again changed its name to *MPLA Newsletter*. Since that date it has been issued bimonthly. State association membership has increased with the years. Today it comprises Arizona, Colorado, Kansas, Montana, Nebraska, Nevada, North and South Dakota, Utah, and Wyoming. Personal as well as corporate memberships are encouraged. Sections in the officers' roster represent academic libraries, children's and school libraries, a junior members round table, public libraries and trustees, state agencies, and technical services. There are committees for awards, bylaws and procedures, continuing education, finance, intellectual freedom, nominations, professional development grants, public relations, and membership. Letters to the editor; personal, state, and regional news items; job listings; conference programs; and proceedings are published, but there are no tables of contents, indexes, or book reviews. Stated objectives include opportunities for professional involvement, continuing education programs, a forum for the exchange of ideas, information on new technology in librarianship, support of regional library efforts, and information on people and programs in member states. The format and printing are readable and attractive, with some illustrations. Recent annual conference issues carry full-color illustrated covers. Full- and partial-page advertising is accepted. While it has not yet attained the bulk and scope of its sister publication, *PNLA Quarterly*, this is a well-edited, well-produced, useful periodical, especially to its individual and association participants.   Jeanne Osborn

592. **NELA Newsletter**, Vol. 1- , No. 1- . Wakefield, Mass., New England Library Association, 1969- . 6 issues/yr. $8.00/yr.; $1.25 (single issue). ISSN 0027-0448.

The *NELA Newsletter* is "published by the New England Library Association for its members." It is a four-page tabloid-sized newspaper; some of the issues are illustrated (mostly with photographs). The front page features one, occasionally two, major articles based on programs from conferences in the New England area or at major national meetings. Some are reports of projects thought to be of general interest to the membership. Subjects covered vary from newspaper indexes using a microcomputer to an evaluation of libraries in China, from the history of the Boston Public Library to CD audio technology to Carnegie libraries. The rest of the four-page newsletter is taken up with shorter accounts of events, legislation, and issues, mostly culled from the newsletters or press releases of the several New England state agencies and library associations. Also usually included are a short "people in the news" column and calendar of events. The Fall issues tend to concentrate on the annual conference.

Suzanne K. Gray

593. **New Jersey Libraries**, Vol. 1- , No. 1- . Trenton, N.J., New Jersey Library Association, 1966- . 4 issues/yr. $12.00/yr.; free with membership; $17.50/yr. (foreign); $3.00 (single issue). ISSN 0028-5811.

594. **New Jersey Libraries Newsletter**, Vol. 1- , No. 1- . Trenton, N.J., New Jersey Library Association, 1982- . 10 issues/yr.; only with membership.

New Jersey Libraries is the official publication of the New Jersey Library Association (NJLA) and is included in the cost of membership. In 1964 it appeared as the *New Jersey Library Association Newsletter* and incorporated two supplements, *New Jersey School Libraries* and *Trustee News*. Since 1966 the publication has been titled *New Jersey Libraries*. At various times in the past it has been issued on a monthly schedule, but for the past several years it has appeared on a quarterly basis supplemented by a monthly newsletter. The periodical is again indexed in *Library Literature* beginning with the Spring 1987 issue (vol. 20, no. 1) after a three-year hiatus.

The present physical format is neat and attractive, usually with a line drawing and one-color-plus-black cover. There are few if any illustrations except for graphs or charts incorporated in text material. It is 5½ by 8½ inches in size and averages twenty-eight to thirty pages including advertising. Regular features include an editorial plus a guest editorial, a "20 Years Ago" column of excerpts from earlier issues highlighting past professional concerns, a "New

Jersey Bibliographer" column, a "message" from the New Jersey State Library emphasizing current activities, and a placement service listing. Each issue concentrates on a particular phase of professional concern or interest, such as research in New Jersey libraries, pay equity and comparable worth, the role of the small library, library administration leadership, and library education in New Jersey. The issue under discussion is considered from several points of view and by various library types (public, university, private college, county, and special). The writing is thoroughly professional although the articles, which are serious and informative, make no pretense at being scholarly.

The *New Jersey Libraries Newsletter*, a four-page 8½-by-11-inch monthly publication (September-June) is available to association membership only. It publishes timely information, including a calendar of events of coming professional meetings and conferences, NJLA executive board reports, professional personnel moves, and a classified job advertisement column.

The library profession of New Jersey on an across-the-board scale is well served by these two publications working in tandem, *New Jersey Libraries* addressing pertinent major current issues and the *Newsletter* focusing on the immediate what's-happening-when information.

G. Joan Burns

595. **NYLA Bulletin**, Vol. 1- , No. 1- . New York, New York Library Association, 1953- . monthly (except July). $6.00/yr.; free with membership. ISSN 0027-7134.

The *NYLA Bulletin* is the official publication of the New York Library Association, dating back to the early 1950s, and is typical of its genre, designed to inform association membership as to what is coming up that they should know about together with an awareness of who is working where in their state. When compared to other state library association publications (example: *Michigan Librarian*), it is no better and no worse.

Somewhat lackluster in general content, style, and appearance, it has nevertheless come a long way in the past year or so. The reviewer was sent thirteen issues dating from January 1986 to April 1987, and it was not difficult to discern an attempt by the new editor, Richard D. Johnson, to make it more visually interesting and more readable. Since Johnson took over in the fall of 1986, there are some positive changes: a masthead appears in each issue, color (single, variable) is used in each issue to relieve what used to be black-and-white print and photographs exclusively, and the type format has gone from standard IBM PC to offset printing. All in all, there is a much more interesting and professional appearance to the publication.

Each issue contains a highlighted cover story. Typical topics are legislative lobbying, state and federal funding for libraries in New York state, library standards, and annual statewide library conferences, both in preview and in retrospect. There are no editorials and no obvious editorializing in the anonymously written stories and news items. Also, there are no reader's forum or letters column, no reviews, and, alas, little attempt at cleverness or wit. Just the facts, ma'am, which may be a boon or a drawback, depending on one's perspective.

What you do get is plenty of names. A lengthy section, aptly titled "People," tells who is working where, who retired, and the like. Committee members are listed frequently, together with their addresses and telephone numbers. Brief news items seem sandwiched in and/or around ads and notices of upcoming events, mostly to make column lengths come out right. You say you want advertising? Issues range from eight to sixteen standard pages, and about one-quarter of a typical issue consists of ads, from full-pagers from Wilson, Bowker, and DIALOG to smaller ones for local personnel agencies and subscription agents.

One supposes that it all comes down to objectives. If it is the purpose of a state library association newsletter to tell who is doing what, without any protracted discussion of why, then the *NYLA Bulletin* does an admirable job of it. If, however, think-pieces, comment from the membership, results of research, and challenges for change belong in these pages, then the publication could stand improvement. To encapsulate: There is nothing wrong with it, but in a state with so many libraries, so much state-level involvement, so much money, and so many talented people, one could reasonably expect that much more could be done to improve this newsletter.   Bruce A. Shuman

596.   **PLA Bulletin**, Vol. 1- , No. 1- . Harrisburg, Pa., Pennsylvania Library Association, 1945- . 8 issues/yr. $20.00/yr.; free with membership. ISSN 0197-9299.

This is the official organ of the Pennsylvania Library Association. It began in 1945 as a quarterly newsletter to the membership. Gradually it expanded to include articles of general interest to librarians and became more of a journal with some scholarly articles. This expansion continued until the middle of the 1970s.

In 1969 it became a bimonthly publication and in 1978 it changed to a monthly. As the number of issues increased per year the size of the bulletin decreased, and it again took on a newsletter format. In November 1984 only eight issues per year seemed adequate for its purposes. It has continued in this manner to the present time.

Throughout its history the scope and purpose has been to communicate to the membership news and official business of the organization. The present editor, however, hopes to broaden the scope once again to include articles of interest to all librarians of the state whether or not they are members. In fact, a journal/bulletin proposal was submitted to the membership in the March 1987 issue by the Committee on Publications and Research Materials to produce two yearly issues of a journal which "would provide a forum for the presentation of ideas and information about developments of interest not only to Pennsylvania libraries but also to a larger library community."

In addition to news items about the organization, each current issue includes the following regular features: "Calendar," "New Members," "People," "Pied Piper" (Youth Services Division page), "Trustee's Tidings," "Conference Plans," and the "President's Message."

The editor is appointed by the president and approved by the Board of Directors. Each editor has changed the publication slightly to reflect his or her own philosophy since there is at present no written and approved publication policy.

Since most articles are contributed by those members concerned with the functioning of the association, the writing quality is uneven but in quite good journalistic style, reflecting the influence of quality editors.

Although the audience for this periodical at present is pretty much limited to the membership, it should attract a wider readership in the near future.   Sara R. Mack

597.   **South Carolina Librarian**, Vol. 1- , No. 1- . Charleston, S.C., South Carolina Library Association, 1956- . semiannual. $3.00/yr.; free with membership. ISSN 0038-3112.

The first issue of the *South Carolina Librarian* was published in November 1956. It was the successor to the *South Carolina Library Bulletin*, published jointly by the South Carolina Library Association (SCLA) and the South Carolina State Library Board since 1945. The new journal provided an opportunity not only for news of the association and membership but also for substantive articles and opinion pieces. During the last thirty years, under the leadership of only five different editors, the journal has maintained a remarkably good balance of these diverse objectives. In recent years, with the publication of the SCLA newsletter, *News and*

Views, news items on SCLA sections, round-tables, and members have decreased and more articles have been published in each of the semi-annual issues. Minutes of the SCLA Executive Board and an annual membership directory were regular features in the journal but now appear in *News and Views.*

The major orientation of the journal has been to South Carolina librarians, and the majority of the contributors over the years have also come from those ranks. A moderately good balance of articles and shorter pieces on all types of libraries (except special libraries) in the state has been maintained over the years. Scholarly articles have not been a strong point with the journal but they do occasionally appear. The predominant focus of articles has been a mixture of SCLA conference presentations, "how to" pieces, and brief historical papers. One mainstay feature published on an irregular basis has been "Recent South Caroliniana—A Partial List," usually compiled by a staff member of the South Caroliniana Library at the University of South Carolina. Book reviews, while not appearing in every issue, are also a regular and useful addition to the journal, since they tend to emphasize South Carolina related publications and reference works.

The physical format of the journal from 1956 to 1968 was 8½ by 11 inches, but it is now a smaller 9-by-6-inch size. The number of pages in each issue has remained fairly constant over the years at about thirty. Good quality photography is regularly used and the most recent editor has begun the practice of featuring, on the cover page as well as on occasional internal pages, reproductions of artwork by South Carolina artists. In the early years no ads appeared in the journal, but these now average about ten per issue.

In general, the journal has met its stated association and editorial objectives. It matches quite well the publications of other state library associations of similar size. The quality of the editing has remained remarkably consistent over the years and has generally been high. Scholarship and critical analysis of library and information science problems have not been strengths, and there is ample room for (and the editors have consistently pleaded for) improvement in these areas. Shorter and informal pieces continue to predominate, and this weakens the impact the journal could have on the library profession within the state as well as beyond its borders.

Robert V. Williams

Part IV
ABSTRACTS OF LIBRARY SCIENCE DISSERTATIONS

Abstracts of Library Science Dissertations

Gail A. Schlachter

INTRODUCTION

Unlike the commercially produced monographs, reference books, and journals described elsewhere in this edition of *Library Science and Information Annual*, doctoral dissertations are cloaked by fragmented and sluggish bibliographic announcements and distribution channels. While it is possible to contact library schools at the end of each year to identify dissertations completed there during that year, the only way to learn about dissertations dealing with library and library-related topics that were prepared outside of library schools is to wait until they are listed in *Dissertation Abstracts International* (*DAI*). However, dissertations completed in the third and fourth quarter of one year are frequently not included in *DAI* until the third or fourth quarter of the next year. As a result, it was impossible to review dissertations completed in 1987 and meet the manuscript submission date for this edition of *LISCA*. Thus, this volume provides a review of the 1986 dissertations and, similarly, each subsequent volume will cover dissertations completed in a previous year.

To date, 74 library, information, and related dissertations completed in 1986 have been identified. To place those doctoral studies in perspective, the following quantitative profile is modeled after the statistical analysis provided in Schlachter and Thomison's *Library Science Dissertations, 1925-1972: An Annotated Bibliography* (Libraries Unlimited, 1974) and

Library Science Dissertations, 1973-1981: An Annotated Bibliography (Libraries Unlimited, 1982).

Completion Data

On the average, 14 dissertations were completed each year between 1925 and 1972. From 1973 through 1981, the yearly average increased 800 percent, to 111 dissertations per year. The number of dissertations completed in 1986 (74) was down substantially from both the 1972 to 1981 yearly average and the totals reported in the previous three editions of the *Annual*: 102 in 1984, 120 in 1985, and 83 in 1986.

Sponsoring Schools

The 74 dissertations reviewed for this edition of the *Annual* were completed at 30 private and public institutions of higher learning in the United States and Canada, less than one-third the number of schools involved in the total production of library and library-related dissertations between 1973 and 1981. The five "top" producing universities, responsible for nearly 45 percent of the doctoral studies reviewed for 1986, are the University of Pittsburgh (12 percent), Case Western Reserve University (10 percent), University of Southern California (8 percent), Florida State University (7 percent), and Indiana University (7 percent). All of the schools, except for the University of Southern

California, were also listed as top producers in this section of the *Annual* analysis last year.

Degrees Received

Following the pattern set between 1925 and 1981, the Ph.D. remained the most commonly earned degree (83 percent) in 1986, followed by the Ed.D. (11 percent), and the D.L.S. (3 percent). Although in past years other degrees (e.g., D.L.A., D.B.A.) were also represented in the dissertations reviewed, to date none have been reported for studies completed in 1986.

Methodology Employed

As in the analyses reported by Schlachter and Thomison in the two volumes of *Library Science Dissertations*, each of the 74 dissertations completed in 1986 was placed into one of seven research categories: citation/content analysis, experimental design, theoretical treatment, operations research (systems analysis and all forms of information storage and retrieval), survey research (case studies, mailed questionnaires, interviews), historical analysis (including biographies and bibliographies), and other (including those dissertations for which insufficient information was available to determine methodology employed). The ranking of research methodologies employed in the 74 dissertations completed during 1986, from most to least used, is survey research (48 percent), historical analysis (15 percent), operations research (12 percent), citation/content analysis (12 percent), experimental design (11 percent), theoretical treatment (1 percent), and other (1 percent). These rankings and percentages differed in two major ways from the approaches used in the 1985 dissertations: (1) while survey research remained the most commonly employed methodology, the percent of dissertations using that technique decreased from 57 percent in 1985 to 48 percent in 1986; and (2) the percentage of dissertations utilizing historical analysis more than doubled, from 6 percent in 1985 to 15 percent in 1986, making historical analysis the second-ranked methodology (compared to the fifth-ranked in 1985).

Sex

Although women have consistently constituted the majority of practicing librarians, they authored only a minority of library, information, and related dissertations from 1925 to 1979. Since that time, however, the field has oscillated. From 1980 to 1982, women were responsible for the first time for over half the dissertations completed. In 1983, 1984, and 1985, the trend reversed; no more than 47 percent of the dissertations in any of those years were written by women. In 1986, the picture changed again; women authored 54 percent of the library, information, and related dissertations completed that year.

Summary

Using the results of this quantitative analysis, it is possible to develop a profile of the library, information, and related dissertations completed in 1986. The typical dissertation was written for the Ph.D. degree by a woman (for the first time since 1982), using survey research methods at one of a handful of major universities in the United States.

The following 37 dissertations have been chosen to be abstracted in the 1987 edition of *Library and Information Science Annual* because they represent the quality, interest, relevance, and/or subjects of the library, information, and related dissertations completed in 1986.

ABSTRACTS

598. Bolt, Janice Ann Havlicek (Ph.D., Florida State University, 1986). **A Study of the Effects of a Bibliographic Instruction Course on Achievement and Retention of College Students.** 240p. Order no. DA8708161.

PURPOSE: In this quasi-experimental study, Bolt examined the relationship between library instruction and the academic success of low-achieving undergraduate students.

PROCEDURE: The "treated group" was composed of a random sample of students at an urban-based public university who had failed university competency examinations in both reading and English and who were enrolled in a three-credit library instruction course designed to teach basic study and reference skills. Using a causal-comparative method, Bolt compared this group to an "untreated" group of students who had passed the university's competency examinations and had not taken the library instruction course. The students in the two groups were compared on three characteristics: academic achievement/grades in undergraduate coursework, continuing enrollment/retention, and graduation.

FINDINGS: No difference in grades, grade point average, or retention was found between the two groups of students (although the untreated group had initially outperformed the treated group in the areas of reading and writing).

599. Browne, Blanche Gutowski (Ph.D., Georgia State University, 1986). **Duplication of Monographic Titles in the Acquisition Process of a School System with Implications for Participation in a Bibliographic Utility.** 133p. Order no. DA8612329.

PURPOSE: This study was conducted to identify factors that might influence a school system's decision to participate in a bibliographic utility.

PROCEDURE: Using stratified random sampling, Browne selected four high schools (two large and two small) to study. She examined each of the school's purchase orders for monographs during a three-year period. A total of 3,306 volumes were ordered. Browne searched for each of these titles in the OCLC database and used descriptive statistics to record duplication.

FINDINGS: Browne found the duplication rate to be 11 percent (with more duplication between the large than the small schools and more duplication between older monographs than the more recent titles). The hit rate for titles included in the OCLC database was 99.99 percent, whether the titles were unique or duplicates.

CONCLUSIONS: The high hit rate for titles in the OCLC database and the uniqueness of acquisitions were important reasons for a school system to consider participating in a bibliographic utility. Duplication rate, based on the findings in this study, was not a major factor.

600. Crowe, William Joseph (Ph.D., Indiana University, 1986). **Verner W. Clapp as Opinion Leader and Change Agent in the Preservation of Library Materials.** 151p. Order no. DA8617800.

PURPOSE: In this historical study, Crowe examined the role played by Verner W. Clapp in the area of preservation of library materials (defined for the purposes of this study to include microphotography, binding, and permanence/durability of paper).

PROCEDURE: In writing this biographical study, Crowe consulted Clapp's papers, records of the organizations with which Clapp was affiliated, and secondary sources dealing with related topics (including the part of social science literature that addresses paradigms of changes, definitions of change agents and opinion leaders, and categorizations of change strategies).

FINDINGS: While he was at the Library of Congress, from 1922 to 1956, Clapp did not take a leadership role in the preservation of library materials. During that period, however, he did serve as a leader in the field of librarianship and, in the process, became interested in the area of preservation. From 1956 through 1972, at the Council on Library Resources, Clapp became both an opinion leader and a change agent in the area of preservation. He was more successful in promoting permanent/durable paper (and preserving existing paper) than he was in the other two areas of preservation: he was unable to effect significant changes in binding methods and he seemed to focus more on the dissemination and economy functions of microphotography than on its utility for preservation.

CONCLUSIONS: Crowe identified three major contributions Clapp made to preservation: his work with Barrow on preserving existing paper, his advocacy of preservation within the library community (particularly during his associations with the American Library Association and the Association of Research Libraries), and his research on the permanence/durability of paper.

601. Dewdney, Patricia Helen (Ph.D., University of Western Ontario, 1986). **The Effects of Training Reference Librarians in Interview Skills.**

PURPOSE: Using techniques developed by Dervin (neutral questioning) and Jennerich (microskills), Dewdney assessed the benefits of trying to train librarians in the communication skills needed in the reference interview.

PROCEDURE: Twenty-four reference librarians from three Ontario public libraries participated in this field experiment. The study was designed as a 2x3 factorial experiment with a control group; this resulted in one group receiving neutral questioning training, one group receiving microskills training, and one group not receiving any specific training. Tape recordings were made of encounters between 334 library users and these librarians, before and after training. Transcripts were made of the encounters and analyzed for evidence of selected questioning and listening skills. After each encounter, users were asked to complete a questionnaire that assessed their satisfaction with the answer received and the librarian's behavior; 236 questionnaires were completed. Data were tested using analysis of variance techniques.

FINDINGS: Librarians trained in neutral questioning provided significantly more helpful answers than librarians trained in microskills or librarians who were not trained at all.

CONCLUSIONS: If a user's perception of service was initially very positive, moderate changes in the librarian's communication behavior may not change the user's perception of service. Training clearly helped the librarians improve their interview skills. Librarians were able to transfer selected skills from training to the work setting.

RECOMMENDATIONS: Dewdney suggested that librarian-user behavior in naturalistic settings be studied further.

602. Dowell, David Ray (Ph.D., University of North Carolina at Chapel Hill, 1986). **The Relation of Salary to Sex in a Female Dominated Profession: Librarians Employed at Research Universities in the South Atlantic Census Region.** 238p. Order no. DA8711107.

PURPOSE: In this study, Dowell examined the relationship between gender and librarians' salaries in south Atlantic research universities.

PROCEDURE: Data were collected on the salaries and activities of librarians employed in research universities in the South Atlantic Census Region. Multiple regression and path analysis were used to examine the possible relationship between sex and salary.

FINDINGS: In the surveyed libraries, women typically had less supervisory responsibility, had completed fewer degrees, had less university service and fewer library professional organization memberships, had less publishing activity, and earned $5,000.00 per year less than men. Moreover, when these factors were held constant, the women in the study still earned $1,200.00 less than men. The best predictors of salary were, in descending order of importance, level of position in the organization (accounted for nearly 60 percent of all variance), years of experience as a librarian, number of librarians supervised, years of service in university-wide organizations, and level of highest degrees in other disciplines. Women tended to view women's contributions (to the library, the university, or the profession) more favorably than men viewed women's contribution—a factor that might affect hiring, promotion, training, initial salary, and raises, since men were more likely to be in the administrative positions where these decisions would be made.

CONCLUSIONS: With women underrepresented in library management, the advancement and rewards of other women may be retarded.

603. Euster, Joanne Reed (Ph.D., University of California, Berkeley, 1986). **The Activities and Effectiveness of the Academic Library Director in the Environmental Context.** 221p. Order no. DA8614756.

PURPOSE: Euster examined the role of the academic library director in a two-pronged environment: the user/consumer environment and the parent organization's control environment.

PROCEDURE: Data were collected from forty-two library directors throughout the United States, a selected group of their dean-level peers, and a group of library middle managers.

FINDINGS: Internal subordinates evaluated academic library directors less favorably than did colleagues external to the library. The subordinates' ratings, however, tended to match their directors' own reports of activity. Only moderate (or weaker) associations were found in the correlation studies conducted.

CONCLUSIONS: Even after leader profiles were developed (based on four key patterns of effectiveness, activity, and change), Euster was unable to find any one characteristic or even combination of characteristics that related directly to effectiveness. She concluded that successful leader behavior for academic library directors is related to their organizational environment.

604. Halperin, Michael Robert (Ph.D., Drexel University, 1986). **The Publications of U.S. Industrial Scientists: A Company and Industry Analysis.** 134p. Order no. DA8616543.

PURPOSE: In this study, Halperin examined the relationship between the volume of scientific/technical publications by industrial scientists and the characteristics of the corporations where they were employed.

PROCEDURE: Halperin collected data from 225 U.S. corporations for 1975 through 1983; the corporations chosen each had a consistent record of supporting research and development.

FINDINGS: Small firms (as measured by their annual sales) produced proportionately more scientific papers than did large firms. R&D "productivity" (the annual number of papers published divided by constant dollar annual R&D expenditures) remained relatively stable from 1975 through 1983. Strong correlations were found between (1) patenting and publication of scientific papers, (2) R&D expenditures and the publication of scientific papers, and (3) the number of elite scientists in a firm and the publication of scientific papers. Little or no correlation was found between (1) R&D and paper publication over time, or (2) the number of elite scientists in a corporation and the publication of patents.

605. Haynes, Kathleen Jean Mavourneen (Ph.D., Texas Woman's University, 1986). **A Study of the Ecological Validity of Procedures in Staging, T-Unit Roles, and Discourse Matrix Diagramming and an Examination of the Criteria for Usability for User Documentation for Microcomputers.** 273p. Order no. DA8626485.

PURPOSE: This study was conducted to answer the following research question: Do the findings of individual studies using discourse analysis procedures have ecological validity when used to evaluate the utility of user documentation?

PROCEDURE: For this study, fifteen subjects with varying levels of microcomputer experience were observed using preselected chunks of a user computer manual. Four descriptive procedures were used to assess the effectiveness of user documentation for microcomputers: staging, t-unit roles, discourse matrix diagramming, and criteria for usability.

FINDINGS: The staging procedure revealed that coordination and new information low in the staging hierarchy tended to result in errors. The t-unit role analysis revealed that difficulty may result from poor placement of rhetorical/sequencing roles and the use of many t-units together (to define, describe, or explain), because the user may not have time to assimilate the information. The discourse matrix diagrams revealed poor writing and important generalizations in the text. The criterion of usability indicated that contextual factors (especially legibility and layout) can influence the interpretation of the text. Both novice and experienced users tended to reread the text, ignore instructions, and skip over topics.

CONCLUSIONS: When discourse analysis procedures are combined with criteria for usability that are based on research, they can have ecological validity.

606. He, Chunpei (Ph.D., Case Western Reserve University, 1986). **Discipline Influence Score: A Method for Determining the Core Journals of a Discipline.** 172p. Order no. DA8627859.

PURPOSE: He proposed a new quantitative method of establishing a core journal list for any discipline: Discipline Influence Score (DIS).

PROCEDURE: Discipline Influence Score involves two steps: (1) start with a small group of "seed" journals, selected on the basis of a journal citation communication graph; and (2) compute the DIS of the identified citation-related journals, based on their relative importance to the discipline. He demonstrated the DIS by starting with 5 seed journals in veter-

inary medicine and ending up with 146 citation-related journals (which he called the "Experimental Journal Set"). He used seventy-four veterinary journals listed in the *Journal Citation Reports* to form the "Veterinary Journal Set." Then the DIS was calculated for each of the publications in the Experimental Journal Set (DIS is calculated by summing the probabilities that a journal could be cited by each of the journals in the Veterinary Journal Set) and the journals were ranked by DIS in descending order.

FINDINGS: Using the DIS method, journals in veterinary medicine, general medicine, agriculture, and basic science were chosen. The DIS journal rankings did not correlate with any of the following four quantitative measures: productivity, citations received, impact factor, or influence measure. The rank correlation between DIS and an evaluation of journal usage by experts in veterinary institutions in the United States and China proved to be statistically significant.

CONCLUSIONS: DIS may be a useful tool for journal selection in specific disciplines.

607. Herron, Nancy Lee (Ph.D., University of Pittsburgh, 1986). **Information Seeking Behavior and the Perceptions of Information Channels by Journalists of Two Daily Metropolitan Newspapers.** 172p. Order no. DA8702068.

PURPOSE: This study focused on the information-seeking behavior of newspaper journalists: how they search for, use, and verify information from inside and outside the newspaper organization.

PROCEDURE: Questionnaires were sent to journalists at the two daily metropolitan Pittsburgh newspapers.

FINDINGS: Over 66 percent of the surveyed journalists preferred to use informal channels (especially personal communications with colleagues) rather than formal channels to gather information. The surveyed journalists showed little diversity in their use of the various source types; they demonstrated more diversity in the ways they looked for and used information sources. Frequency of use was most related to ease of use and accessibility.

CONCLUSIONS: Using the library as an intermediary between electronic networks and the newspaper organization could provide solutions to the problems of accessibility and ease of use.

608. Kosters, Cleo (Ed.D., University of South Dakota, 1986). **A Critical Analysis of Certification Requirements for School Librarians in the Fifty States from 1950 to 1985.** 351p. Order no. DA8622516.

PURPOSE: In this historical study, Kosters traced the training and experience school librarians have been required to have in the library science field, the media field, and both fields.

PROCEDURE: The certification requirements of the fifty states plus the District of Columbia from 1950 through 1985 were compared and analyzed for this study.

FINDINGS: Certification requirements varied greatly from state to state. In 20 percent of the states, there was no mention of the role of school librarians in the certification requirements. In the states with certification requirements that mentioned school librarians (1) there has been an increasing proliferation of terminology and nomenclature in the certification requirements, as more library skills, media skills, and library media skills were specified; and (2) school librarians have been increasingly expected to acquire different kinds of training and experience, to meet the needs of special education children, to participate in the teaching/learning process, and to act as resource persons.

609. Krentz, Roger Franklin (Ph.D., University of Wisconsin at Madison, 1986). **A Study of Selected Competencies of Full-time School District Media Directors as Perceived by Three Groups of Educators.** 260p. Order no. DA 8701854.

PURPOSE: In this study, Krentz compared the perceptions of the competencies of full-time library media directors held by principals, library media specialists, and full-time library media directors themselves.

PROCEDURE: Krentz developed a survey questionnaire based on the competencies established and published by the Wisconsin School Library Media Association and the Wisconsin Educational Media Association in 1984. The competencies studied included: organization, instructional development, library media staff development, research and evaluation, leadership and professionalism, fiscal management, and communication and public relations. Data were collected from principals, library media specialists, and full-time library media directors in Wisconsin school districts.

FINDINGS: All three groups of educators (principals, library media specialists, and full-time library media directors) shared identical perceptions of the competencies of full-time library media directors.

610. Landau, Lucille (Ph.D., Case Western Reserve University, 1986). **Selecting Journals for Publication: A Bibliometric Approach.** 36p. Order no. DA8627870.

PURPOSE: The purpose of this study was to develop an objective and quantitative method for selecting journals in which to publish research papers.

PROCEDURE: Landau developed a matrix for each journal cited by and each journal citing (based on the listings in the *Journal of Citation Reports*) the journal *Critical Care Medicine* from 1978 through 1980. The data were analyzed using the computer program APL. The matrices were multiplied upon themselves until convergence was achieved.

FINDINGS: The most popular/well-known journals in the medical field were also the most popular/well-known ones in the scientific medical community. The most selective journals in the medical field were the *New England Journal of Medicine* and *Lancet*. A middle group of widely read journals that were not considered "junk" and were very acceptable in which to publish also existed.

CONCLUSIONS: Librarians and researchers should use the APL program to identify appropriate journals for publication.

611. Larson, Ray Reed (Ph.D., University of California at Berkeley, 1986). **Workload Characteristics and Computer System Utilization in Online Library Catalogs.** 417p. Order no. DA 8624828.

PURPOSE: In addition to exploring the problems of measuring and evaluating online library catalog system performance, Larson examined the structure and functions of online catalogs and the characteristics and needs of online catalog users.

PROCEDURE: After examining various methodologies for computer performance evaluation, Larson chose "transaction monitoring" (where each command processed by the online catalog record system is recorded along with its associated performance measures) to assess online catalog performance. He applied this methodology to a large online catalog system and used regression techniques to model the performance characteristics of the system.

FINDINGS: In his findings, Larson assessed the importance of system workload in determining performance, examined the role of system and command complexity, and determined the utility and volume of transaction monitoring as an evaluation methodology.

612. Lunardi, Albert Anthony (Ed.D., University of San Francisco, 1986). **The Library Services and Construction Act, Title III: Public School Library Participation within Cooperative Library Networks.** 311p. Order no. DA 8628339.

PURPOSE: This study was undertaken to answer the following research question: What has been the national effect of the Library Services and Construction Act (LSCA) Title III in stimulating public school library participation within cooperative library networks?

PROCEDURE: Questionnaires were sent to fifty-two networks and forty-two public school libraries located in twenty-nine states and Washington, D.C.; responses were received from twenty-four networks and forty-two public school libraries in eighteen states. The data were analyzed using descriptive statistics, a standardized t-test, the chi-square test, and the Spearman rank correlation coefficient.

FINDINGS: The data show that fiscal, legal, attitudinal, governance, planning, evaluation, and technological concerns were not insurmountable barriers to networking. By being parts of networks, public school librarians realized benefits that improved and extended services to the communities they served. Neither public school nor network librarians viewed LSCA Title III as an important federal library program. However, the overall effect of the program has been positive.

CONCLUSIONS: Over the past century, public school librarians have had to adapt to everchanging environments. Their involvement in the networking process is directly related to their dedication to serve and their willingness to share.

613. Marghalani, Mohammed A. (Ph.D., University of Pittsburgh, 1986). **A Systematic Design of a Proposed Model for School Library Media Center Programs in Saudi Arabia.** 234p. Order no. DA8702071.

PURPOSE: The purpose of this study was three-fold: (1) to determine the current condition of secondary and comprehensive school libraries in Saudi Arabia; (2) to explore the attitudes of secondary and comprehensive school principals toward school library media center programs; and (3) to develop a model for school library media center programs in Saudi Arabia.

PROCEDURE: To collect data for this study, Marghalani distributed questionnaires and conducted supplemental interviews. The following statistical techniques were used to analyze the data: frequencies, percentages, measures of central tendency, and t-tests.

FINDINGS: The majority of the media personnel had worked in libraries between one and five years, but only 11 percent of the personnel had library qualifications. Nearly two-thirds of the personnel functioned as teacher-librarians. Few of the school libraries had nonprint materials or equipment. Most also lacked adequate print and nonprint materials for teachers or staff. Nevertheless, more than half of the principals made positive comments about the need for library media centers.

CONCLUSIONS: Even though school libraries have not been adequately supported and have not been able to play a major role in the teaching, learning, or curriculum of secondary and comprehensive schools in Saudi Arabia, principals still have positive attitudes toward school library media center programs.

RECOMMENDATIONS: The analysis, design, implementation, and evaluation (ADIE) model designed by Marghalani is intended to serve as a guide for school library media program development in Saudi Arabia.

614. McCrady, Jacqueline Jane Caldwell (Ph.D., University of Southern California, 1986). **Professional Status and Librarianship: A Study of the Professions and the Process of Social Exchange.** (Copies available exclusively from Micrographics Department, Doheny Library, University of Southern California, Los Angeles, CA 90089-0182).

PURPOSE: In order to better understand librarians' lack of full professional status, McCrady attempted (1) to use the social exchange theory to test the relationship between society and the professions and (2) to study the relationship between librarianship and its public.

PROCEDURE: McCrady collected data from 207 randomly selected members of the general public using a survey instrument, designed specifically for this study, that examined the relationship between the type of service offered by a professional group to the public and the public's perception of the group's professional status. The collected data were compared to relationships found for three other occupational groups: barbers/beauticians, doctors, and teachers.

FINDINGS: The survey population was highly educated: 45 percent of the respondents had four or more years of college. The survey population did not consider the services performed by librarians to be necessary enough to warrant full professional status. When the data were compared to other occupational groups, McCrady found that teachers and doctors had correlations of nearly equal strength, librarians had significant but slight correlations, and barbers/beauticians had almost no correlation on the major variables.

CONCLUSIONS: The social exchange theory proved useful in explaining the professional-public relationship.

615. Mowery, Judith Kay (Ph.D., Indiana University, 1986). **Correlates of Professionalism**

among **Academic Librarians.** 334p. Order no. DA8628077.

PURPOSE: While librarianship has been frequently examined in terms of occupational professionalism this is one of only a few studies to pay attention to the attitudinal aspects of professionalism exhibited by individual librarians.

PROCEDURE: Using the five attitudinal dimensions of the measurement scale developed by sociologist Richard Hall—the use of professional association as a major reference, the belief in service to the public, the belief in self-regulation, the sense of calling to a field, and the sense of autonomy—Mowery prepared a questionnaire to collect data from a sample of academic librarians in Illinois. The data were analyzed using measures of association and multiple regression techniques.

FINDINGS: The surveyed librarians scored highest on the outer-directed attributes of professionalism (the three dimensions having to do with occupational status and self-determination). All the factors studied (including faculty status, collective bargaining, subject specialization, computerized operations in the library environment, administrative responsibility, association membership, and library collection size) proved to be weak predictors of professionalism and its dimensions.

616.   Neuman, Susan Goldstein (Ph.D., University of Pittsburgh, 1986). **The Influence of Management Information Systems in Strategic Planning for Collection Development in Academic Libraries.** 169p. Order no. DA8712571.

PURPOSE: In order to determine the extent to which Management Information Systems (MIS) play a part in academic library collection development, Neuman examined (1) whether or not academic libraries followed MIS, (2) the management tools and the type of data collected to improve collection development planning and decision making, (3) the environmental factors considered for these decisions, and (4) the prevalence of collection/acquisitions plans.

PROCEDURE: Questionnaires were sent to the library directors and collection development officers of those Association of Research Libraries members that were classified as Doctorate-Granting Institutions by the Carnegie Classification of Institutions of Higher Education. Responses were received from eighty library directors (out of ninety-two) and sixty-seven collection development officers or their designates (out of eighty). Only the data received from the sixty-seven schools where both the directors and the collection development officers/designates had responded were used in the final analysis.

FINDINGS: Some automated tools were being used for collection development planning, but generally MIS and Decision Support Systems were not. Environmental factors were usually considered as part of collection development planning. Few libraries had developed collection development plans.

617.   Nimer, Ribhi Mustafa Elayyan (Ph.D., University of Pittsburgh, 1986). **An Investigation into the Use of Sources of Medical Information by the Practicing Jordanian Physicians of Selected Hospitals in Jordan.** 160p. Order no. DA8702070.

PURPOSE: The four main objectives of this study were: (1) to investigate the need for medical sources and libraries in Jordan, (2) to identify the medical sources and libraries used by Jordanian physicians, (3) to determine what methods and sources these physicians used to locate needed information, and (4) to identify the variables that may relate to the frequency of use of library and nonlibrary sources.

PROCEDURE: The questionnaire designed to collect data was first pretested on 12 Arab health professionals and then sent to 410 physicians working in four Jordanian hospitals; 289 usable questionnaires were returned (70.5 percent response rate). One-way analysis of variance and t-tests were used to test the research hypotheses.

FINDINGS: The more extensive the physicians' experience, the more likely they were to use nonlibrary sources of information. No relationship was found between type of physician (e.g., internists, pediatricians, gynecologists) and frequency of use of information. However, specialists were found to use information sources more frequently than general practitioners. Research-oriented physicians were more likely to use library-related sources than were clinically oriented physicians. Similarly, physicians trained in English-speaking countries used library-related sources more frequently than those educated in Jordan, the Arab states, or non-English-speaking countries.

618.   Oksas, Joan K. (Ed.D., Loyola University of Chicago, 1986). **First-, Second-, and Third-Grade Children's Picture Preference of Caldecott Award Winners and Runners-up, 1972-1984 in Selected Schools.** 150p. Order no. DA8613694.

PURPOSE: The purpose of this study was to determine if elementary school children would select Caldecott Award winners as their first choice.

PROCEDURE: Oksas asked 384 children in the first, second, and third grades at three schools in the Chicago, Illinois, area to vote on their picture preferences of the Caldecott winners for 1972, 1978, 1980, 1982, and 1984. Data were also collected on the children's race, sex, grade, reading level, and school system.

FINDINGS: The Caldecott Award winners were not always the children's first choice. Oksas found statistically significant relationships between the books selected and (1) reading level, (2) grade, (3) sex (this showed up in five of the seven-year periods studied), and (4) school system attended; no relationship was found between books selected and race.

619. Paris, Marion (Ph.D., Indiana University, 1986). **Library School Closings: Four Case Studies.** 163p. Order no. DA8628012.

PURPOSE: Since 1978, ten accredited library/information science programs have closed. This dissertation uses a case-study method to examine conditions and possible patterns associated with the closings.

PROCEDURE: A case-study methodology was employed; data were collected from university administrators, executive officers, and faculty from four library schools (two public and two private) that closed.

FINDINGS: While the decisions resulting in the closing of each of the schools were unique, certain common factors associated with the closings emerged during the analysis. Each closing was fiscally motivated, the university administrators had no commitment to offering library education at their institutions, and library school personnel were unable to argue effectively against the closings.

CONCLUSIONS: ALA accreditation does not prevent closings when university administrators seek to eliminate library education programs.

RECOMMENDATIONS: Library administrators must be prepared to justify the existence of their programs. Library school personnel must play more active intellectual and social roles in their parent institutions.

620. Paulk, Betty Douglas (Ph.D., Florida State University, 1986). **The Facilitation of Direct Searching of Online Services by the End User in Academic Libraries.** 282p. Order no. DA8616899.

PURPOSE: In this study, Paulk explored academic librarians' views on the future of (1) end user online searching and (2) the online search librarian's role.

PROCEDURE: Questionnaires were sent to 487 online search librarians at doctoral-level academic institutions in the United States; 431 usable questionnaires (89 percent response rate) were returned.

FINDINGS: Only 10 percent of the respondents were in institutions that allowed end users to access online services directly. Similarly, while more than half of the respondents reported they were offering instructional programs in online searching, few were actually teaching the end user to conduct searches. However, more than half of the surveyed librarians believed that end user searching was inevitable and, as a result, online search librarians would have a more challenging role. They were not clear on exactly what that role would be.

CONCLUSIONS: While academic librarians believed that end users would be conducting their own searches in the near future, they were ambiguous about the role online search librarians should assume in encouraging and training end users to perform online searches.

621. Riechel, Rosemarie (D.L.S., Columbia University, 1986). **Telephone Reference Activity in Large Public Libraries.** 165p. Order no. DA8623594.

PURPOSE: While public libraries have provided telephone reference service throughout this century, this is the first study to explore the role and clientele of this service in suburban as well as urban libraries.

PROCEDURE: Questionnaires were sent to twenty-one public libraries (nineteen responded) in consolidated city and adjacent county systems serving populations of 350,000 or more.

FINDINGS: The respondents reported they recognized the needs of telephoning patrons and that they met these needs using manual tools, microcomputers, and/or automated information retrieval systems.

CONCLUSIONS: Riechel provided guidelines, policies, and procedures for the operation of telephone reference services and assessed the effect of proposed changes in telephone rates and telecommunications charges.

622. Rittenhouse, Robert John (Ph.D., Case Western Reserve University, 1986). **A Composite Measure for Weighting Databases in Defense, Engineering, and Science.** 298p. Order no. DA8702080.

PURPOSE: The purpose of this experimental study was to determine if the measure of closeness (which consists of a relevance factor and a descriptive factor) could be used to select relevant databases in the areas of defense, engineering, and science.

PROCEDURE: The measure of closeness is composed of a relevance factor (the sum of the recall and precision rates) and a descriptive factor (the sum of the weighted properties of subject coverage, thesaurus strength, technical level, subject coding, and length of years searched retrospectively). Searches in seven topics (composites, missiles, rockets, sonar, torpedoes, underwater acoustics, and underwater weapons) were conducted in databases from DIALOG Information Services, Defense Logistics Studies Information Exchange, Defense Technical Information Center, Mead Data Central Nexis, NASA/RECON, and DOE/RECON. These databases were ranked according to their closeness values and compared with their corresponding databases ranked by retrievals from DIALINDEX (a DIALOG multidatabase file). Two experiments were conducted: (1) six randomly selected DIALOG files were compared to DIALOG files subjectively selected for their expected higher relevance to the topics; and (2) the DIALINDEX method was compared to the measure of closeness technique. The data were analyzed using Mann-Whitney two rank and Spearman Rho rank correlation tests.

FINDINGS: Randomly selected files retrieved only a limited number of relevant citations. The DIALINDEX method was not significantly different from use of the weighted measure of closeness alone. DIALINDEX term frequency retrievals appeared to result in ranking relevant databases.

CONCLUSIONS: Artificial intelligence designs might enhance the future modeling of weighting schemes for more effective online search techniques.

623. Robertson, Steven Donald (Ph.D., University of Southern California, 1986). **Public Microcomputing in Southern California Community Libraries.** (Copies available exclusively from Micrographics Department, Doheny Library, University of Southern California, Los Angeles, CA 90089-0182).

PURPOSE: Robertson used a survey research design to identify the extent to which microcomputers were made available for public use in Southern California public libraries.

PROCEDURE: First, two questionnaires were sent to libraries in a ten-county Southern California area to determine the availability of microcomputers for public uses. Seventy-nine sites with computers for public use were identified. Next, three survey sites were selected (based on the hardware and software they had available and the characteristics of their communities) and a patron survey instrument was pretested at one of the sites. Finally, all patrons

at the three facilities were given a survey form during a one-week survey period; over 90 percent of the questionnaires were returned at each of the sites.

FINDINGS: While patrons routinely brought games to the library, they rarely brought other types of software to use on library computers. If nongame software was available in the library, it was used. Younger users were more interested in games and programming; older users were more application-oriented. Game players were more tolerant of louder environments than other users. Most patrons were dissatisfied with the amount of work space available; putting computers in standard audiovisual carrels did not provide enough room. Most of the patrons were library users well before they became library computer users. Most of the library computer users had previous computer experience, either at work or at school.

624. Rodney, Mae Lipscomb (Ph.D., University of North Carolina, 1986). **The Influence of Certain Variables on Collection Use at Three Historically Black Liberal Arts Colleges.** 180p. Order no. DA8618385.

PURPOSE: In this study, Rodney attempted (1) to measure collection use at selected black college libraries and (2) to determine if collection use at those libraries was comparable to the use level at other academic libraries.

PROCEDURE: Rodney collected the following information for materials available at three historically black liberal arts college libraries: subject field, copyright date, and inclusion in such standard selection tools as *Books for College Libraries, Public Library Catalog* (1973), and *Public Library Catalog* (1978). In addition, she measured relative use (i.e., book use in relation to holdings) by sampling shelflist and circulation records. These data were then compared to statistics available from other academic libraries.

FINDINGS: Collection use at black college libraries corresponded to that reported at other academic libraries. Relative use was low (but varied by subject). Older materials were used less frequently. Similarly, titles listed in standard selection tools were used less than those not listed.

CONCLUSIONS: The effectiveness of standard selection tools for small black colleges was questioned.

625. Safrit, Janice Annette (Ed.D., University of North Carolina at Greensboro, 1986). **The Development of an Instrument for Measuring Library Instructional Services and**

Organizational Climate in Academic Libraries. 217p. Order no. DA8718634.

PURPOSE: The purpose of this study was to design, develop, and test an instrument that could be used to diagnose the organizational climates that promote library instruction within academic libraries.

PROCEDURE: The instrument created for this study, based on Alan R. Samuels's Modified Institutional Functioning Inventory, was titled the Academic Library Instructional Services Survey (ALISS). ALISS consisted of five climate scales: innovation, esprit, instruction and utilization, support, and self-study and planning. The instrument was tested at sixteen randomly selected colleges and universities and four criterion institutions. Validity was tested by factor analysis and institutional profile analysis. Reliability was measured by the coefficient Alpha and item analysis using Pearson Produce Moment Correlations.

FINDINGS: ALISS was moderately valid and reliable. Communication, management, and user services were found to play important roles in the relationship between instruction in library use and organizational climate.

CONCLUSIONS: ALISS could be useful in planning library instructional services and in determining if the organizational climate as perceived by librarians and faculty could contribute to the development of a successful program.

RECOMMENDATIONS: The value of ALISS as a predictor of program success should be tested further. An attempt should be made to use ALISS as a diagnostic tool. The possible relationship between curriculum development and organizational climate should be explored.

626. Schwartz, Carolyn Susan (Candy) (Ph.D., Syracuse University, 1986). **A Study of the Application of Post-Retrieval Clustering in Bibliographic Databases.** 144p. Order no. DA 8625849.

PURPOSE: The purpose of this study was to determine an effective way of presenting retrieval results.

PROCEDURE: Two different databases were used in this study: INSPEC and PSYC-INFO. A clustering algorithm was applied to forty-eight retrieved sets in these databases. Schwartz calculated coefficients of ranking effectiveness (CREs) for the results presented in an order derived from the clustering and in reverse accession number order (the order commonly available in commercial search systems). Then, she used a two-alternative t-test to measure significant differences of CRE means.

FINDINGS: Generally, items retrieved from large bibliographic databases were not ordered so that relevant references were presented before nonrelevant references. Post-retrieval clustering provided a more effective presentation of retrieved results.

627. Simmons, Randall Craig (Ph.D., University of Illinois at Urbana-Champaign, 1986). **Relationship between Moral Reasoning and Participation in and Acceptance of Library Theft-Behaviors among Undergraduates in a Large Academic Library.** 353p. Order no. DA 8701620.

PURPOSE: While previous studies have examined the psychological, sociological, and situational factors related to the unauthorized removal of materials from academic libraries, this is the first study that explores the relationship between library theft-behaviors and moral reasoning among undergraduate students.

PROCEDURE: Two questionnaires were used: a three-story version of the Defining Issues Test (which measures the level of moral reasoning) and a questionnaire that examined the subjects' awareness of, acceptance of, and participation in library theft-behaviors. Data were collected from 432 undergraduate students at the University of Illinois at Urbana-Champaign.

FINDINGS: No significant correlation was found between level of moral reasoning and acceptance of or participation in library theft-behaviors. The signal characteristic of participation in library theft-behaviors was acceptance of individual library theft-behaviors. Students were most likely to accept mutilation and theft if the acts were perceived as being done in reaction to library policies. Students were most likely to accept borrowing and hiding of materials when perceived as being done in reaction to library design.

628. Stansbery, Mary Kay Matthew (Ph.D., Texas Woman's University, 1986). **Attitudes of Selected Graduate Faculty toward the Use of Library Funds to Pay for Electronic Access to Scholarly Journals.** 184p. Order no. DA 8715163.

PURPOSE: This study examined (1) the willingness of graduate faculty to support the use of at least some library funds to pay for electronic access to scholarly journals (rather than for the acquisition of hardcopy scholarly journals) and (2) the relationship between this attitude and the following three variables: age/seniority of faculty, discipline, and level/intensity of graduate degree-granting program.

PROCEDURE: Data were collected from faculty at seven academic institutions in the north Texas area.

FINDINGS: Most of the respondents indicated they would miss having local ownership of hardcopy journals in their university library, but they would support the use of library funds to access full-text scholarly journal databases. The most significant factor in accounting for differing faculty attitudes was the discipline in which the faculty member was based (social science-humanities versus pure science).

CONCLUSIONS: This may be the right time for academic libraries to educate faculty about today's technological and fiscal realities in the information field. CD-ROM technologies may bridge the psychological gap between viewing information on a terminal or computer printout and the desire for local ownership of hardcopy scholarly journals.

629. Stocks, Hugh Grant (Ph.D., University of California at Los Angeles, 1986). **The Book of Mormon in English, 1870-1920: A Publishing History and Analytical Bibliography.** 434p. Order no. DA8621140.

PURPOSE: In order to gain a clearer picture of printing and publishing in the Church of Jesus Christ of Latter-Day Saints (LDS), Stocks traced the publishing history of the *Book of Mormon* between 1870 (when the book's printing plates were transferred to Utah) and 1920 (the date of an influential format revision) and then compared LDS publishing practices with those of mainline Protestant, Christian Science, and Seventh-Day Adventist churches.

PROCEDURE: Stocks analyzed each American printing of the *Book of Mormon*, examined relevant documents in the archives of both the LDS church and the Reorganized Church of Jesus Christ of Latter-Day Saints (RLDS) to clarify responsibilities for and relationships between each edition/impression, and prepared a descriptive bibliography using the principles codified by Fredson Bowers.

FINDINGS: Stocks identified three editions, fourteen impressions, and one issue of the *Book of Mormon* that either were listed inaccurately or were not covered in previously issued bibliographic sources. In addition, he found one printing listed by Flake that does not exist.

CONCLUSIONS: LDS's publishing operation—which is highly centralized, informally controlled at the highest ecclesiastical levels, and focused on central church goals—is different from the pattern followed by the other denominations examined in this dissertation.

630. Thomas, Rebecca Lynne (Ph.D., Ohio State University, 1986). **The Influence of a Poetry-Enriched Environment on the Poetry Preferences and Responses of Sixth-Grade Children: A Librarian-Teacher Collaboration.** 194p. Order no. DA8612418.

PURPOSE: Using a nonequivalent control group design method, this study examined the poetry preferences and responses of sixth-grade students.

PROCEDURE: To collect data for this study, Thomas used the nonequivalent control group design developed by Campbell and Stanley and the poetry preference instrument created by Terry in a pretest/posttest situation. Two groups of sixth-grade students from a suburban school district in Ohio were studied. One group (the experimental group) received in-depth poetry instruction during the year; the other group (the control group) did not. The poetry program was planned collaboratively by the school librarian and the classroom teacher.

FINDINGS: Both groups of students expressed preferences for humorous and familiar poems (as opposed to poems about nature, free verse poems, etc.). However, the experimental group demonstrated greater gains in overall preference between the pretest and posttest.

631. Thompson, Paul (Ph.D., University of California at Berkeley, 1986). **Subjective Probability, Combination of Expert Opinion, and Probabilistic Approaches to Information Retrieval.** 184p. Order no. DA8718181.

PURPOSE: Thompson focused on three aspects of applying probability to the problem of information retrieval: identifying the psychological literature on human probability assessment, preparing a computer simulation study to examine how errors in estimation of term probability propagate into the combined probability for each document (and the effect this has on the ranked output of documents), and developing a new mathematical model for probabilistic information retrieval (PIR).

PROCEDURE: As part of his study, Thompson reviewed the literature, developed a computer simulation study, and prepared a new mathematical model for PIR.

FINDINGS: Thompson identified four major difficulties with current PIR theories: (1) small samples, (2) validity of probabilities used, (3) independence/dependence of individual term probabilities, and (4) interpretation of the probability of a single case (i.e., a specific document's relevance to a single retrieval system user). The computer simulation study prepared by Thompson was motivated by a desire to determine the effect on retrieval effectiveness of various levels of input term probability errors. The mathematical model developed by Thompson used a subjective interpretation of probability, probability distributions, and the technique of combination of expert opinion.

CONCLUSIONS: The mathematical model developed by Thompson may overcome the four obstacles to PIR listed above.

632. Udoh, Victoria Weimuna (Ph.D., University of Pittsburgh, 1986). **The Role of State and Federal Ministries in the Development of School Libraries in Nigeria.** 142p. Order no. DA 8712573.

PURPOSE: Although the original purpose of this research was to investigate the relationship between the education, career background, and official attitudes of the Permanent Secretaries of Education and their support of personnel and funds for school libraries in Nigeria, it was changed during the course of the study to be a description of school libraries in Nigeria because the permanent secretaries did not respond to the data collection questionnaire.

PROCEDURE: While data were not supplied by the permanent secretaries, responses were received from Inspectors of Education and school librarians in Nigeria. In addition to the survey instrument, Udoh used personal interviews and document analysis to collect data.

FINDINGS: Approximately half of the states had at least one professional and paraprofessional at the federal level. Half of the states funded libraries in the annual school budgets and slightly less approved levies. Only 5 percent incorporated allocation into their development plans. Most states operated a decentralized pattern.

CONCLUSIONS: School libraries in Nigeria had inadequate funding, administration, and personnel. There were not enough librarians organizing services to schools at the Ministry level and there was no coordination between the federal and state levels. A centralized pattern would best promote school library development in Nigeria.

633. Vaughan, Elinor Folger (Ed.D., University of North Carolina at Greensboro, 1986). **An Examination of Library Involvement in the Literacy Education Programs of the North Carolina Community College System: A Perceptual Analysis.** 280p. Order no. DA8718687.

PURPOSE: Vaughan examined the type and degree of library involvement in the literacy education mission of the North Carolina Community College System.

PROCEDURE: Questionnaires were sent to library program directors and directors of the Adult Basic Education (ABE) programs of fifty-seven member organizations of the North Carolina Community College System (100 percent response rate). The collected data were ranked and observations were noted.

FINDINGS: Students in the ABE programs received only minimal library services. The services they did receive tended to be traditional in nature (ones that required a minimum of library staff time). The directors of both the libraries and the ABE programs were interested in improving communication and working closer together. The respondents perceived functional illiteracy to be widespread in North Carolina and perceived the North Carolina Community College System to be the primary provider for literacy education in the state.

634. Zsiray, Stephen W., Jr. (Ed.D., Utah State University, 1986). **A Study of the Impact of Staffing Patterns in Elementary School Library Media Centers on Program Development.** 201p. Order no. DA8619420.

PURPOSE: In order to explore the relationship between staffing patterns and elementary school library media center program development, Zsiray studied the following program activities: planning, budgeting, purchasing, production, access and delivery, maintenance, public information, and evaluation.

PROCEDURE: Questionnaires were sent to all elementary library media personnel in Utah; nearly 76 percent of the questionnaires were returned. The data were analyzed using content analysis, descriptive statistics, and such statistical techniques as one-way ANOVA and the Scheffe post hoc test of pair-wise comparisons. Both statistical and practical significance were considered in interpreting the data.

FINDINGS: Zsiray found that there was no relationship between either (1) higher levels of professional performance and district-level library media specialist support for building-level library media specialists or (2) professional activities and the presence/absence of district-level supported media specialists.

CONCLUSIONS: There was little difference in the programs offered by certified building-level elementary school library media specialists and those offered by elementary school library media aides.

RECOMMENDATIONS: Future studies should examine the impact of leadership provided by the district-level library media specialist's support on building-level library media programs.

Author/Title Index

Unless otherwise indicated, reference is to entry number. References to page number are identified by a *p* (e.g., p. 4).

Subject Index

Unless otherwise indicated, reference is to entry number. References to page number are identified by a *p* (e.g., p.4).